# Eleventh Workshop on Innovative Use of NLP for Building Educational Applications 2016

Held at the 2016 Conference of the North American Chapter of the Association for Computational Linguistics: Human Language Technologies (NAACL HLT 2016)

San Diego, California, USA
16 June 2016

ISBN: 978-1-5108-2525-3

**Printed from e-media with permission by:**

Curran Associates, Inc.
57 Morehouse Lane
Red Hook, NY  12571

**Some format issues inherent in the e-media version may also appear in this print version.**

Copyright© (2016) by the Association for Computational Linguistics
All rights reserved.

Printed by Curran Associates, Inc. (2016)

For permission requests, please contact the Association for Computational Linguistics
at the address below.

Association for Computational Linguistics
209 N. Eighth Street
Stroudsburg, Pennsylvania 18360

Phone:   1-570-476-8006
Fax:      1-570-476-0860

acl@aclweb.org

**Additional copies of this publication are available from:**

Curran Associates, Inc.
57 Morehouse Lane
Red Hook, NY 12571 USA
Phone:  845-758-0400
Fax:     845-758-2634
Email:  curran@proceedings.com
Web:    www.proceedings.com

NAACL HLT 2016

# The Eleventh Workshop
# on Innovative Use of NLP for
# Building Educational Applications

## Proceedings of the Workshop

June 16, 2016
San Diego, California, USA

# Gold Sponsors

# Silver Sponsors

**This page intentionally left blank.**

# Introduction

We are excited to be holding the 11th edition of the BEA workshop. Since starting in 1997, the BEA workshop, now one of the largest workshops at NAACL/ACL, has become one of the leading venues for publishing innovative work that uses NLP to develop educational applications. The consistent interest and growth of the workshop has clear ties to challenges in education, especially with regard to supporting literacy. The research presented at the workshop illustrates advances in the technology, and the maturity of the NLP/education field that are responses to those challenges with capabilities that support instructor practices and learner needs. NLP capabilities now support an array of learning domains, including writing, speaking, reading, and mathematics. In the writing and speech domains, automated writing evaluation (AWE) and speech assessment applications, respectively, are commercially deployed in high-stakes assessment and instructional settings, including Massive Open Online Courses (MOOCs). We also see widely-used commercial applications for plagiarism detection and peer review. There has been a renewed interest in spoken dialog and multi-modal systems for instruction and assessment as well as feedback. We are also seeing explosive growth of mobile applications for game-based applications for instruction and assessment. The current educational and assessment landscape, especially in the United States, continues to foster a strong interest and high demand that pushes the state-of-the-art in AWE capabilities to expand the analysis of written responses to writing genres other than those traditionally found in standardized assessments, especially writing tasks requiring use of sources and argumentative discourse.

The use of NLP in educational applications has gained visibility outside of the NLP community. First, the Hewlett Foundation reached out to public and private sectors and sponsored two competitions: one for automated essay scoring, and another for scoring of short answer, subject-matter-based response items. The motivation driving these competitions was to engage the larger scientific community in this enterprise. MOOCs are now beginning to incorporate AWE systems to manage the thousands of constructed-response assignments collected during a single MOOC course. Learning@Scale is another venue that discusses NLP research in education. The Speech and Language Technology in Education (SLaTE), now in its seventh year, promotes the use of speech and language technology for educational purposes. Another breakthrough for educational applications within the CL community is the presence of a number of shared-task competitions over the last three years. There have been four shared tasks on grammatical error correction with the last two held at CoNLL (2013 and 2014). In 2014 alone, there were four shared tasks for NLP and Education-related areas. We are pleased to announce a unique shared task at BEA this year: Automated Evaluation of Scientific Writing.

As a community, we continue to improve existing capabilities, and to identify and generate innovative ways to use NLP in applications for writing, reading, speaking, critical thinking, curriculum development, and assessment. Steady growth in the development of NLP-based applications for education has prompted an increased number of workshops, typically focusing on one specific subfield. In this workshop, we present papers from the following subfields: tools for automated scoring of text and speech, automated test-item generation, curriculum development, collaborative problem solving, content evaluation in text, dialogue and intelligent tutoring, evaluation of genres beyond essays, feedback studies, and grammatical error detection.

This year we received a record 46 submissions, and accepted 8 papers as oral presentations and 20 as poster presentation and/or demos, for an overall acceptance rate of 61%. Each paper was reviewed by three members of the Program Committee who were believed to be most appropriate for each paper. We continue to have a very strong policy to deal with conflicts of interest. First, we made a concerted effort to not assign papers to reviewers to evaluate if the paper had an author from their institution. Second, with respect to the organizing committee, authors of papers for which there was a conflict of interest recused themselves from the discussions.

While the field is growing, we do recognize that there is a core group of institutions and researchers who work in this area. With a higher acceptance rate, we were able to include papers from a wider variety of topics and institutions. The papers accepted were selected on the basis of several factors, including the relevance to a core educational problem space, the novelty of the approach or domain, and the strength of the research. The accepted papers were highly diverse – an indicator of the growing variety of foci in this field. We continue to believe that the workshop framework designed to introduce work in progress and new ideas needs to be revived, and we hope that we have achieved this with the breadth and variety of research accepted for this workshop, a brief description of which is presented below:

For *automated writing evaluation*, Meyer & Koch investigate how users of intelligent writing assistance tools deal with correct, incorrect, and incomplete feedback; Rei & Cummins investigate the task of assessing sentence-level prompt relevance in learner essays; Cummins et al focus on determining the topical relevance of L2 essays to the prompt; Loukina & Cahill investigate how well systems developed for automated evaluation of written responses perform when applied to spoken responses; Beigman Klebanov et al address the problem of quantifying the overall extent to which a test-taker's essay deals with the topic it is assigned; King & Dickinson investigate questions of how to reason about learner meaning in cases where the set of correct meanings is never entirely complete, specifically for the case of picture description tasks; Madnani et al present preliminary work on automatically scoring tests of proficiency in music instruction; Rahimi & Litman automatically extract and investigate the usefulness of topical components for scoring the Evidence dimension of an analytical writing in response to text assessment; Ledbetter & Dickinson describe the development of a morphological analyzer for learner Hungarian, outlining extensions to a resource-light system that can be developed by different types of experts.

For *short-answer scoring*, Horbach & Palmer explore the suitability of active learning for automatic short-answer assessment on the ASAP corpus; Banjade et al present a corpus that contains student answers annotated for their correctness in context, in addition to a baseline for predicting the correctness label; and Rudzewitz explores the practical usefulness of the combination of features from three different fields – short answer scoring, authorship attribution, and plagiarism detection – for two tasks: semantic learner language classification, and plagiarism detection for evaluating short answers.

For *grammar and spelling error detection*, Madnani et al discuss a classifier approach that yields higher precision and a language modeling approach that provides better recall; Beinborn et al discuss a model that can predict spelling difficulty with a high accuracy, and provide a thorough error analysis that takes the L1 into account and provides insights into cross-lingual transfer effects; Napoles et al estimate the deterioration of NLP processing given an estimate of the amount and nature of grammatical errors in a text; and, Yuan et al develop a supervised ranking model to re-rank candidates generated from an SMT-based grammatical error correction system.

For *text difficulty and curriculum development*, Xia et al address the task of readability assessment for texts aimed at L2 learners; Reynolds investigates Russian second language readability assessment using a machine-learning approach with a range of lexical, morphological, syntactic, and discourse features; Chen & Meurers study the frequency of a word in common language use, and systematically explore how such a word-level feature is best used to characterize the reading levels of texts; Yoon et al present an automated method for estimating the difficulty of spoken texts for use in generating items that assess non-native learners' listening proficiency; Milli & Hearst explore the automated augmentation of a popular online learning resource – Khan Academy video modules – with relevant reference chapters from open access textbooks; and Chinkina & Meurers present an IR system for text selection that identifies the grammatical constructions spelled out in the official English language curriculum of schools in Baden-Württemberg (Germany) and re-ranks the search results based on the selected (de)prioritization of grammatical forms.

For *item generation*, Hill & Simha propose a method to automatically generate multiple-choice fill-in-the-blank exercises from existing text passages that challenge a reader's comprehension skills and contextual awareness; Wojatzki et al present the concept of bundled gap filling, along with an efficient computational model for automatically generating unambiguous gap bundle exercises, and a disambiguation measure for guiding the construction of the exercises and validating their level of ambiguity; and Pilán explores the factors influencing the dependence of single sentences on their larger textual context in order to automatically identify candidate sentences for language learning exercises from corpora which are presentable in isolation.

For *collaborative problem solving*, Flor et al present a novel situational task that integrates collaborative problem solving behavior with testing in a science domain.

For *accessibility*, Martinez-Santiago et al discuss computer-designed tools in order to help people with Autism Spectrum Disorder to palliate or overcome such verbal limitations.

As noted earlier, this year we are excited to host the first Shared Task in *Automated Evaluation of Scientific Writing* (http://textmining.lt/aesw/index.html). The task involves automatically predicting whether sentences found in scientific language are in need of editing. Six teams competed and their system description papers are found in these proceedings and are presented as posters in conjunction with the BEA11 poster session. A summary report of the shared task (Daudaravicius et al) is also found in the proceedings and will be presented orally.

We wish to thank everyone who showed interest and submitted a paper, all of the authors for their contributions, the members of the Program Committee for their thoughtful reviews, and everyone who attended this workshop. We would especially like to thank our sponsors; at the Gold Level: American Institutes for Research (AIR), Cambridge Assessment, Educational Testing Service, Grammarly, Pacific Metrics and Turnitin / Lightside, and at the Silver Level: Cognii and iLexIR. Their contributions allow us to subsidize students at the workshop dinner, and make workshop t-shirts! We would like to thank Joya Tetreault for creating the t-shirt design (again!).


Joel Tetreault, Yahoo
Jill Burstein, Educational Testing Service
Claudia Leacock, Grammarly
Helen Yannakoudakis, University of Cambridge

**Organizers:**

Joel Tetreault, Yahoo Labs
Jill Burstein, Educational Testing Services
Claudia Leacock, Grammarly
Helen Yannakoudakis, University of Cambridge

**Program Committee:**

Laura Allen, Arizona State University
Rafael Banchs, I2R
Timo Baumann, Universität Hamburg
Lee Becker, Hapara
Beata Beigman Klebanov, Educational Testing Service
Lisa Beinborn, Technische Universität Darmstadt
Kay Berkling, Cooperative State University Karlsruhe
Suma Bhat, University of Illinois, Urbana-Champaign
Serge Bibauw, Université Catholique de Louvain
David Bloom, Pacific Metrics
Chris Brew, Thomson Reuters
Ted Briscoe, University of Cambridge
Chris Brockett, Microsoft Research
Julian Brooke, University of Melbourne
Aoife Cahill, Educational Testing Service
Lei Chen, Educational Testing Service
Min Chi, North Carolina State University
Martin Chodorow, Hunter College and the Graduate Center, CUNY
Mark Core, University of Southern California
Scott Crossley, Georgia State University
Luis Fernando D'Haro, Human Language Technology - Institute for Infocomm Research
Daniel Dahlmeier, SAP
Barbara Di Eugenio, University of Illinois Chicago
Markus Dickinson, Indiana University
Yo Ehara, Tokyo Metropolitan University
Keelan Evanini, Educational Testing Service
Mariano Felice, University of Cambridge
Michael Flor, Educational Testing Service
Thomas François, Université Catholique de Louvain
Michael Gamon, Microsoft Research
Binyam Gebrekidan Gebre, Max Planck Computing and Data Facility
Kallirroi Georgila, University of Southern California
Dan Goldwasser, Purdue University
Cyril Goutte, National Research Council Canada

Iryna Gurevych, Technische Universität Darmstadt
Na-Rae Han, University of Pittsburgh
Andrea Horbach, Saarland University
Chung-Chi Huang, National Institutes of Health
Radu Tudor Ionescu, University of Bucharest
Ross Israel, Factual
Fazel Keshtkar, Southeast Missouri State University
Ekaterina Kochmar, University of Cambridge
Mamoru Komachi, Tokyo Metropolitan University
Bob Krovetz, Lexical Research
Lun-Wei Ku, Academia Sinica
Kristopher Kyle, Georgia State University
John Lee, City University of Hong Kong
Ben Leong, Educational Testing Service
James Lester, North Carolina State University
Diane Litman, University of Pittsburgh
Annie Louis, University of Essex
Anastassia Loukina, Educational Testing Service
Xiaofei Lu, Pennsylvania State University
Wencan Luo, University of Pittsburgh
Nitin Madnani, Educational Testing Service
Shervin Malmasi, Macquarie University
Montse Maritxalar, University of the Basque Country
Julie Medero, Harvey Mudd College
Detmar Meurers, Universität Tübingen
Lisa Michaud, Aspect Software
Rada Mihalcea, University of Michigan
Michael Mohler, Language Computer Corp.
Smaranda Muresan, Columbia University
Courtney Napoles, Johns Hopkins University
Hwee Tou Ng, National University of Singapore
Vincent Ng, University of Texas, Dallas Huy Nguyen, University of Pittsburgh
Rodney Nielsen, University of North Texas
Nobal Niraula, The University of Memphis
Simon Ostermann, Saarland University
Alexis Palmer, Heidelberg University
Ted Pedersen, University of Minnesota, Duluth
Ildikó Pilán, University of Gothenburg
Zahra Rahimi, University of Pittsburgh
Lakshmi Ramachandran, Pearson
Arti Ramesh, University of Maryland, College Park
Marek Rei, University of Cambridge
Robert Reynolds, University of Tromsø
Brian Riordan, Educational Testing Service
Mark Rosenstein, Pearson
Mihai Rotaru, Textkernel

Alla Rozovskaya, Virginia Tech
C. Anton Rytting, University of Maryland, College Park
Keisuke Sakaguchi, Johns Hopkins University
Mathias Schulze, University of Waterloo
Swapna Somasundaran, Educational Testing Service
Helmer Strik, Centre for Language Studies, Centre for Language and Speech Technology, Radboud University, Nijmegen
David Suendermann-Oeft, Educational Testing Service
Sowmya Vajjala, Iowa State University
Giulia Venturi, Institute of Computational Linguistics "Antonio Zampolli" (ILC-CNR)
Elena Volodina, University of Gothenburg
Carl Vogel, Trinity College
Xinhao Wang, Educational Testing Service
Michael White, Department of Linguistics, The Ohio State University
David Wible, National Central University
Alistair Willis, The Open University, UK
Magdalena Wolska, Universität Tübingen
Peter Wood, University of Saskatchewan
Huichao Xue, Google
Helen Yannakoudakis, University of Cambridge
Marcos Zampieri, Saarland University
Klaus Zechner, Educational Testing Service
Torsten Zesch, University of Duisburg-Essen
Fan Zhang, University of Pittsburgh
Xiaodan Zhu, National Research Council Canada

# Table of Contents

**This page intentionally left blank.**

# Conference Program

**Thursday June 16, 2016**

**08:45–09:00**  **_Load Oral Presentations_**

**09:00–09:15**  **_Opening Remarks_**

09:15–09:40  _The Effect of Multiple Grammatical Errors on Processing Non-Native Writing_
Courtney Napoles, Aoife Cahill and Nitin Madnani

09:40–10:05  _Text Readability Assessment for Second Language Learners_
Menglin Xia, Ekaterina Kochmar and Ted Briscoe

10:05–10:30  _Automatic Generation of Context-Based Fill-in-the-Blank Exercises Using Co-occurrence Likelihoods and Google n-grams_
Jennifer Hill and Rahul Simha

**10:30–11:00**  **_Break_**

11:00–11:25  _Automated classification of collaborative problem solving interactions in simulated science tasks_
Michael Flor, Su-Youn Yoon, Jiangang Hao, Lei Liu and Alina von Davier

11:25–11:50  _Computer-assisted stylistic revision with incomplete and noisy feedback. A pilot study_
Christian M. Meyer and Johann Frerik Koch

11:50–12:15  _A Report on the Automatic Evaluation of Scientific Writing Shared Task_
Vidas Daudaravicius, Rafael E. Banchs, Elena Volodina and Courtney Napoles

**12:25–02:00**  **_Lunch_**

**02:00–02:45**  **_Poster and Demo Session A_**

_Topicality-Based Indices for Essay Scoring_
Beata Beigman Klebanov, Michael Flor and Binod Gyawali

_Predicting the Spelling Difficulty of Words for Language Learners_
Lisa Beinborn, Torsten Zesch and Iryna Gurevych

**Thursday June 16, 2016 (continued)**



02:45–03:30     *Poster and Demo Session B*

*Linguistically Aware Information Retrieval: Providing Input Enrichment for Second Language Learners*
Maria Chinkina and Detmar Meurers

*Enhancing STEM Motivation through Personal and Communal Values: NLP for Assessment of Utility Value in Student Writing*
Beata Beigman Klebanov, Jill Burstein, Judith Harackiewicz, Stacy Priniski and Matthew Mulholland

*Cost-Effectiveness in Building a Low-Resource Morphological Analyzer for Learner Language*
Scott Ledbetter and Markus Dickinson

*Automatically Scoring Tests of Proficiency in Music Instruction*
Nitin Madnani, Aoife Cahill and Brian Riordan

*Combined Tree Kernel-based classifiers for Assessing Quality of Scientific Text*
Liliana Mamani Sanchez and Hector-Hugo Franco-Penya

*Augmenting Course Material with Open Access Textbooks*
Smitha Milli and Marti A. Hearst

*Exploring the Intersection of Short Answer Assessment, Authorship Attribution, and Plagiarism Detection*
Björn Rudzewitz

*Sentence-Level Grammatical Error Identification as Sequence-to-Sequence Correction*
Allen Schmaltz, Yoon Kim, Alexander M. Rush and Stuart Shieber

*Combining Off-the-shelf Grammar and Spelling Tools for the Automatic Evaluation of Scientific Writing (AESW) Shared Task 2016*
René Witte and Bahar Sateli

*Candidate re-ranking for SMT-based grammatical error correction*
Zheng Yuan, Ted Briscoe and Mariano Felice

*Spoken Text Difficulty Estimation Using Linguistic Features*
Su-Youn Yoon, Yeonsuk Cho and Diane Napolitano

*Automatically Extracting Topical Components for a Response-to-Text Writing Assessment*
Zahra Rahimi and Diane Litman

**03:30–04:00**   *Break*

# The Effect of Multiple Grammatical Errors on Processing Non-Native Writing


**Courtney Napoles**
Johns Hopkins University
`courtneyn@jhu.edu`

**Aoife Cahill     Nitin Madnani**
Educational Testing Service
`{acahill,nmadnani}@ets.org`



## Abstract

In this work, we estimate the deterioration of NLP processing given an estimate of the amount and nature of grammatical errors in a text. From a corpus of essays written by English-language learners, we extract ungrammatical sentences, controlling the number and types of errors in each sentence. We focus on six categories of errors that are commonly made by English-language learners, and consider sentences containing one or more of these errors. To evaluate the effect of grammatical errors, we measure the deterioration of ungrammatical dependency parses using the labeled F-score, an adaptation of the labeled attachment score. We find notable differences between the influence of individual error types on the dependency parse, as well as interactions between multiple errors.


## 1 Introduction

With the large number of English-language learners and the prevalence of informal web text, noisy text containing grammatical errors is widespread. However, the majority of NLP tools are developed and trained over clean, grammatical text and the performance of these tools may be negatively affected when processing errorful text. One possible workaround is to adapt tools for noisy text, e.g. (Foster et al., 2008; Cahill et al., 2014). However, it is often preferable to use tools trained on clean text, mainly because of the resources necessary for training and the limited availability of large-scale annotated corpora, but also because tools should work correctly in the presence of well-formed text.

Our goal is to measure the performance degradation of an automatic NLP task based on an estimate of grammatical errors in a text. For example, if we are processing student responses within an NLP application, and the responses contain a mix of native and non-native texts, it would be useful to be able to estimate the difference in performance (if any) of the NLP application on both types of texts.

We choose dependency parsing as our prototypic task because it is often one of the first complex downstream tasks in NLP pipelines. We will consider six common grammatical errors made by non-native speakers of English and systematically control the number and types of errors present in a sentence. As errors are introduced to a sentence, the degradation of the dependency parse is measured by the decrease in the F-score over dependency relations.

In this work, we will show that

- increasing the number of errors in a sentence decreases the accuracy of the dependency parse (Section 4.1);
- the distance between errors does not affect the accuracy (Section 4.2);
- some types of grammatical errors have a greater impact, alone or in combination with other errors (Section 4.3).

While these findings may seem self-evident, they have not previously been quantified on a large corpus of naturally occurring errors. Our analysis will serve as the first step to understanding what happens to a NLP pipeline when confronted with grammatical errors.

1


*Proceedings of the 11th Workshop on Innovative Use of NLP for Building Educational Applications*, pages 1–11,
San Diego, California, June 16, 2016. ©2016 Association for Computational Linguistics

## 2 Data

Previous research concerning grammatical errors has artificially generated errors over clean text, such as Foster et al. (2008) and Felice and Yuan (2014), among others. While this is one approach for building a large-scale corpus of grammatical and ungrammatical sentence pairs, we use text with naturally occurring errors so that our analysis covers the types of errors typically seen in non-native writing.

As the source of our data, we use the training section of the NUS Corpus of Learner English (NUCLE),[1] which is a large corpus of essays written by non-native English speakers (Dahlmeier et al., 2013). The NUCLE corpus has been annotated with corrections to the grammatical errors, and each error has been labeled with one of 28 error categories.

We will only consider the following common errors types, which constitute more than 50% of the 44 thousand corrections in NUCLE:

- Article or determiner [*Det*]
- Mechanical (punctuation, capitalization, and spelling) [*Mec*]
- Noun number [*Noun*]
- Preposition [*Prep*]
- Word form [*Wform*]
- Verb tense and verb form [*Verb*]

While other error coding schemes specify the nature of the error (whether the text is unnecessary, missing, or needs to be replaced) in addition to the word class (Nicholls, 2004), the NUCLE error categories do not make that distinction. Therefore we automatically labeled each error with an additional tag for the *operation* of the correction, depending on whether it was *missing* a token, had an *unnecessary* token, or needed to *replace* a token. We labeled all noun, verb, and word form errors as *replacements*, and automatically detected the label of article, mechanical, and preposition errors by comparing the tokens in the original and corrected spans of text. If the correction had fewer unique tokens than the original text, it was labeled *unnecessary*. If the correction had more unique tokens, it was labeled *missing*. Otherwise the operation was labeled a *replacement*. To verify the validity of this algorithm, we reviewed the 100 most frequent error–correction pairs labeled

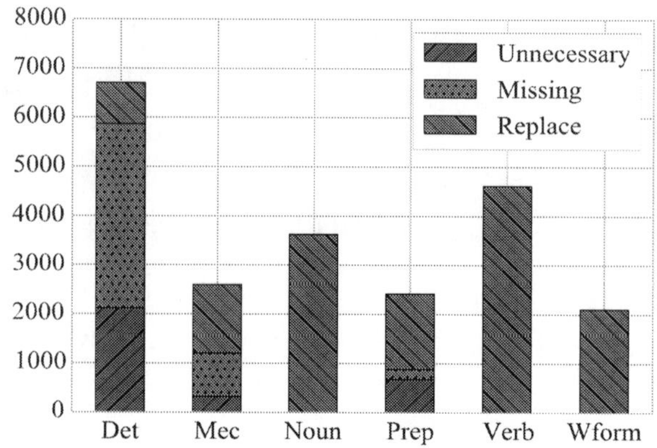



Figure 1: The number of corrections by error type and operation that we used in this study.

with each operation, which encompasses 69% of the errors in the corpus.[2]

To compile our corpus of sentences, we selected all of the corrections from NUCLE addressing one of the six error types above. We skipped corrections that spanned multiple sentences or the entire length of a sentence, as well as corrections that addressed punctuation spacing, since those errors would likely be addressed during tokenization.[3]

We identified 14,531 NUCLE sentences containing errors subject to these criteria. We applied the corrections of all other types of errors and, in the rest of our analysis, we will use the term *errors* to refer only to errors of the types outlined above. On average, each of these sentence has 26.4 tokens and 1.5 errors, with each error spanning 1.2 tokens and the correction 1.5 tokens. In total, there are 22,123 errors, and Figure 1 shows the total number of corrections by error type and operation. Because of the small number of naturally occurring sentences with exactly 1, 2, 3, or 4 errors (Table 1), we chose to generate new sentences with varying numbers of errors from the original ungrammatical sentences.

For each of the NUCLE sentences, we generated ungrammatical sentences with $n$ errors by systematically selecting $n$ corrections to ignore, applying all of the other corrections. We generated sentences

---

[1] Version 3.2

[2] Many error–correction pairs are very frequent: for example, inserting or deleting *the* accounts for 3,851 of the errors and inserting or deleting a plural *s* 2,804.

[3] NLTK was used for sentence and token segmentation (`http://nltk.org`).

| # errors | NUCLE sentences | Generated sentences | Exactly $n$ errors |
|---|---|---|---|
| 1 | 14,531 | 22,123 | 9,474 |
| 2 | 5,030 | 11,561 | 3,341 |
| 3 | 572 | 5,085 | 0 |
| 4 | 570 | 3,577 | 362 |

Table 1: The number of NUCLE sentences containing at least $n$ errors, the number of sentences with $n$ errors that were generated from them, and the number of NUCLE sentences with exactly $n$ errors.

with $n = 1$ to 4 errors, when there were at least $n$ corrections to the original sentence. For example, a NUCLE sentence with 6 annotated corrections would yield the following number of ungrammatical sentences: 6 sentences with one error, $\binom{6}{2} = 15$ sentences with two errors, $\binom{6}{3} = 20$ sentences with three errors, and so on. The number of original NUCLE sentences and generated sentences with each number of errors is shown in Table 1. We also generated a grammatical sentence with all of the corrections applied for comparison.

We parsed each sentence with the ZPar constituent parser (Zhang and Clark, 2011) and generated dependency parses from the ZPar output using the Stanford Dependency Parser[4] and the universal dependencies representation (De Marneffe et al., 2014). We make the over-confident assumption that the automatic analyses in our pipeline (tokenization, parsing, and error-type labeling) are all correct.

Our analysis also depends on the quality of the NUCLE annotations. When correcting ungrammatical text, annotators are faced with the decisions of whether a text needs to be corrected and, if so, how to edit it. Previous work has found low inter-annotator agreement for the basic task of judging whether a sentence is grammatical ($0.16 \leq \kappa \leq 0.40$) (Rozovskaya and Roth, 2010). The NUCLE corpus is no different, with the three NUCLE annotators having moderate agreement on how to correct a span of text ($\kappa = 0.48$) and only fair agreement for identifying what span of text needs to be corrected ($\kappa = 0.39$) (Dahlmeier et al., 2013). Low inter-annotator agreement is not necessarily an indication of the quality of the annotations, since it could

also be attributed to the diversity of appropriate corrections that have been made. We assume that the annotations are correct and complete, meaning that the spans and labels of annotations are correct and that all of the grammatical errors are annotated. We further assume that the annotations only fix grammatical errors, instead of providing a stylistic alternatives to grammatical text.

## 3 Metric: Labeled F-score

To measure the effect of grammatical errors on the performance of the dependency parser, we compare the dependencies identified in the corrected sentence to those from the ungrammatical sentence.

The labeled attachment score (LAS) is a commonly used method for evaluating dependency parsers (Nivre et al., 2004). The LAS calculates the accuracy of the dependency triples from the candidate dependency graph with respect to those of the gold standard, where each triple represents one relation, consisting of the head, dependent, and type of relation. The LAS assumes that the surface forms of the sentences are identical but only the relations have changed. In this work, we require a method that accommodates unaligned tokens, which occur when an error involves deleting or inserting tokens and unequal surface forms (replacement errors).

There are some metrics that compare the parses of unequal sentences, including SParseval (Roark et al., 2006) and TEDeval (Tsarfaty et al., 2011), however neither of these metrics operate over dependencies. We chose to evaluate dependencies because dependency-based evaluation has been shown to be more closely related to the linguistic intuition of good parses compared to two other tree-based evaluations (Rehbein and van Genabith, 2007).

Since we cannot calculate the LAS over sentences of unequal lengths, we instead measure the $F_1$-score of the dependency relations. So that substitutions (such as morphological changes) are not severely penalized, we represent tokens with their index instead of the surface form. First, we align the tokens in the grammatical and ungrammatical sentences and assign an index to each token such that the aligned tokens in each sentence share the same index. Because reordering is uncommon in the NUCLE corrections, we use dynamic programming to find the lowest-

---

[4]Using the EnglishGrammaticalStructure class with the flags `-nonCollapsed -keepPunct`.

cost alignment between a sentence pair, where the cost for insertions and deletions is 1, and substitutions receive a cost proportionate to the Levenshtein edit distance between the tokens (to award "partial credit" for inflections).

We calculate the Labeled F-score (LF) over dependency relations of the form <head index, dependent index, relation>. This evaluation metric can be used for comparing the dependency parses of aligned sentences with unequal lengths or tokens.[5] A variant of the LAS, the Unlabeled Attachment Score, is calculated over pairs of heads and dependents without the relation. We considered the corresponding unlabeled F-score and, since there was no meaningful difference between that and the labeled F-score, we chose to use labeled relations for greater specificity.

In the subsequent analysis, we will focus on the difference in LF before and after an error is introduced to a sentence. We will refer to the LF of a sentence with $n$ errors as $LF_n$. The LF of a sentence identical to the correct sentence is 100, therefore $LF_0$ is always 100. The decrease in LF of an ungrammatical sentence with $n$ errors from the correct parse is $LF_0 - LF_n = 100 - LF_n$, where a higher value indicates a larger divergence from the correct dependency parse.

## 4   Analysis

Our analysis will be broken down by different characteristics of ungrammatical sentences and quantifying their effect on the LF. Specifically, we will examine increasing numbers of errors in a sentence, the distance between errors, individual error types, and adding more errors to an already ungrammatical sentence.

### 4.1   Number of errors

The first step of our analysis is to verify our hypothesis that the absolute LF decrease ($LF_0 - LF_n$) increases as the number of errors in a sentence increases from $n = 1$ to $n = 4$. Pearson's correlation reveals a weak correlation between the LF decrease and number of errors (Figure 2). Since this analysis will be considering sentences generated with only a

[5]Available for download at https://github.com/cnap/ungrammatical-dependencies.

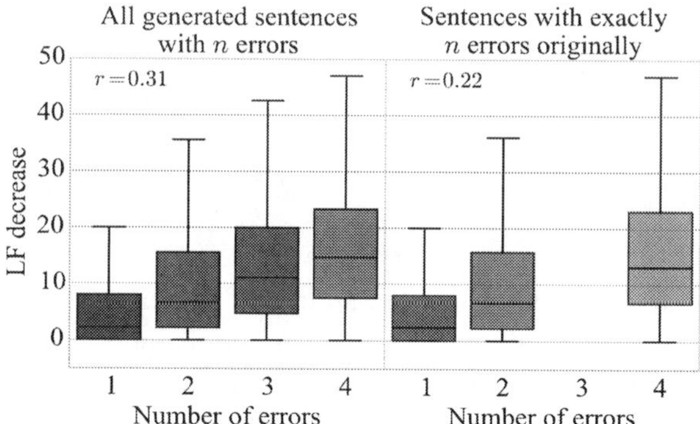

Figure 2:  Mean absolute decrease in LF by the number of errors in a sentence ($100 - LF_n$).

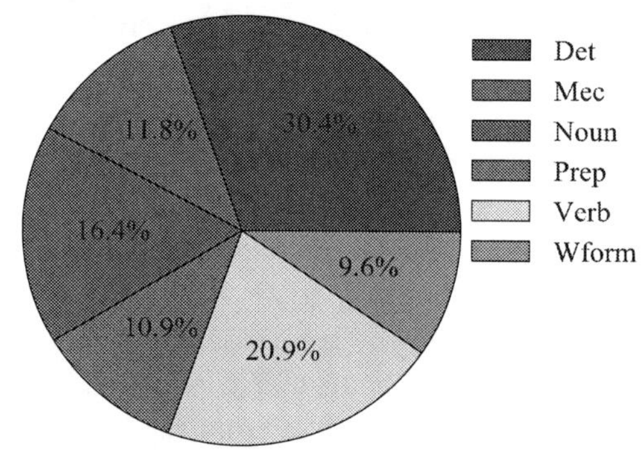


Figure 3:   The distribution of error types in sentences with one error. The distribution is virtually identical ($\pm 2$ percentage points) in sentences with 2–4 errors.

subset of errors from the original sentence, we will verify the validity of this data by comparing the LF decrease of the generated sentences to the LF decrease of sentences that originally had exactly $n$ errors. Since the LF decreases of the generated and original sentences are very similar, we presume that the generated sentences exhibit similar properties as the original sentences with the same number of errors. We further compared the distribution of sentences with each error type as the number of errors per sentence changes, and find that the distribution is fairly constant. The distribution of sentences with one error is shown in Figure 3. We will next investigate whether the LF decrease is due to interaction between errors or if there is an additive effect.

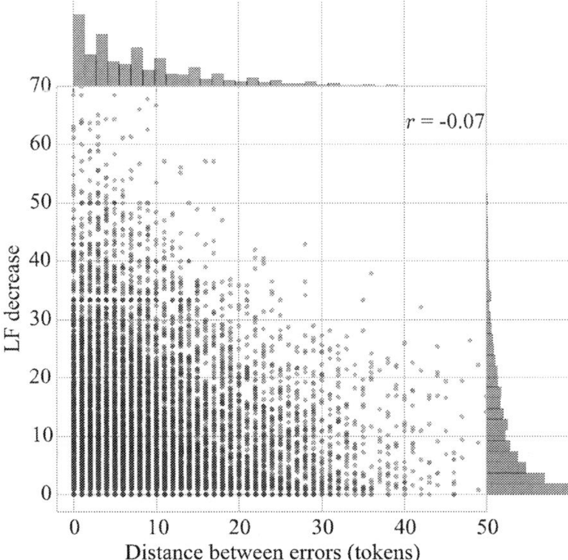


Figure 4: Distance between two errors and the decrease in LF.

## 4.2 Distance between errors

To determine whether the distance between errors is a factor in dependency performance, we took sentences with only two errors and counted the number of tokens between the errors (Figure 4). Surprisingly, there is no relationship between the distance separating errors and the dependency parse accuracy. We hypothesized that errors near each other would either interact and cause the parser to misinterpret more of the sentence, or conversely that they would disrupt the interpretation of only one clause and not greatly effect the LF. However, neither of these were evident based on the very weak negative correlation. For sentences with more than two errors, we calculated the mean, minimum, and maximum distances between all errors in each sentence, and found a weak to very weak negative correlation between those measures and the LF decrease ($-0.15 \leq r \leq -0.04$).

## 4.3 Error type and operation

Next, we considered specific error types and their operation—whether they were missing, unnecessary, or needed replacement. To isolate the impact of individual error types on the LF, we calculated the mean LF decrease ($100 - LF_1$) by error and operation over sentences with only one error (Figure 5).

The mean values by error type are shown in Figure 6, column 1.

Two trends are immediately visible: there is a clear difference between error types and, except for determiner errors, missing and unnecessary errors have a greater impact on the dependency parse than replacements. Nouns and prepositions needing replacement have the lowest impact on the LF, with $100 - LF_1 < 4$. This could be because the part of speech tag for these substitutions does not often change (or only change NN to NNS in the case of nouns), which would therefore not greatly affect a dependency parser's interpretation of the sentence, but this hypothesis needs to be verified in future work. A prepositional phrase and noun phrase would likely still be found headed by that word. Verb replacements exhibit more than twice the decrease in LF than nouns and prepositions. Unlike noun and preposition replacements, replacing a verb tends to elicit greater structural changes, since some verbs can be interpreted as nouns or past participles and gerunds could be interpreted as modifying nouns, etc. (Lee and Seneff, 2008).

Determiner errors also have a low impact on LF and there is practically no difference by the operation of the correction. This can be explained because determiners occur at the beginning of noun phrases, and so deleting, inserting, or replacing a determiner would typically affect one child of the noun phrase and not the overall structure. However, mechanical errors and missing or unnecessary prepositions have a great impact on the LF, with $LF_1$ at least $10\%$ lower than $LF_0$. Inserting or deleting these types of words could greatly alter the structure of a sentence. For example, inserting a missing preposition would introduce a new prepositional phrase and the subsequent noun phrase would attach to that phrase. Regarding *Mec* errors, inserting commas can drastically change the structure by breaking apart constituents, and removing commas can cause constituents to become siblings.

## 4.4 Adding errors to ungrammatical sentences

We have seen the mean LF decrease in sentences with one error, over different error types. Next, we examine what happens to the dependency parse when an error is added to a sentence that is already ungrammatical. We calculated the LF of sen-

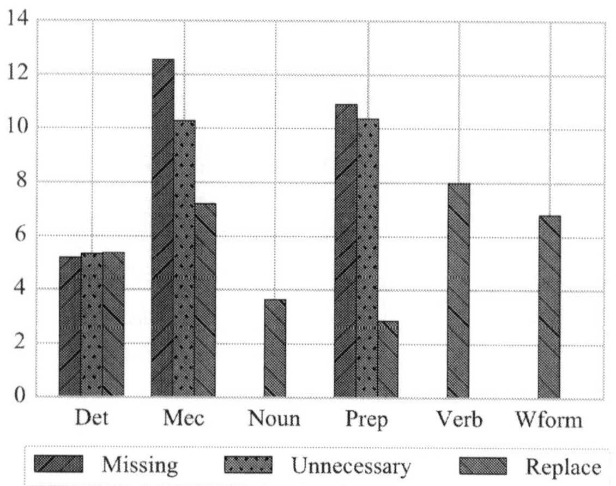

Figure 5: The mean decrease in LF ($100 - LF_1$) for sentences with one error, by error type.

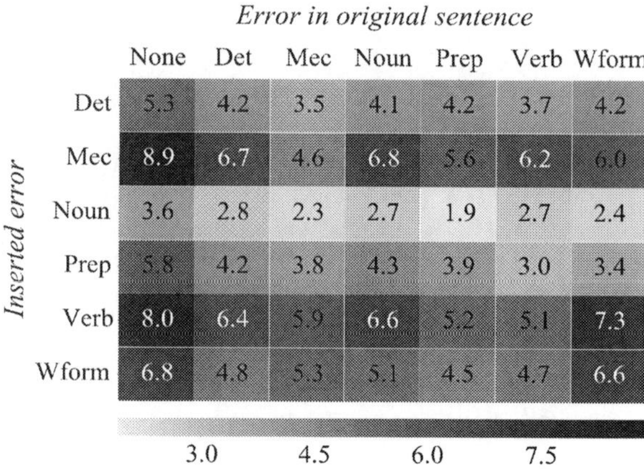


| | None | Det | Mec | Noun | Prep | Verb | Wform |
|---|---|---|---|---|---|---|---|
| Det | 5.3 | 4.2 | 3.5 | 4.1 | 4.2 | 3.7 | 4.2 |
| Mec | 8.9 | 6.7 | 4.6 | 6.8 | 5.6 | 6.2 | 6.0 |
| Noun | 3.6 | 2.8 | 2.3 | 2.7 | 1.9 | 2.7 | 2.4 |
| Prep | 5.8 | 4.2 | 3.8 | 4.3 | 3.9 | 3.0 | 3.4 |
| Verb | 8.0 | 6.4 | 5.9 | 6.6 | 5.2 | 5.1 | 7.3 |
| Wform | 6.8 | 4.8 | 5.3 | 5.1 | 4.5 | 4.7 | 6.6 |

Figure 6: Mean decrease in LF ($LF_1 - LF_2$) for sentences when introducing an error (row) into a sentence that already has an error of the type in the column. The *None* column contains the mean decrease when introducing a new error to a grammatical sentence ($100 - LF_1$).

tences with one error ($LF_1$), introduced a second error into that sentence, and calculated the decrease in LF ($LF_1 - LF_2$). We controlled for the types of errors both present in the original sentence and introduced to the sentence, not differentiating the operation of the error for ease of interpretation. The mean differences by error types are in Figure 6.

Each column indicates what type of error was present in the original sentence (or the *first* error), with *None* indicating the original sentence was grammatically correct and had no errors. Each row represents the type of error that was added to the sentence (the *second* error). Note that this does not indicate the left–right order of the errors. This analysis considers all combinations of errors: for example, given a sentence with two determiner errors $A$ and $B$, we calculate the LF decrease after inserting error $A$ into the sentence that already had error $B$ and vice versa.

Generally, with respect to the error type, the relative magnitude of change caused by adding the second error (column 2) is similar to adding that type of error to a sentence with no errors (column 1). However, introducing the second error always has a lower mean LF decrease than introducing the first error into a sentence, suggesting that each added error is less disruptive to the dependency parse as the number of errors increase.

To verify this, we added an error to sentences with 0 to 3 errors and calculated the LF change ($LF_n - LF_{n+1}$) each time a new error was introduced. Figure 7 shows the mean LF decrease after adding an error of a given type to a sentence that already had 0, 1, 2, or 3 errors.

Based on Figure 7, it appears that the LF decrease may converge for some error types, specifically determiner, preposition, verb, and noun errors. However, the LF decreases at a fairly constant rate for mechanical and word form errors, suggesting that ungrammatical sentences become increasingly uninterpretable as these types of errors are introduced. Further research is needed to make definitive claims about what happens as a sentence gets increasingly errorful.

## 5 Qualifying LF decrease

In the previous analysis, the range of LF decreases are from 1 to around 10, suggesting that approximately 1% to 10% of the dependency parse was changed due to errors. However, this begs the question of what a LF decrease of 1, 5, or 10 actually means for a pair of sentences. Is the ungrammatical sentence garbled after the LF decrease reaches a certain level? How different are the dependencies found in a sentence with a LF decrease of 1 versus 10? To illustrate these differences, we selected an example sentence and calculated the LF decrease

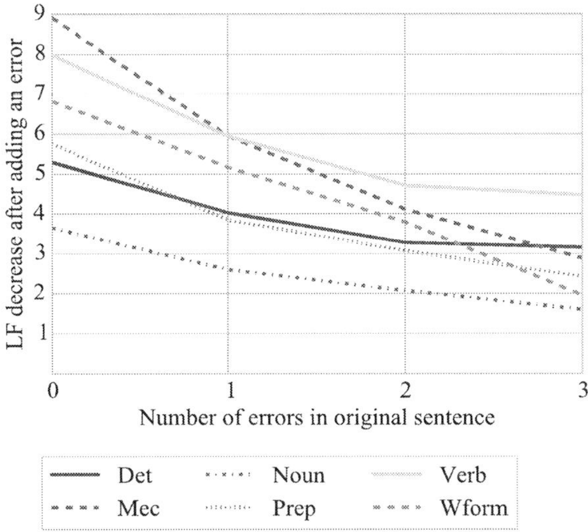

Figure 7: Mean decrease in LF ($LF_n - LF_{n+1}$) when an error of a given type is added to a sentence that already has $n$ errors.

and dependency graph as more errors were added (Table 2, Figure 8, and Figure 9).

Notice that the largest decrease in LF occurs after the first and second errors are introduced (10 and 13 points, respectively). The introductions of these errors result in structural changes of the graph, as does the fourth error, which results in a lesser LF decrease of 5. In contrast, the third error, a missing determiner, causes a lesser decrease of about 2, since the graph structure is not affected by this insertion.

Considering the LF decrease as the percent of a sentence that is changed, for a sentence with 26 tokens (the mean length of sentences in our dataset), a LF decrease of 5 corresponds to a change in 1.3 of the tokens, while a decrease of 10 corresponds to a change in 2.6 tokens. Lower LF decreases ($< 5$ or so) generally indicate the insertion or deletion of a token that does not affect the graph structure, or changing the label of a dependency relation. On the other hand, greater decreases likely reflect a structural change in the dependency graph of the ungrammatical sentence, which affects more relations than those containing the ungrammatical tokens.

## 6    Related work

There is a modest body of work focused on improving parser performance of ungrammatical sentences. Unlike our experiments, most previous work has used small (around 1,000 sentences) or artificially generated corpora of ungrammatical/grammatical sentence pairs.

The most closely related works compared the structure of constituent parses of ungrammatical to corrected sentences: with naturally occurring errors, Foster (2004) and Kaljahi et al. (2015) and evaluate parses of ungrammatical text based on the constituent parse and Geertzen et al. (2013) evaluate performance over dependencies. Cahill (2015) examines the parser performance using artificially generated errors, and Foster (2007) analyzes the parses of both natural and artificial errors. In Wagner and Foster (2009), the authors compared the parse probabilities of naturally occurring and artificially generated ungrammatical sentences to the probabilities of the corrected sentences. They found that the natural ungrammatical sentences had a lower reduction in parse probability than artificial sentences, suggesting that artificial errors are not interchangeable with spontaneous errors. This analysis suggests the importance of using naturally occurring errors, which is why we chose to generate sentences from the spontaneous NUCLE errors.

Several studies have attempted to improve the accuracy of parsing ungrammatical text. Some approaches include self-training (Foster et al., 2011; Cahill et al., 2014), retraining (Foster et al., 2008), and transforming the input and training text to be more similar (Foster, 2010). Other work with ungrammatical learner text includes Caines and Buttery (2014), which identifies the need to improve parsing of spoken learner English, and Tetreault et al. (2010), which analyzes the accuracy of prepositional phrase attachment in the presence of preposition errors.

## 7    Conclusion and future work

The performance of NLP tools over ungrammatical text is little understood. Given the expense of annotating a grammatical-error corpus, previous studies have used either small annotated corpora or generated artificial grammatical errors in clean text.

This study represents the first large-scale analysis of the effect of grammatical errors on a NLP task. We have used a large, annotated corpus of grammatical errors to generate more than 44,000 sentences with up to four errors in each sentence. The ungrammatical sentences contain an increasing number of naturally occurring errors, facilitating the comparison of parser performance as more errors are introduced to a sentence. This is the first step toward a larger goal of providing a confidence score of parser accuracy based on an estimate of how ungrammatical a text may be. While many of our findings may seem obvious, they have previously not been quantified on a large corpus of naturally occurring grammatical errors. In the future, these results should be verified over a selection of manually corrected dependency parses.

Future work includes predicting the LF decrease based on an estimate of the number and types of errors in a sentence. As yet, we have only measured change by the LF decrease over all dependency relations. The decrease can also be measured over individual dependency relations to get a clearer idea of which relations are affected by specific error types. We will also investigate the effect of grammatical errors on other NLP tasks.

We chose the NUCLE corpus because it is the largest annotated corpus of learner English (1.2 million tokens). However, this analysis is relies on the idiosyncrasies of this particular corpus, such as the typical sentence length and complexity. The essays were written by students at the National University of Singapore, who do not have a wide variety of native languages. The types and frequency of errors differ depending on the native language of the student (Rozovskaya and Roth, 2010), which may bias the analysis herein. The available corpora that contain a broader representation of native languages are much smaller than the NUCLE corpus: the Cambridge Learner Corpus–First Certificate in English has 420 thousand tokens (Yannakoudakis et al., 2011), and the corpus annotated by (Rozovskaya and Roth, 2010) contains only 63 thousand words.

One limitation to our method for generating ungrammatical sentences is that relatively few sentences are the source of ungrammatical sentences with four errors. Even though we drew sentences from a large corpus, only 570 sentences had at least four errors (of the types we were considering), compared to 14,500 sentences with at least one error. Future work examining the effect of multiple errors would need to consider a more diverse set of sentences with more instances of at least four errors, since there could be peculiarities or noise in the original annotations, which would be amplified in generated sentences.

## Acknowledgments

We would like to thank Martin Chodorow and Jennifer Foster for their valuable insight while developing this research, and Beata Beigman Klebanov, Brian Riordan, Su-Youn Yoon, and the BEA reviewers for their helpful feedback. This material is based upon work partially supported by the National Science Foundation Graduate Research Fellowship under Grant No. 1232825.

## References

Aoife Cahill, Binod Gyawali, and James Bruno. 2014. Self-training for parsing learner text. In *Proceedings of the First Joint Workshop on Statistical Parsing of Morphologically Rich Languages and Syntactic Analysis of Non-Canonical Languages*, pages 66–73, Dublin, Ireland, August. Dublin City University.

Aoife Cahill. 2015. Parsing learner text: To shoehorn or not to shoehorn. In *Proceedings of The 9th Linguistic Annotation Workshop*, pages 144–147, Denver, Colorado, USA, June. Association for Computational Linguistics.

Andrew Caines and Paula Buttery. 2014. The effect of disfluencies and learner errors on the parsing of spoken learner language. In *Proceedings of the First Joint Workshop on Statistical Parsing of Morphologically Rich Languages and Syntactic Analysis of Non-Canonical Languages*, pages 74–81, Dublin, Ireland, August. Dublin City University.

Daniel Dahlmeier, Hwee Tou Ng, and Siew Mei Wu. 2013. Building a large annotated corpus of learner english: The NUS Corpus of Learner English. In *Proceedings of the Eighth Workshop on Innovative Use of NLP for Building Educational Applications*, pages 22–31, Atlanta, Georgia, June. Association for Computational Linguistics.

Marie-Catherine De Marneffe, Timothy Dozat, Natalia Silveira, Katri Haverinen, Filip Ginter, Joakim Nivre, and Christopher D Manning. 2014. Universal Stanford dependencies: A cross-linguistic typology. In *Proceedings of Language Resources and Evaluation Conference (LREC)*, volume 14, pages 4585–4592.

Mariano Felice and Zheng Yuan. 2014. Generating artificial errors for grammatical error correction. In *Proceedings of the Student Research Workshop at the 14th*

| Num. errors | Inserted error type | LF decrease | Sentence |
|---|---|---|---|
| 0 | n/a | n/a | One of the factors that determines and shapes technological innovation the most is the country 's economic status . |
| 1 | Verb | 10.0 | One of the factors that ***determined*** and shapes technological innovation the most is the country 's economic status . |
| 2 | Mec | 13.1 | One of the factors that determined and shapes technological innovation the most is the ***country*** economic status . |
| 3 | Det | 1.9 | One of the factors that determined and shapes ***the*** technological innovation the most is the country economic status . |
| 4 | Verb | 5.0 | One of the factors that determined and ***shaped*** the technological innovation the most is the country economic status . |

Table 2: An example of a sentence with 4 errors added and the LF decrease ($\text{LF}_{n-1} - \text{LF}_n$) after adding each subsequent error to the previous sentence. Changed text is shown in bold italics.

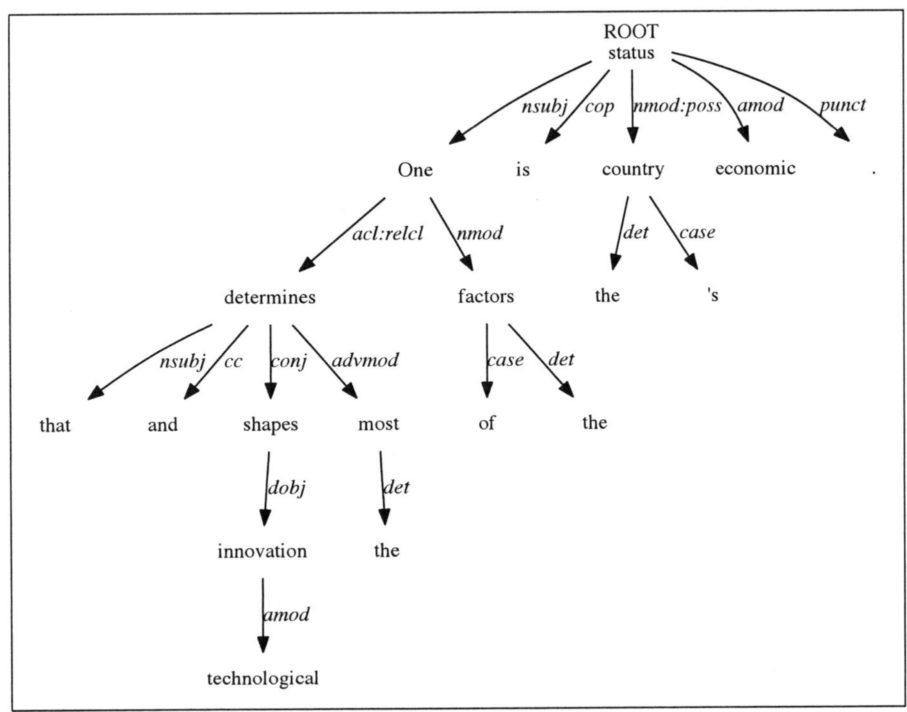

Figure 8: Dependency graph of the correct sentence in Table 2.

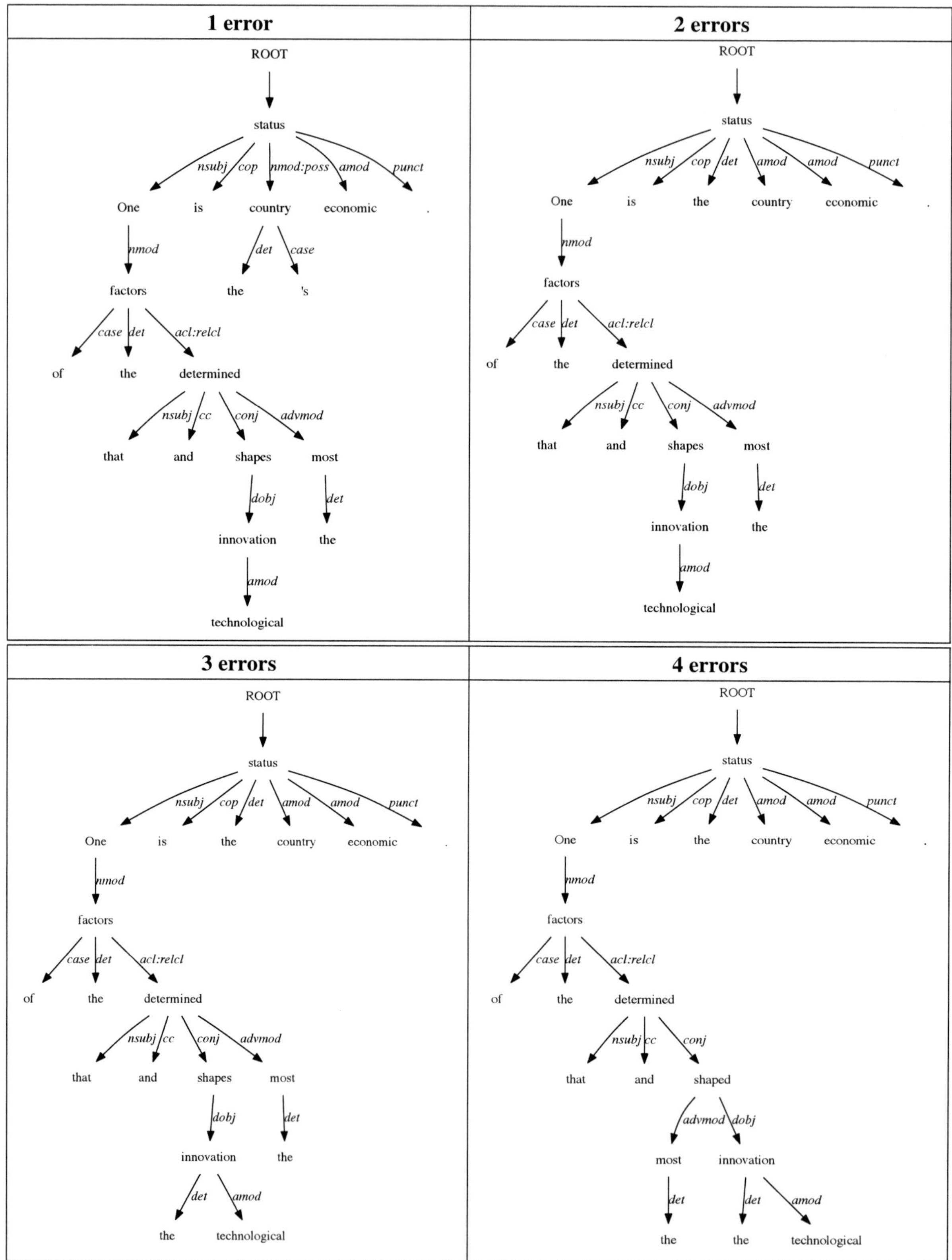

Figure 9: The dependency graphs of the sentence in Table 2 and Figure 8 after each error is introduced.

*Conference of the European Chapter of the Association for Computational Linguistics*, pages 116–126, Gothenburg, Sweden, April. Association for Computational Linguistics.

Jennifer Foster, Joachim Wagner, and Josef Van Genabith. 2008. Adapting a WSJ-trained parser to grammatically noisy text. In *Proceedings of the 46th Annual Meeting of the Association for Computational Linguistics on Human Language Technologies: Short Papers*, pages 221–224. Association for Computational Linguistics.

Jennifer Foster, Özlem Çetinolu, Joachim Wagner, and Josef van Genabith. 2011. Comparing the use of edited and unedited text in parser self-training. In *Proceedings of the 12th International Conference on Parsing Technologies*, pages 215–219, Dublin, Ireland, October. Association for Computational Linguistics.

Jennifer Foster. 2004. Parsing ungrammatical input: an evaluation procedure. In *Proceedings of Language Resources and Evaluation Conference (LREC)*.

Jennifer Foster. 2007. Treebanks gone bad. *International Journal of Document Analysis and Recognition (IJDAR)*, 10(3-4):129–145.

Jennifer Foster. 2010. "cba to check the spelling": Investigating parser performance on discussion forum posts. In *Human Language Technologies: The 2010 Annual Conference of the North American Chapter of the Association for Computational Linguistics*, pages 381–384, Los Angeles, California, June. Association for Computational Linguistics.

Jeroen Geertzen, Theodora Alexopoulou, and Anna Korhonen. 2013. Automatic linguistic annotation of large scale L2 databases: The EF-Cambridge Open Language Database (EFCAMDAT). In *Proceedings of the 31st Second Language Research Forum. Somerville, MA: Cascadilla Proceedings Project*.

Rasoul Kaljahi, Jennifer Foster, Johann Roturier, Corentin Ribeyre, Teresa Lynn, and Joseph Le Roux. 2015. Foreebank: Syntactic analysis of customer support forums. In *Conference on Empirical Methods in Natural Language Processing (EMNLP)*.

John Lee and Stephanie Seneff. 2008. Correcting misuse of verb forms. In *Proceedings of ACL-08: HLT*, pages 174–182, Columbus, Ohio, June. Association for Computational Linguistics.

Diane Nicholls. 2004. The Cambridge Learner Corpus: Error coding and analysis for lexicography and ELT. In *Proceedings of the Corpus Linguistics 2003 Conference*, pages 572–581.

Joakim Nivre, Johan Hall, and Jens Nilsson. 2004. Memory-based dependency parsing. In *HLT-NAACL 2004 Workshop: Eighth Conference on Computational Natural Language Learning (CoNLL-2004)*, pages

49–56, Boston, Massachusetts, USA, May 6–May 7. Association for Computational Linguistics.

Ines Rehbein and Josef van Genabith. 2007. Evaluating evaluation measures. In *Proceedings of the 16th Nordic Conference of Computational Linguistics (NODALIDA)*, pages 372–379.

Brian Roark, Mary Harper, Eugene Charniak, Bonnie Dorr, Mark Johnson, Jeremy G Kahn, Yang Liu, Mari Ostendorf, John Hale, Anna Krasnyanskaya, et al. 2006. SParseval: Evaluation metrics for parsing speech. In *Proceedings of Language Resources and Evaluation Conference (LREC)*.

Alla Rozovskaya and Dan Roth. 2010. Annotating ESL errors: Challenges and rewards. In *Proceedings of the NAACL HLT 2010 Fifth Workshop on Innovative Use of NLP for Building Educational Applications*, pages 28–36. Association for Computational Linguistics.

Joel Tetreault, Jennifer Foster, and Martin Chodorow. 2010. Using parse features for preposition selection and error detection. In *Proceedings of the 48th Annual Meeting of the Association of Computational Linguistics on Human Language Technologies: Short Papers*, pages 353–358, Uppsala, Sweden, July. Association for Computational Linguistics.

Reut Tsarfaty, Joakim Nivre, and Evelina Andersson. 2011. Evaluating dependency parsing: Robust and heuristics-free cross-annotation evaluation. In *Proceedings of the 2011 Conference on Empirical Methods in Natural Language Processing*, pages 385–396, Edinburgh, Scotland, UK., July. Association for Computational Linguistics.

Joachim Wagner and Jennifer Foster. 2009. The effect of correcting grammatical errors on parse probabilities. In *Proceedings of the 11th International Conference on Parsing Technologies*, pages 176–179. Association for Computational Linguistics.

Helen Yannakoudakis, Ted Briscoe, and Ben Medlock. 2011. A new dataset and method for automatically grading esol texts. In *Proceedings of the 49th Annual Meeting of the Association for Computational Linguistics: Human Language Technologies-Volume 1*, pages 180–189. Association for Computational Linguistics.

Yue Zhang and Stephen Clark. 2011. Syntactic processing using the generalized perceptron and beam search. *Computational Linguistics*, 37(1):105–151.

# Text Readability Assessment for Second Language Learners

**Menglin Xia** and **Ekaterina Kochmar** and **Ted Briscoe**
University of Cambridge
William Gates Building
Cambridge, CB3 0FD, UK
{mx223,ek358,ejb1}@cl.cam.ac.uk

## Abstract

This paper addresses the task of readability assessment for the texts aimed at second language (L2) learners. One of the major challenges in this task is the lack of significantly sized level-annotated data. For the present work, we collected a dataset of CEFR-graded texts tailored for learners of English as an L2 and investigated text readability assessment for both native and L2 learners. We applied a generalization method to adapt models trained on larger native corpora to estimate text readability for learners, and explored domain adaptation and self-learning techniques to make use of the native data to improve system performance on the limited L2 data. In our experiments, the best performing model for readability on learner texts achieves an accuracy of 0.797 and $PCC$ of 0.938.

## 1 Introduction

Developing reading ability is an essential part of language acquisition. However, finding proper reading materials for training language learners at a specific level of proficiency is a demanding and time-consuming task for English instructors as well as the readers themselves. To automate the process of reading material selection and the assessment of reading ability for non-native learners, a system that focuses on text readability analysis for L2 learners can be developed. Such a system enhances many pedagogical applications by supporting readers in their second language education.

Text readability, which has been formally defined as the sum of all elements in textual material that affect a reader's understanding, reading speed, and level of interest in the material (Dale and Chall, 1949), is influenced by multiple variables. These may include the style of writing, its format and organization, reader's background and interest as well as various contextual dimensions of the text, such as its lexical and syntactic complexity, level of conceptual familiarity, logical sophistication and so on.

The choice of the criteria to measure readability often depends upon the need and characteristics of the target readers. Most of the studies so far have evaluated text difficulty as judged by native speakers, despite the fact that text comprehensibility can be perceived very differently by L2 learners. In the case of L2 learners, due to the difference in the pace of language acquisition, the focus in readability measures often differs from that for native readers. For example, the grammatical aspects of readability usually contribute more to text comprehensibility for L2 learners than the conceptual cognition difficulty of the reading material (Heilman et al., 2007). A system that is tailored towards learner's perception of reading difficulty can produce more accurate estimation of text reading difficulty for non-native readers and thus better facilitate language learning.

One of the major challenges for a data-driven approach to text readability assessment for L2 learners is that there is not enough significantly sized, properly annotated data for this task. At the same time, text readability assessment in general has been previously studied by many researchers and there are a number of existing corpora aimed at native speakers that can be used. To address the problem, we compiled a collection of texts that are tailored for



*Proceedings of the 11th Workshop on Innovative Use of NLP for Building Educational Applications*, pages 12–22,
San Diego, California, June 16, 2016. ©2016 Association for Computational Linguistics

L2 learners' readability and looked at several approaches to make use of existing native data to estimate readability for L2 learners.

In sum, the contribution of our work is threefold. First, we develop a system that produces state-of-the-art estimation of text readability, exploit a range of readability measures and investigate their predictive power. Second, we focus on readability for L2 learners of English and present a level-graded dataset for non-native readability analysis. Third, we explore methods that help to make use of the existing native corpora to produce better estimation of readability when there is not enough data aimed at L2 learners. Specifically, we apply a generalization method to adapt models trained on native data to estimate text readability for learners, and explore domain adaptation and self-training techniques to improve system performance on the data aimed at L2 learners. To the best of our knowledge, these approaches have not been applied in readability experiments before. The best performing model in our experiments achieves an accuracy ($ACC$) of 0.797 and Pearson correlation coefficient ($PCC$) of 0.938.

## 2 Related Work

### 2.1 Automated Readability Assessment

Many previous studies on text readability assessment have used machine learning based approaches, which enable investigation of a broader set of linguistic features. Si and Callan (2001) and Collins-Thompson and Callan (2004) were among the early works on statistical readability assessment. They applied unigram language models and naïve Bayes classification to estimate the grade level of a given text. Experiments showed that the language modelling approach yields better results in terms of accuracy than the traditional readability formulae, such as the the Flesch-Kincaid score (Kincaid et al., 1975). Schwarm and Ostendorf (2005) extended this method to multiple language models. They combined traditional reading metrics with statistical language models as well as some basic parse tree features and then applied an SVM classifier. Heilman et al. (2007; 2008) expanded the feature set to include certain lexical and grammatical features extracted from parse trees while using a linear regression model to predict the grade level.

Pitler and Nenkova (2008) and Feng et al. (2010) were the first to introduce discourse-based features into the framework. The experiments with discourse features demonstrated promising results in predicting the readability level of text for both classification and regression approaches.

Kate et al. (2010) looked at both the effect of the feature choice and the machine learning framework choice on performance, and found that the improvement resulting from changing the framework is smaller than that from changing the features.

### 2.2 Readability Assessment for L2 Learners

Most previous work on readability assessment is directed at predicting reading difficulty for native readers. Several efforts in developing automated readability assessment that take L2 learners into consideration have emerged since 2007. Heilman et al. (2007) tested the effect of grammatical features for both L1 (first language) and L2 readers and found that grammatical features play a more important role in L2 readability prediction than in L1 readability prediction. Vajjala and Meurers (2012) combined measures from Second Language Acquisition research with traditional readability features and showed that the use of lexical and syntactic features for measuring language development of L2 learners has a substantial positive impact on readability classification. They observed that lexical features perform better than syntactic features, and that the traditional features have a good predictive power when used with other features. Shen et al. (2013) developed a language-independent approach to automatic text difficulty assessment for L2 learners. They treated the task of reading level assessment as a discriminative problem and applied a regression approach using a set of features that they claim to be language-independent. However, most of these studies have used textual data annotated with the readability levels for native speakers of English rather than L2 learners specifically.

While the majority of work on automated readability assessment are for English, studies on L2 readability in other languages, including French (François and Fairon, 2012), Portuguese (Branco et al., 2014), and Swedish (Pilán et al., 2015), are also emerging. These studies generally use textbook materials with readability levels assigned by publishers

| | Level1 | Level2 | Level3 | Level4 | Level5 |
|---|---|---|---|---|---|
| age group | 7-8 | 8-9 | 9-10 | 10-14 | 14-16 |
| original corpus | 629 | 801 | 814 | 1969 | 3500 |
| modified corpus | 529 | 767 | 801 | 1288 | 845 |

**Table 1:** Number of documents in the original and modified WeeBit corpus

| Exams | KET | PET | FCE | CAE | CPE |
|---|---|---|---|---|---|
| targeted level | A2 | B1 | B2 | C1 | C2 |
| # of docs | 64 | 60 | 71 | 67 | 69 |
| avg. len. of text | 14.75 | 19.48 | 38.07 | 45.76 | 39.97 |

**Table 2:** Statistics for the Cambridge English Exams data

or language instructors.

Overall, study of automatic readability analysis for L2 learners is still in its early stages, mainly due to the lack of available well-labelled data annotated with the readability levels for L2 learners.

## 3 Data

### 3.1 Native Data: the WeeBit Corpus

Among the existing publicly available corpora, the WeeBit corpus created by Vajjala and Meurers (2012) is one of the largest datasets for readability analysis. The WeeBit corpus is composed of articles targeted at readers of different age groups from two sources, the Weekly Reader magazine and the BBC-Bitesize website. Within the dataset, the Weekly Reader data consists of texts covering age-appropriate non-fictional content for four grade levels, corresponding to children of ages between 7-8, 8-9, 9-10 and 10-12 years old. The BBC-Bitesize website data is targeted at two grade levels, for ages between 11-14 and 14-16. The two datasets are merged to form the WeeBit corpus, with the targeted ages used to assign readability levels.

A copy of the original WeeBit corpus was obtained from the authors (Vajjala and Meurers, 2012). The texts are webpage documents stored in raw HTML format. We have identified that some texts contain broken sentences or extraneous content from the webpages, such as copyright declaration and links, that correlate with the target labels in a way which is likely to artificially boost performance on the task and would not generalize well to other datasets. To avoid that, we re-extracted texts from the raw HTML and discarded text documents that do not contain proper reading passages. Table 1 shows the distribution of texts in the modified dataset.

### 3.2 L2 Data: the Cambridge Exams dataset

Most work on readability assessment has been done on native corpora with age-specific reading levels (Schwarm and Ostendorf, 2005; Feng et al., 2010).

Such texts are aimed not at L2 learners but rather at native-speaking children of different ages. Therefore, the level annotation in such texts is arrived at using criteria different from those that are relevant for L2 readers. The lack of significantly sized L2 level-annotated data raises a problem for readability analysis aimed at L2 readers. To tackle this, we created a dataset with texts tailored for L2 learners' readability specifically.

We have collected a dataset composed of reading passages from the five main suite Cambridge English Exams (KET, PET, FCE, CAE, CPE).[1] These five exams are targeted at learners at A2–C2 levels of the Common European Framework of Reference (CEFR) (Council of Europe, 2001).[2] The documents are harvested from all the tasks in the past reading papers for each of the exams. The Cambridge English Exams are designed for L2 learners specifically and the A2–C2 levels assigned to each reading paper can be treated as the level of reading difficulty of the documents for the L2 learners.[3] Table 2 shows the number of documents at each CEFR level across the dataset. The data is available at `http://www.cl.cam.ac.uk/~mx223/cedata.html`.

Experimenting on the language testing data annotated with the L2 learner readability levels is one of the contributions of this research. Most previous work on readability assessment for English have relied on the data annotated with readability levels aimed at native speakers. In this work, we use language testing data with the levels assigned based on L2 learner levels, and we believe that this level annotation is more appropriate for text readability assessment for L2 learners than using texts with the level annotation aimed at native speakers.

---

[1] `http://www.cambridgeenglish.org`

[2] The CEFR determines foreign language proficiency at six levels in increasing order: A1 and A2, B1 and B2, C1 and C2.

[3] We are aware that the type of the task may also have an effect on the reading difficulty of the texts, but this is ignored at this stage.

## 4 Readability Measures

This section describes the range of linguistic features explored and the machine learning framework applied to the WeeBit data that constitute a general readability assessment system. The set of features used in our experiments is an extension to those used in previous work (Feng et al., 2010; Pitler and Nenkova, 2008; Vajjala and Meurers, 2012; Vajjala and Meurers, 2014), and their predictive power for reading difficulty assessment is investigated in our experiments. We have extended the feature set with the EVP-based features, GR-based complexity measures and the combination of language modeling features that have not been applied to readability assessment before.

### 4.1 Features

**Traditional Features** The traditional features are easy-to-compute representations of superficial aspects of text. The metrics that are considered include: the number of sentences per text, average and maximum number of words per sentence, average number of characters per word, and average number of syllables per word. Two popular readability formulas are also included: the Flesch-Kincaid score (Kincaid et al., 1975) and the Coleman-Liau readability formula (Coleman and Liau, 1975).

**Lexico-semantic Features** Vocabulary knowledge is one of the most important aspects of reading comprehension (Collins-Thompson, 2014). Lexico-semantic features provide information about the difficulty or familiarity of vocabulary in the text.

A widely used lexical measure is the *type-token ratio* (TTR), which is the ratio of the number of unique word tokens (referred to as types) to the total number of word tokens in a text. However, the conventional TTR is influenced by the length of the text. *Root TTR* and *Corrected TTR*, which take the logarithm and square root of the text length instead of the direct word count as denominator, can produce a more unbiased representation and are included in the experiment.

Part of speech (POS) based lexical variation and lexical density measures (Lu, 2011) are also examined. *Lexical variation* is defined as the type-token ratio of lexical items such as nouns, adjectives, verbs, adverbs and prepositions. *Lexical density* is defined as the proportion of the five classes of lexical items in all word tokens. The percentage of content words (nouns, verbs, adjectives and adverbs) and function words (all the remaining POS types) are two other indicators of lexical density.

Vajjala and Meurers (2012; 2014) reported in their readability classification experiment that the proportion of words in the text that are found in the Academic Word List is one of the most predictive measures among all the lexical features they considered. The Academic Word List (Coxhead, 2000) is comprised of words that frequently occur across all topic ranges in an academic text corpus. The *proportion of academic vocabulary words* in the text can be viewed as another measure of lexical complexity.

A similar but more refined approach to estimate lexical complexity is based on the use of the *English Vocabulary Profile* (EVP).[4] The EVP is an online vocabulary resource that contains information about which words and phrases are acquired by learners at each CEFR level. It is collected from the Cambridge Learner Corpus (CLC), a collection of examination scripts written by learners from all over the world (Capel, 2012). It provides a more fine-grained lexical complexity measure that captures the relative difficulty of each word by assigning the word difficulty to one of the six CEFR levels. Additionally, the EVP indicates the word difficulty for L2 learners rather than native speakers, which makes it more informative in non-native readability analysis. In our experiments, the proportion of words at each CEFR level is calculated and added to the feature set.

**Parse Tree Syntactic Features** A number of *syntactic measures* based on the RASP parser output (Briscoe et al., 2006) are used to describe the grammatical complexity of text, including average parse tree depth, and average number of noun, verb, adjective, adverb, prepositional phrases and clauses per sentence.

*Grammatical relations* (GR) between constituents in a sentence may also affect the judgement of syntactic difficulty. Yannakoudakis (2013) applied 24 GR-based complexity measures in essay scoring and showed good results. These complexity measures capture the grammatical sophistication of the text through the representation of the distance be-

---

[4]http://www.englishprofile.org/

tween the sentence constituents. For instance, these measures calculate the longest/average distance in the GR sets generated by the parser and the average/maximum number of GRs per sentence. A set of 24 GR-based measures used by Yannakoudakis (2013) are generated by RASP for each sentence. We take the average of these measures across the text to incorporate the GR-related aspect of its syntactic difficulty.

Other types of complexity measures that are derived from the parser output include: *cost metric*, which is the total number of parsing actions performed for generating the parse tree; *ambiguity of the parse*, and so on. A total number of 114 non-GR based complexity measures are extracted. These complexity measures are averaged across the text and used to model finer details of the syntactic difficulty of the text.

**Language Modeling Features** Statistical language modeling (LM) provides information about distribution of word usage in the text and is in fact another way to describe the lexical dimension of readability. To avoid over-fitting to the WeeBit data, two types of language modeling based features are extracted using the SRILM toolkit (Stolcke, 2002): (1) *word token n-gram models*, with $n$ ranging from 1 to 5, trained on the British National Corpus (BNC), and (2) *POS n-grams*, with $n$ ranging from 1 to 5, trained on the five levels in the WeeBit corpus itself. The LMs are used to score the text with log-likelihood and perplexity.

**Discourse-based Features** Discourse features measure the cohesion and coherence of the text. Three types of discourse-based features are used.

**(1) Entity density features**

Previous work by Feng et al. (2009; 2010) has shown that entity density is strongly associated with text comprehension. An entity set is a union of named entities and general nouns (including nouns and proper nouns) contained in a text, with overlapping general nouns removed. Based on this, *9 entity density features*, including the total number of all/unique entities per document, the average number of all/unique entities per sentence, percentage of named entities per sentence/document, percentage of named entities in all entities, percentage of overlapping nouns removed, and percentage of unique named entities in all unique entities, are calculated.

**(2) Lexical chain features**

Lexical chains model the semantic relations among entities throughout the text. The lexical chaining algorithm developed by Galley and McKeown (2003) is implemented. The semantically related words for the nouns in the text, including synonyms, hypernyms, and hyponyms, are extracted from the WordNet (Miller, 1995). Then for each pair of the nouns in the text, we check whether they are semantically related. Finally, lexical chains are built by linking semantically related nouns in text. A set of *7 lexical chain-based* features are computed, including total number of lexical chains per document, total number of lexical chains normalized with text length, average/maximum lexical chain length, average/maximum lexical chain span, and the number of lexical chains that span more than half of the document.[5]

**(3) Entity grid features**

Another entity-based approach to measure text coherence is the entity grid model introduced by Barzilay and Lapata (2008). They represented each text by an entity grid, which is a two-dimensional array that captures the distribution of discourse entities across text sentences. Each grid cell contains the grammatical role of a particular entity in the specified sentence: whether it is a subject (S), object (O), neither a subject nor an object (X), or absent from the sentence (-). A local entity transition is defined as the transition of the grammatical role of an entity from one sentence to the following sentence. In our experiments, we used the Brown Coreference Toolkit v1.0 (Eisner and Charniak, 2011) to generate the entity grid for the documents. The *probabilities of the 16 types* of local entity transition patterns are calculated to represent the coherence of the text.

## 4.2 Implementation and Evaluation

In our experiments, we cast readability assessment as a supervised machine learning problem. In particular, a pairwise ranking approach is adopted and compared with a classification method. We believe that the reading difficulty of text is a continuous rather than discrete variable. Text difficulty within a level can also vary. Instead of assigning an abso-

---

[5]The *length* of a chain is the number of entities contained in the chain. The *span* of a chain is the distance between the indexes of the first and the last entities in the chain.

| feature set | Classification | | Ranking | |
|---|---|---|---|---|
| | ACC | PCC | pairwise ACC | PCC |
| traditional | 0.586 | 0.770 | 0.862 | 0.704 |
| lexical | 0.578 | 0.726 | 0.863 | 0.743 |
| syntactic | 0.599 | 0.731 | 0.824 | 0.692 |
| LM | 0.714 | 0.848 | 0.872 | 0.769 |
| discourse | 0.563 | 0.688 | 0.848 | 0.659 |
| all combined | **0.803** | **0.900** | **0.924** | **0.848** |

**Table 3:** Classification and ranking results on the WeeBit corpus with feature sets grouped by their type

lute level to the text, treating readability assessment as a ranking problem allows prediction of the relative difficulty of pairs of documents, which captures the gradual nature of readability better. Because of this, we hypothesize that the ranking model can generalize better to unseen texts and texts with different level annotation.

Support vector machines (SVM) have been used in the past for readability assessment by many researchers and have consistently yielded better results when compared to other statistical models for the task (Kate et al., 2010). We use the LIBSVM toolkit (Chang and Lin, 2011) to implement both multiclass classification and pairwise ranking. Five-fold cross validation is used for evaluation. We report two popular performance metrics, accuracy ($ACC$) and Pearson correlation coefficient ($PCC$), and use pairwise accuracy to evaluate ranking models. Pairwise accuracy is defined as the percentage of instance pairs that the model ranked correctly. It should be noted that accuracy and pairwise accuracy are not directly comparable. Thus, $PCC$ is introduced to compare the results of the classification and the ranking models.

### 4.3   Results

In predicting the text reading difficulty on the WeeBit data, the best result is achieved with a combination of all features and a classification model, with $ACC$=0.803 and $PCC$=0.900. We performed ablation tests and found that all feature sets have contributed to the overall model performance. Although there have been readability assessment studies on similar datasets, the results obtained in our experiments are not directly comparable to those. One of the major reasons is the modifications that we have made to the corpus (as discussed in Sec-

tion 3.1). Vajjala and Meurers (2012) reported that a multilayer perceptron classifier using three traditional metrics alone yielded an accuracy of 70.3% on their version of the WeeBit corpus. Their final system achieved a classification accuracy of 93.3% on the five-class corpus. Nonetheless, the best system in our experiments yields results competitive to most existing studies. For reference, Feng et al. (2010) reported an accuracy of 74.01% using a combination of discourse, lexical and syntactic features for readability classification on their Weekly Reader Corpus and an accuracy of 63.18% when using all feature sets described in Schwarm et al. (2005).

Comparing the classification and the ranking models, we note that the results of the two models vary across feature sets and none of the two models is consistently better than the other. When all features are combined, the classification model outperforms the ranking one. It suggests that a ranking model is not necessarily the best model in predicting readability overall when trained and tested on the same dataset.

## 5   Readability Assessment on L2 Data

So far we have studied the effect of various readability measures on the task of readability assessment and built two different types of models to predict text difficulty. However, the WeeBit corpus consists of texts aimed at native speakers of different ages rather than at L2 readers. Although there are certain similarities concerning reading comprehension between these two groups, the perceived difficulty of texts can be very different due to the difference in the pace and stages of language acquisition. Since the goal of our research is to automatically detect readability levels for language learners, it would be more helpful to work with data that are directly annotated with reading difficulty for L2 learners.

Ideally, it would be good to train a model directly on text annotated with L2 levels and then use this model to estimate readability for the new texts. However, the Cambridge Exams data we have compiled is relatively small, and the model trained on it will likely not generalize well. Therefore, we examined several approaches to make use of the WeeBit corpus for readability assessment on the L2 data.

| | classification | | ranking | |
|---|---|---|---|---|
| | ACC | PCC | pairwise ACC | PCC |
| native data | 0.803 | 0.900 | 0.924 | 0.848 |
| L2 data | 0.233 | 0.730 | 0.913 | 0.880 |

**Table 4:** Generalization results of the classification and ranking models trained on native data applied to language testing data

| Levels | 1 | 2 | 3 | 4 | 5 |
|---|---|---|---|---|---|
| A2 | 4 | 0 | 55 | 4 | 1 |
| B1 | 0 | 0 | 24 | 6 | 30 |
| B2 | 0 | 1 | 1 | 4 | 65 |
| C1 | 0 | 0 | 0 | 3 | 64 |
| C2 | 0 | 0 | 0 | 0 | 69 |

**Table 5:** Confusion matrix of the classification model on the language testing data

## 5.1 Generalization Experiment

First, we tested the generalization ability of the classification and ranking models trained on the WeeBit corpus on the Cambridge Exams data to see if it is possible to directly apply the models trained on native data to L2 data. Table 4 reports the results.

In the case of the multi-class classification model, the accuracy dropped greatly when the model is applied to the L2 dataset, while the correlation remained relatively high. Looking at the confusion matrix of the classifier's predictions on the L2 data (see Table 5), we notice that most of the documents in the L2 data are classified into the higher levels of WeeBit by the model. This is because, on average, the Cambridge Exams texts are more difficult than the WeeBit corpus ones which are generally targeted at children of young ages. Thus, the mismatch between the targeted levels has led to poor generalization of the classification model.

In contrast, for the ranking model, both evaluation measures are relatively unharmed when the model is applied to the L2 data. It shows that, when generalizing to an unseen dataset, the estimation produced by the ranking model is able to maintain a high pairwise accuracy and correlation with the ground truth. We believe that this is because the ranking model does not try to band the documents into one of the levels on a different basis of difficulty annotation. Instead, pairwise ranking captures the relative reading difficulty of the documents, and therefore the resulting ranked positions of the documents are closer to the ground truth compared to the classification model.

## 5.2 Mapping Ranking Scores to CEFR Levels

From the generalization experiment we can conclude that ranking is more accurate in predicting the CEFR levels of unseen learner texts than classification. Therefore, it is more appropriate to make use of the more informative ranking scores produced by the ranking model to learn a function that bands the scores into CEFR levels.

In learning the mapping function, we adopted a five-fold cross-validation approach. We split the Cambridge Exams dataset into five cross validation folds, with approximately equal number of documents at each level in each fold. A mapping function that converts ranking scores into CEFR levels is learnt from training folds and then tested on the validation fold in each run. The final results are averaged across the runs.

We compared three groups of methods to learn the mapping function.

**(1) Regression and rounding**: A regression function is learnt from the ranking scores and the ground truth labels on the training part of the dataset and then applied to the validation part. The mapped CEFR prediction is then rounded to its closest integer and clamped to range $[1, 5]$. Both linear regression and polynomial regression models are considered. The intuition behind using polynomial functions instead of a simple linear function for mapping is that the correlation of ranking scores and CEFR levels is not necessarily linear so a non-linear function might be more suitable for this task.

**(2) Learning the cut-off boundary**: We learn a separation boundary that bands the ranking scores to levels by maximizing the accuracy of such separation. For instance, we consider the ranked documents as a list with descending readability, with their ranking scores following the same order. If we could find a suitable cut-off boundary between each two adjacent levels in the list, then every document above the boundary would fall into the higher level, and all documents below the boundary into the lower level. In this way, the ranked documents are banded into five levels with four separation boundaries learnt.

**(3) Classification on the ranking scores**: The task can also be addressed as a classification problem. The ranking scores can be considered as a sin-

| Mapping functions | ACC | PCC |
|---|---|---|
| linear regression | 0.541 | 0.587 |
| polynomial regression | 0.586 | **0.873** |
| cut-off boundary | 0.562 | 0.872 |
| logistic regression | 0.610 | 0.862 |
| linear SVM | **0.622** | 0.864 |

**Table 6:** Results of mapping ranking scores to CEFR levels

|  | pairwise ACC | PCC |
|---|---|---|
| EasyAdapt | 0.933 | 0.905 |
| native data only | 0.913 | 0.880 |
| L2 data only | 0.943 | 0.913 |

**Table 7:** Results of domain adaptation from native to language testing data

gle dimensional feature and CEFR levels as the target value. Here, two approaches are adopted and compared, logistic regression and a linear SVM. As a matter of fact, the SVM approach can be considered as a variation of learning a separation boundary, as it tries to find an optimal decision boundary between the classes.

Table 6 shows the results of the three mapping methods. Among the three approaches for mapping ranking scores to CEFR levels (regression-based, separation boundary-based, and classification-based), the classification ones showed better results than the others in terms of accuracy. Though not as high in accuracy as the SVM, a polynomial mapping function[6] also yielded very good results in terms of $PCC$. Compared to the other two methods, the separation boundary-based approach performs better than a linear regression function but fails to match the polynomial regression and classification-based methods. Nonetheless, all three approaches considerably outperformed the naive generalization of the classification model from the WeeBit corpus to the Cambridge Exams data. These improvements are statistically significant at $p<0.05$ level.[7]

### 5.3 Domain Adaptation from Native to L2 Data

Another way to make use of the native data is to treat the task as a domain adaptation problem, where the WeeBit corpus is taken as the source domain, and the L2 data as the target domain. The idea behind this is to use out-of-domain training data to boost the performance on limited in-domain data.

EasyAdapt (Daumé III, 2007) is one of the best performing domain adaptation algorithms. It has previously been applied to essay scoring and showed

good results (Phandi et al., 2015). In a two domain case, EasyAdapt expands the input feature space from $\mathbb{R}^F$ to $\mathbb{R}^{3F}$, and then applies two mapping functions $\Phi^S(\mathbf{x}) = \langle \mathbf{x}, \mathbf{x}, \mathbf{0} \rangle$ and $\Phi^T(\mathbf{x}) = \langle \mathbf{x}, \mathbf{0}, \mathbf{x} \rangle$ on source domain data and target domain data input vectors respectively. Here, $\mathbf{0} = \langle 0, ...0 \rangle \in \mathbb{R}^F$ is the zero vector. In this manner, the instance feature vectors from the WeeBit corpus and Cambridge Exams datases are augmented to three times their original dimensionality. The augmented feature space captures both general and domain specific information and is thus capable of generalizing source domain knowledge to facilitate estimation on the target domain. As there is a mismatch between the levels on native and L2 data, the pairwise ranking algorithm needs to be adapted to ensure that the preference pairs are only created from the same domain. A five-fold cross-validation is used as in previous experiments.

Table 7 shows the results of applying EasyAdapt with the ranking model. For comparison, we also present the results obtained when we apply the model trained on the native data to the L2 data directly, and the results obtained when we train the ranking model on the L2 data only. We can see that ranking with EasyAdapt outperforms the naive generalization approach significantly ($p<0.05$), but it does not beat the results obtained when training a model on L2 data directly.

After applying the ranking model with EasyAdapt, the ranking scores can be converted to CEFR levels using the same methods as described in Section 5.2. The best mapped CEFR estimation is achieved with a linear SVM classifier on the ranking score, reaching an $ACC$ of 0.707 and $PCC$ of 0.899. Compared to the naive generalization of the classification model from native to L2 data, the mapped estimation is less influenced by the mismatch between difficulty levels in the two domains (see Table 8).

---

[6]A 4th order polynomial function is adopted because it yields better results compared to other orders.

[7]Throughout this paper, we test significance using $t$-test for $ACC$ and Williams' test (Williams, 1959) for $PCC$.

| Levels | 1 | 2 | 3 | 4 | 5 |
|---|---|---|---|---|---|
| A2 | 11 | 3 | 0 | 0 | 0 |
| B1 | 2 | 9 | 0 | 1 | 0 |
| B2 | 0 | 0 | 13 | 0 | 2 |
| C1 | 0 | 0 | 2 | 9 | 2 |
| C2 | 0 | 0 | 0 | 4 | 10 |

**Table 8:** Confusion matrix of the mapped estimation after EasyAdapt application on one of the cross-validation folds

| Type | ACC | PCC |
|---|---|---|
| L2 data only | 0.785 | 0.924 |
| self-training | 0.797 | 0.938 |

**Table 9:** Results of self-training

## 5.4 Using Self-training to Enhance the Classification Model

In addition to the domain adaptation, we experimented with self-training to boost the performance on the limited L2 data with the native data. To the best of our knowledge, neither of the approaches has been applied to readability assessment before.

Self-training is a commonly used semi-supervised machine learning algorithm that aims to use the large amount of unlabelled data to help build a better classifier on a small amount of labeled data (Zhu, 2005). When using native data to boost model performance on L2 data with self-training, the L2 data is regarded as labeled instances, and the native data as unlabeled ones. A model is trained on the L2 data and then used to score the native data. The most confident $K$ instances as well as their labels are added to the training set. Then the model is re-trained and the procedure is repeated. A five-fold cross-validation is used in evaluation as before.

We have experimented with a grid search on $K$'s and the number of iterations, and found out that whatever the choice of the parameters is, the model performance degrades with self-training when the unlabeled instances are added blindly to all levels of the L2 dataset. Taking into account the mismatch in the difficulty levels between the native and L2 texts, we adapted the algorithm to add the unlabeled data only to the lower three levels of the L2 dataset. The best result is achieved with $K=10$ and 9 iterations, with 270 texts added in total (as shown in Table 9). It seems reasonable to compare the results of this approach to those obtained with a model that is trained directly on the L2 data. Hence, we include the results of this model in Table 9 for comparison.

The results show that self-training can significantly ($p<0.05$) help estimating readability for L2 texts by including a certain amount of unlabeled data (in this case, the native data) in training. However, the range of the reading difficulty covered by the unlabeled data may influence the model performance.

## 6 Conclusions and Future Work

We investigated text readability assessment for both native and L2 learners. We collected a dataset with text tailored for language learners' readability and explored methods to adapt models trained on larger existing native corpora in estimating text reading difficulty for learners. In particular, we developed a system that achieves state-of-the-art performance in readability estimation, with $ACC=0.803$ and $PCC=0.900$ on native data, and $ACC=0.785$ and $PCC=0.924$ on L2 data, using a linear SVM. We compared a ranking model against the classification model for the task and showed that although a ranking model does not necessarily outperform a classification one in readability assessment on the same data, it is more accurate when generalizing to an unseen dataset. Following this, we showed that, by applying a ranking model and then learning a mapping function, the model trained on the native data can be applied to estimate the CEFR levels of unseen text effectively. This model achieves an accuracy of $0.622$ and $PCC$ of $0.864$, and considerably outperforms the naive generalization of the classification model, which achieves an accuracy of $0.233$ and $PCC$ of $0.730$.

In addition, we experimented with domain adaptation and self-training approaches to make use of the more plentiful native data to produce better estimation of readability when the L2 data is limited. When treating the native data as a source domain and L2 data as a target domain, applying the EasyAdapt algorithm for ranking achieves an accuracy of $0.707$ and $PCC=0.899$. The best result is achieved by using self-training to include native data as unlabelled data in training the classification model, with $ACC=0.797$ and $PCC=0.938$.

Future work will focus on the improvement of readability assessment framework for L2 learners and the identification of the optimal feature set that can generalize well to unseen text.

## Acknowledgements

We thank Cambridge Assessment for their assistance in the collection of the language testing data. We would like to express our gratitude to Sowmya Vajjala and Detmar Meurers for sharing the WeeBit corpus with us. We are also grateful to the reviewers for their useful comments.

## References

Regina Barzilay and Mirella Lapata. 2008. Modeling local coherence: An entity-based approach. *Computational Linguistics*, 34(1):1–34.

António Branco, Jose Rodrigues, Francois Costa, Jaime Silva, and Richard Vaz. 2014. Assessing automatic text classification for interactive language learning. In *Information Society (i-Society), 2014 International Conference on*, pages 70–78.

Ted Briscoe, John Carroll, and Rebecca Watson. 2006. The second release of the RASP system. In *Proceedings of the COLING/ACL on Interactive presentation sessions*, pages 77–80.

Annette Capel. 2012. Completing the English Vocabulary Profile: C1 and C2 vocabulary. *English Profile Journal*, 3(e1).

Chih-Chung Chang and Chih-Jen Lin. 2011. LIBSVM: a library for support vector machines. *ACM Transactions on Intelligent Systems and Technology (TIST)*, 2(3):27.

Meri Coleman and Ta Lin Liau. 1975. A computer readability formula designed for machine scoring. *Journal of Applied Psychology*, 60(2):283–284.

Kevyn Collins-Thompson and James Callan. 2004. A Language Modeling Approach to Predicting Reading Difficulty. In *Proceedings of North American Chapter of the Association for Computational Linguistics: Human Language Technologies*, pages 193–200.

Kevyn Collins-Thompson. 2014. Computational assessment of text readability: A survey of current and future research. *ITL - International Journal of Applied Linguistics*, 165(2):97–135.

Council of Europe. 2001. *Common European Framework of Reference for Languages: Learning, Teaching, Assessment*. Cambridge University Press.

Averil Coxhead. 2000. A new academic word list. *TESOL Quarterly*, pages 213–238.

Edgar Dale and Jeanne S. Chall. 1949. The concept of readability. *Elementary English*, 26(1):19–26.

Hal Daumé III. 2007. Frustratingly easy domain adaptation. In *Proceedings of the 45th Annual Meeting of the Association of Computational Linguistics*, pages 256–263.

Micha Eisner and Eugene Charniak. 2011. Extending the entity grid with entity-specific features. In *Proceedings of the 49th Annual Meeting of the Association for Computational Linguistics: Human Language Technologies: short papers-Volume 2*, pages 125–129.

Lijun Feng, Noémie Elhadad, and Matt Huenerfauth. 2009. Cognitively motivated features for readability assessment. In *Proceedings of the 12th Conference of the European Chapter of the Association for Computational Linguistics*, pages 229–237.

Lijun Feng, Martin Jansche, Matt Huenerfauth, and Noémie Elhadad. 2010. A comparison of features for automatic readability assessment. In *Proceedings of the 23rd International Conference on Computational Linguistics: Posters*, pages 276–284.

Thomas François and Cédrick Fairon. 2012. An AI readability formula for French as a foreign language. In *Proceedings of the 2012 Joint Conference on Empirical Methods in Natural Language Processing and Computational Natural Language Learning*, pages 466–477.

Michel Galley and Kathleen McKeown. 2003. Improving word sense disambiguation in lexical chaining. In *International Joint Conference on Artificial Intelligence*, volume 3, pages 1486–1488.

Michael Heilman, Kevyn Collins-Thompson, Jamie Callan, and Maxine Eskenazi. 2007. Combining lexical and grammatical features to improve readability measures for first and second language texts. In *Proceedings of North American Chapter of the Association for Computational Linguistics: Human Language Technologies*, pages 460–467.

Michael Heilman, Kevyn Collins-Thompson, and Maxine Eskenazi. 2008. An analysis of statistical models and features for reading difficulty prediction. In *Proceedings of the Third Workshop on Innovative Use of NLP for Building Educational Applications*, pages 71–79.

Rohit J. Kate, Xiaoqiang Luo, Siddharth Patwardhan, Martin Franz, Radu Florian, Raymond J. Mooney, Salim Roukos, and Chris Welty. 2010. Learning to predict readability using diverse linguistic features. In *Proceedings of the 23rd International Conference on Computational Linguistics*, pages 546–554.

J. Peter Kincaid, Robert P. Fishburne Jr., Richard L. Rogers, and Brad S. Chissom. 1975. Derivation of new readability formulas (Automated Readability Index, Fog Count and Flesch Reading Ease Formula) for Navy enlisted personnel. Technical report, DTIC Document.

Xiaofei Lu. 2011. A Corpus-Based Evaluation of Syntactic Complexity Measures as Indices of College-Level ESL Writers' Language Development. *TESOL Quarterly*, pages 36–62.

George A Miller. 1995. WordNet: a lexical database for English. *Communications of the ACM*, 38(11):39–41.

Peter Phandi, Kian Ming A. Chai, and Hwee Tou Ng. 2015. Flexible Domain Adaptation for Automated Essay Scoring Using Correlated Linear Regression. In *Proceedings of the 2015 Conference on Empirical Methods in Natural Language Processing*, pages 431–439.

Ildikó Pilán, Sowmya Vajjala, and Elena Volodina. 2015. A readable read: Automatic Assessment of Language Learning Materials based on Linguistic Complexity. *To appear in Research in Computing Science*.

Emily Pitler and Ani Nenkova. 2008. Revisiting readability: A unified framework for predicting text quality. In *Proceedings of the Conference on Empirical Methods in Natural Language Processing*, pages 186–195.

Sarah E. Schwarm and Mari Ostendorf. 2005. Reading level assessment using support vector machines and statistical language models. In *Proceedings of the 43rd Annual Meeting on Association for Computational Linguistics*, pages 523–530.

Wade Shen, Jennifer Williams, Tamas Marius, and Elizabeth Salesky. 2013. A Language-Independent Approach to Automatic Text Difficulty Assessment for Second-Language Learners. In *Proceedings of the 2nd Workshop on Predicting and Improving Text Readability for Target Reader Populations*, pages 30–38.

Luo Si and Jamie Callan. 2001. A statistical model for scientific readability. In *Proceedings of the tenth international conference on Information and knowledge management*, pages 574–576.

Andreas Stolcke. 2002. SRILM-an extensible language modeling toolkit. In *Proceedings of the International Conference on Spoken Language Processing*, pages 901–904.

Sowmya Vajjala and Detmar Meurers. 2012. On improving the accuracy of readability classification using insights from second language acquisition. In *Proceedings of the Seventh Workshop on Building Educational Applications Using NLP*, pages 163–173.

Sowmya Vajjala and Detmar Meurers. 2014. Readability assessment for text simplification: From analysing documents to identifying sentential simplifications. *International Journal of Applied Linguistics*, 165(2):194–222.

Evan James Williams. 1959. *Regression analysis*, volume 14. Wiley New York.

Helen Yannakoudakis. 2013. Automated assessment of English-learner writing. Technical Report UCAM-CL-TR-842, University of Cambridge, Computer Laboratory.

Xiaojin Zhu. 2005. Semi-supervised learning literature survey. Technical Report 1530, Computer Sciences, University of Wisconsin-Madison.

# Automatic Generation of Context-Based Fill-in-the-Blank Exercises Using Co-occurrence Likelihoods and Google *n*-grams


**Jennifer Hill** and **Rahul Simha**
The George Washington University
800 22nd Street NW
Washington, DC 20052, USA
`jenhill@gwu.edu`
`simha@gwu.edu`



## Abstract

In this paper, we propose a method of automatically generating multiple-choice fill-in-the-blank exercises from existing text passages that challenge a reader's comprehension skills and contextual awareness. We use a unique application of word co-occurrence likelihoods and the Google $n$-grams corpus to select words with strong contextual links to their surrounding text, and to generate distractors that make sense only in an isolated narrow context and not in the full context of the passage. Results show that our method is successful at generating questions with distractors that are semantically consistent in a narrow context but inconsistent given the full text, with larger $n$-grams yielding significantly better results.


## 1 Introduction

According to the American Library Association, approximately 43% of Americans have reading skills at or below the most basic level of prose literacy, defined as the ability to "search, comprehend, and use information from continuous texts" (Baer et al., 2009). These underdeveloped literacy skills are in many cases the result of poor reading comprehension. Results from a large-scale national survey indicate that most adult learners with low literacy skills have "difficulty integrating and synthesizing information from any but the simplest texts," likely due to a number of factors including poor phonemic awareness, vocabulary understanding, and reading fluency (Krudenier, 2002). It also suggests that adults in basic education programs are more likely to view reading as simply a decoding task rather than a multifaceted skill involving semantic processing, active memory, and inference.

One method of addressing weak reading skills is the cloze, or fill-in-the-blank (FITB), exercise. These exercises involve strategically removing *target words* from a text and requiring the reader to identify the missing word among a list of *distractors*. However, while FITB exercises can be valuable resources for practicing and improving reading skills, they are time consuming to create by hand. The goal of this paper is to suggest a method for automatically creating such exercises from existing text passages. Such a method would allow for significantly faster and less costly exercise creation on a larger scale, and would allow for nearly any desired reading materials to serve as a learning resource.

We propose that, for native English speakers, a good reading comprehension question challenges the reader not with syntactic errors or unusual word senses, but rather with contextual inconsistencies. Figure 1 gives an example of the type of question we wish to generate: when looking at a narrow context, all four of the word choices are logical selections for the blank, but when the meaning implied by the surrounding text is taken into account, only one choice is sensible. This type of exercise encourages engagement and focus while reading: as a well-formed question should not have obvious inconsistencies within a narrow reference frame, a reader must actively construct meaning as they read in order to identify the correct answer.

In this paper, we propose a method of automatically generating FITB questions from existing text

23


*Proceedings of the 11th Workshop on Innovative Use of NLP for Building Educational Applications*, pages 23–30,
San Diego, California, June 16, 2016. ©2016 Association for Computational Linguistics

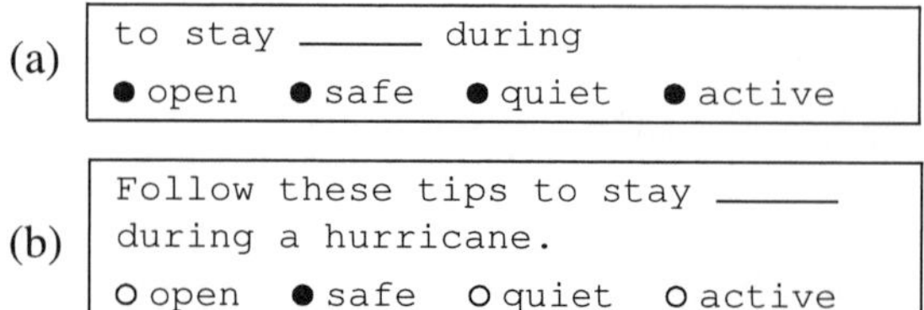



**Figure 1:** An example illustrating the premise behind our exercises: (a) In a narrow context, all four word choices are equally fitting; (b) In the full context, only the target word logically fits

passages that follow this context-specific pattern, using a unique application of word co-occurrence likelihoods and the Google Books $n$-gram corpus (Michel et al., 2010).

## 2 Previous Work

Ours is not the first paper to address the task of generating fill-in-the-blank questions. Many previous studies focus on automatically creating exercises specifically for language learning and vocabulary assessment. Sakaguchi et al. (2013) describe a method of generating distractors for assessing an ESL reader's ability to distinguish semantic nuances between vocabulary words. Brown et al. (2005) utilize WordNet word relations and frequencies to generate distractors for vocabulary words from equally-challenging terms. Pino and Eskenazi (2009) and Goto et al. (2010) both explore different methods of generating distractors of different classes designed to indicate particular deficiencies in phonetic or morphological vocabulary mastery.

Others focus on generating exercises for quizzing or knowledge testing purposes. Agarwal and Mannem (2011) explore generating gap-fill exercises from informative sentences in textbooks, while Karamanis and Mitkov (2006) locate suitable distractors for medical texts from domain-specific documents. Both of these methods choose distractors from other sentences in a constrained set of source texts rather than relying on external corpora.

A few studies have focused on more comprehension-specific exercises, generating distractors that are semantically similar to the target word. Zesch and Melamud (2014) propose a method of generating semantically similar distractors to the target word using context-sensitive lexical inference rules. The distractors generated using this method are contextually and semantically similar to the target word, but not in the context being used in the sentence. Kumar et al.'s RevUP system (2015) utilizes a word vector model trained on the desired text domain to find semantically-similar words and verifies their similarity using WordNet synsets. Aldabe et al. (2009) generate semantically-similar distractors using distributional data obtained from the British National Corpus, and also, like our study, utilize the Google $n$-grams corpus to determine each generated distractor's probability of occurring with its surrounding terms. However, their study differs from ours in that they utilize the Google $n$-grams solely for validating that their chosen distractors make sense, whereas we use the corpus for the actual generation of the distractors.

Perhaps the closest cousin to our proposed method can be found in the DQGen system (Mostow and Jang, 2012). DQGen generates cloze questions designed to test different types of comprehension failure in children, one of which involves creating "plausible" distractors that create contextually sensible sentences in isolation but do not fit in the context of the rest of the text. Their system also utilizes the Google $n$-grams corpus for finding semantically consistent distractors for these sentences. However, they do not address the challenge of choosing strategic target words, and their attempt to generate distractors at the sentence level that are contextually inconsistent at the passage level returned underwhelming results, as most target words were found to be easily distinguishable without needing previous sentences for context. While our paper addresses a similar task of finding distractors that are plausible when external context is excluded, we generate distractors at the narrower phrase level that rely on the surrounding text for context.

## 3 Exercise Creation

The process of automatically generating FITB exercises from an existing text involves three distinct steps: (1) choosing which target words to blank from these sentences, (2) choosing distractors for each target word, and (3) compiling these elements into a full passage-level exercise.

## 3.1 Choosing Target Words

The first step to creating a FITB question from a text passage is to choose which words to replace with blanks. We consider a "good" blanked question to be one in which there are enough context clues in the surrounding text for the reader to understand the text's intended meaning even when the chosen word is removed. If the reader is able to understand the sentence's intended meaning with the target word removed, then the task of replacing the word should be trivial.

We begin by considering every word in the sentence as a potential word to be blanked. However, many words would not make good target words in practice. We discard function words (articles, pronouns, conjunctions, etc.) from the pool due to their closed nature and frequent appearance across documents. However, unlike some other studies (Coniam, 1997) (Shei, 2001), we do not use global word frequencies to find uncommon words from which to create blanks. We propose that even easily-understood target words that successfully challenge comprehension of the surrounding context will implicitly test mastery of the more challenging words in the passage. However, we do consider local word frequencies, eliminating words whose stemmed form appears in the document multiple times, so that readers cannot identify target words simply by recognition due to previous encounters.

Because our exercises are designed to test understanding rather than knowledge, we also do not wish to "quiz" readers on facts, as is the case in several other studies (Karamanis et al., 2006). Therefore we also disregard classes of words that typically present factual information and could be easily exchanged for any other word of the same class (see Figure 2). These include:

- **Named entities** Specific entities, such as people, locations, and organizations
- **Numbers** Digits and their written forms

After this filtering step, the remaining set of words serves as our pool of *potential blanks*.

From this pool, we must then locate the words which relate most closely to their surrounding text. We explore several different "scopes" of context surrounding the potential blanks, and utilize word co-

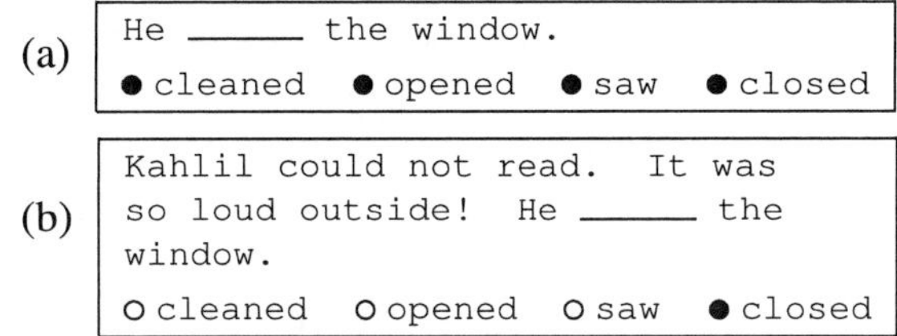



**Figure 2:** Examples of poor target words

occurrence likelihoods to find the potential blanks that have the strongest contextual links to information within that scope. By removing words that have a meaningful contextual relationship to one or more other words in the scope, we aim to ensure that there are enough hints left remaining to enable the reader to make a reasonable inference about the blanked word.

### 3.1.1 Contextual Scope

Though our goal is to generate blanks at the sentence level, individual sentences in a passage are rarely conceptually independent from one another. True understanding of a sentence's meaning often relies on information that has been gathered from previous sentences in the passage. Figure 3 gives an example of a question that relies on previous information to answer correctly.



**Figure 3:** An example of contextual scope influencing answer selection. When the word *closed* is removed (a), the reader must rely on the previous sentences to provide the context clues necessary to fill this blank (b).

Shanahan et al. (1984) found that traditional cloze-style comprehension questions are not good indicators of "intersentential comprehension," the ability to process and apply information across sentence boundaries. We therefore explore several different contextual "scopes" when attempting to find pairs of words with contextual links. Adjusting the scope of included information allows the blanks-selection method to incorporate potentially relevant or necessary context words that a reader has internalized from the sentences they have already read in order to test their intersentential comprehension.

Three scopes were tested in this paper:

**s1**: Context words are chosen only from the target sentence $\{s_t\}$

**s2**: Context words are chosen from the target sentence and the preceding sentence $\{s_{t-1}, s_t\}$

**s3**: Context words are chosen from the target sentence and the two preceding sentences $\{s_{t-2}, s_{t-1}, s_t\}$

The pool of scope words for each sentence is filtered less rigorously than the pool of potential blanks, as many of the word classes that make poor blanks are poor choices specifically because they provide important factual information that we wish to leverage for context. We therefore choose only to remove function words from the pool, leaving named entities, numbers, and frequently-occurring words.

### 3.1.2 Word Co-occurrences

We assume that words that co-occur together regularly are likely to have a contextual and/or semantic relationship to one another. We therefore utilize word co-occurrence likelihoods to select the potential blanks with the strongest relationship to their scope-specific context words.

To represent word co-occurrence likelihoods, we use the word vector space model GloVe (Pennington et al., 2014), trained on 42-billion tokens. The GloVe model formulates word vectors such that the dot product of any two word vectors $\hat{w}_1 \cdot \hat{w}_2$ represents the logarithm of the words' probability of co-occurring together in a document.

Our goal is to find the scope word for each potential blank with the highest likelihood of co-occurring with that blanked word. Using the GloVe model, for each potential blank $b \in B$, we find the closest scope word $c$ in the set of all scope words $S$ for that blank such that $(b, c) = \arg\min(\hat{b} \cdot \hat{s})$ ($\forall s \in S$ such that $s.stem \neq b.stem$). Each of these pairs is added to the pool of blanks to carry to the task of choosing distractors.

### 3.2 Choosing Distractors

To turn a blanked passage into an exercise, each blank is presented as a multiple choice question. The reader is given four words to choose from that

could potentially fit the given blank: the target word and three distractors. For our exercises that specifically target contextual understanding, we specify that a good distractor should make sense both grammatically and logically within a narrow context, but should not make sense within the broader context of the surrounding words.

To accomplish this, we explore a unique application of the Google Books $n$-grams Corpus for generating reasonable distractors for a blanked word. Google $n$-grams is a massive corpus containing frequency counts for all unigrams through 5-grams that occur across all texts in the Google Books corpus.

```
When you step on the pedals of a
bicycle, it causes the wheels to
spin.

        it [causes] the
        [causes] the wheels
  ✗     bicycle it [causes]
```

**Figure 4:** An example of the sentence-level trigrams extracted from a sentence. Note that an $n$-gram cannot occur between two clauses.

We begin by gathering every 2- through 5-gram in the original sentence that contains the target word. If the sentence contains multiple clauses, we consider only the clause which contains the target word. This allows us to avoid selecting $n$-grams of unusual or unintended structure (see Figure 4). We then use a sliding window to gather all $n$-grams ($2 \leq n \leq 5$) within the clause of the form $\{w_1...w_{t-1}, [w_t], w_{t+1}...w_n\}$, where the target word $[w_t]$ occupies each position $1 \leq t \leq n$. We then search the Google corpus for $n$-grams matching each pattern $\{w_1...w_{t-1}, [w_t.pos], w_{t+1}...w_n\}$ ($1 \leq t \leq n$), where $w_t.pos$ represents the part of speech of the target word $w_t$ (obtained using the Stanford Part-Of-Speech Tagger (Toutanova et al., 2003)). If the query returns no results, we attempt to generalize the pattern further by replacing proper names and pronouns with their part of speech (see Figure 5).

We utilize a back-off model when querying for distractors, using $n$-grams of size $n = \{5...2\}$. For each $n$-sized pattern searched, we find the intersection $D$ of all words at index $t$ (limiting our results to the top 100 for the sake of performance).

We do not want any of the generated distractors to fit the blank as well as the target word, so we

```
James Brown [VBD] up   →  ✗
       NNP  [VBD] up   →  Moses lifted up
                         Peter stood up
                         Jill  went  up
                         ...
```

**Figure 5:** When $n$-gram queries return no results, we generalize specific terms to increase the likelihood of finding a match

need to remove all words in $D$ that are likely to make too much sense in context. Because synonyms can often be used interchangeably in the same sentence, we discard all words that are direct synonyms of $w_t$ (using synsets gathered from WordNet[1]). We also remove all words $d \in D$ such that $(\mathbf{\hat{w}_t} \cdot \mathbf{\hat{d}}) < (\mathbf{\hat{w}_t} \cdot \mathbf{\hat{c}})$ (where $c$ is the closest scope word in the pair $(w_t, c)$), because these words have a *higher* likelihood than the target word does of co-occurring with their context words.

If the resulting filtered set $D$ contains fewer than three words (the minimum required to create a multiple choice question), we back off to the next largest value of $n$, continuing this pattern until we have found three or more distractors for the blank. If fewer than three distractors are found after $n = 2$, the word is discarded from the pool of potential blanks. From the final set $D$, we select the three *least*-frequently occurring distractors in the Google corpus.

### 3.3 Exercise Generation

Once we have found all remaining potential blanks that have three or more distractors, we must pare down the list to create the final passage-level exercise. If any one sentence has more than one potential blank, we choose the blank that has the highest co-occurrence likelihood with its paired scope word and discard the other(s). We also discard any blanks whose paired scope word was itself made into a blank (because the context has been removed).

The resulting set of blanks constitutes the set of "best" questions for the passage. We then can present the passage-level exercise in its entirety, replacing each blanked word with a multiple choice question consisting of the target word and its three chosen distractors. Though we choose not to do so,

the number of blanked sentences can also be manually limited by selecting the top $x$ blanks from the set of all word pairs sorted by descending likelihood.

## 4 Evaluation

Our corpus of documents was composed of approximately 1000 reading comprehension text passages obtained from ReadWorks.org[2], ranging in reading level from 100L to 1000L using the Lexile scale. We randomly selected 120 non-unique passages (i.e. one passage could be selected more than once) from which to create questions. For each instance of a selected passage, we generated a single blanked sentence and its top three distractors, to be presented as a multiple choice question.

The questionnaire was separated into two sections, both of which asked participants to answer a set of generated FITB questions. The first section presented each question at the phrase level (i.e. the blanked surrounded by a small subset of the words in the full sentence). The words to include in these phrases were selected by hand to present the blank in a representational narrow context. The second section presented sentence-level FITB questions, surrounded by the context of the entire passage (or, in the case of particularly long passages, by relevant paragraphs from the full text). For both sections, participants were presented with four word choices for each blank, and were asked to select *all* of the words they believed logically fit the blank.

67 native English-speaking volunteers were asked to provide their feedback on each generated blank through an anonymous online questionnaire. Each participant was given a random subset of questions from each section to answer: 20 phrase-level questions, and 10 sentence-level questions. Participants were not aware that the questions were generated automatically and were not informed of the research objectives or what we hoped to obtain from their answers in order to avoid potential feedback bias.

## 5 Results

Alderson et al. (1995) proposed that multiple choice questions be evaluated using two metrics: *reliability* and *validity*. However, because our questions

[1]Princeton University "About WordNet." WordNet. Princeton University. 2010. <http://wordnet.princeton.edu>

[2]http://www.readworks.org/

were not answered by the target audience (i.e. low-literacy readers), we cannot compute reliability using traditional methods (such as Cronbach's alpha). We focus instead on evaluating the validity of our exercises by determining how well they conform to our proposed method of targeting narrow vs. full context.

We assess the validity of our questions and the chosen distractors by examining the proportion of words that fit each blank in a narrow context to words that fit the same blank in the broader context of the surrounding text. In an ideal question, the target word and all distractors should fit in the narrow context, and only the target word should fit given the full context. Thus, for target words, we aim for 100% fit in both contexts; for distractors, we aim for 100% fit in the narrow context and 0% in the full.

|  | Narrow(%) | | Full(%) | |
|---|---|---|---|---|
|  | dist | target | dist | target |
| $n = 2$ | 30.9 | 93.1 | 3.1 | 98.0 |
| $n = 3$ | 57.7 | 92.4 | 7.0 | 93.8 |
| $n = 4$ | 67.1 | 89.9 | 21.9 | 95.5 |
| $n = 5$ | 74.1 | 93.2 | 13.2 | 91.3 |
| ALL | 58.0 | 92.1 | 11.6 | 94.6 |

**Table 1:** The percentage of distractors and target words chosen to fit each blank given the narrow context (left) and the full passage (right)

As can be seen in Table 1, the proportion of distractors deemed to fit the blanks in a narrow context increases substantially as $n$ increases, while the proportion of target words chosen to fit is relatively unaffected. This pattern also holds true given the full context, although to a lesser extent.

On average, 58% of all distractors generated were deemed to fit in their given blanks in a narrow context, although this number is skewed by the poor performance of the bigram model. The 5-gram model was the best-performing for finding distractors that fit in the narrow context, achieving an average fit of approximately 74%. As $n$ increases, more of the syntactic and semantic features of the phrase are able to be incorporated into the distractor selection, increasing the chances of the selected word making both grammatical and contextual sense with *all* of the words in the phrase.

Less than 12% of all distractors on average were deemed to fit the same blanks when given the full context, though the 4-gram model had the worst performance with nearly 22% fit. The bigram model performed best in the full context with approximately 3% fit; however, its poor performance in the narrow context suggests that these words are obviously incorrect and therefore not suitable distractors.

Table 2 compares the proportions of distractors fitting within each context across both $n$-gram model and scope ($s1$ through $s3$). The same pattern of increasing fit with higher values of $n$ can be observed within each scope. However, the scope does not appear to have a significant affect on the quality of the distractors generated.

|  | Narrow(%) | | | Full(%) | | |
|---|---|---|---|---|---|---|
|  | $s1$ | $s2$ | $s3$ | $s1$ | $s2$ | $s3$ |
| $n = 2$ | 29.5 | 31.9 | 27.9 | 3.2 | 3.0 | 3.4 |
| $n = 3$ | 53.7 | 61.2 | 61.0 | 4.6 | 10.2 | 11.1 |
| $n = 4$ | 64.8 | 66.7 | 66.1 | 25.3 | 18.9 | 21.5 |
| $n = 5$ | 75.7 | 74.9 | 75.0 | 13.6 | 13.9 | 20.6 |
| ALL | 56.2 | 59.4 | 56.9 | 10.4 | 11.9 | 13.5 |

**Table 2:** The percentage of distractors fitting each blank given the narrow (left) and full context (right), for each scope.

## 6 Limitations and Future Work

The proportion of words deemed to fit in the narrow contexts is lower than expected for both target words and distractors. We suspect that the concept of words "fitting" in a sentence fragment may not have been fully understood by some participants. For example, many respondents said that the word `went` was not a suitable fit for the phrase `Hidalgo _____ about this`. In this case, some participants may have struggled to identify the phrasal verb "to go about" as being grammatically correct because it clashed with the other choices (`heard`, `agreed`, `said`), where they might have chosen it to fit if it had been presented independently. A future study will explore a less subjective method of evaluating target words within a narrow context.

Perhaps the biggest weakness in our current method lies in filtering out fitting distractors. As indicated in the results above, approximately 12% of all the distractors generated using our algorithm were deemed to make as much sense in context as the target word. Upon observation, we note that the majority of the distractors chosen to fit within their full contexts are "near-synonyms" of the tar-

get word (for example, the words turned and
flushed, which are not obvious synonyms but
are interchangeable given the context of the phrase
her face ______ red.) While we are able to remove direct synonyms using WordNet, we will work
to incorporate a more robust synonym-filtering process in future work, taking advantage of the already-
utilized corpora.

We also wish to further explore the relationship
between scope and the target words chosen. While
we have seen that adjusting the scope has little effect
on the quality of the distractors generated, it remains
to be seen if the target words themselves are of "better" quality for targeting comprehension as the scope
of available context increases.

Alongside improvements to the question generation algorithm's performance, we also wish to prove
the efficacy of these types of exercises in targeting the reading comprehension skills of low-literacy
users. This process will involve further user evaluation, this time involving the target audience.

## 7 Conclusions

In this paper we have discussed a method of automatically generating fill-in-the-blank questions designed to target a reader's comprehension skills and
contextual awareness. We have explored the idea of
using word co-occurrence likelihoods coupled with
scopes of context to find words with strong links to
their surrounding text from which to make blanks.
We have also tested a novel approach to generating
distractors for these words using the Google Books
$n$-grams corpus to find words that are semantically
and logically appropriate for the given blanks in a
narrow context but which do not make sense given
the intention of the passage.

Results suggest that larger $n$-grams are significantly more effective in creating sensible distractors that make sense within a narrow context, and
that a large portion of these distractors become no
longer suitable once the full context of the passage
has been introduced. This suggests that our method
is a promising first step towards the generation of
these types of comprehension-challenging exercises.


## References

Manish Agarwal and Prashanth Mannem. 2011. Automatic gap-fill question generation from text books. In
*Proceedings of the 6th Workshop on Innovative Use
of NLP for Building Educational Applications*, pages
56–64.

Itziar Aldabe, Montse Maritxalar, and Ruslan Mitkov.
2009. A study on the automatic selection of candidate sentences distractors. *Frontiers in Artificial Intelligence and Applications*, 200(1):656–658.

J. Charles Alderson, Caroline Clapham, and Dianne Wall.
1995. *Language Test Construction and Evaluation*.

Justin Baer, Mark Kutner, John Sabatini, and Sheida
White. 2009. Basic reading skills and the literacy of
america's least literate adults: Results from the 2003
national assessment of adult literacy (naal) supplemental studies. *National Center for Education Statistics*.

Jonathan C. Brown, Gwen A. Frishkoff, and Maxine Eskenazi. 2005. Automatic question generation for vocabulary assessment. In *Proceedings of Human Language Technology Conference and Conference on Empirical Methods in Natural Language Processing*, page
826.

David Coniam. 1997. A preliminary inquiry into using
corpus word frequency data in the automatic generation of english language cloze tests. *CALICO Journal*,
14(2):15–33.

Takuya Goto, Tomoko Kojiri, Toyohide Watanabe, To-
moharu Iwata, and Takeshi Yamada. 2010. Automatic
generation system of multiple-choice cloze questions
and its evaluation. *Knowledge Management and E-
Learning*, 2(3):210–224.

Nikiforos Karamanis, Le An Ha, and Ruslan Mitkov.
2006. Generating multiple-choice test items from
medical text: A pilot study. In *Proceedings of the
Fourth International Natural Language Generation
Conference*, number July, pages 111–113.

John Krudenier. 2002. *Research Based Principles for
Adult Basic Education Reading Instruction*.

Girish Kumar, Rafael E. Banchs, and Luis F. D'Haro.
2015. Revup: Automatic gap-fill question generation
from educational texts. In *Proceedings of the 10th
Workshop on Innovative Use of NLP for Building Educational Applications*, pages 154–161.

Jean-Baptiste Michel, Yuan Kui Shen, Aviva Presser
Aiden, Adrian Veres, Matthew K Gray, Joseph P
Pickett, Dale Hoiberg, Dan Clancy, Peter Norvig,
Jon Orwant, Steven Pinker, Martin A Nowak, and
Erez Lieberman Aiden. 2010. Quantitative analysis
of culture using millions of digitized books. *Sciencex-
press*, 331(6014):176–182.

Jack Mostow and Hyeju Jang. 2012. Generating diagnostic multiple choice comprehension cloze questions.

In *Proceedings of the 7th Workshop on Innovative Use of NLP for Building Educational Applications*, pages 136–146.

Jeffrey Pennington, Richard Socher, and Christopher D Manning. 2014. Glove: Global vectors for word representation. *Proceedings of the 2014 Conference on Empirical Methods in Natural Language Processing*, pages 1532–1543.

Juan Pino and Maxine Eskenazi. 2009. Semi-automatic generation of cloze question distractors effect of students 11. *Proceedings of the SLaTE Workshop on Speech and Language Technology in Education*, pages 1–4.

Keisuke Sakaguchi, Yuki Arase, and Mamoru Komachi. 2013. Discriminative approach to fill-in-the-blank quiz generation for language learners. In *Proceedings of the 51st Annual Meeting of the Association for Computational Linguistics*, pages 238–242.

Timothy Shanahan, Michael L. Kamil, and Aileen Webb Tobin. 1984. Cloze as a measure of intersentential comprehension. *Reading Research Quarterly*, 14(2):229.

Chi-Chiang Shei. 2001. Followyou!: An automatic language lesson generation system. *Computer Assisted Language Learning*, 14(2):129–144.

Kristina Toutanova, Dan Klein, and Christopher D Manning. 2003. Feature-rich part-of-speech tagging with a cyclic dependency network. In *Proceedings of the 2003 Conference of the North American Chapter of the Association for Computational Linguistics on Human Language Technology*, pages 252–259.

Torsten Zesch and Oren Melamud. 2014. Automatic generation of challenging distractors using context-sensitive inference rules. In *Proceedings of the 9th Workshop on Innovative Use of NLP for Building Educational Applications*, pages 143–148.

# Automated classification of collaborative problem solving interactions in simulated science tasks

**Michael Flor, Su-Youn Yoon, Jiangang Hao, Lei Liu, Alina A von Davier**
Educational Testing Service, 660 Rosedale Road, Princeton, NJ 08541, USA
{mflor,syoon,jhao,lliu001,avondavier}@ets.org

## Abstract

We present a novel situational task that integrates collaborative problem solving behavior with testing in a science domain. Participants engage in discourse, which is used to evaluate their collaborative skills. We present initial experiments for automatic classification of such discourse, using a novel classification schema. Considerable accuracy is achieved with just lexical features. A speech-act classifier, trained on out-of-domain data, can also be helpful.

## 1 Introduction

Collaborative problem solving (CPS) is a complex activity that involves an interplay between cognitive processes, such as content understanding, knowledge acquisition, action planning and execution (Greiff, 2012; von Davier and Halpin, 2013), non-cognitive processes, such as adaptability, engagement, social regulation, and affect states, such as boredom, confusion, and frustration (Baker et al., 2010; Graesser et al., 2010). Collaborative learning techniques are used extensively in educational practices, from pre-school to higher education. Collaborative activity in learning environments may take place in face-to-face interactions or via online distance-learning platforms (Prata et al., 2009).

Within the domain of educational assessment, there has been a strong recent interest in the evaluation of CPS as a social skill (Griffin et al., 2012; Liu et al., 2015; von Davier and Halpin, 2013). Such interest is informed by analysis of group interactions, which often integrate context, experience, and active engagement of learners (Hatano & Inagaki, 1991; Hmelo-Silver, Nagarajan, & Day, 2000). For

example, Damon and Phelps (1989) pointed out that collaborative discussion provides a rich environment for mutual discovery, reciprocal feedback, and frequent sharing of ideas. Duschl and Osborne (2002) noted that peer collaboration provides opportunities for scientific argumentation – proposing, supporting, criticizing, evaluating, and refining ideas.

To include discursive collaboration in large-scale educational assessments, it is essential to automate the scoring and annotation process of discursive interactions. In our study, we explore an application of natural language processing techniques for annotating group discourses using a novel CPS classification framework.

The rest of this paper is structured as follows. Section 2 presents the experimental task that is used for eliciting collaborative behavior in a controlled setting. Section 3 describes the collected data. Section 4 presents the CPS classification framework and the manual annotation of data according to this framework. Machine learning experiments for automated annotation of collaborative interactions are presented in section 5.

## 2 Task Description

We have designed a research study to explore the relationship between CPS skills and collaboration outcomes (Hao et al., 2015). We focus on measuring collaboration skills within the domain of science. The task was structured as a computer-based simulation, in an interactive game-like environment. Such setting can provide students with opportunities to demonstrate proficiencies in complex interactive environments that traditional assessment formats cannot afford (Klopfer et al., 2009). The simulation



*Proceedings of the 11th Workshop on Innovative Use of NLP for Building Educational Applications*, pages 31–41,
San Diego, California, June 16, 2016. ©2016 Association for Computational Linguistics

task was modified from an existing simulation, Volcano Trialogue (Zapata-Rivera et al., 2014), and delivered over a web-based collaborative platform (see Figure 1). Task participants took the roles of assistants in a virtual seismic measurement laboratory, measuring and monitoring seismic events related to various aspects of (simulated) volcanic activity. They were given various assignments (by a script-controlled virtual scientist agent), and their performance was measured based on their responses to the assignments in the simulation task. In this task, two participants work together via text chat to complete the specific subtasks. All of the turn-by-turn conversations and responses to the questions were recorded in an activity log with time stamps. The conversations were used to measure CPS skills, while responses to the in-simulation test items were used to measure science inquiry skills.

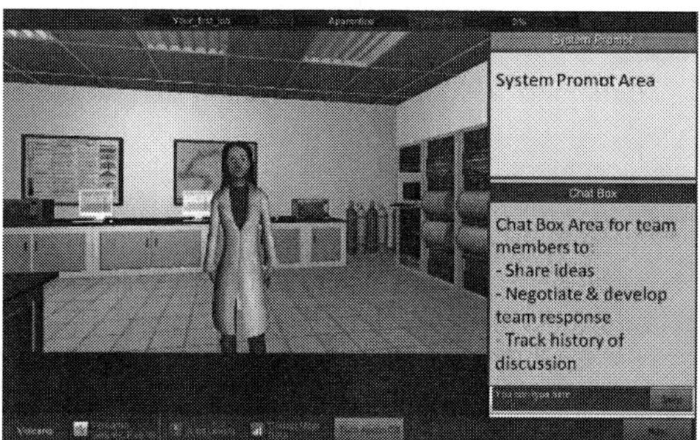


**Figure 1.** Sample screenshot from the Volcano task.

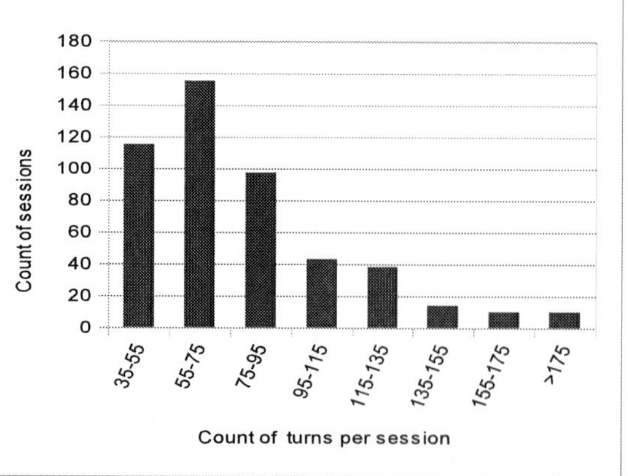


**Figure 2.** Binned distribution of turn counts per session

A session in this simulation task consists of multiple items/subtasks in various formats, such as multiple choice, constructed response, and conversations with virtual agents. There were also action items, such as placing seismometers on a virtual volcano map and making notes of collected seismic data. Pre-designed prompts were displayed in the system prompt area to guide participants through the sequence of subtasks in a session. To capture the evidence for the outcomes of collaboration in the simulation, a three-step response procedure was used for each item. First, each participant was prompted to respond the item individually. Next, each participant was prompted to discuss the item with the partner. Individual response could be revised at this stage and a team-response could be negotiated. Finally, a team-representative was randomly chosen to submit a team answer. The changes in the test-responses before and after the collaboration may indicate how effective the team collaboration was. In a separate paper, we describe how such changes provide insights on which CPS skills are important for better collaboration outcomes (Hao et al., submitted). In the present paper, we focus on developing automated methodologies to classify the conversations in the sessions.

## 3  The CPS chat data

Data was collected through the Amazon Mechanical Turk crowdsourcing data-collection platform. We recruited 1,000 participants with at least one year of college education. Participants were teamed randomly into pairs to take the collaborative science simulation task. After removing sessions with incomplete data, we had complete responses from 482 teams. Figure 2 presents a binned histogram for the amounts of turns taken in the 482 sessions, indicating the amount of dialogue that has occurred. A 'turn' consists of whatever text a participant types before pressing 'Send'. About 80% of the sessions had 35-100 turns. The chattiest session had 300 turns. Sample chat excerpts are presented in Table 2. Overall, there are 38,703 turns in our corpus. The total number of tokens is 189K (213K with punctuation). Average token-count per turn is 4.9 tokens (5.5 with punctuation).

## 4 CPS classification

By analyzing discourse, researchers can make sense of how students collaboratively solve problems. Observable features from the collaborative interaction, such as turn taking, sharing resources and ideas, negotiating, posing and answering questions, etc., may be used for measuring CPS skills.

There are many different ways to annotate interactions, for different purposes. Dialogue acts (DA) are sentence-level units that represent states of a dialogue, such as questions, statements, hesitations, etc. However, classification of dialogue acts differs from CPS classification (Erkens and Janssen, 2008). Whereas dialogue act coding is based on the pragmatic, linguistic features, close to utterance form, the coding of collaborative activities is based on the theoretical interpretation of the content of the utterances – the aim and function of the utterances in the collaboration process. For example, from the DA perspective, "Look at the map" and "Wait for me" are simply directives. From CPS perspective, the former may be considered "Sharing of ideas/resources", the latter – a "Regulating" expression.

Research in the field of collaboration analysis has not settled yet on a single CPS annotation scheme. Hmelo-Silver and Barrows (2008) provide a schema for characterizing collaborative knowledge building for medical students working with an expert facilitator, thus focusing on facilitation aspects. Higgins et al. (2012) present a coding scheme that is focused on the types of interactions between participants (negotiation, elaboration, independence, etc.). Asterhan and Schwarz (2009) describe dual CPS coding of discussion protocols. Kersey et al. (2009) focus on knowledge co-construction in peer interactions. Mercier et al. (2014) describe a coding scheme that focuses on leadership skills in CPS. Lu et al. (2011) describe a coding scheme of discourse moves in online discussions. Weinberger and Fischer (2006) provide a multi-dimensional coding scheme for argumentative knowledge construction in computer-supported collaborative learning.

### 4.1 The CPS Framework

The CPS classification schema used in the present work was developed based on review of computer-supported collaborative learning (CSCL) research findings (Barron, 2003; Dillenbourg and Traum, 2006; Griffin et al., 2012; von Davier and Halpin, 2013) and the PISA 2015 Collaborative Problem Solving Framework (OECD, 2013). Our schema (Liu et al., 2015) is comprised of 33 CPS skills grouped into four major dimensions. The full listing is presented in Table 1. The four dimensions are: sharing ideas, negotiating, regulating problem-solving activities, and maintaining communication. The first dimension – sharing ideas – considers how individuals bring divergent ideas into a collaborative conversation. For instance, participants may share their individual responses to assessment items and/or point out relevant resources that might help resolve a problem. The second dimension – negotiating ideas – is to capture evidence of the team's collaborative knowledge building and construction through negotiating with each other. The categories under this dimension include agreement/disagreement with each other, requesting clarification, elaborating/rephrasing other's ideas, identifying gaps, revising one's own idea. The third dimension – regulating problem-solving activities – focuses on the collaborative regulation aspect of the team discourse. This dimension includes such categories as identifying goals, evaluating teamwork, and checking understanding. The last dimension – maintaining a positive communication atmosphere – is to capture social communications beyond the task-specific interactions.

### 4.2 Human coding of CPS classes

Two human annotators were trained to annotate the chats. Training involved overview of definitions and coding examples for each of the 33 categories of CPS skills. After training, annotators independently coded discourse data from the chat protocols. Seventy seven sessions out of 482 (16%) were coded by both annotators, all other sessions were coded by the same single annotator (H1).

The unit of analysis was each turn of a conversation, i.e. each turn received a label drawn from the 33 categories. Due to complexity of the collaborative process, one turn of chat may have more than one function that can be mapped in the CPS framework. Therefore, an annotator was allowed to assign up to two labels to each turn. A primary label reflects what the annotator considered as the major function in a given turn, and a secondary label reflects an additional, less central function.

Table 2 presents a sample of this annotation. The first column marks speaker-ID, the second column

| CPS skills | Student performance (categories) |
|---|---|
| Sharing ideas | 1. Student gives task-relevant information (e.g., individual response) to the teammate.<br>2. Student points out a resource to retrieve task-relevant information.<br>3. Student responds to the teammate's request for task-relevant information. |
| Negotiating ideas | 4. Student expresses agreement with the teammates.<br>5. Student expresses disagreement with teammates.<br>6. Student expresses uncertainty of agree or disagree.<br>7. Student asks the teammate to repeat a statement.<br>8. Student asks the teammate to clarify a statement.<br>9. Student rephrases/complete the teammate's statement.<br>10. Student identifies a conflict in his or her own idea and the teammate's idea.<br>11. Student uses relevant evidence to point out some gap in the teammate's statement.<br>12. Student elaborates on his or her own statement.<br>13. Student changes his or her own idea after listening to the teammate's reasoning |
| Regulating problem solving | 14. Student identifies the goal of the conversation.<br>15. Student suggests the next step for the group to take.<br>16. Student expresses confusion/frustration or lack of understanding.<br>17. Student expresses progress in understanding.<br>18. Student reflects on what the group did.<br>19. Student expresses what is missing in the teamwork to solve the problem.<br>20. Student checks on understanding.<br>21. Student evaluates whether certain group contribution is useful or not for the problem solving.<br>22. Student shows satisfaction with the group performance.<br>23. Student points out some gap in a group decision.<br>24. Student identifies a problem in problem solving. |
| Maintaining communication | 25. Student responds to the teammate's question (using texts and text symbols).<br>26. Student manages to make the conversation alive (using texts and text symbols, using socially appropriate language).<br>27. Student waits for the teammate to finish his/her statement before taking turns.<br>28. Student uses socially appropriate language (e.g., greeting).<br>29. Student offers help.<br>30. Student apologizes for unintentional interruption.<br>31. Student rejects the teammate's suggestions without an accountable reason.<br>32. Student inputs something that does not make sense.<br>33. Student shows understanding of the teammate's frustration. |

**Table 1:** CPS Framework coding rubric of collaborative problem solving interactions skills

presents the chat text. The fourth column presents the primary classification code assigned by annotator H1. The third column indicates the general dimension for primary label. The fifth column shows the secondary labels given by annotator H1. For example, in the last row of the table, note that the response of participant s8 is classified as primary=category#11 (point out a gap in statement) and secondary=category#2 (suggest information resource).

As the annotation focused on marking only the most prominent CPS functions, a secondary label was used only if the annotator considered that the additional function was prominent enough. Our first annotator assigned a secondary tag (in addition to a primary tag) to 13,404 chat-turns (34% of all cases), while the second annotator used a secondary tag in only 33 cases. Thus, we disregard the secondary tag of the second annotator and compute inter-rater

| ID | Chat text | Dimension | P | S |
|---|---|---|---|---|
| s1 | hi there i'm george! | maintaining communication | 28 | |
| s2 | good morning, I'm j | maintaining communication | 28 | |
| s1 | i think the answer is b | sharing ideas | 1 | |
| s2 | magma approaching crater? | sharing ideas | 1 | 20 |
| s1 | i remember the video saying high frequency waves resulted from rocks cracking | sharing ideas | 2 | 12 |
| s2 | i just reviewed it and you are correct | negotiating ideas | 12 | 4 |
| s2 | c | sharing ideas | 1 | |
| s1 | i chose c as well | sharing ideas | 1 | |
| (some turns omitted here) | | | | |
| s2 | ? | regulating | 16 | |
| s1 | we can keep the first two notes we seemed to have similar answers | regulating | 15 | |
| Example from another session: | | | | |
| s9 | I thought it started low? | sharing ideas | 1 | |
| s8 | nope you can look at the volcanic seismic events in the bottom left corner | negotiating ideas | 11 | 2 |

Table 2: Sample excerpts from some chat sessions, with CPS classifications by annotator H1. P=primary label, S-secondary label. Labels are explained in Table 1.

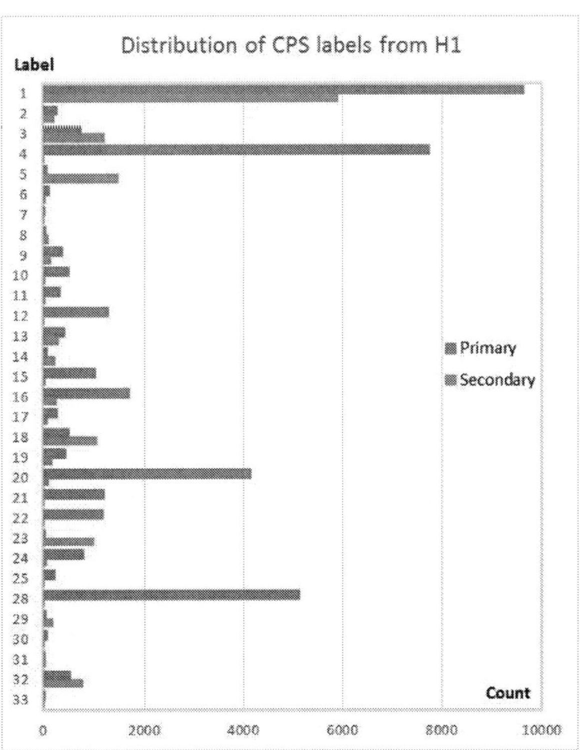


**Figure 3.** Histogram of primary and secondary CPS labels assigned by annotator H1 for the set of 38,703 chat turns.

agreement as follows. The 77 sessions that were processed by both annotators had 6,079 turns. Over those turns, the two annotators agreed in their primary tags in 3,818 cases (62.8% agreement, Cohen's kappa 0.56). We also considered a different criterion, when second annotator's primary tag agreed with either primary or secondary tag given by the first annotator. In this approach, agreement is 72%s and Cohen's kappa is 0.62. According to Landis and Koch (1977) scale, those levels of agreement are somewhere between moderate (kappa 0.41-0.61) and substantial (kappa 0.61-0.80).

Figure 3 presents the distribution of primary and secondary CPS labels assigned by annotator H1 to the whole set of 38,703 turns. The distribution is very uneven. Two categories were never used (#26 and #27).

It is not uncommon to see uneven distribution of categories in collaborative discourse (Chin and Osborne, 2010; Schellens and Valcke, 2005; Lipponen et al. 2003). Given that the task prompted students to share individual responses, it is also not surprising to see categories #1 (give info to partner) and #4 (expresses agreement) as the most frequent codes. Social factors may also be at play. For instance, people often tend to be polite and respectful and express disagreement indirectly. Instead of saying *"no, I disagree"*, very likely a person would say *"my answer is ..."* or *"I think it's ... because"*, and such responses are not coded as expressed disagreement, but rather as sharing or negotiating. This may explain why explicit agreements are five times more frequent than explicit disagreements in our data, the latter also mostly coded as secondary label.

## 5    Automation of CPS classification

Analysis of protocols and logs of communication is an important research technique for investigating collaborative processes. Since such analysis is very time consuming, researchers have turned to automating such analyses by utilizing computational linguistic methods. Discourse Processing is a well-established area in computational linguistics, and there is much research on automatically recognizing and tagging dialogue acts, for spoken or transcribed data (Webb & Liu, 2008; Webb et al., 2005; Serafin & Di Eugenio, 2004; Stolcke et al., 2000; Samuel et al., 1999). De Felice and Deane (2012) describe identifying speech acts in e-mails, as part of a scoring system for educational assessment. Similarly, researchers have developed computational linguistic approaches in analysis of collaboration protocols. Law et al. (2007) presented a mixed system, where manual coding is augmented with automated suggestions, derived from keyword and phrase matching. Erkens and Janssen (2008) describe a rule-based approach for automatic coding of dialogue acts in collaboration protocols. Erkens and Janssen have also stressed the difference between dialogue acts, which are closer to the linguistic form of interaction, and classes of collaborative utterances, which are more context specific and depend on respective theoretical frameworks of collaboration processes. Rosé et al. (2008) and Dönmez et al. (2005) describe a machine learning approach to code collaboration protocols according to the classification system of Weinberger and Fischer (2006).

Here we describe machine learning experiments towards automated coding of collaboration protocols according to the novel CPS framework. In our experiments we attempt to learn directly the 31 categories of the 33 defined in the framework. We chose a multinomial Naive-Bayes and HMM approaches, as starting points to explore assigning CPS tags to chat-turns in our data.

As a pre-processing step, all texts were automatically spell-corrected using a contextually-aware spell checker (Flor, 2012). Slang words and expressions were normalized (e.g. {*ya, yea, yeah, yiss, yisss, yep, yay, yaaaay, yupp*} → *yes*), using a dictionary of slang terms (this functionality is provided in the spell-checker). All texts were then tokenized and converted to lower case.

Following the manual annotation, our goal is to provide a single class-label to each chat turn, which may consist of one or more sentences. All machine learning experiments reported here use five-fold cross-validation with 4:1 train:test ratio. For this purpose the 482 collaboration sessions (described in section 3) were partitioned (once) into five groups: two groups of 97 sessions and three groups of 96 sessions each). This also resulted in unequal (but approximately similar) amount of turns in each fold (7541 turns in the smallest fold, 8032 in the largest).

**Experiment 1.** In our first experiment we train a Naive-Bayes classifier on just the primary labels from human annotator H1. We do not filter features, but rather use all available tokens. We use lexical features (word and punctuation tokens) in several configurations – unigrams, bigrams and trigrams. Performance results (micro-averaged across test-folds) are shown in Table 3. As a baseline, we always predict the most frequent category (CPS category#1), an approach that achieves 24.9% accuracy. The best result, 59.2% classification accuracy, is achieved by using just unigram features (single words and punctuation tokens). It clearly outperforms the baseline by a large margin. Bigrams and trigrams are not useful, their use actually decreases classification accuracy, as compared to using just unigrams.

We also experimented with ignoring the punctuation. A Naïve-Bayes classifier trained on lexical unigrams, but without punctuation, achieves accuracy of 55.5%. This is lower than the 59.2% achieved when punctuation is used. It demonstrates that punctuation is clearly useful for classification, which is consistent with similar results in a different domain (De Felice and Deane, 2012).

**Experiment 2.** Since collaborative interactions in the Volcano task are clearly dialogic, it is reasonable to expect that a CPS label for a given chat-turn may probabilistically depend on the labels of previous turns (as is often the case for dialogue-acts, e.g. Stolcke et al., 2000). Thus, we explore the use of Hidden Markov Model (HMM) classifier in this case (following the approach of Stolcke et al., 2000). We explored a range of parameter settings, using n-best labels from 4 to 7 (for a single chat-turn) and look-back history of one or two turns. Looking back is restricted because the dialogue is usually localized, just a few turns focusing on the specific subtask that participants were working on. Results are presented in Table 3. HMM modeling is clearly not effective in this task, as its results are much lower than those from a Naïve-Bayes classifier. Notably, this result is not without precedent. Serafin & Di Eugenio (2004), working on dialogue act modeling, found that using dialogue history worsens rather than improves performance.

A per-CPS-category performance comparison was conducted between the Naïve-Bayes unigrams-based classifier and the HMM classifier (with n-best=4, lookback=1). The HMM classifier performs worse than NB classifier on all categories, except CPS category #4 (student expresses agreement with the teammates), where HMM is better than NB by 7.34%. This suggests that selective integration of contextual information might be useful.

| Method | Acc.% | Kappa |
|---|---|---|
| Baseline (most frequent class) | 24.9 | 0.01 |
| Experiment 1 | | |
| NB with lexical unigrams | 59.2 | 0.52 |
| NB with unigrams+bigrams | 58.5 | 0.51 |
| NB with 1-,2- & 3-grams | 58.2 | 0.51 |
| NB, unigrams, no punctuation | 55.6 | 0.48 |
| Experiment 2 | | |
| HMM, n-best=4, lookback=1 | 52.5 | 0.42 |
| HMM, n-best=7, lookback=1 | 48.1 | 0.36 |
| HMM, n-best=4, lookback=2 | 46.4 | 0.34 |
| HMM, n-best=7, lookback=2 | 41.7 | 0.28 |
| Experiment 3 | | |
| NB on CPS data, with probabilistic dialog-act tagging trained on out-of-domain data | 44.6 | 0.30 |
| Same as above, +lexical unigrams from CPS data | 60.3 | 0.54 |

**Table 3:** Evaluation results (accuracy and Cohen's kappa) for machine learning classification experiments with 31 CPS Framework tag categories. All results were micro-averaged from five cross-validation test folds (N=38,703 chat turns). NB=Naïve-Bayes, HMM=Hidden Markov Model.

**Experiment 3.** In this experiment we investigated whether automatic dialogue-act detection, trained on out-of-domain data, can be beneficial for CPS classification. Webb & Liu (2008) have demonstrated that using out-of-domain data can contribute to more robust classification of speech acts for in-domain data. Here, we extend this idea even further – use out-of-domain training data and a different classification schema.

In a separate study, we developed an automated speech-act classifier using the ICSI Meeting Recorder Dialogue Act (MRDA) corpus (Shriberg et al., 2004). The dialogue act of each sentence was annotated using MRDA annotation scheme developed for multiparty natural human-human dialogue. It defined a set of primitive communicative actions. In total, it includes 50 tags: 11 general tags and 39 specific tags. General tags include speech act types such as statements and yes/no questions and also make distinctions among syntactically different forms. Specific tags describe the purpose of the utterance, e.g., whether the speaker is making a suggestion or responding positively to a question.

The automated speech-act classifier was trained using a set of linguistic features described in Webb and Liu (2008), including sentence length, sentence initial and final word/POS n-grams, and presence/absence of cue phrases. A Maximum Entropy model-based classifier was trained on randomly selected 40 meetings and tested on the remained 24 meetings. The kappa between the system and human annotator was 0.71 for general tag and 0.61 for specific tag. The inter-rater agreement based on the subset of data was 0.80 for general tag and 0.71 for specific tag.

Notably, the MRDA data – conversations among computer scientists – is different from our CPS data, and the tag-set of dialogue acts is different from the CPS Framework tag-set. For our experiment, we used the out-of-domain-trained speech-act classifier to process CPS chat data and recorded the predicted probabilities of each speech act. Since CPS data was not annotated for speech acts, we do not know how accurate that classifier is. We just took the assigned speech-act tags and used them as probabilistic features in training our Naïve-Bayes CPS classifier, as follows. In training a standard Naïve-Bayes text classifier, each token (e.g. word) is a feature and its basic weight (count) is 1. Thus, the standard approach is to maximize:

$$\operatorname*{argmax}_{c} \log(P(C)) + \sum_{i} \log P(w_i|C)$$

We use the predicted speech-act tags as special features, and their probabilities as feature weights, using the following formula:

$$\operatorname*{argmax}_{c} \log(P(C)) + \sum_{i} \log\left[P(f_i) \times P(f_i|C)\right]$$

where $P(f_i)$ is the probability of speech act $f_i$ in the current chat-turn and $P(f_i|C)$ is the conditional probability of speech act $f_i$ given a specific CPS tag (this part is learned in the training).

A Naïve-Bayes CPS classifier, trained with probabilistic speech-act features, achieves accuracy of 44.6% in assigning CPS tags, which is substantially better than our baseline of 24.9%. We then trained a Naïve-Bayes classifier that integrates both lexical features (unigrams) from CPS training data and probabilistic speech-act features, using the formula:

$$\arg\max_{c} \log(P(C)) + \sum_{j} \log P(w_j|C) + \sum_{i} \log\left[P(f_i) \times P(f_i|C)\right]$$

where $w_j$ are lexical features (tokens). This approach makes the additional naïve assumption that speech acts as features are independent of the words. This classifier achieves 60.3% accuracy in CPS classification, 1% more than lexical-unigrams Naïve-Bayes (significant difference, p<0.000001, McNemar's test for correlated proportions).

We conducted additional investigations, to look how the classifiers perform for each individual CPS category. Table 4 presents the accuracy of the Naïve-Bayes unigram-based classifier on each CPS category. One obvious conclusion is that the larger is the count of a given category, the higher is the classifier accuracy. In fact, the Pearson correlation between tag count and accuracy is 0.701. While this might be expected, there are also some examples that do not follow this trend. The classifier achieves only 9.76% accuracy on label #12 (student elaborates on own statement), although it is a rather frequent category. A possible reason for this might be that elaboration statements are highly heterogeneous in form and lexical content, their status as 'elaborations' requires some abstraction and semantic inference. Another example is label #3 (student responds to the teammate's request for task-relevant information), with only 2.31% classification accuracy. This looks like one of the cases that could benefit from considering content from previous chat-turns, although not always from the immediately preceding turn.

Detailed analysis of classifier performance on each CPS category provides some interesting findings. In experiment 3 we have found that adding probabilistic dialogue act detection as features to a lexical Naïve-Bayes classifier improves overall accuracy by just 1%. However, a detailed view reveals additional information (see last column in Table 4). For some CPS categories, adding dialogue acts considerably improves classifier accuracy: 8% for cat-

egory #20 and 10% for category #22. This is not unexpected – CPS category #20 (student checks on understanding) directly corresponds to dialogue-act category 'understanding-Check'. Another case is CPS category #17 (student expresses progress in understanding), which corresponds rather directly to dialogue-act "acknowledgement". For several other CPS categories, detection of dialogue-acts was not helpful for CPS classification. In future work, we will consider how to use dialogue-act detection selectively in CPS classification.

While the results from our experiments are encouraging, higher levels of accuracy are needed for

| CPS tag | Total Count | Accuracy NB | Accuracy NB DA | Change |
|---|---|---|---|---|
| 1 | 9628 | 66.99 | 67.60 | 0.61 |
| 4 | 7736 | 83.85 | 82.38 | *-1.47* |
| 28 | 5119 | 67.49 | 66.52 | -0.98 |
| 20 | 4136 | 59.99 | 68.01 | **8.03** |
| 16 | 1704 | 44.72 | 46.19 | 1.47 |
| 12 | 1260 | 9.76 | 11.43 | 1.67 |
| 21 | 1189 | 44.66 | 45.33 | 0.67 |
| 22 | 1169 | 49.44 | 59.54 | **10.09** |
| 15 | 1021 | 44.27 | 44.47 | 0.20 |
| 24 | 768 | 50.39 | 51.30 | 0.91 |
| 3 | 735 | 2.31 | 2.31 | 0.00 |
| 32 | 512 | 60.55 | 58.98 | -1.56 |
| 18 | 506 | 29.05 | 28.46 | -0.59 |
| 10 | 498 | 6.83 | 7.43 | 0.60 |
| 19 | 435 | 54.02 | 54.71 | 0.69 |
| 13 | 408 | 30.39 | 29.41 | -0.98 |
| 9 | 359 | 11.98 | 12.81 | 0.84 |
| 11 | 333 | 16.52 | 17.12 | 0.60 |
| 2 | 261 | 45.21 | 42.53 | *-2.68* |
| 17 | 252 | 19.05 | 25.40 | **6.35** |
| 25 | 228 | 11.84 | 7.46 | -4.39 |
| 6 | 115 | 13.91 | 13.04 | -0.87 |
| 5 | 66 | 1.52 | 6.06 | **4.55** |
| 30 | 65 | 16.92 | 23.08 | **6.15** |
| 14 | 57 | 10.53 | 7.02 | *-3.51* |
| 29 | 46 | 8.70 | 4.35 | *-4.35* |
| 8 | 41 | 7.32 | 0.00 | *-7.32* |
| 33 | 26 | 0.00 | 0.00 | 0.00 |
| 23 | 16 | 0.00 | 0.00 | 0.00 |
| 31 | 11 | 0.00 | 0.00 | 0.00 |
| 7 | 3 | 0.00 | 0.00 | 0.00 |

**Table 4:** CPS categories, with counts (primary label by annotator H1), and average automated classification accuracy. (NB)=Naïve-Bayes with unigram features, (NB DA)= Naïve-Bayes with unigram features and Dialogue Act features.

using automated CPS classifiers in operational settings. Beigman-Klebanov and Beigman (2014) and Jamison and Gurevych (2015) have suggested that, in supervised machine learning, the presence of difficult items in the training sets is detrimental to learning performance and that performance can be improved if systems are trained on only easy data. They define 'easy' as less controversial in human annotations. We explore this aspect using the Naïve-Bayes classifier with unigram lexical features.

**Experiment 4.** Our annotator H1 used secondary labels when a chat-turn had two prominent functions (rather than just one). Such cases can be considered ambiguous and more difficult than cases that have only one prominent CPS function. In this experiment we filtered such cases out (reduction of about 34%, to N=25,299), from either training, testing or both. Results are shown in Table 5.

**Experiment 5.** Here we consider as 'easy' only those 3,818 cases where two human annotators agreed on the primary label. We train a new set of classifiers, using the same five-fold cross-validation splits, but filter out from training all cases that lack explicit consensus. Micro-averaged performance for this type of classifier is compared to the classifier that used unfiltered training data. Results are presented in Table 6.

|  |  | Testing | |
|---|---|---|---|
|  |  | Unfiltered data | Cases without secondary tag |
| Training | Unfiltered data | 59.2% <br> *k=0.52* | 69.0% <br> *k=0.62* |
| | Cases without secondary tag | 57.8% <br> *k=0.49* | 70.9% <br> *k=0.63* |

**Table 5:** Classifier accuracy when trained and tested with/without cases that have secondary CPS labels.

|  |  | Testing | |
|---|---|---|---|
|  |  | Unfiltered data | Consensus cases |
| Training | Unfiltered data | 59.2% <br> *k=0.52* | 73.1% <br> *k=0.67* |
| | Consensus cases | 55.3% <br> *k=0.46* | 74.4% <br> *k=0.68* |

**Table 6:** Classifier accuracy when trained and tested with all or just human-rater-consensus cases.

In both experiments 4 and 5 we see that when a classifier is trained on 'easy' data and tested on all data, performance degrades (relative to a classifier that was trained on all data), but degradation is very moderate. In experiment 4, training data was reduced by 30%, but degradation of accuracy was just 1.4%. In experiment 5 training data was reduced by 90%, but degradation of accuracy was just 3.9%. On the other hand, when tested on only easy data, classifiers that were trained on easy data outperform the classifiers that were trained on unfiltered data, but only by a very small margin (1-2%).

## 6 Conclusions

In this paper we presented a novel task that integrates collaborative problem solving behavior with testing in a science domain. For integration in educational assessment, the task would benefit from automated scoring of CPS discourse. We used a complex CPS coding scheme with four major dimensions and 33 classes. In our initial exploration, we sought to obtain a single CPS category-label for each turn in chat dialogues. Our results indicate that considerable accuracy (59.2%) can be achieved by using a simple Naïve-Bayes classifier with unigram lexical features. This result approaches human inter-rater agreement (62.8%).

For future research we consider pursuing several complementary lines of work. One direction is to use more sophisticated machine-learning approaches, such as CRF and SVM, and additional features, such as part-of-speech tags and timing of chat turns. Another direction is to explore the reasons for disagreement in human annotations. Given the complex nature of collaborative discourse, it is usual that some discourse turns carry more than one function mapped in the CPS framework. Thus, another line of exploration is to train a system to decide in which cases it may suggest more than one tag to a given chat turn, i.e. consider multi-label classification of CPS data. Finally, it might be fruitful to provide a bridge between the high-level functionally-defined CPS categories and more linguistically-oriented dialogue acts. We have shown that using a Dialogue Acts classifier, trained on out-of-domain data, can be useful for classifying CPS skills. We will explore whether an explicit mapping between dialogue acts and CPS categories may contribute to better CPS classifications.

## References

Asterhan, C.S.C., and B.B. Schwarz. 2009. Argumentation and Explanation in Conceptual Change: Indications from Protocol Analyses of Peer-to-Peer Dialog. *Cognitive Science*, 33, 374–400.

Baker, R., D'Mello, S.K., Rodrigo, M.M.T. and A.C. Graesser. 2010. Better to Be Frustrated than Bored: The Incidence, Persistence, and Impact of Learners' Cognitive-Affective States during Interactions with Three Different Computer-Based Learning Environments. *International Journal of Human-Computer Studies*, 68, 4, 223-241.

Barron, B. (2003). When smart groups fail. *The Journal of the Learning Sciences*, 12(3):307-359.

Beigman Klebanov, B. and E. Beigman. 2014. Difficult Cases: From Data to Learning, and Back. In Proceedings of the 52nd Annual Meeting of the Association for Computational Linguistics (Short Papers), pages 390–396.

Boyer, K.E., Ha, E.Y., Phillips, R., Wallis, M.D., Vouk, M.A. and J.C. Lester. 2010. Dialogue act modeling in a complex task-oriented domain. In Proceedings of the 11th Annual Meeting of the Special Interest Group on Discourse and Dialogue, pages 297-305. Association for Computational Linguistics.

Chin, C., and J. Osborne. 2010. Students' questions and discursive interaction: Their impact on argumentation during collaborative group discussions in science. *Journal of Research in Science Teaching*, 47(7), 883-908.

Damon, W., and E. Phelps. 1989. Critical distinction among three approaches to peer education. *International Journal of Educational Research*, 13, 9-19.

De Felice R. and P. Deane. 2012. Identifying Speech Acts in E-Mails: Toward Automated Scoring of the TOEIC® E-Mail Task. ETS Research Report RR-12-16. Educational Testing Service, Princeton, NJ.

Dillenbourg, P. and D. Traum. 2006. Sharing solutions: Persistence and grounding in multimodal collaborative problem solving. *The Journal of the Learning Sciences*, 15(1):121-151.

Dönmez, P., Rosé, C., Stegmann, K., Weinberger, A., and F. Fischer. 2005. Supporting CSCL with automatic corpus analysis technology. In T. Koschmann, D.D. Suthers, and T.-W. Chan (Eds.), Proceedings of the 2005 conference on Computer support for collaborative learning: The next 10 years! Mahwah, NJ: Lawrence Erlbaum Associates, pages 125–134.

Duschl, R., and J. Osborne. 2002. Supporting and promoting argumentation discourse. *Studies in Science Education*, 38, 39-72.

Erkens, G. and J. Janssen. 2008. Automatic coding of dialogue acts in collaboration protocols. *Computer-Supported Collaborative Learning*, 3:447–470.

Flor, M. 2012. Four types of context for automatic spelling correction. *Traitement Automatique des Langues* (TAL), 53:3, 61-99

Graesser, A.C., D'Mello, S.K., Craig, S.D., Witherspoon, A., Sullins, J., McDaniel, B. and B. Gholson. 2008. The relationship between affective states and dialog patterns during interactions with AutoTutor. *Journal of Interactive Learning Research*, 19, 2,293-312.

Greiff. S. 2012. From interactive to collaborative problem solving: Current issues in the Programme for International Student Assessment. *Review of Psychology*, 19, 2, 111–121.

Griffin, P., Care, E., and B. McGaw. 2012. The changing role of education and schools. In P. Griffin, B. McGaw, and E. Care (Eds.), *Assessment and teaching 21st century skills*, pages 1-15. Heidelberg, Germany: Springer.

Hao, J., Liu, L., von Davier, A., and P. Kyllonen. 2015. Assessing collaborative problem solving with simulation based tasks. In Proceeding of the 11th international conference on computer supported collaborative learning, Gothenburg, Sweden.

Hao, J., Liu, L., von Davier, A., Kyllonen, P. and C. Kitchen. (Submitted). Collaborative problem solving skills versus collaboration outcomes: findings from statistical analysis and data mining, The 9th International Conference on Educational Data Mining

Hatano, G., and K. Inagaki. 1991. Sharing cognition through collective comprehension activity. In L.B. Resnick, J.M. Levine, & S.D. Teasley (Eds.), *Perspectives on socially shared cognition*, pages 331-348, Washington, DC: American Psychological Association.

Higgins, S., Mercier, E., Burd, L. and A. Joyce-Gibbons. 2012. Multi-touch tables and collaborative learning. *British Journal of Educational Technology*, 43(6), 1041-1054

Hmelo-Silver, C.E., and H.S. Barrows. 2008. Facilitating collaborative knowledge building. *Cognition and Instruction*, 26, 48-94.

Hmelo-Silver, C.E., Nagarajan, A., and R.S. Day. 2000. Effects of high and low prior knowledge on construction of a joint problem space. *Journal of Experimental Education*, 69, 36-57.

Jamison, E.K. and I. Gurevych. 2015. Noise or additional information? Leveraging crowdsource annotation item agreement for natural language tasks. In Proceedings of the 2015 Conference on Empirical Methods in Natural Language Processing, pages 291–297.

Kersey, C., Di Eugenio, B., Jordan, P., and S. Katz. 2009. Knowledge co-construction and initiative in peer learning interactions. In Proceedings of AIED 2009, the 14th International Conference on Artificial Intelligence in Education, pages 325-332. Brighton, UK.

Klopfer, E., Osterweil, S., Groff, J. and J. Haas. 2009. *Using the technology of today, in the classroom today*. The Education Arcade, MIT.

Law, N., Yuen, J., Huang, R., Li, Y., and N. Pan. 2007. A learnable content & participation analysis toolkit for assessing CSCL learning outcomes and processes. In C. A. Chinn, G. Erkens, and S. Puntambekar (Eds.), Mice, minds, and society: *The Computer Supported Collaborative Learning* (CSCL) Conference 2007 (Vol. 8, pp. 408–417). New Brunswick, NJ: International Society of the Learning Sciences.

Landis J.R. and G.G. Koch. 1977. The measurement of observer agreement for categorical data. *Biometrics*, 33:159-174.

Lipponen, L., Rahikainen, M., Lallimo, J., and K. Hakkarainen. (2003). Patterns of participation and discourse in elementary students' computer-supported collaborative learning. *Learning and instruction*, 13(5), 487-509.

Liu, L., Hao, J., von Davier, A.A., Kyllonen, P. and D. Zapata-Rivera. 2015. A tough nut to crack: Measuring collaborative problem solving. Handbook of Research on Technology Tools for Real-World Skill Development, pages 344-359.

Lu, J., Chiu, M. M., and N. Law. 2011. Collaborative argumentation and justifications: A statistical discourse analysis of online discussions. *Computers in Human Behavior*, 27, 946-955.

Mercier, E.M., Higgins, S. and L. da Costa. 2014. Different leaders: Emergent organizational and intellectual leadership in collaborative learning groups. *International Journal of Computer-Supported Collaborative Learning*, 9(4), 397-432.

OECD. 2013. PISA 2015 draft collaborative problem solving assessment framework. OECD Publishing, Organization for Economic Co-operation and Development. http://www.oecd.org/pisa/pisaproducts/Draft%20PISA%202015%20Collaborative%20Problem%20Solving%20Framework%20.pdf

Prata, D.N., Baker, R., Costa, E., Rosé, C.P., Cui, Y. and A.M.J.B. de Carvalho. 2009. Detecting and Understanding the Impact of Cognitive and Interpersonal Conflict in Computer Supported Collaborative Learning Environments. In Proceedings of the 2nd International Conference on Educational Data Mining, 131-140.

Rosé, C.P., Wang, Y.-C., Cui, Y., Arguello, J., Stegmann, K., Weinberger, A. and F. Fischer. 2008. Analyzing collaborative learning processes automatically: Exploiting the advances of computational linguistics in computer-supported collaborative learning. *International Journal of Computer Supported Collaborative Learning*, 3, 237–271.

Samuel, K., Carberry, S., & K. Vijay-Shanker. 1999. Automatically selecting useful phrases for dialogue act tagging. In Proceedings of the Fourth Conference of the Pacific Association for Computational Linguistics, Waterloo, Ontario, Canada.

Schellens, T., and M. Valcke. 2005. Collaborative learning in asynchronous discussion groups: What about the impact on cognitive processing?. *Computers in Human Behavior*, 21(6), 957-975.

Serafin, R., and B. Di Eugenio. 2004. FLSA: Extending Latent Semantic Analysis with features for dialogue act classification s. In Proceedings of the 42nd Annual Meeting on Association for Computational Linguistics, Barcelona, Spain.

Shriberg, E., Dhillon, R., Bhagat, S., Ang, J. and H. Carvey, 2004. The ICSI Meeting Recorder Dialog Act (MRDA) Corpus. In Proceedings of the 5th SIGdial Workshop on Discourse and Dialogue at NAACL-HLT 2004 conference.

Stolcke, A., K. Ries, N. Coccaro, E. Shriberg, R. Bates, D. Jurafsky, P. Taylor, R. Martin, C. Van Ess-Dykema, and M. Meteer. 2000. Dialogue act modeling for automatic tagging and recognition of conversational speech. *Computational Linguistics*, 26(3), pages 339-373.

Von Davier, A.A., and P.F. Halpin. 2013. Collaborative Problem Solving and the Assessment of Cognitive Skills: Psychometric Considerations. ETS Research Report RR-13-41. Educational Testing Service, Princeton, NJ.

Webb, N., Hepple, M., and Y. Wilks. 2005. Dialogue Act Classification Based on Intra-Utterance Features. In Proceedings of the AAAI Workshop on Spoken Language Understanding.

Webb, N., and T. Liu, 2008. Investigating the portability of corpus derived cue phrases for dialogue act classification. In Proceedings of the 22nd International Conference on Computational Linguistics, Vol. 1, pages 977–984, Association for Computational Linguistics.

Weinberger, A., and F. Fischer. 2006. A framework to analyze argumentative knowledge construction in computer-supported collaborative learning. *Computers and Education*, 46(1), 71–95.

Zapata-Rivera, D., Jackson, T., Liu, L., Bertling, M., Vezzu, M., and I.R. Katz. 2014. Assessing science inquiry skills using trialogues. In S. Trausan-Matu, K. Boyer, M. Crosby and K. Panourgia (Eds.), *Intelligent Tutoring Systems* (Vol. 8474, pp. 625-626), Springer International Publishing.

# Computer-assisted stylistic revision with incomplete and noisy feedback
## A pilot study


**Christian M. Meyer**[†‡] **and Johann Frerik Koch**[†]

[†] Ubiquitous Knowledge Processing (UKP) Lab
Technische Universität Darmstadt, Germany
[‡] Research Training Group AIPHES
Technische Universität Darmstadt, Germany
http://www.ukp.tu-darmstadt.de



## Abstract

We investigate how users of intelligent writing assistance tools deal with correct, incorrect, and incomplete feedback. To this end, we conduct an empirical user study around an L1 text revision task for German. Our participants should revise stylistic issues in two given texts using a novel web-based writing environment that highlights potential issues and provides corresponding feedback messages. In comparison to a control group, we find that precision plays a more important role than recall, which confirms previous findings for other languages, issue types, user groups, and experimental setups.


## 1 Motivation

The importance of well-written texts is striking. Research stalls if scientists cannot understand a paper. Technical systems are hardly usable if their documentation is miserable. Job applications may fail due to the use of inadequate registers in a résumé or cover letter. News articles seem carelessly researched if they are full of spelling errors. Even for apparently informal text types, such as microblog posts, authors have to think about a suitable formulation to convey their message in an adequate way to the desired target audience.

To improve a text, authors typically rely on manually provided feedback from friends, colleagues, or professionals as well as on automatically generated feedback from word processors. Since automatic feedback is much less time-consuming and repeatedly available with practically no waiting time, this solution is very attractive.

However, the natural language processing methods generating this kind of feedback are still prone to many errors. Although human feedback might be erroneous as well, automatic methods yet perform significantly worse. The best submission to the 2014 CoNLL shared task on grammatical error correction (Ng et al., 2014) reaches, for example, only 73 % of the average human performance (Bryant and Ng, 2015). A particular issue with automatic feedback is that answers might be embarrassingly wrong (e.g., WATSON considering Toronto a U. S. city during the *Jeopardy!* challenge).

In this paper, we investigate the effects of giving noisy (i.e., partly incorrect) and incomplete feedback on an L1 text revision task. To this end, we conduct a pilot user study with German native speakers, in which we ask them to revise two texts containing a number of stylistic issues. While one group receives feedback about the potential issues, including correct, incorrect, and incomplete feedback, the second group serves as a control group, who revises the texts without any technological help.

Researching how humans deal with the outputs of language processing tools and specifically with automatically generated feedback is long overdue. Though our community achieves much progress in improving the performance on annotated gold standards, we still have limited knowledge about the usefulness of the underlying methods and techniques in a practical setting. We expect that our study makes an important contribution in this direction. From the results of our and similar studies, we envision truly *intelligent* tools that assist writers in their work, rather than forcing them to click repeatedly on "ignore this issue".




*Proceedings of the 11th Workshop on Innovative Use of NLP for Building Educational Applications*, pages 42–52,
San Diego, California, June 16, 2016. ©2016 Association for Computational Linguistics

## 2 State of the Art

There is a vast amount of scientific literature on intelligent writing assistance and automatic text correction methods in natural language processing and especially computer-assisted language learning. To evaluate such methods, we can distinguish data-driven and user-driven approaches discussed below.

### 2.1 Data-driven Evaluation

The most widely accepted evaluation methodology in this area is an intrinsic setup to compare a system's output with annotated reference data. For automatically identifying language-related issues and generating corresponding corrections, the *Helping Our Own* shared tasks (Dale and Kilgarriff, 2010; 2011; Dale et al., 2012) constituted a community around this type of system evaluation, which has successfully continued at the CoNLL conferences (Ng et al., 2013; 2014) and very recently at the BEA workshop (Daudaravicius, 2015). These initiatives are completed by numerous independent evaluation studies, such as the ones by Park and Levy (2011) or Perin et al. (2012) to name just two examples.

Major challenges to this evaluation methodology are: achieving a meaningful comparison of multiple systems, properly interpreting the performance metrics, and ensuring the reliability of the reference data. Chodorow et al. (2012) discuss the comparability of grammatical error detection systems and give recommendations for best practices. Bryant and Ng (2015) pose the highly important question of what is considered high-quality error detection with regard to human performance. Obviously, the quality of the reference data directly affects the evaluation scores. Systems are penalized for detecting an actual error that remained unseen by the human annotators or suggesting a valid correction not covered by the gold standard. Inter-rater agreement measures (Artstein and Poesio, 2008) provide a useful tool to assess the reliability, but as Ng et al. (2014, p. 12) note, metrics such as the kappa coefficient do "not take into account the fact that there is often more than one valid way to correct a sentence".

We believe that data-driven evaluation of intelligent writing assistance systems is vital, but given these issues, we suggest that they should be complemented by user-driven evaluation studies.

### 2.2 User-driven Evaluation

The user-driven evaluation of different types of language feedback has been a major research topic in writing and language learning research, before most automatic writing assistance systems evolved. Jacobs (1989), Owston et al. (1992), and Jacobs et al. (1998) are early works in this direction discussing feedback by teachers and peers, based on different educational resources, and using different media.

More recently, the effects of giving automatically generated feedback became an important research question. Attali (2004) report a large-scale study of the *Criterion* system (Burstein et al., 2003). He automatically scores essays before and after providing automated feedback and notes an overall improvement of the writing quality when providing feedback. The study does, however, not vary the type of feedback in any way. Andersen et al. (2013) distinguish feedback at the text, sentence, and word levels and evaluate different granularities with a questionnaire. Heift and Rimrott (2008) study different ways of formulating feedback messages for spelling errors and find solution suggestions yielding improved results. In a similar line of research, Lavolette et al. (2015) compare immediate and delayed feedback and find that students more likely responded to correct feedback. Madnani et al. (2015) vary the extent of feedback messages about English preposition errors using a crowdsourcing setup. Regardless of the extent of the feedback messages, they find a learning effect in *detecting* errors over multiple writing sessions. But only participants who received correct and detailed feedback were able to *fix* more errors. They, however, note limitations of their study setup due to the unclear distribution of preposition errors and language proficiency of the crowdsourcing population. None of these works systematically varies correct, incorrect, and incomplete feedback.

The work by Nagata and Nakatani (2010) is most closely related to ours. They ask 26 language learners to write a number of essays and revise them under four experimental conditions: without any technological assistance, with recall-oriented automatic feedback, with precision-oriented automatic feedback, and with human feedback. They focus on two types of grammatical errors and find the precision-oriented feedback to maximize the learning effect of the participants. Their work differs from the present paper in multiple ways: First, we consider a revision task of an unknown text instead of a self-written essay, which allows us to control for the number and distribution of errors over all participants. With this setup, we get in a position to compare the users' revisions systematically. Second, we consider German native speakers rather than English learners. Since most previous work is focused on English learners, we believe that addressing native speakers and other languages is an important research gap. Third, we consider stylistic rather than grammatical issues, which has not been extensively discussed before. Fourth, we are interested in the usefulness of intelligent writing assistance systems for improving the text quality rather than the learning effect of the users. Still, we are eager to compare our findings with the previous work and discuss this in section 7.

## 3 Goals and Hypotheses

The motivation for developing intelligent writing assistance systems is that authors get in a position to compose texts of higher quality, ideally with less effort, time, or need for manual feedback. Incomplete and noisy feedback could, however, severely hamper this goal and yield lower quality or higher effort.

To operationalize these thoughts, we simulate an intelligent writing environment that highlights stylistic issues in a text and provides brief feedback messages explaining them. We have the following four hypotheses about the usage of such a system for a text revision task:

1. If users receive correct feedback about a stylistic issue, they will more likely revise the corresponding part of a text than users, who do not receive any feedback.

2. If users receive incorrect feedback about a stylistic issue, they will more likely revise the corresponding part of a text, although this would not be necessary.

3. If users receive incomplete feedback about stylistic issues, they will more likely miss issues, for which they do not receive feedback.

4. The time required for revising the text will not significantly differ between the users of a system with and without technological assistance.

The rationale behind the first hypothesis is that the highlighted text parts direct a user's attention to the stylistic issue. We thus expect a significantly higher number of revised stylistic issues that have been highlighted to the users.

The second hypothesis follows the same motivation as the first one: The users' attention is directed to the highlighted text positions. We believe that a user will more likely revise these highlighted text parts even if this would not be necessary. This would mean that users overtrust the system, even if they are aware of potential errors in the provided feedback. We therefore expect a significantly higher number of revised text positions that do not contain a stylistic issue, but that are highlighted as such.

A different type of overtrust is that users receiving automated feedback will more likely miss issues of similar types if they are not highlighted. We thus believe that the provided feedback causes a shift of focus from the actual revision task to the processing of the highlighted text parts. In this case, we would observe a significantly lower number of unmarked revised stylistic issues if other parts of the text are highlighted and associated with feedback messages.

The fourth hypothesis considers the time required for the revision task. We expect that users receiving feedback and users not receiving feedback will take equally long and therefore no significant difference in the time to complete the task. This would mean that an intelligent writing assistant neither increases nor decreases the required revision time.

## 4 Experimental Design

To test our hypotheses, we conduct an empirical user study, in which we ask our participants to enhance the quality of two given texts. We employ a $2 \times 2$ mixed factorial design. That is, we divide the participants into an experimental and a control group (between-subject variable) and provide them with texts of two different text types (within-subject variable). While the control group does not receive any assistance, the experimental group receives correct, incorrect, and incomplete feedback about stylistic issues in the texts. Below, we first introduce the textual data and the types of issues we consider, before we describe the participants and the overall setup of the study.

## 4.1 Data

For our experiment, we require texts with a predefined set of stylistic issues. Error-annotated learner texts seem an obvious choice. However, we need texts with multiple similar issues in order to systematically compare how users deal with the different types of feedback. Therefore, we turn towards existing high-quality texts and manually introduce a number of similar stylistic issues instead of using pre-annotated (learner) texts.

We select two different text types. The first text $T_1$ is an excerpt of the news article "Die Zaubertafel" (Engl.: "the magical board") about the presentation of the first iPad in 2010, published by the major German newspaper *ZEIT online*.[1] Along the lines of Christensen et al. (2014), we intentionally use an old article to minimize side effects caused by prior knowledge of the participants. As the second text $T_2$, we use a part of the encyclopedic article "Eigentliche Pythons" (Engl.: pythons) from the German Wikipedia.[2] Both texts have about 200 words and exhibit a high text quality. At the same time, both text types also demand for a high quality. This is relevant to control for the expectations of the participants, because text types typically showing lower quality (e.g., learner essays, meeting protocols, personal notes) might not be revised to the same meticulous degree by all participants.

We manually define eleven positions $p \in [1, 11]$ within the texts as our main subjects of analysis. For eight of them, we carefully manipulate the original text to introduce a stylistic issue. The other three remain unchanged. We restrict our manipulations to three issue types:

- *inappropriate registers* (IR), such as using colloquial language in an encyclopedic article,

- *uncommon collocations* (CL), for example when using "yellow" rather than "blond" in the context of hair colors, and

- *insufficient variation* (VA) by repeatedly using the same lexical and syntactic patterns without being a rhetorical device.

---

[1] http://www.zeit.de/2010/06/01-iPad
(published June 1, 2010; last accessed February 4, 2016)

[2] https://de.wikipedia.org/w/?oldid=121124960
(published August 2, 2013; last accessed February 4, 2016)

We choose stylistic issues over spelling and grammar errors, since we expect automatic methods to yield even more false alarms and incorrect suggestions for them than for other issues. We discuss the manipulated texts with multiple colleagues to ensure that the introduced issues can, in principal, be recognized and fixed.

In the next step, we simulate the feedback of an intelligent writing assistance tool. That is, we highlight the words at a position $p$ with yellow background color and we generate a message explaining the issue. Consider for example the IR issue $p = 7$:

> Wie alle Pythonartige sind sie ungiftig und machen ihrer Beute durch Umschlingen den Garaus.

The highlighted phrase "machen [...] den Garaus" is considered colloquial speech meaning to murder someone (i.e., to bump someone off). It is our manipulation of using the verb "töten" (to murder someone, without any register marking). As indicated by the example, we also allow for discontinuous highlights (i.e., a position $p$ might refer to multiple non-adjacent words or phrases).

The corresponding feedback message for this issue is the German equivalent of:

> The phrase "*to bump so. off*" is considered colloquial speech. Check if this phrase is appropriate in the given context.

To keep the cognitive load as small as possible, we limit ourselves to brief feedback messages. The message points out that there *might* be an issue and asks the user to check if a reformulation is necessary. The feedback message does not give suggestions of how to resolve the issue, but leaves the final decision to the user. This is necessary to ensure a fair comparison with the control group with regard to our hypotheses (see section 3).

The main motivation for our work is analyzing how users deal with incomplete and noisy feedback. This is why, we do not give feedback for all issues. Rather, we distinguish between correctly highlighted parts of a text that need revision (TP), incorrectly highlighted parts of a text that do not need revision (FP), and parts of a text that need revision, but are not highlighted to a user (FN). From a tool perspective, the text positions of type TP are a correct system result (i.e., true positives), FP positions

| $p$ | Text | Issue | Manipulated | Highlighted | Feedback |
|---|---|---|---|---|---|
| 1 | $T_1$ | VA | ✓ | ✓ | TP |
| 2 | $T_1$ | IR | ✓ | ✓ | TP |
| 3 | $T_1$ | IR | ✓ | | FN |
| 4 | $T_1$ | CL | ✓ | ✓ | TP |
| 5 | $T_1$ | VA | ✓ | | FN |
| 6 | $T_1$ | VA | | ✓ | FP |
| 7 | $T_2$ | IR | ✓ | ✓ | TP |
| 8 | $T_2$ | CL | | ✓ | FP |
| 9 | $T_2$ | IR | | ✓ | FP |
| 10 | $T_2$ | VA | ✓ | ✓ | TP |
| 11 | $T_2$ | CL | ✓ | | FN |

**Table 1:** Text positions considered for the user study

are detected by a system but false alarms (false positives), and FN positions are errors that remain undetected by the system (false negatives).

Table 1 gives an overview of the eleven relevant text positions $p$. The four TPs, three FPs, and four FNs are roughly equally distributed over the two texts and the three issue types considered. The chosen stylistic issue types, their distribution and position in the text follow practical considerations induced by the underlying texts. That is to say, we aim at making minimal changes to the texts and keep their original content and organization intact, which is necessary to avoid coherence breaks and newly introduced ambiguity.

### 4.2 Participants

We record the revision results of 26 participants. Though finding voluntary users is notoriously difficult, we aim at reducing the bias caused by a single homogeneous user group. This is why, we ask users from three different contexts: students from different programs at our university (31 %), PhD- or Postdoc-level NLP researchers (31 %), and randomly selected volunteers with varying professional backgrounds (38 %). All participants are German native speakers, 62 % of them are male, and their age ranges from 22 to 50 with an average age of $30.2 \pm 6.6$. Of the 26 responses received, 15 participants revised the texts under experimental conditions and 11 were part of the control group.

### 4.3 Procedure

We randomly assign the participants into the two groups. Each participant receives a printout with in-

structions, user credentials for the writing environment, and a usability questionnaire. We first ask the participants to read the instructions, in which we explain the text revision task, the two text types, and our expectations regarding a high text quality. We ask the users to not change the meaning and organization of the texts, but to focus on stylistic issues. Both groups receive the same instruction that the writing environment *might* support the revision task and that this support is not necessarily complete or correct. No additional help or resources should be used to complete the task. To avoid any pressure for the participating students, we made clear that participation is on a voluntary basis and does not affect the grading of any course.

Having read the instructions, the participants access our online writing environment described in section 5 below. The writing environment shows the two selected texts one after another. We randomly shuffle their order to avoid effects based on the order of the two texts. Note that hereafter, we always use the original order ($T_1$ before $T_2$) for our analysis. While participants of the control group can only use common word processor functions to revise the texts, participants of the experimental group additionally see the highlighted text parts and the corresponding feedback messages according to table 1.

For performing the final step of the study, the participants save their revisions in the online system and turn towards the questionnaire printout. We record some demographic data such as age and gender as well as information about the native tongue and a self-assessment of German language skills. The main body of the questionnaire aims at studying the usability of the writing environment in order to control for side effects due to a lack of user-friendliness. In section 6, we analyze these results.

We finalize the details and the formulations of our study by conducting a pretest with a student volunteer, who is not part of the actual study participants. Based on this pretest, we clarify the formulations of the task instructions to avoid misunderstandings.

## 5 Writing Environment

To conduct our user study, we implement a novel web-based writing environment as a secondary contribution of this paper. The writing environment

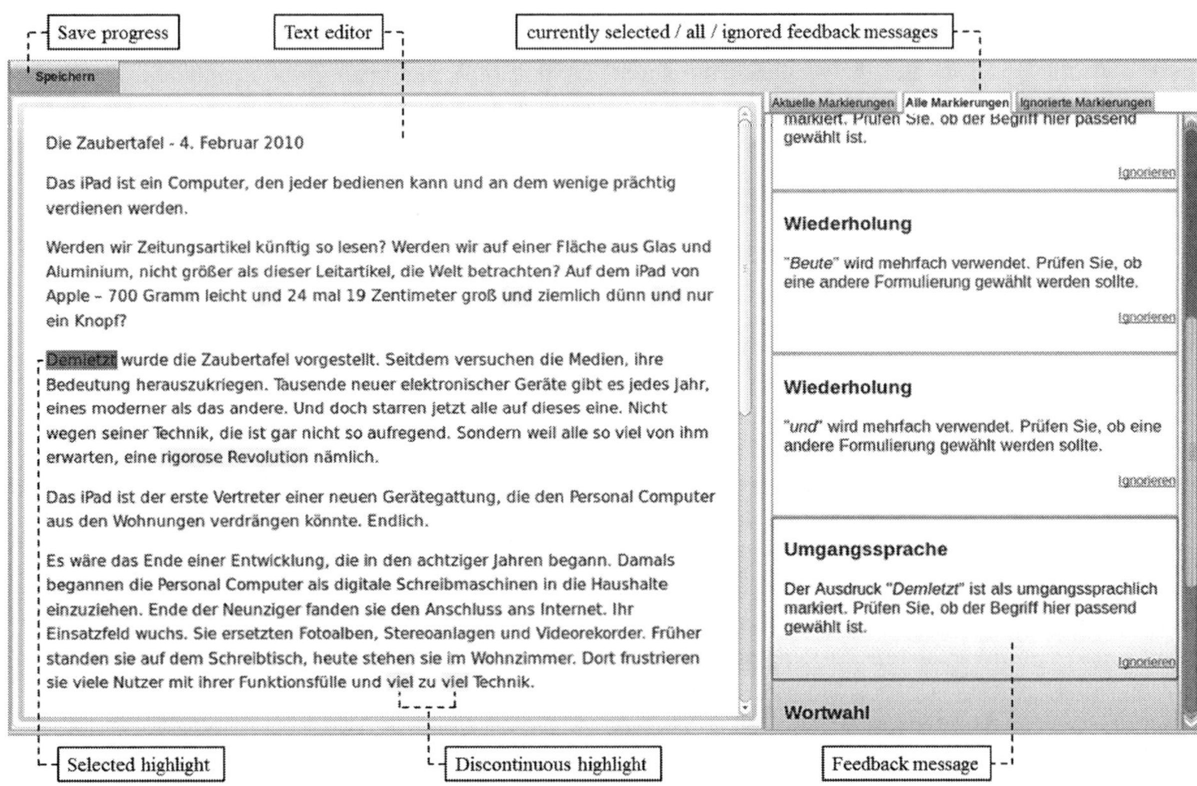



**Figure 1:** Screenshot of our writing environment

features common text edit operations and assists its users by displaying feedback about language-related issues. Although the highlighted text parts and the corresponding feedback messages for the stylistic issues considered in this study could also be modeled as a static webpage, we develop the writing environment with a larger goal in mind: to establish an open research platform for evaluating methods of intelligent writing assistance. The tool is available as open-source software from GitHub.[3] Figure 1 shows a screenshot of the user interface.

The writing environment divides the screen into two parts: a text editor on the left-hand side and a panel for displaying feedback on the right-hand side (about one third of the screen width). The text editor features common edit operations, such as cut/copy/paste, cursor navigation, deleting characters and selections, etc. To draw the user's attention to a certain part of the text, the editor may display words or phrases with a certain background color,

similar to using a marker pen on paper. Our system can properly highlight discontinuous text parts. For the example "machen [...] den Garaus" introduced above, we can highlight the first and the second part individually without losing the link to the same feedback message. This is especially relevant for German, which is rich in separable verbs (i.e., verbs that contain a particle either as a prefix or as a separate word at the end of the sentence). Upon clicking on a highlighted text part, the background color changes to orange, indicating that this issue is currently in the focus. For discontinuous issues, we recolor all highlighted parts linked to the issue.

In the feedback panel on the right-hand side of the screen, the user can choose to view a list of all feedback messages (tab "Alle Markierungen") or only the currently selected ones (tab "Aktuelle Markierungen", default setting). Note that in a real usage scenario, there could be multiple overlapping issues, which is why the current selection may include more than a single feedback message. Clicking on a feedback message has the same effect as

---

[3]https://github.com/UKPLab/
naacl-bea2016-writing-study

clicking on a highlighted text part – the system will mark both the text part and the feedback message in orange. When editing a highlighted text part, the yellow background color will disappear, similar to the spell-checking functionality of common word processors. Users may optionally ignore an issue without editing it. This clears the background color and moves the feedback message to a separate tab "Ignorierte Markierungen", from where it can also be reactivated in case it was ignored by accident or saved for later.

A key feature of our writing environment is that all user–system interactions are recorded and sent to a server instance, where we can analyze and store them. Specifically, we can log the keystrokes, the cursor navigation, and the interaction with the high-lighted text parts and the feedback messages. Since each recorded interaction has a timestamp, we get in a position to determine the time to complete a certain writing task or phase. The recorded user–system interaction data for the revision task described above is the data basis for checking our hypotheses.

## 6 System Usability

To rule out that the measured effects are influenced by a bad design of the writing environment, we ask our participants in the experimental group to rate the system usability.

The *System Usability Scale* (SUS) introduced by Brooke (1996) is among the most widely used measures. The SUS score is based on the user ratings for ten questions using a five point Likert scale each. For a given user $u$, the score is defined as

$$SUS(u) = 2.5 \left( \sum_{i \in \{1,3,5,7,9\}} u_i + \sum_{i \in \{2,4,6,8,10\}} 4 - u_i \right)$$

where $u_i = 0 \ldots 4$ is the user's rating for question $i$. Typically, the individual SUS scores are averaged over all users.

For our study, we use the German SUS translation by Lohmann and Schäfer (2013). One user skipped question 6 ("I thought there was too much inconsistency in this system") and another user skipped the questions 6 and 2 ("I found the system unnecessarily complex") for which we assume the neutral score 2.

Our system achieves an average SUS score of 76.3. While 100 is the maximum score, 68 is considered the threshold between poor and acceptable usability. For scores between 71.4 and 85.5, Bangor et al. (2009) find the highest correlation with the adjective "good", which is why we conclude that the observations made during our study are not affected by a poor system usability.

## 7 Results

For checking our four hypotheses, we identify which participant revised the texts at each of the eleven text positions $p$. All native speaker revisions yielded acceptable texts, which is why we consider a revision at $p$ on a binary scale. This provides us with a total of $11 \cdot 26 = 286$ data points for our analysis; 165 for the experimental group and 121 for the control group. On average, participants of the experimental group revised $\overline{x}_{\mathrm{EG}} = 5.86$ (standard error $SE = 0.53$, min: 2, max: 10) text positions and participants of the control group $\overline{x}_{\mathrm{CG}} = 3.18$ ($SE = 0.74$, min: 0, max: 8). Figure 2 (a) shows a notched boxplot of the total number of revised text positions. In addition to that, we consider the 26 times (in seconds) to complete the task. To test the hypotheses, we use an unpaired two sample Student's $t$-test and a significance level of $\alpha = 0.05$ (i.e., $P \leq 0.05$).

### 7.1 Hypothesis 1: Correct feedback

Our first hypothesis is that participants of the experimental group will more likely revise text parts that are highlighted compared to the control group not receiving any highlights. The corresponding null hypothesis is that $\mu_{\mathrm{EG(TP)}} = \mu_{\mathrm{CG(TP)}}$, where $\mu_{\mathrm{EG(TP)}}$ denotes the expected value of the number of changes at TP positions made by the experimental group and $\mu_{\mathrm{CG(TP)}}$ the corresponding expected value for the control group.

The mean number of revisions of TP positions $\{1, 2, 4, 7, 10\}$ is $\overline{x}_{\mathrm{EG(TP)}} = 4.13$ ($SE = 0.23$) for the experimental group and $\overline{x}_{\mathrm{CG(TP)}} = 1.63$ ($SE = 0.51$) for the control group. All participants in the experimental group revised at least 2 positions, while there are 4 participants of the control group who did not revise a single TP position. Conversely, there are participants of both groups, who revised all 5 TP positions. Figure 2 (b) shows a boxplot indicating a higher number of revisions in the experimental group than in the control group, whereas the control group shows a higher variance.

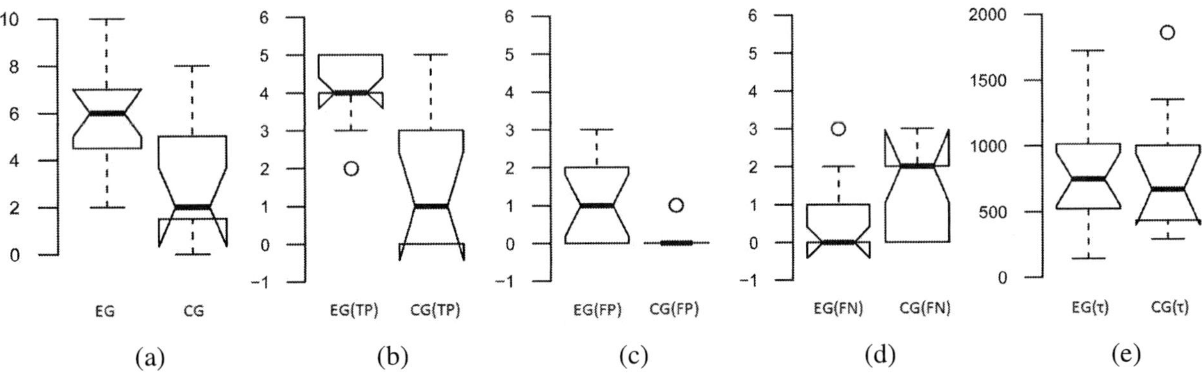

**Figure 2:** Notched boxplots ($\pm 1.57\frac{IQR}{\sqrt{n}}$) comparing all revised positions (a), the revisions at TP positions (b), at FP positions (c), at FN positions (d), and the time to complete the task (e) of the experimental group (EG) and the control group (CG)

The test statistic computes to $t_1 = 4.85$, which is higher than the critical value 2.06 ($P < 0.0001$). We can therefore clearly reject the null hypothesis at the 5 % level in favor of the alternative that highlighting stylistic issues helps the participants with increasing the text quality.

### 7.2 Hypothesis 2: Noisy feedback

Our second hypothesis is that the participants will more likely revise text positions that are mislabeled as stylistic issues. In other words, we expect a significant difference in the number of times the experimental group revises the FP positions $\{6, 8, 9\}$ compared to the control group. The corresponding null hypothesis is that $\mu_{EG(FP)} = \mu_{CG(FP)}$ where $\mu_{EG(FP)}$ denotes the expected value of the number of changes at FP positions made by the experimental group and $\mu_{CG(FP)}$ the corresponding expected value for the control group.

The mean number of revisions of FP positions is $\overline{x}_{EG(FP)} = 1$ ($SE = 0.25$) for the experimental group and $\overline{x}_{CG(FP)} = 0.18$ ($SE = 0.12$ for the control group. There are participants in both groups who did not revise any FP position. In the control group, only two participants revised a single FP position at all. In the experimental group, four participants revised a single, another four revised two, and one participant even revised all three FP positions, which corroborates our hypothesis. Figure 2 (c) shows the boxplot for FP positions.

We compute the test statistic $t_2 = 2.55$, which is higher than the critical value 2.06 ($P = 0.017$). We can therefore reject the null hypothesis at the 5 % level and conclude that highlighting false alarms causes writers to unnecessarily edit their manuscript.

While the results reported so far might be considered obvious, we note that the group difference is less clear than expected and much smaller than the one for the first hypothesis. Since six participants of the experimental group were able to recognize and ignore all false alarms, we suggest that intelligent methods should take the user interaction into account and control for the internal thresholds controlling the precision–recall trade-off. That is to say, users accepting all or most suggestions of a system, including those with a low confidence, should receive a higher precision, whereas users carefully picking out what to revise might be interested in a higher recall. This goes beyond Nagata and Nakatani's (2010) precision-focused suggestion.

### 7.3 Hypothesis 3: Incomplete feedback

Our third hypothesis is that the participants whose texts contain highlighted parts will rather not recognize stylistic issues of a similar type if they are not highlighted as well. In other words, we expect a significant difference in the number of times the participants of either group revise the FN positions $\{3, 5, 11\}$. The corresponding null hypothesis is that $\mu_{EG(FN)} = \mu_{CG(FN)}$ where $\mu_{EG(FN)}$ denotes the expected value of the number of changes at FN positions made by the experimental group and $\mu_{CG(FN)}$ the corresponding expected value for the control group.

The mean number of revisions of FN positions is $\overline{x}_{EG(FN)} = 0.73$ ($SE = 0.28$) for the experimental group and $\overline{x}_{CG(FN)} = 1.36$ ($SE = 0.36$) for the control group. Both groups contain participants, who revised either all three FN positions or none of them. Figure 2 (d) shows the corresponding boxplot.

Although the notches of the boxplot do not overlap (indicating a statistical difference), the test statistic is $t_3 = -1.39$, whose absolute value is clearly lower than the critical value 2.06 ($P = 0.17$). We therefore cannot reject the null hypothesis and thus do not find a significant difference between the two groups. This means that although we note a tendency for users seeing highlighted text parts to overlook unmarked issues of the same type, we do not find a significant difference.

While future studies with a larger number of participants may find a significant difference (mind that we cannot reject the alternative hypothesis based on our results), we note that false positives seem to be a more severe problem when giving automatic writing feedback than false negatives. For the design of an intelligent writing assistance systems, we therefore agree to Nagata and Nakatani (2010) in that we should particularly focus on precision (i.e., avoid false alarms) before aiming at an optimized recall.

### 7.4 Hypothesis 4: Task completion time

Our final hypothesis states that participants of the experimental group do not take significantly longer to complete the task than participants of the control group. We therefore expect that $\mu_{\mathrm{EG}(\tau)} = \mu_{\mathrm{CG}(\tau)}$ where $\mu_{\mathrm{EG}(\tau)}$ is the expected value of the task completion time of the experimental group and $\mu_{\mathrm{CG}(\tau)}$ correspondingly of the control group.

The task completion times range from 2 min, 23 sec to 30 min, 59 sec. The majority of participants require between 7 and 16 min with a mean of $\overline{x}_{\mathrm{EG}(\tau)} = 13$ min, 3 sec ($SE = 104$ sec) for the experimental group and $\overline{x}_{\mathrm{CG}(\tau)} = 13$ min, 27 sec ($SE = 144$ sec) for the control group, which is surprisingly similar. Figure 2 (e) shows again a boxplot.

The test statistic is $t_4 = -0.14$. The absolute value is clearly lower than the critical value 2.06 ($P = 0.89$). We therefore cannot reject the null hypothesis and thus do not find a significant difference between the two groups.

If there is no significant difference in the time that is required to revise a text with and without automatic feedback, this is good news for building intelligent writing assistance tools, as they do not cause additional expenditure of time for the writers.

## 8 Conclusion and Future Work

We conducted an empirical user study to analyze the effects of assisting writers with incomplete and noisy feedback when revising a given text. To this end, we systematically introduced stylistic issues in two texts and asked voluntary participants to enhance the quality of the texts. An experimental group received technological assistance by means of highlighted issues and corresponding feedback messages. We distinguished between highlighted text parts that needed revision (TP), highlighted text parts that did not require revision (FP), and texts parts that required revision without being highlighted (FN). With this setup, we simulated the error types of an actual intelligent writing assistance system. We compared the performance of the experimental group to a control group, who did not receive any technological aids.

Our analysis revealed that highlighting stylistic issues helped the participants to improve the quality of a text. If a text part was highlighted, the participants more likely revised it, even if the given text was already correct. In contrast, we found no significant difference for issues that remained undetected by a system (i.e., incomplete feedback). We concluded that the precision of a system plays a more important role than its recall, as participants tend to overtrust the system output, even though we made clear that the given feedback is not necessarily correct.

As a secondary contribution, we describe a novel writing environment, which we used for our study. We found a good system usability score for the tool and did not find a significant difference in the time to complete the text revision task indicating that neither the tool nor the feedback hinders the task.

We consider the user-driven evaluation of intelligent writing assistance and automatic text correction systems as highly important for assessing their usefulness. Follow-up studies should vary the frequency, order, and distribution of the issues and experiment with different ways of giving feedback. Based on our study results, we consider adaptive and interactive methods highly promising for designing and evaluating intelligent writing assistance tools. Besides writing assistance, future advances are also relevant for automatic essay scoring tools, which could allow for a more fine-grained analysis.

## Acknowledgments

This work has been supported by the DFG-funded research training group "Adaptive Preparation of Information form Heterogeneous Sources" (AIPHES, GRK 1994/1) and by the Volkswagen Foundation as part of the Lichtenberg-Professorship Program under grant № I/82806. We would like to thank the anonymous reviewers for their helpful comments.

## References

Øistein E. Andersen, Helen Yannakoudakis, Fiona Barker, and Tim Parish. 2013. Developing and testing a self-assessment and tutoring system. In *Proceedings of the Eighth Workshop on Innovative Use of NLP for Building Educational Applications*, pages 32–41, Atlanta, GA, USA.

Ron Artstein and Massimo Poesio. 2008. Inter-Coder Agreement for Computational Linguistics. *Computational Linguistics*, 34(4):555–596.

Yigal Attali. 2004. Exploring the Feedback and Revision Features of Criterion. Paper presented at the National Council on Measurement in Education (NCME), April 12–16, 2004, San Diego, CA, USA.

Aaron Bangor, Philip Kortum, and James Miller. 2009. Determining What Individual SUS Scores Mean: Adding an Adjective Rating Scale. *Journal of Usability Studies*, 4(3):114–123.

John Brooke. 1996. SUS: A 'Quick and Dirty' Usability Scale. In Patrick W. Jordan, Bruce Thomas, Bernard A. Weerdmeester, and Ian L. McClelland, editors, *Usability evaluation in industry*, chapter 21, pages 189–194. London//Bristol, PA: Taylor & Francis.

Christopher Bryant and Hwee Tou Ng. 2015. How Far are We from Fully Automatic High Quality Grammatical Error Correction? In *Proceedings of the 53rd Annual Meeting of the Association for Computational Linguistics and the 7th International Joint Conference on Natural Language Processing: Long Papers*, pages 697–707, Beijing, China.

Jill Burstein, Martin Chodorow, and Claudia Leacock. 2003. Criterion Online Essay Evaluation: An Application for Automated Evaluation of Student Essays. In *Proceedings of the Fifteenth Annual Conference on Innovative Applications of Artificial Intelligence*, pages 3–10, Acapulco, Mexico.

Martin Chodorow, Markus Dickinson, Ross Israel, and Joel Tetreault. 2012. Problems in Evaluating Grammatical Error Detection Systems. In *Proceedings of the 24th International Conference on Computational Linguistics*, volume 2, pages 611–628, Mumbai, India.

Janara Christensen, Stephen Soderland, Gagan Bansal, and Mausam. 2014. Hierarchical Summarization: Scaling Up Multi-Document Summarization. In *Proceedings of the 52nd Annual Meeting of the Association for Computational Linguistics (Volume 1: Long Papers)*, pages 902–912, Baltimore, MD, USA.

Robert Dale and Adam Kilgarriff. 2010. Helping Our Own: Text Massaging for Computational Linguistics as a New Shared Task. In *Proceedings of the 6th International Natural Language Generation Conference*, pages 261–265, Dublin, Ireland.

Robert Dale and Adam Kilgarriff. 2011. Helping Our Own: The HOO 2011 Pilot Shared Task. In *Proceedings of the 13th European Workshop on Natural Language Generation*, pages 242–249, Nancy, France.

Robert Dale, Ilya Anisimoff, and George Narroway. 2012. HOO 2012: A report on the Preposition and Determiner Error Correction Shared Task. In *Proceedings of the Seventh Workshop on Building Educational Applications Using NLP*, pages 54–62, Montréal, QC, Canada.

Vidas Daudaravicius. 2015. Automated Evaluation of Scientific Writing: AESW Shared Task Proposal. In *Proceedings of the Tenth Workshop on Innovative Use of NLP for Building Educational Applications*, pages 56–63, Denver, CO, USA.

Trude Heift and Anne Rimrott. 2008. Learner responses to corrective feedback for spelling errors in CALL. *System*, 36(2):196–213.

George M. Jacobs, Andy Curtis, George Braine, and Su-Yueh Huang. 1998. Feedback on student writing: taking the middle path. *Journal of Second Language Writing*, 7(3):307–317.

George M. Jacobs. 1989. Dictionaries Can Help Writing – If Students Know How To Use Them. ERIC Document Reproduction Service ED 316 025, Department of Educational Psychology, University of Hawaii.

Elizabeth Lavolette, Charlene Polio, and Jimin Kahng. 2015. The Accuracy of Computer-Assisted Feedback and Students' Responses to It. *Language Learning & Technology*, 19(2):50–68.

Kris Lohmann and Jörg Schäfer. 2013. System Usability Scale (SUS) – An Improved German Translation of the Questionnaire. Online: http://minds.coremedia.com/2013/09/18/sus-scale-an-improved-german-translation-questionnaire, September, 18, 2013. (accessed: February 4, 2016).

Nitin Madnani, Martin Chodorow, Aoife Cahill, Melissa Lopez, Yoko Futagi, and Yigal Attali. 2015. Preliminary Experiments on Crowdsourced Evaluation of Feedback Granularity. In *Proceedings of the Tenth Workshop on Innovative Use of NLP for Building Educational Applications*, pages 162–171, Denver, CO, USA.

Ryo Nagata and Kazuhide Nakatani. 2010. Evaluating performance of grammatical error detection to maximize learning effect. In *Proceedings of the 23rd International Conference on Computational Linguistics: Poster Volume*, pages 894–900, Beijing, China.

Hwee Tou Ng, Siew Mei Wu, Yuanbin Wu, Christian Hadiwinoto, and Joel Tetreault. 2013. The CoNLL-2013 Shared Task on Grammatical Error Correction. In *Proceedings of the Seventeenth Conference on Computational Natural Language Learning: Shared Task*, pages 1–12, Sofia, Bulgaria.

Hwee Tou Ng, Siew Mei Wu, Ted Briscoe, Christian Hadiwinoto, Raymond Hendy Susanto, and Christopher Bryant. 2014. The CoNLL-2014 Shared Task on Grammatical Error Correction. In *Proceedings of the Eighteenth Conference on Computational Natural Language Learning: Shared Task*, pages 1–14, Baltimore, MD, USA.

Ronald D. Owston, Sharon Murphy, and Herbert H. Wideman. 1992. The Effects of Word Processing on Students' Writing Quality and Revision Strategies. *Research in the Teaching of English*, 26(3):249–276.

Y. Albert Park and Roger Levy. 2011. Automated Whole Sentence Grammar Correction Using a Noisy Channel Model. In *Proceedings of the 49th Annual Meeting of the Association for Computational Linguistics: Human Language Technologies*, pages 934–944, Portland, OR, USA.

Fabrizio Perin, Lukas Renggli, and Jorge Ressia. 2012. Linguistic style checking with program checking tools. *Computer Languages, Systems & Structures*, 38(1):61–72.

# A Report on the Automatic Evaluation of Scientific Writing Shared Task


**Vidas Daudaravicius**
VTeX
`vidas.daudaravicius@vtex.lt`

**Rafael E. Banchs**
Institute for Infocomm Research
`rembanchs@i2r.a-star.edu.sg`

**Elena Volodina**
University of Gothenburg
`elena.volodina@svenska.gu.se`

**Courtney Napoles**
Johns Hopkins University
`courtneyn@jhu.edu`



## Abstract

The Automated Evaluation of Scientific Writing, or AESW, is the task of identifying sentences in need of correction to ensure their appropriateness in a scientific prose. The data set comes from a professional editing company, VTeX, with two aligned versions of the same text – before and after editing – and covers a variety of textual infelicities that proofreaders have edited. While previous shared tasks focused solely on grammatical errors (Dale and Kilgarriff, 2011; Dale et al., 2012; Ng et al., 2013; Ng et al., 2014), this time edits cover other types of linguistic misfits as well, including those that almost certainly could be interpreted as style issues and similar "matters of opinion". The latter arise because of different language editing traditions, experience, and the absence of uniform agreement on what "good" scientific language should look like. Initiating this task, we expected the participating teams to help identify the characteristics of "good" scientific language, and help create a consensus of which language improvements are acceptable (or necessary). Six participating teams took on the challenge.


## 1 Introduction

The vast number of scientific papers being authored by non-native English speakers creates an immediate demand for effective computer-based writing tools to help writers compose scientific articles. Several shared tasks have been organized before that in part addressed this challenge, all with English language learners in mind: Helping Our Own, HOO,

with two editions in 2011 and 2012 (Dale and Kilgarriff, 2011; Dale et al., 2012); and two Grammatical Error Correction Tasks in 2013 and 2014 (Ng et al., 2013; Ng et al., 2014). The four shared tasks focused on grammar error detection and correction, and constituted a major step towards evaluating the feasibility of building novel grammar error correction technologies.

An extensive overview of the automated grammatical error detection for language learners was conducted by Leacock et al. (2010). In subsequent years two English language learner (ELL) corpora were made available for research purposes (Dahlmeier et al., 2013; Yannakoudakis et al., 2011). While these achievements are critical for language learners, we also need to develop tools that support genre-specific writing features. This shared task focused on the genre of scientific writing.

Most scientific publications are written in English by non-native speakers of English. Submitted articles are often returned to the authors with an encouragement to improve the language or have a native speaker proofread the paper. Pierson (2004) lists 10 top reasons why manuscripts are not accepted for publication, with poor writing in the 7th place.

In Section 2, we describe the task and its objectives; Section 3 gives an overview of the data set; Section 4 introduces the participating teams; Section 5 describes the framework used for organizing competitions; Section 6 summarizes the results of the task; Section 7 provides a detailed analysis and discussion of the results; and, finally, Section 8 presents the main conclusions of the Shared Task and our proposed future actions.

53


*Proceedings of the 11th Workshop on Innovative Use of NLP for Building Educational Applications*, pages 53–62,
San Diego, California, June 16, 2016. ©2016 Association for Computational Linguistics

| Institution/Group | Abbreviation | Contact Person |
| --- | --- | --- |
| Harvard University | HU | Allen Schmaltz |
| Heidelberg Institute for Theoretical Studies | HITS | Mohsen Mesgar |
| ImproveSWDublin | ISWD | Liliana Mamani Sanchez |
| Knowlet | Knowlet | René Witte |
| National Taiwan Normal University and Yuan Ze University | NTNU-YZU | Lung-Hao Lee |
| University of Washington + Stanford University | UW-SU | Woodley Packard |

Table 1: The teams that submitted results.

## 2 Task Definition

The goal of the Automated Evaluation of Scientific Writing (AESW) Shared Task was to analyze the linguistic characteristics of scientific writing to promote the development of automated writing evaluation tools that can assist authors in writing scientific papers. More specifically, the task was to predict whether a given sentence requires editing to ensure its "fit" within the scientific writing genre.

The main goals of the task were to

- identify sentence-level features that are unique to scientific writing;
- provide a common ground for development and comparison of sentence-level automated writing evaluation systems for scientific writing;
- establish the state-of-the-art performance in the field.

A few words should be said about the specifics of the *scientific writing* data set. Some proportion of "corrections" in the shared task data are "real error" corrections – i.e. such that most of us would agree that they are errors – for example, wrong pronouns and various other grammatical errors. Others almost certainly represent style issues and similar "matters of opinion", and it seems unfair to expect someone to spot these. This is because of different language editing traditions, experience, and the absence of uniform agreement of what "good" language should look like. The task was organized to create a consensus of which language improvements are acceptable (or necessary) and to promote the use of NLP tools to help non-native writers of English to improve the quality of their scientific writing.

Some interesting uses of sentence-level quality evaluations are the following:

- automated writing evaluation of submitted scientific articles;
- authoring tools for writing English scientific texts;
- identifying sentences that need quality improvement.

The task is defined as a binary classification of sentences, with the two categories *needs improvement* and *does not need improvement*. Two types of predictions are evaluated: Binary prediction (False or True)[1] and Probabilistic estimation (between 0 and 1).

The predictions of the test data set should be reported according to the following format:

- For the *Binary prediction task*:
  ```
  <sentenceID><tab><True|False><new line>
  ```
  e.g., `9.12\tTrue\n`
- For the *Probabilistic estimation task*:
  ```
  <sentenceID><tab><Real number><new line>
  ```
  e.g., `9.12\t0.75212\n`

## 3 The Data Set

The data set is a collection of text extracts from 9,919 published journal articles (mainly from Physics and Mathematics) with data before and after language editing. The data are from selected papers published in 2006–2013 by Springer Publishing Company[2] and edited at VTeX[3] by professional language editors who were native English speakers (Daudaravicius, 2015). Each extract is a paragraph that contains at least one edit made by the language editor. All paragraphs in the data set were randomly ordered from the source text for anonymization. Additionally, identifying parts of the text were replaced with placeholders, specifically authors, institutions, citations, URLs, and mathematical formulas. This

---

[1] Also referred to as *Boolean prediction*.
[2] http://www.springer.com/gp/
[3] http://www.vtex.lt

| Domain | # of paragraphs | | | # of sentences with no changes | | | # of sentences with changes | | | | | |
| | | | | | | | before editing | | | after editing | | |
| | Train | Dev | Test | Train | Dev | Test | Train | Dev | Test | Train | Dev | Test |
|---|---|---|---|---|---|---|---|---|---|---|---|---|
| Mathematics | 78,748 | 9,679 | 9,522 | 218,585 | 27,784 | 28,347 | 353,610 | 44,571 | 44,530 | 353,929 | 44,755 | 44,512 |
| Physics | 55,949 | 7,517 | 7,080 | 169,160 | 23,290 | 19,203 | 291,917 | 39,031 | 35,165 | 291,902 | 38,994 | 35,180 |
| Engineering | 54,370 | 6,360 | 6,785 | 145,013 | 17,309 | 17,722 | 244,900 | 28,997 | 30,398 | 244,518 | 28,942 | 30,347 |
| Computer Science | 36,387 | 4,549 | 4,039 | 103,368 | 12,234 | 11,694 | 164,460 | 19,962 | 18,493 | 164,472 | 19,953 | 18,497 |
| Statistics | 14,724 | 1,755 | 1,613 | 42,390 | 5,283 | 4,475 | 70,121 | 8,607 | 7,329 | 70,139 | 8,604 | 7,342 |
| Economics and Management | 6,961 | 794 | 726 | 25,677 | 2,582 | 2,646 | 37,661 | 3,969 | 4,080 | 37,718 | 3,969 | 4,086 |
| Astrophysics | 3,343 | 389 | 321 | 8,492 | 588 | 858 | 16,571 | 1,392 | 1,676 | 16,630 | 1,384 | 1,694 |
| Chemistry | 2,581 | 278 | 315 | 7,697 | 831 | 1,063 | 13572 | 1,562 | 1,838 | 13,577 | 1,559 | 1,832 |
| Human Sciences | 1,081 | 57 | 70 | 2,358 | 205 | 176 | 4090 | 318 | 295 | 4,055 | 318 | 294 |
| **Total** | **254,144** | **31,378** | **30,471** | **722,740** | **90,106** | **86,184** | **1,196,902** | **148,409** | **143,804** | **1,196,940** | **148,478** | **143,784** |

Table 2: The main statistics of the AESW data-set (version 1.2).

replacement was done automatically and is based on annotation in primary data sources that were LaTeX files[4]. This dataset will be made freely available on the Internet[5] for replications and other studies.

Sentences were tokenized automatically, and then both text versions – *before* and *after* editing – were automatically aligned with a modified `diff` algorithm. Some sentences have no edits, and some sentences have edits that are marked with `<ins>` and `<del>` tags. The text tagged with `<ins>` is the text that was *inserted* by the language editor, and the text tagged with `<del>` is the text *deleted* by the language editor. Substitutions are tagged as insertions and deletions because it is not always obvious which words are substituted with which. Some edits introduce or eliminate sentence boundaries. In such cases, a few sentences are combined into one data set sentence and, therefore, the number of tagged sentences in the data set differs before and after editing (see Table 2).

The training, development and test data sets comprise data from independent sets of articles (see Table 2).

- **The training data**: A fragment of training data is shown in Table 3 where multiple insertions and deletions can be seen.
- **The development data**: The development data is distributionally similar to the training data and the test data with regard to the edited and

---

[4]We used `tex2txt` conversion tool (see demo: `http://textmining.lt:8080/tex2txt.htm`)

[5]More information is available at `http://textmining.lt/aesw/index.html`

| |
|---|
| `<sentence sid="9.1">` For example, separate biasing of the two gates can be used to implement a `<del>capacitor-less</del><ins>capacitorless</ins>` DRAM cell in which information is stored `<del>in</del><ins>at</ins>` the `<del>form</del><ins>back-channel</ins>` `<del>of</del><ins>surface</ins>` `<del>charge</del><ins>near</ins>` `<del>in</del><ins>to</ins>` the `<del>body region,</del><ins>source</ins>` `<del>at</del><ins>in</ins>` the `<del>back channel</del><ins>form</ins>` `<del>surface</del><ins>of</ins>` `<del>near</del><ins>charge</ins>` `<del>to</del><ins>in</ins>` the `<del>source</del><ins>body region</ins>` _CITE_. `</sentence>` |

Table 3: A fragment of training data.

non-edited sentences, as well as the domain.

- **The test data**: Test paragraphs retain texts tagged with `<del>` tags but the tags are dropped. Texts between `<ins>` tags are removed. However, all edits of the test data were provided to the teams after the final results were submitted.

## 3.1 Supplementary Data

To speed up data preparation for training, development and testing, the following supplementary data were accessible to all participants:

*Training, development and test data* split into text before editing and text after editing:

– Tokenized sentences with sentence ID at the beginning of the line.
– POS tags of sentences with sentence ID at the beginning of the line.
– CFG trees of sentences with sentence ID at the beginning of the line.
– Dependency trees of sentences with sentence ID as the first line of each tree.

*Texts from Wikipedia articles* (the dump of April 2015):

– Tokens
– POS tags
– CFG trees of sentences
– Dependency trees of sentences

The data were processed with the Stanford parser with the following parameters:

– model: englishRNN
– type: typedDependencies
– JAVA code for grammatical structure:

```
GrammaticalStructure gs =
  parser.getTLPParams().
    getGrammaticalStructure(tree,
      Filters.acceptFilter(),
      parser.getTLPParams().
        typedDependencyHeadFinder());
```

Shared Task participating teams were allowed to use other publicly available data with the exclusion of proprietary data. All additional data should in that case be specified in the final system reports. The participants were encouraged to share their supplementary data, where relevant.

## 4 Participants

By the time of data release, 18 groups were registered for the task. The data required an agreement which allows its use under the Creative Commons CC-BY-NC-SA 4.0 license with a few extra restrictions. The six groups that submitted results and published system reports are listed in Table 1, with participants spanning several continents.

A high-level summary of the approaches used by each team is provided in Table 5. The most common methods were deep learning (HU and NTNU-YZU) and maximum entropy (Knowlet and UW-SU). The other teams used logistic regression and support vector machines. The deep learning models used only tokens and word embeddings as their

features. NTNU-YZU represented sentences as a sequence of word embeddings to train a convolutional neural network (CNN). HU had a more complex approach, reporting the majority vote of a CNN using word embeddings and stacked character-based and word-based Long Short-Term Memory (LSTM) networks.

Besides tokens and token n-grams, the most common features were parse trees (ISWD and UW-SU). ISWD used tree representations of the sentences as features for a SVM and UW-SU augmented a grammar with a series of "mal-rules", which license ungrammatical properties in sentences, and identified if the mal-rules occurred in the most likely sentence parses. HITS implemented 82 specific features for this task, including counts of word types, patterns found in words (such as contractions), and probabilities. Knowlet tested the efficacy of existing grammar tools for this task by train their model using features extracted from LanguageTool and After the Deadline.

## 5 CodaLab.org

In this section we share our experience of using CodaLab[6] for the AESW Shared Task. CodaLab is an open-source platform that provides an ecosystem for conducting computational research in a more efficient, reproducible, and collaborative manner. On `codalab.org`, we used *Competitions* to bring together all participants of the AESW Shared Task and to automate the result submission process. Each participant had to register on the `codalab.org` system and apply to the task in order to submit results and receive evaluation scores. We created four evaluation phases to distinguish four evaluation tasks:

– Development. Binary decision.
– Development. Probabilistic estimation.
– Testing. Binary decision.
– Testing. Probabilistic estimation.

The training and development data were released on December 7, and the test data and CodaLab evaluation opened on February 29. The deadline for submitting results was March 10.

Participants were allowed to submit results many times (up to 100 submissions per day), with no more

---

[6]`http://codalab.org/`

| | Development | | Testing | |
|---|---|---|---|---|
| | **Binary** | **Probabilistic** | **Binary** | **Probabilistic** |
| HITS | 11 | 9 | 3 | 8 |
| HU | 7 | 0 | 6 | 0 |
| ISWD | 0 | 0 | 8 | 7 |
| Knowlet | 12 | 2 | 5 | 4 |
| NTNU-YZU | 22 | 20 | 238 | 68 |
| UW-SU | 1 | 2 | 2 | 1 |
| #Failed | 23 | 10 | 45 | 16 |
| #Total | 76 | 43 | 307 | 104 |

**Table 4:** The number of result submissions for each shared task phase on `https://competitions.codalab.org`.

than two results for their final submission in each track. Our experience shows that the time span for evaluation can take one minute to a few hours. Table 4 shows the number of successful submissions of each participant for each evaluation phase. The average number of submissions for each evaluation phase was six times except for one participant. In principle, the multiple unlimited number of submissions allows a team to tune their system based on performance against the test set as revealed by the automated scorer. The number of failed uploads is around ten percent. Therefore, our advice for future implementations of similar shared tasks is to limit the number of uploads to five times in the testing phase.

The system allows us to upload scorer programs and reference data to the server such that participants cannot see the reference data, which guarantees that the scorer program runs honestly. The scorer program was initially built using the Haskell programming language, but we could not manage to run the executable on the server despite the documentation describing such a possibility. Therefore, the scorer program was reimplemented in Python. The scorer program written in Python demonstrated unexpected behavior at the end of the testing phase: The `codalab.org` system did not report any errors if participants submitted a truncated list of predictions. One team uploaded a truncated list of predictions that was accepted and scored. The scores were close to a random prediction score. After double checking all submitted results, we discovered that the system accepted results even if the list size of predictions was shorter than its expected size. This happened due to the implementation difference of the `zip` function in Haskell and in Python. In

Haskell, the length of both lists should be equal to apply the `zip` function, otherwise an error is thrown. In Python, the `zip` function merges two lists while a pair of values can be created, and does not throw an exception when the lists are of unequal lengths. One particular team was warned and an additional day was given for correcting their system and re-submitting their results. The lesson learned is that even if a scoring program produces an output score, double checking the final scores should be done manually.

## 6  Results

In this section, we describe the results of both tracks of the shared task.

First, we define the primary evaluation metric for both tracks, the $F_1$ score:

$$F_1 = \frac{2P \cdot R}{P + R}$$

For the Binary decision track, precision and recall are defined as

$$P_{bool} = \frac{TP}{TP + FP} \tag{1}$$

$$R_{bool} = \frac{TP}{TP + FN} \tag{2}$$

where $TP$ (true positive) indicates the number of sentences correctly predicted to need improvement; $FP$ indicates the number of false positives, or the sentences incorrectly predicted to need improvement); and $FN$ (false negative) is the number of sentences incorrectly predicted to *not* need improvement. We additionally report Pearson's correlation coefficient and the agreement calculated with Cohen's kappa.

| Team Acronym | Algorithms | Features | Tools used | Data used |
|---|---|---|---|---|
| HU | CNN, RNN, LSTM | Tokens | Torch, word2vec | AESW 2016, word2vec |
| HITS | HMM, Logistic Regression | CFG trees, POS n-grams, token n-grams, hand-made features | scikit-learn, pyenchant | AESW 2016, American English dictionary, WordNet |
| ISWD | SVM, SubSet Tree kernel | Constituent tree | SVM-Light, SST | AESW 2016 |
| Knowlet | MaxEnt | AtD.rule, AtD.string, LT.rule, LT.string, Token.root n-grams, Token.category n-grams | GATE, After the Deadline (AtD), LanguageTool (LT) | AESW 2016 |
| NTNU-YZU | CNN | Tokens, Bag Of Words | Theano, word2vec | AESW 2016, word2vec, GloVe |
| UW-SU | MaxEnt | Parse trees, mal-rules | DELPH-IN, ERG, ACE parser | AESW 2016 |

**Table 5:** The summary of AESW 2016 Shared Task participant systems.

| Team | Precision | Recall | F-Score | Correlation | Kappa | Mean rank |
|---|---|---|---|---|---|---|
| HU | 0.5444 | 0.7413 | 0.6278 (1) | 0.3760 (1) | 0.3628 (1) | 1 |
| NTNU-YZU | 0.5025 | 0.7785 | 0.6108 (2) | 0.3324 (2) | 0.3070 (2) | 2 |
| ISWD | 0.4482 | 0.7279 | 0.5548 (3) | 0.2168 (5) | 0.1957 (5) | 4.33 |
| UW-SU | 0.4145 | 0.8201 | 0.5507 (4) | 0.1770 (6) | 0.1373 (6) | 5.33 |
| HITS | 0.3765 | 0.9480 | 0.5389 (5) | 0.1037 (7) | 0.0469 (8) | 6.67 |
| ISWD$^\dagger$ | 0.3960 | 0.6970 | 0.5051 (6) | 0.0971 (8) | 0.0835 (7) | 7 |
| NTNU-YZU$^\dagger$ | 0.6717 | 0.3805 | 0.4858 (7) | 0.3282 (3) | 0.3043 (3) | 4.33 |
| Knowlet | 0.6241 | 0.3685 | 0.4634 (8) | 0.2854 (4) | 0.2672 (4) | 5.33 |
| baseline | 0.3607 | 0.6004 | 0.4507 (9) | 0.0001 (9) | 0.0001 (9) | 9 |

**Table 6:** Binary prediction results.

For the Probabilistic estimation track, rankings are calculated based on $F_1$ score using the mean squared error (MSE):

$$P_{prob} = 1 - \frac{1}{n} \sum_i (\pi_i - G_i)^2 \qquad \pi_i > 0.5$$

$$R_{prob} = 1 - \frac{1}{m} \sum_i (\pi_i - G_i)^2 \qquad G_i \in improve$$

For a sentence $i$, $G_i = 1$ if the sentence needs improvement in the gold standard, otherwise $G_i = 0$. $\pi_i$ is the probabilistic estimate that the sentence needs improvement, $n$ is the number of sentences predicted to need improvement ($\pi_i > 0.5$), and $m$ is the number of sentences that actually need improvement. We also calculated the cross-entropy between the predictions and gold standards, defined as

$$H = - \sum_i G_i \log \pi_i$$

Finally, we represented each probability with its corresponding boolean value ($y_i'$ — True if $\pi_i >$ 0.5 else $y_i' = $ False) and calculated the binary-task F-score (with precision and recall calculated as in Equations 1 and 2), the correlation, and agreement statistic.

The results of the Binary decision task are shown in Table 6. The results for the Probabilistic estimation task are provided in Table 7 and the analysis over the corresponding boolean values is shown in Table 8. When a team submitted more than one set of results, we identify the two submissions as TEAM and TEAM$^\dagger$.

## 7 Discussion

All submissions in both tasks have higher F-scores than a random baseline. In the Binary task, the deep learning approaches outperformed the other models, which included support vector machines, maximum entropy models, and logistic regression. HU, which uses a combination of CNN and RNNs, achieves the highest F-score and agreement with the gold standard (Table 6). The second best sys-

| Team | Precision | Recall | F-Score | Correlation | Cross-entropy | Average | STD Dev | Mean rank |
|---|---|---|---|---|---|---|---|---|
| HITS | 0.9333 | 0.7491 | 0.8311 (1) | 0.0600 (8) | 35,992 (5) | 0.4986 | 0.0255 | 4.67 |
| UW-SU | 0.7118 | 0.8748 | 0.7849 (2) | 0.2471 (5) | 22,162 (1) | 0.6276 | 0.0973 | 2.67 |
| ISWD | 0.7062 | 0.8182 | 0.7581 (3) | 0.2690 (4) | 28,385 (2) | 0.5444 | 0.1941 | 3 |
| NTNU-YZU | 0.7678 | 0.7177 | 0.7419 (4) | 0.4043 (2) | 40,716 (6) | 0.3948 | 0.2264 | 4 |
| ISWD[†] | 0.6576 | 0.8014 | 0.7224 (5) | 0.1298 (7) | 32,979 (4) | 0.5743 | 0.2225 | 5.33 |
| HITS[†] | 0.6655 | 0.7889 | 0.7220 (6) | 0.1666 (6) | 30,238 (3) | 0.5441 | 0.2031 | 5 |
| NTNU-YZU[†] | 0.7900 | 0.6166 | 0.6926 (7) | 0.4173 (1) | 54,903 (9) | 0.3033 | 0.2280 | 5.67 |
| Knowlet | 0.7294 | 0.6591 | 0.6925 (8) | 0.3516 (3) | 50,370 (8) | 0.3709 | 0.2942 | 6.33 |
| Baseline | 0.5963 | 0.7163 | 0.6508 (9) | -0.0028 (9) | 44,843 (7) | 0.5511 | 0.2845 | 8.33 |
| Gold standard | | | | | | 0.3606 | 0.4802 | |

**Table 7:** Probabilistic estimation results.

| Team | $Precision_b$ | $Recall_b$ | $F\text{-}Score_b$ | $Correlation_b$ | $Kappa_b$ | Mean rank |
|---|---|---|---|---|---|---|
| HITS | 0.9282 | 0.0065 | 0.0129 (9) | 0.0594 (7) | 0.0079 (7) | 7.67 |
| UW-SU | 0.3606 | 1.0000 | 0.5301 (3) | n/a [a] (9) | 0.0000 (8) | 6.67 |
| ISWD | 0.4482 | 0.7279 | 0.5548 (2) | 0.2168 (4) | 0.1957 (4) | 3.33 |
| NTNU-YZU | 0.5922 | 0.5344 | 0.5618 (1) | 0.3350 (1) | 0.3340 (1) | 1 |
| ISWD[†] | 0.3960 | 0.6970 | 0.5051 (6) | 0.0971 (6) | 0.0835 (6) | 6 |
| HITS[†] | 0.4514 | 0.6070 | 0.5177 (5) | 0.1833 (5) | 0.1775 (5) | 5 |
| NTNU-YZU[†] | 0.6717 | 0.3805 | 0.4858 (7) | 0.3282 (2) | 0.3043 (2) | 3.67 |
| Knowlet | 0.5832 | 0.4778 | 0.5254 (4) | 0.3002 (3) | 0.2969 (3) | 3.33 |
| Baseline | 0.3600 | 0.6000 | 0.4500 (8) | -0.0017 (8) | -0.0015 (9) | 8.33 |

**Table 8:** Probabilistic estimation results, using the corresponding boolean value.

[a] UW-SU reported all probabilities $\pi_i > 0.5$, and therefore $\sigma_\pi = 0$ and $r$ is undefined.

tem is NTNU-YZU, which trained a CNN model. Both of these models used word2vec word embeddings, with NTNU-YZU testing both word2vec and GloVe. The bottom two teams according to the F-score, NTNU-YZU[†] and Knowlet, have the third and fourth strongest agreement with the gold standard, respectively. Compared to the other submissions, these systems have the highest precision of 0.6717 and 0.6241, respectively, with the precision of the other systems ranging from 0.38 to 0.54. They also had the lowest recall (0.3805 and 0.3685) compared to the other teams, with recall between 0.70–0.95. This suggests the importance of precision in this task.

For the Probabilistic estimation track, HITS had the highest precision (0.9333) and F-score (0.8311) (Table 7). The other teams all had precision $>=$ 0.66 and recall $>=$ 0.62. However, the rankings found by the F-score and the correlation diverge significantly for three systems: HITS, NTNU-YZU[†], and Knowlet. While HITS has the highest F-score, it also has the weakest correlation with the gold standard. NTNU-YZU[†] and Knowlet have the lowest F-score but the first and third strongest corre-

lation, respectively. The ranking by cross-entropy is similar to the F-score ranking with the exception of HITS, which has the fifth highest cross-entropy. To address this disparity, we calculated additional rankings of the systems by converting the output probabilities into the corresponding boolean value (True if $\pi_i > 0.5$, and False otherwise) and reporting the values of the same metrics we used to evaluate the Binary prediction task (Table 8). These statistics are indicated with a subscript $b$. In this analysis, the ranking of HITS declines significantly from the original Probabilistic evaluation, with the lowest $F\text{-}score_b$ of all systems. The $precision_b$ of HITS is nearly perfect (0.9282) but $recall_b$ is almost 0 (0.0129), which explains why the $F\text{-}score_b$, $Correlation_b$, and $Kappa_b$ statistics are all so low. Knowlet improves to the fourth-ranked system by $F\text{-}score_b$ from the last. By the correlation and agreement statistics, NTNU-YZU and NTNU-YZU[†] are the best two systems in the converted probabilities analysis.

As demonstrated, different statistics produce dissimilar system rankings. The official scores for both tasks are the F-score, as defined in the workshop description, but there is evidence that the evaluation could be improved in future tasks. UW-SU and HITS pointed out that favoring recall over precision improves their F-score, which increases the system's ranking but decreases its accuracy. Precision has been shown to be more effective when providing feedback on grammatical errors, with less, accurate feedback better than inaccurate feedback (Nagata and Nakatani, 2010). For future shared tasks, additional evaluation methods should be investigated, including $F_{0.5}$, which weights precision more than recall, and a comparison to human evaluation, such as is done by the Workshop on Machine Translation (Bojar et al., 2015).

### 7.1 The trends of system predictions

The initial impetus to organize this competition was to gain insight into the specifics of scientific writing as *a genre* and, with the help of participants, to make an estimation of whether it is possible to offer any robust automatic solutions to support researchers with non-native English background in writing scientific reports. There are several facts and their implications to be considered:

- The first fact deals with formal requirements of the genre. Scientific writing has very clear – and to a certain extent limited – aims, namely to inform other researchers in the field of the latest findings or important issues, usually presented in the form of articles, reports, grant proposals, theses, etc. Each of these follow roughly the same structure comprising more or less obligatory parts (e.g. abstract, data, method). The intended audience – i.e. other researchers – should be familiar with the standard to be able to skim for major findings and conclusions in the document, not wasting time on irrelevant parts. Scientific language is therefore rather rigid to fit this need.
- Another fact we need to consider is that most of the scientific writing is done by mature users of English, who in most cases do not make second-language-learner types of mistakes, at least not frequently. This fact is reflected in the type of edits in our data: they are corrections, mostly reflecting linguistic conventions of the genre. Correct use of punctuation, hyphenation, digits, capitalization, abbreviations,

and domain-appropriate lexical choices are the type of corrections that dominate professionally proofread scientific papers, and are unique to scientific writing. Among more classical second-language type of errors, we can see verb (dis)agreement; (in)appropriate use of articles, prepositions and plurals, (mis)spellings, (in)correct choice of word, etc. However, these traditional error types are much less represented in scientific writing.

To see how successfully our task participants have coped with the challenges of scientific writing, we have analyzed main trends concerning which error types were detected by all algorithms (successfully detected as 'need improvement' by all systems) versus which none were able to capture (i.e. sentences that were annotated as 'need improvement' but no one could detect these sentences).

There are four cases presented in Table 9:

| Prediction of all systems | Gold annotation | | Total |
|---|---|---|---|
| | Correction needed | Correct | |
| Correction needed | 7,899 | 2,663 | 10,563 |
| Correct | 32 | 1,201 | 1,234 |

**Table 9:** Agreement between gold annotations and all systems on test data, in number of sentences

We can observe 7,899 cases of *successful agreement* between the proofreaders and all the teams about sentences that need correction. Most cases of article misuse, punctuation infelicities, diverting capitalization, unconventional usage of digits, abbreviations and hyphenation were detected by all teams, including sentences where lexical choices were not optimal, e.g.:

- *For computations we chose _MATH_ and a spectral interval in the vicinity of the resonance frequency of the mode with radial number _MATH_, _MATH_.*
- *Provided _MATH_ has no zero in its initial data, the ~~log~~ logarithmic singularity at _MATH_ causes the left-~~-~~hand side to blow up at _MATH_, thereby forcing _MATH_ as _MATH_.*
- *Given this reasoning we have evaluated the one one loop and ~~eighteen~~18 two loop vacuum bubble graphs contributing to (_REF_).*

- *Similar**Similarly* to the previous case, we have a line of fixed points with positive slope _MATH_ in (_MATH_, _MATH_) plane as shown in Figure 2.

In 32 cases all the teams have *unanimously disagreed* with the gold standard on the need of correction. These cases cover

- context deficit, where on the sentence level it is impossible to identify the correct need of an article or an adverb, e.g.:
  - *Next, we give ~~the~~a stability analysis.*
  - *The algorithm then terminates.*
- alternative lexical choices, in particular more formal variants or special terminological usages, e.g. ~~notice~~ versus note, ~~fitted parameter~~ versus fit parameter;
- a number of notorious *matters of opinion*, such as replacing this paper for ~~the paper~~ and vice versa, e.g.:
  - *~~The~~This paper is organized as follows.*
  - *Section 5 concludes ~~this~~the paper.*
  - *First, we derive the following: _MATHDISP_.*
- style/tense requirements of the genre, e.g. using present tense referring to the results in tables:
  - *The results ~~were~~are presented in Figure _REF_.*
- use of punctuation in the following cases:
  - *Namely, we observe the following~~:~~:*
  - *Example~~:~~.*
- stylistic preferences:
  - *Since _MATH_ and _MATH_, we ~~can~~easily get _MATH_.*
  - *This error is only limited by the ~~instrument~~ resolution of the instrument.*

It can be argued that in most of those 32 cases corrections are optional.

One conclusion that can be drawn from this task performance analysis is that scientific writing as a genre needs standardization. We have encountered several types of inconsistencies in the data, for example in the case of hyphenation (nonlinear for ~~non-linear~~; and vice versa); or in the case of expressions like this paper for ~~the paper~~ and vice versa. Even though it seems that the area could benefit from standardization, we are well aware that language can never be fully standardized. At most,

there are only and can only be guidelines or consensus on what good language should look like.

Another conclusion is that automatic detection of scientific prose errors as an area of research would benefit from error-type annotation. More rigorous analysis of the data in terms of the type of corrected deviations could give us a better insight into what the genre of scientific writing is and facilitate more error-aware approaches to automatic proofreading of scientific papers.

Yet another conclusion is that stepping outside of a sentence boundary may facilitate recognition of a number of other error types that at the moment go unnoticed due to context deficit, among others inconsistent use of abbreviations, certain cases of article usage, and lacking adverbs, just to name a few.

## 8 Conclusions

In this work we have reported and described the results of the AESW Shared Task (Automatic Evaluation of Scientific Writing), which focuses on the problem of identifying sentences in scientific works that require editing. The main motivation of this task is to promote the use of NLP tools to help non-native writers of English to improve the quality of their scientific writing. From the research perspective, on the other hand, this effort aims at promoting a common framework and standard data set for developing and testing automatic evaluation systems for the scientific writing domain.

From a total of 18 groups registered for the shared task, six of them submitted results and published reports describing their implemented systems. As a consequence, different machine learning paradigms (including neural networks, support vector machines, maximum entropy, and logistic regression) have been tested over the two proposed evaluation modalities (binary and probabilistic estimation). The shared task has helped establish a reference for the state-of-the-art in the automatic evaluation of scientific writing, in which the obtained results demonstrate that there is still room for improvement. The availability of both the data set and the evaluation tools will facilitate the path for future research work in this area.

In the future, we plan to improve on current system performances by implementing and evaluating different system combination strategies. Additionally, as suggested by the observed ranking inconsistencies across the different evaluation metrics in the probabilistic estimation task, we also need to conduct further analysis and take a more detailed look at these results to determine the best evaluation scheme to be used for this modality.

## Acknowledgments

We thank Joel Tetreault for his great support and the other BEA Workshop organizers for including the AESW Shared Task in the BEA11 Workshop. We also appreciate the teams for participating in this new shared task and providing us with helpful feedback. We acknowledge Springer Publishing Company for the permission to publish text extracts that made the AESW Shared Task feasible. This material is based upon work partially supported by the National Science Foundation Graduate Research Fellowship under Grant No. 1232825.

## References

Ondřej Bojar, Rajen Chatterjee, Christian Federmann, Barry Haddow, Matthias Huck, Chris Hokamp, Philipp Koehn, Varvara Logacheva, Christof Monz, Matteo Negri, Matt Post, Carolina Scarton, Lucia Specia, and Marco Turchi. 2015. Findings of the 2015 workshop on statistical machine translation. In *Proceedings of the Tenth Workshop on Statistical Machine Translation*, pages 1–46, Lisbon, Portugal, September. Association for Computational Linguistics.

Daniel Dahlmeier, Hwee Tou Ng, and Siew Mei Wu. 2013. Building a Large Annotated Corpus of Learner English: The NUS Corpus of Learner English. In *Proceedings of the Eighth Workshop on Innovative Use of NLP for Building Educational Applications*, pages 22–31.

Robert Dale and Adam Kilgarriff. 2011. Helping Our Own: The HOO 2011 pilot shared task. In *Proceedings of the 13th European Workshop on Natural Language Generation*, pages 242–249.

R Dale, I Anisimoff, and G Narroway. 2012. A report on the preposition and determiner error correction shared task. In *Proceedings of the NAACL Workshop on Innovative Use of NLP for Building Educational Applications*.

Vidas Daudaravicius. 2015. *Automated Evaluation of Scientific Writing Data Set (Version 1.2) [Data file]*. VTeX, Vilnius, Lithuania.

Claudia Leacock, Martin Chodorow, Michael Gamon, and Joel Tetreault. 2010. Automated grammatical error detection for language learners. *Synthesis lectures on human language technologies*, 3(1):1–134.

Ryo Nagata and Kazuhide Nakatani. 2010. Evaluating performance of grammatical error detection to maximize learning effect. In *Proceedings of the 23rd International Conference on Computational Linguistics: Posters*, pages 894–900. Association for Computational Linguistics.

Hwee Tou Ng, Siew Mei Wu, Christian Hadiwinoto, and Joel Tetreault. 2013. The CoNLL-2013 Shared Task on Grammatical Error Correction. In *Proceedings of the Seventeenth Conference on Computational Natural Language Learning: Shared Task*, pages 1–12.

Hwee Tou Ng, Siew Mei Wu, Ted Briscoe, Christian Hadiwinoto, Raymond Hendy Susanto, and Christopher Bryant. 2014. The CoNLL-2014 Shared Task on Grammatical Error Correction. In *CoNLL Shared Task*, pages 1–14.

David J Pierson. 2004. The top 10 reasons why manuscripts are not accepted for publication. *Respiratory care*, 49(10):1246–1252.

Helen Yannakoudakis, Ted Briscoe, and Ben Medlock. 2011. A new dataset and method for automatically grading ESOL texts. In *Proceedings of the 49th Annual Meeting of the Association for Computational Linguistics: Human Language Technologies-Volume 1*, pages 180–189. Association for Computational Linguistics.

# Topicality-Based Indices for Essay Scoring

**Beata Beigman Klebanov, Michael Flor, and Binod Gyawali**
Educational Testing Service
660 Rosedale Road
Princeton, NJ 08541
`bbeigmanklebanov,mflor,bgyawali@ets.org`

## Abstract

In this paper, we address the problem of quantifying the overall extent to which a test-taker's essay deals with the topic it is assigned (prompt). We experiment with a number of models for word topicality, and a number of approaches for aggregating word-level indices into text-level ones. All models are evaluated for their ability to predict the holistic quality of essays. We show that the best text-topicality model provides a significant improvement in a state-of-art essay scoring system. We also show that the findings of the relative merits of different models generalize well across three different datasets.

## 1 Introduction

The instruction to "stay on topic" oft given to developing writers seems intuitively unproblematic, yet the question of the best way to measure this property of a text is far from settled, and little is known about the interaction of topicality and other properties of text, such as length. We develop text topicality indices and evaluate them in the context of automated scoring of essays. Specifically, we investigate the relationship between the extent to which the essay engages the topic provided in the essay question (prompt) and the quality of the essay as quantified by a human-provided holistic score.

In the existing literature, topicality has been addressed as a control flag to identify off-topic essays or spoken responses (Yoon and Xie, 2014; Louis and Higgins, 2010; Higgins et al., 2006) or as an element in the overall coherence of the essay (Somasundaran

et al., 2014; Higgins et al., 2004; Foltz et al., 1998). Persing and Ng (2014) annotated essays for prompt-adherence, and found that achieving inter-rater reliability was very challenging, reporting Pearson $r = 0.243$ between two raters. We address the relationship between a continuous topicality score and the holistic quality of an essay.

Generally, one can think of the topicality of a given word $w$ on a given topic $T$ as the extent to which $w$ occurs more often in texts addressing $T$ than in otherwise comparable texts addressing a different topic. We consider three models of word topicality from the literature: the significance-test approach as in topic signatures (Lin and Hovy, 2000), the score-product approach as described in the essay scoring literature (Higgins et al., 2006), and a simple cutoff-based approach relying on difference in probabilities.

Given a definition of word topicality, the question arises how to quantify the topicality of the whole text. Specifically, is topicality a property of the vocabulary of a text (of word types) or a property of both the vocabulary and the unfolding discourse (of word tokens)? Thus, do the sentences "I hate restaurants, abhor restaurants, loath restaurants, and love restaurants" and "I hate restaurants, abhor waiters, loath menus, and love food" address the topic of restaurants to the same extent (this would be the prediction of the token-based model), or does the latter sentence address the topic to a greater extent than the former (this would be the prediction of the type-based model)?[1] The second sentence seems to en-

---

[1] Assuming the 4 verbs in the example are off-topic and the nouns are on-topic of restaurants, the token-based model



*Proceedings of the 11th Workshop on Innovative Use of NLP for Building Educational Applications*, pages 63–72,
San Diego, California, June 16, 2016. ©2016 Association for Computational Linguistics

gage more with the topic because it attends to more aspects (or details) of the topic.

In this paper, we implement type-based and token-based approaches to text topicality, using a number of different models for word topicality. All models are evaluated for their ability to predict the holistic quality of an essay.

The contributions of this paper are as follows. First, assuming a number of common definitions of word topicality and an application of predicting holistic quality of essays, we show that text-level topicality is most effectively modeled (a) as a property of word types rather than tokens in the text; (b) taking essay length into account. Second, we show that when word topicality is defined using a simple cutoff-based measure and text-topicality is modeled as in (a),(b) above, we obtain a predictor of essay score that yields a statistically significant improvement in a state-of-art essay scoring system. Third, we show that the characteristics of the best topicality model and its effectiveness in improving essay scoring generalize across different kinds of essays.

## 2  Data

We experiment with three datasets. Two are datasets of essays responding to two different essay tasks written for a large-scale college-level examination in the United States. These essays are scored by professional raters on a 6-point scale. These sets contain tens of thousands of essays responding to dozens different prompt questions (82,500 essays, 76 prompts for each dataset). Their sheer sizes and the variety of topics (prompts) allow for a thorough evaluation of the proposed measures. However, the proprietary nature of these data does not allow for easy replication of the results, or benchmarking; we therefore use a third, publicly available dataset containing 12,100 essays written for the TOEFL test by non-native speakers of English seeking college entrance in the United States, as well as for other purposes. The dataset was originally built for the task of native language identification (Blanchard et al., 2013; Tetreault et al., 2012); however, the distribution provides coarse-grained holistic scores as well

---

says that in both sentences, half the content words are topical, whereas the type-based model says that only 1 out of 5 different content words is topical in the first sentence, and 4 out of 8 in the second.

| Part. | Set 1 | Set 2 | TOEFL |
|---|---|---|---|
| Dev | $76 \times 500$ | $76 \times 500$ | $8 \times 500$ |
| Train | $51 \times 500$ | $51 \times 500$ | $8 \times 760$ (Av) |
| Test | $76 \times 250$ | $76 \times 250$ | $8 \times 253$ (Av) |

**Table 1:** Sizes of the data partitions for each dataset. In the $N \times M$ notation, $N$ = # prompts, $M$ = # essays per prompt. In TOEFL train and test sets, we show average numbers of essays per prompt.

| Score | Set 1 | Set 2 | Score | TOEFL |
|---|---|---|---|---|
| 1 | 0.015 | 0.015 | low | 0.108 |
| 2 | 0.154 | 0.123 | med | 0.546 |
| 3 | 0.384 | 0.412 | high | 0.346 |
| 4 | 0.327 | 0.342 | — | |
| 5 | 0.104 | 0.096 | — | |
| 6 | 0.016 | 0.012 | — | |
| Av. Len. (Std.) | 395 (129) | 405 (134) | Av. Len. (Std.) | 317 (77) |

**Table 2:** Distribution of essay scores, and average (std) of essay length (in words), Train data.

(3-point scale). We describe each of the datasets in detail below. Table 1 shows the sizes of the partitions of the datasets into Dev (used for building topicality models), Train (used for selecting the best topicality model and for training the essay scoring system); Test (used for a blind test of the essay scoring system). Table 2 shows score distributions and mean essay length on Train data.

### 2.1  Set 1

Dataset 1 is comprised of essays written in 2012 and 2013 as part of a large-scale college-level examination in the United States, by a mix of native and non-native speakers of English. The essays respond to a "criticize an argument" task, where a test-taker is given a short prompt text of about 150 words that typically describes a setting where some recommendation is made or a claim is put forward. The task of the test-taker is then to critically evaluate the arguments presented in support of the claim. An example prompt is shown in Figure 1.

### 2.2  Set 2

The second dataset is used for evaluating the generalization of the text-topicality models to a different type of essays. Essays in this dataset are written in

In surveys Mason City residents rank water sports (swimming, boating and fishing) among their favorite recreational activities. The Mason River flowing through the city is rarely used for these pursuits, however, and the city park department devotes little of its budget to maintaining riverside recreational facilities. For years there have been complaints from residents about the quality of the river's water and the river's smell. In response, the state has recently announced plans to clean up Mason River. Use of the river for water sports is therefore sure to increase. The city government should for that reason devote more money in this year's budget to riverside recreational facilities.

Write a response in which you examine the stated and/or unstated assumptions of the argument. Be sure to explain how the argument depends on the assumptions and what the implications are if the assumptions prove unwarranted.

Figure 1: An example Set 1 prompt.

a more open-ended "support your position on an argument" genre, where the prompt is typically a single sentence that puts forward a general claim, such as "As people rely more and more on technology to solve problems, the ability of humans to think for themselves will surely deteriorate." This task is administered on the same test as the one discussed above, and the general properties, such as scale and distribution of scores, are similar.

## 2.3 TOEFL Set

The third dataset will be used to assess generalization of the findings regarding text-topicality models to shorter essays written by non-native speakers of English – a generally less English-proficient population than writers in Sets 1 and 2. This dataset is publicly available from the Linguistic Data Consortium (Blanchard et al., 2013).[2] This set contains 12,100 essays written for the Test of English as a Foreign Language (TOEFL), responding to the question "Do you agree or disagree with the following statement?", a genre similar to that of Set 2. The essays in this set were written in response to

[2]LDC Catalogue No: LDC2014T06

8 different prompts, such as: "A teacher's ability to relate well with students is more important than excellent knowledge of the subject being taught." Only coarse-grained scores are provided, corresponding to low, medium, and high proficiency, which we represent as scores 1, 2, and 3, respectively. The data was partitioned so that 500 essays per prompt are used in Dev to estimate the topical lists; the remaining essays are split 75% (Train) and 25% (Test) within each prompt.

## 3  Models of Word Topicality

Let $T_1 \dots T_m$ be sets of essays responding to $m$ different prompts $t_1 \dots t_m$. For a word $w$ and a prompt $t_k$, we define the following contingency table of counts, where $\neg w$ corresponds to any content word other than $w$ and $\neg T_k$ corresponds to $\cup_{r \neq k} T_r$:

|        | $T_k$    | $\neg T_k$ |
|--------|----------|------------|
| $w$    | $A_{11}$ | $A_{12}$   |
| $\neg w$ | $A_{21}$ | $A_{22}$ |

We define the following word topicality models. The first model, **LH**, due to Lin and Hovy (2000), quantifies the topicality of a word in a topic as a reduction in the entropy of topic distribution achieved by partitioning on the word $w$, scaled so that the resulting value is distributed according to $\chi^2$. Note that to avoid division by zero when $1 - p_1 = 0$, we only consider words with $A_{12} > 0$.

$$LH_{w,k} = -2log\frac{p^{A_{11}+A_{21}}(1-p)^{A_{12}+A_{22}}}{p_1^{A_{11}}(1-p_1)^{A_{12}}p_2^{A_{21}}(1-p_2)^{A_{22}}} \tag{1}$$

where the proportions $p$, $p_1$, and $p_2$ are given by:

$$p = \frac{A_{11} + A_{21}}{A_{11} + A_{21} + A_{12} + A_{22}} \tag{2}$$

$$p_1 = \frac{A_{11}}{A_{11} + A_{12}}; \quad p_2 = \frac{A_{21}}{A_{21} + A_{22}} \tag{3}$$

From this definition, we derive three word topicality weights – the first using the continuous values of topicality mapped to the $[0, 1]$ range, the second – binarized to separate out only words that reach the 0.001 significance, the third – a binarized model with a more permissive threshold for 0.05 significance, which would create larger but noisier sets of topical vocabulary.[3]

$$\alpha_1^{LH}(w, k) = \frac{LH(w, k)}{max_{v \in T_k} LH(v, k)} \quad (4)$$

$$\alpha_2^{LH}(w, k) = \begin{cases} 1 & \text{if } LH(w, k) > 10.83 \\ 0 & \text{otherwise} \end{cases} \quad (5)$$

$$\alpha_3^{LH}(w, k) = \begin{cases} 1 & \text{if } LH(w, k) > 3.84 \\ 0 & \text{otherwise} \end{cases} \quad (6)$$

The second model, **HBA**, due to Higgins et al. (2006), quantifies topicality of a word as the geometric mean of its probability of occurrence in the topic and the complement of its probability of occurrence overall. Thus, the more topical words tend to occur more frequently in the current topic and more rarely in general (this reasoning is similar to tfidf). According to this model, the weight of a word in a topic is defined as follows:[4]

$$\alpha^{HBA} = \sqrt{\frac{A_{11}}{A_{11} + A_{21}} \times \frac{A_{21} + A_{22}}{A_{11} + A_{21} + A_{12} + A_{22}}} \quad (7)$$

Lastly, we define a simple (**S**) cutoff-based binary index, where the word is topical if it is likelier to occur in the current topic than overall:

$$\alpha^S = \begin{cases} 1 & \text{if } \frac{A_{11}}{A_{11} + A_{21}} > \frac{A_{11} + A_{12}}{A_{11} + A_{21} + A_{12} + A_{22}} \\ 0 & \text{otherwise} \end{cases} \quad (8)$$

## 4  Models of Text Topicality

For an essay $e$, let $Y$ be a set of all content word[5] types in $e$ and let $O$ be a set of all content word tokens.[6] Further, let $\alpha_w$ be the topicality value of the word $w \in e$. We then define text topicality as the proportion of topical words (for binary word topicality indices) or mean topicality per word (for continuous word topicality indices), for types and tokens, as follows:

$$TypeTop(e) = \frac{1}{|Y|} \sum_{w \in Y} \alpha_w \quad (9)$$

$$TokTop(e) = \frac{1}{|O|} \sum_{w \in O} \alpha_w \quad (10)$$

We observe that all the word topicality models defined above essentially produce a final list of topical words, based on some estimation set. This introduces a dependence between text length and its topicality, especially under the type-based definition: The longer the text, the less likely it is that the next new word would be topical – simply because there are only so many topical words, and their supply diminishes with every newly chosen word, whereas the (theoretical) supply of non-topical words is infinite. This reasoning suggests that the longer the text, the less topical it would be, on average. Note that we are not implying that longer texts digress more; it is just that the modeling of topicality that is based on a finite list of topical words is inherently biased against longer essays.

Figure 2 shows that this is indeed the case, using a separate set of 3,000 essays responding to the same task as Set 1, using the $\alpha^S$ word topicality index and type-based aggregation. The different series correspond to sets of essays within a certain length band, with color codes ranging from the lightest blue for the shortest essays (shorter than 2 standard deviations below mean length) to the lightest orange for the longest ones (more than 1.5 standard deviation longer than mean length). It is clearly the case that longer essays tend to be less topical, as moving from blue to red to orange generally aligns with moving down the topicality axis. Thus, given that essay length is typically strongly positively correlated with essay scores, we expect that topicality would be negatively correlated with score. However, separating essays by length bands reveals that the relationship between topicality and score is in fact *positive* – when length is held approximately constant, better essays tend to be more topical.[7] These obser-

---

[3]For all indices, we set the value to 0 if $p_2 \geq p_1$, even though a reduction in entropy due to a partition on $w$ could occur when the topic is substantially *less* likely given that $w$ occurred.

[4]In Higgins et al. (2006), the probability of occurrence in general is estimated from a different dataset than that used to estimate prompt-specific probabilities. However, presumably, the general dataset would contain some number of essays responding the current prompt, so we believe our approximation is faithful to the spirit of the original.

[5]We assume function words are irrelevant for topicality.

[6]tYpes vs tOkens

[7]Observe the upward slope of each series in Figure 2.

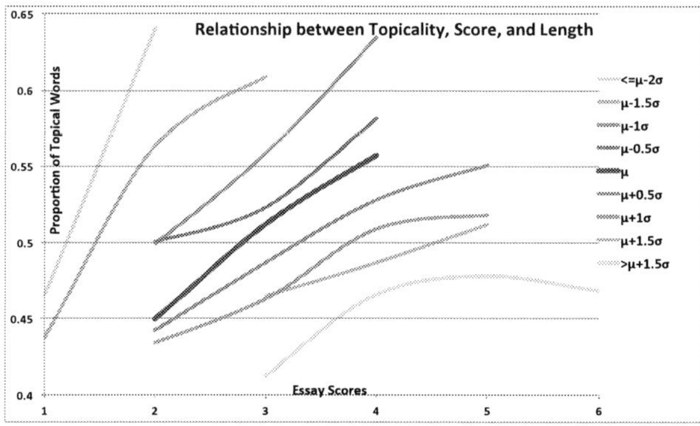


**Figure 2:** Illustration of the relationship between essay score, essay length, and topicality, using $\alpha^S$ index in type aggregation, using an additional sample of 3,000 essays responding to the task in Set 1. The series correspond to length bands, with the lightest blue line showing mean topicality per score level for essays that are more than 2 standard deviations below mean essay length.

vations suggest that the estimated topicality of the essay needs to be scaled to compensate for "baseline" topicality differences that are due to length. We therefore define a length-scaled version of the two indices as follows:

$$TypeTopL(e) = \frac{log(|Y|)}{|Y|} \sum_{w \in Y} \alpha_w \quad (11)$$

$$TokTopL(e) = \frac{log(|O|)}{|O|} \sum_{w \in O} \alpha_w \quad (12)$$

## 5   Selecting Best Topicality Model(s)

We evaluate each of the 5 word-topicality models ($\alpha$) with each of the 4 text-aggregation methods (types/tokens, scaled/unscaled) – 20 models in total – for their ability to predict essay score above and beyond the prediction based on essay length. Essay length is a well-known confounder for essay scoring systems (Page, 1966): It is a strong predictor of essay score ($r$=0.65 for Set 1); yet, an automated essay scoring system needs to capture additional aspects of essay quality construct beyond the basic English production fluency captured by essay length. Our measure of success is therefore **partial correlation** $r_p$ between the feature and the human-provided es-

say score, excluding the effect of essay length.[8] Table 3 shows the results.

We make the following observations based on these results.

First, the relative merits of various topicality models generalize very well across the three sets. We calculated rank-order (Spearman) correlations between the 20 partial correlations for the various models on the three pairs of datasets. Thus, the rank order correlation between column $r_p$ for Set 1 and column $r_p$ for Set 2 in Table 3 is $\rho = 0.92$; Set 1 vs TOEFL $\rho = 0.93$; Set 2 vs TOEFL $\rho = 0.98$.

Second, it is clearly the case that the text topicality indices based on continuous word topicality indices (LH$_1$, HBA) are less effective, their partial correlations with score excluding length being within 0.15 band around zero (lines 1-8 in Table 3). Although some overall correlations with score are reasonable (such as 0.262 in line 4, Set 1; 0.235 in line 2, Set 1), these are mostly accounted for by the even higher correlation with essay length. This suggests that accounting for the nuances of the extent of the topicality of each word is generally not effective – once the word is topical enough, it matters not just how topical it is. Or, at the very least, we have not yet found a way to devise an effective continuous topicality score for a word.

Let us now consider the more effective cutoff-based binary indices (LH$_2$, LH$_3$, SIMPLE), and evaluate the effects of the two manipulations applied across the word topicality models: the log scaling and the use of types vs tokens.

*Log Scaling*: This manipulation is effective in every single case (compare odd lines $n$ to even lines $n+1$ for $n > 8$, for each of the datasets, for a total of 18 comparisons).

*Type vs Token*: Types are better than tokens in every single case (compare lines $n$ to lines $n+2$ within each word topicality model, for $n > 8$, for each of the datasets, for a total of 18 comparisons).

---

[8]Since some of the indices are scaled by log length, we calculated second-order partial correlations excluding the linear effects of both length and log-length on Set 1. The resulting values were very close to the first-order partial correlation values that control for length only, and did not change the comparative standings of the various models. For simplicity, Table 3 reports first-order partial correlations controlling for length for all models.

| ID | Word Model | Tok/ Type | Log Scale? | Set 1 | | | Set 2 | | | TOEFL | | |
|---|---|---|---|---|---|---|---|---|---|---|---|---|
| | | | | $R_s$ | $R_l$ | $r_p$ | $R_s$ | $R_l$ | $r_p$ | $R_s$ | $R_l$ | $r_p$ |
| 1 | HBA | tok | no | -.014 | -.114 | .079 | -.194 | -.217 | -.070 | -.208 | -.216 | -.102 |
| 2 | HBA | tok | yes | .235 | .248 | .099 | .020 | .077 | -.041 | -.041 | .040 | -.080 |
| 3 | HBA | typ | no | .114 | .152 | .020 | -.094 | -.028 | -.101 | -.163 | -.076 | -.146 |
| 4 | HBA | typ | yes | .262 | .358 | .042 | .055 | .169 | -.077 | -.050 | .087 | -.125 |
| 5 | $LH_1$ | tok | no | -.033 | -.102 | .044 | -.138 | -.194 | -.014 | -.124 | -.185 | -.020 |
| 6 | $LH_1$ | tok | yes | .092 | .076 | .056 | -.037 | -.059 | .002 | -.037 | -.052 | -.008 |
| 7 | $LH_1$ | typ | no | .051 | .057 | .018 | -.096 | -.095 | -.045 | -.117 | -.106 | -.068 |
| 8 | $LH_1$ | typ | yes | .148 | .190 | .033 | -.010 | .015 | -.026 | -.044 | -.005 | -.050 |
| 9 | $LH_2$ | tok | no | .049 | -.103 | .154 | .019 | -.014 | .150 | -.054 | -.141 | .035 |
| 10 | $LH_2$ | tok | yes | .304 | .269 | .176 | .235 | .155 | .178 | .139 | .155 | .061 |
| 11 | $LH_2$ | typ | no | -.096 | -.317 | .152 | -.022 | -.255 | .202 | -.072 | -.224 | .074 |
| 12 | $LH_2$ | typ | yes | .135 | -.024 | .199 | .197 | .006 | .257 | .146 | .060 | .137 |
| 13 | $LH_3$ | tok | no | .070 | -.092 | .171 | .042 | -.126 | .169 | -.016 | -.112 | .062 |
| 14 | $LH_3$ | tok | yes | .343 | .310 | .195 | .283 | .206 | .200 | .199 | .219 | .090 |
| 15 | $LH_3$ | typ | no | -.052 | -.279 | .177 | .013 | -.223 | .220 | -.016 | -.177 | .109 |
| 16 | $LH_3$ | typ | yes | .207 | .054 | .227 | .261 | .079 | .280 | .228 | .143 | .179 |
| 17 | SIMPLE | tok | no | .105 | -.073 | .201 | .086 | -.098 | .202 | .078 | -.045 | .129 |
| 18 | SIMPLE | tok | yes | .430 | .418 | .228 | .385 | .324 | .240 | .338 | .368 | .163 |
| 19 | SIMPLE | typ | no | .016 | -.219 | .214 | .080 | -.165 | .256 | .106 | -.070 | .181 |
| 20 | SIMPLE | typ | yes | .349 | .227 | .272 | .396 | .237 | .328 | .399 | .334 | .267 |

**Table 3:** Performance of the different word-topicality models ($\alpha$), with or without log length scaling, in type or token aggregation, on the three datasets, in terms of Pearson correlation with essay score ($R_s$), Pearson correlation with essay length ($R_l$), and partial correlation with score controlling for length ($r_p$). Evaluations are performed on Train data in each dataset.

Finally, we observe that among the cutoff models, the more permissive, the better – the model with a stricter significance threshold for topicality performs worse than the one with a looser threshold, which in turn performs worse than a simple cutoff model with no significance test at all (compare line $n$ to line $n+4$, for $n > 8$, in Table 3). This suggests that richer but noisier topical lists are generally more effective, in the essay scoring context.

Following these observations, we select the type-aggregated log-scaled simple topicality index for evaluation within an essay scoring system for the three datasets.

## 6 Essay Scoring Experiments

In this section, we present an evaluation of the best topicality index for each of the three datasets as a feature in a comprehensive, state-of-art essay scoring system. The baseline engine (e-rater®, described in Burstein et al. (2013)) computes more than 100 micro-features, which are aggregated into macro-features aligned with specific aspects of the writing construct. The system incorporates macro-features measuring grammar, usage, mechanics, organization, development, etc; Table 4 shows the nine macro-features, with examples of micro-features. In addition, we put essay length (number of words) as the 10th macro-feature into the baseline model, to ascertain that any gains observed in the experimental condition are not due to the introduction of length as part of the scaling in the topicality feature.

In the **baseline** condition, a scoring model is built over the ten macro-features using linear regression on the Train set and evaluated on the Test set, for each of the datasets. In the **experimental** condition, the topicality index is added as the 11th macro-feature into the linear regression model; the experimental system is also trained on Train set and evaluated on Test set, for each of the datasets. We evaluate essay scoring performance using Pearson correlation with human holistic score.

To test statistical significance of the improvements, we use Wilcoxon signed-rank test for matched pairs. We calculate the baseline and experimental performance on each prompt separately, and use the 76 pairs of values (for each of Sets 1 and 2) and 8 pairs of values (for TOEFL) as inputs

| Macro-Features | Example Micro-Features |
|---|---|
| Grammar | garbled , run-on, fragmented sentences |
| Usage | determiner-noun agreement errors, noun number errors, missing article |
| Mechanics | spelling, capitalization, punctuation errors |
| Organization | use of discourse elements, such as thesis, support, conclusion |
| Development | size of discourse elements |
| Vocabulary 1 | av. word frequency |
| Vocabulary 2 | av. word length |
| Idiomaticity | use of appropriate prepositions, use of collocational patterns |
| Sentence Variety | use of sentences with various levels of syntactic complexity |
| Length | number of words in the essay |

**Table 4:** Baseline essay scoring system (9 macro-features from a state-of-art essay scoring system, and essay length).

for the test. We use VassarStats for performing the significance tests.[9] Table 5 show the results.

We find that the addition of the topicality feature leads to a statistically significant improvement over the baseline for each of the three datasets. In an additional set of experiments, we removed essay length from both the baseline and the experimental conditions to check whether the topicality feature would improve upon a state-of-art essay scoring system as-is; we found an improvement in all the three datasets, at the same significance levels as those reported in Table 5.

## 7 Related Work

The two approaches that are most closely related to the current work are those of Higgins et al. (2006) and Lin and Hovy (2000), who present word topicality models based on a comparison between the distribution of words in on-topic and off-topic texts. Indeed, these models were the starting point of our work, along with a simpler comparison model based on raw frequencies. Higgins et al. (2006) aggregated the word-level scores using unscaled token-level ag-

---

[9]http://vassarstats.net/

| Data | Performance ($r$) | | Signif. |
| --- | --- | --- | --- |
| | Baseline | Experimental | Level |
| Set 1 | 0.762 | 0.766 | 0.0001 |
| Set 2 | 0.800 | 0.804 | 0.0001 |
| TOEFL | 0.747 | 0.749 | 0.05 |

**Table 5:** Results of essay scoring experiments. Performance is reported in terms of Pearson correlation with human essay score. 2-tailed $p$-values for rejecting the null hypothesis of no improvement are shown in the last column. The Wilcoxon test statistics are: W= 1486, n = 73 (Set 1); W = 2064, n = 71 (Set 2); W = 25, n = 7 (TOEFL).

gregation; our results suggest that this aggregation method can be improved upon by log-length scaling and type-based aggregation. We also showed that Lin and Hovy (2000) topicality models produce better predictions of essay quality, with appropriate scaling and aggregation.

Louis and Higgins (2010) and Higgins et al. (2006) address the task of detecting off-topic essays without on-topic training materials. Persing and Ng (2014) reported a study where essays were scored on an analytic rubric of adherence to the prompt; while this is a promising way to evaluate text-topicality models intrinsically, the reliability of the annotations was low ($r$=0.234). Content scoring was also studied for essays written in response to an extensive reading or listening prompt – quality of content is then related to integrating information from the source materials (Beigman Klebanov et al., 2014; Kakkonen et al., 2005; Lemaire and Dessus, 2001).

A related direction of research implicitly treats topicality as a part of a more generalized notion of "good content," namely, words that are used by good writers. The approach to estimating the quality of content is to compare the content of the current text to sets of training texts that represent various score points (Attali and Burstein, 2006; Kakkonen et al., 2005; Xie et al., 2012). In this approach, there is no differentiation between content that is topical and other words that might be used for other reasons, such as discourse markers used for organizational purposes or spurious, shell-like elements (Madnani et al., 2012); an essay that is dissimilar from high-scoring essays on all or some of these accounts is likely to be viewed as having "bad content." An essay rife with misspellings would like-

wise be seen as having "bad content", because the model high-scoring essays are generally not prone to misspellings. In contrast, our topicality lists are estimated based on a random sample of essays, including low scoring essays; this allows introduction of common misspellings of words frequently used to address the given topic into the topical lists. For example, one of the topical lists includes more than a dozen misspellings of the word *contemporaries*.

There is a large body of work using topic models to capture different topics typically addressed in a corpus of text (Mimno et al., 2011; Newman et al., 2011; Gruber et al., 2007; Blei et al., 2003). In this general framework, each text can address a few different topics and the number and identity of topics for the corpus is typically unknown. In our setting, we assume that each essay is on a single topic, and that topic is known in advance.[10] However, many of these topics are very open-ended, so they might exhibit non-trivial sub-topical structures. For example, a topic about cultural role models might be dealt with by discussing politicians, musicians, sportsmen – each of these could yield a specific sub-topic. In fact, Persing and Ng (2014) used LDA to create sub-topics in this way, and derived features to predict prompt-adherence of an essay. The authors found that in order to make these features more effective, it was beneficial for humans to go over the topics and assign relevance estimates for each sub-topic.

## 8   Conclusion

In this paper, we addressed the problem of quantifying the overall extent to which a test-taker's essay deals with the topic it is assigned (prompt). We experimented with a number of approaches for quantifying the topicality of a word, and with a number of approaches for aggregating word-level topicality into text-level topicality. We found that type-based, log-length scaled aggregation generally works better than the token-based and unscaled one, for the task of predicting the holistic quality of essays. The findings of the effectiveness of log length scaling and of type-based accounting when estimating the topicality of an essay for the purposes of holistic scoring are novel contributions of this work.

---

[10]The high-stakes nature of the examination ensures that these assumptions are rarely wrong.

We also showed that incorporation of text-topicality into essay scoring yields a significant improvement for two different writing tasks over a very strong baseline – a state-of-art essay scoring system augmented with an essay length feature. A significant improvement is also observed on the publicly available set of TOEFL essays, even though the set is smaller, there are only a handful of different prompts, the essays are shorter and less proficiently written, and the scores are given on a coarser-grained scale than for the other two datasets. The demonstration of the excellent generalization of the relative merits of the various topicality models across three datasets and the effectiveness of the topicality feature for improving essay scoring on the three sets is another novel contribution of this work; it suggests robustness of our findings regarding the relationship between topicality, length and quality of essays.

An interesting direction of future work is an intrinsic evaluation of topicality indices against human judgments of topicality. This is a difficult annotation task (Persing and Ng, 2014), and, to our knowledge, no reliable protocol exists for this task.

## References


Yigal Attali and Jill Burstein. 2006. Automated Essay Scoring With e-rater®V.2. *Journal of Technology, Learning, and Assessment*, 4(3).

Beata Beigman Klebanov, Nitin Madnani, Jill Burstein, and Swapna Somasundaran. 2014. Content importance models for scoring writing from sources. In *Proceedings of the 52nd Annual Meeting of the Association for Computational Linguistics (Volume 2: Short Papers)*, pages 247–252, Baltimore, Maryland, June.

Daniel Blanchard, Joel Tetreault, Derrick Higgins, Aoife Cahill, and Martin Chodorow. 2013. TOEFL11: A corpus of non-native english. Educational Testing Service Research Report No. RR-13-24.

David M. Blei, Andrew Y. Ng, and Michael I. Jordan. 2003. Latent Dirichlet Allocation. *Journal of Machine Learning Research*, 3:993–1022.

Jill Burstein, Joel Tetreault, and Nitin Madnani. 2013. The E-rater®Automated Essay Scoring System. In M. Shermis and J. Burstein, editors, *Handbook of Automated Essay Scoring: Current Applications and Future Directions*. New York: Routledge.

Peter Foltz, Walter Kintsch, and Thomas Landauer. 1998. The measurement of textual coherence with latent semantic analysis. *Discourse Processes*, 25(2):285–307.

Amit Gruber, Yair Weiss, and Michal Rosen-Zvi. 2007. Hidden topic markov models. *Journal of Machine Learning Research - Proceedings Track*, 2:163–170.

Derrick Higgins, Jill Burstein, Daniel Marcu, and Claudia Gentile. 2004. Evaluating multiple aspects of coherence in student essays. In *Proceedings of NAACL*, pages 185–192, Boston, Massachusetts, USA, May.

Derrick Higgins, Jill Burstein, and Yigal Attali. 2006. Identifying off-topic student essays without topic-specific training data. *Natural Language Engineering*, 12(2):145–159.

Tuomo Kakkonen, Niko Myller, Jari Timonen, and Erkki Sutinen. 2005. Automatic Essay Grading with Probabilistic Latent Semantic Analysis. In *Proceedings of the Second Workshop on Building Educational Applications Using NLP*, pages 29–36, Ann Arbor, Michigan, June.

Benoît Lemaire and Philippe Dessus. 2001. A System to Assess the Semantic Content of Student Essays. *Journal of Educational Computing Research*, 24:305–320.

Chin-yew Lin and Eduard Hovy. 2000. The automated acquisition of topic signatures for text summarization. In *Proceedings of COLING*, pages 495–501.

Annie Louis and Derrick Higgins. 2010. Off-topic essay detection using short prompt texts. In *Proceedings of the NAACL HLT 2010 Fifth Workshop on Innovative Use of NLP for Building Educational Applications*, pages 92–95, Los Angeles, California, June.

Nitin Madnani, Michael Heilman, Joel Tetreault, and Martin Chodorow. 2012. Identifying high-level organizational elements in argumentative discourse. In *Proceedings of NAACL*, pages 20–28.

David Mimno, Hanna M. Wallach, Edmund Talley, Miriam Leenders, and Andrew McCallum. 2011. Optimizing semantic coherence in topic models. In *Proceedings of the Conference on Empirical Methods in Natural Language Processing*, pages 262–272, Stroudsburg, PA, USA.

David Newman, Edwin Bonilla, and Wray Buntine. 2011. Improving topic coherence with regularized topic models. In J. Shawe-Taylor, R.S. Zemel, P.L. Bartlett, F. Pereira, and K.Q. Weinberger, editors, *Advances in Neural Information Processing Systems 24*, pages 496–504.

Ellis B. Page. 1966. The Imminence of Grading Essays by Computer. *Phi Delta Kappan*, pages 238–243.

Isaac Persing and Vincent Ng. 2014. Modeling prompt adherence in student essays. In *Proceedings of the 52nd Annual Meeting of the Association for Computational Linguistics (Volume 1: Long Papers)*, pages 1534–1543, Baltimore, Maryland, June.

Swapna Somasundaran, Jill Burstein, and Martin Chodorow. 2014. Lexical chaining for measuring discourse coherence quality in test-taker essays. In *Proceedings of COLING*, pages 950–961.

Joel Tetreault, Daniel Blanchard, Aoife Cahill, and Martin Chodorow. 2012. Native tongues, lost and found: Resources and empirical evaluations in native language identification. In *Proceedings of COLING 2012*, pages 2585–2602, Mumbai, India, December.

Shasha Xie, Keelan Evanini, and Klaus Zechner. 2012. Exploring content features for automated speech scoring. In *Proceedings of the 2012 Conference of the North American Chapter of the Association for Computational Linguistics: Human Language Technologies*, pages 103–111, Montréal, Canada, June.

Su-Youn Yoon and Shasha Xie. 2014. Similarity-based non-scorable response detection for automated speech scoring. In *Proceedings of the Ninth Workshop on Innovative Use of NLP for Building Educational Applications*, pages 116–123, Baltimore, Maryland, June.

# Predicting the Spelling Difficulty of Words for Language Learners

Lisa Beinborn$^{\diamond\S}$, Torsten Zesch$^{\ddagger\S}$, Iryna Gurevych$^{\diamond\S}$

$\diamond$ UKP Lab, Technische Universität Darmstadt
$\ddagger$ Language Technology Lab, University of Duisburg-Essen
$\S$ UKP Lab, German Institute for Educational Research
`http://www.ukp.tu-darmstadt.de`

## Abstract

In many language learning scenarios, it is important to anticipate spelling errors. We model the spelling difficulty of words with new features that capture phonetic phenomena and are based on psycholinguistic findings. To train our model, we extract more than 140,000 spelling errors from three learner corpora covering English, German and Italian essays. The evaluation shows that our model predicts spelling difficulty with an accuracy of over 80% and yields a stable quality across corpora and languages. In addition, we provide a thorough error analysis that takes the native language of the learners into account and provides insights into cross-lingual transfer effects.

## 1 Introduction

The irregularities of spelling have been subject to debates for a long time in many languages. Spelling difficulties can lead to substantial problems in the literacy acquisition and to severe cases of dyslexia (Landerl et al., 1997). Learning orthographic patterns is even harder for foreign language learners because the phonetic inventory of their mother tongue might be quite different. Thus, they have to learn both the new sounds and their mapping to graphemes. English is a well-known example for a particularly inconsistent grapheme-to-phoneme mapping. For example, the sequence *ough* can be pronounced in six different ways as in *though,* *through, rough, cough, thought* and *bough.*[1]

In many language learning scenarios, it is important to be aware of the spelling difficulty of a word. In Beinborn et al. (2014), we analyzed that words with high spelling error probability lead to more difficult exercises. This indicates, that spelling difficulty should also be considered in exercise generation. In text simplification tasks (Specia et al., 2012), a quantification of spelling difficulty could lead to more focused, learner-oriented lexical simplification. Spelling problems are often influenced by cross-lingual transfer because learners apply patterns from their native language (Ringbom and Jarvis, 2009). Spelling errors can therefore be a good predictor for automatic natural language identification (Nicolai et al., 2013). Language teachers are not always aware of these processes because they are often not familiar with the native language of their learners. Automatic prediction methods for L1-specific spelling difficulties can lead to a better understanding of cross-lingual transfer and support the development of individualized exercises.

In this paper, we take an empirical approach and approximate spelling difficulty based on error frequencies in learner corpora. We extract more than 140,000 spelling errors by more than 85,000 learners from three learner corpora. Two corpora cover essays by learners of English and the third corpus contains learner essays in German and Italian. We then train an algorithmic

---

[1]IPA pronunciations from https://en.wiktionary.org: /ð o ʊ/, /θ ɹ u/, /ɹ ʌ f/, /k ɔ f/, /θ ɔ t/, and /b a ʊ/

73

*Proceedings of the 11th Workshop on Innovative Use of NLP for Building Educational Applications*, pages 73–83,
San Diego, California, June 16, 2016. ©2016 Association for Computational Linguistics

model on this data to predict the spelling difficulty of a word based on common word difficulty features and newly developed features modeling phonetic difficulties. We make the extracted errors and the code for extraction and prediction publicly available.[2] Our evaluation results show that it is generally possible to predict the spelling difficulty of words. The performance remains stable across corpora and across languages. Common word features such as length and frequency already provide a reasonable approximation. However, if we aim at explaining the processes that cause different spelling errors depending on the L1 of the learner, phonetic features and the cognateness of words need to be taken into account.

## 2  Measuring Spelling Difficulty

Analyses of English spelling difficulties have a long tradition in pedagogical and psycholinguistic literature, but to the best of our knowledge the task of predicting spelling difficulty has not yet been tackled. In this section, we operationalize the analytical findings on spelling difficulty into features that can be derived automatically.

In general, three sources of spelling errors can be distinguished: i) errors caused by physical factors such as the distance between keys on the input device or omitted character repetitions, ii) errors caused by look-ahead and look-behind confusion (e.g. *puclic–public*, *gib–big*), iii) and errors caused by phonetic similarity of letters (e.g. vowel confusion *visable–visible*). Baba and Suzuki (2012) analyze spelling errors committed by English and Japanese learners using keystroke logs and find that the first two types are usually detected and self-corrected by the learner whereas phonetic problems remain unnoticed. In the learner corpora that we analyze, the learners were encouraged to review their essays thoroughly, so we focus on spelling errors that are usually not detected by learners.

In the following, we describe seven features that we implemented for spelling difficulty prediction: two word difficulty features

(length and frequency) and five phonetic features (grapheme-to-phoneme ratio, phonetic density, character sequence probability, pronunciation difficulty and pronunciation clarity).

### 2.1  Word Difficulty Features

Many psycholinguistic studies have shown that frequency effects play an important role in language acquisition (Brysbaert and New, 2009). High-frequency words enable faster lexical access and should therefore be easier to memorize for language learners. For English, the word length is in principle a good approximation of word frequency because frequently used words tend to be rather short compared to more specific terms. Medero and Ostendorf (2009) and Culligan (2015) analyze vocabulary difficulty and find that short length and high frequency are good indicators for simple words. Both features are also highly relevant for spelling difficulty. Put simply, the probability of producing an error is increased by the number of characters that need to be typed. For frequent words, the probability that the learner has been exposed to this word is increased and therefore the spelling difficulty should be lower. We determine the length of a word by the number of characters and the frequency is represented by the unigram log-probability of the word in the Web1T corpus (Brants and Franz, 2006).

### 2.2  Phonetic Difficulty

In addition to the traditional features mentioned above, phonetic ambiguity has been intensely analyzed in the spelling research. Frith (1980) compares the spelling errors of good and poor readers and shows that good readers only produce phonetic misspellings whereas poor readers (which she called 'mildly dyslexic') often produce non-phonetic misspellings. Cook (1997) compares English spelling competence for L1 and L2 users. She confirms that the majority of spelling errors by all three groups (L1 children, L1 adults, L2 adults) are due to ambiguous sound–letter correspondences. Berkling et al. (2015b) study the interplay between graphemes and phonotactics in German in detail and developed a game to teach orthographic patterns

---

[2]https://www.ukp.tu-darmstadt.de/data/spelling-correction/spelling-difficulty-prediction

to children. Peereman et al. (2007) provide a very good overview of factors influencing word difficulty and also highlight the importance of consistent grapheme–phoneme correspondence. It thus seems justified to focus on the phonetic problems. The features described below try to approximate the relationship between graphemes and phonemes from various angles.

**Orthographic Depth** Rosa and Eskenazi (2011) analyze the influence of word complexity features on the vocabulary acquisition of L2 learners and show that words which follow a simple one-to-one mapping of graphemes to phonemes are considered to be easier than one-to-many or many-to-one mappings as in *knowledge*.[3] The orthographic depth can be expressed as the grapheme-to-phoneme ratio (the word length in characters divided by the number of phonemes). For English, we calculate the number of phonemes based on the phonetic representation in the Carnegie Mellon University Pronouncing Dictionary.[4] For Italian and German, a comparable pronunciation resource is not available. However, as the orthography of these two languages is more regular than for English, the pronunciation of a word can be approximated by rules. We use the grapheme-to-phoneme transcription of the text-to-speech synthesis software MaryTTS version 5.1.1 (Schröder and Trouvain, 2003) to determine the phonetic transcription for Italian and German. MaryTTS uses a mixture of resource-based and rule-based approaches. We will refer to transcriptions obtained from these resources as gold transcriptions.

**Phonetic Density** The phonetic density has also been proposed as a potential cause for spelling difficulty, but has not yet been studied extensively (Joshi and Aaron, 2013). It is calculated as the ratio of vowels to consonants. Both extremes—words with high density (e.g. *aerie*) and very low density (e.g. *strength*)—are likely to cause spelling problems.

**Character Sequence Probability** We assume, that the grapheme–phoneme correspondence of a word is less intuitive, if the word contains a rare sequence of characters (e.g. *gardener* vs *guarantee*). To approximate this, we build a language model of character trigrams that indicates the probability of a character sequence using the framework Berkeleylm version 1.1.2 (Pauls and Klein, 2011). The quality of a language model is usually measured as the perplexity, i.e. the ability of the model to deal with unseen data. The perplexity can often be improved by using more training data. However, in this scenario, the model is supposed to perform worse on unseen data because it should model human learners. In order to reflect the sparse knowledge of a language learner, the model is trained only on the 800–1000 most frequent words from each language. We refer to these words as the *Basic Vocabulary*.[5]

**Pronunciation Difficulty** Furthermore, we try to capture the assumption that a spelling error is more likely to occur if the grapheme–phoneme mapping is rare as in *Wednesday*. The sequence *ed* is more likely to be pronounced as in simple past verbs or as in *Sweden*. We approximate this by building a phonetic model using Phonetisaurus, a tool that is based on finite state transducers which map characters onto phonemes and can predict pronunciations for unseen words.[6] Analogous to the character-based language model, the phonetic model is also trained only on words from the *Basic Vocabulary* in order to reflect the knowledge of a language learner. Based on this scarce data, the phonetic model only learns the most frequent character-to-phoneme mappings and assigns higher phonetic scores to ambiguous letter sequences. We use this score as indicator for the pronunciation difficulty.

**Pronunciation Clarity** Even if the learner experiences low pronunciation difficulty, she

---

[3]grapheme length: 9, phoneme length: 5

[4]http://www.speech.cs.cmu.edu/cgi-bin/cmudict

[5]We use the following lists: en: http://ogden.basic-english.org, de: http://www.languagedaily.com/learn-german/vocabulary/common-german-words, it: https://en.wiktionary.org/wiki/Wiktionary:Frequency_lists/Italian1000

[6]http://code.google.com/p/phonetisaurus

might still come up with a wrong pronunciation. For example, many learners are convinced that *recipe* should be pronounced /ɹ ɪ s a ɪ p/. To model the discrepancy between expected and true pronunciation, we calculate the Levenshtein distance between the produced pronunciation by the phonetic model and the gold transcription as pronunciation clarity.

## 3   Spelling Error Extraction

In order to evaluate the described model for predicting spelling difficulty, we need suitable data. For this purpose, we extract spelling errors from corpora of annotated learner essays. The corpora contain annotations for a wide range of errors including spelling, grammar, and style. As the corpora use different annotation formats, we implement an extraction pipeline to focus only on the spelling errors. We apply additional preprocesssing and compute the spelling error probability as an indicator for spelling difficulty.

### 3.1   Corpora

We use learner essays and error annotations from three corpora: EFC, FCE and Merlin. The first two contain essays by learners of English and the Merlin corpus contains essays by learners of German and Italian.[7] We describe them in more detail below.

**EFC**   The EF-Cambridge Open Language Database (Geertzen et al., 2012) contains 549,326 short learner essays written by 84,997 learners from 138 nationalities. The essays have been submitted to *Englishtown*, the online school of *Education First*. 186,416 of these essays are annotated with corrections provided by teachers. We extract 167,713 annotations with the tag *SP* for spelling error.[8] To our knowledge, this is by far the biggest available corpus with spelling errors from language learners.

**FCE**   The second corpus is part of the Cambridge Learner Corpus and consists of learner answers for the *First Certificate in English* (FCE) exam (Yannakoudakis et al., 2011). It contains 2,488 essays by 1,244 learners (each learner had to answer two tasks) from 16 nationalities. The essays have been corrected by official examiners. We extract 4,074 annotations with the tag *S* for spelling error.

**Merlin**   The third corpus has been developed within the EU-project MERLIN (Boyd et al., 2014) and contains learner essays graded according to the Common European Reference Framework. The 813 Italian and the 1,033 German samples have been obtained as part of a test for the European language certificate (TELC). 752 of the German essays and 754 of the Italian essays were annotated with target hypotheses and error annotations by linguistic experts. We extract 2,525 annotations with the tag *O_graph* from the German essays and 2,446 from the Italian essays. Unfortunately, the correction of the errors can only be extracted, if the error annotation is properly aligned to the target hypotheses which is not always the case. We ignore the errors without available correction which reduces the set to 1,569 German and 1,761 Italian errors. In the following, we refer to the German subset as M-DE and the Italian subset as M-IT.

### 3.2   Error Extraction

As the annotation guidelines differed for the three corpora, we first need to apply additional pre-processing steps. In a second step, we aim at quantifying the spelling difficulty for each word by calculating the spelling error probability.

**Pre-processing**   We remove all spelling errors that only mark a change from lowercase to uppercase (or vice versa) and numeric corrections (e.g. *1* is corrected to *one*) as these are rather related to stylistic conventions than to spelling. We lowercase all words, trim whitespaces and only keep words which occur in a word list and consist of at least three letters (to avoid abbreviations like *ms, pm, oz*).[9]

---

[7]It also contains essays by Czech learners, but this subset is significantly smaller than the ones for the other two languages and is therefore not used here.

[8]Some corrections have two different tags; we only extract those with a single *SP* tag.

[9]We use the word list package provided by Ubuntu for spell-checking: http://www.ubuntuupdates.org/package/core/lucid/main/base/\$PACKAGE, packages: wamerican, wngerman, wfrench

|  |  | EFC | FCE | M-DE | M-IT |
|---|---|---|---|---|---|
| Words | All | 7,388,555 | 333,323 | 84,557 | 57,708 |
|  | Distinct | 23,508 | 7,129 | 3,561 | 3,760 |
| Spelling Errors | All | 133,028 | 3,897 | 1,653 | 1,904 |
|  | Distinct | 7,957 | 1,509 | 719 | 747 |
| Ratio Errors/Words | Distinct | .34 | .21 | .20 | .20 |

**Table 1:** Extracted words and spelling errors after pre-processing

**Spelling Error Probability** In this work, we take an empirical approach for quantifying spelling difficulty. A spelling error $s$ is represented by a pair consisting of a misspelling $e$ and the corresponding correction $c$. The error frequency $f_e$ of a word $w$ in the dataset $D$ is then determined by the number of times it occurs as a correction of a spelling error independent of the actual misspelling. The number of spelling errors $S_D$ in the dataset is determined by summing over the error frequencies of all words in the dataset. To quantify the distinct spelling errors, we count all words with $f_e \geq 1$ once.

$$s \quad = (e, c) \tag{1}$$

$$f_e(w) = \sum_{s_i \in D} |w = c_i| \tag{2}$$

$$S_D \quad = \sum_{w_i \in D} f_e(w_i) \tag{3}$$

The number of extracted words and errors are summarized in Table 1. It can be seen that the EFC corpus is significantly bigger than the other corpora. The spelling errors in the EFC corpus are spread over many words leading to a higher ratio of erroneous words over all words.

The pure error frequency of a word can be misleading, because frequently used words are more likely to occur as a spelling error independent of the spelling difficulty of the word. Instead, we calculate the spelling error probability for each word as the ratio of the error frequency over all occurrences of the word (including the erroneous occurrences).

$$p_{err}(w) = \frac{f_{err}(w)}{f(w)} \tag{4}$$

| Corpus | Error Probability | |
|---|---|---|
|  | **high** | **low** |
| EFC | *departmental* | *boy* |
|  | *spelt* | *car* |
|  | *invincible* | *crime* |
| FCE | *synthetic* | *weeks* |
|  | *millennium* | *feel* |
|  | *mystery* | *rainbow* |
| M-DE | *tschüss* | *damit* |
|  | *nächsten* | *machen* |
|  | *beschäftigt* | *gekauft* |
| M-IT | *messagio* | *rossi* |
|  | *lunedí* | *questo* |
|  | *caffè* | *tempo* |

**Table 2:** Examples for high and low spelling error probability

The words are then ranked by their error probability to quantify spelling difficulty.[10] This is only a rough approximation that ignores other factors such as repetition errors and learner ability because detailed learner data was not available for all corpora. In future work, more elaborate measures of spelling difficulty could be analyzed (see for example Ehara et al. (2012)).

### 3.3 Training and Test Data

An inspection of the ranked probabilities indicates that the spelling difficulty of a word is a continuous variable which points to a regression problem. However, the number of spelling errors is too small to distinguish between a spelling error probability of 0.2 and 0.3, for example. Instead, we only focus on the extremes of the scale.

---

[10]In the case of tied error probability, the word with the higher error frequency is ranked higher. In the case of an error frequency of zero for both words, the word with the lower correct frequency is ranked higher.

| | | EFC | FCE | M-DE | M-IT |
|---|---|---|---|---|---|
| | Random Baseline | .500** | .500** | .500** | .500** |
| Individual Features | Orthographic Depth | .482** | .462** | .427** | .622** |
| | Phonetic Density | .483** | .349** | .564** | .508** |
| | Character Sequence Probability | .706** | .642** | .736 | .563** |
| | Pronunciation Clarity | .635** | .677** | .722 | .683 |
| | Pronunciation Difficulty | .792** | .792** | **.828** | .731 |
| | Frequency | .634** | .742** | .778 | .728 |
| | Length | **.809** | **.827** | .747 | **.769** |
| Combined | Length + Frequency + Pronunciation Diff. | .822 | .832 | **.828** | **.792** |
| | All Features | **.835** | **.847** | .814 | **.778** |

**Table 3:** Feature analysis for spelling difficulty using 10-fold cross-validation. The prediction results are expressed as accuracy. Significant differences compared to the result with all features are indicated with **(p<0.01).

The $n$ highest ranked words are considered as samples for high spelling difficulty and the $n$ lowest-ranked words form the class of words with low spelling difficulty. As additional constraint, the errors should have been committed by at least three learners in the EFC dataset and by two learners in the other corpora. For the EFC dataset, we extract 500 instances for each class, and for the FCE dataset 300 instances. 200 instances (100 per class) are used for testing in both cases and the remaining instances are used for training. We find an overlap of 52 words with high spelling error probability in both English corpora. As the Merlin corpus is significantly smaller, we only extract 100 instances per class for German and Italian. 140 instances are used for training and 60 for testing. Table 2 provides examples for high and low error probabilities.

## 4 Experiments & Results

The following experiments test whether it is possible to distinguish between words with high and low spelling error probability using the features described in Section 2. The models are trained with support vector machines as implemented in Weka (Hall et al., 2009). The features are extracted using the DKPro TC framework (Daxenberger et al., 2014).

### 4.1 Feature Analysis

In a first step, the predictive power of each feature is evaluated by performing ten-fold cross-validation on the training set. The results in the upper part of Table 3 are quite similar for the two English corpora. Around 80% of the test words are classified correctly and the most predictive features are the word length and the pronunciation difficulty. It should be noted, that the two features are correlated (Pearson's r: 0.67), but they provide different classifications for 131 of the 800 EFC instances in the cross-validation setting. The results for Italian are slightly worse than for English, but show the same pattern for the different features. For German, the pronunciation difficulty and frequency features perform slightly better than the length feature. The two features orthographic depth and phonetic density are not predictive for the spelling difficulty and only perform on chance level for all four datasets. We additionally train a model build on the three best performing features length, frequency, and pronunciation difficulty as well as one using all features. It can be seen that the results improve slightly compared to the individual features. Due to the rather small datasets and the correlation between the features, the differences between the best performing models are not significant.

In general, the accuracy results are comparable across languages (78–85%) indicating that it is possible to distinguish between words with high and low spelling error probability. In the following, we test whether the models can generalize to the unseen test data.

|              | EFC   | FCE   | M-DE  | M-IT  |
| ------------ | ----- | ----- | ----- | ----- |
| Random       | .500  | .500  | .500  | .500  |
| Len/Freq/Pron | **.840** | .865  | .766  | **.817** |
| All          | **.840** | **.870** | **.800** | .815  |

**Table 4:** Spelling difficulty prediction on the test set for both corpora. The prediction results are expressed as accuracy.

## 4.2 Prediction Results

After these analyses, the two combined models are evaluated on the unseen test data. The results in Table 4 show that the models scale well to the test set and yield accuracy results that are slightly better than in the cross-validation setting. Again, the results of the two combined models are not found to be significantly different. There are two explanations for this. On the one hand, the test set is quite small (200 instances for English, 60 instances for German and Italian) which makes it difficult to measure significant differences. On the other hand, this result indicates that length, frequency and pronunciation difficulty are very predictive features for the spelling difficulty and the other features only have insignificant effects. The finding that longer words are more likely to produce misspellings is not surprising. For deeper psycholinguistic analyses it might be useful to balance the spelling data with respect to the word length. In such a scenario, phonetic aspects would presumably become more important. However, as we want to model the probability that a learner makes a spelling error, we need to take the length effect into account as an important indicator.

## 4.3 Cross-corpus comparison

The above results have shown that the prediction quality is very similar for the two English corpora. To analyze the robustness of the prediction approach, we compare the prediction quality across corpora by training on all instances of one corpus and testing on the instances of another. We also include the German and Italian corpora to this cross-corpus comparison to evaluate the language-dependence of spelling difficulty.

| Train Corpus |         | Test Corpus |      |       |       |
| ------------ | ------- | ----- | ----- | ----- | ----- |
|              |         | EFC   | FCE   | M-DE  | M-IT  |
|              | # inst. | 200   | 200   | 60    | 60    |
| EFC          | 800     | .840  | .772  | .703  | .634  |
| FCE          | 600     | .764  | .870  | .767  | .766  |
| M-DE         | 140     | .659  | .829  | .800  | .796  |
| M-IT         | 140     | .397  | .540  | .780  | .815  |

**Table 5:** Spelling difficulty prediction on the full set across corpora. The prediction results are expressed as accuracy. The number of instances is indicated in brackets for each dataset. The two classes are equally distributed.

The results in Table 5 show that the accuracy for cross-corpus prediction generally decreases compared to the previous results of in-corpus prediction (which are listed in the diagonal of the result matrix), but still remains clearly above chance level for English and German. In contrast, training on the Italian corpus leads to bad results for the two English corpora. It is interesting to note that a model trained on the German spelling errors performs better on the FCE words than a model trained on the English errors from the EFC corpus. The FCE and the Merlin corpus have been obtained from standardized language examinations whereas the EFC corpus rather aims at formative language training. In the second scenario, the learners are probably less prepared and less focused leading to more heterogeneous data which could explain the performance differences across corpora.

## 5 Error Analysis

For a more detailed analysis, we take a closer look at the mis-classifications for the EFC dataset. In a second step, we analyze spelling errors with respect to the L1 of the learners.

### 5.1 Misclassifications

The following words were classified as *high error probability*, but have a low error probability in the learner data: *references, ordinary, universal, updates, unrewarding, incentives, cologne, scarfs, speakers, remained, vocals*. It seems surprising that all those words should have a low error probability. A possible explanation could be that the words had been mentioned in the task description of the essays and are therefore frequently used and spelled correctly. Unfortunately, the task descriptions are not published along with the corpus and we cannot take this factor into account.

The words that were erroneously classified as words with a low spelling error probability are generally shorter: *icy, whisky, cried, curry, spelt, eight, runway, tattoo, daughter, farmers, discreet, eligible, diseases, typical, gallery, genre, mystery, arctic, starters, stretch, rhythm.* In several cases, we see phenomena for which features are available, e.g. a low vowel-consonant ratio in *stretch* and *rhythm*, an infrequent grapheme-to-phoneme mapping in *genre*, a low character sequence probability in *tattoo*. Unfortunately, these features seem to be overruled by the length feature.

In other examples, we observe phenomena that are specific to English and are not sufficiently covered by our features such as irregular morphology (*icy, spelt, cried*). This indicates that features which model language-specific phenomena might lead to further improvements.

## 5.2 Influence of the L1

As phonetic features have a strong influence on spelling difficulty, we assume that the L1 of the learners plays an important role. For example, *arctic* is misspelled as *artic, *gallery* as *galery and *mystery* and *typical* are spelled with *i* instead of *y*. These misspellings correspond to the correct stem of the respective word in Spanish, Italian and Portuguese. In the following, we thus have a closer look at the influence of the L1.

The EFC corpus comprises essays from a very heterogeneous group of learners, but 71% of the annotated essays are written by learners from five nationalities, namely Brazilian, Chinese, German, Mexican, and Russian. For comparative analyses, we also extracted the spelling errors specific to each of these five nationalities. Table 6 shows anecdotal examples of cross-lingual influence on spelling difficulties. For the word *attention*, it can be seen that the Russian learners are tempted to use an *a* as second vowel instead of an *e*. For the Brazilian and Mexican learners, on the other hand, the duplication of the *t* is more problematic because doubled plosive consonants do not occur in their L1.

L1-specific errors are often due to the existence of similar words—so-called cognates—in the native language of the learner. The word *departmental* is particularly difficult for Brazilian and Chinese learners. While most Brazilian learners erroneously insert an *a* due to the cognate *departamento*, none of the Chinese learners commits this error because a corresponding cognate does not exist. The Brazilian and Mexican misspellings of *hamburger* can also be explained with the cognateness to *hamburguesa* and *hambúrguer* respectively. A *g* followed by an *e* is pronounced as a fricative /x/ in Spanish and not as a plosive /g/. This indicates that the phonetic features should model the differences between the L1 and the L2 of the learner.

The word *engineer* provokes a large variety of misspellings. A common problem is the use of *e* as the second vowel, which could be explained with the spelling of the cognates (br: *engenheiro*, de: *Ingenieur*, ru: инженер transliterated as *inzhener*). However, the misspelling by the Mexican learners cannot be explained with cognateness because the Spanish spelling would be *ingeniero*. The spelling of *marmalade* with an *e* seems to be idiosyncratic to German learners.

The above analyses are only performed on an anecdotal basis and need to be backed up with more thorough experimental studies. The examples support the intuitive assumption that cognates are particularly prone to spelling errors due to the different orthographic and phonetic patterns in the L1 of the learner. The cognateness of words can be determined automatically using string similarity measures (Inkpen et al., 2005) or character-based machine translation (Beinborn et al., 2013).

The learners in the EFC corpus also differ in proficiency (e.g. German learners seem to be more advanced than Brazilian learners) which might also have an influence on the spelling error probability of words. However, it is complicated to disentangle the influence of the L1 and

| Correct | Brazilian | Mexican | Chinese | Russian | German |
|---|---|---|---|---|---|
| attention | *atention(27)* <br> *attencion (10)* <br> *atencion (3)* | *atention (13)* <br> *attencion(1)* <br> *attentio (1)* | *attaention (1)* <br> *atttention (1)* <br> - | *attantion (5)* <br> *atantion (1)* <br> *atention (1)* | - <br> - <br> - |
| departmental | *departament (10)* <br> *departamente (1)* <br> *departaments (1)* | *department (1)* <br> - <br> - | *deparment (2)* <br> *deparmental (1)* <br> *deprtment (1)* | - <br> - <br> - | - <br> - <br> - |
| hamburger | *hamburguer (2)* <br> *hamburguers (2)* | *hamburguer (2)* <br> - | *hamburg* <br> *hamburgs (1)* | - <br> - | - <br> - |
| engineer | *engeneer (17)* <br> *ingineer (2)* <br> *ingener (2)* | *enginner (25)* <br> *engeneer (8)* <br> *engenier (4)* | *engneer (5)* <br> *engeneer (4)* <br> *enginner (3)* | *engeneer (14)* <br> *engeener (3)* <br> *ingener (2)* | *ingeneur (2)* <br> *engeneer (2)* <br> *ingeneer (2)* |
| marmalade | - | - | - | - | *marmelade (3)* |

Table 6: Most frequent misspellings for selected examples

of the L2 proficiency based on the current data and we leave this analysis to future work.

## 6 Related work

In section 2, we already discussed psycholinguistic analyses of spelling difficulty. In natural language processing, related work in the field of spelling has focused on error correction (Ng et al., 2013; Ng et al., 2014). For finding the right correction, Deorowicz and Ciura (2005) analyze probable causes for spelling errors. They identify three types of causes (mistyping, misspelling and vocabulary incompetence) and model them using substitution rules. Toutanova and Moore (2002) use the similarity of pronunciations to pick the best correction for an error resulting in an improvement over state-of-the-art spellcheckers. Boyd (2009) build on their work but model the pronunciation of non-native speakers, leading to slight improvements in the pronunciation-based model. Modeling the spelling difficulty of words could also have a positive effect on spelling correction because spelling errors would be easier to anticipate.

Another important line of research is the development of spelling exercises. A popular recent example is the game Phontasia (Berkling et al., 2015a). It has been developed for L1 learners but could probably also be used for L2 learners. In this case, the findings on cross-lingual transfer could be integrated to account for the special phenomena occurring with L2 learners.

## 7 Conclusions

We have extracted spelling errors from three different learner corpora and calculated the spelling error probability for each word. We analyzed the concept of spelling difficulty and implemented common word difficulty features and new phonetic features to model it. Our prediction experiments reveal that the length and frequency features are a good approximation for spelling difficulty, but they do not capture phonetic phenomena. The newly developed feature for pronunciation difficulty can close this gap and complement the word difficulty features for spelling difficulty prediction.

We conclude that the spelling error probability of a word can be predicted to a certain extent. The prediction results are stable across corpora and can even be used across languages. A detailed error analysis indicates that further improvements could be reached by modeling language-specific features (e.g. morphology) and by taking the L1 of the learner into account. We make the spelling errors and our code publicly available to enable further research on spelling phenomena and hope that it will lead to new insights into the processes underlying foreign language learning.

## Acknowledgments

This work has been supported by the Volkswagen Foundation as part of the Lichtenberg-Professorship Program under grant No. I/82806, and by the Klaus Tschira Foundation under project No. 00.133.2008.

## References

Yukino Baba and Hisami Suzuki. 2012. How are spelling errors generated and corrected? A study of corrected and uncorrected spelling errors using keystroke logs. In *Proceedings of the 50th Annual Meeting of the Association for Computational Linguistics: Short Papers*, pages 373–377. Association for Computational Linguistics.

Lisa Beinborn, Torsten Zesch, and Iryna Gurevych. 2013. Cognate Production using Character-based Machine Translation. In *Proceedings of the Sixth International Joint Conference on Natural Language Processing*, pages 883–891. Asian Federation of Natural Language Processing.

Lisa Beinborn, Torsten Zesch, and Iryna Gurevych. 2014. Predicting the difficulty of language proficiency tests. *Transactions of the Association for Computational Linguistics*, 2:517–529.

Kay Berkling, Nadine Pflaumer, and Alexei Coyplove. 2015a. Phontasia—a game for training german orthography. In *Proceedings of the Sixteenth Annual Conference of the International Speech Communication Association*, pages 1874–1875.

Kay Berkling, Nadine Pflaumer, and Rémi Lavalley. 2015b. German Phonics Game using Speech Synthesis-A Longitudinal Study about the Effect on Orthography Skills. In *Proceedings of the Workshop on Spoken Language Technology for Education (SLaTE)*, pages 168–172.

Adriane Boyd, Jirka Hana, Lionel Nicolas, Detmar Meurers, Katrin Wisniewski, Andrea Abel, Karin Schöne, Barbora Štindlová, and Chiara Vettori. 2014. The MERLIN corpus: Learner language and the CEFR. In *Proceedings of the Ninth International Conference on Language Resources and Evaluation (LREC)*.

Adriane Boyd. 2009. Pronunciation Modeling in Spelling Correction for Writers of English As a Foreign Language. In *Proceedings of the Annual Conference of the North American Chapter of the Association for Computational Linguistics: Student Research Workshop and Doctoral Consortium*, pages 31–36. Association for Computational Linguistics.

Thorsten Brants and Alex Franz. 2006. Web 1T 5-gram corpus version 1.1. *Linguistic Data Consortium.*

Marc Brysbaert and Boris New. 2009. Moving beyond Kučera and Francis: A critical evaluation of current word frequency norms and the introduction of a new and improved word frequency measure for American English. *Behavior research methods*, 41(4):977–990.

Vivian Cook. 1997. L2 users and English spelling. *Journal of Multilingual and Multicultural Development*, 18(6):474–488.

Brent Culligan. 2015. A comparison of three test formats to assess word difficulty. *Language Testing*, 32(4):503–520.

Johannes Daxenberger, Oliver Ferschke, Iryna Gurevych, and Torsten Zesch. 2014. DKPro TC: A Java-based Framework for Supervised Learning Experiments on Textual Data. In *Proceedings of the 52nd Annual Meeting of the Association for Computational Linguistics: System Demonstrations*, pages 61–66, Baltimore, Maryland, June. Association for Computational Linguistics.

Sebastian Deorowicz and Marcin G Ciura. 2005. Correcting spelling errors by modelling their causes. *International Journal of Applied Mathematics and Computer Science*, 15(2):275.

Yo Ehara, Issei Sato, Hidekazu Oiwa, and Hiroshi Nakagawa. 2012. Mining words in the minds of second language learners: Learner-specific word difficulty. In *Proceedings of the 24th International Conference on Computational Linguistics*, pages 799–814.

Uta Frith. 1980. Unexpected spelling problems. *Cognitive Processes in Spelling.*

Jeroen Geertzen, Dora Alexopoulou, and Anna Korhonen. 2012. Automatic Linguistic Annotation of Large Scale L2 Databases: The EF-Cambridge Open Language Database (EFCamDat). In Ryan T. Miller, editor, *Selected Proceedings of the 2012 Second Language Research Forum*. MA: Cascadilla Proceedings Project.

Mark Hall, Eibe Frank, Geoffrey Holmes, Bernhard Pfahringer, Peter Reutemann, and Ian H. Witten. 2009. The weka data mining software: An update. *SIGKDD Explorations Newsletter*, 11(1):10–18.

Diana Inkpen, Oana Frunza, and Grzegorz Kondrak. 2005. Automatic identification of cognates and false friends in French and English. In *Proceedings of the International Conference Recent Advances in Natural Language Processing*, pages 251–257.

R.M. Joshi and P.G. Aaron. 2013. *Handbook of Orthography and Literacy*. Taylor & Francis.

K Landerl, H Wimmer, and U Frith. 1997. The impact of orthographic consistency on dyslexia: a German-English comparison. *Cognition*, 63(3):315–34, June.

Julie Medero and Mari Ostendorf. 2009. Analysis of Vocabulary Difficulty using Wiktionary. *Proceedings of the 2nd Workshop on Speech and Language Technology in Education*.

Hwee Tou Ng, Siew Mei Wu, Yuanbin Wu, Christian Hadiwinoto, and Joel Tetreault. 2013. The CoNLL-2013 Shared Task on Grammatical Error Correction. In *Proceedings of the Seventeenth Conference on Computational Natural Language Learning: Shared Task*, pages 1–12.

Hwee Tou Ng, Siew Mei Wu, Ted Briscoe, Christian Hadiwinoto, Raymond Hendy Susanto, and Christopher Bryant. 2014. The CoNLL-2014 Shared Task on Grammatical Error Correction. In *Proceedings of the Eighteenth Conference on Computational Natural Language Learning: Shared Task*, pages 1–12.

Garrett Nicolai, Bradley Hauer, Mohammad Salameh, Lei Yao, and Grzegorz Kondrak. 2013. Cognate and Misspelling Features for Natural Language Identification. In *Proceedings of the Eighth Workshop on Innovative Use of NLP for Building Educational Applications*, pages 140–145.

Adam Pauls and Dan Klein. 2011. Faster and Smaller N-Gram Language Models. *Proceedings of the 49th Annual Meeting of the Association for Computational Linguistics*.

Ronald Peereman, Bernard Lété, and Liliane Sprenger-Charolles. 2007. Manulex-infra: Distributional characteristics of grapheme—phoneme mappings, and infralexical and lexical units in child-directed written material. *Behavior Research Methods*, 39(3):579–589, August.

Håkan Ringbom and Scott Jarvis. 2009. The importance of cross-linguistic similarity in foreign language learning. In Michael H Long and Catherine J Doughty, editors, *The Handbook of Language Teaching*, chapter 7, pages 106–118. John Wiley & Sons.

Kevin Dela Rosa and Maxine Eskenazi. 2011. Effect of word complexity on l2 vocabulary learning. In *Proceedings of the 6th Workshop on Innovative Use of NLP for Building Educational Applications*, pages 76–80. Association for Computational Linguistics.

Marc Schröder and Jürgen Trouvain. 2003. The german text-to-speech synthesis system mary: A tool for research, development and teaching. *International Journal of Speech Technology*, 6(4):365–377.

Lucia Specia, Sujay Kumar Jauhar, and Rada Mihalcea. 2012. SemEval-2012 Task 1: English Lexical Simplification. In *Proceedings of the First Joint Conference on Lexical and Computational Semantics (*SEM)*, pages 347–355. Association for Computational Linguistics.

Kristina Toutanova and Robert C Moore. 2002. Pronunciation modeling for improved spelling correction. *Proceedings of the 40th Annual Meeting of the Association for Computational Linguistics*.

Helen Yannakoudakis, Ted Briscoe, and Ben Medlock. 2011. A New Dataset and Method for Automatically Grading ESOL Texts. In *The 49th Annual Meeting of the Association for Computational Linguistics: Human Language Technologies*.

# Characterizing Text Difficulty with Word Frequencies


**Xiaobin Chen**[*] and **Detmar Meurers**
LEAD Graduate School
Department of Linguistics
Eberhard Karls Universität Tübingen
{xiaobin.chen,detmar.meurers}@uni-tuebingen.de



## Abstract

Natural language processing (NLP) methodologies have been widely adopted for readability assessment and greatly enhanced predictive accuracy. In the present study, we study a well-established feature, the frequency of a word in common language use, and systematically explore how such a word-level feature is best used to characterize the reading levels of texts, a text-level classification problem. While traditionally such word-level features are simply averaged for all words of given text, we show that a richer representation leads to significantly better predictive models.

A basic approach adding a feature for the standard deviation already shows clear gains, and two more complex options systematically integrating more frequency information are explored: (i) encoding separate means for the words of a text according to which frequency band of the language they occur in, and (ii) encoding the mean of each cluster of words obtained by agglomerative hierarchical clustering of the words in the text based on their frequency. The former organizes frequency around general language characteristics, whereas the latter aims to lose as little information as possible about the distribution of word frequencies in a given text. To investigate the generalizability of the results, we compare cross-validation experiments within a corpus with cross-corpus experiments testing on the Common Core State Standards reference texts. We also contrast two different frequency norms and compare frequency with a measure of contextual diversity.


---

[*]Xiaobin Chen is also affiliated with the South China University of Technology, where he holds a lecturer position.

## 1 Introduction

Although readability research has gone through a history of more than one hundred years (DuBay, 2007), the use of Natural Language Processing (NLP) technology in readability research is a recent phenomenon. It has greatly improved the predictive accuracy by enabling a multi-dimensional characterization of a text's reading level (Benjamin, 2012; Collins-Thompson, 2014). For example, Vajjala and Meurers (2012) showed that 46 lexical and syntactic features mostly inspired by complexity measures Second Language Acquisition research support a classification accuracy of 91.3% on WeeklyReader, a collection of texts targeting children in four age groups commonly used in such readability research (Petersen and Ostendorf, 2009; Feng et al., 2010).

The readability of a text is determined by the combination of all text aspects that affects the reader's understanding, reading speed, and level of interest in the text (Dale and Chall, 1949). Recent studies explore lexical, morphological, semantic, psycholinguistic, syntactic, and cognitive features for determining the reading levels of texts (Crossley et al., 2007; Lu et al., 2014; Hancke et al., 2012; Boston et al., 2008; vor der Brück et al., 2008; Heilman et al., 2007; Feng, 2010; McNamara et al., 2014).

Among all these elements, the semantic variable of word difficulty has traditionally been found to account for the greatest percentage of readability variance (Marks et al., 1974). Word difficulty is often associated with word frequency given that the amount of exposure of a reader to the word is believed to be the major predictor of word knowledge (Ryder and Slater, 1988).




*Proceedings of the 11th Workshop on Innovative Use of NLP for Building Educational Applications*, pages 84–94,
San Diego, California, June 16, 2016. ©2016 Association for Computational Linguistics

In the present study, we zoom in to the question how word frequency can best be used to characterize the readability of a text. We experimented with three different methods of using frequency as a word-level feature to inform our predictions of readability at the text-level.

## 2 The Frequency Effect

Reading is a coordinated execution of a series of processes which involve word encoding, lexical access, assigning semantic roles, and relating the information contained in a sentence to earlier sentences in the same text and the reader's prior knowledge (Just and Carpenter, 1980). Successful comprehension of texts depends on the readers' semantic and syntactic encoding abilities (Marks et al., 1974), as well as their vocabulary knowledge in the language (Laufer and Ravenhorst-Kalovski, 2010; Nation, 2006). A general consensus of reading research is that lexical coverage/vocabulary knowledge are good predictors of reading comprehension (Bernhardt and Kamil, 1995; Laufer, 1992; Nation, 2001; Nation, 2006; Qian, 1999; Qian, 2002; Ulijn and Strother, 1990).

A reader's vocabulary knowledge is largely related to the amount of exposure they have received to words—often refered to as *frequency effect*. It is argued to be predictive of word difficulty (Ryder and Slater, 1988) and Leroy and Kauchak (2014) found that word frequency is strongly associated with both actual difficulty (how well people can choose the correct definition of the word) and perceived difficulty (how difficult a word looks). High-frequency words are usually perceived and produced more quickly and more efficiently than low-frequency ones (Balota and Chumbley, 1984; Howes and Solomon, 1951; Jescheniak and Levelt, 1994; Monsell et al., 1989; Rayner and Duffy, 1986). Consequently, a text with many high-frequency words is generally easier to understand than one with a number of rare words. Frequency of word occurrence affects not only the ease of reading, but also its acceptability (Klare, 1968).

The frequency effect is based on a cognitive model assuming a higher base-level of activation for frequently-used words, so they require relatively less additional activation when they are being retrieved from the reader's mental lexicon (Just and Carpenter, 1980). This idea is supported by the findings that high-frequency words are more easily perceived (Bricker and Chapanis, 1953) and readily retrieved by the reader (Haseley, 1957). Going beyond this basic effect, in frequency-based accounts of Second Language Acquisition (Ellis, 2012), the frequency distribution of the input is a key determinant of acquisition, with regularities emerging through the learner's exposure to the distributional characteristics of the language input.

## 3 Word Frequency for Readability Assessment

Figure 1 illustrates how word frequency can be linked to reading comprehension. Based on a model such as this one, it is reasonable to assume that lexical frequencies can inform text-level analyses.

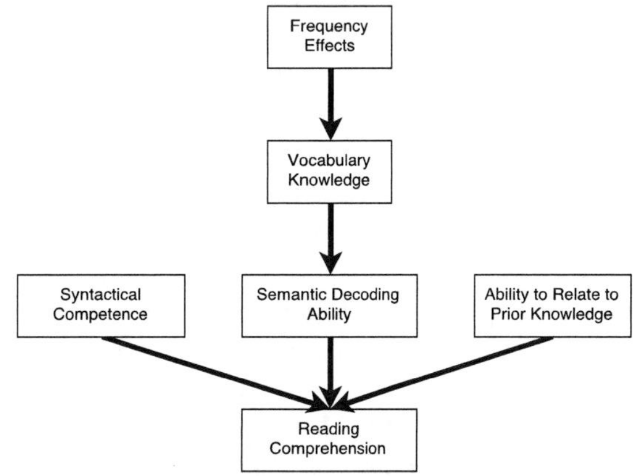


**Figure 1:** The frequency effect on reading comprehension

Traditional readability formulas used measures such as number of "zero-index words" (number of words that are not included in the most frequent words in English), median of index numbers (Lively and Pressey, 1923), average word weighted value (Patty and Painter, 1931), or number of words from the text that are among the first 1,000 and first 2,000 most frequent words (Ojemann, 1934) for predicting reading levels. These measures were found to be highly correlated with difficulty and effective in assessing text readability.

Modern readability assessment systems such as Lexile (Lexile, 2007), ATOS (Milone and Biemiller, 2014), and CohMetrix (McNamara et al., 2014) also made wide use of word frequencies to help determine the reading level of a text, and such systems were found to be relatively effective (Nelson et al., 2012). However, there are several issues concerning the frequency lists used, the nature of the frequency measures, and how they are used to account for text readability that deserve more attention.

The first issue is that the frequency lists adopted by these studies were mostly drawn from written corpora. Spoken language was rarely taken into consideration when frequency lists were being composed. This runs the risk of the frequency values not being a faithful representation of the reader's actual language experience, hence being suboptimal for predicting the ease of perception and retrieval. Fortunately, the SUBTLEX frequency lists (Brysbaert and New, 2009; van Heuven et al., 2014) have been compiled on the basis of spoken language data drawn from movie and TV subtitles to obtain more faithful representations of a language typical user's experience with language. The SUBTLEX frequency lists significantly better predict word processing times than earlier norms such as Kučera and Francis (1967) and Celex (Baayen et al., 1993), or frequencies norms derived from the huge Google books corpus (cf. Brysbaert et al., 2011).

The second issue concerns how frequency is measured. Previous research generally sums up all occurrences of a word in the corpus. Yet some words may be frequent in restricted contexts but are not frequent when considering all contexts of language use. As argued by Adelman et al. (2006), a better method may be to count the Contextual Diversity (CD), the number of contexts in which a word occurs. They found the CD measure to be a better predictor of word frequency effects in lexical decision tasks, a method for probing into the word knowledge in the speaker's mental lexicon. However, to the best of our knowledge, CD measures have never been tested in text-level readability assessment. To address this gap, we experimented with both frequency and CD measures in constructing our readability models.

Finally, as for how to use word frequencies for building readability prediction models, previous research typically employed mean frequencies or the percentage of words from the top frequency bands to characterize text levels. Yet, this loses a lot of information about the distribution of word frequencies in the text. Averaging is easily affected by extreme values, and it loses information about the variabil-ity of the data. Furthermore, averaging over all occurrences of words in a text will minimize the contribution of low-frequency words—yet, it may be precisely these less-frequent words that are causing reading difficulties. In order to explore how word frequency can be better used for readability assessment, we test three different methods for characterizing texts in terms of lexical frequency: (i) complementing the mean frequency with the standard deviation, (ii) encoding separate means for the words of a text according to which frequency band of the language they occur in, and (iii) encoding the mean of each cluster of words obtained by agglomerative hierarchical clustering of the words in the text based on their frequency. The second method organizes the frequency measures around general language characteristics, whereas the third one aims to lose as little information as possible about the distribution of word frequencies in a given text. The goal of the series of experiments is to identify better methods for characterizing texts of different reading levels from the lexical perspective.

In sum, the reviews of the frequency effect on reading comprehension and earlier research on the use of word frequency for readability assessment support the hypothesis that a lexical frequency measure reflecting the reader's language experience can play a substantial role in models of text readability. The research reported here is devoted to testing this hypothesis in a way that addresses the three problems spelled out above: the source of the frequency list, the nature of the frequency measure used, and the method for combining word-level evidence for text-level predictions.

## 4 Experimental Setup

Before turning to the three experiments carried out, let us introduce the resources and the general procedure used. As source of the frequency and CD[1] information, we used the SUBTLEXus (Brysbaert and New, 2009) and the SUBTLEXuk (van Heuven et al., 2014) resources. We ran all experiments with two distinct frequency resources to be able to study the impact of the choice of resource. As corpus for exploring the approach and 10-fold cross validation

---

[1] The CD measure we used is referred to as SUBTLCD in SUBTLEXus and as CD in SUBTLEXuk.

testing we used the leveled text corpus WeeBit (Vajjala and Meurers, 2012). For independent cross-corpus testing, we trained on WeeBit and tested on the exemplar texts from Appendix B of the Common Core State Standards (CommonCore, 2010). For machine learning, we used the basic k-nearest neighbor algorithm implemented in the R package `class` given that in our initial exploration it turned out to perform on a par or better than other commonly used algorithms such as Support Vector Machine or Decision Trees.

### 4.1 The SUBTLEX Lists

The SUBTLEXus (Brysbaert and New, 2009) contains 74,286 word forms with frequency values calculated from a 51-million-word corpus of subtitles from 8,388 American films and television series broadcast between 1900 and 2007. The SUBTLEXuk (van Heuven et al., 2014) is the British counterpart, consisting of 160,022 word forms with frequency values calculated from a 201.7-million-word corpus of subtitles from nine British TV channels broadcast between January 2010 and December 2012. The SUBTLEX resources provide frequency information in several forms motivated in van Heuven et al. (2014); we made use of the frequencies given on the Zipf scale (log10 of the frequency per billion words), as well as the CD values, for which each film or TV program counted as a context.

### 4.2 The WeeBit and Common Core Corpora

The WeeBit corpus used in a number of readability and text simplification studies (Vajjala and Meurers, 2012; Vajjala and Meurers, 2013; Vajjala and Meurers, 2014) was collected from the educational magazine Weekly Reader used in earlier readability research (Petersen and Ostendorf, 2009; Feng et al., 2010) and the BBC-Bitesize website. As summarized in Table 1, it is a 789,926-word corpus of texts labeled with five grade reading levels.

The Common Core corpus consists of exemplar texts from Appendix B of the English Language Arts Standards of the Common Core State Standards. The corpus we use for testing in our experiments is exactly the same as the one used by Nelson et al. (2012). They eliminated the lowest (K–1) level of the original six levels and removed repetition, dra-

| Grade Level | Age Group | # Articles | # Words / Article |
|---|---|---|---|
| WR Level 2 | 7–8 | 616 | 152.63 |
| WR Level 3 | 8–9 | 616 | 190.74 |
| WR Level 4 | 9–10 | 616 | 294.91 |
| BiteSize KS 3 | 11–14 | 616 | 243.56 |
| BiteSize GCSE | 14–16 | 616 | 400.51 |

**Table 1:** Details of the WeeBit corpus

mas, and texts intended for teacher to read aloud, resulting in 168 remaining passages at five levels.

### 4.3 Experimental Procedure

The following basic procedure was followed for each of the experiments carried out:

1. Tokenize corpus texts with CoreNLP Tokenizer (Manning et al., 2014), which had also been used to compose the SUBTLEX frequency lists.

2. Characterize each text using frequency features. The nature of the features differs across the three studies, for which details are given in the following sections.

3. Train classification models on the WeeBit corpus i) in a 10-fold Cross-Validation (CV) setup or ii) using the full corpus when the Common Core data was used as test. The K-nearest neighbors algorithm of the R package `class` was used for model construction and testing.

4. Apply the trained model to the test folds or test corpus to assess model performance.

5. Report results in terms of Spearman's correlation coefficient ($\rho$) to allow comparison of CV and cross-corpus results. We report both 10-fold CV performance on WeeBit and the test performance on Common Core as references for model fit and generalizability. The KNN algorithm results in different models when the parameter K is set differently. The parameter K for each model was decided automatically by testing K from one up to the square root of the number of texts used for training and choosing the value that resulted in the best performing model. In this paper, we report the performance of the best models.

The complete program for feature extraction and experiment settings with R code can be obtained from `http://xiaobin.ch`.

## 5 Study 1: Adding Standard Deviation

In this first study, we tried the most conservative extension: in addition to the mean frequencies of the words in a given document, we computed the standard deviation (SD). So we compared +SD models trained on two frequency features (mean and SD) with the baseline −SD models trained only on the mean frequency. As explained in the previous section, we tested this using the Zipf and CD measures from two different frequency resources, SUBTLEXus and SUBTLEXuk.

We experimented with both token and type models. For token models, we considered the SUBTLEX-frequency of each word instance in a given text. For type models, each distinct word in the document was considered only once.

Table 2 sums up the results for the 10-fold CV in terms of the Spearman rank correlation $\rho$ between model-predicted and actual reading levels of texts.[2] Table 3 shows the performance of the models trained on WeeBit and tested on Common Core.

|         | Token | | Type | |
|---------|-------|-------|-------|-------|
|         | −SD | +SD | −SD | +SD |
| US-ZIPF | -.02 | .40*** | .26** | .42*** |
| US-CD   | -.02 | .46*** | .19* | .44*** |
| UK-ZIPF | .05 | .25*** | .31*** | .38*** |
| UK-CD   | .04 | .26*** | .21** | .29*** |

**Table 2:** 10-fold CV results for models without/with SD

|         | Token | | Type | |
|---------|-------|-------|-------|-------|
|         | −SD | +SD | −SD | +SD |
| US-ZIPF | .03 | .34*** | .33*** | .35*** |
| US-CD   | -.27*** | .28*** | .22** | .33*** |
| UK-ZIPF | -.13 | .26*** | .36*** | .38*** |
| UK-CD   | .00 | .02 | .33*** | .27*** |

**Table 3:** Common Core test results without/with SD

The models trained on frequency mean and SD systematically performed better than those trained

---

[2]Here and throughout, we mark significant differences (from the null hypothesis that there is no correlation) with *** for $p \le .001$, ** for $p \le .01$, and * for $p \le .05$.

with only mean frequencies. While considering both mean and SD of word frequencies seems like an obvious choice, as far as we know no previous research made use of this option providing significantly better performance for text-level readability prediction.

The results also show that the type models uniformly outperform the token models. In order to further explore this finding, in Figure 2 we plotted

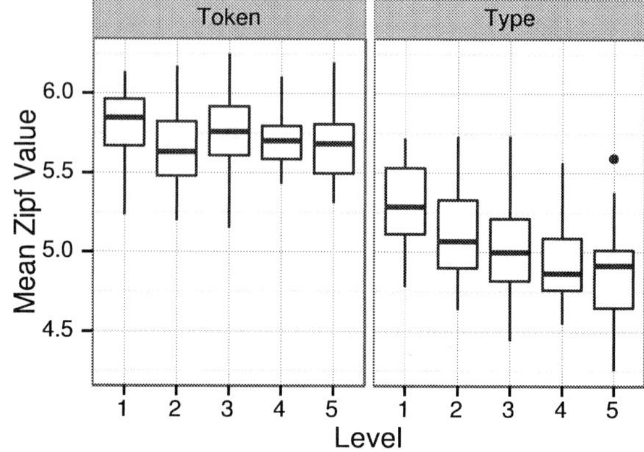


**Figure 2:** Mean token vs. type Zipf by Common Core text level

the mean token and type frequencies of the words in each text of the Common Core corpus by text level. As the reading level increases, the plot shows a clear pattern of decreasing mean type Zipf values. This is not observable for the token averages.

High-frequency tokens usually have multiple occurrence in a given text, inflating the sum of frequency values and obscuring the influence of low frequency words on the mean. The type-based measure eliminates multiple occurrences of tokens so that words across the frequency spectrum contribute equally. The fact that the average type frequencies in Figure 2 are so clearly associated with the readability levels transparently supports the frequency effect.

Comparing the results based on frequency (Zipf) with those using Contextual Diversity (CD), different from the lexical decision tasks (Brysbaert and New, 2009), where CD was more predictive, for text-level readability assessment, frequency performs better for readability assessment.

Finally, Table 3 also showcases that frequency lists calculated from different corpora (here: SUBTLEXus vs. SUBTLEXuk) do result in substantially different model performance. For example, the Zipf measure from the SUBTLEXus corpus resulted in the better 10-fold CV performance than that from the SUBTLEXuk corpus, with a highly significant Spearman's correlation coefficient ($\rho = .42, p \leq .001$) for the type model.

## 6 Study 2: Mean Frequencies of Words from Language Frequency Bands

For the second study, frequency means[3] of words from stratified frequency lists were calculated and used as features to characterize the texts' reading levels. To stratify the frequency list, the words in the SUBTLEX lists were ordered by their frequency values. Then the list was cut into a number of frequency bands, resulting in each word being assigned a band number. Words in the same band thus occur with similar frequency in the language as represented by the corpora the SUBTLEX lists were compiled from. The words in a given text to be analyzed are matched with the words in the frequency list and grouped by the words' band numbers. The text can then be characterized by the average frequencies of the words in each band, i.e., we obtain one average per band. With both SUBTLEX lists, we experimented with up to 100 bands. As before, we used the Zipf frequency and CD measures and tested both token and type models.

Figures 3 and 4 show the performance of token and types models trained with features from both the SUBTLEX lists. The performance is given in terms of 10-fold CV $\rho$s and cross-corpus $\rho$s tested on Common Core. Unlike the results of Study 1, the token models did not perform significantly different from the type models for 10-fold CV. However, the type models generalized better to the Common Core test set than the token models. Word type frequency thus better captures the frequency characteristics of a text. For readability assessment purposes, calculating mean type frequency of words from each frequency band creates better prediction models.

A comparison of the results with those from Study 1 shows that the models constructed using the stratification method clearly outperformed those from Study 1 using only a single mean for all words. When the Zipf measure from the US list is stratified

into 60 bands, the trained model has the best performance among all the models, reaching a 10-fold CV $\rho = .83, p \leq .001$ and a cross-corpus testing $\rho = .39, p \leq .001$). Performance on the test set is rather volatile, though: when the list was cut into 20 bands, the resulting model failed to distinguish between text levels ($\rho = -.11, p \geq .05$) for the test corpus, while the with-in corpus CV correlation coefficient was $\rho = .80, p \leq .001$. The method used in this study thus needs to be fine-tuned with respect to the corpora or resources at hand to achieve the optimal results.

## 7 Study 3: Frequency Cluster Means

The idea behind the third study is the following: The richest frequency representation of a text would be a vector of the frequency of all words in the text. But this is too fine grained to be directly comparable across texts, and texts also differ in length.[4] We therefore incrementally group words together that differ minimally in terms of their frequency values. We can then compute the average frequencies of the words in each group. To realize this idea, we used agglomerative hierarchical clustering to construct a word frequency hierarchical cluster tree for each text in the training corpus. Concretely, we used the `hclust()` function in R with the default complete linkage method and the `dist()` function for calculating Euclidean distances as dissimilarity structure for `hclust()`.

The trees were then cut at different distances from the root to obtain an increasing number of branches, with each branch representing the set of words closest in frequency. The branch means[5] were calculated for each set and used as features to construct the prediction models.

We experimented with the Zipf measure from the SUBTLEXus frequency list with up to 100 clusters and explored type and token models. The performance of the trained models are shown in Figure 5.

---

[3]Without SD; adding SD did not improve performance.

[4]Orthogonal to the number of frequency values compared, note that the order of words in a given text is ignored here. The order may well provide relevant information characterizing the readability of a text. For example, a simple text may well include rare words as long as they are followed by more frequent words explaining the rare ones. This could be interesting to explore in future work.

[5]Without SD; adding SD did not improve model performance either.

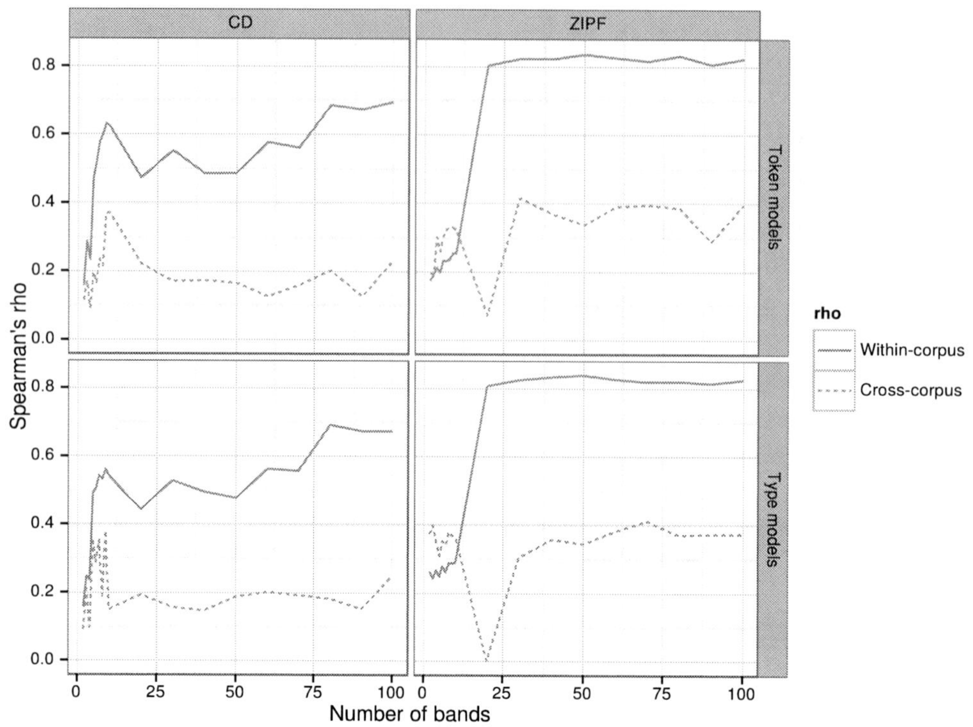

**Figure 3:** 10-fold CV and cross-corpus test $\rho$s between predicted and actual text reading levels by number of SUBTLEXus bands

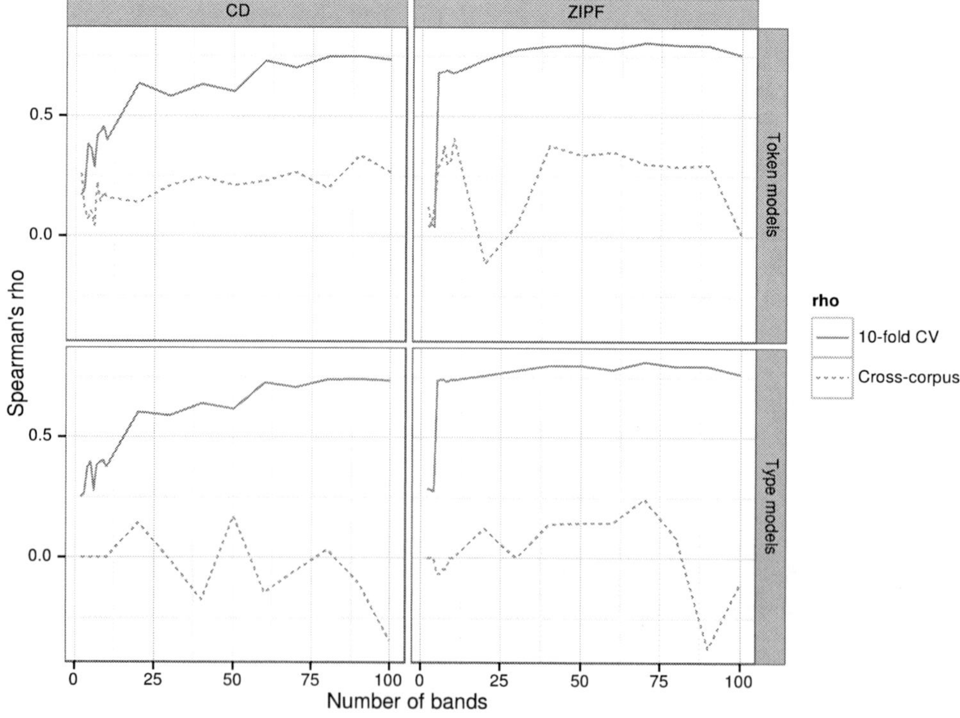

**Figure 4:** 10-fold CV and cross-corpus test $\rho$s between predicted and actual text reading levels by number of SUBTLEXuk bands

90

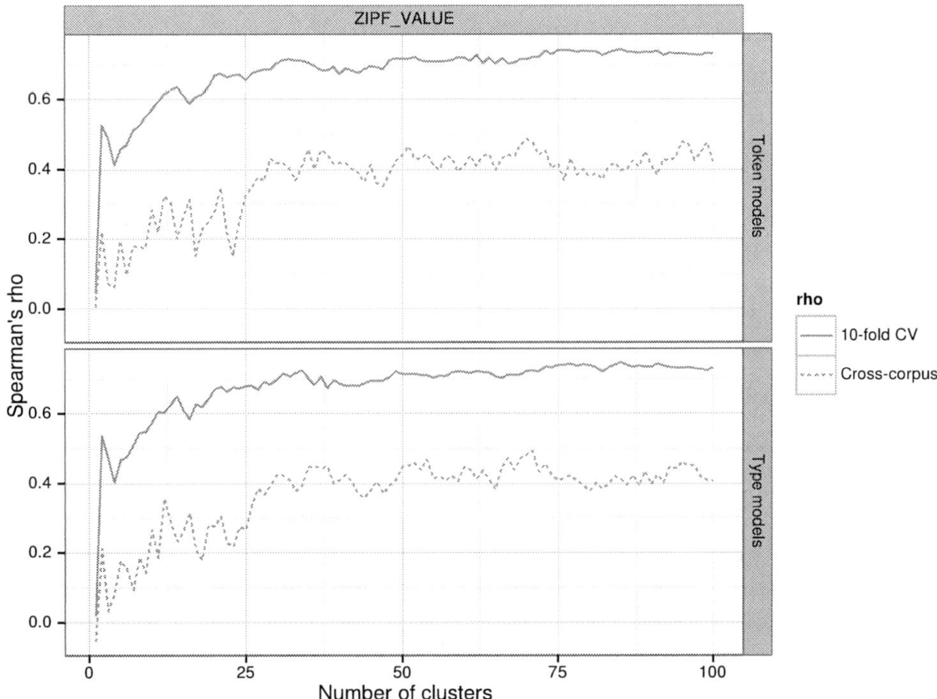

**Figure 5:** 10-fold CV and cross-corpus testing $\rho$s between predicted and actual text reading levels by number of clusters

For most cutting schemes, the token and type models performed comparably. As the number of cluster increased, the trained models improved in performance, with the testing $\rho$s peaking at 70 clusters for all models. Table 4 provides the information for the best performing models from this study.

| Model Type | #Clusters | $\rho$ |
|---|---|---|
| Token Model | | |
|    10-fold CV | 85 | .74*** |
|    Cross-corpus | 70 | .49*** |
| Type Model | | |
|    10-fold CV | 85 | .74*** |
|    Cross-corpus | 71 | .49*** |

**Table 4:** Best-performing models from clustering experiment

The models constructed in this experiments performed significantly better than those from Study 1. Although the models from Study 2 had higher CV $\rho$s, those from this study show a more stable cross-corpus testing performance, which is of major importance for using such a method in practice. It is striking that clustering the words in a text that are similar in word frequency is more reliable across corpora than grouping words by the language frequency bands as a general characteristic of language independent of the texts.

## 8   Comparison with Previous Work

Nelson et al. (2012) assessed the capabilities of six tools for predicting text difficulty: the commercial systems Lexile (MetaMetrics), ATOS (Renaissance Learning), DRP Analyzer (Questar Assessment, Inc.), the Pearson Reading Maturity Metric (Pearson Knowledge Technologies), SourceRater (Educational Testing Service), and the research system REAP (Carnegie Mellon University). Word frequency is a measure that is included in all these systems, though all of them incorporate additional features such as syntactic complexity. One of the evaluations reported by Nelson et al. (2012) was carried out on the freely available Common Core exemplar texts that was also used in Vajjala and Meurers (2014) and the present research, and they reported Spearman's $\rho$, making their results comparable to ours.

The results reported for the best systems clearly

highlight the value of rich feature sets, reaching .76 for SourceRater and .69 for Reading Maturity, which is also the level reached by the Vajjala and Meurers (2014) model.

At the same time, the approach based solely on frequency we discussed in Study 3 with a $\rho$ of .50 is on a par with the results noted by Nelson et al. (2012) for the Lexile system, and only slightly worse than the .53 reported for DRP.

The comparison thus clearly confirms the relevance of considering how lexical frequency information is to be integrated into readability assessment.

## 9   Conclusions

In this paper, we explored the text readability analysis from a word-level perspective, zooming in on lexical frequency. The goal of the three experiments carried out in the research was to investigate how a text-level classification problem can be informed by a word-level feature of the text, namely the frequency of words in general language use. Word frequency is related to the difficulty level of a text given that reading comprehension is partially determined by the reader's vocabulary knowledge, which in turn is related to word frequency. The frequency effect of vocabulary on the reading levels of text is in line with a basic cognitive model positing that words of higher frequencies have a higher level of activation and require less extra effort when they are being retrieved from the reader's mental lexicon. As a result, where frequency lists faithfully represent the reader's language experience, they can predict how difficult the words used in a text are to the reader and in turn inform estimates of the readability of the text.

Three methods of using word frequency lists to predict text readability were tested and confirmed that word frequency is effective in characterizing text difficulty, especially when more than just the average frequency of the words in a text is taken into account. Characterizing text readability in terms of the overall mean and standard deviation of word frequencies performed better than models just using the mean. The model based on the frequencies of the word types occurring in the text (rather than the tokens) were better throughout and generalized much better across corpora. In terms of the nature of the measure itself, the models trained with the Zipf frequency measures were found to outperform those based on measures of Contextual Diversity. The models trained with stratified frequency measures in the second study showed the best performance for the CV evaluation using a single corpus, but generalized less well to the rather different test data set based on the Common Core texts than the clustering approach explored in the third study.

With respect to applying these methods in practical readability assessment contexts, the Zipf frequency measures from the SUBTLEX frequency lists seem to be well-suited, with the overall mean frequency and SD values computed based on the word types being easy and effective. The stratification method improves performance over the simple mean and SD, but it requires fine-tuning of the number of bands. The clustering method has the best model performance and is least sensitive to the use of different frequency lists and measures, but it is also computationally the most expensive.

While the performance of the best frequency models reaches a level that is competitive with systems such as Lexile, clearly a comprehensive approach to readability assessment will integrate a broad range of features integrating more aspects of the linguistic system, language use, and human language processing. Where texts are characterized in terms of observations of smaller units, based our results for lexical frequency it will be advisable to characterize text level readability by more than simple means when aggregating the information obtained, e.g., at the lexical or sentence level.

## Acknowledgments

This research was funded by the LEAD Graduate School [GSC1028], a project of the Excellence Initiative of the German federal and state governments. Xiaobin Chen is a doctoral student at the LEAD Graduate School.

## References

James S. Adelman, Gordon D. A. Brown, and José. F. Quesada. 2006. Contextual diversity, not word frequency, determines word naming and lexical decision times. *Psychological Science*, 17(9):814–23.

R. Harald Baayen, Richard Piepenbrock, and H. van Rijn. 1993. The celex lexical database. CD-ROM.

David A. Balota and James I. Chumbley. 1984. Are lexical decisions a good measure of lexical access? The role of word frequency in the neglected decision stage. *Journal of Experimental Psychology: Human Perception & Performance*, 10(3):340–357.

Rebekah George Benjamin. 2012. Reconstructing readability: recent developments and recommendations in the analysis of text difficulty. *Educational Psychology Review*, 24(1):63–88.

Elizabeth B. Bernhardt and Michael L. Kamil. 1995. Interpreting relationships between L1 and L2 reading: Consolidating the linguistic threshold and the linguistic interdependence hypotheses. *Applied Linguistics*, 16(1):15–34.

Marisa Ferrara Boston, John Hale, Reinhold Kliegl, Umesh Patil, and Shravan Vasishth. 2008. Parsing costs as predictors of reading difficulty: An evaluation using the Potsdam Sentence Corpus. *Journal of Eye Movement Research*, 2(1):1–12.

Peter D. Bricker and Alphonse Chapanis. 1953. Do incorrectly perceived stimuli convey some information? *Psychological Review*, 60(3):181–188.

Marc Brysbaert and Boris New. 2009. Moving beyond Kučera and Francis: A critical evaluation of current word frequency norms and the introduction of a new and improved word frequency measure for American English. *Behavior Research Methods*, 41(4):977–990.

Marc Brysbaert, Emmanuel Keuleers, and Boris New. 2011. Assessing the usefulness of Google Books' word frequencies for psycholinguistic research on word processing. *Frontiers in Psychology*, 2(March):1–8.

Kevyn Collins-Thompson. 2014. Computational assessment of text readability: A survey of past, present, and future research. *International Journal of Applied Linguistics*, 165(2):97–135.

CommonCore. 2010. *Common Core State Standards for English Language Arts and Literacy in History/Social Studies, Science, and Technical Subjects*. Common Core State Standards Initiative.

Scott Crossley, David Dufty, Philip McCarthy, and Danielle McNamara. 2007. Toward a new readability: A mixed model approach. In *Proceedings of the 29th annual conference of the Cognitive Science Society*, pages 197–202, Nashville, Tennessee, USA.

Edgar Dale and Jeanne Chall. 1949. The concept of readability. *Elementary English*, 26(1):19–26.

William H. DuBay. 2007. *Unlocking Language: The Classic Readability Studies*. BookSurge Publishing.

Nick C. Ellis. 2012. Frequency-based accounts of SLA. In Susan M. Gass and Alison Mackey, editors, *Handbook of Second Language Acquisition*, pages 193–210. Routledge.

Lijun Feng, Martin Jansche, Matt Huenerfauth, and Nomie Elhadad. 2010. A comparison of features for automatic readability assessment. In *In Proceedings of the 23rd International Conference on Computational Linguistics (COLING 2010), Beijing, China*.

Lijun Feng. 2010. *Automatic Readability Assessment*. Doctoral dissertation, The City University of New York.

Julia Hancke, Sowmya Vajjala, and Detmar Meurers. 2012. Readability classification for German using lexical, syntactic, and morphological features. In *Proceedings of the 24th International Conference on Computational Linguistics (COLING 2012)*, pages 1063–1080, Mumbai, India.

Leonard Haseley. 1957. *The relationship between cue-value of words and their frequency of prior occurrence*. Unpublished master's thesis, Ohio university.

Michael J. Heilman, Kevyn Collins-Thompson, Jamie Callan, and Maxine Eskenazi. 2007. Combining lexical and grammatical features to improve readability measures for first and second language texts. In *Proceedings of NAACL HLT 2007*, pages 460–467, Rochester, NY. Association for Computational Linguistics.

Dowes H. Howes and Richard L. Solomon. 1951. Visual duration threshold as a function of word-probability. *Journal of Experimental Psychology*, 41(6):401–410.

Jörg D. Jescheniak and Willem J. M. Levelt. 1994. Word frequency effects in speech production: Retrieval of syntactic information and of phonological form. *Journal of Experimental Psychology: Learning, Memory, & Cognition*, 20(4):824–843.

Marcel Adam Just and Patricia A. Carpenter. 1980. A theory of reading: From eye fixations to comprehension. *Psychological review*, 87(4):329–354.

George R. Klare. 1968. The role of word frequency in readability. *Elementary English*, 45(1):12–22.

Henry Kučera and W. Nelson Francis Francis. 1967. *Computational Analysis of Present-day English*. Brown University Press, Providence, RI.

Batia Laufer and Geke Ravenhorst-Kalovski. 2010. Lexical threshold revisited: Lexical text coverage, learners' vocabulary size and reading comprehension. *Reading in a Foreign Language*, 22(1):15–30.

Batia Laufer. 1992. How much lexis is necessary for reading comprehension? In H. Bejoint and P. Arnaud, editors, *Vocabulary and applied linguistics*, pages 126–132. Macmillan, Basingstoke & London.

Gondy Leroy and David Kauchak. 2014. The effect of word familiarity on actual and perceived text difficulty. *Journal of the American Medical Informatics Association*, 21(e1):1–4.

Lexile. 2007. The Lexile Framework for reading: Theoretical Framework and Development. Technical report, MetaMetrics, Inc., Durham, NC.

Bertha A. Lively and Sidney L. Pressey. 1923. A method for measuring the vocabulary burden of textbooks. *Educational Administration and Supervision*, 9:389–398.

Xiaofei Lu, David a. Gamson, and Sarah Anne Eckert. 2014. Lexical difficulty and diversity of American elementary school reading textbooks: Changes over the past century. *International Journal of Corpus Linguistics*, 19(1):94–117.

Christopher D Manning, Mihai Surdeanu, John Bauer, Jenny Finkel, Steven J Bethard, and David McClosky. 2014. The Stanford CoreNLP Natural Language Processing Toolkit. In *Proceedings of 52nd Annual Meeting of the Association for Computational Linguistics: System Demonstrations*, pages 55–60.

Carolyn B. Marks, Marleen J. Doctorow, and M. C. Wittrock. 1974. Word frequency and reading comprehension. *The Journal of Educational Research*, 67(6):259–262.

Danielle S. McNamara, Arthur C. Graesser, Philip M. McCarthy, and Zhiqiang Cai. 2014. *Automated Evaluation of Text and Discourse with Coh-Metrix*. Cambridge University Press, New York, NY.

Michael Milone and Andrew Biemiller. 2014. The development of ATOS: The Renaissance readability formula. Technical report, Renaissance Learning, Wisconsin Rapids.

S. Monsell, M. C. Doyle, and P. N. Haggard. 1989. Effects of frequency on visual word recognition tasks: Where are they? *Journal of Experimental Psychology: General*, 118(1):43–71.

I. S. Paul Nation. 2001. *Learning vocabulary in another language*. Cambridge University Press, Cambridge.

I. S. Paul Nation. 2006. How large a vocabulary is needed for reading and listening? *The Canadian Modern Language Review*, 63(1):59–82.

Jessica Nelson, Charles Perfetti, David Liben, and Meredith Liben. 2012. Measures of text difficulty: Testing their predictive value for grade levels and student performance. Technical report, The Gates Foundation.

Ralph J. Ojemann. 1934. The reading ability of parents and factors associated with reading difficulty of parent education materials. *University of Iowa Studies in Child Welfare*, 8:11–32.

Willard W. Patty and W. I. Painter. 1931. A technique for measuring the vocabulary burden of textbooks. *Journal of Educational Research*, 24(2):127–134.

Sarah E. Petersen and Mari Ostendorf. 2009. A machine learning approach to reading level assessment. *Computer Speech and Language*, 23:86–106.

David Qian. 1999. Assessing the roles of depth and breadth of vocabulary knowledge in reading comprehension. *The Canadian Modern Language Review*, 56(2):282–308.

David Qian. 2002. Investigating the relationship between vocabulary knowledge and academic reading performance: An assessment perspective. *Language Learning*, 52(3):513–536.

Keith Rayner and Susan A. Duffy. 1986. Lexical complexity and fixation times in reading: Effects of word frequency, verb complexity, and lexical ambiguity. *Memory & Cognition*, 14(3):191–201.

Randall James Ryder and Wayne H. Slater. 1988. The relationship between word frequency and word knowledge. *The Journal of Educational Research*, 81(5):312–317.

Jan M. Ulijn and Judith B. Strother. 1990. The effect of syntactic simplification on reading EST texts as L1 and L2. *Journal of Research in Reading*, 13(1):38–54.

Sowmya Vajjala and Detmar Meurers. 2012. On improving the accuracy of readability classification using insights from second language acquisition. In *Proceedings of the Seventh Workshop on Building Educational Applications Using NLP*, pages 163–173, Montréal, Canada. Association for Computational Linguistics.

Sowmya Vajjala and Detmar Meurers. 2013. On the applicability of readability models to Web texts. In *Proceedings of The 2nd Workshop on Predicting and Improving Text Readability for Target Reader Populations*, pages 59–68, Sofia, Bulgaria. Association for Computational Linguistics.

Sowmya Vajjala and Detmar Meurers. 2014. Readability assessment for text simplification: From analyzing documents to identifying sentential simplifications. *International Journal of Applied Linguistics*, 165(2):194–222.

Walter J. B. van Heuven, Pawel Mandera, Emmanuel Keuleers, and Marc Brysbaert. 2014. SUBTLEX-UK: A new and improved word frequency database for British English. *The Quarterly Journal of Experimental Psychology*, 67(6):1176–90.

Tim vor der Brück, Sven Hartrumpf, and Hermann Helbig. 2008. A readability checker with supervised learning using deep syntactic and semantic indicators. In Tomaž Erjavec and Jerneja Žganec Gros, editors, *Proceedings of the 11th International Multiconference: Information Society—IS 2008—Language Technologies*, pages 92–97, Ljubljana, Slovenia.

# Unsupervised Modeling of Topical Relevance in L2 Learner Text


**Ronan Cummins**
ALTA Institute
Computer Lab
University of Cambridge
UK, CB3 0FD
ronan.cummins@cl.cam.ac.uk

**Helen Yannakoudakis**
ALTA Institute
Computer Lab
University of Cambridge
UK, CB3 0FD
helen.yannakoudakis@cl.cam.ac.uk

**Ted Briscoe**
ALTA Institute
Computer Lab
University of Cambridge
UK, CB3 0FD
ejb@cl.cam.ac.uk



## Abstract

The automated scoring of second-language (L2) learner text along various writing dimensions is an increasingly active research area. In this paper, we focus on determining the topical relevance of an essay to the prompt that elicited it. Given the burden involved in manually assigning scores for use in training supervised prompt-relevance models, we develop unsupervised models and show that they correlate well with human judgements.

We show that expanding prompts using topically-related words, via pseudo-relevance modelling, is beneficial and outperforms other distributional techniques. Finally, we incorporate our prompt-relevance models into a supervised essay scoring system that predicts a holistic score and show that it improves its performance.


## 1 Introduction

Given the increase in demand for educational tools and aids for L2 learners of English, the automated scoring of learner texts according to a number of predetermined dimensions (e.g., grammaticality and lexical variety) is an increasingly important research area. While a number of early approaches (Page, 1966; Page, 1994) and recent competitions[1] (Shermis and Hammer, 2012) have sought to assign a holistic score to an entire essay, it is more informative to give detailed feedback to learners by assigning individual scores across each such writing dimension.

This more specific feedback facilitates reflection both on learners' strengths and weaknesses, and focuses attention on the aspects of writing that need improvement. Recent work outlines a number of broad competencies that systems should assess (Kakkonen and Sutinen, 2008). These include *morphology*, *syntax*, *semantics*, *discourse*, and *stylistics*, noting that the specific assessment tasks that might aim to measure these areas of competency may vary. One dimension against which a piece of text is often scored is that of topical relevance. That is, determining if a learner has understood and responded adequately to the prompt. This aspect of automated writing assessment has received considerably less attention than holistic scoring.[2]

Topical relevance is not so much concerned with whether an L2 learner has constructed grammatically correct and well-organised sentences, as it is concerned with whether the learner has understood the prompt and attempted a response with appropriate vocabulary. Other reasons for measuring the topical relevance of a text include the detection of malicious submissions, that is, detecting submissions that have been rote-learned or memorised specifically for assessment situations (Higgins et al., 2006).

In this paper, we employ techniques from the area of distributional semantics and information retrieval (IR) to develop unsupervised prompt-relevance models, and demonstrate that they correlate well with human judgements. In particu-

---

[1]https://www.kaggle.com/c/asap-aes

[2]We note that a recent paper (Persing and Ng, 2014) has referred to this task as *prompt adherence*, while we use the terms *prompt-relevance* and *topical-relevance* interchangeably throughout this paper.

95


*Proceedings of the 11th Workshop on Innovative Use of NLP for Building Educational Applications*, pages 95–104,
San Diego, California, June 16, 2016. ©2016 Association for Computational Linguistics

lar, we study four different methods of expanding a prompt with with topically-related words and show that some are more beneficial than others at overcoming the 'vocabulary mismatch' problem which is typically present in free-text learner writing. To the best of our knowledge, there have been no attempts at a comparative study investigating the effectiveness of such techniques on the automatic prediction of a topical-relevance score in the noisy domain of learner texts, where grammatical errors are common. In addition, we perform an external evaluation to measure the extent to which prompt-relevance *informs* (Rotaru and Litman, 2009) the holistic score.

The remainder of the paper is outlined as follows: Section 2 discusses related work and outlines our contribution. Section 3 presents our framework and four unsupervised approaches to measuring semantic similarity. Section 4 presents both quantitative and qualitative evaluations for all of the methods employed in this paper. Section 5 performs an external evaluation by incorporating the best prompt-relevance model as features into a supervised preference ranking approach. Finally, Section 6 concludes with a discussion and outline of future work.

## 2 Related Research

There are a number of existing automated text-scoring systems (sometimes referred to as *essay scoring systems*). For an overview, the interested reader is directed to reviews and advances in the area (Shermis and Burstein, 2003; Landauer, 2003; Valenti et al., 2003; Dikli, 2006; Phillips, 2007; Briscoe et al., 2010; Shermis and Burstein, 2013). In this section, we review related research on topical-relevance detection for automated writing assessment, and outline the key differences between our approach and that of existing work.

A wide variety of computational approaches (Miller, 2003; Landauer et al., 2003; Higgins et al., 2004; Higgins and Burstein, 2007; Chen et al., 2010) have been used to automatically assess L2 texts. Early work on topical relevance (Higgins et al., 2006) posed the problem as one of binary classification and aimed to identify whether a text was either on or off-topic. The main motivation of the research was to detect off-topic text, text submitted mistakenly (within an online assessment setting), or text submitted in bad faith (i.e., possibly memorised on an unrelated topic). They adopted an unsupervised approach to the problem, where they matched each text to its corresponding prompt using tf-idf weighted content vectors and a similarity function. One of the heuristic approaches employed in that work was to calculate the similarity of an essay to a number of unrelated prompts. If the essay was closer to an unrelated prompt than the relevant one, the essay was deemed to be off-topic.

Briscoe et al. (2010) tackle the problem of off-topic detection using more complex distributional semantic models that tend to overcome the problem of vocabulary mismatch. However, they frame the task as binary classification and evaluate their approach by determining if it can associate a learner text with the correct prompt. The work which is closest in spirit to that of our own is by Louis and Higgins (2010), who expand prompts using morphological variations, synonyms, and words that are distributionally similar to those that appear in the prompt. Their work builds on the earlier work by Higgins et al. (2006), and again pose the problem as one of binary classification.

The most recent work of Persing and Ng (2014) involves scoring L2 learner texts for relevance on a seven-point scale using a feature-rich linear regression approach. While they demonstrate that learning one linear regression model per prompt is a useful supervised approach, it means that substantial training data is needed for each prompt in order to build the models. For the task of determining topical relevance, this places a substantial burden on manually annotating texts for each individual prompt.[3] As a result, supervised prompt-specific approaches are impractical and less flexible in an operational setting; if, for example, a new previously-unseen prompt is required for an upcoming assessment, the model cannot be applied until a sizeable amount of manually-annotated response texts are collected and annotated for that prompt.

A dataset developed from the international corpus of learner data (ICLE) (Granger et al., 2009) consisting of 830 essays measured for relevance against one of 13 prompts on a seven-point scale was re-

---

[3]In fact, it is often the case that there are multiple prompts per exam, which change for every exam sitting.

leased as part of that work (Persing and Ng, 2014).
We make use of this new resource in our work as it
is the *only* such public dataset.[4] We make the following contributions to the automated assessment of
topical relevance:

- We perform the first systematic comparison
  of several unsupervised methods for assessing
  topical relevance in L2 learner text on a publicly available dataset.

- We adopt a new unsupervised pseudo-relevance
  feedback language-modelling approach and
  show that it correlates well with human judgements and outperforms a number of other distributional approaches.

- We perform an external evaluation of our
  best prompt-relevance models by incorporating them into the feature set of a supervised
  prompt-independent text-scoring system, and
  show that they improve its performance.

## 3  Semantic Prompt Relevance

Previous research (Higgins et al., 2006) has shown
that representing a prompt $p$ and an essay $s$ as tf-
idf weighted vectors[5] $p$ and $s$ in the term space $\mathbb{R}^v$
(where $v$ is the vocabulary of the system) yields useful representations for exact matching using cosine
similarity as follows:

$$cos(\boldsymbol{p}, \boldsymbol{s}) = \frac{\sum_{t \in v} p_t \cdot s_t}{\sqrt{\sum_{t \in v} p_t^2 \cdot \sum_{t \in v} s_t^2}} \quad (1)$$

However, it is likely that many L2-learner texts
will use words that are related to the prompt, but
which do not have an exact match to any words contained in the prompt. Therefore, we extend this approach by aiming to expand the prompt $p$ with a set
of topically related expansion terms $e$ using one of a
number of distributional similarity techniques.

### 3.1  Prompt Expansion

As a general method of prompt expansion, we represent the prompt $p$ and each candidate expansion

---

[4] www.hlt.utdallas.edu/~persingq/ICLE/
paDataset.html

[5] We use bold lower-case letters throughout to denote vectors, including probability vectors.

word $w$ as vectors $p$ and $w$ in an $n$-dimensional
space $\mathbb{R}^n$, and then use some measure of similarity between the two vectors (e.g. cosine similarity)
to rank the candidate expansion words according to
how close they are to the original prompt. We then
select the top $|e|$ most similar expansion terms to add
to the original prompt.

Once the $|e|$ closest terms are selected and added
to the original prompt $p$, we create a tf-idf weighted
expanded prompt vector $\boldsymbol{p}_{p+e}$ and compare it to the
tf-idf essay vector $s$ using cosine similarity in the
original space $\mathbb{R}^v$ as per Equation (1). In our approach, we conduct the essay matching in the term
space $\mathbb{R}^v$ as it allows us to analyse the quality of
the expansion terms, and subsequently to understand
the merits and demerits of the various approaches.
We now outline four methods of selecting candidate
prompt expansion terms.

### 3.2  Traditional Distributional Semantics

Our first approach involves building traditional distributional vectors by constructing a matrix of co-
occurrence frequencies. For a specific word $w$, its
vector is constructed by counting the words (its context words $c$) that it co-occurs with in a specified
context (usually a window of a few words). The
row for a specific word $w$ then represents the vector for that word. We weight the vector elements
using the PPMI (positive pointwise mutual information) weighting scheme (Turney et al., 2010).

We build word vectors using a lemmatised version of Wikipedia from 2013. We removed from the
corpus all words that appeared less than 200 times
and used the 96,811 remaining words as both potential expansion words $w$ and as contexts $c$. We used
a 5 word context window (2 words either side of the
target word) and reduced the size of the resultant
vectors by only storing dimensions that had a PPMI
greater than 2.0 (Turney et al., 2010). The resultant
vectors are competitive with the best reported results
for traditional word vectors on a word–word similarity task (Spearman-$\rho = 0.732$ on 3000 word-pairs
from the MEN dataset) (Levy et al., 2015). We cre-
ate a vector representation for the prompt $p$ in $\mathbb{R}^n$ by
summing the PPMI word-vectors of the words oc-
curring in the prompt. Finally, the $|e|$ closest words
to the prompt vector $p$, as measured by cosine similarity, can then be selected as expansion terms.

### 3.3 Random Indexing

*Random Indexing* (RI) (Kanerva et al., 2000) is an approach which incrementally builds word vectors in a dimensionally-reduced space. Words are initially assigned a unique random index vector in a space $\mathbb{Z}^n$, where $n$ is user-defined. These near-orthogonal vectors are updated by iterating over a corpus of text. In particular, the word vector for a specific word $w$ is altered by adding to it the vectors of the words in its contexts. The process proceeds incrementally and therefore only requires one pass over the data. In this way, words that occur in similar contexts will be pushed towards similar points in the space $\mathbb{Z}^n$.

We use *Random Indexing* to build word vectors using the S-Space package[6] using the same preprocessed Wikipedia corpus as outlined in the previous section. We used a dimensionality of 400 with window sizes up to 5 words (finding a window of 5 words to create better vectors for the word-word similarity task). The resultant vectors are not as competitive as those built using the traditional approach on a word-word similarity task (Spearman-$\rho = 0.432$ on 3000 word-pairs from the MEN dataset). Again, we create a vector representation for the prompt $p$ by summing the RI vectors, and find the closest words vectors $w$ to the prompt.

### 3.4 Word Embeddings

The *continuous bag-of-words* architecture (cbow) and the *skip-gram* architectures (skip) in **word2vec** have been shown to be particularly well-suited to learning *word-embeddings* (i.e. low-dimensional vector representations of words) (Mikolov et al., 2013). The **word2vec** package[7] from Mikolov is the original implementation of these models.

We use **word2vec** to learn distributed representations for prompts in a similar manner to that just outlined (in Section 3.2 and Section 3.3). In particular, we learn distributed vectors using both *cbow* and *skip* and the same preprocessed version of Wikipedia as used previously. We used word vectors of length 400 for both architectures with a window of 5 for *cbow* and 10 for *skip-gram* as recommended in the original documentation. For both approaches we use

negative sampling. The performance of these approaches on the word-word MEN dataset are $\rho = 0.737$ and $\rho = 0.764$ for *cbow* and *skip* respectively. As with previous approaches, we create a vector representation for the prompt $p$ by summing the vectors of the words in the prompt.

### 3.5 Pseudo-Relevance Feedback

Pseudo-relevance feedback (PRF) is a technique in IR for expanding queries with topically related words. In PRF, the top $|F|$ ranked documents for a query are deemed relevant and candidate terms occurring in these documents are analysed and selected according to a term-selection function. Each candidate word can be viewed as being described by a vector of contexts of dimensionality $|F|$ (i.e. where the entire document $d \in F$ is the context).

We use this approach by using a prompt analogously to a query. In the popular relevance modelling (RM) framework (Lv and Zhai, 2009), the term-selection value can be viewed as the dot-product of a prompt vector $p$ (the vector of similarities between the initial prompt $p$ and the document contexts $d \in F$) and the candidate word vector $w$ (the vector of weights for word $w$ in its contexts $d \in F$) as follows:

$$PRF(\boldsymbol{p}, \boldsymbol{w}) = \sum_{d \in F} f(w, d) \cdot Pr(p|d) \qquad (2)$$

where $f(w, d)$ is the weight of the candidate word $w$ in document $d$ and $Pr(p|d)$ is the probability that $d$ generated $p$, i.e. the query-likelihood (Ponte and Croft, 1998). Furthermore, by selecting only the most important dimensions (i.e. top $|F|$ documents), dimensional reduction is automatically incorporated in an operationally efficient manner. PRF can be viewed as a dimensionally-reduced probabilistic version of Explicit Semantic Analysis (ESA) (Gabrilovich and Markovitch, 2007). The typical dimensionality used for PRF is usually of around $|F| = 20$.

In the language modelling framework, documents are assumed to have been generated by a mixture of a topical model $\alpha_\tau$ and a background model $\alpha_c$, such that $d \sim (1 - \omega) \cdot \alpha_\tau + \omega \cdot \alpha_c$ where $\omega$ is the mixture parameter. Given a candidate term $w$

---

[6]https://github.com/fozziethebeat/S-Space
[7]https://code.google.com/p/word2vec/

appearing in $d$, the probability that it was generated by the topical model is as follows:

$$f(w, d) = p(\boldsymbol{\alpha}_\tau | w) = \frac{(1 - \omega) \cdot \boldsymbol{\alpha}_\tau}{(1 - \omega) \cdot \boldsymbol{\alpha}_\tau + \omega \cdot \boldsymbol{\alpha}_c} \quad (3)$$

and therefore, we use this probability of topicality $f(w, d)$ as the vector weights for $w$. Assuming that documents have been generated by a multivariate Pólya distribution (Cummins et al., 2015), $f(w, d)$ is as follows:

$$f(w, d) = \frac{tf_{w,d}}{tf_{w,d} + \frac{\omega \cdot m_c \cdot df_w}{(1-\omega) \cdot \sum_{w'} df_{w'}} \cdot \frac{|d|}{m_d}} \quad (4)$$

where $tf_{w,d}$ is the term-frequency, $df_w$ is the document frequency of $w$ in the collection being searched, $m_d$ is the number of unique terms in the document, $m_c$ is the background mass (Cummins et al., 2015), and $\omega = 0.8$ is a stable hyper-parameter that controls the belief in the background model. Essentially, this approach (denoted $PRF$) selects terms that occur more frequently in the top $|F|$ documents than they should by chance. As our documents, we use the same preprocessed Wikipedia corpus as outlined previously.

## 4   Evaluation of Expansion Methods

In this section, we present results on the effectiveness of the unsupervised approaches for the task of assessing the prompt relevance of an essay.

### 4.1   Data and Experimental Setup

For the first set of experiments, we use 830 L2 learner essays from the ICLE dataset that are assessed for prompt relevance across 13 prompts. This corpus consists of essays written by higher intermediate to advanced learners of English, which corresponds to approximately B2 level, or above, of the CEFR (Common European Framework of Reference for Languages). The scores assigned to the essays range from 1.0 to 4.0 in increments of 0.5 (although all essays received a score of 2.0 or more in the dataset as seen in Table 1). The essays were double-marked and the linear correlation[8] between

| score | 1.0 | 1.5 | 2.0 | 2.5 | 3.0 | 3.5 | 4.0 |
|---|---|---|---|---|---|---|---|
| # of essays | 0 | 0 | 8 | 44 | 105 | 230 | 443 |

**Table 1:** Distribution of ICLE essays over score grades.

the assessors was 0.243 (a weak correlation). The distribution of essays per prompt is included in Table 2. We lemmatised all prompts and essays using RASP (Briscoe et al., 2006). A point worth noting is that there are minimal essay-length effects in operation on this dataset. The Spearman correlation between the length of the essay and the human-assigned prompt-relevance score across all 830 essays is $\rho = 0.007$.

As a baseline approach, we use the cosine similarity between the original prompt (unexpanded) and the essay $cos(p, s)$. For all expansion approaches, we set the number of expansion terms $|e| = 200$ and use the weight of association between the prompt and the expansion term as the expansion term's frequency $tf$ value in the expanded prompt. We evaluate the approaches by calculating Spearman's rank ($\rho$) correlation coefficient between each method's predicted similarity score and the scores assigned by the assessors.

### 4.2   Results for Prompt Relevance

Table 2 (Top) shows the performance of the approaches over 11 prompts.[9] On average, all approaches increase over the baseline. We can see that the most consistent approach is the PRF approach as it improves over the baseline in 10 out of 11 prompts. The RI approach also performs well and is the best approach on many of the prompts.

However, to measure the topical quality of the expansion words selected by each approach in isolation, we removed the original prompt words from the expanded prompts and again calculated the performance of the different approaches. This more rigorous evaluation in Table 2 (Bottom) shows that the topical quality of the expansion words from the PRF approach tends to be better than the other approaches. We next look at the actual expansion words selected for two prompts.

---

[8]While this seems to suggest that the upper-bound on this dataset is quite low, the original work notes that 89% of the time, assessors graded within a point of each other. Furthermore, correlation is affected by scale (Yannakoudakis and Cummins, 2015).

[9]The two remaining prompts have only three essays associated with them.

| Prompt | 1 | 2 | 3 | 4 | 5 | 6 | 7 | 8 | 9 | 10 | 11 | Mean |
|---|---|---|---|---|---|---|---|---|---|---|---|---|
| # of essays | 237 | 53 | 64 | 58 | 131 | 43 | 80 | 28 | 49 | 71 | 13 | |
| length | -0.113 | -0.026 | -0.062 | 0.211 | -0.023 | -0.111 | 0.103 | -0.115 | -0.056 | **0.171** | 0.520 | 0.045 |
| $cos(p,s)$ | 0.324 | 0.120 | **0.195** | 0.122 | 0.205 | -0.019 | 0.333 | 0.511 | 0.268 | 0.064 | 0.637 | 0.251 |
| $ds_{p+e}$ | 0.328 | 0.141 | 0.182 | 0.114 | 0.208 | -0.011 | 0.340 | 0.519 | 0.280 | 0.082 | 0.637 | 0.256 |
| $RI_{p+e}$ | **0.372** | 0.098 | 0.103 | **0.214** | 0.192 | **0.093** | **0.398** | **0.720** | 0.259 | 0.116 | 0.449 | 0.274 |
| $cbow_{p+e}$ | 0.345 | 0.125 | 0.131 | 0.114 | 0.209 | 0.068 | 0.328 | 0.581 | 0.265 | -0.024 | 0.637 | 0.253 |
| $skip_{p+e}$ | 0.359 | 0.160 | 0.183 | 0.139 | 0.245 | 0.026 | 0.363 | 0.571 | 0.278 | -0.064 | 0.677 | 0.267 |
| $PRF_{p+e}$ | 0.348 | **0.188** | 0.126 | 0.145 | **0.260** | 0.034 | 0.340 | 0.598 | **0.335** | 0.078 | **0.679** | **0.285** |

| Prompt | 1 | 2 | 3 | 4 | 5 | 6 | 7 | 8 | 9 | 10 | 11 | Mean |
|---|---|---|---|---|---|---|---|---|---|---|---|---|
| # of essays | 237 | 53 | 64 | 58 | 131 | 43 | 80 | 28 | 49 | 71 | 13 | |
| $ds_{e\backslash p}$ | 0.008 | 0.043 | -0.098 | -0.073 | -0.017 | -0.092 | 0.126 | 0.619 | **0.202** | 0.029 | 0.375 | 0.102 |
| $RI_{e\backslash p}$ | **0.097** | 0.016 | -0.195 | 0.326 | 0.061 | 0.091 | **0.206** | 0.572 | 0.030 | **0.185** | -0.082 | 0.119 |
| $cbow_{e\backslash p}$ | 0.080 | 0.025 | -0.209 | 0.165 | 0.071 | **0.266** | 0.088 | **0.677** | -0.079 | -0.118 | 0.239 | 0.110 |
| $skip_{e\backslash p}$ | 0.087 | 0.133 | **-0.052** | 0.167 | 0.149 | 0.188 | 0.173 | 0.592 | 0.000 | -0.171 | 0.222 | 0.135 |
| $PRF_{e\backslash p}$ | 0.079 | **0.184** | -0.055 | **0.363** | **0.151** | 0.155 | 0.157 | 0.612 | 0.161 | 0.125 | **0.455** | **0.217** |

**Table 2:** Correlation (Spearman's $\rho$) between prompt–essay similarity scores and human annotations for each prompt (higher values indicate a better approach) for expansion methods when including original prompt terms (Top – denoted $p + e$) and when removing original prompt terms from the expanded prompt (Bottom – denoted $e \setminus p$). Best result in bold.

| # 2 – Most University degrees are theoretical and do not prepare us for the real life. Do you agree or disagree? | | | | | | | | | |
|---|---|---|---|---|---|---|---|---|---|
| university degree theoretical prepare real life | | | | | | | | | |
| ds | | RI | | cbow | | skip | | PRF | |
| faculty | 0.222 | accept | 0.948 | accept | 0.598 | however | 0.677 | theory | 0.544 |
| graduate | 0.214 | while | 0.919 | psychology | 0.558 | nevertheless | 0.677 | study | 0.444 |
| professor | 0.21 | experience | 0.918 | understand | 0.553 | indeed | 0.675 | science | 0.414 |
| phd | 0.204 | idea | 0.915 | study | 0.551 | insist | 0.672 | differ | 0.396 |
| mathematics | 0.199 | from | 0.913 | teach | 0.55 | accept | 0.671 | student | 0.396 |
| philosophy | 0.195 | work | 0.912 | philosophy | 0.549 | fact | 0.67 | philosophy | 0.394 |
| theory | 0.194 | acknowledge | 0.911 | knowledge | 0.545 | s | 0.67 | topic | 0.392 |
| sociology | 0.189 | nevertheless | 0.911 | argument | 0.538 | would | 0.664 | educate | 0.372 |
| science | 0.185 | notice | 0.91 | discuss | 0.538 | while | 0.66 | academy | 0.361 |
| study | 0.182 | nonetheless | 0.909 | theory | 0.528 | nonetheless | 0.656 | argue | 0.354 |

| # 9 – Feminists have done more harm to the cause of women than good. | | | | | | | | | |
|---|---|---|---|---|---|---|---|---|---|
| feminist harm cause women | | | | | | | | | |
| ds | | RI | | cbow | | skip | | PRF | |
| symptom | 0.310 | likewise | 0.883 | feminism | 0.612 | feminism | 0.671 | feminism | 0.910 |
| disease | 0.275 | consequence | 0.882 | sexual | 0.583 | landdyke | 0.632 | sex | 0.896 |
| risk | 0.270 | furthermore | 0.879 | violence | 0.577 | woman | 0.617 | sexual | 0.896 |
| chronic | 0.266 | affect | 0.875 | stigmata | 0.573 | affect | 0.594 | oppress | 0.883 |
| treatment | 0.260 | response | 0.873 | perceive | 0.573 | twwa | 0.580 | argument | 0.875 |
| infect | 0.256 | moreover | 0.871 | affect | 0.564 | argue | 0.580 | rape | 0.800 |
| diagnosis | 0.255 | hinder | 0.871 | detriment | 0.553 | provoke | 0.578 | men | 0.787 |
| patient | 0.255 | expose | 0.869 | homosexual | 0.547 | believe | 0.574 | gender | 0.762 |
| induce | 0.253 | lastly | 0.866 | consequence | 0.545 | consequence | 0.573 | anti | 0.749 |
| disorder | 0.247 | perceive | 0.863 | oppress | 0.545 | sexism | 0.573 | right | 0.740 |

**Table 3:** The top 10 non-prompt words and their similarity to the prompt in a lemmatised Wikipedia corpus of 4.4M documents.

## 4.3 Qualitative Evaluation of Expansion Terms

Table 3 shows the expansion words selected by each approach for two prompts (prompts # 2 and # 9). For prompt # 2 we can see the top words selected for RI and *skip* do not seem topically similar to the prompt. The top words for *ds*, *cbow*, and PRF seem on-topic and might be part of useful feedback to a learner writing for this prompt.

For prompt # 9, *ds* and RI do not tend to promote topically related words. The words for the *ds* approach seem to be related to topic of *diseases* as it may have been mislead by some of the prompt words. In fact, the top terms promoted by the RI approach are not particularly on-topic for any of the 11 prompts, despite the empirical evaluation in the previous section. This could be because some topical words appear further down the ranking for RI.

We believe the main reason that the PRF approach outperforms the others is that topicality is a quality that spans larger segments of text (e.g. documents). For the other approaches, the words that are promoted are very close in proximity to the prompt words (due to the smaller context sizes), and this is more likely to capture local aspects of word usage. Furthermore, in the PRF approach the most important contexts are those in which *all* prompt words appear together, and this aids automatic disambiguation. Regardless, due to the empirical results in the previous section and the perceived topical quality of the terms from the PRF approach, we make use of the PRF approach as a feature in the next experiment.

## 5   Prompt-Relevance for Holistic Scoring

We now evaluate the effectiveness of a supervised essay scoring system that incorporates tf-idf similarity features and the PRF approach for the task of predicting an overall essay quality score.

### 5.1   Data and Experimental Setup

For this experiment, we used a dataset consisting of 2,316 essays written for the IELTS (International English Language Testing System) English examination from 2005 to 2010 (Nicholls, 2003). The examination is designed to measure a broad proficiency continuum ranging from an intermediate to a proficient level of English (A2 to C2 in the CEFR levels). The essays are associated with 22 prompts that are similar in style (i.e. essay style) to those in the ICLE dataset. Candidates are assigned an overall score on a scale from 1 to 9. Prompt relevance is an aspect that is present in the marking criteria, and it is identified as a determinant of the overall score. We therefore hypothesise that adding prompt-relevance measures to the feature set of a prompt-independent essay scoring system (i.e. that is designed to assess linguistic competence only) would better reflect the evaluation performed by examiners and improve system performance.

The baseline system is a linear preference ranking model (Yannakoudakis et al., 2011; Yannakoudakis and Briscoe, 2012) and is trained to predict an overall essay score based on the following set of features:

- word unigrams, bigrams, and trigrams
- POS (part-of-speech) counts
- grammatical relations
- essay length (# of unique words)

- counts of cohesive devices
- max-word length and min-sentence length
- number of errors based on a presence/absence trigram language model

We divided the dataset into 5-folds in two separate ways. First, we created *prompt-dependent* folds, where essays associated with all 22 prompts appear in both the training and test data in the appropriate proportions. This scenario allows the system to learn from essays that were written in response to the prompt. Second, we created *prompt-independent* folds, where all essays associated with a specific prompt appear in only one fold. This second dataset is a more realistic real-world scenario (see Section 2) whereby the system learns on one set of prompts (possibly from previous years) and aims to predict the score for essays associated with different prompts. For both of these supervised experiments, we measured system performance using Spearman's and Pearson's correlation between the output of the system and the gold essay scores (human judgements).

In order to examine the effect of prompt relevance on these datasets, we added to our baseline system two sets of features. The first set of features labelled PR includes the cosine similarity between the essay and the prompt $cos(p, s)$, the fraction of essays words that appear in the prompt $cov(p, s)$, and the fraction of prompt words that appear in the essay $cov(s, p)$. The second set of features labelled semPR is the same as the first set except that the prompt is expanded using the PRF method from earlier.

### 5.2   Results for Overall Scoring

The results of the experiment are outlined in Table 4. Firstly, we observe that the effectiveness of the baseline system is higher on the *prompt-dependent* folds ($\rho = 0.661$) than on the *prompt-independent* folds ($\rho = 0.637$). This confirms expectations as the *prompt-dependent* folds allow the baseline model to learn useful features from essays written specifically for those prompts. When adding the exact matching prompt-relevance features – referred to as PR in Table 4 – we observe an increase in performance on the *prompt-independent* folds. When we add the semantic prompt-relevance models – referred to as semPR in Table 4 – we again observe a modest increase in

| Prompt-Dependent Folds | | |
|---|---|---|
| System | Spearman-$\rho$ | Pearson-$r$ |
| Baseline | 0.661 | 0.686 |
| + PR | 0.659 | 0.685 |
| + semPR | 0.662 | 0.691 |

| Prompt-Independent Folds | | |
|---|---|---|
| System | Spearman-$\rho$ | Pearson-$r$ |
| Baseline | 0.637 | 0.665 |
| + PR | 0.650† | 0.678† |
| + semPR | 0.656† | 0.687† |

**Table 4:** Performance of systems using 5-fold cross-validation on prompt-dependent folds (top) and prompt-independent folds (bottom) when adding unsupervised prompt-relevance (PR) features and semantic prompt-relevance features (semPR) on a set of 2316 essays. † means statistically significant compared to the baseline using Steiger's test (1980).

performance on the *prompt-independent* folds. We can see that both Spearman and Pearson correlations approach the performance of the baseline system on the *prompt-dependent* folds.

On the other hand, there is little or no increase in performance when adding the PR and semPR features on the *prompt-dependent* folds. One suspected reason for this is that it is likely that the lexical features in the *prompt-dependent* folds are performing prompt-relevance modelling (by learning appropriate weights for lexical features in essays written for that prompt). Overall, this is an interesting result as it shows that the features developed in this paper are useful and contribute to the holistic score in real-world examinations.

## 6  Discussion

Firstly, the results from Section 4 are not directly comparable with previous research using the ICLE dataset, as that work (Persing and Ng, 2014) reported metrics averaged over all essays where each prompt was not isolated individually. Ignoring prompt effects may lead to favouring systems that perform well only on a few prompts, and that are not robust across the types of prompt that may be used operationally. Table 5 shows the results of the approaches outlined in this paper against those from the original research using the ICLE dataset that used supervised models. Importantly, we achieve

these correlations without any training data.

| System | Baseline* | tf-idf | PRF | Persing* |
|---|---|---|---|---|
| Pearson's-$r$ | 0.233 | 0.261 | 0.277 | 0.360 |

**Table 5:** Pearson correlation of systems over all 830 essays. * means from original paper.

Interestingly, we have shown that the PRF prompt expansion is effective and is easily analysable. In an operational setting, prompt expansion is likely to be a highly important feature. Observing non-prompt words, that are related to the prompt, in a learner text is likely to be indicative of a learner who has a good understanding of the vocabulary of the topic.

The expansion step issues the entire prompt to a Wikipedia index to gather candidate expansion terms. While this has been shown to be a useful approach on average, there may be cases when aspects of the prompt are not adequately reflected by the candidate expansion terms. In such cases it may be better to *partition* the prompt into useful phrases that can be expanded in isolation, or to manually rephrase the prompt before expanding it with related terms.

### 6.1  Conclusion and Future Work

We have shown that using an unsupervised pseudo-relevance language modelling approach to measuring relevance in learner texts is beneficial as it correlates with human annotators. The expansion terms in isolation have been shown to be useful and we argue that they are an important feature for overcoming vocabulary mismatch in learner text.

The estimation of an L2 learner's language model from lexemes produced by the learner is an intuitive and theoretically-motivated way to assess many lexical aspects of writing. However, compositionally-motivated language modelling approaches exist (Mitchell and Lapata, 2009), and it would be interesting to investigate these across different areas in assessment.

The approaches developed herein may also be useful for providing feedback and/or suggestions to learners during the process of writing. Future work will look at supplying feedback in pedagogically sound ways.

## Acknowledgements

We would like to thank Cambridge English Language Assessment for supporting this research, and the anonymous reviewers for their useful feedback.

## References

Ted Briscoe, John Carroll, and Rebecca Watson. 2006. The second release of the rasp system. In *Proceedings of the COLING/ACL on Interactive presentation sessions*, pages 77–80. ACL.

Ted Briscoe, Ben Medlock, and Øistein Andersen. 2010. Automated assessment of esol free text examinations. *University of Cambridge Computer Laboratory Technical Reports*, UCAM-CL-TR-790.

Y. Y. Chen, C. L. Liu, T. H. Chang, and C. H. Lee. 2010. An Unsupervised Automated Essay Scoring System. *IEEE Intelligent Systems*, 25(5):61–67.

Ronan Cummins, Jiaul H. Paik, and Yuanhua Lv. 2015. A Pólya urn document language model for improved information retrieval. *ACM Transactions of Informations Systems*, 33(4):21.

Semire Dikli. 2006. An overview of automated scoring of essays. *Journal of Technology, Learning, and Assessment*, 5(1).

Evgeniy Gabrilovich and Shaul Markovitch. 2007. Computing semantic relatedness using wikipedia-based explicit semantic analysis. In *Proceedings of the 20th International Joint Conference on Artifical Intelligence*, IJCAI'07, pages 1606–1611, San Francisco, CA, USA. Morgan Kaufmann Publishers Inc.

Sylviane Granger, Estelle Dagneaux, Fanny Meunier, Magali Paquot, et al. 2009. The international corpus of learner english. version 2. handbook and cd-rom. *Louvain- la- Neuve:Presses universitaires de Louvain*.

Derrick Higgins and Jill Burstein. 2007. Sentence similarity measures for essay coherence. In *Proceedings of the 7th International Workshop on Computational Semantics*, pages 1–12.

Derrick Higgins, Jill Burstein, Daniel Marcu, and Claudia Gentile. 2004. Evaluating multiple aspects of coherence in student essays. In *Proceedings of the Human Language Technology Conference of the North American Chapter of the Association for Computational Linguistics*, pages 185–192. ACL.

D. Higgins, J. Burstein, and Y. Attali. 2006. Identifying off-topic student essays without topic-specific training data. *Natural Language Engineering*, 12(2):145–159.

Tuomo Kakkonen and Erkki Sutinen. 2008. Evaluation criteria for automatic essay assessment systems–there is much more to it than just the correlation. In *International Conference on Computers in Education (ICCE)*, pages 111–116.

Pentti Kanerva, Jan Kristoferson, and Anders Holst. 2000. Random indexing of text samples for latent semantic analysis. In *In Proceedings of the 22nd Annual Conference of the Cognitive Science Society*, pages 103–6. Erlbaum.

Thomas K Landauer, Darrell Laham, and Peter W Foltz. 2003. Automated scoring and annotation of essays with the intelligent essay assessor. *Automated essay scoring: A cross-disciplinary perspective*, pages 87–112.

Thomas K Landauer. 2003. Automatic essay assessment. *Assessment in education: Principles, policy & practice*, 10(3):295–308.

Omer Levy, Yoav Goldberg, and Ido Dagan. 2015. Improving distributional similarity with lessons learned from word embeddings. *Transactions of the Association for Computational Linguistics*, 3:211–225.

Annie Louis and Derrick Higgins. 2010. Off-topic essay detection using short prompt texts. In *Proceedings of the NAACL HLT 2010: Fifth Workshop on Innovative Use of NLP for Building Educational Applications*, pages 92–95. ACL.

Yuanhua Lv and ChengXiang Zhai. 2009. A comparative study of methods for estimating query language models with pseudo feedback. In *Proceedings of the 18th ACM Conference on Information and Knowledge Management*, CIKM '09, pages 1895–1898, New York, NY, USA. ACM.

Tomas Mikolov, Ilya Sutskever, Kai Chen, Greg S Corrado, and Jeff Dean. 2013. Distributed representations of words and phrases and their compositionality. In *Advances in neural information processing systems*, pages 3111–3119.

Tristan Miller. 2003. Essay assessment with latent semantic analysis. *Journal of Educational Computing Research*, 29(4):495 – 512.

Jeff Mitchell and Mirella Lapata. 2009. Language models based on semantic composition. In *Proceedings of the 2009 Conference on Empirical Methods in Natural Language Processing*, pages 430–439. ACL.

Diane Nicholls. 2003. The cambridge learner corpus: Error coding and analysis for lexicography and elt. In *In Proceedings of the Corpus Linguistics 2003 conference*, pages 572–581.

Ellis B Page. 1966. The imminence of grading essays by computer. *Phi Delta Kappan*, 47:238–243.

Ellis Batten Page. 1994. Computer grading of student prose, using modern concepts and software. *The Journal of experimental education*, 62(2):127–142.

Isaac Persing and Vincent Ng. 2014. Modeling prompt adherence in student essays. In *Proceedings of the 52nd Annual Meeting of the Association for Computational Linguistics*, pages 1534–1543, Baltimore, Maryland, June. ACL.

Susan Phillips. 2007. *Automated essay scoring: A literature review*, volume 30. Society for the Advancement of Excellence in Education (SAEE).

Jay M. Ponte and W. Bruce Croft. 1998. A language modeling approach to information retrieval. In *Proceedings of the 21st Annual International ACM SIGIR Conference on Research and Development in Information Retrieval*, SIGIR '98, pages 275–281, New York, NY, USA. ACM.

Mihai Rotaru and Diane J Litman. 2009. Discourse structure and performance analysis: Beyond the correlation. In *Proceedings of the SIGDIAL 2009 Conference: The 10th annual meeting of the special interest group on discourse and dialogue*, pages 178–187. Association for Computational Linguistics.

Mark D Shermis and Jill C Burstein. 2003. *Automated essay scoring: A cross-disciplinary perspective*. Routledge.

Mark D Shermis and Jill Burstein. 2013. *Handbook of automated essay evaluation: Current applications and new directions*. Routledge.

M Shermis and B Hammer. 2012. Contrasting state-of-the-art automated scoring of essays: analysis. Technical report, The University of Akron and Kaggle.

James H Steiger. 1980. Tests for comparing elements of a correlation matrix. *Psychological bulletin*, 87(2):245.

Peter D Turney, Patrick Pantel, et al. 2010. From frequency to meaning: Vector space models of semantics. *Journal of artificial intelligence research*, 37(1):141–188.

Salvatore Valenti, Francesca Neri, and Alessandro Cucchiarelli. 2003. An overview of current research on automated essay grading. *Journal of Information Technology Education*, 2:3–118.

Helen Yannakoudakis and Ted Briscoe. 2012. Modeling coherence in esol learner texts. In *Proceedings of the Seventh Workshop on Building Educational Applications Using NLP*, pages 33–43. Association for Computational Linguistics.

Helen Yannakoudakis and Ronan Cummins. 2015. Evaluating the performance of automated text scoring systems. In *Proceedings of the 10th Workshop on Innovative Use of NLP for Building Educational Applications*.

Helen Yannakoudakis, Ted Briscoe, and Ben Medlock. 2011. A New Dataset and Method for Automatically Grading ESOL Texts. In *Proceedings of the 49th Annual Meeting of the Association for Computational Linguistics: Human Language Technologies*.

# UW-Stanford System Description for AESW 2016 Shared Task on Grammatical Error Detection


**Dan Flickinger**
Stanford University

**Michael Goodman**
University of Washington

**Woodley Packard**
University of Washington



## Abstract

This is a report on the methods used and results obtained by the UW-Stanford team for the Automated Evaluation of Scientific Writing (AESW) Shared Task 2016 on grammatical error detection. This team developed a symbolic grammar-based system augmented with manually defined *mal-rules* to accommodate and identify instances of high-frequency grammatical errors. System results were entered both for the probabilistic estimation track, where we ranked second, and for the Boolean decision track, where we ranked fourth.


## 1 Introduction

Over the past several years, a series of shared tasks have been organized to foster research on the automatic detection of grammatical errors in compositions from a variety of genres. In this year's task, the organizers invited participants to "analyze the linguistic characteristics of scientific writing to promote the development of automated writing evaluation tools that can assist authors in writing scientific papers. The task is to predict whether a given sentence requires editing to ensure its 'fit' within the scientific writing genre." This Automated Evaluation of Scientific Writing (AESW) Shared Task 2016 is described in more detail, along with descriptions of the seven teams and their system results, in Daudaravicius et al. (2016).

This paper provides a description of the system adapted for this task by a team of collaborators from the University of Washington and from Stanford University, The system is based on a symbolic grammar augmented with a set of manually constructed *mal-rules* (Schneider and McCoy, 1998; Bender et al., 2004) designed to license and identify ungrammatical or stylistically deprecated sentence properties in running text. We used an efficient parser to analyze the training and development sets repeatedly with successively refined versions of augmented grammar, producing for each sentence a derivation which recorded any use of mal-rules, thus triggering the "needs editing" flag relevant for the shared task. In the end, we applied the best-performing of these grammar versions to the test data in order to produce the results submitted for scoring.

## 2 Resources and methods

Our basic approach to this task has much in common with the one used in the Stanford system participating in the 2013 CoNLL Shared Task on Grammatical Error Correction (Flickinger and Yu, 2013), again employing a current version of the English Resource Grammar (ERG: Flickinger (2000), Flickinger (2011)) and a task-specific inventory of mal-rules, but this time using a more efficient parser (ACE: `moin.delph-in.net/AceTop`). As with the earlier task, we used the most likely derivation licensed by the grammar and produced by the parser for each sentence, to identify any use of one or more of these mal-rules in the analysis.

For the Boolean decision track, we predicted an error if the top-ranked analysis has an error or does not exist, if the probability of using a mal-rule was at least 1%, or if this sentence was the most likely




*Proceedings of the 11th Workshop on Innovative Use of NLP for Building Educational Applications*, pages 105–111,
San Diego, California, June 16, 2016. ©2016 Association for Computational Linguistics

sentence in the paragraph to require a mal-rule. For the probabilistic track, our estimator also included several parameters hand-tuned on the training data.

## 2.1 Existing resources

Most of the components used in the UW-Stanford system were drawn from the inventory of resources developed and maintained by members of the DELPH-IN (Deep Linguistic Processing with HPSG) consortium (`www.delph-in.net`). These components include the ACE parser, the ERG, the Redwoods treebank (Oepen et al., 2004), and a set of Python libraries for the processing of DELPH-IN components' data (`github.com/delph-in/pydelphin`).

For the grammar, we used a modified version of the "1214" release of the ERG, with substantially the same core linguistic coverage, but with the important addition of a separate set of rules and lexical entries dubbed *mal-rules*, to explicitly characterize frequently occurring ill-formed phrasal constructions and words observed in the data for this shared task. This extended grammar enabled full analyses of roughly 92% of the sentences in each of the training and development data sets provided for the task. Of the 8% of the sentences not covered by this grammar, nearly half failed to parse due to reaching externally imposed (though generous) resource limits before yielding any analysis. Lacking any guidance from the grammar, all of these unparsable sentences were tagged by the system as in need of editing, for the purposes of scoring.

ACE is a modern unification-based chart parser, using an agenda-driven variant of the CKY algorithm. Efficiency is enhanced by aggressive ambiguity packing (Oepen and Carroll, 2000) and selective unpacking (Carroll and Oepen, 2005), and disambiguation is performed using a maximum entropy ranker trained on the Redwoods treebank. ACE's integrated preprocessing and support for clustered computing made it easy to use for parsing the large bodies of text in the training and development data.

Since for this task we only wanted the most likely analysis for each sentence, we used the best available statistical parse selection model for the ERG, one trained using the Redwoods treebank, a manually annotated corpus of some 1.4 million words of text across multiple genres. Crucially, and to the

disadvantage of our use for this task, the treebank does not contain any analyses using the mal-rules which of course figure prominently in the derivations of many of the sentences in the AESW corpus. We hypothesize that the system could have been improved in both precision and recall if the parse selection model had contained information about the relative likelihoods of these mal-rules, but a methodical test of this hypothesis will have to await further study.

## 2.2 Error Discovery

In order to focus our efforts we performed a series of basic searches over the training corpus. Table 1 shows the number of deletes (not followed by inserts), inserts (not preceded by deletes), and substitutions (delete followed by insert) in the corpus. With the training set consisting of about 1.2 million sentences, roughly one of every three sentences contains one or more error corrections.

| Error Type | Count | % Sentences |
|---|---|---|
| del-only | 124,919 | 9.03% |
| ins-only | 267,465 | 17.89% |
| del-ins | 341,108 | 28.68% |
| total | 733,492 | 39.24% |

**Table 1:** Basic error types: unique counts and percentage of sentences affected

Table 2 shows the ten most frequent token-specific insertions, deletions, and substitutions made by the editors in the training corpus. Changes to commas, hyphens, and colons together comprise more than half of all of the edits in the corpus in each of the three types of changes, and the frequency of these is reflected in the choices of phrasal and lexical mal-rules added to the grammar for this task. Changes to the English articles *the* and *a*, while much less frequent than punctuation edits, are the next most significant category. The substitution of *section* to *Section* is the most frequent instance of a class of capitalization edits which collectively account for roughly 5.91% of substitutions. Edits in this category are highly dependent on their context (e.g., the initial capital is generally preferred in *Section _REF_*, but not in *this section*).

| | | | | | | |
|---|---|---|---|---|---|---|
| <del>,</del> | 40.09% | <ins>,</ins> | 52.94% | <del> </del><ins>-</ins> | 13.03% |
| <del>the </del> | 9.19% | <ins>the </ins> | 12.66% | <del>-</del><ins> </ins> | 5.10% |
| <del>:</del> | 8.96% | <ins>.</ins> | 4.78% | <del>,</del><ins>;</ins> | 1.92% |
| <del>-</del> | 3.14% | <ins>a </ins> | 4.03% | <del>.</del><ins>,</ins> | 0.74% |
| <del>.</del> | 1.94% | <ins>:</ins> | 2.87% | <del>section</del><ins>Section</ins> | 0.66% |
| <del>'s</del> | 1.84% | <ins>that </ins> | 2.14% | <del>:</del><ins>.</ins> | 0.60% |
| <del>that </del> | 1.49% | <ins>and </ins> | 1.92% | <del>the</del><ins>a</ins> | 0.59% |
| <del>a </del> | 1.45% | <ins>an </ins> | 0.78% | <del>a</del><ins>the</ins> | 0.56% |
| <del>'</del> | 1.29% | <ins>is </ins> | 0.63% | <del>which</del><ins>that</ins> | 0.54% |
| <del>"</del> | 0.91% | <ins>of </ins> | 0.63% | <del>is</del><ins>are</ins> | 0.54% |

**Table 2:** Top ten deletions, insertions, and substitutions

## 2.3 Symbolic methods

The system relies on the analyses licensed by the grammar to identify sentences containing an error, by finding, in the most likely analysis of an ill-formed sentence, one or more occurrences of mal-rules that permit specific types of ungrammatical constituents. For example, in (1) we show the analysis produced for the sentence "Another important point to note is the problem of unknown SNR situation." where the rule used to admit the phrase *unknown SNR situation* is a mal-rule (hdn_bnp_c_rbst) recording the omission of an obligatory article for the noun phrase.

(1) Sample derivation tree with mal-rule

```
(sb-hd_mc_c
 (sp-hd_n_c
  (another "another")
  (hd-cmp_u_c
   (aj-hdn_norm_c
    (hd_optcmp_c
     (j_tough_dlr (important_a2 "important")))
     (n_sg_ilr (point_n2 "point")))
    (hd-cmp_u_c
     (to_c_prop "to")
     (hd_xcmp_c
      (v_n3s-bse_ilr (note_v1 "note")))))))
 (hd-cmp_u_c
  (be_id_is "is")
  (sp-hd_n_c
   (the_1 "the")
   (hd-cmp_u_c
    (n_sg_ilr (problem_n1 "problem"))
    (hd-cmp_u_c
     (of_prtcl "of")
     ( hdn_bnp_c_rbst
      (aj-hdn_norm_c
       (j_j-un_dlr
        (v_j-nb-pas-tr_dlr
         (v_pas_odlr (know_v1 "unknown"))))
       (np-hdn_cpd_c
        (hdn_bnp-pn_c
         (n_sg_ilr (generic_proper_ne "SNR")))
        (w_period_plr
         (n_sg_ilr
          (situation_n1 "situation."))))))))))))
```

In order to identify frequently occurring error phenomena as candidates to motivate the addition of mal-rules for this task, we carried out a manual analysis and classification of the types of insertion and deletion editing operations annotated in the training and development corpora. As each good candidate emerged, we added a corresponding mal-rule to the grammar, and evaluated the resulting behavior of the system on sample data sets drawn from both training and development. Not all of the rules survived in the final system, either because a particular rule interacted poorly with the rest of the grammar, or because the annotations in the corpus for that phenomenon showed more variation than the rule anticipated. In the final system, the grammar included thirteen phrasal mal-rules, seventeen lexical mal-rules, and about 350 robust lexical entries. Examples of each are given in (2).

(2) Sample mal-rules added to the ERG

a. Syntactic: Comma-spliced sentences

```
cl-cl_runon-cma_c_rbst
```

*Multi-biometrics may address the problem of nonuniversality, e.g., in a speaker recognition system, the individuals who cannot speak cannot be enrolled.*

b. Lexical: Subject-verb agreement mismatch

```
third_sg_fin_v_rbst
```

*In what follow, this letter investigates mixed synchronization of fractional-order Lorenz-like system*

c. Lexical entry: Missing obligatory direct object

```
allow_v1_rbst
```

*The LHC will be a top quark factory, allowing to study several of its properties in great detail.*

A large number of the editorial annotations in the AESW corpora addressed errors in the use of punctuation marks, and thus several of the mal-rules were added to the grammar to permit ill-formed or stylistically deprecated uses of commas and hyphens. For example, several of the phrasal coordination rules were adapted as mal-rules to identify the missing final comma in a multi-part conjoined structure, as in the phrase *such as _MATH_, _MATH_ or _MATH_*.

The process of refining the choices and definitions of these mal-rules included a frequently repeated cycle of manual inspection of the corpus annotations, modifications to the mal-rule inventory, parsing of three 1000-item samples taken from the training and development data sets, and examination of the resulting precision and recall performance of the system on these sample sets.

## 2.4 Statistical methods

The ERG nearly always produces multiple candidate analyses for a given input. Since not all analyses are equally likely, the ERG supplies a maximum entropy model which defines a probability distribution over the set of analyses of any given input:

$$P(a|I) = \frac{1}{Z}e^{\sum_{f\in a}\lambda_f}$$

$$Z = \sum_{b\in\text{analyses}(I)} e^{\sum_{f\in b}\lambda_f}$$

By virtue of ambiguity packing, the parser is able to represent vast sets of analyses in a compact form known as a packed forest. Typically, a user of the ERG wants a single parse tree out, and to this end the ACE parser is capable of efficiently selecting the single tree from the packed forest without enumerating the rest of the analyses (selective unpacking). For the task at hand, however, we were interested not in the complete structure of the best tree, but in whether or not it used any mal-rules. This Boolean quantity can be evaluated directly on the top-ranked tree, but its expected value with respect to the probability distribution defined by the maximum entropy model can also be evaluated over the entire packed forest.

To compute this expectation, we defined a *root*

*symbol*[1] which matches[2] all and only trees that include mal-rules. These are conceptually similar to unary rules which can only appear at the root of the derivation tree. The parser computes the normalization factor $Z_r$ for the set of analyses[3] dominated by each root symbol, using an algorithm similar to the inside algorithm for PCFGs, but keeping track of grandparent contexts as required by the maximum entropy model in a fashion similar to that used by the selective unpacking algorithm. The expected value of the mal-rule indicator (i.e. the probability that a tree drawn according to the maximum entropy distribution uses mal-rules) is then:

$$P(\text{mal-rules}|I) = \frac{Z_{\text{mal}}(I)}{Z_{\text{mal}}(I) + Z_{\text{ordinary}}(I)}$$

Thus we have two signals for use in producing the output value for the shared task: the Boolean indicator for the top-ranked tree:

$$B_{\text{top}}(I) = \begin{cases} 1 & \text{best tree uses mal-rules} \\ 0 & \text{best tree does not use mal-rules} \end{cases}$$

and the real-valued expectation of that indicator:

$$E(B|I) = P(\text{mal-rules}|I)$$

We use both of these signals in both the Boolean and probabilistic tracks. Specifically, our Boolean estimator for an input $I$ in a paragraph $P$ is:

$$\text{output}_{\text{boolean}}(I) = \begin{cases} 1 & \text{no parse was found} \\ 1 & B(I) = 1 \\ 1 & E(B|I) > 0.01 \\ 1 & E(B|I) = \max_{S\in P} E(B|S) \\ 0 & \text{otherwise} \end{cases}$$

That is, we predict an error if the top-ranked tree has an error or does not exist, if the probability of using a mal-rule was at least 1%, or if this sentence was

---

[1] In fact, we have multiple root symbols for mal-rule trees and multiple root symbols for ordinary trees.

[2] The fact that a mal-rule has been used is passed up through the feature structures by the grammar.

[3] Actually, the factor computed can in some cases include probabilities for trees which are not fully-consistent with all of the constraints in the grammar, depending on the aggressiveness of the ambiguity packing optimizations employed; however, we hypothesize that this does not have a large effect on the accuracy of the system.

the most likely sentence in the paragraph to require a mal-rule.

For the probabilistic track, our estimator included several parameters hand-tuned on the training and development data. An obvious approach would be to directly use $P(\text{mal-rules}|I)$ as our probabilistic estimate, but this does not produce very good results, because the task's evaluation metric is a kind of $F$-score on errors, rather than a balanced measure over the entire data set. Indeed, we noticed that results are penalized for ever guessing a probability less than 0.5, and indeed always guessing 0.63 yields an $F$-score that outperforms all but 2 of the participating teams. This is arguably a deficiency in the probabilistic track evaluation metric. Instead of using $P(\text{mal-rules}|I)$ directly, we applied a simple nonlinear transformation:

$$\text{output}_{\text{probabilistic}}(I) =$$

$$\begin{cases} 0.75 & \text{no parse was found} \\ 0.72 + 0.1 \cdot (E(B) - 0.5) & B = 1 \\ 0.70 + 0.12 \cdot E(B)^{0.2} & \substack{B=0 \text{ and} \\ E(B)>0.01} \\ 0.70 & \text{otherwise} \end{cases}$$

The various "magic" numbers in these formulae were determined by manual search on the training and development data.

## 3   Results

Roughly one in three sentences in the training corpus was annotated with an error. The probabilistic track and the Boolean track both used varieties of F-score over error sentences as the evaluation metric. Our system tended to be somewhat conservative about identifying errors; as a result, we found that skewing our outputs towards recall in exchange for some precision improved F-score, although accuracy suffered substantially.

### 3.1   Probabilistic track

Our system ranked second of eight entrants in F-score in the probabilistic track. The probabilistic F-score was defined as the harmonic mean of two related quantities, dubbed precision and recall, defined as follows:

$$P_{\text{prob}} = 1 - \frac{1}{n} \sum_{\substack{i \\ \pi_i > 0.5}} (\pi_i - G_i)^2$$

$$R_{\text{prob}} = 1 - \frac{1}{m} \sum_{\substack{i \\ G_i = 1}} (\pi_i - G_i)^2$$

F-scores ranged from 0.6925 to 0.8311 on the evaluation data, with our system achieving 0.7849. Table 3 shows the relative F-score of the entrants on the official evaluation data, alongside the correlation coefficient between their outputs and the gold standard.

| Team | F-Score | Correlation |
|---|---|---|
| 1 | 0.8311 | 0.0600 |
| UW-SU | 0.7849 | 0.2471 |
| 2 | 0.7581 | 0.2690 |
| 3 | 0.7419 | 0.4043 |
| 4 | 0.7224 | 0.1298 |
| 5 | 0.7220 | 0.1666 |
| 6 | 0.6926 | 0.4173 |
| 7 | 0.6925 | 0.3516 |

**Table 3:** Results for the probabilistic track

It is interesting (and a bit concerning) to note that the F-score metric defined for the task has a strong negative correlation (-0.60) with the more intuitively interpretable correlation coefficient. As mentioned above, we modified the intuitively more appropriate estimator $E(B|I)$ to fit the F-score metric better. Table 4 shows the result of this modification, on the development data (as well as the baseline of always guessing 0.63):

| Estimator | F-Score | Correlation |
|---|---|---|
| $P = E(B|I)$ | 0.5644 | 0.2414 |
| $P = \text{output}_{\text{probabilistic}}$ | 0.7902 | 0.2602 |
| $P = 0.63$ | 0.7756 | – |

**Table 4:** Comparison of estimators (probabilistic track)

As can be seen, rearranging our results with a simple nonlinear transformation had almost no effect on the correlation with gold scores, but improved our F-score tremendously. We wonder what effect a similar simple transformation might have for a team like NTNU-YZU or Knowlet, whose correlation with gold substantially exceeds ours.

### 3.2   Boolean track

Our Boolean track system ranked number four of nine entrants. The evaluation metric for the binary track was the F-score for identifying error sentences, defined in a normal way. The relative performance of the nine entrants on the official evaluation data is shown in Table 5.

| Team | Prec | Rec | F-score |
|---|---|---|---|
| 1 | 0.5444 | 0.7413 | 0.6278 |
| 2 | 0.5025 | 0.7785 | 0.6108 |
| 3 | 0.4482 | 0.7279 | 0.5548 |
| UW-SU | 0.4145 | 0.8201 | 0.5507 |
| 5 | 0.3851 | 0.9241 | 0.5436 |
| 6 | 0.3765 | 0.9480 | 0.5389 |
| 7 | 0.3960 | 0.6970 | 0.5051 |
| 8 | 0.6717 | 0.3805 | 0.4858 |
| 9 | 0.6241 | 0.3685 | 0.4634 |

**Table 5:** Results for the Boolean track

This evaluation metric, while somewhat different in focus from a simple accuracy measure, did not exhibit the disconcerting behaviors observed with the probabilistic track metric; for instance, the correlation coefficient between F-score and system-to-gold correlation was 0.31, which is far less alarming than the -0.60 observed in the probabilistic track.

Again, we found that using the raw grammar output (i.e. the $B$ indicator variable described above) was less effective in terms of the evaluation metric than the thresholded and transformed $output_{boolean}$, as demonstrated in Table 6 (computed over the development data):

| Estimator | F-Score | Accuracy |
|---|---|---|
| $B$ | 0.5411 | 0.6333 |
| $output_{boolean}$ | 0.5854 | 0.5322 |
| no errors | – | 0.6111 |
| all errors | 0.5600 | 0.3889 |

**Table 6:** Comparison of estimators (Boolean track)

The raw $B$ estimator achieves much higher accuracy than the transformed $output_{boolean}$, but somewhat lower F-score—lower in fact than the baseline of guessing that every sentence contains an error.

## 4   Discussion

We encountered several challenges while developing and tuning our system for this task, both in the consistency of the error annotations in the corpus, and in the grammatically lossy method of substituting the single tokens _MATH_, _MATHDISP_, etc. in place of formulaic sequences of tokens. It is not surprising that a corpus of this size would reflect inconsistencies due to the use of multiple "annotators" (editors), and also some number of overlooked errors due to the complexity and scale of the editorial task. Yet for our rule-based approach to error detection, judging the benefit of a newly added mal-rule was not easy, since it might perform as intended on the data, but fail to have a positive impact on the final F-score because of a substantial number of missing or inconsistent error annotations. For example, an error was often signaled for adjective-noun compounds used as modifiers if there was no hyphen connecting the two tokens, as with *second order derivatives* vs. the corrected *second-order derivatives*; however, in the training set, we find the following frequency counts for the three different patterns:

| | |
|---|---|
| " second order " | 636 |
| " second<del> </del><ins>-</ins>order " | 710 |
| " second-order " | 952 |

Clearly, the dominant intended pattern is for these adjective-noun compounds to be hyphenated, but a significant percentage of occurrences without the hyphen were left unedited for many such compounds, and this made the calculation of whether or not to globally impose the regularity via mal-rule a murky one. We saw similar wide variation in error annotation for other hyphenation conventions, such as with the insertion or deletion of hyphen with the *non-* prefix as in *non-linear*.

A second set of challenges to our grammar-based method arose from effects of the quite reasonable and useful decision to replace certain complex expressions in the text with single placeholder tokens, such as _MATH_ for mathematical expressions, or _CITE_ for citations. Because these tokens could stand in for a variety of grammatically distinct phrase types, such as singular or plural noun phrases, declarative clauses, or numerical adjectives, the parsing task could quickly become costly when explicitly representing these ambiguities for each occurrence of each such placeholder token, particularly when a sentence included a series of such terms. A more useful representation might have been to preserve the original literal string as markup on the token that replaced it.

## 5 Conclusions

The grammar-based method we adopted for this task
gave us quite fine-grained control over the types of
errors that our system would attend to, but many of
the more linguistically interesting error phenomena
occurred with low enough frequency in the training
and development corpora that their accurate identification had little noticeable effect on system scoring,
given the preponderance of punctuation-oriented edits. Overall, we remain optimistic about the utility
of the kind of grammar-based approach we adopted
here, when applied to real-world grammar-checking
where fully consistent execution of a particular set
of editorial principles should be welcomed by the
scientific writer.


## References

Emily M. Bender, Dan Flickinger, Stephan Oepen, An-
nemarie Walsh, and Timothy Baldwin. 2004. Arbore-
tum. Using a precision grammar for grammar checking
in CALL. In *Proceedings of the InSTIL Symposium on
NLP and Speech Technologies in Advanced Language
Learning Systems*, Venice, Italy, June.

John Carroll and Stephan Oepen. 2005. High efficiency
realization for a wide-coverage unification grammar.
In Robert Dale and, editor, *Proceedings of the 2nd
International Joint Conference on Natural Language
Processing*, Springer Lecture Notes in Computer Sci-
ence. Jeju, Republic of Korea.

Vidas Daudaravicius, Rafael E. Banchs, Elena Volodina,
and Courtney Napoles. 2016. A report on the automatic evaluation of scientific writing shared task. In
*Proceedings of the Eleventh Workshop on Innovative
Use of NLP for Building Educational Applications*,
San Diego, CA, USA, June. Association for Computational Linguistics.

Dan Flickinger and Jiye Yu. 2013. Toward more precision in correction of grammatical errors. In *Proceedings of the 17th Conference on Natural Language
Learning*, pages 68–73, Sofia, Bulgaria.

Dan Flickinger. 2000. On building a more efficient
grammar by exploiting types. *Natural Language Engineering*, 6 (1) (Special Issue on Efficient Processing
with HPSG):15 – 28.

Dan Flickinger. 2011. Accuracy vs. robustness in grammar engineering. In Emily M. Bender and Jennifer E.
Arnold, editors, *Language from a Cognitive Perspective: Grammar, Usage, and Processing*, pages 31–50.
Stanford: CSLI Publications.

Stephan Oepen and John Carroll. 2000. Ambiguity pack-
ing in constraint-based parsing – practical results. In
*Proceedings of NAACL 2000*, pages 162–169, Seattle,
USA.

Stephan Oepen, Daniel Flickinger, Kristina Toutanova,
and Christopher D. Manning. 2004. LinGO Redwoods. A rich and dynamic treebank for HPSG.
*Journal of Research on Language and Computation*,
2(4):575 – 596.

David Schneider and Kathleen McCoy. 1998. Recognizing syntactic errors in the writing of second language
learners. In *Proceedings of Coling-ACL 1998*, pages
1198 – 1204, Montreal.

# Shallow Semantic Reasoning from an Incomplete Gold Standard for Learner Language

**Levi King** and **Markus Dickinson**
Indiana University
Bloomington, IN
{leviking,md7} @indiana.edu

## Abstract

We investigate questions of how to reason about learner meaning in cases where the set of correct meanings is never entirely complete, specifically for the case of picture description tasks (PDTs). To operationalize this, we explore different models of representing and scoring non-native speaker (NNS) responses to a picture, including bags of dependencies, automatically determining the relevant parts of an image from a set of native speaker (NS) responses. In more exploratory work, we examine the variability in both NS and NNS responses, and how different system parameters correlate with the variability. In this way, we hope to provide insight for future system development, data collection, and investigations into learner language.

## 1 Introduction and Motivation

Although much current work on analyzing learner language focuses on grammatical error detection and correction (e.g., Leacock et al., 2014), there is a growing body of work covering varying kinds of semantic analysis (e.g., Meurers et al., 2011; Bailey and Meurers, 2008; King and Dickinson, 2014, 2013; Petersen, 2010), including assessment-driven work (e.g., Somasundaran et al., 2015; Somasundaran and Chodorow, 2014). One goal of such work is to facilitate intelligent language tutors (ILTs) and language assessment tools that maximize communicative interaction, as suggested by research in second language instruction (cf. Celce-Murcia, 1991, 2002; Larsen Freeman, 2002). Whether for feedback or for assessment, however, there are lingering questions about the semantic analysis to address. We investigate questions of how to reason about learner meaning in cases where the set of correct meanings is never entirely complete.

Focusing on semantic analysis requires a sense of what counts as a semantically appropriate utterance from a language learner. Consider when a learner has to describe the contents of a picture (see section 3). There are a number of questions to address in such a situation: 1) Does a semantically correct answer have to sound nativelike or only convey the correct facts? 2) Which facts from the picture are more or less relevant? 3) Are responses strictly correct or not, or is it better to treat correctness as a gradable phenomenon? Additionally, a gold standard of correct responses cannot capture all possible variations of saying the correct content (cf. paraphrases, Barzilay, 2003). We thus must address the specific question of how one can reason about semantic correctness from a (necessarily) incomplete gold standard of answers.

In this paper, we build from our previous work (King and Dickinson, 2013, 2014) and move towards finding a "sweet spot" of semantic analysis (cf. Bailey and Meurers, 2008) for such image-based learner productions. In particular, using available NLP tools, we move away from specific correct semantic representations and an exact definition of correctness, to more abstract data representations and more gradable notions of correctness (section 4). A benefit of more abstract representations is to allow correct and relevant information to be derived from a relatively small set of native speaker responses, as opposed to deriving them by hand, in



*Proceedings of the 11th Workshop on Innovative Use of NLP for Building Educational Applications*, pages 112–121,
San Diego, California, June 16, 2016. ©2016 Association for Computational Linguistics

addition to allowing for a range of sentence types.

We should note, in this context, that we are discussing semantic analysis given a gold standard of native sentences. Image description tasks can often rely on breaking images into semantic primitives (see, e.g., Gilberto Mateos Ortiz et al., 2015, and references therein), but for learner data, we want to ensure that we can account not just for correct semantics (the *what* of a picture), but natural expressions of the semantics (the *how* of expressing the content). In other words, we want to reason about meaning based on specific linguistic forms.

A second issue regarding semantic analysis, beyond correctness, stems from using an incomplete gold standard, namely: assessing the degree of semantic variability, both for native speakers (NSs) and non-native speakers (NNSs). In addition to providing insight into theoretical research on variability in learner language (cf. Ellis (1987), Kanno (1998)), analyzing variability can help determine the best parameters for an NLP system for different kinds of responses. That is, different types of image content might require different mechanisms for processing. Additionally, knowing how different pictures elicit different kinds of content can provide feedback on appropriate types of new data to collect. We approach this issue by clustering responses in various ways (section 5) and seeing how the clusters connect to system parameters.

For both the experiments involving the accuracy of different system parameters (section 4) and the clustering of different responses (section 5), we present results within those sections that show the promise of moving to abstract representations, but in different ways for different kinds of data.

## 2 Related Work

In terms of the overarching goals of developing an interactive ILT, a number of systems exist (e.g., TAGARELA (Amaral et al., 2011), e-Tutor (Heift and Nicholson, 2001)), but few focus on matching semantic forms. *Herr Komissar* (DeSmedt (1995)) is one counter-example; in this game, German learners take on the role of a detective interviewing suspects and witnesses. The system relies largely on a custom-built database of verb classes and related lexical items. Likewise, Petersen (2010) has a sys-

tem to provide feedback on questions in English, extracting meanings from the Collins parser (Collins, 1999). We also rely on reusing modern NLP software, as opposed to handcrafting a system.

The basic semantic analysis in this paper parallels work on content assessment (e.g., c-rater (Leacock and Chodorow, 2003)). These systems are mostly focused on relatively open-ended short answer scoring, with some systems employing task-based restrictions. As one example, Meurers et al. (2011) evaluate English language learners' short answers to reading comprehension questions, constrained by the topic at hand. Their approach performs multiple levels of annotation, including dependency parsing and lexical analysis from Word-Net (Fellbaum, 1998), then aligns elements of the sentence with those of the (similarly annotated) reading prompt, the question, and target answers to determine whether a response is adequate. We explore here a looser notion than alignment for matching NNS responses to a gold standard.

In research closer to our own image-based work, Somasundaran and Chodorow (2014) analyze learner responses to a PDT where the responses were constrained by requiring the use of specific words. The pictures were annotated by experts, and the relevance of responses was calculated through the overlap of the response and annotation contents. Somasundaran et al. (2015) present similar work analyzing responses to sequences of pictures. While they score via a machine learning system, we stick closer to the original forms in trying to find an appropriate way to analyze the data; the notion of overlap for relevance, however, is very similar in spirit to our count-based methods (section 4.2).

We build directly from King and Dickinson (2013, 2014), where the method to obtain a semantic form from a NNS production is: 1) obtain a syntactic dependency representation from the off-the-shelf Stanford Parser (de Marneffe et al., 2006; Klein and Manning, 2003), and 2) obtain a semantic form from the parse, via a small set of hand-written rules. It is this method we attempt to generalize (section 4).

## 3 Data Collection

Because our approach requires both NS and NNS responses and necessitates constraining both the form and content of responses, we previously assembled a small corpus of NS and NNS responses to a PDT (King and Dickinson, 2013). Research in SLA often relies on the ability of task design to induce particular linguistic behavior (Skehan et al., 1998), and the PDT should induce context-focused communicative behavior. Moreover, the use of the PDT as a reliable language research tool is well-established in areas of study ranging from SLA to Alzheimer's disease (Ellis, 2000; Forbes-McKay and Venneri, 2005).

We rely on visual stimuli here for a number of reasons. First, an overarching goal of our work is the development of an ILT that feels like more like a computer game than a grammar drill, and visual stimuli are essential to many games. Secondly, by using images, the information the response should contain is limited to the information contained in the image. Relatedly, particularly simple images should restrict elicited responses to a tight range of expected contents. The current visual stimuli present events that are mainly transitive in nature and likely to elicit responses with an unambiguous subject, verb and object, thereby restricting form in addition to content. Finally, this format allows one to investigate pure interlanguage without the influence of verbal prompts and shows learner language being used to convey meaning and not just manipulate forms.

The PDT consists of 10 items (8 line drawings and 2 photographs[1]) intended to elicit a single sentence each; an example is given in Figure 1. Participants were asked to view the image and describe the action in past or present tense. The data consist of responses from 53 informants (14 NSs, 39 NNSs), for a total of 530 sentences, with the NNSs being intermediate and upper-level adult English learners in an intensive English as a Second Language program. The distribution of first languages (L1s) is: 14 English, 16 Arabic, 7 Chinese, 2 Japanese, 4 Korean, 1 Kurdish, 1 Polish, 2 Portuguese, and 6 Spanish.

Responses were typed by the participants themselves, with spell checking disabled in some cases. Even among the NNSs that used spell checking, a number of spelling errors resulted in real words. To address this, we use a spelling correction tool to obtain candidate spellings for each word, prune the

---

[1]We have not observed substantial differences between responses for the drawings and the photographs.

| Response (L1) |
| --- |
| The man killing the beard. (Arabic) |
| A man is shutting a bird. (Chinese) |
| A man is shooting a bird. (English) |
| The man shouted the bird. (Spanish) |

**Figure 1:** Example item and responses

candidates using word lists from the NS responses, recombine candidate spellings into candidate sentences, and evaluate these with a trigram language model (LM) to select the most likely intended response (King and Dickinson, 2014).

Once the responses had been collected, the NNS responses were annotated for correctness, with respect to the content of the picture. The lead author marked spelling and meaning errors which prevent a complete mapping to correct information (see King and Dickinson, 2013). On the one hand, minor misspellings are counted as incorrect (e.g., *The artiest is drawing a **portret***), while, on the other hand, the annotation does not require distinguishing between between spelling and meaning errors. In the future, we plan on fine-tuning the annotation criteria.

## 4 Generalizing the Methods

The previous work assumed that the assessment of NNS responses involves determining whether the gold standard (GS) contains the same semantic triple that the NNS produced, i.e., whether a *triple* is *covered* or *non-covered*. In such a situation the GS need only be comprised of *types* of semantic triples. But the GS is comprised of the small set of NS responses and is thus incomplete—meaning that exact matching is going to miss many cases, and indeed in King and Dickinson (2013), we note that GS coverage is only at 50.8%. Additionally, relying on matching of triples limits the utility of the method to specific semantic requirements, namely transitive sentences. By moving to bags of dependencies and tallying the counts of (NS) responses in the GS, we can move into a gradable, or ranking, approach to NNS responses.

We want to emphasize the degree to which a response conveys the same meaning as the GS, necessitating an approach which can automatically determine the importance of a piece of information in the GS. We break this down into how we represent the information (section 4.1) and then how we compare NNS information to GS information (section 4.2), allowing us to rank responses from least to most similar to the GS.[2] We also discuss the handling of various other system parameters (section 4.3).

## 4.1 Representation

To overcome the limitations of an incomplete GS, we represent each response as a list of *terms* taken from the dependency parse (de Marneffe et al., 2006), the terms referring to individual dependencies (i.e., relations between words). This eliminates the complications of extracting semantic triples from dependency parses, which could only handle a very restricted set of grammatical forms and resulted in errors in 7–8% of cases (King and Dickinson, 2013). Operating directly on individual dependencies from the overall tree also means the system can allow for "partial credit"; it distributes the matching over smaller, overlapping pieces of information rather than a single, highly specific triple.

Specifically, representations take one of five forms. We first tokenize and lemmatize the response to a list of lemmas that represents the response. The five term representations are then variations on dependencies. The full form concatenates the label, head and dependent, as in `subj#boy#kick`. We call this **ldh** (label, dependent, head). The remaining four forms abstract over either the label, head and/or dependent, as in `X#boy#kick`. We refer to

---

<sup></sup>

[2]Although rankings often go from highest to lowest, we prioritize identifying problematic cases, so we rank accordingly.

these forms as **xdh**, **lxh**, **ldx**, and **xdx**. The `xdx` model is on a par with treating the sentence as a bag of lemmas, except that some function words not receiving parses (e.g., prepositions) are not included (see King and Dickinson, 2013). In our current experiments, we test each of these term representations separately, but we expect to ultimately make use of some weighted combination. Future representations may also incorporate WordNet relations or semantic role labeler output.

## 4.2 Scoring Responses

Taking the term representations from the previous section, the next task is to combine them in a way which ranks responses from least to most appropriate. Responses are scored with one of four approaches, using one of two methods to **weight** response terms combined with one of two methods to **compare** the weighted NNS terms with the GS.

For weighting, we use either a simple frequency measure (**F**) or one based on **tf-idf** (**T**) (Manning et al., 2008, ch. 6). We explore tf-idf as a measure of a term's importance with the hope that it is able to reduce the impact of semantically unimportant terms—e.g., determiners like *the*, frequent in the GS, but unimportant for evaluating the semantic contents of NNS responses—and to upweight terms which may be salient but infrequent, e.g., only used in a handful of GS sentences. For example, for an item depicting a man shooting a bird (see Table 1 and Figure 1), of 14 GS responses, 12 described the subject as *man*, one as *he* and one as *hunter*. Since *hunter* is infrequent in English, even one instance in the GS should get upweighted via tf-idf, and indeed it does. This is valuable, as numerous NNS responses use *hunter*.

Calculating tf-idf relies on both *term frequency* ($tf$) and *inverse document frequency* ($idf$). Term frequency is simply the raw count of an item, and for tf-idf of terms in the GS, we take this as the frequency within the GS. Inverse document frequency is derived from some reference corpus, and it is based on the notion that appearing in more documents makes a term less informative with respect to distinguishing between documents. The formula is in (1) for a term $t$, where $N$ is the number of documents in the reference corpus, and $df_t$ is the number of documents featuring the term ($idf_t = \log \frac{N}{df_t}$).

A term appearing in fewer documents will thus obtain a higher *idf* weight, and this should readjust frequencies based on semantic importance.

$$(1) \quad tfidf(t) = tf_{GS} \log \frac{N}{df_t}$$

After counting/weighting, the frequencies are then either **averaged** to yield a response score (**A**), or NNS term weights and GS term weights are treated as vectors and the response score is the **cosine distance** (**C**) between them. This yields:

**Frequency Average (FA).** Within the GS, the frequency of each term is calculated. Each term in the NNS response is then given a score equal to its frequency in the GS; terms missing from the GS are scored zero. The response score is the average of the term scores, with higher scores closer to the GS.

**Tf-idf Average (TA).** This involves the exact same averaging as with model FA, but now the terms in the GS are assigned tf-idf weights before averaging.

**Frequency Cosine (FC).** The frequency of each term is calculated within the GS and (separately) within the NNS response. The term scores are then treated as vectors, and the response score is the cosine distance between them, with lower scores being closer to the GS.

**Tf-idf Cosine (TC).** This involves the exact same distance comparison as with model FC, but now the terms of both the GS and NNS responses are assigned tf-idf weights before comparison.

## 4.3 System Parameters

In addition to the four approaches, we have term representations and two sets of parameters, listed below, to vary, resulting in a total of 60 settings for processing responses (see also Table 2).

**Term form.** As discussed in section 4.1, the terms can take one of five representations: `ldh`, `xdh`, `lxh`, `ldx`, or `xdx`.

**Scoring approach.** As discussed in section 4.2, the NNS responses can be compared with the GS via models FA, TA, FC, or TC.

**Reference corpus.** The reference corpus for deriving tf-idf scores can be either the Brown Corpus (Kucera and Francis, 1967) or the Wall Street Journal (WSJ) Corpus (Marcus et al., 1993). These are abbreviated as B and W in the results below; na indicates the lack of a reference corpus, as this is only relevant to approaches TA and TC. The corpora are divided into as many documents as originally distributed (W: 1640, B: 499). The WSJ is larger, but Brown has the benefit of containing more balance in its genres (vs. newstext only). Considering the narrative nature of PDT responses, a reference corpus of narrative texts would be ideal, but we choose manually parsed reference corpora as they are more reliable than automatically parsed data.

**NNS source.** Each response has an original version (NNSO) and the output of a language model spelling corrector (NNSLM) (see section 3).

## 4.4 Results

### 4.4.1 Evaluation metrics

We ran 60 response experiments, each with different system settings (section 4.3). Within each experiment, we rank the 39 scored NNS responses from least to most similar to the GS. For assessing these settings themselves, we rely on past annotation, which counted unacceptable responses as errors (see section 3).[3] As the lowest rank indicates the greatest distance from the GS, a good system setting should ideally position the unacceptable responses among those with the lowest rankings. Thus, we assign each error-containing response a score equal to its rank, or, if necessary, the average rank of responses sharing the same score.

In Table 1, an excerpt of sentence responses is shown for one item, ranked from lowest to highest. To take one example, the third-ranked sentence, *the man is hurting duck*, has a score of 0.996, and it is annotated as an error (1 in the *E* column). Thus, the evaluation metric adds a score of 3 to the overall sum. The sentence ranked 18, by contrast, is not an error, and so nothing is added. In the case of the top rank, two responses with errors are tied, covering rank 1 and 2, so each adds a score of 1.5.

---

[3]The source of the error is also labeled—stemming from NNS unintelligibility or a system error (from spelling correction, parsing, or some downstream component)—but we do not currently use this annotation.

| $R$ | $S$ | Sentence | $E$ | $V$ |
|---|---|---|---|---|
| 1 | 1.000 | she is hurting. | 1 | 1.5 |
| | 1.000 | man mull bird | 1 | 1.5 |
| 3 | 0.996 | the man is hurting duck. | 1 | 3.0 |
| 4 | 0.990 | he is hurting the bird. | 1 | 3.0 |
| 11 | 0.865 | the man is trying to hurt a bird | 1 | 11.0 |
| 12 | 0.856 | a man hunted a bird. | 0 | 0.0 |
| 17 | 0.775 | the bird not shot dead. | 1 | 17.0 |
| 18 | 0.706 | he shot at the bird | 0 | 0.0 |
| 19 | 0.669 | a bird is shot by a un | 1 | 19.0 |
| 20 | 0.646 | the old man shooting the birds | 0 | 0.0 |
| 37 | 0.086 | the old man shot a bird. | 0 | 0.0 |
| 38 | 0.084 | a old man shot a bird. | 0 | 0.0 |
| 39 | 0.058 | a man shot a bird | 0 | 0.0 |
| Total (Raw) | | | 17 | 169 |
| Average Precision | | | | 0.75084 |

Table 1: Rankings for Item 10 from the best system setting (TC_B_NNSLM_ldh) based on average precision scores. $R$: rank; $S$: sentence score; $E$: error; $V$: rank value.

The sum of these scores is taken as the **Raw** metric for that experimental setting. In many cases, one version of a response (NNSO or NNSLM) contains an error, but the other version does not. Thus, for example, an NNSO experiment may result in a higher error count than the NNSLM equivalent, and in turn a higher Raw score. In this sense, Raw scores emphasize error reduction and incorporate item difficulty.

However, it is possible that the NNSO experiment, even with its higher error count and Raw score, does a better job ranking the responses in a way that separates good and erroneous ones. To account for this, we also use **(mean) average precision ((M)AP)** (Manning et al., 2008, ch. 8), which emphasizes discriminatory power.

For average precision (AP), one calculates the precision of error detection at every point in the ranking, lowest to highest. In Table 1, for example, the precision for the first cut-off (1.000) is 1.0, as two responses have been identified, and both are errors ($\frac{2}{2}$). At the 11th- and 12-ranked response, precision is 1.0 ($\frac{11}{11}$) and 0.917 ($=\frac{11}{12}$), respectively, precision dropping when the item is not an error. AP averages over the precisions for all $m$ responses ($m = 39$ for our NNS data), as shown in (2), with each response notated as $R_k$. Averaging over all 10

items results in the Mean AP (MAP).

$$(2) \quad AP(item) = \frac{1}{m} \sum_{k=1}^{m} Precision(R_k)$$

As mentioned, the Raw metric emphasizes error reduction, as it reflects not just performance on identifying errors, but also the effect of the overall number of errors. In this way, it may be useful for predicting future system performance, an issue we explore in the evaluation of clustering items (section 5.3). MAP, on the other hand, emphasizes finding the optimal separation between errors and non-errors and is thus more of the focus in the evaluation of the best system parameters next.

### 4.4.2 Best system parameters

To start the search for the best system parameters, it may help to continue our single example, in Table 1. The best setting, as determined by the Normalized metric, uses the tf-idf cosine (TC) approach with the Brown Corpus (B), the spelling corrected response (NNSLM), and the full form of the dependencies (ldh). It ranks highest because errors are well separated from non-errors; the highest ranked of 17 total errors is at rank 19. Digging a bit deeper, we can see in this example how the verb *shoot* is common in all the highest-ranked cases shown (#37–39), but absent from all the lowest, showing both the effect of the GS (as all NSs used *shoot* to describe the action) and the potential importance of even simple representations like lemmas. In this case, the ldh representation is best, likely because the word *shoot* is not only important by itself, but also in terms of which words it relates to, and how it relates (e.g., dobj#bird#shoot).

Table 3 shows the five best and five worst system settings averaged across all 10 PDT items, as ranked by MAP. Among the trends that pop out is a favoritism towards NNSLM models (i.e., spelling correction). This is due to the fact that higher numbers of errors inflate the MAP scores, and somewhat counterintuitively, the spelling correction module introduces more errors than it corrects, meaning there are more errors present overall in the NNSLM responses than in the NNSO responses.[4]

---

[4]Note that among the remaining parameter classes, variation does not effect the number of errors.

| Approach | | Term Form | | Ref. Corpus (TA/TC) | | NNS Source | |
|---|---|---|---|---|---|---|---|
| 0.51577 | TC | xdh | 0.51810 | Brown | 0.51534 | NNSLM | 0.51937 |
| 0.50780 | FC | ldh | 0.51677 | WSJ | 0.50798 | NNSO | 0.49699 |
| 0.50755 | TA | lxh | 0.51350 | | | | |
| 0.49464 | FA | xdx | 0.49901 | | | | |
| | | ldx | 0.49352 | | | | |

**Table 2:** Approaches and parameters ranked by mean average precision for all 10 PDT items.

Another feature among the best settings is the inclusion of heads in the dependency representations. In fact, the top 17 ranked settings all include heads (lxh, xdh, ldh); xdx first enters the rankings at 18, and xdx and ldx are common among the worst performers. This is likely due to the salience of the verbs in these transitive sentences; they constitute the heads of the subjects and objects, in relatively short sentences with few dependencies. Furthermore, the tf-idf weighted models dominate the rankings, especially TC. It is also clear that for our data tf-idf works best with the Brown Corpus (B).

| Rank | MAP | Settings |
|---|---|---|
| 1 | 0.5534 | TC_B_NNSLM_lxh |
| 2 | 0.5445 | TA_B_NNSLM_lxh |
| 3 | 0.5435 | TC_W_NNSLM_lxh |
| 4 | 0.5422 | TC_B_NNSLM_xdh |
| 5 | 0.5368 | TC_B_NNSLM_ldh |
| 56 | 0.4816 | TA_B_NNSO_xdx |
| 57 | 0.4796 | FA_na_NNSLM_ldx |
| 58 | 0.4769 | FC_na_NNSO_lxh |
| 59 | 0.4721 | TA_W_NNSO_xdx |
| 60 | 0.4530 | FA_na_NNSO_lxh |

**Table 3:** Based on Mean Average Precision, the five best and five worst settings across all 10 PDT items.

We also summarize the rankings for the individual parameter classes, presented in Table 2, confirming the trends in Table 3. For a given parameter, e.g., ldh, we averaged the experiment scores from all settings including ldh across all 10 items. Notably, TC outperforms the other models, with FC and TA close behind (and nearly tied). Performance falls for the simplest model, FA, which was in fact intended as a baseline. With TC>FC and TA>FA, tf-idf weighting seems preferable to basic frequencies.

Again, the importance of including heads in de-pendencies is apparent here; the three dependency representations containing heads constitute the top three, with a sizable drop in performance for the remaining two forms (xdx and ldx). Moreover, given the content and narrative style of the PDT responses, it is unsurprising that the Brown Corpus serves as a better reference corpus than the WSJ Corpus for tf-idf. Finally, the NNSLM source significantly outperforms the NNSO source.

Despite the strength of these overall trends, variability does exist among the best settings for different items, a point obscured in the averages. In Tables 4 and 5, we present the best and worst ranked settings for two of the least similar items, 1 and 5. Their dissimilarity can be seen at a glance, simply from the range of the AP scores (0.05–0.31 for item 1 vs. 0.52–0.81 for item 5), which in itself reflects a differing number of erroneous responses (2 [NNSO] or 6 [NNSLM] for item 1 vs. 23 or 24 for item 5).

For item 1, a drawing of a boy kicking a ball, we see considerable variability in the best approach just within the top five settings: all four approaches are in the top five. Contrary to the overall trends, we also see the ldx form—without any head information—in the two best settings. Note also that, even though tf-idf weighting (TA/TC) is among the best settings, it is consistently the worst setting, too.

For item 5 in Table 5, a drawing of a man raking leaves, the most noticeable difference is that of xdx being among three of the top five settings. We believe that part of the reason for the superior performance of xdx (cf. lemmas), is that for this item, all the NSs use the verb *rake*, while none of the NNSs use this word. For item 1 (the boy kicking a ball), there is lexical variation for both NSs and NNSs.

These types of differences—for these items and others—lead us to explore the clustering of item patterns, in order to leverage these differences and auto-

| Rank | AP | Settings |
|---|---|---|
| 1 | 0.30997 | TC_B_NNSLM_ldx |
| 2 | 0.30466 | TA_B_NNSLM_ldx |
| 3 | 0.30015 | TA_B_NNSLM_xdh |
| 4 | 0.29704 | FC_na_NNSLM_xdh |
| 5 | 0.29650 | FA_na_NNSLM_ldh |
| 56 | 0.06474 | TC_B_NNSO_ldx |
| 57 | 0.06174 | TC_W_NNSO_ldx |
| 58 | 0.06102 | TA_W_NNSO_lxh |
| 59 | 0.05603 | TA_W_NNSO_xdx |
| 60 | 0.05094 | TA_W_NNSO_ldx |

**Table 4:** Based on Average Precision, the five best and five worst settings for item 1.

| Rank | AP | Settings |
|---|---|---|
| 1 | 0.80965 | FA_na_NNSLM_xdx |
| 2 | 0.80720 | TA_B_NNSLM_lxh |
| 3 | 0.80473 | TC_B_NNSLM_lxh |
| 4 | 0.79438 | TC_B_NNSLM_xdx |
| 5 | 0.78108 | TC_W_NNSLM_xdx |
| 56 | 0.56495 | FC_na_NNSO_xdh |
| 57 | 0.56414 | TC_B_NNSO_lxh |
| 58 | 0.55890 | TC_W_NNSO_lxh |
| 59 | 0.54506 | FC_na_NNSO_lxh |
| 60 | 0.52013 | FA_na_NNSO_lxh |

**Table 5:** Based on Average Precision, the five best and five worst settings for item 5.

matically choose the optimal settings for new items; we turn to this next.

## 5 Clustering

Given the variability of NS and NNS responses, and the possible correlation with different system parameters, we have begun exploring connections by clustering the different items. The clustering uses, for one set, *response features*, i.e., features observable from the responses, and, separately, *performance features*, i.e., the performance of different system settings on the responses. Although the work is very exploratory, our goal is to get a handle on learner variability for different items and explore correlations between response and performance clusters.

### 5.1 Response Clustering

We cluster the 10 PDT items using simple features taken from the responses themselves. Specifically, we use various combinations of type counts, token counts, and type-to-token ratios for each term form (ldh, xdh, lxh, ldx, xdx), taken from each response source (GS, NNSO, NNSLM).

### 5.2 Performance Clustering

From the system output, we cluster items using per-item Raw scores for various settings. That is, for each of the 10 items, we calculate an average error score for each approach (FA, TA, FC, TC), each term form (ldh, xdh, lxh, ldx, xdx), each reference corpus (B, W), and each response source (NNSO, NNSLM). As mentioned in section 4.4.1, Raw scores should account for the number of errors produced by NNSs for each item, which should correlate with future system performance.

### 5.3 Results

Although there is noise in some experiments, some patterns do seem to emerge in many of the clusterings; we present some of the most common patterns here. Figure 2 shows a clustering based on response features that shares some characteristics with Figure 3, a clustering based on performance features. (Note that clustering heights are not to scale.) In both examples, items 5 and 9 form a cluster attaching to the root. These are described in the GS as *A man is raking leaves* and *Two boys are rowing a boat*. These were also the two most difficult items for NNSs. While other items involved common verbs like *kick*, *paint* and *cut*, the actions depicted in these items were more specific and required words outside the vocabulary of many participants. For example, while all 14 NSs used either *row* or *paddle*, only five of 39 NNSs used these verbs; the rest used verbs like *boat*, *sail*, *sit*, *play* or *ride*.

Items 1 and 4 also appear as a cluster in both cases. In GS examples, these are described as *The boy is kicking a ball* and *A man is reading a newspaper*. The images portray actions that language learners often learn in beginner courses, and in fact, these were the easiest items for NNSs. The simple actions and objects mean that both token counts and type counts are relatively low. With regard to fea-

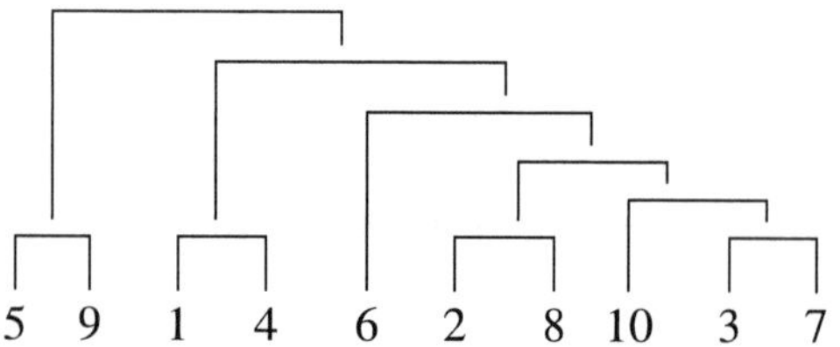

**Figure 2:** PDT items clustered by type and token counts of all NS, NNSO and NNSLM responses.

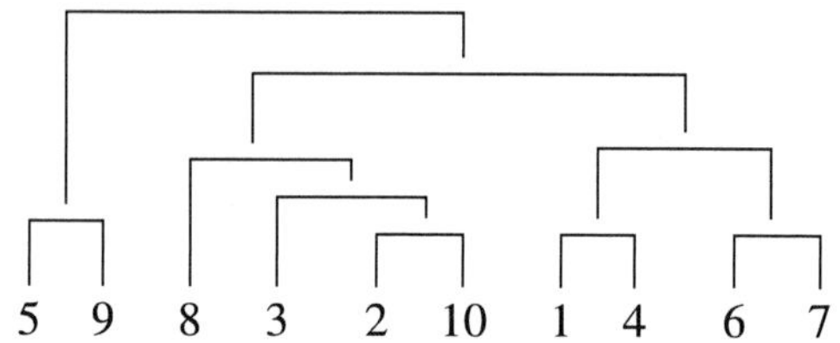

**Figure 3:** PDT items clustered by parameter performance.

ture performance, for both items the same parameters perform highly (TC/TA, ldx/ldh/xdh), suggesting that a future item which clusters with these two would benefit from the same processing.

## 6 Summary and Outlook

We have investigated ways to reason about learner meaning in cases where the set of correct meanings is incomplete, namely in the case of picture description tasks (PDTs). Specifically, we have explored different models of representing and scoring NNS responses to a picture—different linguistic representations, term weighting schemes, reference corpora, and use of spelling correction—in order to automatically determine the relevant parts of an image from a set of NS responses. In more exploratory work, we have also examined the variability in both NS and NNS responses, and how different system parameters correlate with the variability.

Already, the results are providing insight for future system development, data collection, and investigations into learner language. A big next step of the work is to collect more data, and examining the variability in the NS/NNS data has provided feedback on the types of new data to gather, to better ensure a wide range of behavior from NNSs. Getting a range of items, with different sentence types and variability in responses, will help us properly

find our envisioned sweet spot of semantic analysis. In that vein, we plan on exploring more parameters (e.g., semantic role information) and holding out data to better gauge the impact of clustering a new item with the existing items and selecting the processing parameters on that basis. Beyond that loom large questions about how to annotate gradability in learner responses and how to map system processing to accurate semantic feedback.

## Acknowledgments

We would like to thank the members of the CLingDing discussion group and the three anonymous reviewers for their helpful feedback.

## References

Luiz Amaral, Detmar Meurers, and Ramon Ziai. 2011. Analyzing learner language: Towards a flexible NLP architecture for intelligent language tutors. *Computer Assisted Language Learning* 24(1):1–16.

Stacey Bailey and Detmar Meurers. 2008. Diagnosing meaning errors in short answers to reading comprehension questions. In *The 3rd Workshop on Innovative Use of NLP for Building Educational Applications (ACL08-NLP-Education)*. Columbus, OH, pages 107–115.

Regina Barzilay. 2003. *Information Fusion for Multidocument Summarization: Paraphrasing and Generation*. Ph.D. thesis, Columbia University.

Marianne Celce-Murcia. 1991. Grammar pedagogy in second and foreign language teaching. *TESOL Quarterly* 25:459–480.

Marianne Celce-Murcia. 2002. Why it makes sense to teach grammar through context and through discourse. In Eli Hinkel and Sandra Fotos, editors, *New perspectives on grammar teaching in second language classrooms*, Lawrence Erlbaum, Mahwah, NJ, pages 119–134.

Michael Collins. 1999. *Head-Driven Statistical Models for Natural Language Parsing*. Ph.D. thesis, University of Pennsylvania, Philadelphia, PA.

Marie-Catherine de Marneffe, Bill MacCartney, and Christopher D. Manning. 2006. Generating typed dependency parses from phrase structure parses. In *Proceedings of LREC 2006*. Genoa, Italy.

William DeSmedt. 1995. Herr Kommissar: An ICALL conversation simulator for intermediate German. In V. Melissa Holland, Jonathan Kaplan, and Michelle Sams, editors, *Intelligent Language Tutors: Theory Shaping Technology*, Lawrence Erlbaum, Mahwah, NJ, pages 153–174.

Rod Ellis. 1987. Interlanguage variability in narrative discourse: Style shifting in the use of the past tense. *Studies in Second Language Acquisition* 9:1–19.

Rod Ellis. 2000. Task-based research and language pedagogy. *Language Teaching Research* 4(3):193–220.

Christiane Fellbaum, editor. 1998. *WordNet: An Electronic Lexical Database*. The MIT Press, Cambridge, MA.

Katrina Forbes-McKay and Annalena Venneri. 2005. Detecting subtle spontaneous language decline in early Alzheimer's disease with a picture description task. *Neurological Sciences* 26(4):243–254.

Luis Gilberto Mateos Ortiz, Clemens Wolff, and Mirella Lapata. 2015. Learning to interpret and describe abstract scenes. In *Proceedings of the 2015 Conference of the North American Chapter of the Association for Computational Linguistics: Human Language Technologies*. Association for Computational Linguistics, Denver, Colorado, pages 1505–1515.

Trude Heift and Devlan Nicholson. 2001. Web delivery of adaptive and interactive language tutoring. *International Journal of Artificial Intelligence in Education* 12(4):310–325.

Kazue Kanno. 1998. Consistency and variation in second language acquisition. *Second Language Research* 14(4):376–388.

Levi King and Markus Dickinson. 2013. Shallow semantic analysis of interactive learner sentences. In *Proceedings of the Eighth Workshop on Innovative Use of NLP for Building Educational Applications*. Atlanta, Georgia, pages 11–21.

Levi King and Markus Dickinson. 2014. Leveraging known semantics for spelling correction. In *Proceedings of the Third Workshop on NLP for Computer-Assisted Language Learning*. Uppsala, Sweden, pages 43–58.

Dan Klein and Christopher D. Manning. 2003. Accurate unlexicalized parsing. In *Proceedings of ACL-03*. Sapporo, Japan.

Henry Kucera and W. Nelson Francis. 1967. *Computational Analysis of Present-Day American English*. Brown University Press, Providence, RI.

Diane Larsen-Freeman. 2002. Teaching grammar. In Diane Celce-Murcia, editor, *Teaching English as a second or foreign language*, Heinle & Heinle, Boston, pages 251–266. 3rd edition.

Claudia Leacock and Martin Chodorow. 2003. C-rater: Automated scoring of short-answer questions. *Computers and Humanities* pages 389–405.

Claudia Leacock, Martin Chodorow, Michael Gamon, and Joel Tetreault. 2014. *Automated Grammatical Error Detection for Language Learners*. Synthesis Lectures on Human Language Technologies. Morgan & Claypool Publishers, second edition.

Christopher D. Manning, Prabhakar Raghavan, and Hinrich Schütze. 2008. *Introduction to Information Retrieval*. CUP.

Mitchell P. Marcus, Beatrice Santorini, and Mary Ann Marcinkiewicz. 1993. Building a large annotated corpus of english: The penn treebank. *Computational Linguistics* 19(2):313–330.

Detmar Meurers, Ramon Ziai, Niels Ott, and Stacey Bailey. 2011. Integrating parallel analysis modules to evaluate the meaning of answers to reading comprehension questions. *Special Issue on Free-text Automatic Evaluation. International Journal of Continuing Engineering Education and Life-Long Learning (IJCEELL)* 21(4):355–369.

Kenneth A. Petersen. 2010. *Implicit Corrective Feedback in Computer-Guided Interaction: Does Mode Matter?*. Ph.D. thesis, Georgetown University, Washington, DC.

Peter Skehan, Pauline Foster, and Uta Mehnert. 1998. Assessing and using tasks. In Willy Renandya and George Jacobs, editors, *Learners and language learning*, Seameo Regional Language Centre, pages 227–248.

Swapna Somasundaran and Martin Chodorow. 2014. Automated measures of specific vocabulary knowledge from constructed responses ('Use these words to write a sentence based on this picture'). In *Proceedings of the Ninth Workshop on Innovative Use of NLP for Building Educational Applications*. Baltimore, Maryland, pages 1–11.

Swapna Somasundaran, Chong Min Lee, Martin Chodorow, and Xinhao Wang. 2015. Automated scoring of picture-based story narration. In *Proceedings of the Tenth Workshop on Innovative Use of NLP for Building Educational Applications*. Association for Computational Linguistics, Denver, Colorado, pages 42–48.

# The NTNU-YZU System in the AESW Shared Task: Automated Evaluation of Scientific Writing Using a Convolutional Neural Network


**Lung-Hao Lee[1], Bo-Lin Lin[2,3], Liang-Chih Yu[2,3], Yuen-Hsien Tseng[4]**
[1]Information Technology Center, National Taiwan Normal University
[2]Department of Information Management, Yuan Ze University
[3]Innovation Center for Big Data and Digital Convergence, Yuan Ze University
[4]Office of Research and Development, National Taiwan Normal University
[1,4]No. 162, Sec. 1, Heping E. Rd., Taipei 106, Taiwan
[2,3]No. 135, Yuan-Tung Rd., Chung-Li 320, Taiwan
{lhlee, samtseng}@ntnu.edu.tw, s1046253@mail.yzu.edu.tw, lcyu@saturn.yzu.edu.tw



## Abstract

This study describes the design of the NTNU-YZU system for the automated evaluation of scientific writing shared task. We employ a convolutional neural network with the Word2Vec/GloVe embedding representation to predict whether a sentence needs language editing. For the Boolean prediction track, our best F-score of 0.6108 ranked second among the ten submissions. Our system also achieved an F-score of 0.7419 for the probabilistic estimation track, ranking fourth among the nine submissions.


## 1 Introduction

Automated grammatical error detection and correction are important tasks and research topics in computational linguistics. A number of competitive tasks have been organized to encourage innovation in this direction (Leacock et al., 2014). For examples, Helping Our Own (HOO) was a series of shared tasks used for correcting grammatical errors of English texts written by non-native speakers (Dale and Kilgarriff, 2011; Dale et al., 2012). The CoNLL 2013/2014 shared tasks aimed to correct grammatical errors among learners of English as a foreign language in the educational application (Ng et al., 2013; 2014). The first NLP-TEA workshop featured a shared task on grammatical error diagnosis for learners of Chinese as a foreign lan-

guage (Yu et al., 2014). The following year, a similar Chinese grammatical error diagnosis shared task was held in the second NLP-TEA workshop in conjunction with ACL-IJCNLP 2015 (Lee et al., 2015). These competitions reflect the need for automated writing assistance for various applications.

The Automated Evaluation of Scientific Writing (AESW) shared task seeks to promote the use of NLP tools to help improve the quality of scientific writing in English by predicting whether a given sentence needs language editing or not. The AESW shared task contains two tracks: (1) a Boolean prediction track in which a sentence in need of editing will result in a binary classifier outputting true; otherwise the system should return false; and (2) a probabilistic estimation track in which the system estimates the editing probability (between 0 and 1) of each input sentence. A sentence is assigned 1 if it requires editing, and 0 otherwise. Each participating team can submit multiple results using different approaches for evaluation, but the final performance comparisons are limited to two designated submissions for each track.

This study describes the joint efforts between National Taiwan Normal University and Yuan Ze University (NTNU-YZU) in the AESW shared task. We introduce a convolutional neural network and its use for predicting language editing of scientific writing at the sentence level. The input sentence is represented as a sequence of words using distributed vectors looked up in a word embedding matrix. The datasets provided by the AESW organizers are used to train the neural network for the prediction




*Proceedings of the 11th Workshop on Innovative Use of NLP for Building Educational Applications*, pages 122–129,
San Diego, California, June 16, 2016. ©2016 Association for Computational Linguistics

task. The output is a value for probabilistic estimation. If the output value exceeds a certain threshold, it is considered as true for binary decision. Our best results in terms of F-score are 0.6108 (ranked at 2/10) and 0.7419 (4/9), respectively for the Boolean prediction track and the probabilistic estimation track.

The rest of this paper is organized as follows. Section 2 introduces existing studies for grammatical error detection and correction. Section 3 describes the details of the NTNU-YZU system architecture for the AESW shared task. Section 4 presents the evaluation results and their performance comparison. Section 5 elaborates on the implications and lessons learned. Conclusions are finally drawn in Section 6.

## 2 Related Work

Automated grammatical error detection and correction for second/foreign language learners has attracted considerable research attention. Although commercial products such as Microsoft Word have long provided grammatical checking for English, researchers in NLP have found that there is still much room for improvement in this area. A number of techniques have recently been proposed to deal with various types of writing errors. A novel approach based on alternating structure optimization was proposed to correct article and preposition errors (Dahlmeier and Ng, 2011). A linguistically motivated approach was also proposed to correct verb errors (Rozovskaya et al., 2014). A classifier was designed to detect word-ordering errors in Chinese sentences (Yu and Chen, 2012). Linguistic structures with interacting grammatical properties were identified to address such dependencies via joint inference and learning (Rozovskaya and Roth, 2013). A set of linguistic rules with syntactic information was handcrafted for detecting errors in Chinese sentences (Lee et al., 2013). A sentence judgment system was developed using both rule-based linguistic analysis and an n-gram statistical method for detecting grammatical errors (Lee et al., 2014). A penalized probabilistic first-order inductive learning algorithm was presented for Chinese grammatical error diagnosis (Chang et al., 2012). Relative position and parse template language models were proposed to correct grammatical errors (Wu et al., 2010). Dependency trees were used to train a language model for correcting grammatical errors at the tree level (Zhang and Wang, 2014). A classification-based system and a statistical machine translation-based system were combined to improve correction quality (Susanto et al., 2014). Different from correcting grammatical errors independently, integer linear programming was used to model the inference process considering all possible errors (Wu and Ng, 2013). The theory of contrastive analysis was formalized to demonstrate that language-specific error distributions could be predicted from the typological properties of the native language and its relation to English (Berzak et al., 2015).

Chodorow et al. (2012) presented the evaluation scheme for mapping writer, annotator, and system output onto traditional evaluation metrics for grammatical error detection. In addition to the choice of metric, they argued that the data skew is an important factor that should be considered. Evaluation methods from WMT human evaluation campaigns were also adapted to grammatical error correction (Grundkiewicz et al., 2015). The evaluation method based on globally optimal alignment between the source, a system hypothesis, and a reference was used to provide scores for both detection and correction (Felice and Briscoe, 2015). Inter-annotator agreement statistics in grammatical error correction was analyzed (Bryant and Ng, 2015). They found that the human upper bound is roughly 73% in terms of the F-score between human annotators.

More recently, deep learning techniques have been widely applied to problems in natural language processing with promising results. This trend motivates us to explore convolutional neural networks to automatically evaluate scientific writing at the sentence level.

## 3 The NTNU-YZU System

Figure 1 shows our Convolutional Neural Network (CNN) architecture for the AESW shared task. An input sentence is represented as a sequence of words. Each word refers to a row looked up in a word embedding matrix generating from Word2Vec (Mikolov et al., 2013) or GloVe (Pennington et al., 2014). We use convolutions over the sentence matrix to extract the features. A single convolution layer is adopted. The sliding window is called a filter in the CNN. We obtain the full convolutions by sliding the filters over the whole

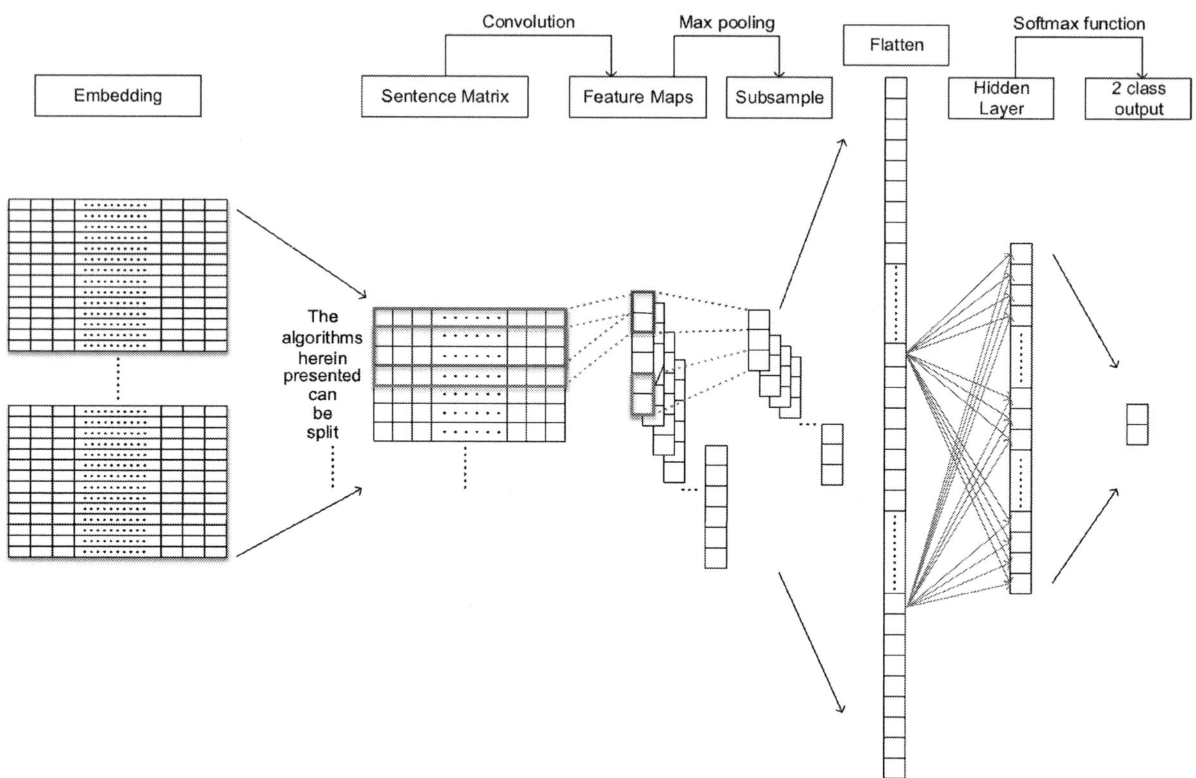


**Figure 1:** The illustration of our convolutional neural network architecture for the AESW shared task.

matrix. Each filter performs the convolution operation on the sentence matrix and generates a feature map. A pooling layer is then used to subsample features over each map. The most common approach to pooling is to apply a max operation to reduce the dimensionality for keeping the most salient features, which are then concatenated to form the flatten for neural computing. The final softmax layer then receives this flatten as input and uses it to classify the sentence.

During the training phase, a CNN automatically learns the values of its filters. If a sentence needs language editing to improve its grammaticality, the class is assigned as 1, and 0 otherwise. All training sentences accompanying their classes are used for learning in our CNN model.

To classify a sentence during the testing phase, we directly use the probability of the class 1 (*i.e.*, needs improvements) as the result for probabilistic estimation track. For the Boolean prediction track, if this probability exceeds a predefined threshold, then its output will be considered as true.

## 4 Evaluations

### 4.1 Data

The datasets for the AESW shared task were provided by task organizers (Daudaravicius, 2016), including a collection of texts extracted from 9,919 selected papers published in 2006-2013 by Springer Publishing Company and edited at VTex by native English speaking editors. The training, development and test datasets were comprised of data from an independent set of articles. After editing, the training and development sets respectively consists of 1,196,940 and 148,478 sentences, for designing and implementing the system. In total, 143,804 sentences in the test dataset were used for final performance evaluation.

The pre-trained word vectors we used are publicly available for download at the official Word2Vec and GloVe web sites. For Word2Vec representation, the model was trained on part of the Google News dataset, producing 300 dimensional vectors for 3 millions words and phrases as a result. For the GloVe representation, we adopted 4 different datasets for training the vectors including one from Wikipedia 2014 and Gigaword 5 (400K vocabulary), two common crawl datasets (uncased 1.9M vocabulary, and cased 2.2M vocabulary) and one Twitter dataset (1.2M vocabulary).

To implement the system, a python library Theano (Bastien et al., 2012) was used. The abovementioned datasets and linguistic resources were used to construct a convolutional neural network for this shared task.

## 4.2 Scores

For performance evaluation, this shared task adopted three metrics: precision, recall, and F-score. The scores were calculated for both tracks individually.

For the Boolean prediction track, precision measures the proportion of the gold standard sentences among all sentences reported by the system as positive examples. Recall measures the proportion of gold standard sentences correctly identified as needing improvement. F-score is the harmonic means of precision and recall.

For the probabilistic estimation track, the Mean Squared Error (MSE) is used. The precision (denoted as P), recall (R), and F-score (F) are defined in the following equations:

$$P = 1 - \frac{1}{n}\Sigma_i(q_i - s_i)^2, if \ q_i > 0.5 \quad (1)$$

$$R = 1 - \frac{1}{m}\Sigma_i(q_i - s_i)^2, if \ s_i = 1 \quad (2)$$

$$F = \frac{2*P*R}{P+R} \quad (3)$$

where $q_i$ is the probabilistic estimation, $s_i$ is the gold standard, n is the number of sentences predicted as requiring improvement, and m is the number of gold standard sentences needing improvement.

## 4.3 Experiments

In the first set of experiments, we fine-tuned several parameter combinations to obtain the Convolutional Neural Network (CNN). Three main parameters may affect system performance: (1) Number of epochs, which is the number of iterations required to learning the network parameters (set from 3 to 5); (2) Number of filters, which is regarded as the number of features used to train the network (100 and 250 in this experiment); and (3) Filter length, which denotes the number of contexts for convolution (set from 2 to 4). We used mini-batches to train the network. The size of each mini-batch was set as 100. We also considered the number of learning instances. In addition to adopting training instances used only for network learning, we incorporate sentences from the development datasets for model training. To optimize training CNN efficiently, this set of experiments adopts the conventional bag-of-word vectors used to index a word as vocabulary. In addition, the default threshold was set as 0.5 for binary decisions.

In the second set of experiments, we compared the effects of different word embedding methods including Word2Vec and Glove. We also evaluated the influence of the number of dimensions used for word representation.

In the third set of experiments, we adopted the best settings generated from the above experiments to fine-tune the threshold for Boolean decision. We increase the threshold from 0.1 to 0.9 in increments of 0.1, and then fine tune in increments of 0.01 to obtain approximately optimal performance for the CNN model.

## 4.4 Results

Table 1 shows the Boolean results with different parameter settings. A greater number of epochs do not always produce the better results. A smaller number of filters obtained better outcomes in more than two-thirds of testing cases with the same settings. Similarly, a longer filter length does not guarantee better results. In more than half of testing cases, using more sentences from the development dataset in model training did not produce better F-scores. In summary, 4 epochs, 100 filters, and a filter length of 3 achieved the best recall of 0.5251 and an F-score of 0.5526. We used these parameter settings for the following experiments.

Table 2 shows the results of our CNN model with different word embedding methods for the Boolean prediction track. Within the GloVe representation, the Twitter dataset (only 200 dimensions) does not achieve good results, possibly due to the poor suitability of textual usages of social media for the automated evaluation of scientific writing. With 300 dimensions each, trained word vectors from Wikipedia and Gigaword obtained relatively better effects than that from common crawl data. In addition, more dimensions usually lead to better

| Number of Epochs | Number of Filters | Filter Length | Training | | | Training + Development | | |
|---|---|---|---|---|---|---|---|---|
| | | | Precision | Recall | F-score | Precision | Recall | F-score |
| 3 | 100 | 2 | 0.5964 | 0.4567 | 0.5173 | 0.5908 | 0.482 | 0.5309 |
| 3 | 100 | 3 | 0.6058 | 0.4751 | 0.5325 | 0.6285 | 0.4294 | 0.5102 |
| 3 | 100 | 4 | 0.6151 | 0.4388 | 0.5122 | 0.5942 | 0.5006 | 0.5434 |
| 4 | 100 | 2 | 0.5876 | 0.4692 | 0.5218 | 0.5959 | 0.4534 | 0.515 |
| 4 | 100 | 3 | 0.6049 | 0.4558 | 0.5199 | 0.5832 | **0.5251** | **0.5526** |
| 4 | 100 | 4 | 0.6099 | 0.4441 | 0.5139 | 0.6026 | 0.465 | 0.525 |
| 5 | 100 | 2 | 0.5644 | 0.5167 | 0.5395 | 0.5851 | 0.466 | 0.5188 |
| 5 | 100 | 3 | 0.5952 | 0.4769 | 0.5295 | 0.6064 | 0.4569 | 0.5211 |
| 5 | 100 | 4 | 0.5981 | 0.4451 | 0.5103 | 0.6132 | 0.4156 | 0.4954 |
| 3 | 250 | 2 | 0.6081 | 0.4381 | 0.5093 | 0.6085 | 0.4363 | 0.5082 |
| 3 | 250 | 3 | 0.6222 | 0.4466 | 0.5199 | 0.6102 | 0.4726 | 0.5327 |
| 3 | 250 | 4 | 0.632 | 0.4007 | 0.4904 | 0.6067 | 0.4702 | 0.5298 |
| 4 | 250 | 2 | 0.5828 | 0.4874 | 0.5308 | 0.5944 | 0.4558 | 0.516 |
| 4 | 250 | 3 | 0.6187 | 0.4362 | 0.5116 | 0.626 | 0.4263 | 0.5072 |
| 4 | 250 | 4 | 0.6091 | 0.4479 | 0.5162 | 0.6325 | 0.3995 | 0.4897 |
| 5 | 250 | 2 | 0.5929 | 0.4325 | 0.5001 | 0.6 | 0.4388 | 0.5069 |
| 5 | 250 | 3 | 0.6052 | 0.4427 | 0.5113 | 0.5972 | 0.4725 | 0.5276 |
| 5 | 250 | 4 | 0.6413 | 0.3431 | 0.4471 | **0.6424** | 0.3545 | 0.4569 |

**Table 1:** Boolean results of our CNN model with different parameters.

results. Comparing the representations of GloVe and Word2Vec, the GloVe achieves better recall and a higher F-score than Word2Vec, while Word2Vec provides higher precision. Again, using more sentences to train the CNN does not result in better performance in this set of experiments. In summary, the Word2Vec training from the Google News data obtains the best precision at 0.6717. The best recall 0.5344 and F-score 0.5618 were achieved using the GloVe representation learning from Wikipedia and Gigaword (300 dimensions).

Compared with the default threshold of 0.5, evaluation results showed that the F-score obtained using the Word2Vec representation could be improved to 0.6108 by setting the threshold to 0.21. Similarly, the F-score of the GloVe representation learning from Wikipedia and Gigaword (300 dimensions) can be slightly improved to 0.6046 with a threshold of 0.34. We also analyzed why the low thresoulds resulting the better results. In our obserations, the class (0/1) in the training set is imbalanced. The number of instances with class 0 (*i.e.*, without needing improvements) is about 1.5 times than that with the class 1, which may affect

the model favors the class 0 and generates a low probability of the class 1.

Table 3 shows the results of our CNN model with different word embedding methods for the probabilistic estimation track. Similar outcomes are obtained for the probabilistic estimation track. Our CNN using the Word2Vec representation achieved the best precision of 0.79. Also, using the CNN model with the GloVe representation trained from Wikipedia and Gigaword (300 dimensions) obtained the best recall of 0.7177 and the highest F-score of 0.7419.

### 4.5 Comparisons

In this shared task, each participant can submit up to two results as final submissions for each track. Our submission selected the result with best F-score and the result with relatively better precision without obviously bad recall. For the Boolean prediction track, we selected the best F-score of 0.6108 (with a precision at 0.5025 and recall at 0.7785) achieved by the Word2Vec representation with a threshold 0.21, and a precision of 0.6717

| Word Embedding | Training | | | Training + Development | | |
|---|---|---|---|---|---|---|
| | Precision | Recall | F-score | Precision | Recall | F-score |
| Word2Vec (Google News, 300d) | **0.6717** | 0.3805 | 0.4858 | 0.6279 | 0.4871 | 0.5486 |
| GloVe (Wikipedia 2014 + Gigaword 5, 50d) | 0.5956 | 0.4539 | 0.5152 | 0.6084 | 0.437 | 0.5086 |
| GloVe (W. 2014 + G. 5, 100d) | 0.6357 | 0.3968 | 0.4886 | 0.6178 | 0.451 | 0.5214 |
| GloVe (W. 2014 + G. 5, 200d) | 0.6234 | 0.4548 | 0.5259 | 0.6303 | 0.4422 | 0.5198 |
| GloVe (W. 2014 + G. 5, 300d) | 0.5923 | **0.5344** | **0.5618** | 0.6164 | 0.4842 | 0.5424 |
| GloVe (Common Crawl, uncased, 300d) | 0.6222 | 0.4843 | 0.5447 | 0.6293 | 0.4584 | 0.5304 |
| GloVe (Common Crawl, cased, 300d) | 0.6129 | 0.508 | 0.5555 | 0.6328 | 0.4634 | 0.535 |
| GloVe (Twitter, 200d) | 0.6532 | 0.3925 | 0.4903 | 0.6419 | 0.4301 | 0.5151 |

Table 2: Boolean results of our CNN model with different word embedding methods.

| Word Embedding | Training | | | Training + Development | | |
|---|---|---|---|---|---|---|
| | Precision | Recall | F-score | Precision | Recall | F-score |
| Word2Vec (Google News, 300d) | **0.79** | 0.6166 | 0.6926 | 0.7759 | 0.6805 | 0.7251 |
| GloVe (Wikipedia 2014 + Gigaword 5, 50d) | 0.7675 | 0.6865 | 0.7248 | 0.7714 | 0.6853 | 0.7258 |
| GloVe (W. 2014 + G. 5, 100d) | 0.779 | 0.6552 | 0.7117 | 0.7744 | 0.6818 | 0.7252 |
| GloVe (W. 2014 + G. 5, 200d) | 0.7767 | 0.6819 | 0.7262 | 0.7785 | 0.6775 | 0.7245 |
| GloVe (W. 2014 + G. 5, 300d) | 0.7678 | **0.7177** | **0.7419** | 0.7745 | 0.6938 | 0.7319 |
| GloVe (Common Crawl, uncased, 300d) | 0.7755 | 0.6916 | 0.7311 | 0.7784 | 0.68 | 0.7259 |
| GloVe (Common Crawl, cased, 300d) | 0.773 | 0.704 | 0.7369 | 0.779 | 0.6789 | 0.7255 |
| GloVe (Twitter, 200d) | 0.784 | 0.649 | 0.7102 | 0.7817 | 0.668 | 0.7204 |

Table 3: Probabilistic results of our CNN model with different word embedding methods.

and recall of 0.3805 (the F-score of 0.4858 as a result) with the same word embedding method at the default threshold 0.5. For the probabilistic estimation track, we submitted a result with an F-score of 0.7419 (with a precision at 0.7678 and recall of 0.7177) using the GloVe representation trained from Wikipedia and Gigaword at 300 dimensions, and the result with best precision at 0.79 and recall at 0.6166 (the F-score was 0.6926) using the Word2Vec embedding.

The official results of this shared task for the Boolean prediction track and probabilistic estimation track can be found in the organizers' task report (Vidas et al., 2016). The organizers also provided the baseline method using random guess. If the F-score is considered, our first NTNU-YZU submission for the Boolean track ranked a close second (the best is 0.6278) among the ten submissions. The second NTNU-YZU submission achieved the best precision among all submissions with a moderate F-score. For the probabilistic estimation track, the F-score of our first NTNU-YZU submission ranked fourth among the nine submissions. In terms of precision, our second NTNU-YZU submission ranked second among all submissions.

## 5   Lessons

The CodaLab is used to evaluate this competition-based shared task. This open-source system is very helpful for automating such competitions, but is still in development. About 12%(=31/269) of our submissions for the Boolean prediction track failed with/without error information. Similarly, 16%(=13/81) of submissions for the probabilistic estimation track failed.

Based on our experience in organizing or participating in shared tasks, all participants should independently complete the systems and their evaluation. The CodaLab automatically keeps the last submission of each participant in the leaderboard. All participants have access to the current leaderboard results during the testing phrase, which may affect system development and the final result selection.

For the shared task, only about three months are allowed for system design and implementation, and some participants were unable to complete the task in time, or withdrew because of unsatisfactory results. The schedule left our team time to only explore one of possible machine learning models. Allowing more time to complete the task, may produce better results.

In addition to using precision, recall, and F-score as evaluation metrics, we suggest evaluating the false positive rate, which is the proportion of sentences that incorrectly identified as needing improvement. Although high precision usually implies a low error rate, a low false positive rate is still considered as an important metric in the real world, because frequently and incorrectly identifying sentences as in need of improvement may cause user frustration.

## 6   Conclusions and Future Work

This study describes the NTNU-YZU system in the AESW shared task, including system design, implementation, and evaluation. We trained a convolutional neural network using two embedding methods (Word2Vec and GloVe) for the automated evaluation of scientific writing. Our system achieved an F-score of 0.6108, ranking second among the ten submissions for the Boolean prediction track. For the probabilistic estimation track, our best F-score of 0.7419 ranked fourth among the nine submissions.

This is our first exploration for this research topic and future work will explore other machine learning approaches to improve system performance. In addition to predicting whether a given English sentence needs language editing or not, we will focus on detecting/correcting grammatical errors in sentences written by Chinese learners.

## Acknowledgments

This study was partially supported by the Ministry of Science and Technology, under the grant MOST 102-2221-E-155-029-MY3, MOST 103-2221-E-003-013-MY3, MOST 104-2911-I-003-301 and the "Aim for the Top University Project" and "Center of Learning Technology for Chinese" of National Taiwan Normal University, sponsored by the Ministry of Education, Taiwan.

We thank all organizers for their great work to hold this shared task. Our thanks also go to the anonymous reviewers for their valuable comments.

## References

Bastien, Frédéric, Pascal Lamblin, Razvan Pascanu, James Bergstra, Ian Goodfellow, Arnaud Bergeron, Nicolas Bouchard, Daivd Warde-Farley, and Yoshua Bengio. 2012. Theano: new features and speed improvements. In *Proceedings of NIPS 2012 Workshop on Deep Learning and Unsupervised Feature Learning*, pages 1-10.

Berzak, Yevgeni, Roi Reichart, and Boris Katz. 2015. Contrastive analysis with predictive power: typology driven estimation of grammatical error distributions in ESL. In *Proceedings of CoNLL-15*, pages 94-102.

Bryant, Christopher, and Hwee Tou Ng. 2015. How far are we fully automatic high quality grammatical error correction? In *Proceedings of ACL-IJCNLP-15*, pages 697-707.

Chang, Ru-Ying, Chung-Hsien Wu, and Philips K. Prasetyo. 2012. Error diagnosis of Chinese sentences using inductive learning algorithm and decomposition-based testing mechanism. *ACM Transactions on Asian Language Information Processing*, 11(1): Article 3.

Chodorow, Martin, Markus Dickinson, Ross Israel, and Joel Tetreault. 2012. Problems in evaluating grammatical error detection systems. In *Proceedings of COLING-12: Technical Papers*, pages 611-628.

Dahlmeier, Daniel, and Hwee Tou Ng. 2011. Grammatical error correction with alternating structure optimization. In *Proceedings of ACL-11*, pages 915-923.

Dale, Robert, and Adam Kilgarriff. 2011. Helping our own: The HOO 2011 pilot shared task. In *Proceedings of the 13th European Workshop on Natural Language Generation*, pages 1–8.

Dale, Robert, Ilya Anisimoff, and George Narroway. 2012. HOO 2012: A report on the preposition and determiner error correction shared task. In *Proceedings of the 7th Workshop on the Innovative Use of NLP for Building Educational Applications*, pages 54–62.

Daudaravicius, Vidas. 2016. Automated evaluation of scientific writing data set (version 1.2) [data file]. VTex.

Daudaravicius, Vidas, Rafael E. Banchs, Elena Volodina, and Courtney Napoles. 2016. A report on the automated evaluation of scientific writing shared task. In *Proceedings of the 11th Workshop on the Innovative Use of NLP for Building Educational Applications*.

Felice, Mariano, and Ted Briscoe. Towards a standard evaluation method for grammatical error detection and correction. In *Proceedings of NAACL-HLT-15*, pages 578-587.

Grundkiewicz, Roman, Marcin Junczys-Dowmunt, and Edward Gillian. 2015. Human evaluation of grammatical error correcting systems. In *Proceedings of EMNLP-15*, pages 461-470.

Leacock, Claudia, Martin Chodorow, Michael Gamon, and Joel Tetreault. 2014. *Automated Grammatical Error Detection for Language Learners*, Second edition. Morgan & Claypool Publishers.

Lee, Lung-Hao, Liang-Chih Yu, and Li-Ping Chang. 2015. Overview of the NLP-TEA 2015 shared task for Chinese grammatical error diagnosis. In *Proceedings of the 2nd Workshop on Natural Language Processing Techniques for Educational Applications*, pages 1-6.

Lee, Lung-Hao, Liang-Chih Yu, Kuei-Ching Lee, Yuen-Hsien Tseng, Li-Ping Chang, and Hsin-Hsi Chen. 2014. A sentence judgment system for grammatical error detection. In *Proceedings of COLING-14: Demonstration*, pages 67-70.

Lee, Lung-Hao, Li-Ping Chang, Kuei-Ching Lee, Yuen-Hsien Tseng, and Hsin-His Chen. 2013. Linguistic rules based Chinese error detection for second language learning. In *Work-in-Progress Poster Proceedings of the 21st International Conference on Computers in Education*, pages 27-29.

Mikolov, Tomas, Ilya Sutskever, Kai Chen, Greg Corrado, and Jeffrey Dean. 2013. Distributed representations of words and phrases and their compositionality. In *Proceedings of NIPS-13*, pages 1-10

Ng, Hwee Tou, Siew Mei Wu, Ted Briscoe, Christian Hadiwinoto, Raymond Hendy Susanto, and Christopher Bryant. 2014. The CoNLL-2014 shared task on grammatical error correction. In *Proceedings of CoNLL-14 Shared Task*, pages 1-14.

Ng, Hwee Tou, Siew Mei Wu, Yuanbin Wu, Christian Hadiwinoto, and Joel Tetreault. 2013. The CoNLL-2013 shared task on grammatical error correction. In *Proceedings of CoNLL-13 Shared Task*, pages 1-12.

Pennington, Jeffrey, Richard Socher, and Christopher D. Manning. 2014. GloVe: Global vectors for word representation. In *Proceedings of EMNLP-14*, pages 1532-1543.

Rozovskaya, Alla, Dan Roth, and Vivek Srikumar. 2014. Correcting grammatical verb errors. In *Proceedings of EACL-14*, pages 358-367.

Rozovskaya, Alla, and Dan Roth. 2013. Joint learning and inference for grammatical error correction. In *Proceedings of EMNLP-13*, pages 791-802.

Susanto, Raymond Hendy, Peter Phandi, and Hwee Tou Ng. 2014. System combination for grammatical error correction. In *Proceedings of EMNLP-14*, pages 951-962.

Wu, Chung-Hsien, Chao-Hung Liu, Matthew Harris, and Liang-Chih Yu. 2010. Sentence correction incorporating relative position and parse template language model. *IEEE Transactions on Audio, Speech, and Language Processing*, 18(6): 1170-1181.

Wu, Yuanbin, and Hwee Tou Ng. 2013. Grammatical error correction using integer linear programming. In *Proceedings of ACL-13*, pages 1456-1465.

Yu, Chi-Hsin, and Hsin-Hsi Chen. 2012. Detecting word ordering errors in Chinese sentences for learning Chinese as a foreign language. In *Proceedings of COLING-12*, pages 3003-3018.

Yu, Liang-Chih, Lung-Hao Lee, and Li-Ping Chang. 2014. Overview of grammatical error diagnosis for learning Chinese as a foreign language. In *Proceedings of the 1st Workshop on Natural Language Processing Techniques for Educational Applications*, pages 42-47.

Zhang, Longkai, and Houfeng Wang. 2014. Go climb a dependency tree and correct the grammatical errors. In *Proceedings of EMNLP-14*, pages 266-277.

# Automated Scoring Across Different Modalities

**Anastassia Loukina and Aoife Cahill**
Educational Testing Service
660 Rosedale Rd
Princeton, NJ 08541, USA
aloukina@ets.org, acahill@ets.org

## Abstract

In this paper we investigate how well the systems developed for automated evaluation of written responses perform when applied to spoken responses. We compare two state of the art systems for automated writing evaluation and a state of the art system for evaluating spoken responses. We find that the systems for writing evaluation achieve very good performance when applied to transcriptions of spoken responses but show degradation when applied to ASR output. The system based on sparse $n$-gram features appears to be more robust to such degradation. We further explore the role of ASR accuracy and the performance and construct coverage of the combined model which includes all three engines.

## 1 Introduction

In this paper we evaluate how well the systems developed for automated evaluation of *written* responses perform when applied to *spoken* responses. We use a corpus of spoken responses to an English language proficiency test and compare the performance of two state-of-the-art systems for evaluating writing and a state of the art system for evaluating spoken responses.

Automated speech scoring, until recently, primarily focused on evaluating pronunciation and prosody of highly constrained read speech (Bernstein et al., 1990; Neumeyer et al., 1996; Witt and Young, 2000). With the improvement in automatic speech recognition technology, automated scoring has lately also been applied to constructed responses where the content of the response may not be known

in advance (Zechner et al., 2009; Cheng et al., 2014). Earlier scoring systems for such responses still primarily evaluated delivery aspect of the response, but there has also been a growing amount of work on automatic evaluation of grammar, vocabulary and content of spoken responses (Bernstein et al., 2010; Chen and Zechner, 2011; Xie et al., 2012; Bhat and Yoon, 2015).

While automatic evaluation of these high-level aspects of language proficiency is a relatively new field in automated speech scoring, there exists a substantial body of research on evaluating these constructs in written responses including several systems already used operationally for scoring responses to high-stakes language proficiency tests (see Shermis (2014) for a comprehensive overview).

Automated scoring systems for spoken and written responses generally share a common structure: they extract a set of features measuring different aspects of language proficiency and use a machine learning algorithm to map those features to a human score. There is also a substantial overlap in the criteria used to score grammar and vocabulary of spoken and written responses. Therefore, it is not unreasonable to expect that some of the features developed for evaluating writing will also be applicable to scoring spoken responses (cf. Crossley and McNamara (2013)).

On the other hand, the performance of such features can be affected by a number of factors. First of all, many grammatical features rely on knowledge of sentence boundaries in order to parse the response into syntactic constituents. In written responses the sentence boundaries can be established



*Proceedings of the 11th Workshop on Innovative Use of NLP for Building Educational Applications*, pages 130–135,
San Diego, California, June 16, 2016. ©2016 Association for Computational Linguistics

based on punctuation. In spoken responses, however, these have to be estimated using machine learning algorithms such as the ones described in Chen and Yoon (2011). Furthermore, sentence boundaries in speech are often ambiguous. These factors may lead to a decrease in feature performance.

Second, in automated speech scoring the transcription of the spoken responses necessary to evaluate grammar and vocabulary is obtained using automated speech recognition (ASR) (Higgins et al., 2011). These systems may incorrectly recognize certain words introducing additional noise into the feature input and consequently lowering their performance.

Finally, spoken and written discourse differ in what is considered appropriate in terms of language use (Chafe and Tannen, 1987; Biber and Gray, 2013). Thus, for example, sentence fragments typically considered inappropriate for written language are generally very common in unscripted spoken responses. This may also impact how well the features developed for written responses perform on spoken responses.

We first introduce three state-of-the-art operational systems for automated scoring. We then apply the engines for evaluating writing to a corpus of spoken responses. Finally, we evaluate whether combining different engines leads to further improvement in system performance and construct coverage.

## 2 Automated scoring systems

### 2.1 e-rater®

*e-rater®* (*E*) is an engine that can automatically provide feedback on students' writing, as well as automatically assign a score to that writing. Using statistical and rule-based NLP methods, *E* identifies and extracts several feature classes for model building and essay scoring (Attali and Burstein, 2006; Burstein et al., 2013)). Individual feature classes typically represent an aggregate of a larger feature set and are designed to capture a specific aspect of the construct being measured. The feature classes used in this paper include the following: (a) grammatical errors (e.g., subject-verb agreement errors), (b) word usage errors (e.g., their versus there), (c) presence of essay-based discourse elements (e.g., thesis statement, main points, supporting details,

and conclusions), (d) development of essay-based discourse elements, (e) a feature that considers correct usage of prepositions and collocations (Futagi et al., 2008), and (f) sentence variety. To train a new scoring model, features are extracted from a training data set, and a linear model (roughly equivalent to non-negative least squares regression) is learned.

### 2.2 c-rater-ML

c-rater-ML (*C*) is an automated scoring engine originally designed to evaluate the content of a student response. It is typically applied to short responses ranging from a few words to a short paragraph. Therefore, in contrast to *E* and *S* many of the features used in the *C* engine are sparse lexicalized features similar to the ones described in Heilman and Madnani (2013). In addition to word and character $n$-gram features, the models also include syntactic dependency features. As a result of the large number of sparse features, the modeling technique for this kind of feature set needs to be different from a straightforward linear model. *C* employs a Support Vector Regressor with a radial basis function kernel. We use this alternative approach to scoring (with many sparse lexical features and a non-linear learning function) to contrast with the typical scoring models used for evaluating speech or writing quality.

### 2.3 SpeechRater

*SpeechRater*[sm] (*S*) (Zechner et al., 2009) is an automated scoring engine that is designed to evaluate the quality of spontaneous spoken responses. Using signal processing as well as NLP techniques, *S* extracts features for evaluating both the delivery characteristics (e.g. fluency, pronunciation) and the language use characteristics (e.g. grammar, vocabulary) of each response.

The features are extracted from the sound recording of the response using the two stage method described in Higgins et al. (2011) where the transcription of the responses is obtained using automated speech recognition technology. The ASR engine incorporated into *S* was trained on over 800 hours of non-native speech from the same assessment used in this study with no speaker overlap. The ASR system uses a GMM-based crossword triphone acoustic model and a 4-gram language model with a vocabulary size of 65,000 words.

The $S$ model used in this study contained 18 features. Of these, 15 features covered various aspects of delivery such as fluency, pronunciation and rhythm. Three features measured language use. These feature were: (1) average log of the frequency of all content words (Yoon et al., 2012), (2) CVA-based comparison between the lexical content of each response and the reference corpus (based on Xie et al. (2012)) and (3) a CVA-based comparison computed based on part-of-speech tags (Bhat and Yoon, 2015). As in case of $E$, the final score is computed as a linear combination of these features.

## 3 Data and methodology

### 3.1 Corpus of spoken responses

The study is based on a corpus of 5,884 spoken responses to an English language proficiency test obtained from 996 speakers. The corpus contains up to six responses from each speaker. Each response was unscripted and around 1 minute long.

The corpus was equally split into training and evaluation sets (2,941 responses each). There was no overlap of speakers or prompts in the two sets. All responses were assigned a holistic proficiency score by expert raters. The scores ranged from 1 (low proficiency) to 4 (high proficiency). The raters evaluated the overall intelligibility of responses, grammar, the use of vocabulary, and topic development. To obtain human benchmarks, 136 responses from the evaluation set were scored by two raters. The agreement between the two raters was Pearson's $r = 0.56$.

All responses were transcribed by a professional transcription agency. The average length of transcribed responses was 104 words ($\sigma = 30$) with the length of 50% of the responses falling between 84 and 124 words. The responses from more proficient speakers were generally longer: the number of words in the response was moderately correlated with proficiency score with Pearson's $r = 0.51$ ($p < 0.0001$). Table 1 shows the number of responses in the evaluation set assigned to each score category as well as the mean and standard deviation of the number of words in the transcriptions of these responses.

Finally, we computed the word error rate (WER)

| Score | 1 | 2 | 3 | 4 |
|---|---|---|---|---|
| N responses | 104 | 1005 | 1485 | 347 |
| Average N words | 51.5 | 91.0 | 111.9 | 126.5 |
| Std. N words | 25.4 | 24.7 | 25.5 | 28.9 |
| Average WER | 48% | 36% | 31.5% | 30% |

**Table 1:** The total number of responses in each score category, the average number of words/standard deviation of transcribed responses and the average ASR word error rate for responses in each category.

for the ASR output for each response in our corpus. The average WER for the whole corpus was 34% ($\sigma = 13.7$). The ASR was somewhat more accurate for more proficient speakers with the correlation between response WER and response score Pearson's $r = -0.24$ ($p < 0.0001$). As can be seen from Table 1, the relationship between WER and proficiency scores was non-linear: the WER was substantially greater for speakers with the lowest proficiency level (score 1), the difference between the rest of the speakers was smaller.

### 3.2 Method

#### 3.2.1 Feature extraction

We used each of the three engines to extract the corresponding features for each response. Features for $S$ were extracted following the operational pipeline from the sound recording of the response with all features including those related to language use computed on the ASR output. For $E$ and $C$ the features were extracted using three different inputs: (1) the ASR output (the same as used in $S$), (2) the expert human transcription which included punctuation, and (3) the human transcription after removing all punctuation. All transcriptions were processed to remove fillers such as 'uhm' and 'uh', word fragments and repeated words.

#### 3.2.2 Model building

We then used various combinations of features to compare the performance of the engines. For $S$ and $E$ we used the actual feature values returned by each system (18 $S$ features and 9 $E$ features). Since $C$ is based on numerous sparse features we used a stacking approach (Wolpert, 1992) to combine it with the other two engines: we used 10-fold cross-validation to generate predicted scores for all responses in the training set and used these predicted scores as a single "$C$" feature. For the evaluation set this feature corresponded to scores predicted for the evaluation set using the $C$ model trained on the training set.

We then trained a series of models based on different combinations of features from the three engines. The coefficients for all models were estimated on the training set using non-negative least squares regression. The models were then used to generate predictions on the evaluation set. Finally, in all cases the predictions were re-scaled using a normal transformation to match the distribution of human scores on the training set.

## 4   Results

Table 2 shows the performance of all 19 models in terms of correlation (Pearson's $r$) between predicted and observed scores for the evaluation set. We used Steiger's method for comparing dependent correlations (Steiger, 1980)[1] to evaluate whether the differences between models are statistically significant. Unless stated otherwise, all reported differences are significant at $\alpha = 0.01$ after applying Bonferroni correction for multiple comparisons.

### 4.1   Performance of $E$ and $C$ on transcriptions

When used with human transcription, both $E$ and $C$ performed close to the $S$ baseline ($r = 0.61$ for $E$, 0.61 for $C$ and 0.63 for $S$, the differences are not significant). There was a small improvement from combining the two automated writing evaluation engines ($EC$) with $r$ increasing to 0.64.

### 4.2   Performance of $E$ and $C$ on ASR output

There was a decrease in performance of both writing engines when the features were computed on ASR output. The degradation was larger for $E$ (from 0.61 to 0.52). $C$ appeared to be more robust to the noise introduced by ASR with the performance decreasing from 0.61 to 0.58. The model based on the combination of both engines computed on ASR output achieved $r = 0.60$.

We further explored the reason for degradation between the features computed on transcription and ASR output. As discussed in the introduction, ASR

output does not contain sentence boundaries necessary for the computation of some of the features. To evaluate the impact of this factor we computed a new set of features using human transcriptions with punctuation removed. We found that this had no significant effect on model performance.

We next looked at the effect of response WER on the accuracy of the scoring engine for this response. We first hypothesized that the scoring error may be greater for responses with higher WER. To test this hypothesis we computed the correlation between the scoring error (the absolute difference between predicted and observed score) and the WER for each response. As expected, there was no significant correlation when automated scores were computed on transcriptions with or without punctuation. Surprisingly, the correlations between WER and scoring error for scores computed on ASR output were very low: $r = 0.09$ ($p < 0.00001$) for $E$ and $r = 0.07$, $p = 0.0001$ for $C$. In other words, there was no linear relationship between the response WER and the scoring error.

We also tested whether the relationship between the scoring error and WER was further obscured by training the models on already "noisy" ASR outputs. We retrained the $E$, $C$ and $EC$ models using the features computed on transcriptions and then evaluated them using features computed on ASR outputs. We found that the performance of these new models was similar ($E$) or slightly lower ($C$ and $EC$) than the performance of the models trained on ASR outputs. Furthermore, the correlation between the WER and scoring error for these models were as low as the correlations observed for ASR-trained models.

### 4.3   Combined performance of all three engines

Finally, we evaluated the performance and construct coverage of the model based on the combination of all three engines.

We found that the performance improved if $S$ features were combined with writing features computed based on transcriptions. This is not surprising considering that all $S$ features were computed on ASR output and therefore the new features computed on transcriptions most likely contained the information lost due to inaccurate ASR.

For features computed on ASR output, we found that there was no further gain in performance from

---

[1]We used the Python implementation from https://github.com/psinger/CorrelationStats

| Model | Description | Org N feats | trans | trans-no-punct | asr |
|---|---|---|---|---|---|
| *S* | Baseline model containing *S* features only | 18 | | | 0.63 |
| *E* | The model containing only *E* features | 9 | 0.61 | 0.60 | 0.52 |
| *C* | The original *C* model | (see text) | 0.61 | 0.62 | 0.58 |
| *EC* | The model which combined *E* features and predictions from *C* (see main text) | 10 | 0.64 | 0.64 | 0.60 |
| *SE* | The combination of *S* and *E* features | 27 | 0.67 | 0.66 | 0.63 |
| *SC* | The combination of *S* features and predictions from *C* (see main text) | 19 | 0.66 | 0.66 | 0.64 |
| *SEC* | The combination of *S* and *E* features and predictions from *C* | 28 | 0.67 | 0.67 | 0.64 |

**Table 2:** Summary of performance (Pearson's $r$ between the predicted and human score) of all 19 models evaluated in this study. The table shows the original number of features and the model performance for different types of input (see section 3.2.1). The final number of features in the model may be less than the original number of features since all coefficients were set to be positive.

combining *S* and *E* (*SE*), *C* (*SC*) or all three engines (*SEC*).

We also evaluated which features had the biggest contribution to the final score in different models. In the baseline *S* model, delivery features (fluency, pronunciation, and prosody) accounted for 80% of the final score. The language use features accounted for the remaining 20%. In the combined model, the relative contribution of language use features increased to 38% for *SE*, 37% for *SC* and 44% for *SEC*. Thus in the combined model the delivery and language use features are more evenly balanced.

## 5 Discussion

In this paper we explored how well state-of-the-art engines for evaluating written responses perform when applied to transcriptions of spoken responses. Surprisingly, we found that the writing engines achieve relatively high agreement with human scores even though they do not measure some fundamental aspects of spoken language proficiency: fluency and pronunciation. At the same time, there was no improvement between the baseline *S* system and a system that combines all three engines.

Furthermore, the drop in performance of writing engines when moving from well-formed transcribed text to ASR output is not as high as one might initially expect given the relatively high WER in this data set. We also found that the relationship between the ASR accuracy and scoring error was not straightforward and deserves further study. Finally, lack of sentence boundaries had no effect on the engine per-formance.

*C* engine showed good agreement with human scores even though there was no overlap between prompts in training and evaluation sets and therefore the model could not learn any specifics relevant to particular prompts and had to rely on general patterns of word use.

Our results highlight the complex role of construct in automated scoring. The majority of speakers who show good performance along one of the dimensions of language proficiency generally also score high along other dimensions. This is exemplified by our result that writing engines which measured only one aspect of spoken responses still showed relatively high agreement with holistic scores. Consequently, as shown in this study, the gain in performance from combining different engines is small or non-existent. However, a system which heavily relies on features measuring a single aspect of proficiency is sub-optimal both in terms of validity of the final score and the system vulnerability to various gaming behaviours.

We showed that combining the speech scoring engine with the existing features developed for scoring written responses produces a model where the contribution of different proficiency aspects to the final score is more balanced leading to a more valid system, which is potentially more robust to gaming. In future study we will investigate the individual contribution of different features in these engines.

## Acknowledgments

We thank Keelan Evanini, Su-Youn Yoon, Brian Riordan, Klaus Zechner and two anonymous BEA reviewers for their comments and suggestions.

## References

Yigal Attali and Jill Burstein. 2006. Automated essay scoring with e-rater®v.2. *Journal of Technology, Learning, and Assessment*, 4(3).

Jared Bernstein, Michale Cohen, Hy Murveit, Dimitry Rtischev, and Mitchel Weintraub. 1990. Automatic Evaluation and Training in English Pronunciation. In *Proceedings of ICSLP 90*, pages 1185–1188.

Jared Bernstein, Jian Cheng, and Masanori Suzuki. 2010. Fluency and Structural Complexity as Predictors of L2 Oral Proficiency. *Proceedings of Interspeech 2010, Makuhari, Chiba, Japan*, pages 1241–1244.

Suma Bhat and Su-Youn Yoon. 2015. Automatic assessment of syntactic complexity for spontaneous speech scoring. *Speech Communication*, 67:42–57.

Douglas Biber and Bethany Gray. 2013. Discourse Characteristics of Writing and Speaking Task Types on the TOEFL iBT Test: A Lexico-Grammatical Analysis. *ETS Research Report*, RR-13-04.

Jill Burstein, Joel Tetreault, and Nitin Madnani. 2013. The e-rater automated essay scoring system. In Mark D. Shermis and Jill Burstein, editors, *Handbook of automated essay evaluation: Current applications and new directions*. Routledge, New York, NY.

Wallace Chafe and Deborah Tannen. 1987. The relation between written and spoken language. *Annual Review of Anthropology*, 16:383–407.

Lei Chen and Su-Youn Yoon. 2011. Detecting structural events for assessing non-native speech. *Proceedings of the 6th workshop on Innovative Use of NLP for Buidling Educational Applications*, pages 38–45.

Miao Chen and Klaus Zechner. 2011. Computing and Evaluating Syntactic Complexity Features for Automated Scoring of Spontaneous Non-Native Speech. *Proceedings of the 49th Annual Meeting of the Association for Computational Linguistics*, pages 722–731.

Jian Cheng, Yuan Zhao D'Antilio, Xin Chen, and Jared Bernstein. 2014. Automatic Assessment of the Speech of Young English Learners. *Proceedings of the 9th Workshop on Innovative Use of NLP for Building Educational Applications*, pages 12–21.

Scott Crossley and Danielle McNamara. 2013. Applications of Text Analysis Tools for spoken response grading. *Language Learning & Technology*, 17(2):171–192.

Yoko Futagi, Paul Deane, Martin Chodorow, and Joel Tetreault. 2008. A computational approach to detecting collocation errors in the writing of non-native speakers of english. *Computer Assisted Language Learning*, 21:353–367.

Michael Heilman and Nitin Madnani. 2013. ETS: Domain adaptation and stacking for short answer scoring. In *Second Joint Conference on Lexical and Computational Semantics (*SEM), Volume 2: Proceedings of the Seventh International Workshop on Semantic Evaluation (SemEval 2013)*, pages 275–279.

Derrick Higgins, Xiaoming Xi, Klaus Zechner, and David Williamson. 2011. A three-stage approach to the automated scoring of spontaneous spoken responses. *Computer Speech & Language*, 25(2):282–306.

Leonardo Neumeyer, Horacio Franco, Mitchell Weintraub, and Patti Price. 1996. Automatic text-independent pronunciation scoring of foreign language student speech. *Proceeding of Fourth International Conference on Spoken Language Processing. ICSLP '96*, 3:1457–1460.

Mark D. Shermis. 2014. State-of-the-art automated essay scoring: Competition, results, and future directions from a United States demonstration. *Assessing Writing*, 20:53–76.

James H Steiger. 1980. Tests for comparing elements of a correlation matrix. *Psychological Bulletin*, 87(2):245.

Silke M. Witt and Steve J. Young. 2000. Phone-level pronunciation scoring and assessment for interactive language learning. 30(2):95–108.

David H. Wolpert. 1992. Stacked generalization. *Neural Networks*, 5:241–259.

Shasha Xie, Keelan Evanini, and Klaus Zechner. 2012. Exploring content features for automated speech scoring. In *NAACL HLT '12 Proceedings of the 2012 Conference of the North American Chapter of the Association for Computational Linguistics: Human Language Technologies*, pages 103–111.

Su-Youn Yoon, Suma Bhat, and Klaus Zechner. 2012. Vocabulary profile as a measure of vocabulary sophistication. *Proceedings of the Seventh Workshop on the innovative use of NLP for Building Educational Applications*, pages 180–189.

Klaus Zechner, Derrick Higgins, Xiaoming Xi, and David M. Williamson. 2009. Automatic scoring of non-native spontaneous speech in tests of spoken english. *Speech Communication*, 51(10):883–895.

# Model Combination for Correcting Preposition Selection Errors[*]


**Nitin Madnani**     **Michael Heilman**     **Aoife Cahill**

660 Rosedale Road
Princeton, NJ 08541, USA
`{nmadnani,mheilman,acahill}@ets.org`



## Abstract

Many grammatical error correction approaches use classifiers with specially-engineered features to predict corrections. A simpler alternative is to use $n$-gram language model scores. Rozovskaya and Roth (2011) reported that classifiers outperformed a language modeling approach. Here, we report a more nuanced result: a classifier approach yielded results with higher precision while a language modeling approach provided better recall. Most importantly, we found that a combined approach using a logistic regression ensemble outperformed both a classifier and a language modeling approach.


## 1   Introduction

In this paper, we compare methods for correcting grammatical errors. Much of the previous work on grammatical error detection and correction has studied methods based on statistical classifiers (Tetreault and Chodorow, 2008; De Felice and Pulman, 2009; Tetreault et al., 2010; Rozovskaya and Roth, 2010; Dahlmeier and Ng, 2011; Seo et al., 2012; Cahill et al., 2013). In particular, Tetreault and Chodorow (2008) and Tetreault et al. (2010) found that classifiers based on a variety of contextual linguistic features performed well, especially in terms of precision (i.e., avoiding false positives). Gamon (2010), however, reported that a language modeling approach substantially outperformed a classifier using contextual features. Finally, Rozovskaya and Roth (2011) found that a classifier outperformed a language modeling approach on different data, making it unclear which approach is best.

Much of the previous work has used well-formed text when training contextual classifiers due to the lack of large error-annotated corpora. Han et al. (2010) conducted experiments with a relatively small error-annotated corpus and showed that it outperformed a contextual classifier trained on well-edited text. More recently, Cahill et al. (2013) mined Wikipedia revisions to produce a large, publicly available error-annotated corpus and reported similar results on multiple, publicly available data sets.

Our goal in this paper is *not* to build a state-of-the-art system but rather to investigate the following research questions:

- Does a contextual classifier trained on error-annotated data outperform a language modeling approach?

- Can a classifier trained on error-annotated data and the language modeling approach be effectively combined?

With respect to the second question, Gamon (2010) previously reported that a combination of a contextual classifier trained on well-edited text and a language modeling approach outperformed each individual method. However, given that the performance of his classifier was lower than what has been reported on other datasets (Tetreault and Chodorow, 2008; Rozovskaya and Roth, 2011), we believe it is worth reinvestigating the merits of system combination but with publicly available data sets and with a classifier trained on error-annotated data instead of on well-edited text. This work differs from Susanto et al. (2014) in that we are interested in combining statistical models in order to more accurately correct individual preposition errors, while their work

---

[*]Michael Heilman is now a data scientist at Civis Analytics.




*Proceedings of the 11th Workshop on Innovative Use of NLP for Building Educational Applications*, pages 136–141,
San Diego, California, June 16, 2016. ©2016 Association for Computational Linguistics

combined — at the sentence level — the outputs of multiple systems designed to correct *different types* of grammatical errors.

## 2 Task Description

In this paper, we focus on the task of detecting and correcting preposition selection errors in English writing — that is, errors where the writer selects the incorrect preposition for a given context. We consider 36 different prepositions (§3.1).

### 2.1 Evaluation Datasets

We use two data sets for evalution: (a) The CLC **FCE** dataset, which contains exam scripts written by English language learners for the Cambridge ESOL First Certificate in English (Yannakoudakis et al., 2011), with 20% held out for development, and (b) The **HOO** 2011 shared task data set, which contains excerpts of ACL papers manually annotated for grammatical errors (Dale and Kilgarriff, 2011). No HOO data was used for development.

### 2.2 Metrics

To evaluate performance, we compute precision, recall, and $F_1$ score for each dataset. Precision is the percentage of system corrections that are correct according to the gold standard, and recall is the percentage of the gold standard corrections that were correctly marked by the system. Our evaluation metric can be viewed as similar to a micro-averaged $F_1$ score for a multi-class document classification task where documents are the original prepositions, classes are the possible corrections, and only documents for ungrammatical prepositions have class labels. Our $F_1$ score is similar to the WAS evaluation scheme of Chodorow et al. (2012), except that we treat cases where the original preposition, system prediction, and gold standard all differ as false negatives. Chodorow et al. (2012) instead treat such cases as both false positives and false negatives, and as a result, the sum of true positives, false positives, true negatives, and false negatives does not equal the number of examples.

## 3 Methods

This section describes our implementations of the classifier, language modeling, and system combina-

tion approaches to preposition error correction.

### 3.1 Classifier

Our first system is a classifier trained on error-annotated data, following Cahill et al. (2013). The classifier uses logistic regression to solve a 36-way classification problem with one class per preposition (Tetreault and Chodorow, 2008). It includes 25 lexical and syntactic contextual features. It also includes a feature indicating the writer's original preposition. The classifier learns a conditional probability distribution $p_{CLS}(w|x)$ over prepositions $w$ given the context $x$ in which they appear.

To train this classifier, we used the preposition error corpus mined from revisions in an XML snapshot of Wikipedia (Cahill et al., 2013). The snapshot contained 8,735,890 articles and 288,583,063 revisions. The resulting data set consists of 7,125,317 prepositions and their sentence contexts. Of these prepositions, 1,027,643 were marked as errors and annotated with corrections.

We include a threshold parameter $\lambda_{CLS}$, tuned to maximize $F_1$ score on the development set. Let $w_{orig}$ be the writer's preposition, let $Q$ be the set of prepositions, and let $w_{alt} = \text{argmax}_{y \in Q - \{w_{orig}\}} p_{CLS}(y|x)$ (i.e., the best alternative that differs from the original). If $p_{CLS}(w_{alt}) - p_{CLS}(w_{orig}) > \lambda_{CLS}$, then the alternative is predicted (i.e., a correction is made). Otherwise, no change is made. We explored values ranging from 0 to 1, with steps of size .001.

### 3.2 Language Model

Our second system uses a language modeling approach. We use KenLM (Heafield, 2011) to estimate an unpruned model for $n = 6$ with modified Kneser-Ney smoothing (Chen and Goodman, 1998) on the text of all articles contained in a snapshot of English Wikipedia from June 2012 (68,356,743 sentences). We use this $n$-gram language model to obtain scores $g_{LM}(w, s, i) = \frac{\log_{10} p_{LM}(f(w,s,i))}{|s|+1}$, where $w$ is the preposition to be scored, $s$ is the writer's original sentence, $i$ is the position of the original preposition in $s$, $f$ is a function that returns a variant of $s$ with the preposition at $i$ replaced with $w$, and $p_{LM}$ returns the probability for a sentence. We divide the language model log probability by $|s| + 1$, where $|s|$ is the number of tokens in the sentence, to account for differences in sentence lengths.[1]

Again, we include a threshold $\lambda_{LM}$ for deciding whether to replace the writer's original preposition with the best alternative preposition. This works similarly, except that it works with differences in the language model scores $g_{LM}$ rather than differences in probabilities. We explored a grid with 45 manually selected points obtained by examining the percentiles for $g_{LM}$ on the development set.[2]

### 3.3  System Combinations

We examine three methods for combining the language modeling and classifier approaches.

### 3.3.1  Heuristic

The first method is a simple heuristic combination intended to increase the recall of the classifier approach. We first tune the $\lambda_{CLS}$ and $\lambda_{LM}$ thresholds individually for the classifier and language model approaches to optimize $F_1$ score, as described above. Then, if the classifier predicts a correction, we return that as the final correction. If the classifier did not predict a correction but the language model did, then we return the language model's suggested correction. If neither predicts a correction, then we return the original preposition.

### 3.3.2  Interpolation

The second method combines the scores from the classifier and the language model, finds the best alternative to the original (i.e., a potential correction), and then applies a threshold to decide whether or not to make the correction.

Let $g_{LM}(w, s, i)$ be the language model score (§3.2) for the sentence $s$ containing the preposition of interest $w$ at position $i$, and let $g_{CLS}(w, s, i) = \log_{10} p_{CLS}(w|f_{CLS}(s, i))$, computed using the classifier, where $f_{CLS}$ is a function that returns the contextual features for the classifier.[3]

For each original preposition $w_{orig}$, this method computes the difference between its classifier or language model score and the corresponding score for each alternative preposition $w_{alt}$:

$$\Delta_{CLS}(w_{orig}, w_{alt}, s, i) = g_{CLS}(w_{alt}, s, i)$$
$$- g_{CLS}(w_{orig}, s, i)$$
$$\Delta_{LM}(w_{orig}, w_{alt}, s, i) = g_{LM}(w_{alt}, s, i)$$
$$- g_{LM}(w_{orig}, s, i)$$

The method then computes an interpolated score for each alternative preposition as follows:

$$g_{INT}(w_{orig}, w_{alt}, s, i) =$$
$$\alpha * \Delta_{CLS}(w_{orig}, w_{alt}, s, i)$$
$$+ (1 - \alpha) * \Delta_{LM}(w_{orig}, w_{alt}, s, i)$$

It then finds the best alternative $\hat{w}_{INT}$ to the writer's original preposition $w_{orig}$ based on that score, i.e.,

$$\hat{w}_{INT} = \arg\max_{w_{alt}} g_{INT}(w_{orig}, w_{alt}, s, i),$$

and then predicts it as the final correction if $g_{INT}(w_{orig}, \hat{w}_{INT}, s, i) > \lambda_{INT}$. The interpolation parameter $\alpha$ and the threshold parameter $\lambda_{INT}$ are tuned to maximize $F_1$ on the development set, with a search grid for $\alpha$ and $\lambda_{INT}$ ranging from 0 to 1 with steps of size .01.

### 3.3.3  Ensemble Classifier

Finally, we evaluate an ensemble that uses scores from the classifier and language model as features.

Specifically, we use a logistic regression classifier to make binary predictions about whether or not to accept potential corrections from the revision classifier (§3.1). We give priority to the classifier since it had higher precision on the development set. Given an original preposition $w_{orig}$ in a sentence $s$ at position $i$, with $\hat{w}_{CLS}$ being the best alternative according to the revision classifier, the following features are considered by the logistic regression:

- binary features for each of the 36 possible values of the writer's original preposition. The feature for $w_{orig}$ is set to 1, and the rest are set to 0.

- binary features for each of the 36 possible values of the best alternative to the writer's original preposition, according to the revision classifier. The feature for $\hat{w}_{CLS}$ is set to 1, and the rest are set to 0.

---

[1]Our language modeling approach differs from that of Rozovskaya and Roth (2011). We use a language model to compute probabilities for whole sentences, whereas they use one to derive feature weights for contexts around the writer's original preposition, which are used in a separate model.

[2]We also evaluated language models for $n=3, 4, 5$ on the development set, but we do not include them here since their performance was not as good as the 6-gram model.

[3]We take the logarithm of the classifier probability here to put it on a similar scale to the language model score.

- $\Delta_{CLS}(w_{orig}, \hat{w}_{CLS}, s, i)$ (see §3.3.2)

- $\Delta_{LM}(w_{orig}, \hat{w}_{CLS}, s, i)$

Once trained, we obtain the probability of making a change for any given preposition $p(\text{change} = 1 | w_{orig}, s, i)$ according to the logistic regression. We output $\hat{w}_{CLS}$ as the final prediction if $p(\text{change} = 1 | w_{orig}, s, i) > \lambda_{ENS}$.

To tune $\lambda_{ENS}$, we use a procedure based on 10-fold cross-validation to obtain probabilities for the development set. Each fold (i.e., tenth) of the development set is iteratively held out, and the ensemble is trained on the remaining folds. The ensemble is then used to obtain probabilities of corrections for the examples in the held-out fold. Once we have probabilities for the whole set, we tune $\lambda_{ENS}$ to maximize $F_1$ score, using a search grid ranging from 0 to 1 with steps of .001.

## 4 Results

Figure 1 shows the development set precision-recall curves for the revision classifier, the language modeling approach, the interpolation approach, and the ensemble approach. The heuristic approach is shown as a single point in the figure since there is no threshold to tune. For each curve, the figure also shows the point corresponding to the threshold that yields the optimal $F_1$ score. From these results, all system combination approaches seem useful for combining the outputs of the classifier and language model to balance precision and recall. The ensemble appears particularly effective: the ensemble system's precision is generally higher than the classifier and language model systems at the same levels of recall, and the ensemble's recall is generally higher at the same levels of precision.

Table 1 shows the performance of all methods on the FCE and HOO test sets. Note that to apply the ensemble method to a test set, we trained the ensemble on the entire development set and then computed probabilities of corrections for the test set instances. We observe the following:

1. For both the FCE and the HOO test sets, the classifier approach yields results with higher precision whereas language model approach provides better recall.

2. For the FCE test set, we find that the ensemble approach attains the best $F_1$ score and that it

| Dataset | System | P | R | $F_1$ | Sig. |
|---|---|---|---|---|---|
| FCE | Classifier | **65.63** | 17.77 | 27.97 | * |
| | LM | 28.42 | 30.39 | 29.37 | * |
| | Heuristic | 30.91 | 37.26 | 33.79 | * |
| | Interpolation | 50.67 | 36.30 | 42.30 | * |
| | Ensemble | 51.72 | **38.35** | **44.04** | |
| HOO | Classifier | **59.26** | 19.75 | 29.63 | |
| | LM | 12.90 | 14.81 | 13.79 | * |
| | Heuristic | 21.24 | 29.63 | 24.74 | * |
| | Interpolation | 34.29 | 29.63 | 31.79 | |
| | Ensemble | 32.93 | **33.33** | **33.13** | |

**Table 1:** P, R and $F_1$ scores for the FCE and HOO test sets. Bold indicates the best result for each metric. "*" indicates that the $F_1$ score for a system was significantly different ($p < .05$) from that of the ensemble system as per the $BC_a$ Bootstrap (Efron and Tibshirani, 1993) test with 10,000 replications.

performs significantly better than all other approaches, including both the classifier and the language model.

3. For the HOO test set — which is quite different from the FCE data in both its genre (ACL papers) and the distribution of grammatical errors — the ensemble approach still attains the best performance and is significantly better than the language model and the heuristic system combination approach.

Finally, we also compared the ensemble approach to a current state-of-the-art preposition error correction system. To do this, we evaluated on the CoNLL 2013 shared task test set (Ng et al., 2013), which contains essays written by students at the National University of Singapore and manually annotated with grammatical errors. We use the "revised" version of the annotations that includes revisions submitted by participants after the initial evaluation and only evaluate preposition selection errors. We did not use any of this data for development. We compared our ensemble system to the system submitted by the team that performed best on preposition errors ("NAIST, PC"). Our ensemble obtained $F_1 = 14.24$, whereas the NAIST system obtained $F_1 = 7.56$. This difference is statistically significant ($p < 0.05$).

Note that these results are not directly comparable with the official results of the preposition error correction component of the CoNLL shared task. First, we only measured the performance of the two systems on preposition selection errors since our system is

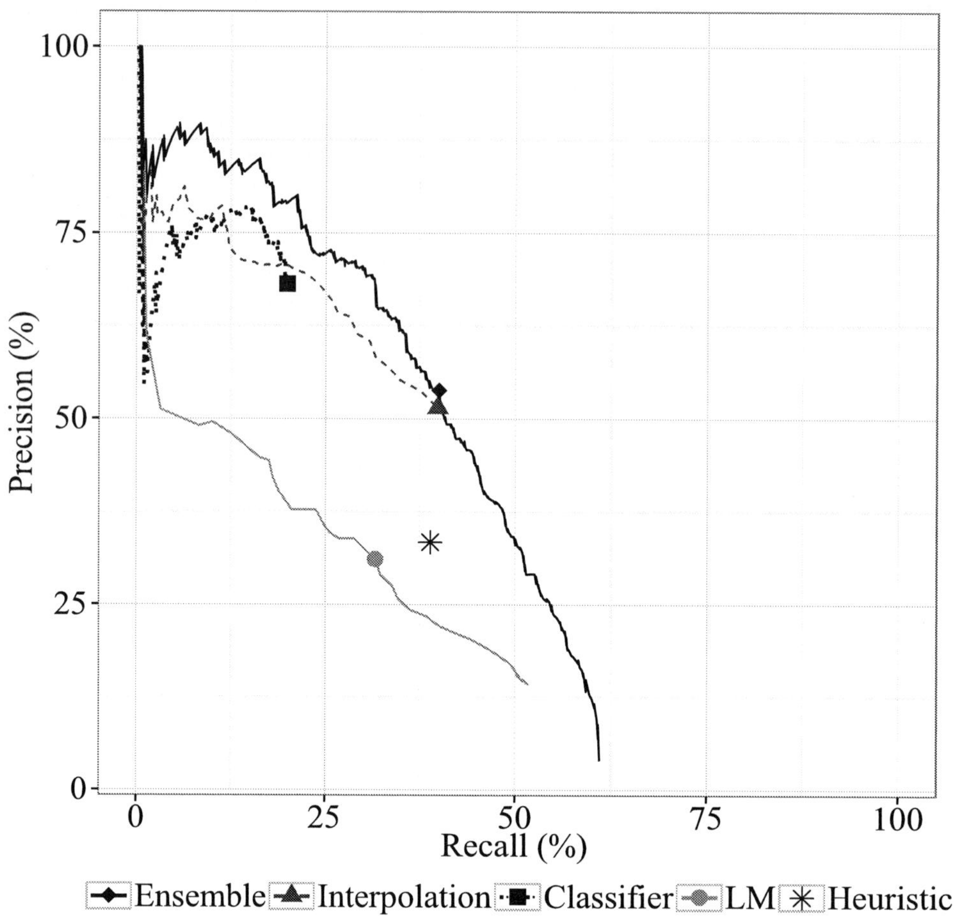



**Figure 1:** P and R values for the development set. Curves indicate performance at various values for the threshold $\lambda$ for making a correction. Corresponding shaped dots indicate points at which $F_1$ is highest for each method.

not designed to correct either extraneous or missing preposition errors. Secondly, the F1 results on the CoNLL shared task used estimated types for computing precision, while were were certain of our error type. It is also not possible to compare to the published results on the HOO 2012 shared task (Dale et al., 2012) which used CLC-FCE data, because results for the three types of preposition errors were combined in one overall score.

## 5   Conclusions

Our goal in this paper was *not* to build a state-of-the-art preposition error correction system but rather to re-examine how well a simple language modeling approach performs on the task of correcting preposition selection errors, compared to the more typical approach that uses a classifier trained on a large error-annotated corpus (Cahill et al., 2013). We found that a language model does not generally perform as well as a classifier in terms of $F_1$, similar to a previous finding from Rozovskaya and Roth (2011). In addition, we also found that while the classifier has higher precision, the language model yields higher recall.

We also examined several methods for combining the classification and the language modeling approaches and found that a logistic regression ensemble is particularly effective. This ensemble significantly outperformed both the classifier and language modeling approaches on two publicly available test sets which indicates that more hybrid approaches should be investigated for grammatical error correction.

## Acknowledgments

We would like to thank Lyle Ungar for his original suggestion, Kenneth Heafield for help with KenLM, Lei Chen, Anastassia Loukina, and the BEA reviewers.

## References

Aoife Cahill, Nitin Madnani, Joel Tetreault, and Diane Napolitano. 2013. Robust systems for preposition error correction using wikipedia revisions. In *Proceedings of NAACL*, pages 507–517.

Stanley F. Chen and Joshua Goodman. 1998. An Empirical Study of Smoothing Techniques for Language Modeling. Technical Report TR-10-98, Harvard University.

Martin Chodorow, Markus Dickinson, Ross Israel, and Joel Tetreault. 2012. Problems in Evaluating Grammatical Error Detection Systems. In *Proceedings of COLING 2012*, pages 611–628.

Daniel Dahlmeier and Hwee Tou Ng. 2011. Grammatical Error Correction with Alternating Structure Optimization. In *Proceedings of ACL*, pages 915–923.

Robert Dale and Adam Kilgarriff. 2011. Helping Our Own: The HOO 2011 Pilot Shared Task. In *Proceedings of the Generation Challenges Session at the 13th European Workshop on Natural Language Generation*, pages 242–249.

Robert Dale, Ilya Anisimoff, and George Narroway. 2012. Hoo 2012: A report on the preposition and determiner error correction shared task. In *Proceedings of the Seventh Workshop on Building Educational Applications Using NLP*, pages 54–62, Montréal, Canada, June. Association for Computational Linguistics.

Rachele De Felice and Stephen G. Pulman. 2009. Automatic detection of preposition errors in learner writing. *CALICO Journal*, 26(3):512–528.

Bradley Efron and Robert J. Tibshirani. 1993. *An Introduction to the Bootstrap*. Chapman and Hall/CRC, Boca Raton, FL.

Michael Gamon. 2010. Using Mostly Native Data to Correct Errors in Learners' Writing. In *Proceedings of HLT-NAACL*, pages 163–171.

Na-Rae Han, Joel Tetreault, Soo-Hwa Lee, and Jin-Young Ha. 2010. Using Error-Annotated ESL Data to Develop an ESL Error Correction System. In *Proceedings of LREC*.

Kenneth Heafield. 2011. KenLM: faster and smaller language model queries. In *Proceedings of the EMNLP 2011 Sixth Workshop on Statistical Machine Translation*, pages 187–197.

Hwee Tou Ng, Siew Mei Wu, Yuanbin Wu, Christian Hadiwinoto, and Joel Tetreault. 2013. The CoNLL-2013 Shared Task on Grammatical Error Correction. In *Proceedings of CoNLL*.

Alla Rozovskaya and Dan Roth. 2010. Training Paradigms for Correcting Errors in Grammar and Usage. In *Proceedings of HLT-NAACL*, pages 154–162.

Alla Rozovskaya and Dan Roth. 2011. Algorithm Selection and Model Adaptation for ESL Correction Tasks. In *Proceedings of ACL: HLT*, pages 924–933.

Hongsuck Seo, Jonghoon Lee, Seokhwan Kim, Kyusong Lee, Sechun Kang, and Gary Geunbae Lee. 2012. A Meta Learning Approach to Grammatical Error Correction. In *Proceedings of ACL (Short Papers)*, pages 328–332.

Raymond Hendy Susanto, Peter Phandi, and Hwee Tou Ng. 2014. System combination for grammatical error correction. In *Proceedings of the 2014 Conference on Empirical Methods in Natural Language Processing (EMNLP)*, pages 951–962, Doha, Qatar, October. Association for Computational Linguistics.

Joel R. Tetreault and Martin Chodorow. 2008. The Ups and Downs of Preposition Error Detection in ESL Writing. In *Proceedings of COLING*, pages 865–872.

Joel Tetreault, Jennifer Foster, and Martin Chodorow. 2010. Using Parse Features for Preposition Selection and Error Detection. In *Proceedings of ACL (Short Papers)*, pages 353–358.

Helen Yannakoudakis, Ted Briscoe, and Ben Medlock. 2011. A New Dataset and Method for Automatically Grading ESOL Texts. In *Proceedings of ACL*, pages 180–189.

# Pictogrammar: an AAC device based on a semantic grammar


**Fernando Martínez-Santiago**
dofer@ujaen.es

**Arturo Montejo-Ráez**
amontejo@ujaen.es

**Miguel Ángel García-Cumbreras**
magc@ujaen.es

**Manuel Carlos Díaz-Galiano**
mcdiaz@ujaen.es

Computer Science Department
University of Jaén
Jaén, 23071, Spain



## Abstract

As many as two-thirds of individuals with an Autism Spectrum Disorder (ASD) also have language impairments, which can range from mild limitations to complete non-verbal behavior. For such cases, there are several Augmentative and Alternative Communication (AAC) devices available. These are computer-designed tools in order to help people with ASD to palliate or overcome such limitations, at least partially. Some of the most popular AAC devices are based on pictograms, so that a pictogram is the graphical representation of a simple concept and sentences are composed by concatenating a number of such pictograms. Usually, these tools have to manage a vocabulary made up of hundreds of pictograms/concepts, with no or very poor knowledge of the language at semantic and pragmatic level. In this paper we present Pictogrammar, an AAC system which takes advantage of SUpO and PictOntology. SUpO (Simple Upper Ontology) is a formal semantic ontology which is made up of detailed knowledge of facts of everyday life such as simple words, with special interest in linguistic issues, allowing automated grammatical supervision. PictOntology is an ontology developed to manage sets of pictograms, linked to SUpO. Both ontologies make possible the development of tools which are able to take advantage of a formal semantics.


## 1 Introduction

Language acquisition and comprehension is difficult for people with certain language impairments. Communications based on modern technologies could play a relevant role in helping with such processes. This papers introduces one of those potential technologies with important novelties.

Autism and autism spectrum disorders (ASD), such as Asperger syndrome, are neurodevelopmental conditions diagnosed on the basis of a triad of behavioral impairments: impaired social interaction, impaired communication and restricted and repetitive interests and activities (American Psychiatric Association, 2004). Thus, communication is severely impaired in persons with acute autism. What the individual understands (receptive language) as well as what is actually spoken by the individual (expressive language) are significantly delayed or nonexistent. Deficits in language comprehension include the inability to understand simple directions, questions or commands (Lim, 2011). Furthermore, the absence of verbal communication is common or, when present, it is often very immature: "want water" instead of "I want some water, please". Some of the most popular tools used to palliate, at least partially, severe communication impairments are the so-called Systems of Augmentative and Alternative Communication (SAAC). Augmentative and Alternative Communication (AAC) involves the study and proposal of alternative communication mechanisms and, when needed, to compensate for temporary or permanent impairments, activity limitations, and participation restrictions of individuals with severe disorders of speech-language production and/or comprehension, including spoken and written modes of communication (Beukelman and Mirenda, 2005).

Some of the most popular SAACs are based on




*Proceedings of the 11th Workshop on Innovative Use of NLP for Building Educational Applications*, pages 142–150,
San Diego, California, June 16, 2016. ©2016 Association for Computational Linguistics

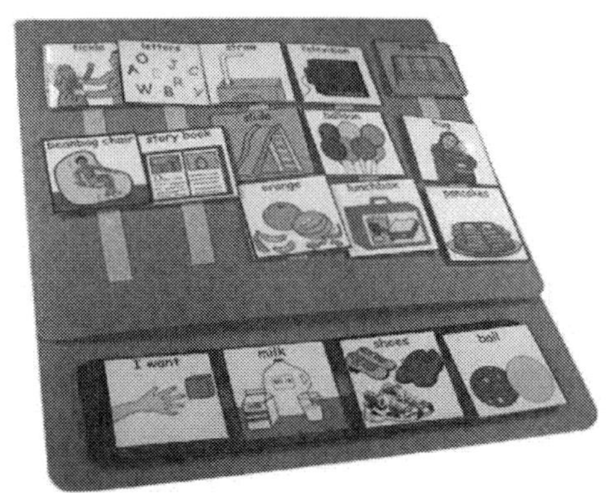

Figure 1: PECS book

Figure 2: Some examples of PECS pictograms

pictograms, such the Pictograms Exchange Communication System (PECS) (Andy and Lori, 1994; Andy and Lori, 2001) (Figures 1 and 2). Pictograms are images which are used to support text, making the meaning clearer and easier to understand. PECS is not only a SAAC, but a method for teaching young children or any individual with communication impairment a way to communicate within a social context. PECS has a very remarkable influence on development of most of SAACs based on pictograms.

In the most advanced phases, individuals are taught to answer questions and to comment. Additionally, descriptive language concepts such as size, shape, color, number, etc. are also taught so the student can make her message more specific by combining picture symbols. For example, "I want a big yellow ball" (Figure 3).

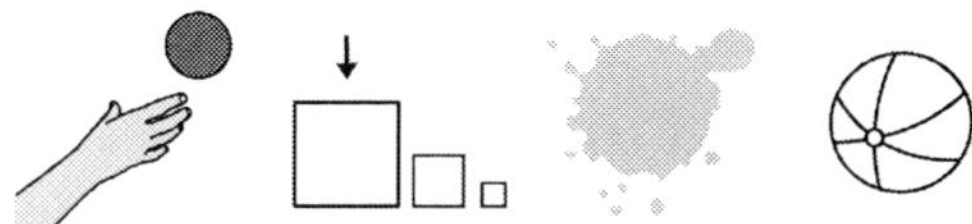

Figure 3: "I want big yellow ball" using ARASAAC pictograms

There are several communicators inspired by PECS, such as Speak4Yourself[1], ARaSuite[2], SC@UT[3], CPA[4], e-Mintza[5] or Mind-Express[6]. The pictograms are usually categorized under families of words. The way such families are defined is a bit vague and it varies across applications. For example, the pictograms in e-Mintza are sometimes categorized according to the most usual part-of-speech of the word such as verbs or adjectives, while other words are categorized based on meaning, such as food or friends. With this application, the user chooses every pictogram from the full set of pictograms available which is made up of several hundred or even thousands of pictograms in some cases.

Figure 4: A simplified diagram of the working hypothesis

The main objective of this paper is to describe Pictogrammar, a complete AAC system within a framework under the following hypothesis: an upper ontology which includes a formal representation of a

---

[1] http://speakforyourself.org

[2] http://sourceforge.net/projects/arasuite/

[3] http://scaut.ugr.es/scaut/

[4] http://prezi.com/jcpr9qcmcnr-/cpa/

[5] http://fundacionorange.es/emintza.html

[6] http://fundacionorange.es/emintza.html

controlled natural language is an adequate framework for developing therapeutic and palliative tools for severe language impairments in general, and beginning communicators in particular, which refers to those people (mainly children) learning how to communicate. This idea is depicted in a very simplified way in Figure 4.

Pictogrammar is described in section 2. Sections 3 and 4 describe both SUpO and PictOntology ontologies. Then, an overview of an ontology to manage collections of pictograms, called PictOntology, is given, along with how it works with SUpO, an ontology that models the piece of language which is supported by Pictogrammar. Section 5 provides a more detailed view of the issues regarding the integration of these ontologies into Pictogrammar. We finish with some conclusions and future work.

## 2 Pictogrammar

Pictogrammar is an AAC device that follows the scheme outlined in figure 4. It is therefore necessary to define the three components: a controlled language, the ontology to model, at a conceptual level, this language, and an authoring tool to obtain access to the ontology. In the end, this authoring tool makes communication possible. More specifically, the elements involved in the platform are described as follows:

- The controlled natural language is the piece of symbolic communication to be learned/mastered.

- The users are the student and a number of people such as language pathologists, family and caregivers. The student is the person to be introduced into symbolic communication, i.e. a beginning communicator.

- Simple Upper Ontology, SUpO, is the upper ontology, a semantic grammar with regard to the world in which it is suitable to communicate within a controlled language. This ontology is feasible because the size of the core vocabulary of the controlled language is relatively small and it is used to make straightforward assertions (Martínez-Santiago et al., 2015). PictOntology is an ontology linked to SUpO (described in section 4).

- The authoring tool is Pictogrammar, a system of Augmentative and Alternative Communication (SAAC) based on pictograms. Pictogrammar uses as input a vocabulary made up of a set of pictograms contained in PictOntology.

Since Pictogrammar is linked to an ontology with linguistic knowledge, it provides several benefits and novel issues in *message generation* (when the user "writes the message by using the pictograms) and in *message communication* (when the system "reads" what the user wrote to transmit this message to a counterpart). These are the benefits expected:

1. In message generation:

   (a) Expandable. By using ontology authoring tools, it is possible to increase the knowledge of the world as the user requires.

   (b) Predictive semantic grammar: given the construction of a sentence, the SAAC filters pictograms based on the context of the sentence.

   (c) Only syntactically correct sentences are allowed, by means of a controlled grammar where words are related to syntactic categories (`part of speech`). For instance, the pictogram related to *dog* could not be used as a verb.

   (d) Only meaningful sentences are allowed, due to syntactic correctness and topic-based relations.

   (e) Adaptive. The syntax and systems of meanings are adapted to the user's linguistic skills. For example, a given user could be ready to use articles and prepositions whereas other users could use just a few nouns.

2. In message communication:

   (a) Sentences generated using the SAAC are grammatically correct, so they are more natural. This is achieved by means of:

      i. Correction at the morphosyntactic level: genre and number concordance, or correct conjugation of verbal tenses. The more inflective the term is, the more impact this aspect produces.

ii. Compensating for syntactic deficiencies in the input, as much as possible. For example, the user omits pictograms about articles or prepositions, but in some cases the grammar could assign "default" values.

(b) It is easy to translate to other languages and means of communication.

3. A common ontology makes it possible to share knowledge about the language model that users are able to understand and produce. In this way, a teacher (usually a language therapist) uses a computer-aid system in order to improve the verbal behavior of a given student (therapeutic software).

In addition, the same student could use an augmentative and adaptive communicator (palliative software). If the language of the student is formally modeled then it is possible that both the therapeutic and palliative software share the same knowledge, creating a homogeneous learning ecosystem. For example, if the teacher is teaching the expression I want (also know as a *mand* according to Skinner (Chomsky, 1959)), then the student will have access to specific exercises for this expression and, in addition, she could use the expression in her own communicator. This is the case of Pictogrammar as a system rather than as a standalone communicator: the language therapist defines every detail of the vocabulary for every student by using a cloud-based application (an application program that functions in the cloud) that, in the end, is an authoring tool used to produce new knowledge. Meanwhile, the student learns and uses such a language by using their own Android device (smartphone or tablet) with our communication app, an authoring tool to make use of the same piece of knowledge (see Figure 5).

Some of these components are detailed in section 5 when explaining the integration of Pictogrammar, SUpO and PictOntology.

## 3 SUpO, a simple upper Ontology

SUpO (Martínez-Santiago et al., 2015) models generic and basic knowledge about the world such as the main properties and uses of everyday concepts: food, toys, places, persons, etc. On the other hand,

there are several upper ontologies available such as DOLCE (Masolo et al., 2003) (Descriptive Ontology for Linguistic and Cognitive Engineering), SUMO (Pease, 2006) (Suggested Upper Merged Ontology) or OpenCyC [7]. All of them formally define concepts of the world and are filled with axioms and rules for tasks which concern reasoning and planning, but they have no semantic detail, especially predicate-argument structure. Since one of the highlights of SUpO is the provision of support tools to improve communicative skills, this ontology has special interest in modeling the semantic level of the language. Thus, SUpO is oriented to a more suitable form for language modeling: FrameNet (Baker et al., 1998) and the Resource Grammar Library of Grammatical Framework (GF) (Ranta, 2011).

The semantic model of SUpO is an adaptation and specialization of a small piece of FrameNet, which provides the taxonomy of concepts on which SUpO is designed.

The syntactic and morphosyntactic modules are implemented with Grammatical Frameworks and Grammatical Framework Resource Grammar Library, which is available for more than 20 languages, including English and Spanish.

An important property of Grammatical Frameworks is that they are designed to support multilingual grammars, and the translation between grammars which share the same representation of meanings is automatic. From this point of view, it is possible to define PictOntology as the SUpO version whose vocabulary is concreted by means of pictograms.

## 4 PictOntology

This section is a brief description of PictOntology, a straightforward ontology to manage a collection of pictograms linked to SUpO. PictOntology is part of Pictogrammar, but it could be reused in future applications where pictograms are involved.

Pictograms provide a visual representation of a concept. We have chosen pictograms as the visual representation of every concept included in SUpO. Thus, our ontology is made up of 621 pictograms belonging to SymbolStix[8] collection. We have chosen

---

[7]available at http://sw.opencyc.org/

[8]https://www.n2y.com/products/symbolstix

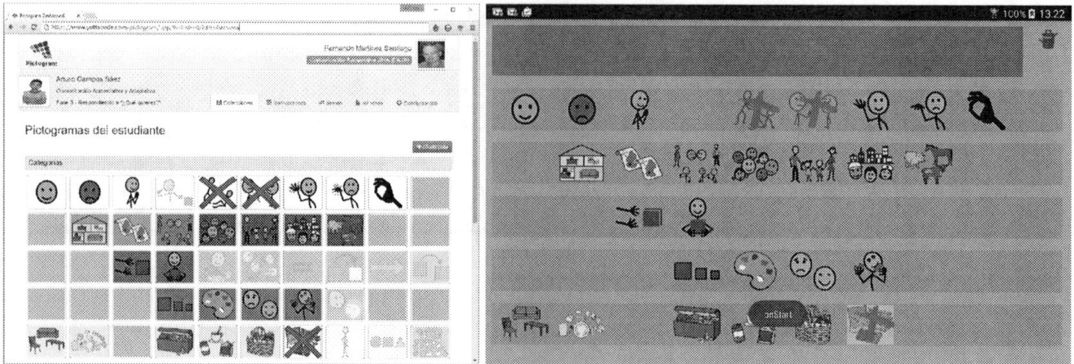

**Figure 5:** Shared vocabulary between teacher(left) and student(right).

SymbolStix because it is a comprehensive collection of symbols (about 12,000 symbols) which covers a wide range of categories such as Geography, Sports, Logos, People, Health, Technology, Food and Drink, and many others.

The construction of PictOntology is mainly an integration process with the ontology for media resources, which is a recommendation of the W3C (the Media Resource Ontology (Champin et al., 2012)). The intent of the ontology for media resources is to bridge the different descriptions of media resources, and to provide a core set of descriptive properties. It defines a core set of metadata properties for media resources, along with their mappings to elements from a set of existing metadata formats. PictOntology reuses several concepts and attributes concerning Exchangeable Image File Format (EXIF), authoring and creator. Thus, PictOntology could be defined as a specialization of the ontology for media resources where we have established additional properties and a taxonomy of the pictograms (see Table 1).

The definition of each category in PictOntology is similar to the SUMO (Niles and Pease, 2001) idea of category: a category is made up of words which are intended to be used as constituents of the same semantic role. In any case, the PictOntology definition of category is more restrictive: a PictOntology category groups together pictograms which naturally evoke multiple ideas about the same concept (the category) and, moreover, share the same part of speech. In this way, we have defined 35 different categories. Some examples are shown in Table 2. The goals behind it are:

- To simplify and make intuitive the location of every pictogram as much as possible.

- The integration of PictOntology whitin SUpO. It is possible to define PictOntology as the concretion of SUpO by using a vocabulary based on pictograms so that every PictOntology category has a one-to-one relation with a SUpO category.

- To group together similar categories, if needed. Categories are pictograms themselves, thus a category could be part of a more general category. This is useful, for example, for adapting the rendering of categories to different screen resolution (the bigger the screen, the more categories)[9].

Since PictOntology is based on Media Resource Ontology, we have formalized PictOntology in the same way that Media Resource Ontology is formalized, i.e. by using the Web Ontology Language (OWL) (Horrocks et al., 2012).

## 5 Improving communication strategies using Pictogrammar

In this section we outline some available communicative strategies by using Pictogrammar which are possible by means of both SUpO and PictOntology.

---

[9]The current version of the AAC device of Pictogrammar is optimized to be used on 7 inches displays. It makes possible to include 50 categories x 50 concepts per category approximately. It provides access up to 2500 concepts by implementing a two-click *category + concept* pattern

| Name | DataType | Description |
| --- | --- | --- |
| ma:identifier | identifier:URI, type:String | The file which contains the pictogram |
| ma:title | title:String, type:String | The English name of the pictogram. This name is usually equivalent to its expression in English. |
| ma:language | String | Usually, pictograms are language-independent but sometimes are localized for a given language or culture, e.g. calendars. |
| ma:creator | String | The creator of the resource |
| ma:contributor | identifier:URI—String, role:String | The ID of the person who added the pictogram to the ontology |
| ma:collection | URI—String | Name of the collection it belongs to |
| ma:relation | identifier:URI, relation:String | "is-a" relation between a pictogram and its category |
| pt:expressions | List of lang:String, expression: String | The textual translation of the pictogram in the group of supported languages |
| pt:level | {"transparent" "learned" "abstract"} | <ul><li>"transparent" symbols are very obvious depictions of the concepts that they illustrate.</li><li>"learned": the meaning needs to be learned. The consistent nature of learned symbols means that the concepts they represent become obvious when they are shown together.</li><li>"abstracts": symbols that have no obvious meaning when viewed on their own, and typically represent determiners or adpositions.</li></ul> |
| pt:learned_group | String | If a pictogram is learned, then it is consistent with other pictograms relative to the same concept. This label is shared for the learned pictograms relative to the same concept. For example, *in*, *on*, *under* and *behind* are all about "relative position" |
| pt:SUpO_concepts | { identifier:URI, type:List of Strings } | The ID of SUpO concepts depicted by the pictogram |

**Table 1:** Examples of properties of PictOntology

| Category | Description | Examples |
| --- | --- | --- |
| Flavours | Usual adjectives regarding food | tasty, spicy, salty, sweet |
| Moving | verbs related to movement | come, climb, dance, drive, drop, fly, follow, kick, quit, run |
| Professions | Names of well-known jobs | teacher, bus driver, doctor, nurse |

**Table 2:** Examples of categories in PictOntology

The American Speech Language Hearing Association recommends that an AAC should be thought of as a system comprising four components: *symbols, aids, strategies*, and *techniques* (American Psychiatric Association, 2004). Strategy is defined to be the way in which symbols can be conveyed most effectively and efficiently. During the writing of a sentence, Pictogrammar improves the strategy by reducing the number of pictograms that the user has available at a given moment. This makes possible the implementation of three complementary strategies: predictive grammar, Language Acquisition Motor Planning (LAMP) and Motor Planning overload.

## 5.1 Semantic predictive parser

Because of the use of a semantic grammar, the construction of phrases using Pictogrammar is supported by a predictive parser(Angelov, 2009). Note that this predictive parser is different to usual predictive text tools which are applied to the prediction of possible words when typing the first letters of the word, or the word taking into account just the grammatical role, not the semantic role. Since Pictogrammar predicts by taking into account the semantics of the phrase, the predictions are much more accurate. Moreover, the number of pictograms available while the phrase is being constructed is reduced because the user only has access to the pictograms which make sense in the sequence. For example, if a user writes "I want to eat" then Pictogrammar only shows the most popular foods, other categories of foods and properties of food. Pictogrammar knows this from the patterns and categories found in SUpO.

In addition, since semantic predictive grammar only allows her to write meaningful sentences, the user receives feedback of the correct use of language at the pragmatic level, which could be relevant from a therapeutic point of view, although we have no evidence for this at the moment.

## 5.2 Language acquisition motor planning

A usual criticism of AAC systems based on pictograms is the high number of pictograms required as the communicative user's skills grows. Since every word has its own pictogram, the user has to spend a lot of time at first learning every pictogram, and then finding out where the pictogram is located

in the SAAC. Language Acquisition Motor Planning (LAMP) (Baker, 1982),(Halloran and Emerson, 2006) is a suitable strategy for dealing with a growing vocabulary. In short, praxis or motor planning is the planning and execution of a series of movements. Language Acquisition through Motor Planning (LAMP) is a therapeutic approach based on motor planning principles that can be reinterpreted according to our purposes as follows:

- The motor patterns used to "speak" with the SAAC must be consistent and unique, that is, the user should not have variants in the way she clicks and dives into categories in order to select the same pictogram in different situations.

- Each consistent pattern of one, two or three "clicks" on the SAAC must always result in the same term.

- These motor patterns are meant to reflect the consistent and unique motor patterns that result in the production of speech.

- The vocabulary sets in LAMP are organized to maintain consistent and unique motor patterns.

Consistent motor patterns for word selection allow the development of automaticity in communication but they are difficult to implement in a low-tech SAAC because of the number of pictograms. In such a case, consistently searching for the location of desired symbols and the placement of those individual symbols on a strip requires more motor planning and cognitive attention to the communication process.

Thus, the LAMP strategy is implemented in Pictogram as follows:

1. The predictive parser allows the user to hold a reduced number of icons on the main screen.

2. The only way to communicate with Pictogrammar are pictograms (even categories are pictograms)

3. Every PictOntology concept is associated with a unique motor pattern.

Furthermore, motor planning is usually implemented in systems which are not based on pictograms but on icons with several meanings depending on every motor pattern which the icon forms. But using pictograms which represent a concept or idea is a valuable resource if you are interested in teaching literacy (Flewitt, Nind, A Payler, 2009) (Lacey, Layton, Miller, Goldbart, A Lawson, 2007).

### 5.3 Motor planning overload

Another advantage of using motor planning by means of a predictive parser is that we are able to design more compact boards by overloading motor patterns, and this is not a minor issue because makes it possible to implement Pictogrammar for smaller screens which would make it easier to carry a device. Thanks to SUpO, it is possible to infer words which are mutually exclusive, for example apple and happy. Thus, two pictograms share the same motor pattern only if such pictograms cannot be simultaneously available. For example, two words which both represent fruits have to have necessarily different motor patterns, but if one word is about a fruit and another word is about feelings, they could share the same motor pattern since there is no way to choose between both words in a given state of the construction of a phrase. This issue is what we call motor planning overload.

## 6  Conclusion and future work

In this paper we present Pictogrammar, a SAAC based on PictOntology which has some remarkable properties from a therapeutic and palliative point of view, such as: (a) sharing of a common ontology among students, language pathologists, family and caregivers, (b) implementation of an effective predictive parser, (c) motor planning overload and (d) generation of natural language which is grammatically correct even if the input is not. We also describe PictOntology, an ontology developed to manage sets of pictograms. PictOntology is linked with SUpO, a formal semantic which is made up of detailed knowledge of facts of everyday life as simple words, with special interest in linguistic roles. In addition, it is a model of correct use of the language at the pragmatic level, since Pictogrammar only allows the user to write meaningful sentences.

As future work, we want to measure the effectiveness of this system in terms of speed of learning and size of the vocabulary acquired, evaluating the system with real users. The application this approach to other disorders regarding literacy development and oral acquisition of language is also under study. Regarding oral acquisition of language, we are encouraged in following this line since (Kasari et al., 2014) showed that speech-generating-devices improve the acquisition of oral, spontaneous, and communicative utterances in school-aged, minimally verbal children with autism.

## Acknowledgments

This work has been partially supported by the Spanish Government (grant TIN2015-65136-C2-1-R)

## References

American Psychiatric Association. 2004. Diagnostic and statistical manual of mental disorders (DSM). *Washington, DC: American psychiatric association*, pages 143–7.

B. Andy and F. Lori. 1994. The picture exchange communication system. *Focus on Autism and Other Developmental Disabilities*, 9(3):1–19.

B. Andy and F. Lori. 2001. The picture exchange communication system. *Behavior modification*, 25(5):725–744.

Krasimir Angelov. 2009. Incremental parsing with parallel multiple context-free grammars. In *Proceedings of the 12th Conference of the European Chapter of the Association for Computational Linguistics*, pages 69–76. Association for Computational Linguistics.

Collin F Baker, Charles J Fillmore, and John B Lowe. 1998. The Berkeley FrameNet project. In *Proceedings of the 17th international conference on Computational linguistics-Volume 1*, pages 86–90. Association for Computational Linguistics.

Bruce Baker. 1982. Minspeak. *Byte*, 7(9).

David Beukelman and Pat Mirenda. 2005. Augmentative and alternative communication: Supporting children and adults with complex communication needs.

Pierre-Antoine Champin, Tobias Bürger, Thierry Michel, John Strassner, WonSuk Lee, Werner Bailer, Joakim Söderberg, Florian Stegmaier, Jean-Pierre EVAIN, Véronique Malaisé, and Felix Sasaki. 2012. Ontology for media resources 1.0. W3C recommendation, W3C, February. http://www.w3.org/TR/2012/REC-mediaont-10-20120209/.

Noam Chomsky. 1959. A review of bf skinner's verbal behavior. *Language*, 35(1):26–58.

John Halloran and M Emerson. 2006. Lamp: language acquisition through motor planning. *Wooster (OH): Prentke Romich Company*.

Ian Horrocks, Markus Krötzsch, Birte Glimm, and Michael[tm] Smith. 2012. OWL 2 web ontology language conformance (second edition). W3C recommendation, W3C, December. http://www.w3.org/TR/2012/REC-owl2-conformance-20121211/.

Connie Kasari, Ann Kaiser, Kelly Goods, Jennifer Nietfeld, Pamela Mathy, Rebecca Landa, Susan Murphy, and Daniel Almirall. 2014. Communication interventions for minimally verbal children with autism: A sequential multiple assignment randomized trial. *Journal of the American Academy of Child & Adolescent Psychiatry*, 53(6):635–646.

H. A. Lim. 2011. *Developmental speech-language training through music for children with autism spectrum disorders: Theory and clinical application.* Jessica Kingsley Publishers.

F. Martínez-Santiago, M.C. Díaz-Galiano, L.A. Ureña-López, and R. Mitkov. 2015. A semantic grammar for beginning communicators. *Knowledge-Based Systems*, 86:158–172.

Claudio Masolo, Stefano Borgo, Aldo Gangemi, Nicola Guarino, Alessandro Oltramari, and Luc Schneider. 2003. *The WonderWeb Library of Foundational Ontologies Preliminary Report.*

Ian Niles and Adam Pease. 2001. Towards a standard upper ontology. In *Proceedings of the international conference on Formal Ontology in Information Systems-Volume 2001*, pages 2–9. ACM.

Adam Pease. 2006. Formal representation of concepts: The Suggested Upper Merged Ontology and its use in linguistics. In *Ontolinguistics: How Ontological Status Shapes the Linguistic Coding of Concepts*. Mouton de Gruyter, New York.

Aarne Ranta. 2011. *Grammatical framework: Programming with multilingual grammars.* CSLI Publications, Center for the Study of Language and Information.

# Detecting Context Dependence in Exercise Item Candidates Selected from Corpora

**Ildikó Pilán**
Swedish Language Bank, University of Gothenburg
Gothenburg, 405 30, Sweden
`ildiko.pilan@svenska.gu.se`



## Abstract

We explore the factors influencing the dependence of single sentences on their larger textual context in order to automatically identify candidate sentences for language learning exercises from corpora which are presentable in isolation. An in-depth investigation of this question has not been previously carried out. Understanding this aspect can contribute to a more efficient selection of candidate sentences which, besides reducing the time required for item writing, can also ensure a higher degree of variability and authenticity. We present a set of relevant aspects collected based on the qualitative analysis of a smaller set of context-dependent corpus example sentences. Furthermore, we implemented a rule-based algorithm using these criteria which achieved an average precision of 0.76 for the identification of different issues related to context dependence. The method has also been evaluated empirically where 80% of the sentences in which our system did not detect context-dependent elements were also considered context-independent by human raters.


## 1 Introduction

Extracting single sentences from corpora with the use of Natural Language Processing (NLP) tools can be useful for a number of purposes including the detection of candidate sentences for automatic exercise generation. Such sentences are also known as *seed sentences* (Sumita et al., 2005) or *carrier sentences* (Smith et al., 2010) in the Intelligent Computer-Assisted Language Learning (ICALL) literature. Interest for the use of corpora in language learning has arisen already in the 1980s, since the increasing amount of digital text available enables learning through authentic language use (O'Keeffe et al., 2007). However, since sentences in a text form a coherent discourse, it might be the case that for the interpretation of the meaning of certain expressions in a sentence, previously mentioned information, i.e. a *context*, is required (Poesio et al., 2011). Corpus sentences whose meaning is hard to interpret are less optimal to be used as exercise items (Kilgarriff et al., 2008), however, having access to a larger linguistic context is not possible due to copy-right issues sometimes (Volodina et al., 2012).

In the followings, we explore how we can automatically assess whether a sentence previously belonging to a text can also be used as a stand-alone sentence based on the linguistic information it contains. We consider a sentence *context-dependent* if it is not meaningful in isolation due to: (i) the presence of expressions referring to textual content that is external to the sentence, or (ii) the absence of one or more elements which could only be inferred from the surrounding sentences.

Understanding the main factors giving rise to context dependence can improve the trade-off between discarding (or penalizing) sub-optimal candidates and maximizing the variety of examples and thus, their authenticity. Such a system may not only facilitate teaching professionals' work, but it can also aid the NLP community in a number of ways, e.g. evaluating automatic single-sentence summaries, detecting ill-formed sentences in machine translation output or identifying dictionary examples.

Although context dependence has been taken into

151


*Proceedings of the 11th Workshop on Innovative Use of NLP for Building Educational Applications*, pages 151–161,
San Diego, California, June 16, 2016. ©2016 Association for Computational Linguistics

consideration to some extent in previous work, we offer an in-depth investigation of this research problem. The theoretical contribution of our work is a set of criteria relevant for assessing context dependence of single sentences based on a qualitative analysis of human evaluators' comments. This is complemented with a practical contribution in the form of a rule-based system implemented using the proposed criteria which can reliably categorize corpus examples based on context dependence both when evaluated using relevant datasets and according to human raters' judgments. The current implementation of the system has been tested on Swedish data, but the criteria can be easily applied to other languages as well.

## 2   Background

### 2.1   Corpus Examples Combined with NLP for Language Learning

In a language learning scenario, corpus example sentences can be useful both as exercise items and as vocabulary examples. Previous work on exercise item generation has adopted different strategies for carrier sentence selection. In some cases, sentences are mainly required to contain a lexical item or a linguistic pattern that constitutes the target of the exercise, but context dependence is not explicitly addressed (Sumita et al., 2005; Arregik, 2011). Another alternative has been using dictionary examples as carrier sentences, e.g. from WordNet (Pino and Eskenazi, 2009). Such sentences are inherently context-independent, however, they pose some limitations on the linguistic aspects to target in the exercises. In Pilán et al. (2014) we presented and compared two algorithms for carrier sentence selection for Swedish, using both rule-based and machine learning methods. Context dependence, which had not been specifically targeted in that phase, emerged as a key issue for sub-optimal candidate sentences during an empirical evaluation.

Identifying corpus examples for illustrating lexical items is the main purpose of the GDEX (Good Dictionary Examples) algorithm (Husák, 2010; Kilgarriff et al., 2008) which has also inspired a Swedish algorithm for sentence selection (Volodina et al., 2012). GDEX incorporates a number of linguistic criteria (e.g. sentence length, vocabulary

frequency) based on which example candidates are ranked. Some of these are related to context dependence (e.g. incompleteness of sentences, presence of personal pronouns), but they are somewhat coarser-grained criteria not focusing on syntactic aspects. A system using GDEX for carrier sentence selection is described in Smith et al. (2010) who underline the importance of the well-formedness of a sentence and who determine a sufficient amount of context in terms of sentence length. Segler (2007) focuses on vocabulary example identification for language learners. Teachers' sentence selection criteria has been modeled with logistic regression, the main dimensions examined being syntactic complexity and similarity between the original context of a word and an example sentence.

### 2.2   Linguistic Aspects Influencing Context Dependence

The relationship between sentences in a text can be expressed either explicitly or implicitly, i.e. with or without specific linguistic elements requiring extra-sentential information (Mitkov, 2014). The explicit forms include words and phrases that imply structural discourse relations or are anaphoric (Webber et al., 2003). In a text, the way sentences are interconnected can convey an additional relational meaning besides the one which we can infer from the content of each sentence separately. Examples of such elements include *structural connectives*: conjunctions, subjunctions and "paired" conjunctions (Webber et al., 2003).

Another form of reference to previously mentioned information is *anaphora*. The phenomenon of anaphora consists of a word or phrase (*anaphor*) referring back to a previously mentioned entity (*antecedent*). Mitkov (2014) outlines a number of different anaphora categories based on their form and location, the most common being pronominal anaphora which has also been the focus of recent research within NLP (Poesio et al., 2011; Ng, 2010; Nilsson, 2010). A number of resources available today have noun phrase coreference annotation, such as the dataset from the SemEval-2010 Task (Recasens et al., 2010) and SUC-CORE for Swedish (Nilsson Björkenstam, 2013).

Besides the anaphora categories described in Mitkov (2014), Webber et al. (2003) argue that adverbial connectives (*discourse connectives*), e.g. *istället* 'instead', also behave anaphorically, among others because they function more similarly to anaphoric pronouns than to structural connectives. A valuable resource for developing automatic methods for handling discourse relations is the Penn Discourse Treebank (Prasad et al., 2008) containing annotations for both implicit and explicit discourse connectives. Using this resource Pitler and Nenkova (2009) present an approach based on syntactic features for distinguishing between discourse and non-discourse usage of explicit discourse connectives (e.g. *once* as a temporal connective corresponding to "as soon as" vs. the adverb meaning "formerly"). Another phenomenon connected to context dependence is *gapping* where the second mention of a linguistic element is omitted from a sentence (Poesio et al., 2011).

## 3   Datasets

Instead of creating a corpus specifically tailored for this task with gold standard labels assigned by human annotators, which can be a rather time- and resource-intensive endeavor, we explored how different types of existing data sources which contained inherently context-(in)dependent sentences could be used for our purposes.

Language learning coursebooks contain not only texts, but also single sentences in the form of exercise items, lists and language examples illustrating a lexical or a grammatical pattern. We collected sentences belonging to these two latter categories from COCTAILL (Volodina et al., 2014), a corpus of coursebooks for learners of Swedish as a second language. Most exercises contained gaps which might have misled the automatic linguistic annotation, therefore they have not been included in our dataset.

Dictionaries contain example sentences illustrating the meaning and the usage of an entry. One of the characteristics of such sentences is the absence of referring expressions which would require a larger context to be understood (Kilgarriff et al., 2008), therefore they can be considered suitable representatives of context-independent sentences. We collected instances of good dictionary example sentences from two Swedish lexical resources: SALDO

(Borin et al., 2013) and the Swedish FrameNet (SweFN) (Heppin and Gronostaj, 2012). These sentences were manually selected by lexicographers from a variety of corpora.

Sentences explicitly considered dependent on a larger context are less available due to their lack of usefulness in most application scenarios. Two previous evaluations of corpus example selection for Swedish are described in Volodina et al. (2012) and Pilán et al. (2013), we will refer to these as EVAL1 and EVAL2 respectively. In the former case, evaluators including both lexicographers and language teachers had to provide a score for the appropriateness of about 1800 corpus examples on a three-point scale. In EVAL2, about 200 corpus examples selected with two different approaches were rated by a similar group of experts based on their understandability (readability) for language learners, as well as their appropriateness as exercise items and as good dictionary examples. The data from both evaluations contained human raters' comments explicitly mentioning that certain sentences were context-dependent. We gathered these instances to create a negative sample. Since comments were optional, and context dependence was not the focus of these evaluations, the amount of sentences collected remained rather small, 92 in total. It is worth noting that this data contains spontaneously occurring mentions based on raters' intuition, rather than being labeled following a description of the phenomenon of context dependence as it would be customary in an annotation task.

The sentences from all data sources mentioned above constituted our development set. The amount of sentences per data source is presented in Table 1, where CIND indicates positive, i.e. context-independent samples, and CDEP the negative, context-dependent ones. The suffix -LL stands for sentences collected from language learning materials while -D represents dictionary examples.

| Source | Code | Nr. sent | Total |
|---|---|---|---|
| COCTAILL | CIND-LL | 1739 | |
| SALDO | CIND-D | 4305 | **8729** |
| SweFN | CIND-D | 2685 | |
| EVAL1 | CDEP | 22 | |
| EVAL2 | CDEP | 70 | **92** |

**Table 1:** Number of sentences per source.

## 4 Methodology

As the first step in developing the algorithm, we aimed at understanding the presence or absence of which linguistic elements make sentences dependent on a larger context by analyzing our negative sample. Although the number of instances in the context-independent category was considerably higher, certain linguistic characteristics of such sentences could have been connected to aspects not relevant to our task. Negative sentences on the other hand, although modest in number, were explicit examples of the target phenomenon. Information about the cultural context may also be relevant for this task, however, we only concentrated on linguistic factors which can be effectively captured with NLP tools.

We aimed at covering a wide range of potential application scenarios, therefore we developed a method that was independent of: (i) information from surrounding sentences and (ii) the exact intended use for the selected sentences. The first choice was motivated by the fact that, even though most previous related methods (see section 2.2) rely on information from neighboring sentences as well, sometimes a larger context might not be available either due to the nature of the task (e.g. output of single-sentence summarization systems) or copyright issues. Secondly, for a more generalizable approach, we aimed at assessing sentences based on whether their information content can be treated as an autonomous unit rather than according to whether they provide the appropriate amount and type of context to, for example, be solved as exercise items of a certain type. This way the method could serve as a generic basis to be tailored to specific applications which may pose additional requirements on the sentences.

Being that the amount of negative samples was rather restricted, we opted for the qualitative method of *thematic analysis* (Boyatzis, 1998; Braun and Clarke, 2006) aiming at discovering *themes*, i.e. categories, in our negative sample. Once we collected a set of context-dependent sentences, we started coding our data, in other words, manually labeling the instances with *codes*, a word or a phrase shortly describing the type of element that inhibited the interpretation of the sentence in isolation (for some examples see Table 2 on the next page). In the subsequent phases, we grouped together codes into themes, i.e. broader categories, according to their thematic similarity in a mixed deductive-inductive fashion. We started out with an initial pool of themes inspired by phenomena proposed in previous literature relevant to context dependence. Some of the codes, however, could not be placed in any of these themes. For part of these we have found a theme candidate in the literature after the pattern emerged during the code grouping phase. In other cases, in absence of an existing category matching some instances of the CDEP data, we created our own theme labels.

Besides thematic analysis, we carried out also a quantitative analysis based on the distribution of part of speech tags in both our positive and negative sample in order to identify potential differences that could support and complement the information emerged in the themes.

In the following step, we implemented a rule-based algorithm for handling context dependence using the findings from the qualitative and quantitative analyses. Since most emerged aspects could be translated into rather easily detectable linguistic clues, and a sufficiently large dataset annotated with the different context-dependent phenomena was not available for Swedish, we opted for a heuristic-based system. We applied the algorithm and observed its performance on our development data. Our primary focus was on evaluating how precisely are context-dependent elements identified in CDEP, but we complemented this also with observing the percentage of false positives for context dependence in our positive sample.

Finally, in order to test candidate selection empirically, a new set of sentences has been retrieved from different corpora. These sentences were then first given to our system for assessment, then the subset of candidates not containing context dependent elements were given to evaluators for an external validation.

| Theme | ID | Nr | Example code | Example CDEP sentence |
|---|---|---|---|---|
| Incomplete sentence | INCOMPSENT | 12 | incorrect sent. tokenization | *"piper hon och alla skrattar .* '"' she whines and everyone laughs.' |
| Implicit anaphora | IMPANAPHORA | 11 | omitted verb | *Till jul skulle hon [X].* 'For Christmas she should have [X].' |
| Pronominal anaphora | PNANAPHORA | 23 | pronoun as subject | *Eller också sitter **den** i taket.* 'Or **it** sits on the roof.' |
| Adverbial anaphora 1 (Temporal and locative) | ADVANAPHORA1 | 12 | locative adverb | ***Då** ska folk kunna lämna området .* '**Then** people can leave the area.' |
| Adverbial anaphora 2 (Discourse connectives) | ADVANAPHORA2 | 22 | adv. anaphora | *Vissa gånger sover hon inte **heller**.* 'Sometimes she does not sleep **either**.' |
| Structural connectives | STRUCTCONN | 17 | coordinating conjunction | ***Men** de pratade inte på samma ställe.* '**But** they did not talk at the same place.' |
| Answers to closed ended questions | CEQANSWER | 11 | yes/no answer | ***Ja**, men det är ju jul.* '**Yes,** but it is of course Christmas.' |
| Context-depend properties of concepts | CDPC | 8 | unusual noun-noun comb. | *Du lämnar **planen, tolvan**!* 'You leave the **field, twelve**!' |

**Table 2:** Thematic analysis results.

## 5  Data Analysis Results

### 5.1  Qualitative Results Based on Thematic Analysis

The list of themes collected during our qualitative analysis is presented in Table 2. For each theme, we provide an identifier (*ID*), the number of occurrence in the CDEP dataset (*Nr*[1]) together with an example code and an example sentence[2].

The total number of codes emerged from the data was 22, which we mapped to 8 themes. Some of the themes were related to the categories mentioned in previous literature which we described in section 2. These included pronominal anaphora (Mitkov, 2014), adverbial anaphora (Webber et al., 2003), connectives (Miltsakaki et al., 2004). Incomplete sentences (Didakowski et al., 2012) contained incorrectly tokenized sentences, titles and headings. Moreover, we distinguished three themes among different anaphoric expressions: pronominal anaphora, adverbial anaphora (with temporal and locative adverbs) and discourse connectives, i.e. adverbials expressing logical relations. Under the implicit anaphora theme we grouped different forms of gapping.

Two themes that emerged from the data during the thematic analysis were answers to closed ended questions and context-dependent properties of concepts. In the case of the former category, answers were mostly of the yes/no type. As for the latter theme, our data showed that the unexpectedness of the context of a word (especially if this is short, such as a sentence) can also play a role in whether a sentence is interpretable in isolation. Previous literature (Barsalou, 1982) defines this phenomenon as "context-dependent properties of concepts". While the "core meanings" of words are activated "independent of contextual relevance", context-dependent properties are "only activated by relevant contexts in which the word appears" (Barsalou, 1982, p. 82). In (1) we provide an example of both context-independent and context-dependent properties of the noun *tak* 'roof', from the EVAL2 data.

(1)  (a)  *Troligen berodde olyckan på all snö som låg på taket.*
'The accident probably depended on all the snow that covered the roof.'

(b)  *Fler än hundra levande kunde dras fram under taket .*
'More than a hundred [people] were pulled out from under the roof alive.'

Sentence (1b) was considered context-dependent by human raters, while (1a) was not. Being covered in snow (1a) appears a more easily interpretable property of roof without a larger context than having

---

[1] Occasionally sentences included more than one theme.

[2] Tokens relevant to each theme are in bold and [X] indicates the position of an omitted element.

something being pulled out from under it. The context that activates the context-dependent property of roof in (1b) is that the roof had collapsed, which, however, is missing from the sentence.

Finally, for 7 sentences in our CDEP data, no clear elements causing context dependence could have been clearly identified, these are omitted from Table 2, but they have been preserved in the experiments.

### 5.2 Quantitative Comparison of Positive and Negative Samples

Besides carrying out a thematic analysis, we compared our positive and negative samples also based on quantitative linguistic information in search of additional evidence for the emerged themes and to detect further aspects that could be potentially worth targeting. Overall part of speech (POS) frequency counts showed some major differences between the CDEP and CINDEP sentences. There was a tendency towards a nominal content in context-independent sentences, where 21.6% of all POS tags were nouns. However, this value was 9% lower for context-dependent sentences, which would suggest a preference for a higher density of concepts in context-independent sentences. Pronouns, on the other hand, were more frequent in context-dependent sentences (12.6% in total) than in context-independent ones (7% less frequent).

The qualitative analysis revealed that elements responsible for context dependence commonly occurred at the beginning of the sentence. Therefore, we compared the percentage of POS categories for this position in the two groups of sentences. Context-independent sentences showed a strong tendency towards having a noun in sentence-initial position, almost one fourth of the sentences fit into this category. On the other hand, only 3% of the positive examples started with a conjunction, but 16% of context-depend items belonged to this group.

## 6 An Algorithm for the Assessment of Context Dependence

Inspired by the results of the thematic analysis and the quantitative comparison described above, we implemented a heuristics-based system for the automatic detection of context dependence in single sentences. For retrieving example sentences the system uses the concordancing API of Korp (Borin et al., 2012), a corpus-query system giving access to a large amount of Swedish corpora. All corpora were annotated for different linguistic aspects including POS tags and dependency relation tags which served as a basis for the implementation. The system scores each sentence based on the amount of phenomena detected that match an implemented context dependence theme. Users can decide whether to *filter*, i.e. discard sentences that contain any element indicating context dependence. Alternatively, sentences can be *ranked* according to the amount of context-dependent issues detected: sentences without any such elements are ranked highest, followed by instances minimizing these aspects. All themes have an equal weight of 1 when computing the final ranking score, except for pronominal anaphora in which case, if pronouns have antecedent candidates, the weight is reduced to 0.5. In the followings, we provide a detailed description of the implementation of the themes listed in Table 2.

**Incomplete sentence.** To detect incomplete sentences the algorithm scans instances for the presence of an identified dependency root, the absence of which is considered to cause context dependence. Moreover, orthographic clues denoting sentence beginning and end are inspected. Sentence beginnings are checked for the presence of a capital letter optionally preceded by a parenthesis, quotation mark or a dash, frequent in dialogues. Sentences beginning with a digit are also permitted. Sentence end is checked for the presence of major sentence delimiters (e.g. period, exclamation mark).

**Implicit anaphora.** Candidate sentences are checked for gapping, in other words, omitted elements. Our system categorizes as gapped (elliptic) a sentence which either lacks a finite verb or a subject. Finite verbs are all verbs that are not infinite, supine or participle. Modal verbs are considered finite in case they form a verb group with another verb. Subjects include also logical subjects, and in the case of a verb in imperative mode, no subject is required.

**Explicit pronominal anaphora.** We considered in this category the third person singular pronouns *den* 'it' (common gender) and *det* 'it' (neuter gender) as well as demonstrative pronouns (e.g. *denna* 'this', *sådan* 'such' etc.). We did not include here the animate third person pronouns *han* 'he' and *hon* 'she' since corpus-based evidence suggests that these are often used in isolated sentences in coursebooks (Scherrer and Lindemalm, 2007) as well as in conversation (Mitkov, 2014). Similarly to the English pronoun *it*, the Swedish equivalent *det* can also be used non-anaphorically in expositions, clefts and expressions describing a local situation, such as time and weather (Holmes and Hinchliffe, 2003; Li et al., 2009; Gundel et al., 2005) as the examples in (2) show.

(2)    (a)  *det* with weather-related verbs
            *Det regnar.*
            'It is raining.'
    (b)  Cleft
            *Det är sommaren (som) jag älskar.*
            'It is the summer (that) I like.'
    (c)  Exposition
            *Det är viktigt att du kommer.*
            'It is important that you come.'

Our system treats as non-anaphoric the pronoun *det* if it is expletive (pleonastic) syntactically according to the output of the dependency parser which covers expositions and clefts. To handle cases like (2a), weather-related verbs have been collected from lexical resources. The list currently comprises 14 items. First, verbs related to the class *Weather* in the Simple+ lexicon (Kokkinakis et al., 2000) have been collected. Then for each of these, the child nodes from the SALDO lexicon have been added. Finally, the list has been complemented with a few manual additions.

For potentially anaphoric pronouns, the system tries to identify antecedent candidates in a similar way to the robust pronoun resolution algorithm proposed in Mitkov (1998). We count proper names and nouns occurring with the same gender and number to the left of the anaphora. This is complemented with an infinitive marker headed by a verb as potential candidate for *det*. Since certain types of information useful for antecedent disambiguation were not available through our annotation pipeline or lexical resources for Swedish (e.g. gender for named entities, animacy), the final step for scoring and choosing candidates is not applied in this initial version of the algorithm. Lastly, pronouns followed by a relative clause introduced by *som* 'which' were considered non-anaphoric.

**Explicit adverbial anaphora.** Adverbs emerged as an undesirable category during both EVAL1 and EVAL2. However, a deeper analysis of our development data revealed that not all adverbs have equal weight when determining the suitability of a sentence. Some are more anaphoric then others. We collected a list of anaphoric adverbs based on Teleman et al. (1999). Certain time and place adverbials, also referred to as demonstrative pronominal adverbs (Webber et al., 2003) are used anaphorically (e.g. *där* 'there', *då* 'then'). Sentences containing these adverbs are considered context-independent only when: (i) they are the head of an adverbial of the same type that further specifies them, e.g. *där på landet* 'there on the countryside'; (ii) they appear with a determiner, which in Swedish builds up a demonstrative pronoun, e.g. *det där huset* 'that house'.

**Discourse connectives.** Discourse connectives, i.e. adverbs expressing logical relations, fall usually into the syntactic category of conjunctional adverbials in the dependency parser output. Several conjunctional adverbials appear in the context-dependent sentences from EVAL1 and EVAL2. Our system categorizes a sentence containing a conjuctional adverb context-independent when a sentence contains: (i) at least 2 coordinate clauses; (ii) coordination or subordination at the same dependency depth or a level higher, that is, a sibling node that is either a conjunction or a subjunction.

**Structural connectives.** Sentences with conjunctions as dependency roots are considered context-dependent unless they are paired conjunctions with both elements included (e.g. *antingen … eller* 'either … or'). Conjunctions in sentence initial position are also treated as an indication of context dependence except when there are at least two clauses or conjuncts in the sentence.

**Answers to closed ended questions.** To identify sentences that are answers to closed ended questions, the algorithm tries to match POS-tag patterns of sentence-initial interjections (e.g. *ja* 'yes', *nej* 'no') and adverbs surrounded by minor delimiters (e.g. dash), the initial delimiter being optional in the case of interjections.

**Context-dependent properties of concepts.** Apart from the theme implementations described above, we are currently investigating the usefulness of word co-occurrence information for this theme. The corpus query tool Korp for instance offers an API providing mutual information scores. The intuition behind this idea is that the frequency of words appearing together is positively correlated with the unexpectedness of the association between them.

## 7 Performance on the Datasets

We evaluated our system both on the hand-coded negative example sentences collected from EVAL1 and EVAL2 (CDEP) and the positive samples comprised of the good dictionary examples (CINDEP-D) and the coursebook sentences (CINDEP-LL). The performance when predicting different aspects of context dependence is presented in Table 3.

| Theme | Precision | Recall | F1 |
|---|---|---|---|
| INCOMPSENT | 0.75 | 0.5 | 0.6 |
| IMPANAPHORA | 0.33 | 0.36 | 0.35 |
| PNANAPHORA | 0.75 | 0.78 | 0.77 |
| ADVANAPHORA1 | 0.91 | 0.83 | 0.87 |
| ADVANAPHORA2 | 0.87 | 0.59 | 0.70 |
| STRUCTCONN | 0.7 | 0.82 | 0.76 |
| CEQANSWER | 1.0 | 0.55 | 0.71 |
| Average | **0.76** | 0.63 | 0.60 |

**Table 3:** Theme prediction performance in CDEP sentences.

We focused on maximizing precision, i.e. on correctly identifying as many themes as possible in the hand-coded CDEP sentences, recall values were of lower importance since we aimed at avoiding every context-dependent sentence rather than retrieving them all. Most themes were correctly identified, all themes except one was predicted with a precision of at least 0.7 and above. The only theme that yielded a lower result was that of implicit anaphoras. The error analysis revealed that these cases were mostly connected to an incorrect dependency parse of the sentences, mainly subjects tagged as objects in sentences with an inverted (predicate-subject) word order.

As mentioned previously, we strived for minimizing sub-optimal sentences in terms of context dependence, while trying to avoid being excessively selective to maintain a varied set of examples. To assess performance with respect to this latter aspect, we inspected also the percentage of sentences identified as context-dependent in dictionary examples (CIND-D) and coursebook sentences (CIND-LL). The percentage of predicted themes per dataset is shown in Table 4 where *Total* stands for the percentage of sentences with at least one predicted theme.

| Theme | CIND-D | CIND-LL |
|---|---|---|
| IncompSent | 2.37 | 3.39 |
| ImpAnaphora | 4.61 | 5.80 |
| PNAnaphora | 9.39 | 11.0 |
| AdvAnaphora1 | 3.59 | 2.93 |
| AdvAnaphora2 | 9.95 | 3.74 |
| StructConn | 3.70 | 0.92 |
| CEQAnswer | 0.37 | 2.59 |
| Total | 33.35 | 26.74 |

**Table 4:** Percentage of sentences with a predicted theme in the CIND datasets.

We can observe that even though all sentences are expected to be context-independent, our system labeled as context-dependent about three out of ten good dictionary examples and coursebook sentences. The error analysis revealed that some of these instances did indeed contain context-dependent elements, e.g. the conjunction *men* 'but' in sentence-initial position. In CIND-LL in the case of some sentences containing anaphoric pronouns an image provided the missing context in the coursebook, thus not all predicted cases were actual false positives, but rather, they indicated some noise in the data. As for dictionary examples, the presence of such sentences may also suggest that the criterion of context dependence can vary somewhat depending on the type of lexicon or lexicographers' individual decisions.

Some sentences exhibited more than one phenomenon connected to context dependence. Multiple themes were predicted in 30.43% of the CDEP sentences, but only 6.54% and 7.25 of the CIND-D and CIND-LL sentences respectively.

## 8   User-based Evaluation Results

The algorithm was tested also empirically during an evaluation of automatic candidate sentence selection for the purposes of learning Swedish as a second language. The evaluation data consisted of 338[3] sentences retrieved from a variety of modern Swedish corpora and classified as not containing context dependence themes according to our algorithm (with the exception of 4 control sentences that were context-dependent). These were all unseen sentences not present in the datasets described in section 3. In the evaluation setup, all implemented themes were used as filters, i.e. sentences containing any recognized element connected to context dependence, described in section 6, were discarded. Besides context dependence, the evaluated system incorporated also other selection criteria (e.g. readability), but for reasons of relevance and space these aspects and the associated results are not discussed here.

The selected sentences were given for evaluation to 5 language teachers who assessed the suitability of these sentences based on 3 criteria: (i) their degree of being independent of context, (ii) their CEFR[4] level and (iii) their overall suitability for language learners. Teachers were required to assess this latter aspect without a specific exercise type in mind, but considering a learner reading the sentence instead. Sentences were divided into two subsets, each being rated by at least 2 evaluators. Teachers had to assign a score between 1 to 4 to each sentence according to the scale definition in Table 5.

| | The sentence... |
|---|---|
| 1 | ... doesn't satisfy the criterion. |
| 2 | ... satisfies the criterion to a smaller extent. |
| 3 | ... satisfies the criterion to a larger extent. |
| 4 | ... satisfies the criterion entirely. |

**Table 5:** Evaluation scale.

The results were promising, the average score

over all evaluators and sentences for context independence was 3.05, and for overall suitability 3.23. For context-independence, 61% of the sentences received score 3 or 4 (completely satisfying the criterion) from at least half of the evaluators, and 80% of the sentences received an average score higher than 2.5. This latter improves significantly on the percentage of context-dependent sentences that we reported previously in Pilán et al. (2013), where about 36% of all selected sentences were explicitly considered context-dependent by evaluators.

Furthermore, we computed the Spearman correlation coefficient for teachers' scores of overall suitability and context dependence to gain insight into how strongly associated these two aspects were according to our evaluation data. The correlation over all sentences was $\rho$=0.53, which indicates that not being context-dependent is positively associated with overall suitability. Therefore, context dependence is worth targeting when selecting carrier sentences.

## 9   Conclusion and Future Work

We described a number of criteria that influence context dependence in corpus examples when presented in isolation. Based on the thematic analysis of a set of context-dependent sentences, we implemented a rule-based algorithm for the automatic assessment of this aspect which has been evaluated not only on our datasets but also with the help of language teachers with very positive results.

About 76% of themes were correctly identified in context-dependent sentences, while the amount of false positives in the context-independent data was maintained rather low. Approximately 80% of candidate sentences selected with a system incorporating the presented algorithm were deemed context-independent in our user-based evaluation. The results also showed a positive correlation between sentences being context-independent and overall suitable for language learners.

In the future, we are planning to explore the extension of the algorithm to other languages as well as to experiment with machine learning approaches for this task using, among others, the resources mentioned in this paper.

---

[3]We excluded 8 sentences with incomplete evaluator scores during the calculation of the results.

[4]The Common European Framework of Reference for Languages (CEFR) is a scale describing proficiency levels for second language learning (Council of Europe, 2001).

## References

Itziar Aldabe Arregik. 2011. *Automatic Exercise Generation Based on Corpora and Natural Language Processing Techniques*. Ph.D. thesis, Universidad del País Vasco.

Lawrence W Barsalou. 1982. Context-independent and context-dependent information in concepts. *Memory & Cognition*, 10(1):82–93.

Lars Borin, Markus Forsberg, and Johan Roxendal. 2012. Korp-the corpus infrastructure of Språkbanken. In *Proceedings of LREC*, pages 474–478.

Lars Borin, Markus Forsberg, and Lennart Lönngren. 2013. SALDO: a touch of yin to WordNet's yang. *Language Resources and Evaluation*, 47(4):1191–1211.

Richard Eleftherios Boyatzis. 1998. *Transforming qualitative information: Thematic analysis and code development*. Sage.

Virginia Braun and Victoria Clarke. 2006. Using thematic analysis in psychology. *Qualitative research in psychology*, 3(2):77–101.

Council of Europe. 2001. *Common European Framework of Reference for Languages: Learning, Teaching, Assessment*. Press Syndicate of the University of Cambridge.

Jörg Didakowski, Lothar Lemnitzer, and Alexander Geyken. 2012. Automatic example sentence extraction for a contemporary German dictionary. In *Proceedings EURALEX*, pages 343–349.

Jeanette K Gundel, Nancy Hedberg, and Ron Zacharski. 2005. Pronouns without explicit antecedents: how do we know when a pronoun is referential. *Anaphora processing: linguistic, cognitive and computational modelling*, pages 351–364.

Karin Friberg Heppin and Maria Toporowska Gronostaj. 2012. The Rocky Road towards a Swedish FrameNet-Creating SweFN. In *Proceedings of LREC*, pages 256–261.

Philip Holmes and Ian Hinchliffe. 2003. *Swedish: A comprehensive grammar*. Psychology Press.

Miloš Husák. 2010. *Automatic retrieval of good dictionary examples*. Bachelor Thesis, Brno.

Adam Kilgarriff, Miloš Husák, Katy McAdam, Michael Rundell, and Pavel Rychlỳ. 2008. GDEX: Automatically finding good dictionary examples in a corpus. In *Proceedings of Euralex*.

Dimitrios Kokkinakis, Maria Toporowska-Gronostaj, and Karin Warmenius. 2000. Annotating, disambiguating & automatically extending the coverage of the Swedish SIMPLE lexicon. In *Proceedings of LREC*.

Yifan Li, Petr Musilek, Marek Reformat, and Loren Wyard-Scott. 2009. Identification of pleonastic it

using the web. *Journal of Artificial Intelligence Research*, pages 339–389.

Eleni Miltsakaki, Rashmi Prasad, Aravind Joshi, and Bonnie Webber. 2004. Annotating discourse connectives and their arguments. In *Proceedings of the HLT/NAACL Workshop on Frontiers in Corpus Annotation*, pages 9–16. Boston, MA.

Ruslan Mitkov. 1998. Robust pronoun resolution with limited knowledge. In *Proceedings of the 17th international conference on Computational linguistics-Volume 2*, pages 869–875. Association for Computational Linguistics.

Ruslan Mitkov. 2014. *Anaphora resolution*. Routledge.

Vincent Ng. 2010. Supervised noun phrase coreference research: The first fifteen years. In *Proceedings of the 48th annual meeting of the Association for Computational Linguistics*, pages 1396–1411. Association for Computational Linguistics.

Kristina Nilsson Björkenstam. 2013. SUC-CORE: A Balanced Corpus Annotated with Noun Phrase Coreference. *Northern European Journal of Language Technology NEJLT*, 3:19–39.

Kristina Nilsson. 2010. Hybrid methods for coreference resolution in Swedish.

Anne O'Keeffe, Michael McCarthy, and Ronald Carter. 2007. *From corpus to classroom: Language use and language teaching*. Cambridge University Press.

Ildikó Pilán, Elena Volodina, and Richard Johansson. 2014. Rule-based and machine learning approaches for second language sentence-level readability. In *Proceedings of the Ninth Workshop on Innovative Use of NLP for Building Educational Applications*, pages 174–184.

Ildikó Pilán, Elena Volodina, and Richard Johansson. 2013. Automatic Selection of Suitable Sentences for Language Learning Exercises. In *20 Years of EURO-CALL: Learning from the Past, Looking to the Future. Proceedings of EUROCALL.*, pages 218–225.

Juan Pino and Maxine Eskenazi. 2009. Semi-automatic generation of cloze question distractors effect of students' L1. In *SLaTE*, pages 65–68.

Emily Pitler and Ani Nenkova. 2009. Using syntax to disambiguate explicit discourse connectives in text. In *Proceedings of the ACL-IJCNLP 2009 Conference Short Papers*, pages 13–16. Association for Computational Linguistics.

Massimo Poesio, Simone Ponzetto, and Yannick Versley. 2011. Computational models of anaphora resolution: A survey. http://wwwusers.di.uniroma1.it/~ponzetto/pubs/poesio10a.pdf.

Rashmi Prasad, Nikhil Dinesh, Alan Lee, Eleni Miltsakaki, Livio Robaldo, Aravind K Joshi, and Bonnie L Webber. 2008. The Penn Discourse TreeBank 2.0. In *Proceedings of LREC*.

Marta Recasens, Lluís Màrquez, Emili Sapena, M Antònia Martí, Mariona Taulé, Véronique Hoste, Massimo Poesio, and Yannick Versley. 2010. Semeval-2010 task 1: Coreference resolution in multiple languages. In *Proceedings of the 5th International Workshop on Semantic Evaluation*, pages 1–8. Association for Computational Linguistics.

Paula Levy Scherrer and K. Lindemalm. 2007. *Rivstart: A1+ A2,Textbok*. Natur & Kultur, Stockholm.

Thomas M Segler. 2007. *Investigating the selection of example sentences for unknown target words in ICALL reading texts for L2 German*. PhD Thesis. University of Edinburgh.

Simon Smith, PVS Avinesh, and Adam Kilgarriff. 2010. Gap-fill tests for language learners: Corpus-driven item generation. In *Proceedings of ICON-2010: 8th International Conference on Natural Language Processing*, pages 1–6.

Eiichiro Sumita, Fumiaki Sugaya, and Seiichi Yamamoto. 2005. Measuring non-native speakers' proficiency of English by using a test with automatically-generated fill-in-the-blank questions. In *Proceedings of the second workshop on Building Educational Applications Using NLP*, pages 61–68. Association for Computational Linguistics.

Ulf Teleman, Staffan Hellberg, and Erik Andersson. 1999. *Svenska akademiens grammatik*. Svenska Akademien/Norstedts ordbok (distr.).

Elena Volodina, Richard Johansson, and Sofie Johansson Kokkinakis. 2012. Semi-automatic selection of best corpus examples for Swedish: Initial algorithm evaluation. In *Proceedings of the SLTC 2012 workshop on NLP for Computer-Assisted Language Learning*, volume 80 of *Linköping Electronic Conference Proceedings*, pages 59–70. Linköping University Electronic Press.

Elena Volodina, Ildikó Pilán, Stian Rødven Eide, and Hannes Heidarsson. 2014. You get what you annotate: a pedagogically annotated corpus of coursebooks for Swedish as a Second Language. In *Proceedings of the third workshop on NLP for Computer-Assisted Language Learning*, volume 107 of *Linköping Electronic Conference Proceedings*, pages 128–142. Linköping University Electronic Press.

Bonnie Webber, Matthew Stone, Aravind Joshi, and Alistair Knott. 2003. Anaphora and discourse structure. *Computational linguistics*, 29(4):545–587.

# Feature-Rich Error Detection in Scientific Writing Using Logistic Regression


**Madeline Remse, Mohsen Mesgar** and **Michael Strube**
Heidelberg Institute for Theoretical Studies gGmbH
Schloß-Wolfsbrunnenweg 35
69118 Heidelberg, Germany
`(madeline.remse|mohsen.mesgar|michael.strube)@h-its.org`



## Abstract

The goal of the Automatic Evaluation of Scientific Writing (AESW) Shared Task 2016 is to identify sentences in scientific articles which need editing to improve their correctness and readability or to make them better fit within the genre at hand. We encode many different types of errors occurring in the dataset by linguistic features. We use logistic regression to assign a probability indicating whether a sentence needs to be edited. We participate in both tracks at AESW 2016: *binary prediction* and *probabilistic estimation*. In the former track, our model (HITS) gets the fifth place and in the latter one, it ranks first according to the evaluation metric.


## 1 Introduction

The AESW 2016 Shared Task is about predicting if a given sentence in a scientific article needs language editing. It can therefore be pictured as a binary classification task. Two types of prediction are evaluated: binary prediction (*false* or *true*) and probabilistic estimation (between 0 and 1). These types of prediction form the two tracks of the shared task, both of which we participate in.

We solve both problems by applying a logistic regression model. We design a variety of features based on a thorough analysis of the training data. We choose the set of features that yields the highest performance on training and development sets.

Accounting for the imbalance of numbers of wrong and correct sentences in the training data during feature selection we obtain a model for the probabilistic task that outranks our competitors' systems.

However, a detailed analysis of the results shows that the model takes advantage of the evaluation metric and that our less informed system produces results that are, although not yielding a top evaluation score, more meaningful.

In the course of a profound analysis of the training data we encounter both linguistic errors, which likely occur in diverse genres, and such errors that are intrinsic to scientific writing and thus rank among the major challenges of this task. As pointed out on the AESW 2016 webpage[1], correcting problems concerning diction and style is a matter of opinion. It depends on factors that are not necessarily deducible from linguistic properties. Common abbreviations are an example. There are cases where they are accepted by an editor, and there are cases where they are corrected. That is, sometimes *e.g.* is left as is and sometimes it is changed to *for instance* or *for example* without any obvious reason. There are even words that are corrected in opposite directions. For example, the first letter of the name prefix *van* has been corrected to be uppercase in some sentences and also has been corrected to be lowercase in other sentences. Especially abbreviations that are not common within one particular domain, but are used in isolated documents are problematic. This is due to limitations of the dataset, which provides only paragraphs, but not documents as contexts for sentences. For example, we may assume that *R-G* has been introduced as a technical term at some point in a document. But since we do not know which paragraphs belong to this document, we cannot be sure that this is the case.

---

[1] `http://textmining.lt/aesw/index.html`

162


*Proceedings of the 11th Workshop on Innovative Use of NLP for Building Educational Applications*, pages 162–171,
San Diego, California, June 16, 2016. ©2016 Association for Computational Linguistics

Section 2 gives an overview of the types of errors we encountered. In Section 3 we introduce our system design, detail on how we derive features from our data analysis, what kinds of language models we apply, give a short outline on logistic regression and describe the implementation of our system. In Section 4 we describe our training steps, followed by reporting results in Section 5, a discussion of lessons learned in Section 6 and related work in Section 7.

## 2  Data Analysis[2]

### 2.1  Simple Errors

SPELLING ERRORS are frequent and many concern using hyphens in compounds. Another common error is the wrong usage of ARTICLES. Definite articles are missing or unnecessarily inserted before generic nouns, (for instance *over the formula _REF_*). Indefinite articles are erroneous with respect to the subsequent phoneme, (e.g. *a open neighborhood*). Some errors concern descriptions of REFERENCES, which are usually capitalized (*table _REF_* or *figures _REF_ and _REF_*). NUMERALS are spelled out when they should not be, and vice-versa (*2* or *seventy-three*). It is correct to spell numerals out if they are smaller than 10, otherwise they are often spelled in digits. CONTRACTIONS, such as *doesn't* and *what's*, are considered too colloquial for scientific writing. Dots behind ABBREVIATIONS are omitted, and also common abbreviations such as *e.g.*, *i.e.* and *vs.* are written wrongly. Other errors include incorrect PLURALIZATION of decades (*1980's*), regular past tense generation of IRREGULAR VERBS (*lighted*) and the modification of words by the wrong PREPOSITION (*very different to the correction*). Words are unnecessarily REPEATED sometimes (*The the*).

### 2.2  Complex Errors

All errors described above can easily be categorized by means of simple patterns. Other errors are harder to capture, for example wrong word order or missing words. The most common errors that we come across are mistakes in the PUNCTUATION of a sentence, especially unnecessary or missing commas.

---

[2]All examples in this section have been drawn from the training data.

NUMBER DISAGREEMENT is a common grammatical error. It occurs in passive or active clauses (e.g. *the system are assumed to be the following form* and *the counter variables goes on changing*) and in nominal phrases (e.g. *Three class of boundary conditions* and *these new set of Lyapunov terms*).

WORK-SPECIFIC ABBREVIATIONS such as the insertion of *R-G* for the compound *recombination-generation* are errors that occur in individual situations. Detecting issues with DICTION AND STYLE is probably the most intricate problem in this task.

## 3  System Design

### 3.1  Formally Capturing Error Types

Simple errors can mostly be captured by binary features that formalize rules. For example, if a sentence contains an incorrect ABBREVIATION of *id est*, such as *ie.*, then it needs correction. Similar rules can be applied to the spelling mode of cardinal numbers and the CONTRACTION of auxiliary words, such as *'s*, *'ve*, etc. Also, when finding a four digit number starting with 1 and ending with 0, it is likely to denote a decade. If it is directly followed by *'s*, an incorrect PLURALIZATION is detected.

Some rules formulated that way need additional information. To assert that *seventeen* should not be spelled out the system must be aware that it denotes a NUMERAL greater than 10. This information can be made available through appropriate mappings. Lists of wrongly generated past tense forms of IRREGULAR VERBS can be created with managable effort, just like lists of common abbreviations.

SPELLING ERRORS can be detected by looking up words in a dictionary. Whether or not a compound requires being joined by a hyphen cannot be determined that way. Compounds can be created productively and are not necessarily in a dictionary.

NUMBER DISAGREEMENTS are easy to detect by means of dependencies between head and modifiers within phrases and part-of-speech tags, which often carry information about the number of words. However, that means that recognizing these errors heavily depends on the correctness of the dependency trees and the part-of-speech tags.

Other error types are ascertainable by language modeling. PREPOSITIONS often occur in combination with the same words. Thus an appropriately trained language model learns that the word *different* occurs with *from* much more frequently than with *to*. Classic n-gram models account for unusual sequences of words and faulty word orderings. Language models based on co-occurrences of constituents in syntax trees can reveal grammatical errors and indicate positions where a comma or article is likely to be inserted.

### 3.2  Language Models

To capture more complex errors we use a variety of language models that we compute on correct sentences in the training data.

The n-gram probability of the $i^{th}$ linguistic unit of a sentence $l_i$, being a token $w$ or a part-of-speech tag $t$, given its $n-1$ predecessors is defined as

$$p(l_i \mid l_{i-n+1}^{i-1}) = \frac{c(l_{i-n+1}^{i})}{c(l_{i-n+1}^{i-1})},$$

where $c(x)$ is the number of occurrences of $x$ throughout the dataset (Jurafsky and Martin, 2009, pp. 117–147).

Language modeling is not limited to a language unit and its direct predecessors. The probability of the occurrence of a word or part-of-speech tag can be computed depending on whatever might be appropriate to model a linguistic phenomenon. Therefore we compute the probability of a linguistic unit given the subsequent $n-1$ linguistic units:

$$p(l_i \mid l_{i+1}^{i+n-1}) = \frac{c(l_i^{i+n-1})}{c(l_{i+1}^{i+n-1})}.$$

The following formula for the probability of a word $w$ accounts for the relation between part-of-speech tags and lexicals:

$$p(w_i \mid t_i) = \frac{c(w_i, t_i)}{c(t_i)}.$$

In order to identify words that are typically preceded by a particular part-of-speech, we compute

$$p(t_i \mid w_{i+1}) = \frac{c(t_i, w_{i+1})}{c(w_{i+1})}.$$

Given a syntax tree, let $succ(g)$ be the right sibling of a node $g$, let $pred(g)$ be the left sibling of a node $g$, and let $child(g)$ be the set of children of a node $g$. We define:

$$p(pred(h) = g \mid h) = \frac{c(pred(h) = g)}{\sum_{g' \in C} c(pred(h) = g')},$$

$$p(succ(h) = g \mid h) = \frac{c(succ(h) = g)}{\sum_{g' \in C} c(pred(h) = g')},$$

$$p(g \in child(h) \mid h) = \frac{c(g \in child(h))}{\sum_{g' \in C} c(g' \in child(h))},$$

where $C$ is the set of constituents.

Other sets of features address the probability of prepositional phrases as modifiers of words. Let $nmod(v)$ be a preposition that modifies a word $v$:

$$p(nmod(v) = w) = \frac{c(nmod(v) = w)}{\sum_{w' \in V} c(nmod(v) = w')}.$$

**Smoothing:** Since the purpose of our language models is to identify unusual combinations and orderings of words, part-of-speech tags, and chunks, we go without strong smoothing measures and leave it to machine learning to reveal the point where a language construct qualifies as unacceptably improbable. Also, we do not prune the vocabulary, because technical terms which are limited to very specific scientific fields or even to only few documents are characteristic for scientific writing. For practical reasons we apply the very basic add-$\delta$ smoothing (Jurafsky and Martin, 2009, p. 134), choosing $\delta = 0.1$ in order to prevent zero-division.

### 3.3  Features

We implement a total of 82 features based on the data analysis described in Section 2. These features can be classified into three sets, depending on their range. Features 1–14 (see Table 1) are integer-valued, features 15–55 (see Table 2) are binary, and features 56–82 (see Table 3) are real-valued.

Most of the integer-valued features originate in readability research and address the coherence of documents, but they may also be helpful to assess sentence quality (Pitler and Nenkova, 2008). It is plausible that long sentences or sentences with a very high parse tree should be shortened or split into more sentences in order to simplify their syntax. Thus they account for those cases where phrases are deleted in favor of conciseness. Many occurrences of constituents such as *VP*, *SBAR* or *NP* are likely to

| ID | Definition |
|----|------------|
| 1 | number of definite articles (token *the* with POS-tag *DT*) |
| 2 | number of pronouns (tokens with POS-tag *PRP*) |
| 3 | number of SBAR (subtrees of syntax tree with root *SBAR*) |
| 4 | number of VP (subtrees of syntax tree with root *VP*) |
| 5 | number of NP (subtrees of syntax tree with root *NP*) |
| 6 | sentence length (number of tokens) |
| 7 | parse tree height (edges on the longest path between the root and a leaf of the syntax tree) |
| 8 | number of constituents (subtrees of the syntax tree) |
| 9 | number of words not in vocabulary (tokens never seen in training) |
| 10 | number of words unknown to WordNet (ignores stop words, compounds with hyphens, tokens with digits) |
| 11 | number of words unknown to `pyenchant`-package using en_US-dictionary (ignores stop words, compounds with hyphen, tokens with digits) |
| 12 | maximal number of verb forms in a row (longest row of POS-tags starting with 'VB') |
| 13 | number of dots (ignores period at the end of a sentence) |
| 14 | number of abbreviations in paragraph (feature 13, summed over all sentences of a paragraph) |

**Table 1:** Integer-valued features.

occur in too complex sentences. Many pronouns are indicative for ambiguity, since it is more difficult to identify the corresponding antecedents.

The binary features are mostly designed for specific error types, looking for patterns or exact strings found to be frequently corrected in the training data.

Abbreviations sometimes are and sometimes are not accepted (Section 2). In order to capture more information on their usage we added Features 13 and 14. They count the number of abbreviations in the sentence and in the whole paragraph respectively. The general idea is that if an author has a tendency to use abbreviations, an editor does not perceive an individual abbreviation as inconsistent.

Features 47–55 recognize domain-related errors. Although the domain is unlikely to be directly decisive for distinguishing correct from incorrect sentences, some kinds of errors might coincide with individual domains. Our model does not take into account dependencies between features (Jurafsky and Martin, 2009, p. 238). However we examine their impact on the model's performance. They could be beneficial for other machine learning algorithms.

In order to detect spelling errors, some of the binary features check if all words in a sentence are present within specific sets, such as the vocabulary used in the correct training data, an American English dictionary[3], or WordNet[4]. We implement

integer-valued counterparts for these features, because an absolute decision might be too restrictive.

Most of the real-valued features consist of probabilities computed in our language models. We compute maximum likelihood estimates of sentences based on different models. We use part-of-speech n-grams and token n-grams for $n \in \{1, 2, 3\}$ and a Hidden Markov Model. We also capture those n-grams in a sentence that yield the lowest probability compared to all other n-grams. Furthermore there are features that detect the position where a comma is most likely to be inserted with respect to the preceding and succeeding tokens and part-of-speech tags as well as the preceding, succeeding and superordinate constituents in the syntax tree. The same is done for inserting and deleting articles and substituting prepositions by other prepositions. Mostly we do not compute an isolated probability, but rather connect it with comparative probabilities. For instance, feature 82 does not only compute the probability of a comma before a pair of words, but returns the factor by which a comma is more likely than the word actually preceding the pair. That way the feature does depend on the subsequent word pair and also on the word to be substituted.

### 3.4 Machine Learning Approach

We participate in the binary and the probabilistic track using a logistic regression model. Logistic regression is capable of performing both probabilistic estimation and binary classification. Its training

---

[3]We used the `pyenchant` package:
http://pythonhosted.org/pyenchant/
[4]https://wordnet.princeton.edu/

| ID | Definition |
|---|---|
| 15 | contains *Van* |
| 16 | contains *van* |
| 17 | contains *n't* |
| 18 | contains is or us contraction (*where's, what's, that's, it's, let's*) |
| 19 | contains *'ve* |
| 20 | contains *'d* |
| 21 | first word not capitalized |
| 22 | dot after MATH or MATHDISP |
| 23 | wrong decade pluralization (*1**0's*) |
| 24 | reference description not capitalized (token *table, figure, lemma*, etc. before token *REF*) |
| 25 | abbreviation without dot (token *Tab, Fig, Figs, Eq*, etc. not ended or followed by .) |
| 26 | contains word unknown to `pyenchant`-package (binary version of Feature 11) |
| 27 | contains word not in vocabulary (binary version of Feature 9) |
| 28 | contains word unknown to WordNet (binary version of Feature 10) |
| 29 | two nouns connected by hyphen (parts of compound are all in WordNet as nouns) |
| 30 | contains small cardinal number in digits (e.g. *2*) |
| 31 | contains high cardinal number in letters (e.g. *seventeen, thirty*) |
| 32 | contains two cardinal numbers in letters, joined by a hyphen (e.g. *seventy-three*) |
| 33 | contains two cardinal numbers in letters in a row (e.g. *fifty two, one zero*) |
| 34 | wrong first letter after indefinite article<br>(to a limited extent recognizes excepions: *an honest, a one-dimensional space, an SVM*, etc.) |
| 35 | contains the same token twice in a row (e.g. *The the*) |
| 36 | number mismatch between passive auxiliary verb and subject<br>(number of nsubjpass and number of auxpass of a verb do not match according to the POS-tags.) |
| 37 | number mismatch between verb and subject<br>(number of verb and nsubj do not match according to the POS-tags.) |
| 38 | number mismatch between article and head of a noun phrase |
| 39 | number mismatch between number modifier and head of a noun phrase |
| 40 | contains *vs* (not followed by .) |
| 41 | contains *vs* (ended with or followed by .) |
| 42 | contains *ie* or *ie.* |
| 43 | contains *i.e.* |
| 44 | contains *eg* or *eg.* |
| 45 | contains irregular verb with regular suffix (*lighted, builded*, etc.) |
| 46 | contains token *based* not followed by *on* |
| 47–55 | occurs in domains: Astrophysics, Chemistry, Computer Science, Economics/Management, Engineering, Human Sciences, Mathematics, Physics, Statistics |

Table 2: Binary Features

phase is also not very time-consuming, which is beneficial for our feature selection procedure. It derives the probability of an observation $x$ to belong to a particular class $y$ from a linear combination of the observed feature vector $f$ and a weight vector $w$ (Jurafsky and Martin, 2009, pp. 231–239). It applies a logistic function to map the result of this linear combination to lie between 0 and 1. In the training phase the parameters in $w$ are chosen to maximize the probability of the observed $y$ values. During testing unseen samples are classified according to their probability computed by linearly combining their feature vectors with the very weight vector $w$ that was determined in training.

## 3.5 Implementation

Our system is based on an object-oriented data model that provides information on the different datasets. Sentence objects comprise every piece of information at hand, including the actual tagged data and supplementary information such as lists of tokens and part-of-speech tags, a graph-like structure implementing the syntax tree, and a dictionary mapping tuples of indices in the token list to the

| ID | Definition |
| --- | --- |
| 56 | average word length |
| 57 | max. gain of changing a preposition ($nmod(w)$ denotes preposition that modifies $w$): $\max(\{\frac{p_{modify}(w',w_i)}{p_{modify}(nmod(w_i),w_i)} : 1 \leq i \leq \|S\| \text{ AND } w' \in V \text{ AND } \exists j [1 \leq j \leq \|S\| \wedge nmod(w_i) = w_j]\})$, |
| 58 | max. gain of swapping the case of a first letter ($swap(w)$ is $w$ with case of first letter swapped)): $\max(\{\frac{p_{ngram}(w_{i-2},w_{i-1},swap(w_i))}{p_{ngram}(w_{i-2},w_{i-1},w_i)} : 1 \leq i \leq \|S\| \})$, |
| 59 | maximum likelihood estimate (token unigrams): $\prod_{1 \leq i \leq \|S\|} p(w_i)$ |
| 60 | maximum likelihood estimate (POS-tag unigrams): $\prod_{1 \leq i \leq \|S\|} p(t_i)$ |
| 61 | maximum likelihood estimate (token bigrams): $\prod_{1 \leq i \leq \|S\|} p(w_i \mid w_{i-1})$ |
| 62 | maximum likelihood estimate (POS-tag bigrams): $\prod_{1 \leq i \leq \|S\|} p(t_i \mid t_{i-1})$ |
| 63 | maximum likelihood estimate (token trigrams): $\prod_{1 \leq i \leq \|S\|} p(w_i \mid w_{i-2}w_{i-1})$ |
| 64 | maximum likelihood estimate (POS-tag trigrams): $\prod_{1 \leq i \leq \|S\|} p(t_i \mid t_{i-2}t_{i-1})$ |
| 65 | maximum likelihood estimate (Hidden Markov Model): $\prod_{1 \leq i \leq \|S\|} p(t_i \mid t_{i-1}) \cdot p(w_i \mid t_i)$ |
| 66 | min. probability of any POS-tag trigram: $\min(\{p(t_i \mid t_{i-2}t_{i-1}) : 1 \leq i \leq \|S\|\})$ |
| 67 | min. probability of any POS-tag bigram: $\min(\{p(t_i \mid t_{i-1}) : 1 \leq i \leq \|S\|\})$ |
| 68 | min. probability of any POS-tag unigram: $\min(\{p(t_i) : 1 \leq i \leq \|S\|\})$ |
| 69 | min. probability of any token trigram: $\min(\{p(w_i \mid w_{i-2}w_{i-1}) : 1 \leq i \leq \|S\|\})$ |
| 70 | min. probability of any token bigram: $\min(\{p(w_i \mid w_{i-1}) : 1 \leq i \leq \|S\|\})$ |
| 71 | min. probability of any token unigram: $\min(\{p(w_i) : 1 \leq i \leq \|S\|\})$ |
| 72 | min. lexical probability of any token: $\min(\{p(w_i \mid t_i) : 1 \leq i \leq \|S\|\})$ |
| 73 | fraction of tokens that are commas: $\frac{\|\{i : w_i =, 1 \leq i \leq \|S\|\}\|}{\|S\|}$ |
| 74 | max. gain of inserting comma after chunk: $\max(\{p(succ(g) =, \mid g) : g \in Tree(S) \text{ AND } succ(g) \neq ,\})$ |
| 75 | max. gain of inserting comma before chunk: $\max(\{p(pred(g) =, \mid g) : g \in Tree(S) \text{ AND } pred(g) \neq ,\})$ |
| 76 | max. gain of inserting comma within subtree: $\max(\{p(, \in g \mid g) : g \in Tree(S) \text{ AND }, \notin child(g)\})$ |
| 77 | max. gain of inserting article: $\max(\{\frac{p(\mathbf{DT} \mid w_i)}{p(t_{i-1},w_i)} : 1 \leq i \leq \|S\| \text{ AND } t_{i-1} \neq \mathbf{DT}\})$ |
| 78 | max. gain of deleting article: $\max(\{\frac{p(t_{i-2},w_i)}{p(\mathbf{DT} \mid w_i)} : 1 \leq i \leq \|S\| \text{ AND } t_{i-1} = \mathbf{DT}\})$ |
| 79 | max. gain of inserting comma after pair of POS-tags: $\max(\{\frac{p(, \mid t_{i-2}t_{i-1})}{p(t_i \mid t_{i-2}t_{i-1})} : 1 \leq i \leq \|S\|\})$ |
| 80 | max. gain of inserting comma after pair of words: $\max(\{\frac{p(, \mid w_{i-2}w_{i-1})}{p(w_i \mid w_{i-2},w_{i-1})} : 1 \leq i \leq \|S\|\})$ |
| 81 | max. gain of inserting comma before pair of POS-tags: $\max(\{\frac{p(, \mid t_{i+1}t_{i+2})}{p(t_i \mid t_{i+1}t_{i+2})} : 1 \leq i \leq \|S\|\})$ |
| 82 | max. gain of inserting comma before pair of words: $\max(\{\frac{p(, \mid w_{i+1}w_{i+2})}{p(w_i \mid w_{i+1}w_{i+2})} : 1 \leq i \leq \|S\|\})$ |

**Table 3:** Real-valued features

dependency relation between the corresponding tokens. The object can hold both its correct and its incorrect versions. The Sentence class also implements all features and methods needed for data analysis. The purpose of the Corpus class is to gather and manipulate sentence information and transfer it to convenient output formats. It also holds a static object that encapsulates all functionality regarding language modeling.

Each step on the way to the final system is then implemented in a seperate script that accesses the data model described above. These steps can be combined to form a closed system or be extended to do further data analysis or to use machine learning approaches other than logistic regression.

For machine learning we used the `scikit-learn`[5] implementation of logistic regression.

## 4 Training

All sentences in the training set are used for training, that is, a sentence that needs correction enters the training set with both its original and its corrected version and thus introduces two samples with different labels to the training data, namely $-1$ for the correct version and $+1$ for the wrong version. Sentences that do not need modification have the label $-1$. To prevent single features from being predominant we scale all feature vectors using the `scikit-learn MaxAbsScaler`. It maps all our

[5] http://scikit-learn.org/stable/

values to lie between 0 and 1 by dividing by the largest absolute value that occurs in each feature during training. That way binary features and 0 values remain unaffected. Note that test data samples can still end up with feature values greater than 1, but all features will still be cut to reasonable sizes.

## 4.1 Feature Selection

In order to determine which of the features are helpful in an actual system, we first extract a small subset of binary features that all yield a high precision when classifying sentences of the development set solely based on their value. Seven of the features yield a precision of more than 90%, namely 17, 18, 19, 22, 23, 32, and 42. We train a logistic regression model using only these features. We evaluate the predictions of the model using the F1-scores for both tracks of the shared task, as defined in (Daudaravičius, 2015). Then we add each of the remaining features and keep the one that improves the F1-score most. We repeat that process until none of the features improves the score anymore. We perform this process on both training and development data seperately. Note that we do not include the features which encode the domain of a sentence. Instead, their combined impact is tested at the end of the procedure. If and only if adding them all yields an improvement, they are kept in the final model.

After having determined the most informative features, we account for distributional properties of our training set by adjusting some parameters. The training set is heavily biased towards correct sentences, because for each sentence (even with error) there is a correct version, but there is not necessarily a wrong version for each sentence. In order to make up for this imbalance we set the class weights inversely proportional to their respective proportions in the training data, as suggested by the `scikit-learn`-documentation[6]. Applying L1 regularization instead of L2 regularization gives us a minor performance boost, too. Table 4 shows the feature sets determined by the feature selection process along with the performances of the models on the different datasets with weighted classes and using L1 regularization.

---

<sup>6</sup>`http://scikit-learn.org/stable/
modules/generated/sklearn.linear_model.
LogisticRegression.html`

| Model | precision | recall | F1 |
|---|---|---|---|
| **prob.u.L2** | 0.6655 | 0.7889 | 0.722 |
| **prob.w.L1** | 0.9333 | 0.7491 | 0.8311 |
| **bool.w.L1** | 0.3765 | 0.9480 | 0.5389 |

**Table 6:** Results on test data

Seeing how setting the right parameters can improve the performance of logistic regression, we do another feature selection on the development data. This time we weight the classes as described above and apply L1 regularization from the outset. That way we obtain the feature sets reported in Table 5.

## 5 Results

Since the results in Table 5 yield very promising results on the development data, we apply the two models to the test data, which yields comparable results (see models **bool.w.L1** and **prob.w.L1** in Table 6). Taking a closer look at the individual outcomes, however, reveals that they are by no means expressive. In the binary task our system almost always assigns *true* and thereby ensures the high recall. The precision on the other hand is relatively low and roughly matches the proportion of spurious sentences in the data. Hence our system would be outperformed by one that assigns *true* to all samples.

Our results on the probabilistic track look similar. Apart from a few instances to which our model assigns a probability around 95%, the estimations are always very close to 50%.

In order to examine the effects of a larger set of features we also apply the model resulting from feature selection on the training data to the test data for the probabilistic task. We expect that thanks to the multitude of features this model (**prob.u.L2**) will eventuate in a more diverse result. Despite the fact that as reported in Table 6 the F1-score drops by 11 points compared to our other system, the individual outcomes in fact seem to be much more expressive. The results still have a tendency to range around 50% but there are considerably more outliers and a lot more probabilities greater than 95%.

## 6 Discussion

### 6.1 Lessons learned

It is noticeable that we end up with very few features when performing the feature selection process

|  | features | F1-score |
|---|---|---|
| **bool: training data** | 1, 7, 8, 9, 13, 14, 17, 18, 19, 20, 21, 22, 23, 24, 25, 29, 30, 31, 32, 34, 40, 42, 43, 44, 45, 46, 57, 58, 73, 77, 78, 79, 81, 82 | 0.4251 |
| **prob: training data** | 7, 9, 11, 14, 17, 18, 19, 22, 23, 32, 42, 47, 48, 49, 50, 51, 52, 53, 54, 55, 56, 60, 66, 67, 69, 70, 73, 74, 75 | 0.7500 |
| **bool: development data** | 1, 3, 8, 9, 13, 14, 17, 18, 19, 22, 23, 24, 25, 30, 31, 32, 34, 35, 41, 42 43, 45, 46, 57, 58, 77, 82 | 0.5264 |
| **prob: development data** | 11, 14, 17, 18, 19, 22, 23, 26, 30, 32, 39, 42, 56, 66, 67, 69, 70, 74, 75 | 0.7547 |

**Table 4:** F1-scores resulting from feature selection, weighting classes and applying L1 regularization afterwards

|  | features | F1-score |
|---|---|---|
| **bool: development data** | 17, 18, 19, 22, 23, 32, 42, 69, 79 | 0.5701 |
| **prob: development data** | 17, 18, 19, 22, 23, 32, 42, 44, 72 | 0.8477 |

**Table 5:** F1-scores resulting from feature selection with classes weighted and L1 regularization applied from the outset

weighting the classes beforehand. By weighting the classes inversely proportional to their proportions in the training data, the system is immediately biased towards high probabilities for *true* labels, trying to compensate the superior number of *false* labels in the training data. Starting the feature selection process with high-precision features, the probability spikes whenever these features are 1. So both the model for the boolean track and the one for the probabilistic track start out with very high precisions. Due to the strong *true*-bias, all other probabilities are close to but still smaller than 50%, yielding a relatively high recall in the probabilistic system, which results in a very good performance according to the provided evaluation metric. The boolean system, on the other hand, has a very low recall, so in order to increase its F1-score, the precision is sacrificed during feature selection in favor of a better recall.

The feature selection processes show which features are more useful than others. We see that most of the integer-valued features that are valuable for readability assessment are never chosen for any model. A possible reason is that readability ease in scientific writing is not as important as in other domains, since the target readers are highly educated. A high linguistic complexity is rather characteristic for scientific writing and is possibly not perceived as a deficiency as much.

Interestingly the WordNet features (10, 28) do not work well, in contrast to the features using the `pyenchant`-package (11, 26).

The number of abbreviations in a paragraph (14) is chosen by every model so it is possible that an author's writing style throughout the rest of a document affects the editor's acceptance of individual sentences. It is worth considering to design more features that account for consistency in a paragraph.

Binary features often manage to improve the models, except for features 15 and 16, which is not surprising, given the fact that they denote exactly opposite properties and the model is not able to account for dependencies between features. Features 36–39 try to detect number disagreements and seem to perform poorly. Being based on both dependency trees and part-of-speech tags, these features rely on the correctness of the supplementary data, which in this case has been generated automatically, and hence cannot be guaranteed to be correct.

Our results also show that the domain-related features are not very helpful in combination with logistic regression. We can report that they only make a minor difference in the one model they entered.

Especially the models for probabilistic estimation are improved by features 66, 67 and 69, which are supposed to detect the most unlikely n-grams in a sentence. They are better in detecting local discrepancies in a sentence than the maximum likelihood estimation features 59–65, because an unlikely n-gram does not have much impact on the likelihood estimation of a sentence, so even a major error reflected in a very low n-gram probability can possibly go unnoticed. That cannot happen in the features 66–72.

The remaining features, dealing with the effects of insertion, deletion, and substitution of commas, articles, and prepositions, have positive impact on some of the models, which is why we are confident that language modeling is the key to other helpful features yet to be found.

## 6.2 Evaluation Metric

The evaluation score works well for a system whose only purpose is the identification of erroneous sentences, so for the binary classification task the F1-score is perfectly suitable. However, it may be worth considering whether the information that a sentence is fine could be valuable, too. That might be the case whenever sentences must be further processed. In that case the accuracy metric might be the better choice, because it takes all correct classifications into account, whereas the F1-score does not reward instances correctly classified as *false*.

As for the probabilistic task, our results show that the evaluation score is not strict enough, and that it is prone to misjudge the expressiveness of the results. In fact, correctly assigning 1.0 to only one faulty sentence and 0.5 to all other sentences yields a score of 0.8571. The result is not as extreme if precision and recall are computed based on the mean absolute error, which results in 0.6667. This, still, clearly overestimates the quality of the results.

## 7   Related Work

As Daudaravičius (2015) states, a lot of scientists authoring scientific papers are nonnative English speakers. This insight suggests a relation of automatic evaluation of scientific writing to the field of language learner systems. Gamon (2010) mainly addresses article and preposition errors, which have shown to be frequent errors in the dataset provided for the AESW 2016 Shared Task, too. He uses language models on both a lexical and a syntactical level to find more likely alternatives for prepositions and articles with respect to the linguistic environment they occur in. He also bases some features on ratios of language model outcomes, rather than on individual probabilities, which is an approach that underlies many of our real-valued features.

Tetreault et al. (2010) examine how helpful parser output features are when modeling preposition usage. They present several phrase structure and dependency-based features, including left and right contexts of constituents in parse trees and the lexicals modified by a prepositional phrase.

For our features we extract those ideas from these works that seem the most promising for the challenge we encounter. But they both hold inspiration for even more features than those we implement in the course of our participation in the shared task and will be reconsidered in future work.

## 8   Conclusions

To detect spurious sentences in scientific writing we trained a logistic regression model. After a thorough data analysis, which gave us some profound insight into the types of errors occurring in scientific writing, we designed a number of features to detect these errors. We identified the most meaningful features by performing an incremental feature selection. Some of the resulting features show that corrections which seemed arbitrary might be justified by means of consistency of a text. We also used the probabilities of sentences according to language models as features, which our feature selection process determined to be helpful. Using the selected features our regression model achieved respectable results compared to our competitors' systems. Weighting our classes during the feature selection procedure, we accomplished a score to rank highest according to the evaluation metric in the probabilistic track of the task. However, we discovered that these results are very homogeneous and thus not expressive enough for a real life system. For future improvements of our system, we plan on developing an evaluation metric that takes the diversity of result data into account.

## Acknowledgements

This work has been funded by the Klaus Tschira Foundation, Heidelberg, Germany. The second author has been supported by a HITS Ph.D. scholarship. We would like to thank Mark-Christoph Müller for giving feedback on earlier drafts of this report.

## References

Vidas Daudaravičius. 2015. Automated evaluation of scientific writing: AESW shared task proposal. In *Proceedings of the Tenth Workshop on Innovative Use of NLP for Building Educational Applications,* Denver, Col., 4 June 2015, pages 56–63.

Michael Gamon. 2010. Using mostly native data to correct errors in learners' writing: A meta-classifier approach. In *Proceedings of Human Language Technologies 2010: The Conference of the North American Chapter of the Association for Computational Linguistics,* Los Angeles, Cal., 2–4 June 2010, pages 163–171.

Daniel Jurafsky and James H. Martin. 2009. *Speech and Language Processing.* Pearson Education, Upper Saddle River, N.J., second edition.

Emily Pitler and Ani Nenkova. 2008. Revisiting readability: A unified framework for predicting text quality,. In *Proceedings of the 2008 Conference on Empirical Methods in Natural Language Processing,* Waikiki, Honolulu, Hawaii, 25–27 October 2008, pages 186–195.

Joel Tetreault, Jennifer Foster, and Martin Chodorow. 2010. Using parse features for preposition selection and error detection. In *Proceedings of the ACL 2010 Conference Short Papers,* Uppsala, Sweden, 11–16 July 2010, pages 353–358.

# Bundled Gap Filling:
## A New Paradigm for Unambiguous Cloze Exercises


**Michael Wojatzki**
Language Technology Lab
University of Duisburg Essen
Duisburg, Germany
michael.wojatzki@uni-due.de

**Oren Melamud**
Computer Science Department
Bar-Ilan University
Ramat-Gan, Israel
melamuo@cs.biu.ac.il

**Torsten Zesch**
Language Technology Lab
University of Duisburg Essen
Duisburg, Germany
torsten.zesch@uni-due.de



## Abstract

Cloze tests, also known as gap-fill exercises, are a popular tool for acquiring and evaluating language proficiency. A major challenge in the way of automating scoring of cloze tests is the yet unsolved problem of gap filler ambiguity. To address this challenge, we present the concept of *bundled gap filling*, along with (1) an efficient computational model for automatically generating unambiguous *gap bundle* exercises, and (2) a disambiguation measure for guiding the construction of the exercises and validating their level of ambiguity. Our evaluation shows that our proposed exercises achieve a dramatic reduction in gap filler ambiguity, while our disambiguation measure can be effectively used to discard exercises that are nevertheless too ambiguous.


## 1 Introduction

Cloze-tests (or gap-fill tasks) (Taylor, 1953) are a frequently used exercise type, where a target word in a sentence is hidden and replaced with a gap. The learner is then asked to figure out the hidden word based on its context. While gap-fill tasks are quite easy to generate, automated scoring is difficult as gaps are often significantly ambiguous (Chavez-Oller et al., 1985). For example, in the sentence *'The students have to ___ the test'* most people would accept *do*, *take*, or *pass* as valid gap-fillers. However, for reasons of practicability, in common test scenarios this ambiguity is often ignored, which may result in high error-rates even when testing native speakers (Klein-Braley and Raatz, 1982).

The ambiguity of gap-fill tasks can be countered by providing a set of answer candidates for the learner to choose from. The candidates include a single correct solution and a set of incorrect *distractors* that are –in theory– used to control the difficulty of the task. However, providing answer candidates encourages guessing and changes the nature of the task from producing a solution to recognizing a solution (Wesche and Paribakht, 1994).

Furthermore, in practice, it is far from trivial to find good distractors and to resolve the trade-off between task difficulty and task ambiguity. Distractors that have little relatedness with the sentential context of a gap are easy to reject and therefore usually yield unambiguous but very easy tasks. Alternatively, distractors that fit well into the gap are hard to tell from the correct solution, but may be in fact also valid solutions themselves, resulting in an ambiguous exercise with more than one correct answer.

In this paper, we propose a new paradigm for addressing the ambiguity problem in gap-fill exercises, which we call *bundled gap filling*. A *gap bundle* is a set of gaps in different sentences, all hiding the exact same single word. In a gap bundle exercise, the learner is presented with all of the gaps in a bundle at the same time and asked to find the single word behind all of them. Figure 1 illustrates this approach (last row) in comparison to the traditional ones (upper rows).

As generating gap bundle exercises manually would be tedious, we propose a probabilistic gap bundle disambiguation measure based on language models (Chen and Goodman, 1999). Guided by this measure, we can both automatically generate gap bundle exercises, such that ambiguity is minimized, and discard the ones that are nevertheless too ambiguous.

Proficient English speakers are expected to get (near) perfect scores in non-ambiguous gap fill exercises, but much lower scores in ambiguous exer-




*Proceedings of the 11th Workshop on Innovative Use of NLP for Building Educational Applications*, pages 172–181,
San Diego, California, June 16, 2016. ©2016 Association for Computational Linguistics

| Type | Example | Ambiguity | Automatability | Nature of Task |
|---|---|---|---|---|
| gap-fill | The students have to ___ the test. | high | high | production |
| multiple-choice gap-fill | The students have to ___ the test.<br>a) take<br>b) fold<br>c) entertain<br>d) fry | low to moderate depending on selected distractors | low as it's hard to control both ambiguity and difficulty | recognition |
| bundled gap-fill | The students have to ___ the test.<br>Their cook will ___ three salmons.<br>All passengers should ___ their seats.<br>Both authors ___ credit for this. | low to moderate depending on selected gaps | high using the scheme proposed in this paper | production |

**Figure 1:** Comparison of three types of gap-fill exercises: (a) gap-fill, (b) gap-fill + distractors, (c) bundled gap-fill

cises. In our empirical evaluation, native and near-native English speakers achieved a mean success rate of .78 on bundled gap exercises compared to .27 on single gap exercises in an identical setting. This suggests that indeed the ambiguity of our gap bundles is dramatically lower than that of traditional single gaps.

## 2 Bundled Gap Filling Exercises

In this section, we describe (i) our proposed bundled gap filling exercises, (ii) a probabilistic model for estimating their level of ambiguity, and (iii) a scheme to automatically construct exercises, such that ambiguity is minimized.

### 2.1 Motivation

For a gap-fill exercise to be unambiguous, we wish to ensure that any word other than the given target word would be considered a highly unlikely solution by a proficient speaker under a common-sense interpretation. Unfortunately, as previously mentioned, this is commonly not the case for a single gap, e.g. *'The students have to ___ the test'* has multiple solutions including *take* and *do*. Similarly, *take* is not the only valid gap filler in the sentence *'All passengers should ___ their seats'*. However, in this case *do* would not be considered as a likely alternative, while *find* would. Therefore, when asked to find a single word that fits both gaps, a skilled speaker would probably be able to reject both *do* and *find*. In bundled gap filling exercises, we wish to take ad-

vantage of this variance in the ambiguity patterns of gaps.

### 2.2 General Approach

We make the following approximated assumptions regarding the reader of the gap-fill exercise. First, in the mind of the reader there exists some probabilistic distribution of the likely solutions of any given gap. The more ambiguous the gap, the wider this distribution is. Second, when asked to find a single word that fits two or more gaps bundled together, the reader attempts to 'compute' the joint distribution, which is the likelihood of any word to be a gap filler for all of these gaps at the same time. For a skilled reader, if the likelihood of the original target word in this joint distribution is significantly higher than any other word, then this bundled gap filling exercise in unambiguous. While impossible to predict precisely, we approximate the likelihood distribution in a speaker's mind using an $n$-gram language model, which predicts the likelihood of a gap-filler based on similar word sequences statistics observed in a large corpus.

To construct a gap bundle for a given target word, we start with a random seed sentence containing a gap hiding this word. We compute an approximation for the probabilistic distribution of its most likely gap-fillers, and then we iteratively add more sentences with gaps hiding the same target word to the bundle to make the bundle less ambiguous. To do this effectively, at each step we try to add the gap that would make the original target word stand out most in the resulting joint distribution of the gap bundle.

## 2.3 Probabilistic Modeling of Gap Ambiguity

We denote the probabilistic distribution for gap-filler words of a single gap in a sentence as:

$$P_{w \in V}(F(g) = w) = p_g(w) \tag{1}$$

$$\sum_{w \in V} p_g(w) = 1 \tag{2}$$

where $V$ is the vocabulary containing all words, $w$ is a single word, and $F(g)$ is the gap filler for gap $g$. This distribution can be estimated using a language model as we show later in Section 2.5.

Next, we make the following approximation for the joint probabilistic distribution of the word $w$ filling the gaps in a gap bundle, given that it must be the same word filling all of these gaps:

$$
\begin{aligned}
P_{w \in V}(F(b) &= w) \\
= P_{w \in V}(g_1 = w, &..., g_n = w) \\
\propto \prod_{i \in 1..n} &p_{g_i}(w),
\end{aligned}
\tag{3}
$$

where $b$ is a gap bundle that comprises the gaps $\{g_1, ..., g_n\}$.

Finally, we define our measure $D(b)$ for the disambiguation level of a gap bundle $b$, as the log of the ratio between the probability of the target word $t$ and the probability of the most likely word $w$ other than $t$:

$$D(b) = log \frac{P(F(b) = t)}{\max\limits_{w \in V \setminus \{t\}} P(F(b) = w)} \tag{4}$$

The greater this ratio, the more likely the target word compared to any other word, and accordingly we consider the gap bundle less ambiguous.[1] Based on this formalization, in the next section, we propose a scheme that can automatically construct gap bundles with high disambiguation measure values.

Figure 2 illustrates the log probability distributions of gap-filler words for two single gaps hiding the target word *take*, as well as the joint distribution

---

[1]We use the log of the ratio for convenience and arithmetic stability.

of the gap bundle comprising these two gaps. The ambiguity measure is illustrated as the difference between the log probability of the word *take* and the other most probable word in the distribution. As can be seen, the combination of the two gaps in a bundle yields a much higher disambiguation level than each of its constituents.

## 2.4 Constructing Disambiguated Gap Bundles

We next describe a scheme to automatically construct disambiguated gap bundles based on our model. As input to this process we assume the following: (1) for each desired gap bundle, a given random seed sentence with a gap, $g_1$, hiding some target word $t$; (2) a given size $m$ for the desired gap bundle; and (3) a corpus $G$, where $G_t$ is the set of gaps in $G$ hiding the target word $t$.

A straightforward approach to construct a disambiguated gap bundle for $g_1$ would be to evaluate all possible gap bundles that include $g_1$ and $(m-1)$ additional gaps from $G_t$, and choose the one with the highest disambiguation measure. By restricting the bundle to gaps only from $G_t$, we make sure that $t$ is a correct answer to the exercise (i.e. a valid gap filler), and by optimizing our disambiguation measure we wish to increase the chances of a skilled speaker to identify $t$ as the *only* correct answer.

Unfortunately, the exhaustive search described above is not useful from a practical point of view as it would require $O(m^{|G_t|} \cdot |V|)$ computations. We therefore propose instead a greedy algorithm with complexity $O(m \cdot |G_t| \cdot |V|)$ that successively selects the next gap to be added to the bundle, such that its ambiguity is reduced the most:

$$g_{i+1} = \arg\max_{g \in G_t \setminus b_i}(D(b_i \cup g)), \tag{5}$$

where $b_i$ is the gap bundle after step $i$, and $g_{i+1}$ is the gap to be added in step $(i + 1)$.

Finally, a threshold on the disambiguation level of the resulting gap bundle can be used to discard bundles for which our algorithm failed to reach a satisfactory level of disambiguation.

## 2.5 Estimating Gap-filler Distributions

A critical element of our proposed approach is the ability to efficiently estimate the distribution of gap-filler words for a given gap in a sentence. Probably

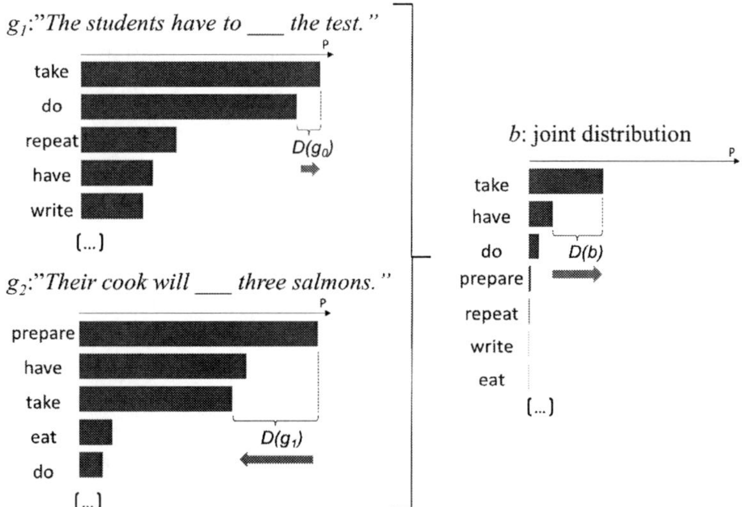



**Figure 2:** Two single gaps (top) combined into a gap bundle (bottom) for the target word *take*. The diagrams illustrate the respective gap-filler words log probability distributions. $D(g_0)$ and $D(g_1)$ are the disambiguation measures of the single gaps - note that $D(g_1)$ has a negative value. $D(b)$ is the improved disambiguation measure of the gap bundle.

the most natural choice to do this is by using probabilistic language modeling techniques, widely used in NLP for various applications (Chen and Goodman, 1999). Language models are learned from large corpora of text and used to estimate the probability of a given sequence of words, such as a sentence.

A straightforward approach to use a language model to estimate the gap-filler distribution is to fill the gap in a sentence with every possible word in the vocabulary and use the language model to estimate the probability of each resulting sentence. The probability of the gap-filler would be proportional to the probability of its respective sentence.

The problem with the above approach is that it becomes computationally intensive with large vocabularies, which may include hundreds of thousands of words. Therefore, we use instead the FASTSUBS tool (Yuret, 2012), which can efficiently compute a pruned distribution of the top-$k$ most probable gap fillers, using an $n$-gram language model. The probability of all the words below the top-$k$ is considered to be zero. For this computation to be efficient, $k$ needs to be much smaller than the size of the vocabulary. However, in practice gap fillers not in the top 1000 are usually estimated with near-zero probabilities anyway. Using pruned distributions, also brings

down the complexity of our gap bundle construction algorithm from $O(m \cdot |G_t| \cdot |V|)$ to $O(m \cdot |G_t| \cdot k)$.

The main risk with pruning the distributions as described above, is that once a word is assigned with zero probability in a given gap, it will have a zero probability estimate in any bundle containing this gap, no matter how probable it is in the other gaps in the bundle. This is because the joint probability is a product of single gap probabilities. To mitigate this we use a simple form of *additive smoothing* (Chen and Goodman, 1999), that adds the probability mass of the $k$-th gap-filler to all words in the vocabulary including the ones in the top-$k$.[2]

## 3 Exercise Generation Settings

When actually generating exercises following our proposed scheme, one needs to make a few practical choices, including: (1) the corpus $C$ for training the language model, (2) the corpus $G$ from which the gaps are sampled, (3) the set of target words $T$, and (4) the number of gaps (or sentences) in a bundle.

Note that $C$ and $G$ can be the same, but $C$ would preferably be a very large corpus in order to derive a high quality language model, and $G$ would be a possibly smaller, higher quality corpus containing sen-

---

[2]We do not normalize the probability distributions as for our purposes we are only interested in probability ratios.

tences that are more suitable for learners.

In this section we describe some considerations related to these choice, as well as the settings used for generating the exercises in our experiments.

### 3.1 Language Model

Melamud et al. (2015) used gap-filler distributions (also known as *substitute vectors*), which are based on a language model, achieving state-of-the-art performance in lexical substitution tasks. Following their settings, we trained a 5-gram language model using the KenLM toolkit[3] (Heafield et al., 2013) with modified Kneser-Ney smoothing on the two billion word ukWaC English web corpus (Baroni et al., 2009). We then used this language model with the FASTSUBS tool[4] (Yuret, 2012) to generate the probability distribution of gap-filler words, pruned to the top 1000 most probable gap fillers.

Using a large web corpus, such as ukWaC, entails good coverage of diverse language styles for our language model, at some acceptable cost of noisy low quality texts.

### 3.2 Gap Bundle Corpus

While our algorithm can generate bundles given any set of input sentences, the quality of the exercises might vary strongly according to the corpus, from which the sentences are selected.

By selecting a corpus focused on a certain domain, a teacher may tune the generated bundles to the desired learning goals. For example, Sasaki (2000) show that participants perform better in a cloze exercise if it contains familiar cultural issues.

The corpus should be sufficiently large to offer enough distinct gaps for each target word to choose from. In contrast, if the corpus exceeds a certain size, it makes computation expensive without adding much value. In addition, the quality of exercises depends on the length of the sentences in the bundle. Short sentences provide little context for disambiguating the gap, while too long sentences are hard to parse for the learner.

As an example for a gap bundle corpus, we select the GUM corpus[5] (Zeldes, 2016) that is sufficiently large (44,000 tokens) and contains a good variety of

topics. The corpus is created from 54 articles extracted from the collaboration platforms *Wikinews*, *Wikivoyage*, and *wikiHow*. The articles contain interviews, news-articles, travel guides and 'how-to' instructions, and represent a good trade-off between formal and everyday language.

### 3.3 Target Words

In principle, our algorithm works with any target word. However, as with the choice of the gap bundle corpus, the selection of target words will influence the nature of the resulting exercises.

According to Abraham and Chapelle (1992) the difficulty of a gap is influenced by whether the omitted word is a function word or a content word. In this work we choose to focus on content words.

Another major influencing factor is the frequency of the selected target words (Kobayashi, 2002). For our study, we select words from the middle of the frequency distribution avoiding the extreme ends. For very infrequent words our gap corpus will not contain enough gaps to choose from. Very frequent words are mostly function words, which may behave differently and are out of scope.

As there might still be frequency effects, we sample the target words from different frequency classes. We compute the frequency class $\hat{f}$ of a word $w$ in a given vocabulary $V$ by using:

$$\hat{f}(w) = \lfloor 0.5 - \log_2(\frac{f(w)}{f_{max}(V)}) \rfloor,$$

where $f_{max}(V)$ is the frequency count of the most frequent word in $V$. Table 1 shows the selected target words and their frequency classes.

There are additional attributes that influence the resulting gaps. For example, longer target words result in increased difficulty in traditional gap-fill tasks (Abraham and Chapelle, 1992; Brown, 1989). We leave the examination of such factors to future work.

### 3.4 Gap Bundle Size

We hypothesize that generally the more sentences with gaps we add to a bundle the less ambiguous it would be. However, larger bundle sizes may result in cognitive overload or shift the nature of the task towards a test of working memory capacity. Previous work investigating multiple-choice gap-fill exercises has shown that three distractors plus the correct

---

| Target Words | Frequency Class | Word Class |
|---|---|---|
| new | 5 | |
| best | 6 | |
| full | 7 | Adjectives |
| final | 8 | |
| people | 5 | |
| language | 6 | |
| information | 7 | Nouns |
| room | 8 | |
| make | 5 | |
| want | 6 | |
| add | 7 | Verbs |
| give | 8 | |

**Table 1:** List of target words

| | Average Success Rate | Average Disambiguation Measure |
|---|---|---|
| Single Gap | .27 | -0.50 |
| $Bundle_2$ | .59 | 4.00 |
| $Bundle_3$ | .68 | 7.75 |
| $Bundle_4$ | .78 | 11.06 |

**Table 2:** Comparison of average success rate and our estimated disambiguation measure $D(b)$ for different bundle sizes.

answer is the optimal number to provide (Graesser and Wisher, 2001). Therefore, in this work we consider gap bundles that include up to four sentences.

## 4 User Study

We conducted the user study described in this section to evaluate our hypothesis that bundled gap exercises are less ambiguous than the traditional single sentence cloze items. We note that the evaluation of other educational aspects, such as learner proficiency level discrimination, were left to future work.

Gap-fill exercises are typically used with language learners, such as non-native speakers or children. However, the premise behind our study is that fully proficient speakers should be able to achieve (near) perfect scores on such exercises, provided that they are not ambiguous, i.e. that the correct answer is much more likely than any other possible solution. Accordingly, we consider high scores for proficient speakers as evidence for low levels of ambiguity in gap-fill exercises and vice versa.

### 4.1 Setup

We implement the user study using an online survey with 35 participants (20 female). To ensure a high level of language proficiency, participants either have to be native speakers of English or report a high self-assessment score (e.g. C2 CEFR level).

To measure the impact of bundle size, for each target word, we start with a single seed sentence (as in the traditional cloze test scenario) and then successively present the next sentence, chosen by our automatic algorithm for the bundle, until we reach a bundle size of four. In each step, the participant is asked to provide a single word which fits best to all of the gaps presented thus far. This setup is exemplified in Figure 3, where we show the four test steps for the target word *new*. Overall, we test this for all 12 target words (see Table 1).

For each test step, we measure average *success rate* as the ratio of participants that provided the correct target word, out of all participants. As we conducted this study with highly proficient speakers, we assume that participants who fail to provide the correct answer, have a competing answer in mind, which is also valid.

### 4.2 Results

We now report and discuss the results of the user study. We address the two major points: (1) how well gap-fill bundles resolve the ambiguity of cloze tasks, and (2) whether we can automatically discard low-quality gap bundles for quality assurance.

**Exercise Ambiguity** Our main finding is that the average success rate for single sentence cloze items is .27, while it steadily rises with every added sentence reaching .78 for a four sentence bundle - see Table 2. We also find that our average disambiguation measure grows with the size of the bundle and the success rate. These results suggests that our approach is extremely effective in reducing the ambiguity of cloze items. Still, even with four-sentence bundles we observe a non-negligible (.22) error rate. Part of this could be attributed to human performance errors, but it could also be the case that some of the bundles are still somewhat ambiguous even with four sentences.

To get more insights into this phenomenon, we conducted a detailed analysis of success rate per

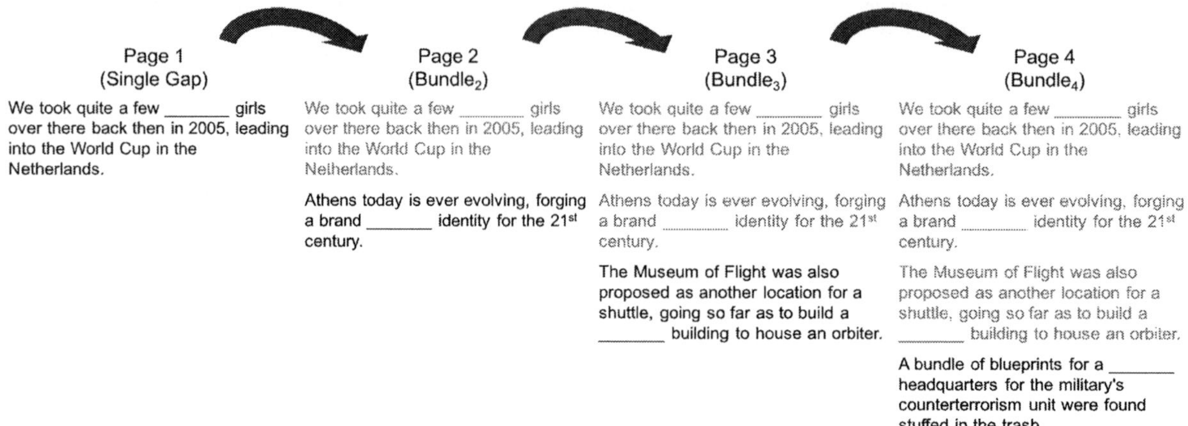


**Figure 3:** Example of the setup of the user study for the target word *new*. In the first step we present a regular single sentence cloze item, which was randomly selected. Then, we successively present larger bundles to reduce ambiguity. The subsequent sentences are selected by our algorithm.

item and bundle size - see Figure 4. On average, the biggest impact on success rate of about 30 points is observed between the single gap and the first bundle with two sentences. For some targets (*best, people, add,* and *new*) this improvement exceeds even 50 points. On the other hand, there are a few exceptions to the monotonous growth in success rate for some targets (e.g. *give, best* and *final*), where we observe a decline for an increased bundle size. Nevertheless, this decline is only local and does not exceed 11 points. The target *give* is particularly extraordinary as it has very high success rate across all bundle sizes. A deeper analysis shows that its randomly selected seed sentence uses the target in a quite idiomatic way ("*whales come to these protected waters to give birth.*"), which makes the gap unambiguous right from the start.

A further notable exception is the target word *final*, for which our algorithm does not manage to significantly dissolve the ambiguity (the overall improvement is just 12 points). An analysis of the variety of answers given by the study participants shows that they tended to include more adjectives that are highly related to *final* (e.g. *last* or *first*) when presented with the larger bundles. Here, the algorithm fails to provide a sentence that removes this ambiguity. We manually checked all sentences containing the word *final* in the gap bundle corpus and found that none of them could be used to really rule out *last* or *first*. This could indicate that our gap sentence corpus is not diverse enough, as it doesn't include a sentence, such as: "*This is the last and final call for flight 123 to San Diego*". However, we must also acknowledge that some words may have very close synonyms (as in *final* and *last*) that could be very hard to distinguish. In such cases, where our algorithm generates an ambiguous exercise, we wish to be able to automatically detect and discard it for quality assurance, as discussed next.

**Quality Assurance** In this analysis, we try to answer the question whether it is possible to automatically reject gap bundles that are likely to yield a low success rate due to ambiguity. We propose to use a threshold on our ambiguity measure $D(b)$ and analyze our study results to estimate the threshold value.

In Figure 5, we visualize the relationship between success rate in a given exercise and our model's corresponding disambiguation estimate $D(b)$. The estimated correlation between these two variables is decent ($r = 0.66$) though not perfect. However, a nice property with respect to thresholding is that our measure is rather conservative and does not overestimate the ambiguity reduction. This means that, for example, by discarding all items with $D(b) < 4.0$ we can remove almost all items with success rate below 50%, while keeping more than 80% of the items with success rate above 50%. This suggests that we are able to guarantee high-quality gap bundles, as long as we are allowed to reject some items (e.g. by flagging the teacher that for a certain seed sentence

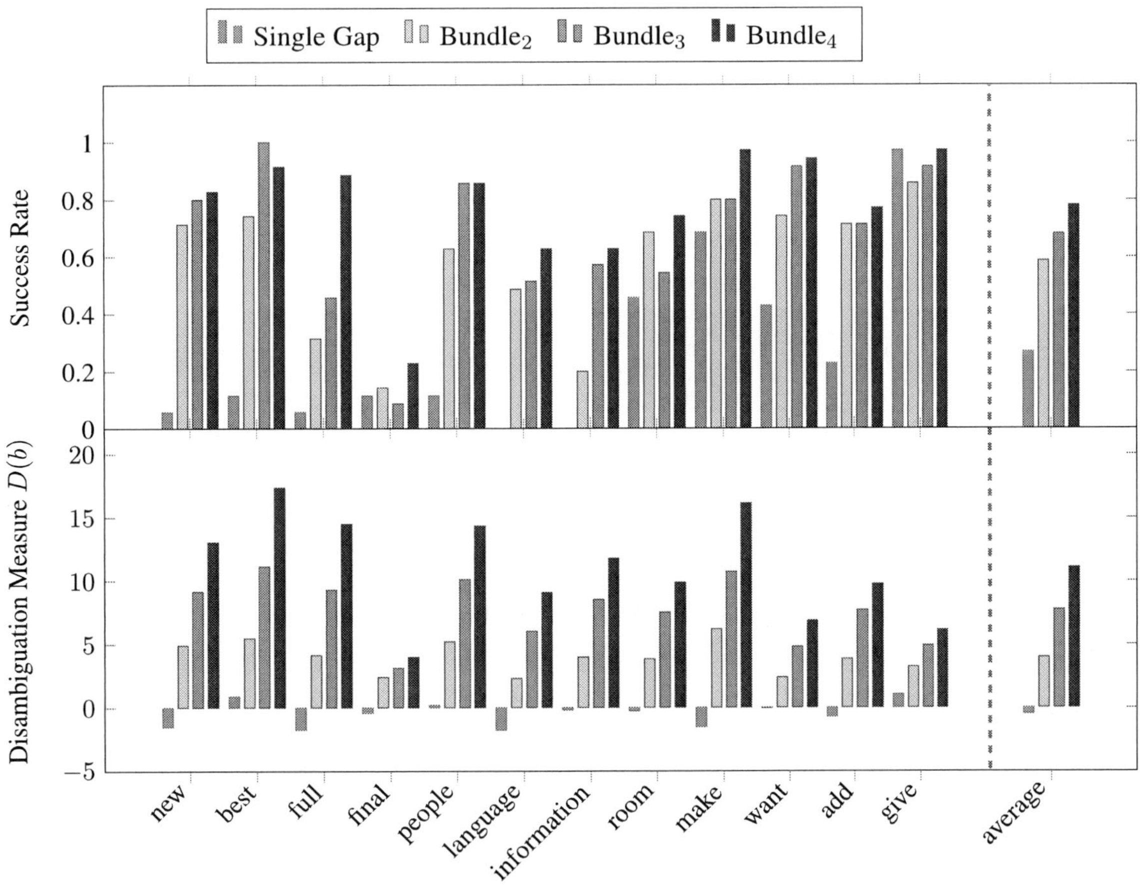



**Figure 4:** Success rate and disambiguation measure per item.

no good gap bundle can be generated).

## 5   Related Work

To the best of our knowledge, bundled gap filling is introduced in this work for the first time. Therefore, there is no directly related previous work.

However, in a broader sense, our work continues research on automated handling of ambiguity in cloze tests. Horsmann and Zesch (2014) control for ambiguity of cloze tests by selecting low ambiguity sentences based on a series of (dis-)ambiguity indicators. However, they fail to reduce the ambiguity to a sufficient degree and limit the practical relevance, as a user is limited to a narrow set of gaps that fit their approach.

As mentioned before, probably the most popular method for resolving ambiguity is to use a multiple-choice format, providing a set of distractors that may be generated automatically. These distractors may be generated from common confusions (Lee and Seneff, 2007), typical learner errors (Sakaguchi et al., 2013) or by selecting words with the same word-class or frequency in a reference corpus (Hoshino and Nakagawa, 2007).

A major problem of gap-fill exercises with distractors is that they are often too easy – especially for advanced learners –, as the generated distractors do not make sense in the context of the gap. Therefore, some approaches go one step further considering distractor candidates that are highly compatible with the context of the gaps. Then they need to automatically judge that such distractors are not in fact correct answers themselves, e.g. by considering collocations of targets and distractors (Pino and Eskenazi, 2009; Smith et al., 2010; Sumita et al., ). For example, Sumita et al. () check whether replacing the target with the distractor results in a sentence that exists on the web. If so, they conclude that the

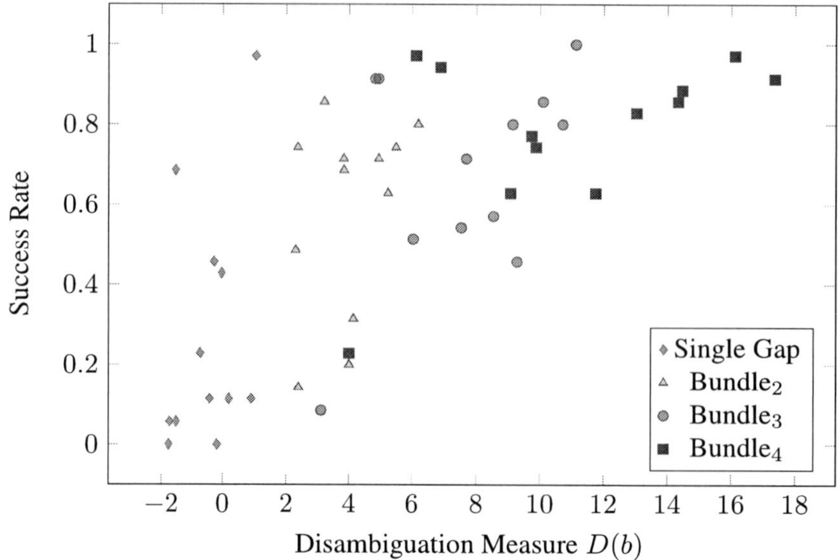


**Figure 5:** Relationship between our disambiguation measure and success rate. Each point represents a single item in the user study.

distractor is invalid. However, their approach seems to be limited, as it relies on finding exact matches of sentences which even on the web is rather unlikely. Zesch and Melamud (2014) generate distractors that are semantically similar to the target word in some sense, but not in the particular sense induced by the gap-fill context. While their approach points in a promising direction it fails to model a sufficiently large difficulty continuum, especially when targeting a group with high level of language proficiency.

Ultimately, a disadvantage of gap-fill tests with distractors is that the test is a recognition task rather than a production task and therefore considerably easier. In contrast, our *bundled gap-filling* approach has the advantage that there is no recognition stimuli and therefore the test remains a production task.

## 6   Conclusions & Future Work

In this work, we presented *bundled gap-filling* exercises and an efficient algorithm for automatically generating them. Our evaluation provides evidence that gap bundles are significantly less ambiguous than regular gap-fill exercises. This gives our approach the important advantage of supporting high automation for both generation and scoring of the exercises.

We see two main directions of research for future work. First, we want to improve the quality of the generated exercises by optimizing different parameters of the model. For example, we expect that using a larger gap sentence base or using a better language model, such as a recurrent neural network (RNN) language model, could improve the results. Second, although our bundled gap filling test is basically still a cloze test, the format change might alter the nature of the required knowledge. Consequently, we want to determine what kind of knowledge the gap bundles are actually measuring by applying it to real-life testing scenarios and examining the relations to other established measures of language proficiency. Thereby, we also want to examine the test's ability to discriminate learners with different proficiency levels by considering relations to other established measures of language proficiency and variations of the cloze test paradigm.

## Acknowledgments


This work was partially supported by the Deutsche Forschungsgemeinschaft (DFG) under grant No. GRK 2167, Research Training Group "User-Centred Social Media", by the Israel Science Foundation grant 880/12, and by the German Research Foundation through the German-Israeli Project Cooperation (DIP, grant DA 1600/1-1).

# References


Roberta G. Abraham and Carol A. Chapelle. 1992. The meaning of cloze test scores: An item difficulty perspective. *The Modern Language Journal*, 76(4):468–479.

Marco Baroni, Silvia Bernardini, Adriano Ferraresi, and Eros Zanchetta. 2009. The WaCky wide web: a collection of very large linguistically processed web-crawled corpora. *Language resources and evaluation*, 43(3):209–226.

James Dean Brown. 1989. Cloze item difficulty. *JALT journal*, 11:46–67.

Mary Anne Chavez-Oller, Tetsuro Chihara, Kelley A. Weaver, and John W. Oller. 1985. When are cloze items sensitive to constraints across sentences? *Language Learning*, 35(2):181–206.

Stanley F. Chen and Joshua Goodman. 1999. An Empirical Study of Smoothing Techniques for Language Modeling. *Computer Speech & Language*, 13(4):359–393.

Arthur C. Graesser and Robert A. Wisher. 2001. Question generation as a learning multiplier in distributed learning environments. Technical report, DTIC Document.

Kenneth Heafield, Ivan Pouzyrevsky, Jonathan H. Clark, and Philipp Koehn. 2013. Scalable modified Kneser-Ney language model estimation. In *Proceedings of the 51st Annual Meeting of the Association for Computational Linguistics*, pages 690–696, Sofia, Bulgaria.

Tobias Horsmann and Torsten Zesch. 2014. Towards Automatic Scoring of Cloze Items by Selecting Low-Ambiguity Contexts. In *NEALT Proceedings Series Vol.22*, pages 33–42.

Ayako Hoshino and Hiroshi Nakagawa. 2007. Assisting cloze test making with a web application. In *Proceedings of the Society for Information Technology and Teacher Education International Conference*, pages 2807–2814.

Christine Klein-Braley and Ulrich Raatz. 1982. Der C-Test: ein neuer Ansatz zur Messung allgemeiner Sprachbeherrschung. *AKS-Rundbrief*, 4:23–37.

Miyoko Kobayashi. 2002. Cloze tests revisited: Exploring item characteristics with special attention to scoring methods. *The Modern Language Journal*, 86(4):571–586.

John Lee and Stephanie Seneff. 2007. Automatic generation of cloze items for prepositions. In *Proceedings of INTERSPEECH*, pages 2173–2176, Antwerp, Belgium.

Oren Melamud, Ido Dagan, and Jacob Goldberger. 2015. Modeling Word Meaning in Context with Substitute Vectors. In *Proceedings of the NAACL*, Denver, Colorado, USA.

Juan Pino and Maxine Eskenazi. 2009. Semi-Automatic Generation of Cloze Question Distractors Effect of Students' L1. In *SLaTE Workshop on Speech and Language Technology in Education*.

Keisuke Sakaguchi, Yuki Arase, and Mamoru Komachi. 2013. Discriminative Approach to Fill-in-the-Blank Quiz Generation for Language Learners. In *Proceedings of the 51st Annual Meeting of the Association for Computational Linguistics (Volume 2: Short Papers)*, pages 238–242, Sofia, Bulgaria.

Miyuki Sasaki. 2000. Effects of cultural schemata on students' test-taking processes for cloze tests: a multiple data source approach. *Language Testing*, 17(1):85–114.

Simon Smith, PVS Avinesh, and Adam Kilgarriff. 2010. Gap-fill Tests for Language Learners: Corpus-Driven Item Generation. In *Proceedings of ICON-2010: 8th International Conference on Natural Language Processing*, pages 1–6, Kharagpur, India.

Eiichiro Sumita, Fumiaki Sugaya, and Seiichi Yamamoto. In *Proceedings of the second workshop on Building Educational Applications Using NLP*, pages 61–68, Stroudsburg, PA, USA.

Wilson L. Taylor. 1953. "Cloze Procedure": A New Tool For Measuring Readability. *Journalism Quarterly*, 30(4):415–433.

Marjorie Wesche and Sima T. Paribakht. 1994. Enhancing Vocabulary Acquisition through Reading: A Hierarchy of Text-Related Exercise Types. Paper presented at the AAAL '94 Conference.

Deniz Yuret. 2012. Fastsubs: An efficient and exact procedure for finding the most likely lexical substitutes based on an n-gram language model. *Signal Processing Letters, IEEE*, 19(11):725–728.

Amir Zeldes. 2016. The GUM Corpus: Creating Multilayer Resources in the Classroom. *Language Resources and Evaluation*, pages 1–32.

Torsten Zesch and Oren Melamud. 2014. Automatic Generation of Challenging Distractors Using Context-Sensitive Inference Rules. In *Proceedings of the 9th Workshop on Innovative Use of NLP for Building Educational Applications at ACL*, pages 143–148, Baltimore, USA.

# Evaluation Dataset (DT-Grade) and Word Weighting Approach towards Constructed Short Answers Assessment in Tutorial Dialogue Context


**Rajendra Banjade, Nabin Maharjan, Nobal B. Niraula, Dipesh Gautam,**
**Borhan Samei, Vasile Rus**
Department of Computer Science / Institute for Intelligent Systems
The University of Memphis
Memphis, TN, USA
{rbanjade, nmharjan, nbnraula, dgautam, bsamei, vrus}@memphis.edu



## Abstract

Evaluating student answers often requires contextual information, such as previous utterances in conversational tutoring systems. For example, students use coreferences and write elliptical responses, i.e. incomplete but can be interpreted in context. The DT-Grade corpus which we present in this paper consists of short constructed answers extracted from tutorial dialogues between students and an Intelligent Tutoring System and annotated for their correctness in the given context and whether the contextual information was useful. The dataset contains 900 answers (of which about 25% required contextual information to properly interpret them). We also present a baseline system developed to predict the correctness label (such as correct, correct but incomplete) in which weights for the words are assigned based on context.


## 1  Introduction

Constructed short answers are responses produced by students to questions, e.g. in a test or in the middle of a tutorial dialogue. Such constructed answers are very different form answers to multiple choice questions where students just choose an option from the given list of choices. In this paper, we present a corpus called DT-Grade[1] which contains constructed short answers generated during interaction with a state-of-the-art conversational Intelligent Tutoring System (ITS) called DeepTutor (Rus et al., 2013; Rus et al., 2015). The main instructional task during tutoring was conceptual problem

---

[1] Available at http://language.memphis.edu/dt-grade

solving in the area of Newtonian physics. The answers in our data set are shorter than 100 words. We annotated the instances, i.e. the student generated responses, for correctness using one of the following labels: correct, correct-but-incomplete, contradictory, or incorrect. The student answers were evaluated with respect to target/ideal answers provided by Physics experts while also considering the context of the student-tutor interaction which consists of the Physics problem description and the dialogue history related to that problem. In fact, during annotation we only limited our context to the immediately preceding tutor question and problem description. This decision was based on previous work by Niraula and colleagues (2014) that showed that most of the referring expressions can be resolved by looking at the past utterance; that is, looking at just the previous utterance could be sufficient for our task as considering the full dialogue context would be computationally very expensive.

Automatic answer assessment systems typically assess student responses by measuring how much of the targeted concept is present in the student answer. To this end, subject matter experts create target (or reference) answers to questions that students will be prompted to answer. Almost always, the student responses depend on the context (at least broadly on the context of a particular domain) but it is more prominent in some situations. Particularly in conversational tutoring systems, the meanings of students' responses often depend on the dialogue context and problem/task description. For example, students frequently use pronouns, such as *they, he, she*, and *it*, in their response to tutors' questions or other prompts.




*Proceedings of the 11th Workshop on Innovative Use of NLP for Building Educational Applications*, pages 182–187,
San Diego, California, June 16, 2016. ©2016 Association for Computational Linguistics

In an analysis of tutorial conversation logs, Niraula et al. (2014) found that 68% of the pronouns used by students were referring to entities in the previous utterances or in the problem description. In addition to anaphora, complex coreferences are also employed by students.

Also, in tutorial dialogues students react often with very short answers which are easily interpreted by human tutors as the dialogue context offers support to fill-in the blanks or untold parts. Such elliptical utterances are common in conversations even when the speakers are instructed to produce more syntactically and semantically complete utterances (Carbonell, 1983). By analyzing 900 student responses given to DeepTutor tutoring systems, we have found that about 25% of the answers require some contextual information to properly interpret them.

---

**Problem description**: A car windshield collides with a mosquito, squashing it.
**Tutor question**: How do the amounts of the force exerted on the windshield by the mosquito and the force exerted on the mosquito by the windshield compare?
**Reference answer**:
The force exerted by the windshield on the mosquito and the force exerted by the mosquito on the windshield are an action-reaction pair.
**Student answers**:
**A1**. *Equal*
**A2**. *The force of the bug hitting the window is much less than the force that the window exerts on the bug*
**A3**. *they are equal and opposite in direction*
**A4**. *equal and opposite*

---

Table 1: A problem and student answers to the given question.

As illustrated in the Table 1, the student answers may vary greatly. For instance, answer A1 is elliptical. The *"bug"* in A2 is referring to the mosquito and *"they"* in A3 is referring to the amount of forces exerted to each other.

In order to foster research in automatic answer assessment in context (also in general), we have annotated 900 student responses gathered from an experiment with the DeepTutor intelligent tutoring system (Rus et al., 2013). Each response was annotated for:

(a) their correctness, (b) whether the contextual information was helpful in understanding the student answer, and (c) whether the student answer contains important extra information. The annotation labels, which are similar to the ones proposed by Dzikovska et al. (2013), were chosen such that there is a balance between the level of specificity and the amount of effort required for the annotation.

We also developed a baseline system using semantic similarity approach with word weighting scheme utilizing contextual information.

## 2 Related Work

Nielsen et al. (2008) described a representation for reference answers, breaking them into detailed facets and annotating their relationships to the learners answer at finer level. They annotated a corpus (called SCIENTSBANK corpus) containing student answers to assessment questions in 15 different science domains. Sukkarieh and Bolge (2010) introduced an ETS-built test suite towards establishing a benchmark. In the dataset, each target answer is divided into a set of main points (called content) and recommended rubric for assigning score points.

Mohler and Mihalcea (2009) published a collection of short student answers and grades for a course in Computer Science. Most recently, a Semantic Evaluation (SemEval) shared task called Joint Student Response Analysis and 8th Recognizing Textual Entailment Challenge was organized (Dzikovska et al., 2013) to promote and streamline research in this area. The corpus used in the shared task consists of two distinct subsets: BEETLE data, based on transcripts of students interacting with BEETLE II tutorial dialogue system (Dzikovska et al., 2010), and SCIENTSBANK data. Student answers, accompanied with their corresponding questions and reference answers are labeled using five different categories. Basu et al. (2013) created a dataset called Powergrading-1.0 which contains responses from hundreds of Mechanical Turk workers to each of 20 questions from the 100 questions published by the USCIS as preparation for the citizenship test.

Our work differs in several important ways from previous work. Our dataset is annotated paying special attention to context. In addition to the tutor question, we have provided the problem description as well which provides a greater amount of contextual information and we have explicitly marked whether the contextual information was important to properly interpret/annotate the answer. Furthermore, we have annotated whether the student answer contains important extra information. This information is also very useful in building and evaluating natural language tools for automatic answer assessment.

## 3   Data Collection and Annotation

**Data Collection**: We created the DT-Grade dataset by extracting student answers from logged tutorial interactions between 40 junior level college students and the DeepTutor system (Rus et al., 2013). During the interactions, each student solved 9 conceptual physics problems and the interactions were in the form of purely natural language dialogues, i.e., with no mathematical expressions and special symbols. Each problem contained multiple questions including gap-fill questions and short constructed answer questions. As we focused on creating constructed answer assessment dataset with sentential input, we filtered out other types of questions and corresponding student answers. We randomly picked 900 answers for the annotation.

**Annotation**:   The annotation was conducted by a group of graduate students and researchers who were first trained before being asked to annotate the data. The annotators had access to an annotation manual for their reference. Each annotation example (see Figure 1) contained the following information: (a) problem description (describes the scenario or context), (b) tutor question, (c) student answer in its natural form (i.e., without correcting spelling errors and grammatical errors), (d) list of reference answers for the question. The annotators were asked to read the problem and question to understand the context and to assess the correctness of the student answer with respect to reference answers. Each of the answers has been assigned one of the following labels.

**Correct**: Answer is fully correct in the context. Extra information, if any, in the answer is not contradicting with the answer.

**Correct-but-incomplete**: Whatever the student provided is correct but something is missing, i.e. it is not complete. If the answer contains some incorrect part also, the answer is treated as incorrect.

**Contradictory**:  Answer is opposite or is very contrasting to the reference answer.  For example, "equal", "less", and "greater" are contradictory to each other.  However, Newton's first law and Newton's second law are not treated as contradictory since there are many commonalities between these two laws despite their names.

**Incorrect**: Incorrect in general, i.e. none of the above three judgments is applicable. Contradictory answers can be included in the incorrect set if we want to find all kinds of incorrect answers.

```
<Instance ID="386">
<MetaInfo StudentID ="DTSU017"
TaskID="LP03  PR09.bLK.sh"
DataSource="DeepTutorSummer2014"/>
<ProblemDescription>A car windshield collides with a
mosquito, squashing it.</ProblemDescription>
<Question>How does Newton's third law apply to this
situation?</Question>
<Answer>both objects exert the same amount of force on each
other</Answer>
<Annotation
Label="correct(0)|correct_but_incomplete(0)|contradictory(0)|i
ncorrect(0)">
<AdditionalAnnotation ContextRequired="0|1"
ExtraInfoInAnswer="0|1"/>
<Comments Watch="0|1"> </Comments>
</Annotation>
<ReferenceAnswers>
1:  The action is the windshield squashing the mosquito, and
the equal and opposite reaction is the mosquito hitting the
windshield.
</ReferenceAnswers>
</Instance>
```

**Figure 1:** An annotation example.

As shown in Figure 1, annotators were asked to assign one of the mutually exclusive labels - correct, correct-but-incomplete, contradictory, or incorrect. Also, annotators were told to mark whether contextual information was really important to fully understand a student answer. For instance, the student answer in the Figure 1 contains the phrase *"both forces"* which is referring to the force of windshield and the force of mosquito in problem description. Therefore, contextual information is useful to fully understand what both forces the student is referring to. As shown in Table 1 (in Section 1), a student answer could be an elliptical sentence (i.e., does not contain complete information on its own). In such

| Parameter | Value |
| --- | --- |
| All | 900 |
| Correct | 365 (40.55%) |
| Correct but incomplete | 209 (23.22%) |
| Contradictory | 84 (9.33%) |
| Incorrect | 242 (26.88%) |
| Requiring context | 223 (24.77%) |
| Containing extra info | 102 (11.33%) |

Table 2: Summary of DT-Grade dataset.

cases, annotators were asked to judge the student response based on the available contextual information and reference answers and nothing more; that is, they were explicitly told not to use their own science knowledge to fill-in the missing parts.

If a student response contained extra information (i.e., more information than in the reference/ideal answer provided by experts), we asked annotators to ignore the extra parts unless it expressed a misconception. However, we told annotator to indicate whether the student answer contains some additional important information such as a detailed explanation of their answer. The annotators were encouraged to write comments and asked to set the 'watch' flag whenever they felt a particular student response was special/different. Such 'to watch' instances were considered for further discussions with the entire team to either improve the annotation guidelines or to gain more insights regarding the student assessment task.

The dataset was divided equally among 6 annotators who then annotated independently. In order to reach a good level of inter-annotator agreement in annotation, 30 examples were randomly picked from each annotation subset and reviewed by a supervisor, i.e. one of the creators of the annotation guidelines. The agreements (in terms of Cohen's kappa) in assigning correctness label, identifying whether the context was useful, and identifying whether the student answer contained extra information were 0.891, 0.78, and 0.82 respectively. In another words, there were significant agreements in all components of the annotation. The main disagreement was on how to use the contextual information. The disagreements were discussed among the annotators team and the annotations were revised in few cases.

**The Dataset**: We have annotated 900 answers. Table 2 offers summary statistics about the dataset. The 40.55% of total answers are correct whereas 59.45% are less than perfect. We can see that approximately 1 in every 4 answers required contextual information to properly evaluate them.

## 4 Alignment Based Similarity and Word Weighting Approach

**Approach**: Once the dataset was finalized we wanted to get a sense of its difficulty level. We developed a semantic similarity approach in order to assess the correctness of student answers. Specifically, we applied optimal word alignment based method (Banjade et al., 2015; Rus and Lintean, 2012) to calculate the similarity between student answer and the reference answer and then used that score to predict the correctness label using a classifier. In fact, the alignment based systems have been the top performing systems in semantic evaluation challenges on semantic textual similarity (Han et al., 2013; Agirre et al., 2014; Sultan et al., 2015; Agirre et al., 2015).

The challenge is to address the linguistic phenomena such as ellipsis and coreferences. An approach can be to use off-the-shelf tools, such as coreference resolution tool included in Stanford CoreNLP Toolkit (Manning et al., 2014). However, we believe that such NLP tools that are developed and evaluated in standard dataset potentially introduce errors in the NLP pipeline where the input texts, such as question answering data, are different from literary style or standard written texts.

As an alternative approach, we assigned a weight for each word based on the context: we gave a low weight to words in the student answer that were also found in the previous utterance, e.g. the tutoring systems question, and more weight to new content. This approach gives less weight to answers that simply repeat the content of the tutors question and more weight to the answers that add the new, asked-for information; as a special case, the approach provides more weight to concise answers (see A1 and A2 in Table 1). The same word can have different weight based on the context. Also, it partially addresses the impact of coreferences in answer grading because the same answer with and without coreferences will be more likely to get comparable scores. The reference answers are usually self contained, i.e. without using coreferring expressions and only those student answers which are also self-contained and similar to reference answer will get higher score. On the other hand, answers using coreferences (such as: they, it) will get lower score unless they are resolved and the student answer becomes similar to reference answer. Giving lower weights to the words, if present in the student answer, for which student could use coreferences makes these two types of answers somewhat equivalent.

Finally, the similarity score was calculated as:

$$sim(A, R) = 2 * \frac{\sum_{(a,r)\in OA} w_a * w_r * sim(a,r)}{\sum_{a\in A} w_a + \sum_{r\in R} w_r}$$

Where A/R refers to student/reference answer and a/r is a token in it. The $sim(a,r)$ referes to the similarity score between a and r calculated using word2vec model (Mikolov et al., 2013). OA is optimal alignment of words between A and R obtained using Hungarian algorithm as described in Banjade et al. (2015). The $0 \leq w_a \leq 1$ and $0 \leq w_r \leq 1$ refer to weight of the word in A and R respectively.

**Experiments and Results**: In order to avoid noisy alignments, the word-to-word similarity score below 0.4 was set to 0.0 (empirically set). The $sim(A, R)$ was then used with Multinomial Logistic Regression (in Weka) to predict the correctness label. If there were more than one reference answers, we chose one with the highest similarity score with the student answer. We then set different weights (from 1.0 to 0.0) for the words found in tutor utterance (we considered a word was found in the previous utterance if its base form or the synonym found in WordNet 3.0 (Miller, 1995) matched with any of the words in the previous utterance). We changed the weight in the student answer as well as in the reference answer and the impact of weight change in the classification results were assessed using 10-fold cross validation approach. The changes in classification accuracy with changing weights are presented in Figure 2.

Giving weight of 1.0 to each word is equivalent to aligning words in student answer with the reference

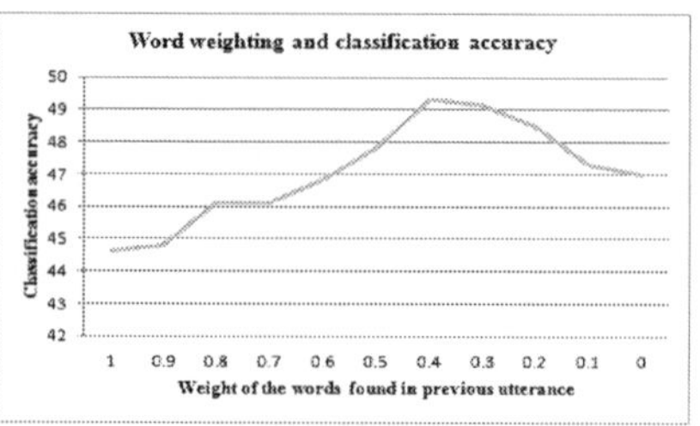

**Figure 2:** Classification accuracy and weight of the words that are found in the last utterance.

answer without looking at the context. But we can see the improvement in classification accuracy after reducing word weights up to 0.4 (accuracy 49.33%; kappa = 0.22) for the words found in the previous utterance and then decreases. It indicates that the words found in previous utterance should get some weight but new words should get more importance. This approach is somewhat intuitive. But deeper semantic understanding is required in order to improve the performance. For instance, sometimes this word weighting approach infers more information and gives higher weight to the incomplete utterance where students true understanding of the context is hard to predict. Furthermore, it is non-trivial to use additional context, such as problem description including assumptions and graphical illustrations.

## 5   Conclusion

We presented a corpus called DT-Grade which contains student answers given to the intelligent tutoring system and annotated for their correctness in context. We explicitly marked whether the contextual information was required to properly understand the student answer. We also annotated whether the answer contains extra information. That additional information can be correct or incorrect as there is no specific reference to compare with but the answer grading systems should be able to handle them.

We also presented a baseline system in which we used semantic similarity generated using optimal alignment with contextual word weighting as feature in the classifier for predicting the correctness label. However, there is enough room for the improvements and using additional features in the classifier or developing a joint inference model such as Markov Logic Network incorporating different linguistic phenomena can be two future directions.

## Acknowledgments

This research was supported by the Institute for Education Sciences (IES) under award R305A100875 to Dr. Vasile Rus. All opinions and findings presented here are solely the authors'.

## References

Eneko Agirre, Carmen Banea, Claire Cardie, Daniel Cer, Mona Diab, Aitor Gonzalez-Agirre, Weiwei Guo, Rada Mihalcea, German Rigau, and Janyce Wiebe. 2014. Semeval-2014 task 10: Multilingual semantic textual similarity. In *Proceedings of the 8th international workshop on semantic evaluation (SemEval 2014)*, pages 81–91.

Eneko Agirre, Carmen Baneab, Claire Cardiec, Daniel Cerd, Mona Diabe, Aitor Gonzalez-Agirrea, Weiwei Guof, Inigo Lopez-Gazpioa, Montse Maritxalara, Rada Mihalceab, et al. 2015. Semeval-2015 task 2: Semantic textual similarity, english, spanish and pilot on interpretability. In *Proceedings of the 9th international workshop on semantic evaluation (SemEval 2015)*, pages 252–263.

Rajendra Banjade, Nobal B Niraula, Nabin Maharjan, Vasile Rus, Dan Stefanescu, Mihai Lintean, and Dipesh Gautam. 2015. Nerosim: A system for measuring and interpreting semantic textual similarity. *SemEval-2015*, page 164.

Sumit Basu, Chuck Jacobs, and Lucy Vanderwende. 2013. Powergrading: a clustering approach to amplify human effort for short answer grading. *Transactions of the Association for Computational Linguistics*, 1:391–402.

Jaime G Carbonell. 1983. Discourse pragmatics and ellipsis resolution in task-oriented natural language interfaces. In *Proceedings of the 21st annual meeting on Association for Computational Linguistics*, pages 164–168. Association for Computational Linguistics.

Myroslava O Dzikovska, Johanna D Moore, Natalie Steinhauser, Gwendolyn Campbell, Elaine Farrow, and Charles B Callaway. 2010. Beetle ii: a system for tutoring and computational linguistics experimentation. In *Proceedings of the ACL 2010 System Demonstrations*, pages 13–18. Association for Computational Linguistics.

Myroslava O Dzikovska, Rodney D Nielsen, Chris Brew, Claudia Leacock, Danilo Giampiccolo, Luisa Bentivogli, Peter Clark, Ido Dagan, and Hoa T Dang. 2013. Semeval-2013 task 7: The joint student response analysis and 8th recognizing textual entailment challenge. Technical report, DTIC Document.

Lushan Han, Abhay Kashyap, Tim Finin, James Mayfield, and Jonathan Weese. 2013. Umbc ebiquity-core: Semantic textual similarity systems. In *Proceedings of the Second Joint Conference on Lexical and Computational Semantics*, volume 1, pages 44–52.

Christopher D Manning, Mihai Surdeanu, John Bauer, Jenny Rose Finkel, Steven Bethard, and David McClosky. 2014. The stanford corenlp natural language processing toolkit. In *ACL (System Demonstrations)*, pages 55–60.

Tomas Mikolov, Kai Chen, Greg Corrado, and Jeffrey Dean. 2013. Efficient estimation of word representations in vector space. *arXiv preprint arXiv:1301.3781*.

George A Miller. 1995. Wordnet: a lexical database for english. *Communications of the ACM*, 38(11):39–41.

Michael Mohler and Rada Mihalcea. 2009. Text-to-text semantic similarity for automatic short answer grading. In *Proceedings of the 12th Conference of the European Chapter of the Association for Computational Linguistics*, pages 567–575. Association for Computational Linguistics.

Rodney D Nielsen, Wayne Ward, James H Martin, and Martha Palmer. 2008. Annotating students' understanding of science concepts. In *LREC*.

Nobal B Niraula, Vasile Rus, Rajendra Banjade, Dan Stefanescu, William Baggett, and Brent Morgan. 2014. The dare corpus: A resource for anaphora resolution in dialogue based intelligent tutoring systems. In *LREC*, pages 3199–3203.

Vasile Rus and Mihai Lintean. 2012. A comparison of greedy and optimal assessment of natural language student input using word-to-word similarity metrics. In *Proceedings of the Seventh Workshop on Building Educational Applications Using NLP*, pages 157–162. Association for Computational Linguistics.

Vasile Rus, Sidney DMello, Xiangen Hu, and Arthur Graesser. 2013. Recent advances in conversational intelligent tutoring systems. *AI magazine*, 34(3):42–54.

Vasile Rus, Nobal Niraula, and Rajendra Banjade. 2015. Deeptutor: An effective, online intelligent tutoring system that promotes deep learning. In *Twenty-Ninth AAAI Conference on Artificial Intelligence*.

Jana Z Sukkarieh and Eleanor Bolge. 2010. Building a textual entailment suite for the evaluation of automatic content scoring technologies. In *LREC*. Citeseer.

Md Arafat Sultan, Steven Bethard, and Tamara Sumner. 2015. Dls@cu: Sentence similarity from word alignment and semantic vector composition. In *Proceedings of the 9th International Workshop on Semantic Evaluation*, pages 148–153.

# Linguistically Aware Information Retrieval:
# Providing Input Enrichment for Second Language Learners

**Maria Chinkina**     **Detmar Meurers**
LEAD Graduate School
Department of Linguistics
Eberhard Karls Universität Tübingen
{maria.chinkina,detmar.meurers}@uni-tuebingen.de

## Abstract

How can second language teachers retrieve texts that are rich in terms of the grammatical constructions to be taught, but also address the content of interest to the learners? We developed an Information Retrieval system that identifies the 87 grammatical constructions spelled out in the official English language curriculum of schools in Baden-Württemberg (Germany) and reranks the search results based on the selected (de)prioritization of grammatical forms. In combination with a visualization of the characteristics of the search results, the approach effectively supports teachers in prioritizing those texts that provide the targeted forms.

The approach facilitates systematic input enrichment for language learners as a complement to the established notion of input enhancement: while input enrichment aims at richly representing the selected forms and categories in a text, input enhancement targets their presentation to make them more salient and support noticing.

## 1   Introduction

Acquisition of a language directly depends on the learner's exposure to it. Hence, the importance of *input* in second language (L2) learning is systematically emphasized in Second Language Acquisition (SLA) research (Krashen, 1977; Swain, 1985; Gass and Varonis, 1994). Krashen even proposed the *input hypothesis* arguing that exposing learners to language input containing target structures is *the* single most important component of both first and second language learning. While later SLA approaches are more balanced in terms of considering input, output, and interaction (as well as implicit and explicit learning), they also further advanced our understanding of the role of input in terms of the frequency and perceptual salience of constructions needed for L2 learners to acquire a second language (e.g., Slobin, 1985; Schmidt, 1990).

We will refer to a method ensuring that a targeted structure is frequently represented in a text as *input enrichment*. While the isolated positive effect on L2 acquisition of the related notion of *input flooding* (Trahey and White, 1993) remains to be empirically substantiated (Reinders and Ellis, 2009; Loewen et al., 2009), input enrichment clearly is a meaningful component of the repertoire of language teachers. At the same time, manually searching for such reading material takes a lot of time and effort so that teachers often fall back on schoolbook texts designed to introduce the relevant constructions. This limits the choice of texts, and schoolbook texts typically are less up-to-date and in line with student interests than other authentic texts could be.

We therefore investigated how we can support teachers in selecting reading material that is (i) at the learner's level of language proficiency, (ii) in line with the teacher's pedagogical goal, and (iii) offers content of interest to the learner. The paper motivates input enrichment and presents *FLAIR*[1] (Form-focused Linguistically Aware Information Retrieval), a web search system striving to provide a balance of form and content in the search for appropriate reading material.

---

[1] http://purl.org/icall/flair



*Proceedings of the 11th Workshop on Innovative Use of NLP for Building Educational Applications*, pages 188–198,
San Diego, California, June 16, 2016. ©2016 Association for Computational Linguistics

In terms of envisaged use cases, in the most straightforward case, FLAIR helps the teacher identify reading materials appropriate for a class or individual students in terms of form, content, and reading level. The system can also feed into platforms providing input enhancement such as *WERTi* (Meurers et al., 2010) or generating exercises from text such as *Language Muse$^{SM}$* (Burstein et al., 2012), ensuring that the form targeted by enhancement or exercise generation is as richly represented as possible given the text base used.

In scenarios putting more value on learner autonomy or data-driven learning, FLAIR makes it possible to distribute the specification of the form and content criteria between teacher and the learner: The teacher uses their pedagogical background in foreign language teaching and learning and their knowledge of the learner's abilities and needs to configure FLAIR in a way that prioritizes (i.e., reranks highly) the texts that best satisfy these form specifications. Using the teacher-configured FLAIR, the learner then takes control and enters search queries in line with their personal interests or information needs. The outcome is a collection of documents that was retrieved based on the learner's search query, with the results ranked according to the pedagogical language learning needs defined by the teacher.

## 2  FLAIR Architecture

The *FLAIR* functionality is realized using a pipeline architecture with four modules, the Web Searcher, the Text Extractor, the Parser and the Ranker:

1. *The Web Crawler* utilizes Microsoft Bing search engine[2] to retrieve the top *N* results given a query.

2. *The Text Extractor* integrates the HttpURLConnection Java library[3] to retrieve the full html code of each page and take care of redirects. The Boilerpipe library[4] then extracts plain text from it.

   The choice of Boilerpipe is motivated by the high performance of the library compared to other text extraction techniques (Kohlschütter et al., 2010).

It provides several algorithms for the extraction of the main textual content from different types of web pages. We tested the DefaultExtractor, the ArticleExtractor and the LargestContentExtractor on a development collection of 50 documents, which established DefaultExtractor as the best choice for our task; the other two options extracted too little text in some cases when the main content was divided into several parts.

3. *The Parser* module employs Stanford CoreNLP[5] (Manning et al., 2014) to identify numerous linguistic forms using the syntactic category and dependency information obtained from it. We discuss this step further in the next section. Long sentences are quite frequent in web texts, so we employed the Stanford Shift-Reduce Parser, which is less sensitive to sentence length. The parser has also been reported to outperform the older Stanford constituency parsers.

4. *The Ranker* is responsible for reranking the top *N* results based on the statistical analysis of the data received from the previous modules. We chose the classical IR algorithm BM25 (Robertson and Walker, 1994) as the basis for our ranking model. An advantage of BM25 is the fact that it allows for any normalization unit and readily balances a multitude of query components. The final score of each document determining its place in the ranking is calculated as

$$G(q, d) = \sum_{t \in q \cap d} \frac{(k+1) \times \mathrm{tf}_{t,d}}{\mathrm{tf}_{t,d} + k \times (1 - b + b \times \frac{|d|}{avdl})} \times log \frac{N+1}{df_t}$$

where $q$ is a *FLAIR query* containing one or more linguistic forms, $t$ is a linguistic form, $d$ is a document, $\mathrm{tf}_{t,d}$ is the number of occurrences of $t$ in $d$, $|d|$ is document length, $avdl$ is the average document length in the collection, and $b$ and $k$ are free parameters we set to 0 and 1.7 respectively. The free parameter $b$ specifies the importance of the document length. We used it to give the user control over the importance of document length (implemented in the interface using a slider that can take values from 0 to 1).

---

[2] http://www.bing.com
[3] http://docs.oracle.com/javase/7/docs/api/java/net/HttpURLConnection.html
[4] https://code.google.com/p/boilerpipe/

[5] http://nlp.stanford.edu/software/corenlp.shtml

# 3 Identification of Linguistic Forms

We based the identification of linguistic forms on the official school curriculum for English in the state of Baden-Württemberg (Germany).[6] The taxonomy of topics in the official curriculum defines the language skills and knowledge that the pupils are expected to acquire in the course of their studies at school; it is not tailored to one particular textbook or approach. Overall, we implemented the identification of 87 grammatical constructions integrating a broad range of morphological, lexical and syntactic properties – the full set of constructions is listed in Appendix A. As constructions motivated by language teaching and learning, they do not necessarily map directly to the standard categories that NLP tools typically identify and are evaluated on. How the two worlds were linked is discussed next.

## 3.1 Between shallow and deep analysis

NLP makes use of different approaches for characterizing language data, from shallow matching to deep grammar formalisms, which are equally well-motivated in language learning as application domain (Meurers, 2015, sec. 3.2). While string matching can work for some basic cases (e.g., identification of articles), the detection of other constructions requires analyses going well beyond the surface level, such as an analysis based on syntactic dependencies. Even for the seemingly simple case of distinguishing different types and cases of **pronouns** to retrieve subjective, objective, reflexive as well as possessive pronouns, a lexical look-up has to be supplemented with dependency parsing in order to distinguish the subjective from the objective *you* or the objective from the possessive *her*.

Taking things one step further, consider what is needed to detect the **used to** construction referring to a habitual action in the past. After making sure that the following word is a to-infinitive, and thus, excluding the option of misidentifying the different constructions *to be used to doing* and *to get used to doing*, one is still left with an ambiguous structure that can be either interpreted as the target construction, as in (1), or as a passive structure, as in (2):

(1)  I *used to come* here every day.

(2)  It is *used to build* rockets.

This ambiguity can be resolved by checking which POS tag was assigned to the verb *used*.

While some of the 87 grammatical constructions in the English language curriculum of Baden-Württemberg support relatively straightforward characterizations based on the syntactic analysis provided by the Stanford CoreNLP, others turned out to require more thought, so that we illustrate some of those in the next section.

## 3.2 Challenges and solutions

The identification of **conditional sentences** offers some interesting challenges. Narayanan et al. (2009) discuss a POS-based approach for identifying conditional types for the task of Sentiment Analysis. It mapped sequences of POS tags to tenses (VBD + VBN = Past Perfect) and further to conditional types (If + Past perfect, MD + Present Perfect = Third Conditional). However, two different types of conditionals can be used in the same sentence, producing a mixed conditional sentence, a common type not covered by this taxonomy. Puente and Olivas (2008) proposed a more granular classification of conditional sentences and an algorithm for detecting them. However, they point out that authentic texts containing conditionals pose a challenge since some retrieved sentences do not conform to their taxonomy. In order to be able to classify every conditional sentence, *FLAIR* limits itself to distinguishing two broad classes relevant for the curriculum, real and unreal conditionals.

Where two constructions are identical in form, additional analysis of the target form in context can be required. For instance, Meurers et al. (2010) employ about 100 Constraint Grammar rules to disambiguate **gerunds** and **participles**, posing a challenge both for English language learners and parsers.

**Real conditionals** (3) and **answers to indirect questions** (4) are another example of ambiguity.

(3)  I don't *come* if he is coming.

(4)  (Do you know if he is coming?)
     I don't *know* if he is coming.

In terms of the constituency and dependency structure provided by the parser, the two cannot be distin-

---

[6]The curricula for grades 2, 4, 6, 8, and 10 are accessible on the education portal website of the state of Baden-Württemberg: `http://www.bildung-staerkt-menschen.de`

guished. A simple solution based on a list of verbs followed by an *if*-clause (e.g., *know*) can help tackle this case but will not generalize to other ambiguous cases, such as different usages of ***Present Progressive*** demonstrated in (5) and (6).

(5)  We are *waiting* for you.

(6)  We are *leaving* next week.

Considering these two sentences, one may assume that a temporal phrase should be an indicator of the time, as in (6). There can be sentential time expressions (7), though a clause introduced by *when* will not always be a future marker (8).

(7)  We are *leaving* when you are done.

(8)  You are constantly *complaining* when things go poorly.

Richer NLP analyses are evidently needed to properly distinguish such cases. Either one targets relevant distinctions with specialized Constraint Grammars or supervised machine-learning approaches (e.g., Boyd et al., 2005), or one attempts a more global analysis using a linguistically rich grammar (HPSG, LFG, TAG, ...).

In the education context, not differentiating between such ambiguous structures can mean exposing the learner to unfamiliar constructions far beyond their current level. According to the English curriculum we targeted, *Present Progressive* is introduced in the second grade, while it is only six years later, in the eighth grade, that school children are expected to use this linguistic form to express an arranged action in the future. The same applies to *real conditionals* as opposed to *answers to indirect questions* (Grades 6 and 8), *adjectives* and *quantifiers* (Grades 2 and 6), or different parts of speech ending in *-ing*, such as *gerunds* and *present participle* forms (Grades 2, 8 and 10). The *FLAIR* interface includes a reading view shown in Figure 1 that highlights and identifies the targeted constructions in a given text, so that at least for the teacher it is possible to judge on a case-by-case basis, which of the uses of an ambiguous form is part of a given text and whether it therefore requires additional explanation – or choice of another text for the envisaged audience.

## 3.3   Pilot evaluation of target identification

Before evaluating the identification of the linguistic target forms, we inspected the performance of the Stanford Shift-Reduce Parser for the constructions our patterns depend on. Among the biggest challenges were *gerunds* that got annotated as either nouns (*NN*) or gerunds/present participles (*VBG*). *Phrasal verbs*, such as *settle in*, also turned out to be difficult for the parser.

Turning to the target form identification performed by FLAIR on the basis of the parsed output, we conducted a pilot study using news articles as a common type of data analyzed by *FLAIR*. We submitting three search queries and saved the top three results for each of them, obtaining nine news articles with an average length of 28 sentences. Table 1 shows the precision, recall, and F-measure for selected linguistic constructions identified by *FLAIR* and the medians and means across the 81 constructions, for which details are included in Appendix A.

| Linguistic target | Prec. | Rec. | $F_1$ |
|---|---|---|---|
| Yes/no questions | 1.00 | 1.00 | 1.00 |
| Irregular verbs | 1.00 | 0.96 | 0.98 |
| *used to* | 0.83 | 1.00 | 0.91 |
| Phrasal verbs | 1.00 | 0.61 | 0.76 |
| Tenses (Present Simple, ...) | 0.95 | 0.84 | 0.88 |
| Conditionals (real, unreal) | 0.65 | 0.83 | 0.73 |
| **Mean** (81 targets) | 0.94 | 0.90 | 0.91 |
| **Median** (81 targets) | 1.00 | 0.97 | 0.95 |

**Table 1:** Evaluating identification of targets by FLAIR

As the numbers show, some constructions are easily detectable (yes/no questions) while others are less reliably identified by the parser (phrasal verbs). There are different reasons for lower performance: the ambiguity of the construction (*real conditionals*) and problems of the Stanford Parser (*-ing verb forms*) discussed above, as well as problematic output of the text extractor module and some limitations of the *FLAIR* patterns used for identification (*unreal conditionals*). *Conditionals* were identified with an average low F score of 0.73 due to the difficulty of their disambiguation partially discussed in section 3.2 and a particular choice we made: In order to avoid exposing learners to an unknown grammatical construction, we disambiguated all unclear cases of conditionals as the one appearing later in

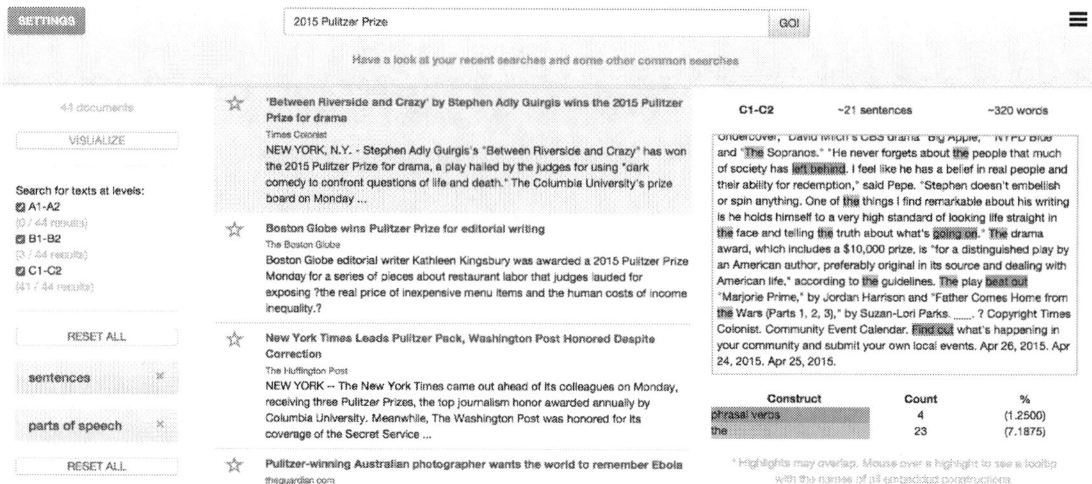

**Figure 1:** *FLAIR* interface: the settings panel, the list of results and the reading interface.

the curriculum, *unreal conditionals* (Grade 8). This way, any potential instances of this construction in texts at a lower level can be avoided (e.g., in Grade 6, when *real conditionals* are introduced).

## 4   Exploring FLAIR in use

Let us start with an example for the kind of distribution of grammatical patterns detected by *FLAIR* when analyzing the top 55 web search results returned for the query term "2016 US presidential elections". Figure 2 shows a heat map with selected constructions sorted in the ascending order by variance in their frequencies across the top 55 web search results. The figure showcases the high variability with which many of the grammatical constructions occur, which is in line with the result reported in Vajjala and Meurers Vajjala and Meurers (2013) that top web search results also differ significantly in terms of readability. This confirms that it is meaningful to rerank the top web search results in order to ensure a rich representation of specific constructions or prioritize a particular reading level.

For a more systematic exploration of the distribution of linguistic forms in web documents, we retrieved the top 60 documents for each of 40 queries using the Bing interface. In total, 2400 documents were retrieved and run through FLAIR. Among the most frequent constructions were *prepositions*, *regular* and *irregular verbs*, and *the simple verb aspect*, all of which appeared in more than 98% of the doc-

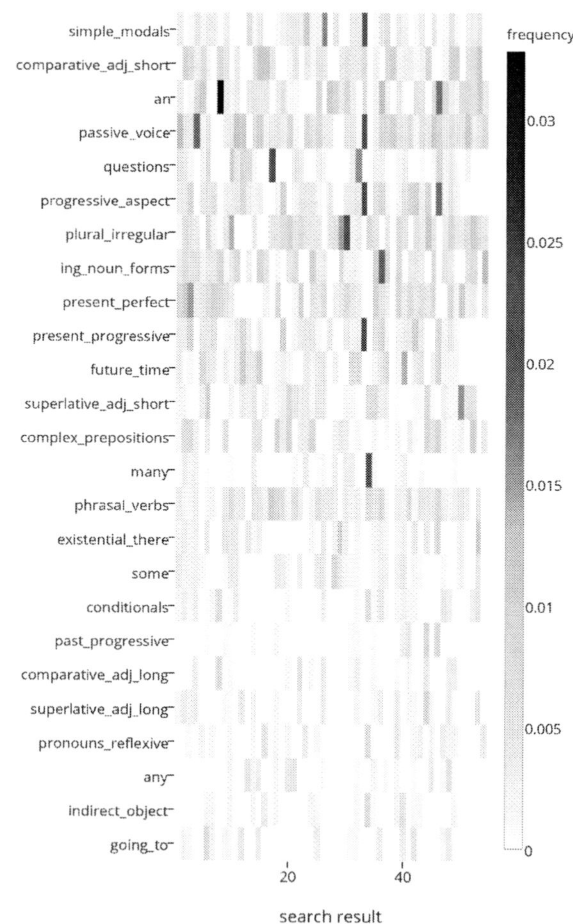

**Figure 2:** A heat map showing the distribution of grammatical construction across the top 55 results for the query "2016 US presidential elections" (normalization unit: document length)

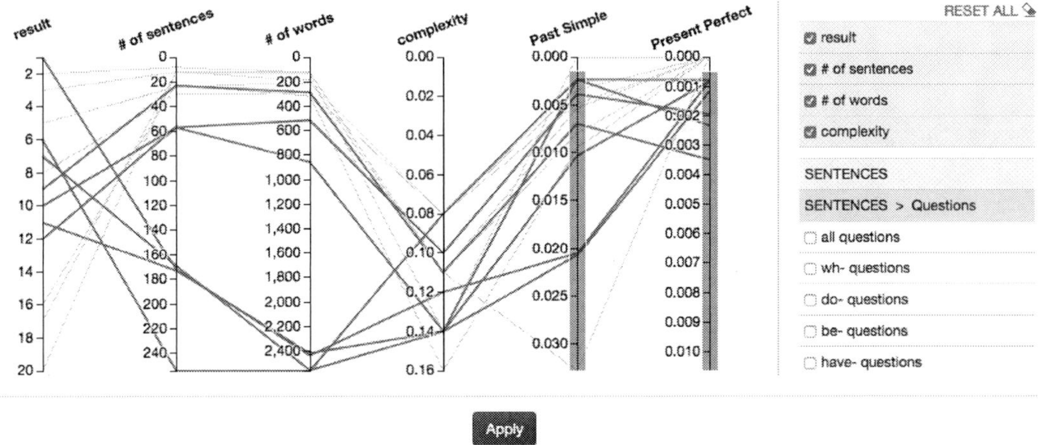


**Figure 3:** Interactive visualization in *FLAIR* with each line representing a document and vertical axes showing characteristics

uments. The least frequent linguistic constructions were *tag questions* (0.8%), *Past Perfect Progressive* (2.6%), and *imperatives* (3.2%).

Turning to a particular use case, it is a common teaching practice to not only expose the learners to one linguistic form but to contrast it with another one in the same context, e.g., *regular* vs. *irregular verbs*. We therefore selected 70 pairs of grammatical constructions from the book *English in Use* (Murphy, 2012) that are known to be challenging for English learners. We then calculated the document frequency for their pairwise co-occurrence in the collection of 2400 web texts. Among the most frequent construction pairs (i.e., where both forms occurred in many documents) were the following ones: *adjectives* vs. *adverbs* (96.7%), *the definite article* vs. *the indefinite article* (95.7%), *irregular verbs* vs. *regular verbs* (95.2%), and *Present Simple* vs. *Past Simple* (93.2%). Some construction pairs are not so easily found within the top retrieved results – either because of the low frequency of at least one of them or due to the fact that they occur in different documents. Among such construction pairs that had a document frequency of less than 10% were *degrees of comparison of adverbs, real conditionals* vs. *unreal conditionals*, and *wh- questions* vs. *yes/no questions*. The highest scoring pair of modal verbs, *can* vs. *could*, appeared in 20% of documents, with other modal pairs scoring significantly lower.[7]

---

[7]A more detailed analysis going beyond the space available here could use *odds ratios* to quantify how strongly the presence and absence of constructions are associated.

## 4.1 Interactive visualization

The *FLAIR* tool includes an interactive visual component that makes it possible to inspect and further select documents based on the multi-faceted nature of the retrieved documents. The interface illustrated in Figure 3 is based on the visualization technique of parallel coordinates used for visualizing multivariate data. Vertical axes represent parameters: any linguistic forms selected by the user, the number of sentences, the number of words and a global readability score. Each polyline stands for a document and records its linguistic characteristics by going through different points on the parameter axes. The interface supports mouse interaction allowing the user to restrict the range of values permitted for particular parameters, with other documents becoming greyed out in the interface and removed from the search results. In the figure, only documents with a non-zero frequency for both *Past Simple* and *Present Perfect* are selected. The numbers on the vertical axes for the grammatical constructions correspond to their relative frequencies in documents. Once the Apply button is selected, the search result list is restricted to those documents satisfying the constraints specified in the visualization module.

The visualization makes it possible to get an overview of the distribution of linguistic characteristics in the set of documents to be reranked. The interface also supports interaction with the visualization, providing fine-grained control over a user-selected set of linguistic characteristics. Users can

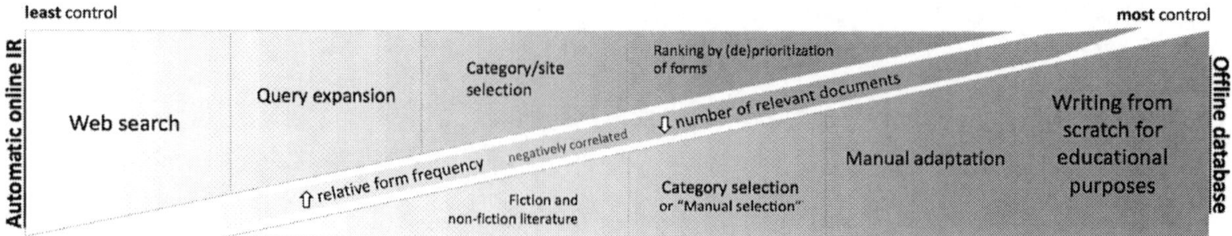


**Figure 4:** Strategies for input enrichment of an already existing corpus or during web search. The font size of the more common strategies is larger than that of the less common ones.

select a range of values for one or more constructions to precisely identify and retrieve documents.

## 4.2 Towards evaluating FLAIR in practice

Depending on a number of parameters, from the internet connection to the nature of the retrieved documents, the current *FLAIR* version takes 10 to 45 seconds to retrieve and analyze 20 web documents, making real-life use possible. Web crawling, text extraction, and NLP analysis are performed on the server in parallel for several documents, depending on the available memory and CPU power. It takes more than half of the total time (from entering the query till displaying a list of results) to fetch the results and extract the text. 20-30% of the total time are used for the NLP. Ranking is performed on the client side and takes 10-20% of the time.

As a pilot exploring whether *FLAIR* can support teachers in real-life scenarios, we asked three foreign language teachers to rank a list of six short documents taking into account the occurrences of two target forms, *the definite article* and *phrasal verbs*. We selected the documents by searching for news about the *Pulitzer Prize*, and we made sure that the distribution of the target constructions was different in each document. The teachers were completing this task on paper and did not have access to *FLAIR*.

Our assumption, in line with the common IR practice, was that high-ranked documents should balance the occurrences of all the items in the search query. That is, the most relevant document would ideally contain the same number of occurrences of all query items. Documents containing all query items but considerably more instances of one than the others would be ranked lower. Finally, the documents containing only one item, even if the number of occurrences is higher than in any other document, would

be considered the least relevant.

In the pilot exploration with the three teachers, the general preferences of each of them confirmed these assumptions underlying the scoring algorithm implemented in *FLAIR*. For the *Pulitzer Prize* query results, the teachers agreed on the most relevant document, which was also ranked highly by *FLAIR*. In future work, we plan to follow up on this pilot with a study of *FLAIR* being used by teachers of English as a foreign language at the university level.

## 5 Input Enrichment Strategies

The analyses in section 4 confirmed a high variability in the occurrence of many of the targeted structures in the web documents retrieved, making a search reranking approach promising. At the same time, we also found that some (combinations of) constructions do not commonly occur in web documents. Figure 4 spells out a spectrum of input enrichment strategies for ensuring sufficient representation of the targeted linguistic forms in reading material. As an input enrichment tool originally designed with web search in mind, *FLAIR* can equally well be used to search through *Project Gutenberg*[8], the oldest digital library containing more than 50 thousand books, or in hand-curated text repositories for children or serving as resources for language teachers such as Time for Kid[9], BBC Bitesize[10], Newsela[11], or OneStopEnglish[12].

---

[8]https://www.gutenberg.org
[9]http://www.timeforkids.com/news
[10]http://www.bbc.co.uk/bitesize
[11]https://newsela.com
[12]http://onestopenglish.com

| | REAP (Brown and Eskenazi, 2004) | TextFinder (Bennöhr, 2005) | LAWSE (Ott and Meurers, 2011) | FLAIR |
|---|---|---|---|---|
| **Database** | offline | offline | Web | Web |
| **Third party tools** | AltaVista | Lucene | Lucene | Bing API, Boilerpipe, Stanford Parser |
| **Learner model** | + | + | − | − |
| **Reading interface** | + | − | − | + |
| **Text complexity** | + | + | + | + |
| **Vocabulary load** | + | − | + | +/− |
| **Grammar** | − | +/− | − | + |
| **Coverage of curriculum** | − | − | − | + |
| **Stated future work** | grammar, cohesiveness | readability formula | syntactic features, grammar | vocabulary, large-scale testing |

Table 2: Comparison of Information Retrieval systems for language learning.

## 6 Related Work

The computational linguistic research targeting the provision of reading material to learners has generally focused on vocabulary and lexical properties or readability (Miltsakaki and Troutt, 2008; Collins-Thompson et al., 2011; Vajjala and Meurers, 2014), with some of the researchers mentioning the integration of grammar modules as future work (Brown and Eskenazi, 2004; Ott and Meurers, 2011).

Table 2 puts our *FLAIR* approach into the context of three learner-oriented IR systems: *REAP* (Brown and Eskenazi, 2004), *TextFinder* (Bennöhr, 2005), and *LAWSE* (Ott and Meurers, 2011). While each of the four systems implements a text complexity module, they differ in how they treat vocabulary and grammar. Vocabulary models are built using either word lists (*LAWSE*) or the information from the learner model (*REAP*). Grammar is given little attention, apart from Bennöhr (2005) taking into account the complexity of different conjunctions as an aspect related to discourse coherence that she directly integrates into her readability formula.

A distinguishing feature of FLAIR aimed at making it usable in real-life language teaching and learning is the comprehensive coverage of the grammatical phenomena contained in a complete curriculum of English, as spelled out in the real-life English curriculum for schools in the state of Baden-Württemberg (Germany).

Finally, most of the IR tools delegate full control over the reading material to one user – either the learner or the educator. This can also be justified for language test developers (cf., *SourceFinder*; Sheehan et al., 2007), but many language learning contexts include more of a mixture of teacher-led and learner-driven, data-driven learning. *FLAIR* addresses this issue by allowing teachers to configure the linguistic form preferences determining the reranking, while letting the learner enter queries based on their content interests to identify the base set of texts being reranked.

## 7 Conclusion and Outlook

The paper presented *FLAIR*, a linguistically aware IR approach supporting automatic input enrichment maximizing exposure of language learners to constructions currently being taught or likely to be learned next. The *FLAIR* tool can be characterized in terms of (i) the coverage of 87 linguistic constructions implemented to meet the requirements of the official curriculum for the English language in German schools, (ii) the use of efficient IR methods for the retrieval and reranking of relevant documents based on the occurrences of selected linguistic constructions in them, and (iii) the option to pre-configure the settings to direct rather than control learners' choice of reading material.

While in this paper we have mainly focused on supporting language teachers in their search for reading material richly representing the forms to be taught, what a language learner is likely to learn next is heavily researched in Second Language Acquisition Research in terms of Krashen's $i + 1$, Vygotsky's *Zone of Proximal Development*, or Pienemann's *Teachability*, so that future research could explore combining input enrichment with learner models determining the construction to be enriched.

Based on the feedback obtained from the foreign language teachers taking part in the discussed pilot studies, we identified several strands for future development. Teachers requested expanding the functionality of the tool to include more linguistic, cultural and social text characteristics that would help them get a more complete grasp of each text retrieved by *FLAIR*. Such factors as a language variety, text register, and the use of formulaic language were prominently mentioned. As a first step, we will integrate a vocabulary module: Integration of the Academic Word List (Coxhead, 2000) is currently being implemented to estimate aspects of text register. An alternative approach we are considering is to check the percentage of words from the core general vocabulary (Brezina and Gablasova, 2013). Yet another type of word list functionality, in line with Krashen's (1977) input hypothesis and similar to the learner model implemented in the *REAP* system (Brown and Eskenazi, 2004), could keep track of the words that the learner has already encountered and take this into account in ranking the retrieved documents.

Full user studies with language teachers and learners will be necessary to evaluate the overall approach as well as the effectiveness of distinct components of *FLAIR*, including what the interactive visualization offers to the teacher. On the technical side, it would be worthwhile to explore other IR algorithms that could be more directly linked to the lexical and grammatical aspects of the linguistic system we are focusing on. On the quantitative side, the analysis of linguistic forms identified by *FLAIR* could be taken one step further by running large text corpora through the parsing module of our system. Analyzing texts in Project Gutenberg, for instance, could show whether it is possible to identify appropriate reading passages from its collection of thousands of books and shed light on the linguistic nature of such collections. Considering FLAIR in the broader research context, the system also holds promise for conducting SLA research on *input enrichment* and *input enhancement*.

## Acknowledgments

This research was funded by the LEAD Graduate School [GSC1028], a project of the Excellence Initiative of the German federal and state governments. Maria Chinkina is a doctoral student at the LEAD Graduate School.

Special thanks to Madeeswaran Kannan, a computational linguistics student and research assistant at the University of Tübingen, for his excellent support in optimizing the *FLAIR* prototype, making the system useful in real life.

## References

Jasmine Bennöhr. 2005. A web-based personalised textfinder for language learners. Master's thesis, University of Edinburgh.

Adriane Boyd, Whitney Gegg-Harrison, and Donna Byron. 2005. Identifying non-referential it: A machine learning approach incorporating linguistically motivated patterns. In *Proceedings of the ACL Workshop on Feature Engineering for Machine Learning in Natural Language Processing*, pages 40–47, Ann Arbor, Michigan, June. Association for Computational Linguistics.

Vaclav Brezina and Dana Gablasova. 2013. Is there a core general vocabulary? Introducing the New General Service List. *Applied Linguistics*, page amt018.

Jonathan Brown and Maxine Eskenazi. 2004. Retrieval of authentic documents for reader-specific lexical practice. In *InSTIL/ICALL Symposium 2004*.

Jill Burstein, Jane Shore, John Sabatini, Brad Moulder, Steven Holtzman, and Ted Pedersen. 2012. The language musesm system: Linguistically focused instructional authoring. *ETS Research Report Series*, 2012(2):i–36.

Kevyn Collins-Thompson, Paul N Bennett, Ryen W White, Sebastian de la Chica, and David Sontag. 2011. Personalizing web search results by reading level. In *Proceedings of the 20th ACM international conference on Information and knowledge management*, pages 403–412. ACM.

Averil Coxhead. 2000. A new academic word list. *TESOL quarterly*, 34(2):213–238.

Susan M Gass and Evangeline Marlos Varonis. 1994. Input, interaction, and second language production. *Studies in second language acquisition*, 16(03):283–302.

Christian Kohlschütter, Peter Fankhauser, and Wolfgang Nejdl. 2010. Boilerplate detection using shallow text features. In *Proceedings of the third ACM international conference on Web search and data mining*, pages 441–450. ACM.

Stephen Krashen. 1977. Some issues relating to the monitor model. *On Tesol*, 77(144-158).

Shawn Loewen, Rosemary Erlam, and Rod Ellis. 2009. The incidental acquisition of third person-s as implicit and explicit knowledge. *Implicit and explicit knowledge in second language learning, testing and teaching*, pages 262–280.

Christopher D. Manning, Mihai Surdeanu, John Bauer, Jenny Finkel, Steven J. Bethard, and David McClosky. 2014. The Stanford CoreNLP natural language processing toolkit. In *Proceedings of 52nd Annual Meeting of the Association for Computational Linguistics: System Demonstrations*, pages 55–60.

Detmar Meurers, Ramon Ziai, Luiz Amaral, Adriane Boyd, Aleksandar Dimitrov, Vanessa Metcalf, and Niels Ott. 2010. Enhancing authentic web pages for language learners. In *Proceedings of the NAACL HLT 2010 Fifth Workshop on Innovative Use of NLP for Building Educational Applications*, pages 10–18. Association for Computational Linguistics.

Detmar Meurers. 2015. Learner corpora and natural language processing. In Sylviane Granger, Gatanelle Gilquin, and Fanny Meunier, editors, *The Cambridge Handbook of Learner Corpus Research*, pages 537–566. Cambridge University Press.

Eleni Miltsakaki and Audrey Troutt. 2008. Real-time web text classification and analysis of reading difficulty. In *Proceedings of the Third Workshop on Innovative Use of NLP for Building Educational Applications*, pages 89–97. Association for Computational Linguistics.

Raymond Murphy. 2012. *English grammar in use*. Ernst Klett Sprachen.

Ramanathan Narayanan, Bing Liu, and Alok Choudhary. 2009. Sentiment analysis of conditional sentences. In *Proceedings of the 2009 Conference on Empirical Methods in Natural Language Processing: Volume 1- Volume 1*, pages 180–189. Association for Computational Linguistics.

Niels Ott and Detmar Meurers. 2011. Information retrieval for education: Making search engines language aware. *Themes in Science and Technology Education*, 3(1-2):pp–9.

Manfred Pienemann. 1989. Is language teachable? psycholinguistic experiments and hypotheses. *Applied Linguistics*, 10(1):52–79.

Cristina Puente and José A Olivas. 2008. Analysis, detection and classification of certain conditional sentences in text documents. In *Proceedings of the 12th International Conference on Information Processing and Management of Uncertainty in Knowledge-Based Systems, IPMU*, volume 8, pages 1097–1104.

Hayo Reinders and Rod Ellis. 2009. The effects of two types of input on intake and the acquisition of implicit and explicit knowledge. *Implicit and explicit knowledge in second language learning, testing and teaching*, pages 281–302.

Stephen E Robertson and Steve Walker. 1994. Some simple effective approximations to the 2-poisson model for probabilistic weighted retrieval. In *Proceedings of the 17th annual international ACM SIGIR conference on Research and development in information retrieval*, pages 232–241. Springer-Verlag New York, Inc.

Richard W Schmidt. 1990. The role of consciousness in second language learning1. *Applied linguistics*, 11(2):129–158.

M Kathleen Sheehan, Irene Kostin, and Yoko Futagi. 2007. Sourcefinder: a construct-driven approach for locating appropriately targeted reading comprehension source texts. In *SLaTE*, pages 80–83. Citeseer.

Dan I Slobin. 1985. Crosslinguistic evidence for the language-making capacity. *The crosslinguistic study of language acquisition*, 2:1157–1256.

Merrill Swain. 1985. Communicative competence: Some roles of comprehensible input and comprehensible output in its development. *Input in second language acquisition*, 15:165–179.

Martha Trahey and Lydia White. 1993. Positive evidence and preemption in the second language classroom. *Studies in second language acquisition*, 15(02):181–204.

Sowmya Vajjala and Detmar Meurers. 2013. On the applicability of readability models to web texts. In *Proceedings of the Second Workshop on Predicting and Improving Text Readability for Target Reader Populations*, pages 59–68.

Sowmya Vajjala and Detmar Meurers. 2014. Assessing the relative reading level of sentence pairs for text simplification. In *Proceedings of the 14th Conference of the European Chapter of the Association for Computational Linguistics (EACL-14)*, Gothenburg, Sweden. Association for Computational Linguistics.

Lev Semenovich Vygotsky. 1986. *Thought and Language*. MIT Press, Cambridge, MA.

# A Evaluation of the identification of the 87 linguistic constructions

| Linguistic form | P | R | $F_1$ |
|---|---|---|---|
| to- infinitives | 1.00 | 0.98 | 0.99 |
| simple prepositions (in, at, on, with, after) | 1.00 | 0.97 | 0.98 |
| copular verbs | 1.00 | 0.97 | 0.98 |
| auxiliary verbs | 1.00 | 0.96 | 0.98 |
| irregular verbs (past participle) | 1.00 | 0.96 | 0.98 |
| advanced modals (might, ought to,able, etc.) | 1.00 | 0.94 | 0.97 |
| regular plural nouns (cats) | 0.99 | 0.94 | 0.96 |
| comparative d. of short adj. (nicer) | 0.71 | 1.43 | 0.95 |
| positive d. of adv. (fast) | 0.91 | 1.00 | 0.95 |
| Past Simple Tense | 1.00 | 0.90 | 0.95 |
| Past Time | 1.00 | 0.90 | 0.95 |
| existential there | 0.90 | 1.00 | 0.95 |
| regular verbs (past participle) | 0.98 | 0.91 | 0.94 |
| positive d. of adj. (nice) | 0.94 | 0.93 | 0.94 |
| full verb forms (am, have, etc.) | 0.88 | 1.00 | 0.94 |
| direct object | 0.91 | 0.93 | 0.92 |
| advanced prepositions (during, through, etc.) | 0.90 | 0.93 | 0.91 |
| used to | 0.83 | 1.00 | 0.91 |
| Present Simple Tense | 0.94 | 0.87 | 0.90 |
| wh- questions | 0.92 | 0.88 | 0.90 |
| Past Perfect Tense | 0.82 | 1.00 | 0.90 |
| complex sentences (with subordinate clauses) | 0.85 | 0.95 | 0.90 |
| Present Time | 0.97 | 0.83 | 0.90 |
| -ing verb forms (gerund and pr. participle) | 0.86 | 0.92 | 0.89 |
| be- questions | 0.80 | 1.00 | 0.89 |
| subjective pronouns (I, you) | 1.00 | 0.79 | 0.88 |
| subordinate clauses reduced | 0.83 | 0.94 | 0.88 |
| Simple Aspect | 0.85 | 0.92 | 0.88 |
| ing- noun forms | 0.90 | 0.82 | 0.86 |
| Past Progressive Tense | 1.00 | 0.75 | 0.86 |
| comparative d. of long adv. (more often) | 1.00 | 0.75 | 0.86 |
| Progressive Aspect | 1.00 | 0.73 | 0.84 |
| adverbial clauses | 0.83 | 0.83 | 0.83 |
| Present Progressive Tense | 1.00 | 0.71 | 0.83 |
| superlative d. of long adv. (most often) | 1.00 | 0.71 | 0.83 |
| incomplete sentences | 1.00 | 0.67 | 0.80 |
| imperative verb forms | 1.00 | 0.67 | 0.80 |
| have- questions | 0.67 | 1.00 | 0.80 |
| real conditionals | 0.68 | 0.96 | 0.79 |
| passive voice | 1.00 | 0.64 | 0.78 |
| absolute possessive pronouns | 1.00 | 0.63 | 0.77 |
| relative clauses | 0.71 | 0.83 | 0.77 |
| Perfect Aspect | 0.89 | 0.67 | 0.76 |
| phrasal verbs | 1.00 | 0.61 | 0.76 |
| Present Perfect Tense | 0.88 | 0.64 | 0.74 |
| complex prepositions (according to, etc.) | 0.56 | 0.83 | 0.67 |
| comparative d. of short adv. (faster) | 1.00 | 0.50 | 0.67 |
| indirect object | 1.00 | 0.50 | 0.67 |
| unreal conditionals | 0.63 | 0.71 | 0.67 |
| comparative d. of long adj. (more interesting) | 1.00 | 0.40 | 0.57 |
| simple sentences | 0.80 | 0.44 | 0.57 |
| Degrees of comparison (adj) | 0.93 | 0.95 | 0.89 |
| Tenses | 0.95 | 0.84 | 0.88 |
| Conditionals | 0.65 | 0.84 | 0.73 |
| **Mean** (81 targets) | 0.94 | 0.90 | 0.91 |
| **Median** (81 targets) | 1.00 | 0.97 | 0.95 |

**Data**: nine news articles with an average length of 28 sentences.

28 constructions with $\mathbf{F_1}$ **of 1**:

questions, do- questions, yes-no questions, tag questions, Future Simple Tense, Future Time, going to, irregular plural of nouns (*children*), emphatic *do*, contracted verb forms, simple modals (*can, must, need, may*), short negation (no, not, never, n't), partial negation (hardly, barely), simple conjunctions (*and, but, or*), advanced conjunctions, objective pronouns, possessive pronouns, reflexive pronouns, some, any, many, much, a, an, the, superlative form of short adjectives (*nicest*), superlative form of long adjectives (*most interesting*), superlative form of short adverbs (*fastest*).

As the texts for the evaluation were selected randomly, we found **few to no instances** of the following six constructions:

Present Perfect Progressive Tense, Past Perfect Progressive Tense, Future Perfect Progressive Tense, Perfect Progressive Tense, Future Progressive Tense, Future Perfect Tense.

# Enhancing STEM Motivation through Personal and Communal Values: NLP for Assessment of Utility Value in Student Writing

**Beata Beigman Klebanov**[1]    **Jill Burstein**[1]    **Judith M. Harackiewicz**[2]
**Stacy J. Priniski**[2]    **Matthew Mulholland**[1]
[1]Educational Testing Service
[2]University of Wisconsin, Madison
`bbeigmanklebanov,jburstein,mmulholland@ets.org`
`jmharack,spriniski@wisc.edu`

## Abstract

We present, to our knowledge, the first experiments on using NLP to measure the extent to which a writing sample expresses the writer's *utility value* from studying a STEM subject. Studies in social psychology have shown that a writing intervention where a STEM student is asked to reflect on the value of the STEM subject in their personal and social life is effective for improving motivation and retention of students in STEM in college. Automated assessment of UV in student writing would allow scaling the intervention up, opening access to its benefits to multitudes of college students. Our results on biology data suggest that expression of utility value can be measured with reasonable accuracy using automated means, especially in personal essays.

## 1 Introduction

Motivational factors, such as goals, confidence, interest and values have been shown to be important in supporting continuing engagement and success in academic pursuits at all age levels (Pintrich, 2003).

In recent years a number of promising interventions have been developed in the field of empirical social psychology to promote student motivation. Among the most successful of these interventions in college classes is the Utility Value Intervention (**UVI**) (Harackiewicz et al., 2014; Harackiewicz et al., 2015). Grounded in Eccles' Expectancy-Value Theory (Eccles et al., 1983; Eccles, 2009), the UVI, in which students write about the personal relevance of course material, helps students discover connections between course topics and their lives –

in their own terms. Discovering these connections helps students appreciate the value of their course work, leading to a deeper level of engagement with course topics that, in turn, improves performance. The effectiveness of these UVI writing assignments has been demonstrated with experimental laboratory studies and field experiments in college and high school (Canning and Harackiewicz, 2015; Harackiewicz et al., 2015; Gaspard et al., 2015; Hulleman et al., 2010; Hulleman and Harackiewicz, 2009). These UVIs are most effective for promoting motivation among those most at risk for dropping out (Harackiewicz et al., 2015; Hulleman and Harackiewicz, 2009; Hulleman et al., 2010).

A large-scale application of UVI in college and other school contexts is hindered by the need to train and employ humans to score students' writing samples for utility value. Our goal is to assess the potential of NLP to provide an automated UV evaluation that could, in turn, support scaling up the UVIs to reach many more struggling college freshmen. An automatically delivered and scored UVI would allow STEM faculty to assign UVI as homework; the automatic scores would be delivered to faculty, and students whose writing samples had insufficient expression of utility would be routed to a one-on-one session with the instructor or a teaching assistant, to discuss their plans and values to help find personal utility in studying STEM.

## 2 Data

Materials used in our experiments come from the study by Harackiewicz et al. (2015).[1]  They col-

---

[1]For data contact Prof. Harackiewicz, jmharack@wisc.edu.



*Proceedings of the 11th Workshop on Innovative Use of NLP for Building Educational Applications*, pages 199–205,
San Diego, California, June 16, 2016. ©2016 Association for Computational Linguistics

lected writing samples from first-year students enrolled in introductory biology courses at University of Wisconsin, Madison, 2012-2014. Students were asked to pose a question related to the recently studied module and answer it while incorporating utility value (**UV**), that is, explaining how the biology topic was related to their own or other people's lives. Six different biology topics are covered in the dataset (e.g., cell biology, ecology).

The utility value and control writing assignments were coded by research assistants for the level of utility value articulated in each essay, on a scale of 0-4, based on how specific and personal the utility value connection was to the individual. A "0" on this scale indicates no utility; a "1" indicates general utility applied to humans generically; a "2" indicates utility that is general enough to apply to anyone, but is applied to the individual; a "3" indicates utility that is specific to the individual; and a "4" indicates a strong, specific connection to the individual that includes a deeper appreciation or future application of the material. Inter-rater reliability with this coding rubric was high, with two independent coders providing the same score on 91% of essays. Disagreements were resolved by discussion.

Students were given 5 days to complete the assignment. Each student contributed 3 writing samples, in same or different genres, as described below.

*Genre Variation*

Students were assigned one of the following four genres, or given a choice (usually between Essay and Letter). The Essay, Letter, and Society genres are UVI genres, in that they request reference to utility value, whereas Summary is a control genre that only asks for a summary of the course material.

Assignment (common to all genres): Select a concept or issue that was covered in lecture and formulate a question.

**Letter** Write a 1-2 page letter to a family member or close friend, addressing this question and discuss the relevance of this specific concept or issue to this other person. Be sure to include some concrete information that was covered in this unit, explaining why the information is relevant to this person's life, or useful for this person. Be sure to explain how the information applies to this person and give examples.

**Essay** Write an essay addressing this question and discuss the relevance of the concept or issue to your own life. Be sure to include some concrete information that was covered in this unit, explaining why this specific information is relevant to your life or useful for you. Be sure to explain how the information applies to you personally and give examples.

**Society** Write an essay addressing this question and discuss the relevance of the concept or issue to people or society. Be sure to include some concrete information that was covered in this unit, explaining why this specific information is relevant to people's lives and/or useful for society and how the information applies to humans. Be sure to give examples.

**Summary** Select the relevant information from class notes and the textbook, and write a 1-2 page response to your question. You should attempt to organize the material in a meaningful way, rather than simply listing the main facts or research findings. Remember to summarize the material in your own words. You do not need to provide citations.

To exemplify UV-rich writing, consider the following excerpt from a Letter on Ecology:

> I heard that you are coming back to America after retirement and are planning on starting a winery. I am offering my help in choosing where to live that would promote the growth of grapes the best. Grapes are best grown in climates that receive large amounts of sunlight during the growing season, get moderate to low amounts of water, and have relatively warm summers. I highly recommend that you move to the west coast, and specifically the middle of the coast in California, to maximize the efficiency of your winery. **Letter, Ecology**

Table 1 shows data partition sizes and average essay length per genre. We note that the test set contains writing samples from unseen students.[2] Table 2 shows the UV score distributions in the training data.

---

[2]not unseen essays from students who contributed another writing sample to the train set

| Genre | Number of Samples | | | Av. Length |
|---|---|---|---|---|
| | TRAIN | DEV | TEST | (words) |
| Essay | 2,766 | 840 | 329 | 508 |
| Letter | 2,457 | 867 | 266 | 508 |
| Society | 273 | 84 | 44 | 492 |
| Summary | 3,353 | 1,160 | 345 | 486 |

**Table 1:** Summary of data, by genre

| Genre | UV Score | | | | |
|---|---|---|---|---|---|
| | 0 | 1 | 2 | 3 | 4 |
| Essay | .04 | .15 | .09 | .38 | .34 |
| Letter | .02 | .03 | .04 | .32 | .59 |
| Society | .03 | .75 | .02 | .16 | .04 |
| Summary | .59 | .38 | .00 | .02 | .01 |

**Table 2:** Distributions of utility value score, by genre

## 3 Features

For measuring utility value in a writing sample, we developed a set of features that address the form and the content of personalized writing.

### 3.1 Pronouns

We expect grammatical categories that signal reference to self, addressee, or other humans to occur frequently in UV-rich writing. We calculate log frequency per 1,000 words for the following categories:

- PRO_SG1: First person singular pronouns

- PRO_PL1: First person plural pronouns

- PRO_2: Second person pronouns

- DET_POS: Possessive determiners (e.g., their)

- PRO_INDEF: Indefinite pronouns (e.g., anyone)

### 3.2 General Vocabulary

Since expression of UV is likely to refer to everyday concerns and activities, we expect essays rich in UV to be less technical, on average, than essays that only summarize the technical content of a biology course, and therefore use shorter, more common, and more concrete words, as well as a larger variety of words. We define the following:

- WORDLN: Average word length (in letters)

- WF_MEDIAN: Median word frequency

- ACADEMICWL: Proportion of academic words (Coxhead, 2000) in content words in the essay

- CONCRETE: Log frequency per 1,000 words of words from the MRC concreteness database (Coltheart, 1981)

- TYPES: # of different words (types count)

### 3.3 Genre-Topic Vocabulary

We define a feature that captures use of language that is common for the given genre in the given topic, under the assumption that, for example, different personal essays on ecology might pick similar subtopics in ecology and also possibly present similar UV statements. For a given writing sample in genre G on topic T, we identify words that are typical of the genre G for the topic T (genre-topic words). A word is typical of genre G for the topic T if it occurs more frequently in genre G on topic T than in all other genres taken together on topic T.[3] The estimation of typical genre-topic vocabulary is done on training and development data.

- GENREVOC: Log type proportion of genre-topic words.

### 3.4 Argumentative and Narrative Elements

While summaries of technical biology material are likely to be written in an expository, informational style, one might expect the UV elements to be more argumentative, as the writer needs to put forward a claim regarding the relationship between their own or other people's lives and biology knowledge, along with necessary qualifications. We therefore defined lists of expressions that could serve to develop an argument (based on Burstein et al. (1998)) and a list of expressions that qualify or enhance a claim (based on Aull and Lancaster (2014)). The features use log token count for each category.

- ARGDEV: Words that could serve to develop an argument, such as *plausibly*, *just as*, *not enough*, *specifically*, *for instance*, *unfortunately*, *doubtless*, *for sure*, *supposing*, *what if*.

---

[3]This is similar to Lin and Hovy (2000) topic signatures approach (or, rather, genre-topic signatures here), without the transformation that supports significance thresholds. This simpler approach was found to be effective in our work on topicality for essay scoring (Beigman Klebanov et al., 2016).

- HEDGEBOOST: Hedging and boosting expressions, such as: *perhaps, probably, to some extent, not entirely true, less likely, roughly* (hedges); *naturally, can never, inevitably, only way, vital that* (boosters).

In addition, in order to connect the biology content to the writer's own life, the writer might need to provide a personal mini-narrative – background with details about the events in his or her life that motivate the particular UV statement. Since heavier reliance on verbs is a hallmark of narrativity, we define the following features (using log frequency per 1,000 words):

- COMVERBS: Common verbs (*get, go, know, put, think, want*)

- PASTTENSEVERBS: VBD part-of-speech tags

### 3.5 Likely UV content

Building on our observations of common UV content in the training data and on previous work by Harackiewicz et al. (2015), we capture specific content and attitude using dictionaries from LIWC (Pennebaker et al., 2007). In particular, UV statements often mention the benefit of scientific knowledge for improving understanding and for avoiding unnecessary harm and risk; specific themes often include considerations of health and diet. For each category, we use log proportion of words belonging to the category in the given writing sample as a feature.

- AFFECT: Words expressing positive and negative affect, such as *love, nice, sweet* and *hurt, ugly, nasty*, respectively.

- SOCIAL PROCESSES: Words expressing social relations and interactions, such as *talk, mate, share, child*, as well as words in the LIWC categories of *Family, Friends*, and *Humans*.

- INSIGHT: Words that signify cognitive engagement, such as *think, know, consider*.

- HEALTH: Words that refer to matters of health and disease, such as *clinic, flu, pill*.

- RISK: Dangers and things to avoid.

- INGESTION: Example words: *eat, dish, pizza*.

## 4  Evaluation

### 4.1  Feature Families

We evaluated each of the five feature families on its own for predicting the UV score, as well as the added value of each feature family over the combination of all the other families. On the development set, we experimented with a number of machine learning algorithms using scikit-learn toolkit (Pedregosa et al., 2011) via SKLL:[4] random forest regressor, elastic net regressor, linear regression, linear support vector regression, ridge regression, support vector regression with RBF kernel. Random forest was selected as it showed the best average performance across the four genres. Pearson correlation ($r$) is the objective function. Table 3 presents the results on the development set: The first 5 rows show each feature family on its own, followed by ALL (all families together) and by models where one family was ablated at a time.

| Feature Family | Essay | Letter | Soc. | Sum. |
|---|---|---|---|---|
| Pronouns | .759 | .442 | .527 | .544 |
| General Voc | .302 | .200 | *.165* | .260 |
| GenreVoc | .219 | .378 | *.186* | .377 |
| ArgNarr | .289 | .286 | .249 | .195 |
| UV content | .306 | .313 | *.025* | .318 |
| ALL | .784 | .543 | .527 | .622 |
| – Pronouns | .451 | .450 | .309 | .450 |
| – General Voc | .777 | .536 | .527 | .611 |
| – GenreVoc | .787 | .500 | .527 | .586 |
| – ArgNarr | .774 | .529 | .527 | .622 |
| – UV content | .768 | .542 | .527 | .622 |

**Table 3:** Pearson correlations with UV score for various feature families. Italicized correlations are not significant ($p > 0.05$).

We observe that all feature families attained statistically significant correlations with utility value scores in Essay, Letter, and Summary genres. With a single exception (GenreVoc in Essay), the correlation attained by the feature set that contains all the families (ALL) was the same or higher than in cases where a feature family was ablated. For Society, all features apart from Pronouns are quite weak, though not detrimental to performance. We decided to keep all features for the benchmark evaluation.

---

[4]https://github.com/EducationalTestingService/skll, version 1.1.1.

## 4.2 Benchmark Evaluations

We compare the effectiveness of our feature set designed specifically for this task with word ngrams (n=1,2,3) baseline. Using the development data, we evaluated ngrams using the same set of machine learning algorithms as for the experimental features (see section 4.1), and selected elastic net regression due to best average performance across the genres. Table 4 shows the performance of the experimental system and the baseline, on the blind test set, per genre. The experimental feature set (containing the total of 21 features) is on par with the baseline, on average, while showing worse performance on Letters, and better performance on Society, the dataset with the smallest number of instances.

Next, we combined the baseline and the experimental feature sets, using the elastic net regressor. Table 4 row Baseline+Exp shows the performance of the combined feature set on test data. The combination yields an average relative improvement of 4% over the baseline and 5.7% – over the experimental system. Generally, the combination matches the better performance between baseline and experimental features on Essay, Summary, and Society genres, and improves over the best performance in the most difficult Letters genre (6.8% relative improvement over baseline).

| System | Essay | Letter | Soc. | Sum. | Av. |
|---|---|---|---|---|---|
| Baseline | .788 | .437 | .731 | .662 | .655 |
| Experimental | .786 | .358 | .799 | .633 | .644 |
| Baseline+Exp | .798 | .467 | .796 | .663 | .681 |

**Table 4:** Evaluation vs ngrams baseline on test data.

## 5 Related Work

Harackiewicz et al. (2015) performed an exploratory analysis of UV writing versus control (Summary) writing, using a subset of categories from LIWC. They found that the categories of personal pronouns, words referencing family, friends, and other humans, as well as words describing social processes were used in significantly higher proportions in UV writing. They also found that words of cognitive involvement and insight are used more in UV writing.

In recent years, NLP techniques have increasingly been applied to studying a variety of social and psychological phenomena. In particular, NLP research has been used to detect language that reflects certain traits of the authors' disposition or thinking, such as detection of deception, sentiment and affect, flirtation, ideological orientation, depression, and suicidal tendencies (Mihalcea and Strapparava, 2009; Abouelenien et al., 2014; Hu and Liu, 2004; Ranganath et al., 2009; Neviarouskaya et al., 2010; Beigman Klebanov et al., 2010; Greene and Resnik, 2009; Pedersen, 2015; Resnik et al., 2013; Mulholland and Quinn, 2013). Such studies have a tremendous potential to help measure, understand, and ultimately enhance personal and societal well being. We believe that the line of inquiry initiated by the current study that is focused on motivation in college likewise promises important potential benefits.

## 6 Conclusion & Future Work

We presented the first experiments, to our knowledge, on using NLP to measure the extent to which a writing sample contains expression of the writer's utility value from studying a STEM subject. Studies in social psychology have shown that a writing intervention where a STEM student is asked to reflect on the value of the STEM subject in their personal and social lives is effective for improving motivation and retention of students in STEM subjects in college. However, the need for a trained human reader to score the writing samples has so far hindered an application of the intervention on a large scale. Our results on biology data are encouraging, suggesting that utility value can be measured with reasonable accuracy using automated means, especially in personal essays.

A direction of future work that would enable further progress in scaling up the UV writing intervention involves development of a support system for scaffolding the process of writing about UV. In particular, once the automated measurement has determined that a draft of an essay lacks sufficient expression of UV, more specific feedback and dedicated writing activities could be automatically suggested to facilitate the student's thinking and writing about the utility value of the STEM subject, which would help boost the student's motivation and success in STEM education.

# 7 Acknowledgement

We would like to thank Su-Youn Yoon and Diane Napolitano for their help with feature generation; Keelan Evanini, Jesse Sparks and Michael Flor for their comments on an earlier draft of this paper.

# References

M. Abouelenien, V. Perez-Rosas, R. Mihalcea, and M. Burzo. 2014. Deception detection using a multimodal approach. In *Proceedings of the 16th ACM International Conference on Multimodal Interaction*, pages 58–65, New York. ACM.

Laura L. Aull and Zak Lancaster. 2014. Linguistic markers of stance in early and advanced academic writing: A corpus-based comparison. *Written Communication*, 31:151–183.

Beata Beigman Klebanov, Eyal Beigman, and Daniel Diermeier. 2010. Vocabulary choice as an indicator of perspective. In *Proceedings of the 48th Annual Meeting of the Association for Computational Linguistics*, pages 253–257, Uppsala, Sweden, July. Association for Computational Linguistics.

Beata Beigman Klebanov, Michael Flor, and Binod Gyawali. 2016. Topicality-based indices for essay scoring. San Diego, CA, June. Association for Computational Linguistics.

Jill Burstein, Karen Kukich, Susanne Wolff, Ji Lu, and Martin Chodorow. 1998. Enriching automated essay scoring using discourse marking. In *Proceedings of the ACL Workshop on Discourse Relations and Discourse Marking*, pages 15–21, Montréal, Canada, August. Association for Computational Linguistics.

E. Canning and J. Harackiewicz. 2015. Teach it, don't preach it: The differential effects of directly communicated and self-generated utility-value information. *Motivation Science*, 1:47–71.

M. Coltheart. 1981. The MRC psycholinguistic database. *Quarterly Journal of Experimental Psychology*, 33A:497–505.

Averil Coxhead. 2000. A new academic word list. *TESOL Quarterly*, 34(2):213–238.

J. Eccles, T. Adler, R. Futterman, S. Goff, Kaczala C., and J. Meece. 1983. Expectations, values and academic behaviors. In J. T. Spence, editor, *Perspective on achievement and achievement motivation*, pages 75–146. San Francisco, CA: W. H. Freeman.

J. Eccles. 2009. Who am I and what am I going to do with my life? Personal and collective identities as motivators of action. *Educational Psychologist*, 44:78–89.

H. Gaspard, A. Dicke, Flunger B., M. Brisson, I. Hafner, B. Nagengast, and U. Trautwein. 2015. Fostering adolescents' value beliefs for mathematics with a relevance intervention in the classroom. *Developmental Psychology*, 51:1226–1240.

Stephan Greene and Philip Resnik. 2009. More than words: Syntactic packaging and implicit sentiment. In *Proceedings of Human Language Technologies: The 2009 Annual Conference of the North American Chapter of the Association for Computational Linguistics*, pages 503–511, Boulder, Colorado, June. Association for Computational Linguistics.

J. Harackiewicz, Y. Tibbetts, E. Canning, and J. Hyde. 2014. Harnessing values to promote motivation in education. volume 18, pages 71–105. Bingley, UK: Emerald Group Publishing Limited.

J. Harackiewicz, E. Canning, Y. Tibbetts, S. Priniski, and J. Hyde. 2015. Closing achievement gaps with a utility-value intervention: Disentangling race and social class. *Journal of Personality and Social Psychology, http:// dx.doi.org/10.1037/pspp0000075*.

M. Hu and B. Liu. 2004. Mining and summarizing customer reviews. In *Proceedings of the tenth ACM SIGKDD International Conference on Knowledge Discovery and Data Mining*, pages 168–177, Seattle, Washington. ACM.

C. Hulleman and J. Harackiewicz. 2009. Promoting interest and performance in high school science classes. *Science*, 326:1410–1412.

C. Hulleman, O. Godes, B. Hendricks, and J. Harackiewicz. 2010. Enhancing interest and performance with a utility value intervention. *Journal of Educational Psychology*, 102:880–895.

C. Lin and Eduard Hovy. 2000. The automated acquisition of topic signatures for text summarization. In *Proceedings of COLING*, pages 495–501.

R. Mihalcea and C. Strapparava. 2009. The lie detector: Explorations in the automatic recognition of deceptive language. In *Proceedings of the 47th Annual Meeting of the Association for Computational Linguistics*, pages 309–312, Singapore. Association for Computational Linguistics.

Matthew Mulholland and Joanne Quinn. 2013. Suicidal tendencies: The automatic classification of suicidal and non-suicidal lyricists using nlp. In *Proceedings of the Sixth International Joint Conference on Natural Language Processing*, pages 680–684, Nagoya, Japan, October. Asian Federation of Natural Language Processing.

Alena Neviarouskaya, Helmut Prendinger, and Mitsuru Ishizuka. 2010. Recognition of affect, judgment, and appreciation in text. In *Proceedings of the 23rd International Conference on Computational Linguistics*

*(Coling 2010)*, pages 806–814, Beijing, China, August. Coling 2010 Organizing Committee.

T. Pedersen. 2015. Screening twitter users for depression and ptsd with lexical decision lists. In *Proceedings of the 2nd Workshop on Computational Linguistics and Clinical Psychology: From Linguistic Signal to Clinical Reality*, pages 46–53, Denver, Colorado. Association for Computational Linguistics.

F. Pedregosa, G. Varoquaux, A. Gramfort, V. Michel, B. Thirion, O. Grisel, M. Blondel, P. Prettenhofer, R. Weiss, V. Dubourg, J. Vanderplas, A. Passos, D. Cournapeau, M. Brucher, M. Perrot, and E. Duchesnay. 2011. Scikit-learn: Machine Learning in Python. *Journal of Machine Learning Research*, 12:2825–2830.

J. Pennebaker, R. Booth, and M. Francis. 2007. *Linguistic Inquiry and Word Count: LIWC (Computer software)*. Austin, TX: LIWC.net.

P. Pintrich. 2003. A motivational science perspective on the role of student motivation in learning and teaching contexts. *Journal of Educational Psychology*.

Rajesh Ranganath, Dan Jurafsky, and Dan McFarland. 2009. It's not you, it's me: Detecting flirting and its misperception in speed-dates. In *Proceedings of the 2009 Conference on Empirical Methods in Natural Language Processing*, pages 334–342, Singapore, August. Association for Computational Linguistics.

Philip Resnik, Anderson Garron, and Rebecca Resnik. 2013. Using topic modeling to improve prediction of neuroticism and depression in college students. In *Proceedings of the 2013 Conference on Empirical Methods in Natural Language Processing*, pages 1348–1353, Seattle, Washington, USA, October. Association for Computational Linguistics.

# Cost-Effectiveness in Building a Low-Resource Morphological Analyzer for Learner Language


**Scott Ledbetter**
Indiana University
Bloomington, IN, USA
saledbet@indiana.edu

**Markus Dickinson**
Indiana University
Bloomington, IN, USA
md7@indiana.edu



## Abstract

In this paper, we describe the development of a morphological analyzer for learner Hungarian, outlining extensions to a resource-light system that can be developed by different types of experts. Specifically, we discuss linguistic rule writing, resource creation, and different system settings, and our evaluation showcases the amount of improvement one gets for differing levels and kinds of effort, enabling other researchers to spend their time and energy as effectively as possible.


## 1 Introduction

There is much work on developing technology and corpora for lesser-resourced languages (LRLs), involving varying assumptions about the amount of available data (e.g., Feldman and Hana, 2010; Duong et al., 2015; McDonald et al., 2011; Garrette et al., 2013; Garrette and Baldridge, 2013; Lynn et al., 2013; Smith and Dickinson, 2014). To our knowledge, though, there has been very little work focusing on tools for automatically analyzing learner language. Yet LRLs present many challenges and opportunities, not least of which is the chance, through language learning, to increase awareness and usage of the language. In that light, we build from our work in Ledbetter and Dickinson (2015) to develop a morphological analyzer for learner Hungarian in a resource-light way, extending the framework to handle a wider range of phenomena and to increase accuracy, addressing the trade-offs between effort and performance.

Part of the purpose in Ledbetter and Dickinson (2015) is to push for the automatic analysis of learner language beyond English, incorporating a wider range of linguistic and error patterns. But there is little indication about how much effort is required to build a system of sufficient accuracy. Garrette and Baldridge (2013) point out exactly the time spent in annotation, and we follow in that vein of estimating time costs, here for analyzing learner language, to foster resource-light development (cf. Smith and Dickinson, 2014).

Indeed, there is a convenient connection between LRLs and the automatic analysis of learner language, one enabling a rule-based approach. In a low-resourced setting, there is a lack of data for data-driven modeling, and one can write rules in a short amount of time; because such rules are linguistically motivated, they are relatively easy to connect to tasks such as providing feedback on learner input or modeling learner behavior, i.e., tasks requiring linguistic analysis. Systems for learner language are also amenable to low-resource development in that the vocabulary is often restricted and the requirement for high precision dovetails nicely with using linguistic rules. Such an approach allows for quick, transparent development, helping identify parts of the linguistic system that the tool gets (in)correct.

Given the need to interact with NLP researchers, educators, and learners, this linguistic transparency is a key property (cf. Loukina et al., 2015). In this work, we propose a number of different kinds of extensions to a system, appropriate for different aspects of analysis. The system is rule-based, which—in addition to being appropriate for Hungarian mor-




*Proceedings of the 11th Workshop on Innovative Use of NLP for Building Educational Applications*, pages 206–216,
San Diego, California, June 16, 2016. ©2016 Association for Computational Linguistics

phology in a resource-light setting—makes it feasible to plug in different components and thus allows one to test the effect of different extensions. We envision different kinds of experts (linguists, teachers, NLP researchers, etc.) being able to contribute within such a paradigm, thus broadening the range of who can contribute to successful analyzer design.

Corresponding to different types of knowledge, we propose four kinds of system improvements: 1) writing linguistic rules (e.g., exception marking); 2) creating resources (e.g., name dictionary); 3) optimizing system settings (e.g., automatic ranking); and 4) analyzing system output. Seeing the effects of these improvements can help contribute to a broader discussion of which components are most in need of development for learner data (cf. constraint relaxation (Reuer, 2003; Schwind, 1995)). The main contribution of this work is thus to outline and identify the benefits of different kinds of resources for building a transparent analyzer, highlighting the best gains for the amount of time one has available.

In section 2 we cover the basics of Hungarian, turning to learner Hungarian and the general framework in section 3. In section 4 we outline the types of improvement, detailing specific modifications to the system and the amount of effort involved in each one. Section 5 then shows the results for tagging accuracy, and we provide general advice on prioritizing effort in section 6. Although our current results are below the state-of-the-art, we have spent little time in getting a workable system. We do not address in this paper how accurate an analyzer needs to be in order to be deployed for providing learner feedback, but it is important to note: a) we highlight starting points for development, not a finished product; and b) for some purposes—such as assisting in the semi-automatic annotation of a learner corpus or targeting subparts of the grammar (for which the system is more accurate) for learner modeling—even the current system can be of benefit.

## 2  Hungarian

Hungarian is a Finno-Ugric language known for its rich agglutinative morphology, in which words are formed by joining morphemes together, as shown in (1). Morphemes convey information such as num-

ber and case (e.g., INESSive) for nouns (1a), number, person, tense, and definiteness for verbs (1b), or changes to part-of-speech (1c). Hungarian also exhibits vowel harmony, which requires that the backness of vowels (represented by the feature [+/-BK]) matches during affixation (Törkenczy, 2008); e.g., the front vowel variant -ben is inappropriate for (1a).

(1)    a.  fá        -k  -ban
           tree[+BK] -PL -INESS[+BK]
           'in trees'
       b.  felejt        -ett         -em
           forget[-BK] -PST[-BK] -1SG.INDEF[-BK]
           'I forgot'
       c.  álm          -atlan              -ság
           sleep[+BK] -NEG.ADJ[+BK] -NOM[+BK]
           'sleeplessness/insomnia'

## 3  Framework

We build from the analyzer in Ledbetter and Dickinson (2015). Given the nature of Hungarian, the morphological analyzer follows in the tradition of rule-based approaches (Prószéky and Kis, 1999; Megyesi, 1999; Trón et al., 2005, 2006), as a statistical approach relying on large amounts of data for training would be more challenging in a resource-light setting. Data sparsity, common with agglutinative languages in which a given wordform appears few times in training data, compounds this problem. The amount and type of resources necessary for our work is comparable to other research on morphologically-rich languages in low-resource settings, e.g. for some Indian languages (Singh et al., 2006; Shrivastava and Bhattacharyya, 2008; Alfter, 2014). Details of the system are in section 3.2.

### 3.1  Data

To develop and evaluate a system, we rely on both native language and learner data. The corpus of learner data was collected from L1 English students of Hungarian, divided into three levels of proficiency (Beginner, Intermediate, Advanced) as determined by course placement in one of three two-semester sequences. The corpus consists of journal entries, each a minimum of ten sentences in length on a topic selected by the student. The data and error annotation are described in Dickinson and Ledbetter

(2012). For native data, we use the Szeged Corpus of Hungarian (Csendes et al., 2004).

For development of all our improvements, we use the same 1000 words of native data and 1024 words of learner data that were used in Ledbetter and Dickinson (2015). The native data is taken from compositions, so as to be relatively comparable to the journal entries found in the learner corpus. For evaluation (section 5), we use new approximately same-sized (1000, 1032) sections of data, i.e., the test sets are comprised of new compositions never before seen by the analyzer. Note that there is no training data, as we are assuming a small set of resources.

## 3.2  Morphological analyzer

The morphological analyzer is affix-driven and works simply by using a small set of known affixes to derive a final analysis. For example, with a suffix *-at* in the grammar that takes a noun stem (N) to the left to derive a cased noun phrase (KP)—notated KP\N—the word *házat* ('house+ACC') obtains a KP analysis, segmented as *ház+at*.

The analyzer supports using features, too, e.g., KP\N {vh:bk} to indicate that vowel harmony (*vh*) requires back (*bk*) vowels here. Error detection can thus be performed on top of morphological analysis simply by allowing for and storing feature clashes (instead of requiring feature unification). In this paper, we focus on providing correct morphological tags, as this is the tool's most primary function.

The baseline performance of the morphological analyzer assumes the minimum of resources required to function: a knowledge base of grammatical affixes and the analyzer (i.e., rule compiler) itself. In section 5, we report two baseline scores, with 10 and then with 50 affixes. Although Ledbetter and Dickinson (2015) also start with a dictionary, we assume no other resources for our baseline; with only affixes, the resulting scores are accordingly low. Each improvement to the analyzer (section 4) is then evaluated separately with respect to this baseline.

Since we are concerned about time, we should note that the rule compiler is around 3000-4000 lines of Python code (depending on how one counts comments, data handling, printing of intermediate output, system-internal checks, etc.). We estimate it

would take 1–2 months for someone to build, but as it relies on a CYK parser (see details in Ledbetter and Dickinson, 2015) and as one may choose different kinds of rule compilers for the same effect (e.g., a constraint grammar compiler (Didriksen, 2016) or an FST-based system (Hulden, 2009)), this time could be significantly less.

## 4  Improvements

The morphological analyzer is designed with low-resource scenarios in mind, starting with as little as a rule compiler and however much grammatical information one has time to specify in rules (i.e., affixes). We want to improve beyond this simple design, but we need to determine the best ways to improve. Ideal improvements: a) require little time to implement; b) contribute (significantly) to better performance; and c) are as transparent as possible.

As mentioned in section 1, improvements to the analyzer are divided into four categories. For ease of implementation and development, each category can represent a different person or team, based on the resources and expertise available.

In each subsection below, we discuss a series of related improvements we have completed and estimate the time required to implement them to the same degree we have. We assume 1 day = 8 hours of work for one person. For these estimates, we do not strictly follow our own experience, as we did not precisely log the time and, more importantly, we expect future users to require less time to choose and implement changes. We also assume someone of moderate expertise in the area for which the improvements need to be made—e.g., someone familiar with Hungarian linguistics enriching the knowledge base (section 4.1) vs. someone familiar with corpus linguistics extracting a most frequent word list (section 4.2). The improvements in section 4.4 are more likely than any other to involve discussion and cooperation among the different people, as it involves incremental changes in the other areas.

## 4.1  Linguistic rule writing

The first set of improvements involves writing rules that correspond to linguistic generalizations. These come in different levels of granularity, e.g., general rules (#1) vs. exceptions (#3).

**1. Enrich the knowledge base (KB):** The morphological analyzer relies primarily on grammatical rules encoded in the knowledge base (KB) of affixes, all of which can be obtained from a traditional grammar reference or language textbook. The size of the KB can vary, and the system's performance increases with richer and more complete grammatical information. The baseline systems detailed in section 3.2 assume a modest base of either 10 or 50 affixes.

Although we experiment with small KBs, it is possible to obtain over 200 affixes for Hungarian using a grammar reference (Törkenczy, 2008), such as the derivational suffix in (2). Here, the affix *-ság* creates a noun (N) when combined with an adjective (A) to its left. Furthermore, the adjective stem must contain back vowels to match the harmonizing suffix (indicated by the feature *vh* and its required value *bk* in braces). An example word can be found in (3). The adjective *boldog* ('happy') can combine with the nominalizing suffix *ság* because it contains back vowels, as specified in the knowledge base. Thus, the completed derivation is the noun *boldogság* ('happiness'). **Time estimate:** 2 days.

    (2)   *-ság*: N\A{vh:bk}

    (3)   *boldog   -ság*
           A{vh:bk} N\A{vh:bk}
           "happiness" (N)

**2. Modify knowledge base features:** The KB can be augmented with grammatical features, used to constrain, i.e., eliminate certain combinations of morphemes. (In the case of learner language, features may only disfavor analyses—see the *Free* setting in section 4.3.) As seen in (2), the feature *vh* constrains a derivation based on vowel harmony. Features also supply key information during derivation to increase the accuracy of morphological tags. In (4), the feature *k* indicates that the noun stem (N) suffixed with *-t* will become a cased noun phrase (KP) in the accusative case (*acc*).

    (4)   *-t*: KP{k:acc}\N

Note that modifications to grammatical features are included in all results presented in section 5, as removing a single feature from each entry in the KB to measure its effectiveness would take a long time and provide little in the way of guidance for future researchers. **Time estimate:** 1-2 days.

**3. Encode exceptions (Except):** Any target language will have exceptions to grammatical rules. A list of the most frequent grammatical exceptions (even as few as 5–10), including handling of irregulars, may provide a boon to performance. In Hungarian, irregular stem changes during verb conjugation, for example, can mask the relatedness of different forms in the paradigm, and only one stem will be found in a dictionary (when a dictionary is used). Forms like those in (5) can be linked to a single stem—the dictionary form of 'to be,' *van*—to facilitate a complete paradigm. The analyzer makes use of only five such cases, targeting the most frequent irregular verb stem changes. **Time estimate:** 1 day.

    (5)   a.  *vagy -ok*        b.  *van -nak*
               be   -1SG          be  -3PL
               '[I] am.'        '[they] are.'

## 4.2 Resource creation

The next improvements involve building resources, generally corresponding to finding data that fits the context under which the language is being produced (e.g., learners with a first language (L1) of English).

**1. Obtain a language dictionary (Dict):** A dictionary of attested target language words is a straightforward improvement. If available digitally, a target language dictionary is simple to add; otherwise, one must be built by hand or via transcription. In the latter case, a minimal list of words can be obtained from a grammar reference or language textbook and then digitized. Our analyzer accesses an English-Hungarian dictionary of 161,000 entries (Vonyó, 1998) with words only (i.e., no part-of-speech or other grammatical information). **Time estimate:** 1 day (electronic resource).

**2. Obtain a list of common names (Names):** A common problem for morphological analysis is the treatment of unknown words. A list of names common to the source (when known) and target languages is often easy to acquire or create and could alleviate a frequent cause of unknown words. The analyzer has access to a list of 400 common first names, 200 from English (L1 in our data) and 200 from Hungarian (L2), obtained from *behindthename.com*. **Time estimate:** 1 day.

**3.    Obtain a list of the most frequent words (Freq):**   A small number of words (e.g., function words) appear very frequently in written data, independent of domain, while the vast majority of words appear only a few times.   With access to corpus data, a list of the most frequent words in the language with the proper morphological tags (added by hand) can ensure that the analyzer is accurate for a large amount of written data.   Of the 100 most frequent words in the Hungarian National Corpus (Oravecz et al., 2014), 50 were selected and placed in a database for the analyzer along with the appropriate morphological tags. Selection proceeded one word at a time, beginning with the most frequent, using several criteria, including familiarity to learners, opaque rather than transparent morphology, and appropriateness to genre. **Time estimate:** 1 day.

### 4.3    System settings

The third set of improvements focus on implementation, deriving ways to obtain the best analysis from among many possible ones or in cases where little-to-no information is known.

**1.    Devise a method to rank analyses (Rank):** Morphological analysis for learner data must be more flexible than similar methods for native language data.   Misspelled words, clashes of grammatical features, and a non-targetlike distribution of morphological affixes can all cause failure for rules designed to analyze the standard target language. Overgeneration is accordingly a significant problem for any system that attempts to account for such differences.   A method for prioritizing one possible analysis over another is essential for reducing ambiguity, which in turn has a direct effect on precision.

We created a simple method to rank analyses in the output of the analyzer. First, any analysis that makes use of a stem found in the dictionary is ranked higher than one that doesn't.   Second, an analysis is ranked higher than another if it exhibits fewer clashes of grammatical features during derivation (section 3.2).   If neither of the above rules applies, analyses are ranked in the order they were created. Future work can explore more sophisticated methods of ranking. **Time estimate:** 1 week.

**2.    Determine a default tag for unknown words (Def):**   As indicated earlier, unknown words can reduce accuracy during analysis, and learners are prone to innovate new forms.   This problem can be minimized by assigning a default analysis to unknown words.   Our analyzer proposes a single tag *Nc-sn* (noun: common, singular, nominative case) when it fails to produce a derivation. Following standard practice in POS tagging, this default tag specifically targets the most likely open class of words. **Time estimate:** 1 day.

**3.   Hypothesize roots (Hyp):**   The design of the analyzer emphasizes flexibility to account for the differences between learner data and standard target language data. In order to make the system more robust, a derivation can hypothesize a potential stem after an affix from the knowledge base has been recognized.   This allows for non-standard roots (e.g., those that have been misspelled) during derivation, even if the system is relying on dictionary lookup.

(6)    **haz  -ban*
     house -INESSIVE
     'in [a] house.'

In (6), for example, a system built to analyze standard Hungarian may not recognize *haz* as part of a valid word, as *ház* ('house') is the likely intended form. By completing a derivation when possible, on the basis of the suffix (e.g., $N_{hyp}$ + KP\N), the analyzer can be more robust—though, it can also over-posit analyses. **Time estimate:** 2 days.

**4.   Relax constraints (Free):**   Another method for introducing flexibility into the analyzer involves the features associated with the affixes in the KB. When analyzing target language data, the features of stems and affixes should unify, resulting in a complete derivation. In learner data, on the other hand, we expect feature clashes as learners have not yet mastered the rules of the target language grammar. By relaxing the unification of features to allow clashes, we can more often obtain complete derivations.

(7)  *ház  -ben{vh:fr}
     house -INESSIVE

     'in [a] house.'

Consider the example in (7). The suffix *-ben* requires a stem with front vowels (the value of the feature *vh* must be *fr*), but the stem *ház* contains back vowels. With the appropriate setting, our analyzer permits the derivation and provides the correct morphological tag. **Time estimate:** 2 days.

The last two modifications (Hyp, Free) are proposed in Ledbetter and Dickinson (2015), but need to be evaluated within the space of other settings.

### 4.4  System analysis

The improvement in this section is relevant to the whole system, relying on other settings and not easily isolated to a single area of expertise. No evaluation of this improvement is provided, as it was undertaken at several stages during development.

**1. Perform a system/error analysis:**  Time can be spent on an analysis of system performance, using a small set of (annotated) development data. At any stage of development, it is useful to inspect the output of the analyzer and investigate potential mistakes in rules, affixes, features, improvements, or the underlying code itself. Thus, creating a small set of annotated data is important for this stage.

Indeed, some of the time for the other improvements is "hidden" in this task. In our experience, we were able to identify a number of ways in which the system was not functioning as expected. We identified affixes omitted from the KB, discovered new features to restrict spurious analyses, and developed the initial ideas for ranking analyses—in addition, of course, to debugging the underlying code. Resolving each of these led to an increase in accuracy. **Time estimate**: 1 month (or more).

## 5  Evaluation

After devising the improvements on the development data, we evaluate the morphological analyzer first on native Hungarian data and then on learner data, recording precision, recall, and accuracy measures. Each improvement to the system is first considered individually, assessing its value apart from all others, and then combined with other improvements to determine the overall effectiveness.

The test sets, as mentioned in section 3, are new excerpts from the target (1000 tokens) and learner corpora (1032 tokens). The analyzer produces as output one or more morphological tags for each word in the input. During evaluation, this list of output tags is compared to a list of gold standard tags. For native data, the gold tag list from the target language corpus contains the correct context-specific tag as well as a list of possible tags based on morphology. The annotation of the target language corpus uses corrected output from the *magyarlanc* (Zsibrita et al., 2013) tool. For learner data, we annotate a single gold standard tag for each word.

We evaluate how many tags from the analyzer match possible tags from the gold standard and whether the correct context-specific tag appears in the output. Specifically, we report:

- **Precision (P)**: the number of tags in the output that appear in the gold standard, divided by the number of tags in the output.

- **Recall (R)**: the number of tags in the output that appear in the gold standard, divided by the number of tags in the gold standard.

- **Accuracy (A)**: the number of correctly identified context-specific tags divided by the total number of words in the input.

### 5.1  Individual improvements

The precision, recall, and accuracy measures for each individual improvement are given in Table 1 for native data and Table 2 for learner data. The top half of the table, labeled *KB-10*, indicates that the analyzer used a knowledge base of ten affixes, and the lower half of *KB-50* indicates 50 affixes. All other improvements are identified by columns with

| KB-10 | ML | Base | Except | Dict | Names | Freq | Rank | Def | Hyp | Free |
|---|---|---|---|---|---|---|---|---|---|---|
| P | 0.970 | 0.018 | 0.023 | 0.107 | 0.018 | 0.385 | 0.018 | 0.221 | 0.145 | 0.018 |
| R | 0.413 | 0.008 | 0.010 | 0.051 | 0.008 | 0.182 | 0.008 | 0.094 | 0.070 | 0.008 |
| A | 0.930 | 0.018 | 0.023 | 0.089 | 0.018 | 0.303 | 0.018 | 0.058 | 0.125 | 0.018 |
| KB-50 | ML | Base | Except | Dict | Names | Freq | Rank | Def | Hyp | Free |
| P | 0.970 | 0.037 | 0.041 | 0.213 | 0.037 | **0.401** | 0.037 | 0.239 | 0.221 | 0.037 |
| R | 0.413 | 0.016 | 0.018 | 0.115 | 0.016 | **0.190** | 0.016 | 0.103 | 0.146 | 0.016 |
| A | 0.930 | 0.036 | 0.041 | 0.194 | 0.036 | **0.321** | 0.036 | 0.076 | 0.245 | 0.036 |

**Table 1:** Evaluation for each improvement (native data)

| KB-10 | ML | Base | Except | Dict | Names | Freq | Rank | Def | Hyp | Free |
|---|---|---|---|---|---|---|---|---|---|---|
| P | 0.850 | 0.003 | 0.016 | 0.062 | 0.003 | 0.290 | 0.003 | 0.104 | 0.079 | 0.003 |
| R | 0.850 | 0.003 | 0.016 | 0.068 | 0.003 | 0.311 | 0.003 | 0.105 | 0.091 | 0.003 |
| A | 0.850 | 0.003 | 0.016 | 0.068 | 0.003 | 0.311 | 0.003 | 0.105 | 0.091 | 0.003 |
| KB-50 | ML | Base | Except | Dict | Names | Freq | Rank | Def | Hyp | Free |
| P | 0.850 | 0.011 | 0.024 | 0.147 | 0.011 | **0.297** | 0.011 | 0.112 | 0.162 | 0.011 |
| R | 0.850 | 0.011 | 0.024 | 0.184 | 0.011 | **0.319** | 0.011 | 0.112 | 0.240 | 0.011 |
| A | 0.850 | 0.011 | 0.024 | 0.184 | 0.011 | **0.319** | 0.011 | 0.112 | 0.240 | 0.011 |

**Table 2:** Evaluation for each improvement (learner data). Recall (R) = Accuracy (A) since only one gold standard tag is annotated.

labels matching their descriptions in section 4. The *ML* column provides a comparison with a native language tool, *magyarlanc* (Zsibrita et al., 2013).

For native data (Table 1), *magyarlanc* attains nearly perfect precision and very high accuracy. This is to be expected, given that the tool was used in creating the gold standard annotation of the test corpus. Recall, naturally, is less, as *magyarlanc* disambiguates among all the context-independent tags. These figures provide a rough estimate of the difficulty of morphological analysis for Hungarian. As expected, the baseline performance of our analyzer is extremely low, at 2% precision and less than 1% recall with a meager knowledge base, and about double that with a slightly richer one.

For every improvement, the size of the knowledge base increases performance. Three different improvements (Names, Rank, and Free), however, make no difference in performance as compared to Base, irrespective of the difference in size of the KB. By far, the most effective improvement is Freq (most frequent word list), attaining the highest performance (e.g., precision above 40%) with 50 affixes in the KB. The Dict, Def, and Hyp improvements also exhibit noteworthy gains for all three metrics.

There is a slight gain from the addition of Except, but no more than 1%—unsurprising, given the small number of encoded cases.

For learner data (Table 2), performance is lower across the board. The *magyarlanc* tool loses about 13% in precision and 8% in accuracy, illustrating the increased difficulty of the task of analyzing learner language. Our analyzer begins with baseline scores at 1% or lower for both KB-10 and KB-50. The results for learner data parallel those for native data: the Names, Rank, and Free improvements provide no increase in performance, while Freq provides the greatest gains, reaching nearly 30% precision and 32% recall and accuracy. Likewise, the Dict, Def, and Hyp improvements provide noticeable gains, with Except providing small gains.

While no single improvement on its own results in very high scores, the evaluation highlights the most effective improvements. The Freq improvement alone, for example, contributes nearly 40% to precision for native language data.

## 5.2 Improvements in combination

We now turn to an evaluation of the system in successive iterations, beginning with the baseline system and adding one new improvement each time. Table 3 shows the results for native data, while Table 4 shows the results for learner data. The last column in each table gives the results of a final test with all improvements added. In each series of tests, a knowledge base of 50 affixes is used.

|   | Base | +Dict | +Freq | +Def | +Hyp | All |
|---|------|-------|-------|------|------|-----|
| P | 0.037 | 0.213 | 0.497 | **0.579** | 0.472 | 0.451 |
| R | 0.016 | 0.115 | 0.281 | 0.323 | 0.350 | **0.363** |
| A | 0.036 | 0.194 | 0.479 | 0.517 | 0.567 | **0.594** |

**Table 3:** Evaluation for stepwise improvements in combination, moving left to right (KB 50, native data)

|   | Base | +Dict | +Freq | +Def | +Hyp | All |
|---|------|-------|-------|------|------|-----|
| P | 0.011 | 0.147 | 0.378 | **0.457** | 0.384 | 0.370 |
| R | 0.011 | 0.184 | 0.492 | 0.592 | 0.631 | **0.661** |
| A | 0.011 | 0.184 | 0.492 | 0.592 | 0.631 | **0.661** |

**Table 4:** Evaluation for stepwise improvements in combination, moving left to right (KB 50, learner data)

Note that the order of added improvements is based on both practical concerns and effectiveness in the individual evaluations discussed above. The first improvement added to the system is Dict (a target language dictionary): though this did not provide the greatest gains in the evaluation metrics, it is the most central resource and one of the easiest to obtain. The next improvements (Freq, Def, and Hyp) were selected for their contributions during individual evaluations, and each is added in an order corresponding to its impact on performance. Finally, the other modules (Except, Names, Rank, Hyp) are added for the *All* model.

For native data (Table 3), the system displays a general trend of increasing precision, recall, and accuracy as improvements are added. Precision reaches its peak at 58% with the addition of the default tag (Def) improvement, while recall and accuracy continue to increase. Both recall and accuracy reach their maximum with all improvements added. Precision at its maximum remains well below that of *magyarlanc*'s 97%, but recall reaches 36% with all improvements, just 5% short of *magyarlanc*. The *All* model, despite making use of every improvement, exhibits a drop in precision; an inspection of the data reveals that this is due to the increased number of proposed analyses. The system is outputting more tags that are correct (thus, the increase in recall), but the number of proposed analyses increases by a larger margin, and thus precision falls.

For learner data (Table 4), the trends are nearly identical for the successive improvements. The Dict, Freq, and Def improvements obtain a precision of 46%, compared to *magyarlanc*'s 85%, while recall and accuracy rise to 66% with all improvements added, about 20% from *magyarlanc*'s 85%. As with native data, precision falls with the *All* model, even though the number of correct tags is at its highest. The figures for maximum recall and accuracy are encouraging, considering that *magyarlanc* makes use of contextual information for disambiguating possible morphological tags. Our analyzer currently uses no contextual information, analyzing one word at a time. With the incorporation of additional information such as syntactic frames, the results could be more competitive with those for native data. It is also important to note that the *magyarlanc* tool is based on the *morphdb* database (Trón et al., 2006), which represents years of work, while many of our system improvements require less than a month.

It may seem surprising that recall and accuracy for learner data surpass the results for native data. This stems from the fact that the gold standard annotation for learner data has only one correct tag. Similarly, for the calculation of precision, multiple analyses proposed by the system adversely affect the score, even if alternatives may be correct for a word.

Although the evaluation data is different, we can roughly compare accuracies of 0.594 and 0.661 to corresponding accuracies of 0.505 and 0.478 in Ledbetter and Dickinson (2015). This gain is in spite of using 205 affixes in the KB in Ledbetter and Dickinson (2015) vs. 50 here, highlighting the point that some improvements (e.g., Freq) are more time-effective than others (e.g., expanding the KB).

## 6 Discussion and Outlook

Concerning ourselves with the balance between improving analyzer accuracy and/or coverage and spending time to do so, the most valuable improvement for the analysis of L2 Hungarian morphology is a list of the most frequent words and the corresponding tags. Other notable improvements include incorporating a method for hypothesizing stems, a dictionary of Hungarian words, and a default tag for analysis. Finally, some rich knowledge base of grammatical information is essential, and even small KB sizes can have moderate performance with other improvements in place.

With the exceptions of enriching the knowledge base and creating a method for hypothesizing stems, each improvement is estimated to need only a single day to implement (to the level we have). Together, all these improvements would require just over a single work week. Additional time, when available, may be spent on further improvements or system analysis, as discussed in section 4.4.

The recommended improvements are spread across several areas of expertise, and many require at least some existing resources. In some settings, it may not be possible to implement even these few. With these restrictions in mind, we propose the following prioritization of improvements:

1. Target language dictionary. While not the largest improvement, it is hard to envision adequate analysis without a dictionary. For many languages, the ease of acqusition and widespread availability of this resource make it quick and effective to obtain. In the absence of an electronic dictionary, it is possible to extract some lexicon from a grammar resource or language textbook; much more time will then be spend in digitization.

2. Frequent word list. This improvement provides the greatest benefit for performance, requiring a moderate amount of target language data to ascertain the most common words. It may also be necessary to add morphological information if the corpus isn't annotated. If no corpus data is available, one could also use intuition to derive something akin to the most common, or most salient, words in a language.

3. Default tag. One of the simplest methods to improve the analyzer, a default tag requires very little knowledge of coding to implement.

4. Knowledge base. The size of the knowledge base directly affects performance, though it

takes longer to implement. We have shown that as few as 10 affixes may be used to begin analysis, and 50 shows great promise.

5. Hypothesized stems. This requires knowledge of the underlying code of the analyzer and may need fine-tuning for different target languages.

6. System analysis. System analysis should be a part of every stage of development, but it also requires the most time of any improvement.

Performance of the system with these improvements does not reach the level of a tool designed for native language morphological analysis. However, our work illustrates that significant gains can be made with fewer resources, most of which are easily accessible, assuming only a grammar reference or language textbook to begin. With the prioritized list of improvements above, time and energy can be used efficiently to streamline the development of a low-resource morphological analyzer.

There is still much to do to get a better handle on the impact of different improvements to obtain a better analyzer. We envision exploring larger knowledge bases and their effect on increasing ambiguity, developing more methods for ranking analyses—perhaps incorporating trends from any possible available learner data—and experimenting with resources (dictionaries, name lists) which are targeted towards particular domains or learning contexts. Additionally, one question has still not been addressed by our evaluation: how good is good enough? Utilizing other evaluation measures that probe into real-world usage, e.g., for error detection and grammar extraction (Ledbetter and Dickinson, 2015), will be crucial in that respect.

## Acknowledgments

We would like to thank the three anonymous reviewers for their helpful feedback.

## References

David Alfter. 2014. *Morphological analyzer and generator for Pali*. Ph.D. thesis, University of Trier, Trier, Germany.

Dóra Csendes, János Csirik, and Tibor Gyimóthy. 2004. The szeged corpus: A pos tagged and syntactically annotated hungarian natural language corpus. In *Text,*

*Speech and Dialogue: 7th International Conference, TSD*, pages 41–47.

Markus Dickinson and Scott Ledbetter. 2012. Annotating errors in a hungarian learner corpus. In *Proceedings of the 8th Language Resources and Evaluation Conference (LREC 2012)*.

Tino Didriksen. 2016. *Constraint Grammar Manual: 3rd version of the CG formalism variant*. GrammarSoft ApS.

Long Duong, Trevor Cohn, Steven Bird, and Paul Cook. 2015. Low resource dependency parsing: Cross-lingual parameter sharing in a neural network parser. In *Proceedings of the 53rd Annual Meeting of the Association for Computational Linguistics and the 7th International Joint Conference on Natural Language Processing (Volume 2: Short Papers)*, pages 845–850. Beijing, China.

Anna Feldman and Jirka Hana. 2010. *A resource-light approach to morpho-syntactic tagging*. Rodopi, Amsterdam/New York, NY.

Dan Garrette and Jason Baldridge. 2013. Learning a part-of-speech tagger from two hours of annotation. In *Proceedings of the 2013 Conference of the North American Chapter of the Association for Computational Linguistics: Human Language Technologies*, pages 138–147. Association for Computational Linguistics, Atlanta, Georgia.

Dan Garrette, Jason Mielens, and Jason Baldridge. 2013. Real-world semi-supervised learning of pos-taggers for low-resource languages. In *Proceedings of the 51st Annual Meeting of the Association for Computational Linguistics (Volume 1: Long Papers)*, pages 583–592. Association for Computational Linguistics, Sofia, Bulgaria.

Mans Hulden. 2009. Foma: a finite-state compiler and library. In *Proceedings of the 12th Conference of the European Chapter of the Association for Computational Linguistics*, pages 29–32. Association for Computational Linguistics.

Scott Ledbetter and Markus Dickinson. 2015. Automatic morphological analysis of learner hungarian. In *Proceedings of the Tenth Workshop on Innovative Use of NLP for Building Educational Applications*, pages 31–41. Denver, CO.

Anastassia Loukina, Klaus Zechner, Lei Chen, and Michael Heilman. 2015. Feature selection for automated speech scoring. In *Proceedings of the Tenth Workshop on Innovative Use of NLP for Building Educational Applications*, pages 12–19. Denver, CO.

Teresa Lynn, Jennifer Foster, Mark Dras, and Josef van Genabith. 2013. Working with a small dataset semi-supervised dependency parsing for irish. In *Proceedings of SPMRL 2013*. Seattle.

Ryan McDonald, Slav Petrov, and Keith Hall. 2011. Multi-source transfer of delexicalized dependency parsers. In *Proceedings of the 2011 Conference on Empirical Methods in Natural Language Processing*, pages 62–72. Association for Computational Linguistics, Edinburgh, Scotland, UK.

Beata Megyesi. 1999. Improving Brill's POS tagger for an agglutinative language. In *Proceedings of the Joint SIGDAT Conference on Empirical Methods in Natural Language Processing and Very Large Corpora*, pages 275–284.

Csaba Oravecz, Tamás Váradi, and Bálint Sass. 2014. The hungarian gigaword corpus. In *Proceedings of LREC 2014*.

Gabor Prószéky and Balazs Kis. 1999. A unification-based approach to morpho-syntactic parsing agglutinative and other (highly) inflectional languages. In *Proceedings of the 37th annual meeting of the Association for Computational Linguistics on Computational Linguistics*, pages 261–268.

Veit Reuer. 2003. Error recognition and feedback with lexical functional grammar. *CALICO Journal*, 20(3):497–512.

Camilla B. Schwind. 1995. Error analysis and explanation in knowledge based language tutoring. *Computer Assisted Language Learning*, 8(4):295–324.

Manish Shrivastava and Pushpak Bhattacharyya. 2008. Hindi pos tagger using naive stemming: Harnessing morphological information without extensive linguistic knowledge. In *Proceedings of ICON-2008: 6th International Conference on Natural Language Processing*, pages 1–8. ICON.

Smriti Singh, Kuhoo Gupta, Manish Shrivastava, and Pushpak Bhattacharyya. 2006. Morphological richness offsets resource demand: Experiences in constructing a pos tagger for hindi. In *Proceedings of the COLING/ACL 2006 Main Conference Poster Sessions*, pages 779–786. Association for Computational Linguistics.

Amber Smith and Markus Dickinson. 2014. Evaluating parse error detection across varied conditions. In *Proceedings of the 13th International Workshop on Treebanks and Linguistic Theories (TLT13)*. Tübingen, Germany.

Miklós Törkenczy. 2008. *Hungarian Verbs and Essentials of Grammar, 2nd ed.* McGraw-Hill, New York.

V. Trón, Gy. Gyepesi, P. Halácsy, A. Kornai, L. Németh, and D. Varga. 2005. Hunmorph: Open source word analysis. In *Proceedings of the Workshop on Software*, pages 77–85. Association for Computational Linguistics.

V. Trón, P. Halácsy, P. Rebrus, A. Rung, P. Vajda, and E. Simon. 2006. Morphdb. hu: Hungarian lexical database and morphological grammar. In *Proceedings of 5th International Conference on Language Resources and Evaluation (LREC)*, pages 1670–1673.

Attila Vonyó. 1998. A magyar elektronikus könyvtár.

János Zsibrita, Veronika Vincze, and Richárd Farkas. 2013. Magyarlanc: A toolkit for morphological and dependency parsing of hungarian. In *Proceedings of RANLP*, pages 763–771.

# Automatically Scoring Tests of Proficiency in Music Instruction

**Nitin Madnani**     **Aoife Cahill**     **Brian Riordan**

Educational Testing Service
Princeton, NJ, 08541 USA
{nmadnani,acahill,briordan}@ets.org

## Abstract

We present preliminary work on automatically
scoring constructed responses elicited as part
of a certification test designed to measure the
effectiveness of the test-taker as a K-12 music
teacher. This content scoring differs from most
previous work in that the responses are relatively long and are written by an adult population of generally proficient English writers. We
obtain reasonably good scoring performance
for all the test questions using simple features.
We carry out some initial error analysis and
show that there is still room for improvement.

## 1 Introduction

In this paper, we examine the feasibility of automatically scoring content-based questions from a teacher
certification test which measures the test-taker's effectiveness as a K-12 music teacher. The test was designed by experts with extensive experience in music
education, who consult regularly with music teachers and music education professors throughout the
USA to ensure the appropriateness and validity of
individual test questions.

Specifically, this test measures indicators of the
beginning educator's professional readiness to teach
K-12 music in each of the three major music education specialties: general, instrumental, and vocal
music education. The typical test population consists
of undergraduates who have completed, or nearly
completed, a music education program. Materials
appearing on the test reflect instrumental, vocal, jazz,
and general music instruction specialties across the
K-12 grade range. Note that the test contains a combination of multiple-choice as well as constructed

response (essay-style) questions. A final score for
the test is computed by combining the scores for all
questions and *only* that score is reported to the test-
takers, not individual question scores. In this paper,
we focus on building automated scoring models for
the essay-style questions.

## 2 Data

We obtained test-taker responses written between
2013 and 2015 to multiple administrations of the test.
Each student wrote answers to three essay-style questions. We look at a total of six different essay-style
questions across all test forms. Although we cannot
disclose the actual questions for reasons of test secu-
rity, Figure 1 shows a sample question from the test.
It asks the prospective teacher to examine a given
vocal music sample and answer questions relevant
to teaching the sample to a hypothetical class of students. Overall scores are assigned on a 0–3 scale,
based on the degree to which the test-taker accurately
responds to the three subparts of the question. Figure 3a shows the total number of scored responses
available ($N$) for each of the six questions.

The responses to all six questions on the test are
scored by two human experts on a 0–3 scale.[1] Figure 2 shows the distributions of the response lengths
and the scores assigned to the responses by the first
human expert (hereafter referred to as the H1 score).

## 3 Related Work

The test we examine here has been designed primarily
to elicit content knowledge from prospective teachers
in the context of instruction. Our work can be consid-

---

[1]For each response, the two experts are chosen randomly
from a pool of 9 experts.



*Proceedings of the 11th Workshop on Innovative Use of NLP for Building Educational Applications*, pages 217–222,
San Diego, California, June 16, 2016. ©2016 Association for Computational Linguistics

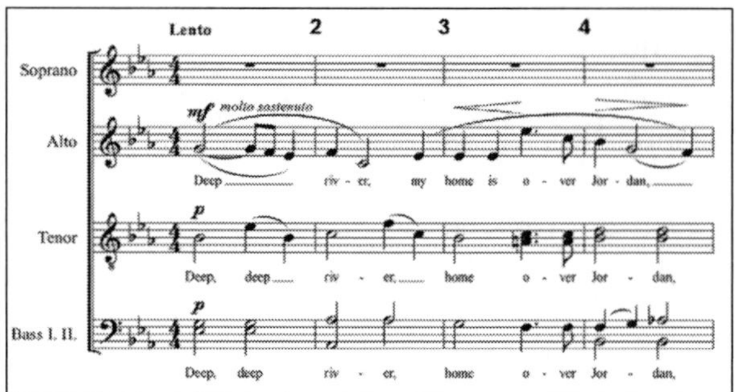




Figure 1: A sample question from the music teaching proficiency test. Note that only a part of the entire music sample included with the question is shown here.

ered similar in spirit to some of the previous work on short-answer scoring, where the focus is on scoring content-driven responses to math, biology, or computer science questions (Sukkarieh and Stoyanchev, 2009; Sukkarieh et al., 2011; Mohler et al., 2011; Dzikovska et al., 2013; Ramachandran et al., 2015; Sakaguchi et al., 2015; Zhu et al., 2016).[2] However, we claim that there is very little in that body of previous work that focuses on responses exhibiting *all* of the following characteristics:

- The responses we examine are written by a population of adults that are generally proficient English writers. This is different from most previous work where the population is generally composed of middle- and high-school students with varying levels of English proficiency.

- The average length of these responses is approximately 220 words which is much longer than the responses considered in much of the previous work (10-100 words long, on average).

- These responses are from a high-stakes test (teacher certification) whereas previous work has focused mostly on responses from low-

to medium-stakes tests (in-class discussions, homework assignments, placement tests, etc.).

The work that could be considered most similar to ours is that of Alfonseca and Pérez (2004) (further described by Pérez-Marín and Pascual-Nieto (2011)) which focuses on scoring responses to computer science questions (50-130 words long, on average) written by undergraduate students. However:

1. Their responses were written to tests that lacked the instructional context — tests that assessed content comprehension but *not* how that content can best be taught to a class of K-12 students. Although both types of responses might require understanding the same concepts, they are likely to be expressed differently. For example, the following is an excerpt from a sample response to the question in Figure 1.

*"This example is best suited for a high school mixed chorus. One performance challenge that would be likely for a HS chorus performing this work would be the octave leap in the alto part in measure 3. (This is also found in measure 11.) This passage needs to maintain the legato phrasing marked throughout and needs to crescendo smoothly without a loss of tone and without accenting the top E-flat. Students may tend to restrict their throats in order to*

---

[2]See Table 3 in Burrows et al. (2015) for a comprehensive list.

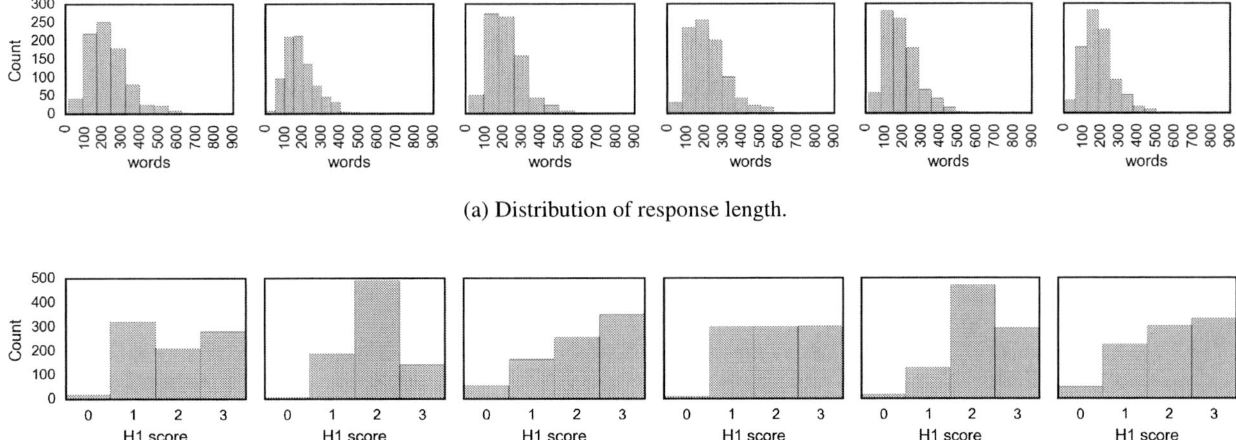

(a) Distribution of response length.

(b) Distribution of the response scores assigned by the first human expert (H1 scores).

Figure 2: The response length and H1 score distributions of all six questions from the test.

*reach the high note. With insufficient breath support, the crescendo and legato phrasing will not be musical. ... "*

2. Their responses were scored by comparing to human-authored reference answers whereas our scoring approach does not require any reference answers.

To the best of our knowledge, there has not been any work that uses a machine-learned model to automatically score questions that measure content-based teaching ability.

## 4 Content Scoring Model

We split the data available for each of the questions into training and test sets with 70% for training and 30% for test. We then build an automated scoring model for each question separately using the H1 score as our target. Each scoring model uses support vector regression (Smola and Schölkopf, 2004) to estimate a function that predicts human scores from vectors of binary linguistic features. We use the implementation from the *scikit-learn* package (Pedregosa et al., 2011), with default parameters except for the complexity parameter, which is tuned using cross-validation on the data provided for training.

As features in the model, we start with the set of features that have generally been used for scoring content-based short answers in the literature:

- lowercased word $n$-grams ($n$=1,2), including punctuation

- lowercased character $n$-grams ($n$=2,3,4,5)
- syntactic dependency triples computed using the ZPar parser (Zhang and Clark, 2011))
- length bins (specifically, whether the log of 1 plus the number of characters in the response, rounded down to the nearest integer, equals $x$, for all possible $x$ from the training set)

A salient characteristic of this test and its constituent questions, as described by its designers, is that they measure content knowledge from prospective teachers, but not writing proficiency. There is a separate test that measures the writing proficiency of prospective teachers, that is required for all test-takers taking the music test.

In order to empirically confirm the minimal impact of writing proficiency, we build a second automated scoring model for writing proficiency using features inspired by Attali and Burstein (2006) and train it on the responses written by the same population of test-takers for the general writing proficiency test (*not* the music teaching proficiency test). Note that this model is generic, i.e., not question specific. We then use this trained model to assign scores to the responses from the music teaching proficiency test. A low agreement of these proficiency scores with the H1 scores assigned to the music questions should be sufficient evidence to indicate that the writing proficiency of the test-takers is not an important factor. There will obviously be some agreement because good writers

| Q | N | QWK | | | Adjacent Agreement | | | Exact Agreement | | |
|---|---|---|---|---|---|---|---|---|---|---|
| | | H1-H2 | H1-WP | H1-CS | H1-H2 | H1-WP | H1-CS | H1-H2 | H1-WP | H1-CS |
| 1 | 1162 | .702 | .306 | .566 | .937 | .817 | .958 | .705 | .389 | .470 |
| 2 | 1160 | .764 | .217 | .570 | .988 | .892 | 1.00 | .846 | .434 | .714 |
| 3 | 1154 | .695 | .245 | .515 | .955 | .809 | .945 | .573 | .358 | .476 |
| 4 | 1272 | .647 | .253 | .500 | .959 | .854 | .962 | .665 | .398 | .530 |
| 5 | 1270 | .757 | .089 | .619 | .983 | .840 | .994 | .810 | .330 | .680 |
| 6 | 1267 | .669 | .196 | .426 | .950 | .831 | .928 | .597 | .359 | .464 |

(a) Scoring performance on the test set for the six questions. $N$ indicates the total number of responses available for each question, with 70% used to train the content scoring model, the H1-H2 columns denote the agreements between the two experts, the H1-WP columns denote the agreements between the H1 scores and those assigned by the generic writing proficiency model, and the H1-CS columns denote the agreements between the H1 scores and the question-specific content scoring model.

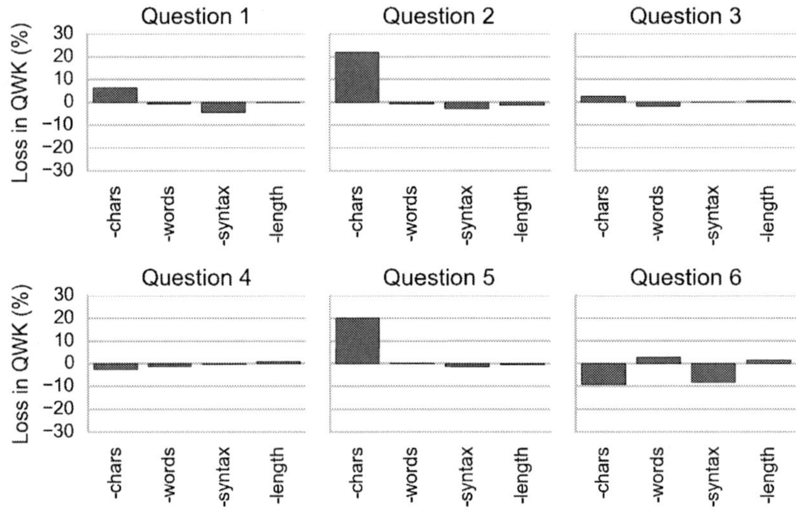

(b) The impact of ablating each of the four feature types on the overall scoring performance on the test set (*chars* = character $n$-grams, *words* = word $n$-grams, *syntax* = dependency triples, and *length* = log length features). Values $> 0$ indicate loss in performance when the feature is ablated and vice versa.

Figure 3: Scoring performance and ablation results.

are also likely to be better students.

## 5   Results

Figure 3a shows the performance of our content scoring model on the test set for all six questions (the H1-CS columns). We present three different metrics that measure the agreement of our model's predictions with the H1 scores. Although quadratic weighted kappa (QWK) is generally the standard metric of performance for short-answer scoring, we also compute the exact as well as adjacent agreement of the predictions with the H1 scores. The exact agreement shows the rate at which our model and H1 awarded the same score to a response. The adjacent agreement shows the rate at which scores given by our model and H1 were no more than one score point apart (e.g., the model assigned a score of 2 and the human rater assigned a score of 1 or 3). All three metrics were computed after rounding the raw predictions obtained from the SVR.

As an upper bound on automatic scoring performance, we also present the same agreement metrics between the H1 scores and the scores assigned by the second human expert (H2).

The table also includes the same agreement metrics for the predictions made by the generic writing proficiency model (the H1-WP columns). As expected, its performance is significantly worse than our content scoring model. This empirically confirms that the writing proficiency of the test-taker is not a factor in the human expert's assessment of their music teaching proficiency.

## 6   Discussion

Our model's predictions have high adjacent agreement with H1 scores. In fact, many adjacent agreement values are higher than the corresponding H1-H2 values. However, the exact agreement and QWK values are quite a bit lower than their H1-H2 counterparts. These observations tell us that although our content scoring model often predicts scores within 1 score point of the H1 score, it also either over-predicts or under-predicts the H1 score by more than 1 score point more often than H2 does.

Further spot-checking of sample responses in the training data indicated that sometimes it was possible that there was more than one correct answer to a question. For example, in the sample question from Section 2, it could be possible that there is more than one challenging aspect of the piece. As long as the test-taker articulates a valid challenge, along with an appropriate rehearsal technique, it is possible to obtain a score of 3. In situations where there is limited training data available, and not all valid challenging aspects have been sufficiently represented, for example, this may cause problems for automated scoring models. We cannot say with any certainty whether that caused the human-machine QWK scores to be lower than the corresponding human-human scores in our experiments, but it is an avenue of research that we intend to explore in future work.

We also wanted to examine how much each of the individual feature types contributes to the model's performance. To do so, we ablated each of the four feature types one at a time and re-ran the scoring model on the test set. Figure 3b shows the percentage loss in overall QWK for each of the six questions as we ablate each feature type. A value above zero indicates that removing a feature family led to a loss in performance and a value below zero indicates that removing a feature family actually led to an increase in performance.

We observe that including the *syntax* feature type almost always hurts the overall performance. At first, we hypothesized that this could be due to poor parser performance on these texts since they contain a lot of specialized musical terms (e.g., *glissando*, *embouchure* etc.) To confirm this hypothesis, we selected a few responses at random from the training data and looked at their dependency parses. Although we noticed some inaccuracies (e.g., *dotted* being interpreted as a verb in the phrase *rhythm dotted quarter note*), we did not find any evidence of significantly poor parsing performance. This means that the parsing feature representation itself seems to be deficient. We plan to experiment with other types of syntactic features in the future.

## 7   Conclusion

In this paper, we examined the feasibility of automatically scoring a unique content-based assessment - a test to measure the proficiency of teaching musical concepts to K-12 students. We first presented the characteristics that make the responses for this assessment different from almost all other previous work and then presented our approach to building an automated content scoring model. Our model performs moderately well on all six essay-style questions from the test but is prone to over- or under-predicting the true score by more than 1 point. As part of future work, we hope to explore the following in order to improve the model's performance:

- Increase the size of the training data to account for the relatively open-ended nature of the questions.
- Improve the representation of the syntactic features.
- Experiment with a hybrid approach (Sakaguchi et al., 2015) that combines our response-based approach with another approach that uses overlap with reference answers to assign scores.
- Experiment with some music- and instruction-specific features, including discourse/argumentation features.

### Acknowledgments

We would like to thank Beata Beigman Klebanov, Matt Mulholland, Sunny Singh, Isaac Bejar, Seth Weiner, Kevin Cureton, Diane Bailey, and the anonymous BEA reviewers.

## References

Enrique Alfonseca and Diana Pérez. 2004. Automatic assessment of open ended questions with a bleu-inspired algorithm and shallow nlp. In *Advances in Natural Language Processing*, pages 25–35. Springer.

Yigal Attali and Jill Burstein. 2006. Automated essay scoring with e-rater V. 2. *The Journal of Technology, Learning and Assessment*, 4(3):1–30.

Steven Burrows, Iryna Gurevych, and Benno Stein. 2015. The eras and trends of automatic short answer grading. *International Journal of Artificial Intelligence in Education*, 25(1):60–117.

Myroslava Dzikovska, Rodney Nielsen, Chris Brew, Claudia Leacock, Danilo Giampiccolo, Luisa Bentivogli, Peter Clark, Ido Dagan, and Hoa Trang Dang. 2013. Semeval-2013 task 7: The joint student response analysis and 8th recognizing textual entailment challenge. In *Second Joint Conference on Lexical and Computational Semantics (*SEM), Volume 2: Proceedings of the Seventh International Workshop on Semantic Evaluation (SemEval 2013)*, pages 263–274, Atlanta, Georgia, USA, June. Association for Computational Linguistics.

Michael Mohler, Razvan Bunescu, and Rada Mihalcea. 2011. Learning to grade short answer questions using semantic similarity measures and dependency graph alignments. In *Proceedings of the 49th Annual Meeting of the Association for Computational Linguistics: Human Language Technologies*, pages 752–762, Portland, Oregon, USA, June. Association for Computational Linguistics.

F. Pedregosa, G. Varoquaux, A. Gramfort, V. Michel, B. Thirion, O. Grisel, M. Blondel, P. Prettenhofer, R. Weiss, V. Dubourg, J. Vanderplas, A. Passos, D. Cournapeau, M. Brucher, M. Perrot, and E. Duchesnay. 2011. Scikit-learn: Machine Learning in Python. *Journal of Machine Learning Research*, 12:2825–2830.

Diana Pérez-Marín and Ismael Pascual-Nieto. 2011. Willow: a system to automatically assess students free-text answers by using a combination of shallow nlp techniques. *International Journal of Continuing Engineering Education and Life Long Learning*, 21(2-3):155–169.

Lakshmi Ramachandran, Jian Cheng, and Peter Foltz. 2015. Identifying patterns for short answer scoring using graph-based lexico-semantic text matching. In *Proceedings of the Tenth Workshop on Innovative Use of NLP for Building Educational Applications*, pages 97–106, Denver, Colorado, June. Association for Computational Linguistics.

Keisuke Sakaguchi, Michael Heilman, and Nitin Madnani. 2015. Effective feature integration for automated short answer scoring. In *Proceedings of the 2015 Conference of the North American Chapter of the Association for Computational Linguistics: Human Language Technologies*, pages 1049–1054, Denver, Colorado, May–June. Association for Computational Linguistics.

Alex J. Smola and Bernhard Schölkopf. 2004. A Tutorial on Support Vector Regression. *Statistics and Computing*, 14(3):199–222.

Jana Z Sukkarieh and Svetlana Stoyanchev. 2009. Automating model building in c-rater. In *Proceedings of the 2009 Workshop on Applied Textual Inference*, pages 61–69. Association for Computational Linguistics.

Jana Z Sukkarieh, Ali Mohammad-Djafari, Jean-Francois Bercher, and Pierre Bessiére. 2011. Using a maxent classifier for the automatic content scoring of free-text responses. In *AIP Conference Proceedings-American Institute of Physics*, volume 1305, page 41.

Yue Zhang and Stephen Clark. 2011. Syntactic Processing Using the Generalized Perceptron and Beam Search. *Computational linguistics*, 37(1):105–151.

Mengxiao Zhu, Ou L. Liu, Liyang Mao, and Amy Pallant. 2016. Use of Automated Scoring and Feedback in Online Interactive Earth Science Tasks. In *Proceedings of the 2016 IEEE Integrated STEM Education Conference*, Princeton, NJ.

# Combined Tree Kernel-based classifiers for Assessing Quality of Scientific Text [*]


**Liliana Mamani Sanchez**
Trinity College Dublin
`mamanisl@tcd.ie`

**Hector Franco-Penya**
Dublin Institute of Technology
`hector.franco@dit.ie`



## Abstract

This document describes Tree Kernel-SVM based methods for identifying sentences that could be improved in scientific text. This has the goal of contributing to the body of knowledge that attempt to build assistive tools to aid scientist improve the quality of their writings. Our methods consist of a combination of the output from multiple support vector machines which use Tree Kernel computations. Therefore, features for individual sentences are trees that reflect their grammatical structure. For the AESW 2016 Shared Task we built systems that provide probabilistic and binary outputs by using these models for trees comparisons.


## 1 Introduction

The system described in this article was submitted to the Automated Evaluation of Scientific Writing (AESW) Shared Task (Daudaravicius et al., 2016).

English is the most common language used for scientific writing across the world. Other things being equal, many scientific writers are non-native English speakers, what leads to a demand for assisting tools that employ "grammar error correction technologies" to compose scientific articles (Daudaravicius, 2015).

Several competitions similar to the one this article addresses have been organized, namely: the Helping Our Own (HOO) Shared Task (Dale and Kilgarriff, 2011; Dale et al., 2012), The CoNLL-2014 shared task on Grammatical Error Correction (Ng et

al., 2014). Those evaluations make use of human annotated examples of correct and incorrect grammar (Dahlmeier et al., 2013; Yannakoudakis et al., 2011).

Particularly, Leacock et al. (2010) provide a comprehensive overview of various aspects related to grammar error detection research.

This paper is organized as follows: Section 2 briefly describes the goals of the task our models attempt to address, Section 3 describes our experiments including the proposed Tree Kernel models, whose results are reported in Section 4. Section 5 further comments on the results, and Section 6 concludes with some summarizing remarks.

## 2 The task

The task consists in identifying sentences that need improvement or correction. This is done by classifying sentences into ones that do need amendments and those that do not. The training dataset provided by the organizers comprises sentences pairs $(S_o, S_e)$, where $S_o$ is a sentence presented as written by a non-native individual, these sentences contain at least one grammatical or lexical mishap that can be corrected. The corresponding $S_e$ has been edited as to make $S_o$ to look as a sentence with good academic style. For instance, example (2), shows a sentence that is an improved version of the one in example (1).

(1)   This is called as sub-additivity property of von-Neumann entropy.

(2)   This is called a sub-additivity property of von Neumann entropy.

---

[*] Both authors contributed equally to the contents and experiments described in this paper.




*Proceedings of the 11th Workshop on Innovative Use of NLP for Building Educational Applications*, pages 223–228,
San Diego, California, June 16, 2016. ©2016 Association for Computational Linguistics

The intuition behind this task is that systems that automatically identify sentence candidates for improvement may be built. The core solution would be provided by keeping track of common pitfalls committed by non-native individuals in their writing as in (1). Subsequently, such a system would learn how these pitfalls have been addressed as to emulate text produced by native writers.

The training dataset also comprises a set of sentences written by native English academics; they constitute a body of text that is representative of good academic writing style.

## 3 Experiments

For our experiments we used constituent trees corresponding to the examples from the training dataset. This dataset provided by the shared task organizers comprises parse tree structures which were generated by using the Stanford parser (Klein and Manning, 2003).

### 3.1 Tree Kernels

The tree structures were used to train Support Vector Machines using the SVM-light implementation by Joachims (1999) and SubSet Tree kernel (SST) computation tool (Collins and Duffy, 2002a; Moschitti, 2004; Moschitti, 2006) built on top of the former.

In essence, a Tree Kernel classifier computes a kernel function between two trees by comparing subtrees extracted from them. Since the number of possible comparisons between subtrees is exponential, we restricted the choice of subtrees to SubSet Trees (SSTs) (Collins and Duffy, 2002b). A SST is a tree where the leaves may comprise non-terminal symbols and the rules that these trees reflect should be well formed according to the rules of the target language grammar, in this case English.

Tree Kernel methods over Support Vector Machine have been successfully used on many other natural language processing applications, such as Semantic Role Labelling (Moschitti et al., 2008), question answer classification (Moschitti et al., 2007) or relational text categorization (Moschitti, 2008).

Figure 1b illustrates some SubSet trees[1] extracted

---

<sup></sup>[1]For reasons of brevity, the whole set of SubSet Trees that is

by the SST kernel from the full syntactic tree structure for (2), which is shown in Figure 1a. Such subtrees will be used as features for the Support Vector Machine model.

Our intuition behind using parse trees comparisons to identify candidate text for correction is that non-native writers will regularly use spurious lexical grammatical structures across their writings. Therefore, given a new sentence to classify, its underlying grammatical structure will be compared to a collection of tree structures built out of a training dataset.

### 3.2 Models for sentence quality assessment

Our overall strategy was to build models that use tree representations of sentences to be used in Support Vector Machines-based systems for sentence quality assessment. SVMs work with training examples labelled as either positive (1) or negative (-1). Therefore, sentences in need of edition are labelled as positive examples while sentences which do not need edition are labelled as negative examples. A machine learning system trained on these examples aims to predict a positive one.

Labelling examples as either positive or negative was translated into labelling tree structures corresponding to these examples with the respective label; for instance, the tree in Figure 1a is deemed a positive example. Internally, the SST tree tool assigns these labels to the corresponding subtrees: following from this, features such as the subtrees in 1b, are labelled as positive examples for the kernel computation.

To prepare the datasets for the training stage, we divided the dataset provided by the organizers in tree groups: $D_o$: sentences as written by non-native speakers and need edition; $D_e$ are sentences that have a counterpart in $D_o$ which were edited to have an improvement in good academic writing style; and $D_n$: sentences written by native English academic writers which do not have counterparts in $D_o$ and do not need edition.

We wanted to experiment with different conditions on how the identification of sentences in need of improvement may occur. Therefore, considering these three subdatasets $D_o$, $D_e$ and $D_n$, three models were built.

---

extracted from the full parse tree is not shown here.

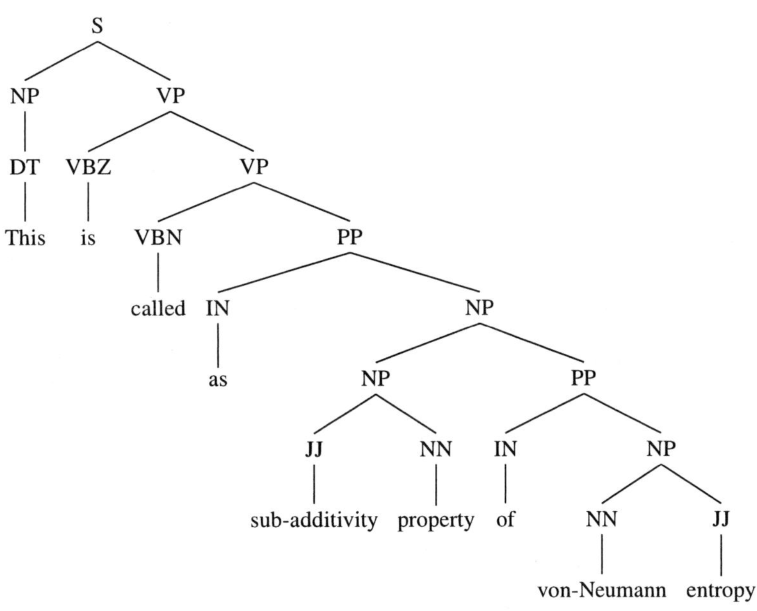

(a) Constituent tree from the sentence in example (1).

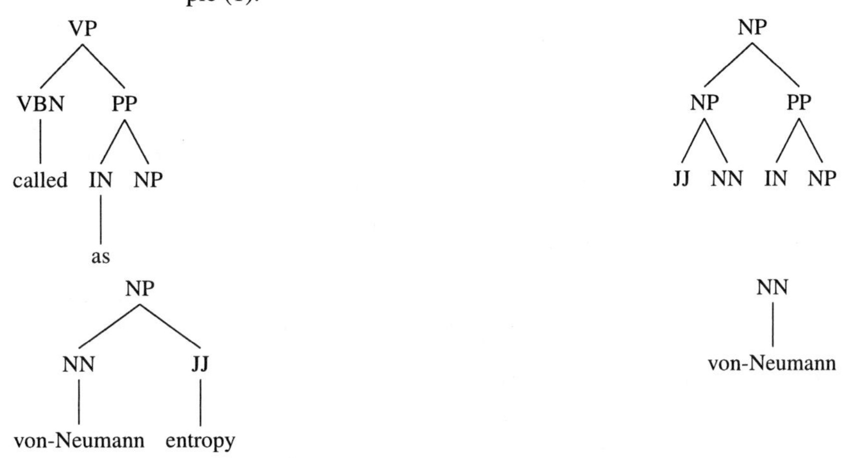

(b) SubSet Trees (SST) extracted from (a).

Figure 1: Example of how SubSet Trees (SST) extract sub trees as features from constituent tree structures.

- $\mathcal{MO}$: uses uniquely sentences in $D_o$ as positive examples, and sentences from $D_e$ as negative examples.

- $\mathcal{ZM}$: uses sentences from $D_o$ as positive examples, and sentences from $D_n$ as negative examples.

- $\mathcal{ZMO}$: uses sentences from $D_o$ as positive samples and sentences from both $D_e$ and $D_n$ as negative samples.

$\mathcal{MO}$ depicts a scenario where the identification would be better for sentence that keep close similarity to the sentences in the training dataset and high precision is paramount. $\mathcal{ZM}$ favours situations where sentences to be assessed do not keep high similarity to the set of positive training examples but the model is able to generalize by contrasting with sentences with good academic style. Ultimately, $\mathcal{ZMO}$ should enclose advantages of the two previous models.

The training dataset of parse trees provided by the organizers contained 475,473 trees for $D_o$, 476,142 trees for $D_e$ and 725,374 for $D_n$. Due to their length some sentences were unsuitable for processing by the TK-SVMLight tool, therefore examples whose length was above 1,400 characters were dropped out from the training set. This meant dropping 1,489 examples from $D_o$, 1,433 from $D_e$, and 283 from $D_n$. Thus, 948,693 training examples were used for $\mathcal{MO}$, 1,199,075 examples for $\mathcal{ZM}$, and 1,673,784 examples for $\mathcal{ZMO}$.

Another reason why we chose Tree Kernels computation as a basis for our systems is that we think this sort of classification task should rely uniquely on sentence-level features. Other non-linguistic candidate features could have been taken into account such as the relative position of an individual sentence within a paragraph or document. However, a system built comprising such a feature might not work properly on individual sentences that need classification.

### 3.3 Training and evaluation procedures

Unfortunately, the computation of kernels for all SubSet Trees is highly demanding in terms of computation time. Due to hardware limitations, for all three models the training data set was split into 100 sub-datasets, and a Support Vector Machine model was trained for each sub-dataset. Then, predictions were computed by using each of those hundred Support Vector Machine models over the unlabelled test dataset provided by the task organizers. The overall numerical categorization value for a system was calculated by averaging over these predictions. This categorization value was normalized to generate the probability of a sentence needing improvement $OutputProb$ using formula(1), where $OutputSVMmodel_i \in [-1, 1]$.

$$OutputProb = \frac{\sum_{i=1}^{100} OutputSVMmodel_i}{200} + 0.5 \tag{1}$$

Because the formula aims to estimate probabilities, if $OutputProb > 1$ then it is floored down to one, if $OutputProb < 0$, then it is rounded up to zero.

Some issues related to the use Stanford parser emerged during the evaluation stage. The parsing procedure for examples from the testing set was expected to produce a parse tree per example, which thereafter would be formatted properly for testing our systems. However, the parser failed to identify the boundaries of some sentences, particularly if there was an abbreviation with a period or a colon symbol occurring in them. For instance, abbreviations such as "etc." or "i e." caused the parser produce two parse trees for a single sentence.

This issue was overcame by running a script that matches the tree structure with the original sentence if the tree structure contained at least 50% of the words in the original sentence, for which no more than 10 consecutive sentences or consecutive trees can be unmatched.

This procedure left 188 sentences without a match (which is negligible amount of the total testing set: 0.13%). For these sentences a probability of 0.5 or a label 'false' was assigned.

## 4 Results

Table 1 shows the results for the systems submitted to the task organizers.

The system was evaluated according to the predicted label (bin) and according to the predicted probability (prob).

Table 1: Results in terms of Precision, Recall and F-measure for systems that produce either a probabilistic (prob) or binary (bin) prediction. The number in parenthesis points to the relative ranking compared to other systems.

| System | Precision | Recall | $F_1$ |
| --- | --- | --- | --- |
| $\mathcal{ZM}$ bin | 0.4482 (4) | 0.7279 (6) | 0.5548 (3) |
| $\mathcal{ZM}$ prob | 0.7062 (6) | 0.8182 (2) | 0.7581 (3) |
| $\mathcal{MO}$ bin | 0.3960 (8) | 0.6970 (7) | 0.5051 (7) |
| $\mathcal{MO}$ prob | 0.6576 (8) | 0.8014 (3) | 0.7224 (3) |

$\mathcal{ZMO}$ results are not reported as the system did not produce any positive prediction ($F_1 = 0$).

For the competition of binary output systems, our $\mathcal{ZM}$ system performs better than $\mathcal{MO}$ system for $F-$score, resulting ranked in third place. This is 0.073 points behind the best system score (HU), but 0.1041 points better than the baseline system from the task organizers.

Regarding the probabilistic output systems competition, our $\mathcal{MO}$-based system was ranked third. Similarly, this system is 0.073 points behind the best system (HITS) and 0.1073 points above the baseline. Also, this system's results seem to keep correlation with the results from the systems provided by the team NTNU-YZU.

## 5   Discussion

It is unfortunate the dataset size prompted us to split the training set into a hundred sub-datasets to train their corresponding Support Vector Machine models. This split was done according to the order in which sentences appear on the training set, expecting that indirectly each modified sentence will provide the negative and the positive examples (this is the sentence before and after being edited, $S_o$ and $S_e$ respectively ) is likely to fall within same sub-set. While this is a simplified strategy to split the training set, the effectiveness of other methods is an open research question to explore. Clustering algorithms could provide a better split.

The distribution of positive and negative examples for $\mathcal{MO}$ was perfectly balanced as 50% of samples were positive while the other 50% were negative. The $\mathcal{ZM}$ model was fairly balanced, the $\mathcal{ZMO}$ was not balanced (475,473 positive examples in contrast to 952,284 negative examples) and this lead to the

corresponding systems produce only negative predictions.

It seems that the F1 measure is proportional to how well balanced each data set is, this could be due to not using the development set to tune the threshold for binary predictions, or to re-arrange probabilities.

Systems trained using the $\mathcal{ZM}$ perform better than the ones using $\mathcal{MO}$. We think a reason for this is that in $\mathcal{MO}$ a positive example shares various subtrees with its corresponding negative example. Therefore, this may affect the classifier ability to calculate predictions for some examples in the test set. It would be ideal to make use of the test set gold standard to have more conclusive insights in this respect.

## 6   Conclusions

We described in this paper machine learning-based systems for identifying sentences that need amendments to improve their academic style. Our four systems have a Support Vector Machines computations as a core, they were built having tree representations of target sentences as features. The best systems of these four are the ones that use a model where sentences needing improvement are deemed as positive examples, and as negative examples sentences that were not edited and do not correspond to the positive examples are taken into account. This may be due to various reasons such as the distribution of positive and negative examples, or entropy of the datasets. We intend to address these and other issues in our systems in future work.

We think these systems' performance can be improved by modifying: the combination of models, and the software implementation, the representation of features. So far, we have implemented an empirical combination of sub-models output to have a global prediction output.

Making changes in the implementation of tree kernels computation may help to create models that meet scalability requirements. The final prediction would benefit of having less sub-models while keeping computation time reasonable.

Finally, we expect these attempts and future work to contribute to the state of the art of assistive writing technologies.

# References

Michael Collins and Nigel Duffy. 2002a. New ranking algorithms for parsing and tagging: Kernels over discrete structures, and the voted perceptron. In *Proceedings of the 40th annual meeting on association for computational linguistics*, pages 263–270. Association for Computational Linguistics.

Michael Collins and Nigel Duffy. 2002b. New ranking algorithms for parsing and tagging: Kernels over discrete structures, and the voted perceptron. In *Proceedings of 40th Annual Meeting of the Association for Computational Linguistics*, pages 263–270, Philadelphia, Pennsylvania, USA, July. Association for Computational Linguistics.

Daniel Dahlmeier, Hwee Tou Ng, and Siew Mei Wu. 2013. Building a large annotated corpus of learner english: The nus corpus of learner english. In *Proceedings of the Eighth Workshop on Innovative Use of NLP for Building Educational Applications*, pages 22–31.

Robert Dale and Adam Kilgarriff. 2011. Helping Our Own: The HOO 2011 Pilot Shared Task. *the Generation Challenges Session at the 13th European Workshop on Natural Language Generation,*, pages 242–249.

Robert Dale, Ilya Anisimoff, and George Narroway. 2012. HOO 2012: A report on the Preposition and Determiner Error Correction Shared Task. *the Seventh Workshop on Building Educational Applications Using NLP*, pages 54–62.

Vidas Daudaravicius, Rafael E. Banchs, Elena Volodina, and Courtney Napoles. 2016. A report on the automatic evaluation of scientific writing shared task. In *Proceedings of the Eleventh Workshop on Innovative Use of NLP for Building Educational Applications*, San Diego, CA, USA, June. Association for Computational Linguistics.

Vidas Daudaravicius. 2015. Automated Evaluation of Scientific Writing: AESW Shared Task Proposal. *Silver Sponsor*, pages 56–63.

Thorsten Joachims. 1999. Making large scale svm learning practical. Technical report, Universität Dortmund.

Dan Klein and Christopher D. Manning. 2003. Accurate Unlexicalized Parsing. *Proceedings of the 41st Annual Meeting on Association for Computational Linguistics - ACL '03*, 1:423–430.

Claudia Leacock, Martin Chodorow, Michael Gamon, and Joel Tetreault. 2010. Automated grammatical error detection for language learners. *Synthesis lectures on human language technologies*, 3(1):1–134.

Alessandro Moschitti, Silvia Quarteroni, Roberto Basili, and Suresh Manandhar. 2007. Exploiting syntactic and shallow semantic kernels for question answer classification. In *Annual meeting-association for computational linguistics*, volume 45, page 776.

Alessandro Moschitti, Daniele Pighin, and Roberto Basili. 2008. Tree kernels for semantic role labeling. *Computational Linguistics*, 34(2):193–224.

Alessandro Moschitti. 2004. A study on convolution kernels for shallow semantic eing. *Proceedings of the 42nd Annual Meeting on Association for Computational Linguistics - ACL '04*, pages 335–es.

Alessandro Moschitti. 2006. Making tree kernels practical for natural language learning. In *EACL*, volume 113, page 24.

Alessandro Moschitti. 2008. Kernel methods, syntax and semantics for relational text categorization. In *Proceedings of the 17th ACM conference on Information and knowledge management*, pages 253–262. ACM.

Hwee Tou Ng, Siew Mei Wu, Yuanbin Wu, Christian Hadiwinoto, and Joel Tetreault. 2014. *Shared Task on Grammatical Error Correction*.

Helen Yannakoudakis, Ted Briscoe, and Ben Medlock. 2011. A new dataset and method for automatically grading esol texts. In *Proceedings of the 49th Annual Meeting of the Association for Computational Linguistics: Human Language Technologies-Volume 1*, pages 180–189. Association for Computational Linguistics.

# Augmenting Course Material with Open Access Textbooks

**Smitha Milli** and **Marti A. Hearst**
University of California, Berkeley
Berkeley, CA 94720
smilli@berkeley.edu, hearst@berkeley.edu

## Abstract

Online, open access, high-quality textbooks are an exciting new resource for improving the online learning experience. Because textbooks contain carefully crafted material written in a logical order, with terms defined before use and discussed in detail, they can provide foundational material with which to buttress other resources. As a first step towards this goal, we explore the automated augmentation of a popular online learning resource – Khan Academy video modules – with relevant reference chapters from open access textbooks. We show results from standard information retrieval weighting and ranking methods as well as an NLP-inspired approach, achieving F1 scores ranging from 0.63, to 0.83 on science topics. Future work includes taking into account the difficulty level and prerequisites of a textbook to select sections that are both relevant and reflect the concepts that the reader has already encountered.

## 1 Introduction

A learner who is studying material from an online course, such as a video from a Khan academy physics sequence, may desire additional reading material to supplement the current video or exercise. It can be distracting to do a web search to find relevant material, and furthermore, the material that is found may be described at the wrong level or may assume prerequisite knowledge that the learner does not have. To this point, Mathew et al. (2015) note that online encyclopedic resources, such as Wikipedia, are not pedagogically organized and tend to have many cyclic dependencies among articles.

Textbooks written for students are specifically designed for learning. Material is carefully organized to define terms before use or to point the reader to the location in which the material will be discussed in more detail. Content is described at a consistent reading level and notation and formatting are also consistent.

However, to date, textbooks have not been widely used for automated online recommendations, most likely because they have not been freely available online for many subjects. This situation is changing with the advent of projects like OpenStax (Pitt, 2015)[1] for which respected educators are writing and vetting free online textbooks in major subject categories.

In this work we explore the potential of augmenting online course materials – specifically Khan Academy modules[2] – with relevant supplemental reading from textbooks. We show that even very simple algorithms can go a long way towards making effective recommendations.

## 2 Related Work

There has been some related work in aligning textbook content to other content. Contractor et al. (2015) identify the need to automatically label instructional materials with learning standards, which are defined hierarchically from general goals down to lists of instructions that define the skills that students should learn during a course or within a curriculum. They develop an algorithm for representing the content within a list of learning standards

---

[1] https://openstaxcollege.org
[2] https://www.khanacademy.org



*Proceedings of the 11th Workshop on Innovative Use of NLP for Building Educational Applications*, pages 229–234,
San Diego, California, June 16, 2016. ©2016 Association for Computational Linguistics

for high school math and science curricula and label corresponding portions of "educational documents" and Khan academy video transcripts. They use an unsupervised method that models each instruction as a collection of terms that are relevant to that instruction and use external resources including Wikipedia, Wordnet, and a word vector embedding algorithm trained on Wikipedia and news text for term expansion. They allow a match between a text and an instruction only if the higher level goals also match. When associating learning goals with educational documents, they achieve accuracy of 81% for math and 71% for science.

Textbooks often refer to the same concept in multiple locations, and require the reader to make digressions to other parts of the text to understand concepts that they are not familiar with. Agrawal et al. (2013) address the problem of automatically determining which concepts described elsewhere in the textbook are most relevant to what the reader is viewing at the current juncture. They create a model of the structure of references to concepts within sections of the textbook and model the manner in which readers would navigate these references based on their structure within the book. The model does not examine the text itself.

Agrawal et al. (2011), working with substandard textbooks (written in a developing nation), identify the sections can be enriched by better written content. They define a syntactic complexity score that makes use of the maturity of the text and a semantic dispersion score based on the observation that sections that discussed concepts with respect to one another were of higher quality. Their earlier work (Agrawal et al., 2010) linked textbook content to web resources. Our intent starts with the opposite assumption: that the textbooks are authoritative and are to be linked to other content.

Mathew et al. (2015) distinguish between pedagogic and general resources such as thesauri, noting that the latter have good coverage but are not structured to aid in learning. They assess a graph-theoretic algorithm for collapsing word definitions into more compact forms.

# 3  Methods

Khan Academy *modules* are courses that cover broad subjects such as "Physics", "Chemistry", "Biology" and are broken down into *submodules* focusing on more specific topics within the subject. Each submodule consists of some combination of videos, readings and interactive exercises presented within a dynamic web interface. For example, within the physics module on Khan Academy, submodules include "Force and Newton's laws of motion", "Magnetic forces and fields", etc. See Figure 1 for a screenshot.

Our goal specifically is: Given a Khan Academy module and a textbook, for each submodule in the Khan Academy module, assign the chapters from the textbook that teach the same concepts as the submodule. We wish to label each of these submodules with relevant chapters for reading. We present three methods to do so.

## 3.1  Method 1: TF-IDF document similarity

We use a standard method for document similarity comparison from information retrieval: weighting terms with tf-idf scores, converting documents into vectors with these weights, and comparing documents by taking the cosine similarity of the vectors (Baeza-Yates et al., 2010). Each submodule is represented using the text from its main page, which only consists of titles and short descriptions of videos, readings, and exercises. The text from the exercises and video transcripts were not used.

The vocabulary of words extracted consists of all words in the submodules excluding stopwords and terms with a document frequency over 0.9. Each submodule and chapter is encoded as a vector of these words using tf-idf weights computed on the set of submodules. Let $D$ be the set of submodules, $N_d$ be the number of words in submodule $d$, $f_d(t)$ be the number of times term $t$ appears in submodule $d$. Term frequency is computed as the raw frequency of a term in all submodules, i.e. $\frac{\sum_{d \in D} f_d(t)}{\sum_{d \in D} N_d}$. The inverse document frequency for a term is computed as $\log \frac{|D|}{|\{d \in D : t \in D\}|}$. For each submodule the chapter with the highest cosine similarity is selected.

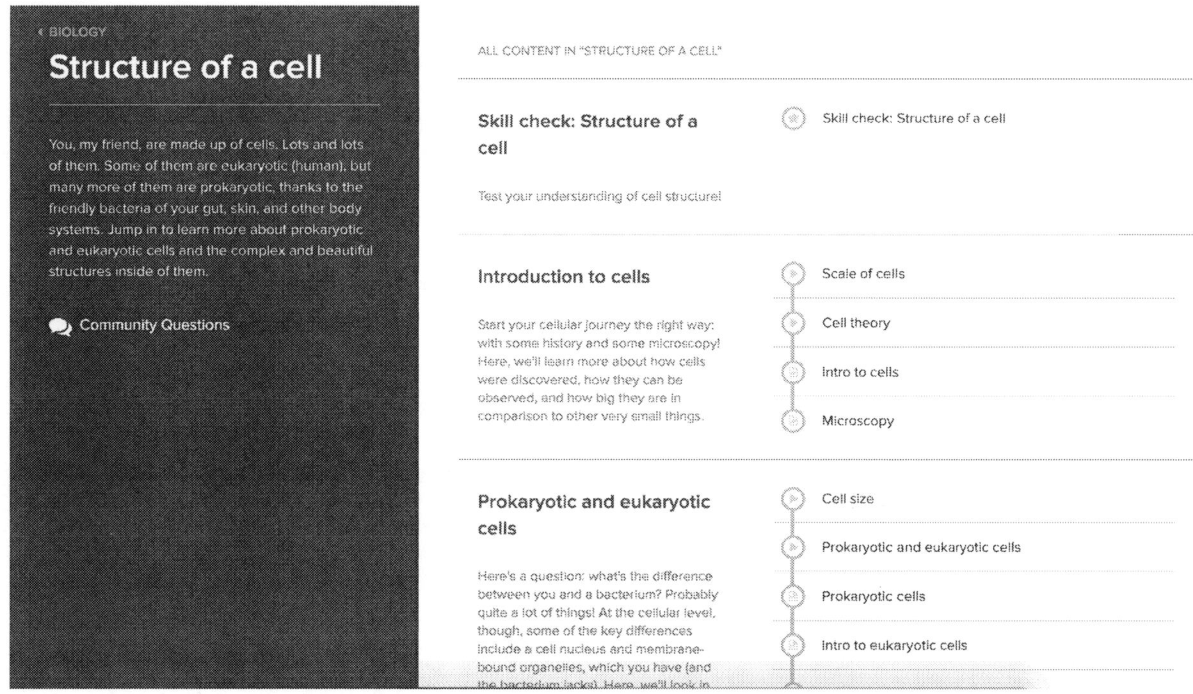


**Figure 1:** A screenshot of the "Structure of a cell" submodule from the Khan Academy biology module.

## 3.2 Method 2: Learning objective frequencies

Although computing document similarity works well when we assume a 1-1 correspondence between a submodule and chapter in a textbook, some submodules may span multiple chapters or no chapters at all.

To address this issue we create a method based on learning objectives. A *learning objective* for a submodule is a concept that is taught in the submodule with the goal of being understood by a learner after completion of the submodule. In this work we assume that learning objectives can be represented by key phrases corresponding to new terms that are taught to the learner such as acceleration, cell division, photosynthesis, etc. This is a very simple representation compared to, say, a knowledge-based method.

Our method extracts learning objectives from a Khan Academy submodules and searches for which chapter teaches those learning objectives with the understanding that different learning objectives may be taught in different chapters. Essentially we are reducing the assumption of a 1-1 correspondence between a submodule and chapter to a 1-1 correspondence between a learning objective and a chapter.

For each submodule a list of learning objectives is extracted. The chapters assigned to the submodule consists of the set of chapters assigned to each learning objective. The pseudocode for this general algorithm is the *augmentSubmodule* procedure in Algorithm 1. *augmentSubmodule* depends on two components: the extraction of learning objectives, *extractLearningObjectives*, and the assignment of chapters to learning objectives, *pickChapterForObj*.

In this work *extractLearningObjectives* is implemented as a keyphrase extraction. The keyphrase extraction is a rule-based approach that breaks up lists and terms that are separated by the word 'and'. For example, the submodule of the physics module titled "Electric charge, electric force, and voltage" contains the keyphrases "electric charge", "electric force", and "voltage", which the algorithm extracts.

In addition, the words in the title are tagged with parts of speech, so that the pattern *"JJ$_1$ and JJ$_2$ NN"* extracts both *"JJ$_1$ NN"* and *"JJ$_2$ NN"*. For example, both the phrases 'balanced forces' and 'unbalanced forces' are extracted from 'balanced and unbalanced forces'. Terms can be filtered to those that occur at least a minimum frequency in the textbook.

Our implementation of *pickChapterForObj* is the

procedure *pickChapterForObjFreq* as shown in Algorithm 1. Let the set of chapters be denoted $C$. $f(t, c_i)$ is the frequency of a term $t$ in chapter $c_i$. The chapter picked for a learning objective $t$ is the chapter with the highest frequency, $\mathrm{argmax}_i f(t, c_i)$ for $i \in \{1, 2, \ldots, |C|\}$.

### 3.3 Method 3: Learning objective spikes

Method 3 is based on the notion of learning objective spikes and is the same as Method 2 except with a change in how a chapter is assigned to a learning objective. We say a learning objective has a *spike* in chapter $i$ if it has a sudden increase in probability in chapter $i$ compared to any of the previous chapters. The threshold for what counts as a "sudden increase" can be tuned. In Method 3 the chapter picked for a learning objective is the chapter with the first spike (if any exist) for the learning objective.

The motivation for this spike-based method is that because textbooks are written to teach, in most cases, when a new term is first discussed in detail is where it is defined and explained best. The assumption of the spike method is that this definition chapter in most cases most useful to show to a learner, even though some following chapters may use that term more frequently in the context of describing some more advanced concepts.

For example, as shown in Figure 2, the word "voltage" is defined in chapter 19, where a spike is seen, and then used many times in chapter 21 in a discussion of circuits. However, "voltage" is mentioned only in passing in chapters 17 and 18, and so those are not the best chapters to show the learner as compared to chapter 19, which has a spike in usage. Thus in Figure 2, Method 3 performs better than Method 2.

Let the set of chapters be denoted $C$. $f(t, c_i)$ is the frequency of a term $t$ in chapter $c_i$. The probability of chapter $c_i$ given a term $t$ is $p(t, c_i) = \frac{f(t, c_i)}{\sum_{j=1}^{|C|} f(t, c_j)}$. The score for a chapter is $s(t, c_i) = p(t, c_i) - \max_{1 < j < i} p(t, c_j)$. Finally, the chapter assigned to a term is chosen by picking the smallest $i$ such that $s(t, c_i) > P$ is true where $P$ is a tunable threshold. The algorithm fails to identify a chapter for the term if $\forall i\ s(t, c_i) \leq P$. The final algorithm for Method 3 is the *augmentSubmodule* procedure using the *pickChapterForObjSpike* procedure

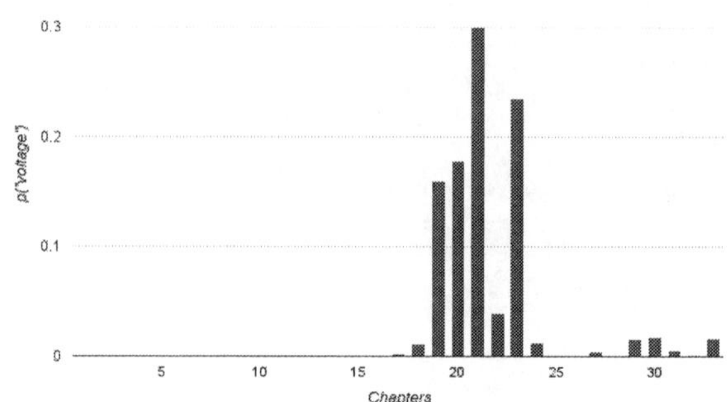



**Figure 2:** The probability of the term voltage over all chapters. The correct chapter (19) is the first spike, but not the chapter with the highest frequency (21).

| Khan Academy Module | Textbook |
| --- | --- |
| Physics | *College Physics* by OpenStax |
| Physics | *Mechanics* by Benjamin Crowell |
| Biology | *Biology* by OpenStax |
| Chemistry | *Chemistry* by OpenStax |

**Table 1:** Test materials; the first row was used for training hyperparameters.

as *pickChapterForObj* (see Algorithm 1).

## 4 Evaluation and Results

All tuning of hyperparameters (tf-idf filtering, the minimum frequency of a learning objective term and the threshold for a spike) was done on augmentation of the Khan Academy physics module with the OpenStax physics textbook. Dataset details appear in Table 1.

For each of the three test modules, we picked a random subset of 10 submodules and split this into two disjoint sets with 5 submodules for each. We recruited four judges and had two judges label each of these disjoint sets, so in total all submodules were labeled twice. For every Khan Academy submodule, the judges were told to select any and all chapters in the textbook that explained the same concepts as that submodule. A fifth judge (one of the authors) broke ties between any discrepancies in answers from the first two judges.

Precision was calculated as $\frac{\sum_{i=0}^{M} N_i}{N}$ where $M$ is the number of submodules, $N_i$ is the number of chapters that were correctly matched for submodule $i$, and $N$ is the total number of chapters that were

| Biology | | | |
|---|---|---|---|
| Method | Precision | Recall | F1 |
| Tf-idf | **1.0** | 0.53 | 0.69 |
| Term freq | 0.88 | **0.74** | **0.80** |
| Spikes | 0.87 | 0.68 | 0.76 |
| Chemistry | | | |
| Method | Precision | Recall | F1 |
| Tf-idf | **1.0** | 0.71 | **0.83** |
| Term freq | 0.58 | **0.79** | 0.67 |
| Spikes | 0.67 | 0.71 | 0.69 |
| Physics | | | |
| Method | Precision | Recall | F1 |
| Tf-idf | **0.60** | 0.67 | **0.63** |
| Term freq | 0.50 | 0.67 | 0.57 |
| Spikes | 0.46 | 0.67 | 0.55 |

**Table 2:** The results of the tf-idf (Method 1), Term frequency (Method 2), and Spikes (Method 3) Keywords methods.

output. Recall was calculated as $\frac{\sum_{i=0}^{M} N_i}{K}$ where $K$ is the total number of gold-standard chapter annotations for the entire module. F1 was the harmonic mean of the precision and recall scores.

The results for the three methods are shown in Table 2. The tf-idf document similarity method (Method 1) achieves high precision, but lower recall because it only selects one chapter per module. Surprisingly the spikes method (Method 3) performed worse than the term frequency method (Method 2). We believe that this is because there were few occasions in the test set where the chapter with the highest frequency of a term did not correspond to the chapter that a term was explained in.

## 5   Limitations

Textbooks that are organized differently from the Khan Academy module are more difficult to attain good results on. For example, our methods get much lower results on the physics module because the physics textbook used does not cover certain topics in the Khan Academy physics module, and our methods do not recognize when a term is not being taught.

In addition, the frequency and spike methods have trouble recognizing where a term is explained for terms such as "force" that occur with high frequency throughout a textbook. Both methods also make the simplifying assumption that the learning objectives

**Algorithm 1** Augmenting Submodules with Chapters

```
 1: procedure AUGMENTSUBMODULE
 2:     learningObjectives ← extractLearningObjectives()
 3:     relevantChapters = [ ]
 4:     for objective in learningObjective do
 5:         chapter ← pickChapterForObj(objective)
 6:         append chapter to relevantChapters
 7:     return relevantChapters
 8: procedure PICKCHAPTERFOROBJFREQ(term)
 9:     return argmax_i f(term, c_i) for i ∈ {1, 2, ..., |C|}
10: procedure PICKCHAPTERFOROBJSPIKE(term)
11:     for i ∈ {1, 2, ..., |C|} do
12:         if s(objective, c_i) > P then return i
13:     return None
```

for a module can be represented by keyphrases extracted from submodule titles.

## 6   Conclusions and Future Work

We have presented three simple methods for augmenting Khan Academy modules with textbook chapters. The tf-idf method achieves high precision but lower recall, so we also showcased two methods (term frequency and spikes) that extract learning objectives and attempt to determine which chapters the learning objectives are located in. These results show great promise for using textbooks to automatically improve online learning materials developed for other purposes.

However, so far we have only evaluated our methods in science domains. Our methods may work less well in other domains where the important terms are less technical, and learning objectives cannot be as well represented by such terms.

In addition, for this work, it was known in advance which textbooks were to be aligned to a module. In a more realistic setting, the application must first select an appropriate textbook for the module, perhaps based on both the subject of the textbook and its level of complexity.

Lastly, our current work provides a coarse augmentation by showing entire relevant chapters to the learner; a useful next step will be to extract relevant excerpts from the chapters.

**Acknowledgements** This research is supported in part by a Google Social Interactions Grant.

## References

Rakesh Agrawal, Sreenivas Gollapudi, Krishnaram Kenthapadi, Nitish Srivastava, and Raja Velu. 2010. Enriching textbooks through data mining. In *Proceedings of the First ACM Symposium on Computing for Development*, page 19. ACM.

Rakesh Agrawal, Sreenivas Gollapudi, Anitha Kannan, and Krishnaram Kenthapadi. 2011. Identifying enrichment candidates in textbooks. In *Proceedings of the 20th international conference companion on World wide web*, pages 483–492. ACM.

Rakesh Agrawal, Sreenivas Gollapudi, Anitha Kannan, and Krishnaram Kenthapadi. 2013. Studying from electronic textbooks. In *Proceedings of the 22nd ACM international conference on Conference on information & knowledge management*, pages 1715–1720. ACM.

Ricardo Baeza-Yates, Berthier Ribeiro-Neto, et al. 2010. *Modern information retrieval, 2nd Edition*. Addison Wesley.

Danish Contractor, Kashyap Popat, Shajith Ikbal, Sumit Negi, Bikram Sengupta, and Mukesh K Mohania. 2015. Labeling educational content with academic learning standards. In *Proceedings of the 2015 SIAM International Conference on Data Mining*. SIAM, April.

Ditty Mathew, Dhivya Eswaran, and Sutanu Chakraborti. 2015. Towards creating pedagogic views from encyclopedic resources. In *Proceedings of the Tenth Workshop on Innovative Use of NLP for Building Educational Applications*, pages 190–195.

Rebecca Pitt. 2015. Mainstreaming open textbooks: Educator perspectives on the impact of openstax college open textbooks. *The International Review of Research in Open And Distributed Learning*, 16(4).

# Exploring the Intersection of Short Answer Assessment, Authorship Attribution, and Plagiarism Detection

**Björn Rudzewitz**
University of Tübingen
Nauklerstrasse 35
72074 Tübingen, Germany
`brzdwtz@sfs.uni-tuebingen.de`

## Abstract

In spite of methodological and conceptual parallels, the computational linguistic applications short answer scoring (Burrows et al., 2015), authorship attribution (Stamatatos, 2009), and plagiarism detection (Zesch and Gurevych, 2012) have not been linked in practice. This work explores the practical usefulness of the combination of features from each of these fields for two tasks: short answer assessment, and plagiarism detection. The experiments show that incorporating features from the other domain yields significant improvements. A feature analysis reveals that robust lexical and semantic features are most informative for these tasks.

## 1 Introduction

Despite different ultimate goals, Short Answer Assessment, Plagiarism Detection, and Authorship Attribution are three domains of Computational Linguistics that share a range of methodology. However, these parallel have not been compared across domains. This work explores the intersection of these areas in a practical context.

In the domain of authorship attribution, a set of texts and potential authors is given, and the goal is to "distinguish between texts written by different authors" (Stamatatos, 2009, page 1). In the domain of short answer assessment, tools are designed to assess the meaning of a short answer by comparing it to a reference answer (Burrows et al., 2015; Ziai et al., 2012), and thereby to its semantic appropriateness. In the domain of Plagiarism Detection, two main goals can

be pursued (Clough and Stevenson, 2011): in extrinsic plagiarism detection, a source and potentially plagiarized texts are compared as a whole unit with methods from the domain of authorship attribution (Grieve, 2007). The goal of intrinsic plagiarism detection is to detect stylistic changes within one document (Zu Eissen and Stein, 2006).

All three areas use textual similarity features on various levels of linguistic abstraction for nominal classifiers, but the distribution of features over three related dimensions differs (Zesch and Gurevych, 2012): style, content, and structure. While (learner language) short answer assessment systems put emphasis on content and ignore stylistic aspects, authorship attribution focuses on stylistic features. Plagiarism detection systems use both content, structural, and stylistic similarity features to classify texts as plagiarizing other documents or not. The main task for short answer assessment and plagiarism detection is to evaluate the existence and quality of paraphrases of a source text. This work explores the effect of features used in the field of authorship attribution and plagiarism detection features for short answer assessment, as well as the effect of short answer assessment features for plagiarism detection.

## 2 Data

For the experiments in the domain of short answer assessment, the Corpus of Reading comprehension Exercises in German (Ott et al., 2012) was used. For the experiments in the domain of plagiarism detection, the Wikipedia Reuse Corpus (Clough and Stevenson, 2011) was selected for the experiments.

235

*Proceedings of the 11th Workshop on Innovative Use of NLP for Building Educational Applications*, pages 235–241,
San Diego, California, June 16, 2016. ©2016 Association for Computational Linguistics

These resources were chosen since they are standard shared evaluation resources in these domains (Burrows et al., 2015; Zesch and Gurevych, 2012).

## 2.1 CREG

CREG-1032 is a short answer learner corpus containing student and reference answers to questions about reading comprehension texts. The longitudinal data was collected at two German programs in the United States at the Ohio State University (OSU) and the Kansas University (KU). The corpus exhibits a high variability of surface forms and semantic content in the student answers due to a variety of proficiency levels represented. Each student answer was annotated by two independent annotators with a binary diagnosis indicating the semantic correctness of the answer, independent of surface variations such as spelling mistakes or agreement errors. The corpus is balanced with respect to this diagnosis. Table 1 shows the distribution of student answers, target answers, and questions, as described in (Meurers et al., 2011b), who also showed that the OSU answers are significantly longer (average token length of 9.7 for KU versus 15.0 for OSU).

## 2.2 Wikipedia Reuse Corpus

The Wikipedia Reuse Corpus (WRC, (Clough and Stevenson, 2011)) represents different types of text reuse imitating different plagiarism types: copy and paste, light and heavy revision, and non-plagiarism. The plagiarism samples vary in the amount of revision and paraphrasing performed by participants. Table 1 shows the corpus' data distribution. The texts were not exclusively written by English native speakers and show similar surface/semantic variation as the CREG answers. With an average of 208 tokens in length, the answers are nearly 20 times as long as the answers in the CREG corpus, but referred to as "short answers" (Clough and Stevenson, 2011, page 1). Since Zesch and Gurevych (2012) showed empirical deficits in the text reuse conditions, all plagiarism labels were collapsed into a single category, rendering the task a binary classification, parallel to the CREG binary diagnoses. In this setting, the data is unbalanced: the majority class is the plagiarism class with 57 instances, whereas there are only 38 non-plagiarized documents.

|  | CREG-1032-KU | CREG-1032-OSU | WRC |
|---|---|---|---|
| # student answers | 610 | 422 | 95 |
| # target answers | 136 | 87 | 5 |
| # questions | 117 | 60 | 5 |

Table 1: Data distribution in the CREG-1032 and Wikipedia Reuse Corpus data set.

## 3 Baseline Short Answer Assessment System

The UIMA-based CoMiC system (Meurers et al., 2011a; Meurers et al., 2011b) served as a framework for the experiments. It is an alignment-based short answer assessment system which aligns student to reference answers on different levels of linguistic abstraction in order to classify learner answers as (in)correct based on the quantity of different alignment types. CoMiC proved to be highly effective for both German and English (Burrows et al., 2015). The CoMiC system follows a three-stage pipeline architecture (Bailey and Meurers, 2008; Meurers et al., 2011a): alignment, annotation, diagnosis.

First, the system enriches the raw answer texts with linguistic annotation. Table 2 from (Meurers et al., 2011b) shows the different annotation tasks together with the respective tools.

| Task | NLP Tool |
|---|---|
| Sentence Detection | OpenNLP (Baldridge, 2005) |
| Tokenization | OpenNLP (Baldridge, 2005) |
| Lemmatization | TreeTagger (Schmid, 1994) |
| Spell Checking | Edit distance (Levenshtein, 1966) igerman98 word list |
| POS Tagging | TreeTagger (Schmid, 1994) |
| NP Chunking | OpenNLP (Baldridge, 2005) |
| Lexical Relations | GermaNet (Hamp and Feldweg, 1997) |
| Similarity Score | PMI-IR (Turney, 2001) |
| Dependency Parsing | MaltParser (Nivre et al., 2007) |

Table 2: NLP tools used in the CoMiC system.

In the second step, a globally optimal alignment configuration is selected by the Traditional Marriage Algorithm (Gale and Shapley, 1962). The system aligns tokens, NP chunks, and dependency triples. Tokens are aligned when they match on the surface, lowercased surface, synonym, semantic type, or lemma level. Only new elements (not verbatim given in the corresponding question) are aligned.

In the final step, a range of features (Table 3, (Meurers et al., 2011b)) are extracted and fed to a machine learning component. In contrast to the original

CoMiC system, predictions are made with WEKA's (Hall et al., 2009) memory based learner instead of the TiMBL memory based learner (Daelemans et al., 2007). The features denote directionalized quantities of alignments on different linguistic levels ('pct' = 'percentage of').

| Feature | Description |
|---|---|
| 1. Keyword Overlap | pct keywords aligned |
| 2. Target Token Overlap | pct aligned target tokens |
| 3. Learner Token Overlap | pct aligned student tokens |
| 4. Target Chunk Overlap | pct aligned target chunks |
| 5. Learner Chunk Overlap | pct aligned student chunks |
| 6. Target Triple Overlap | pct aligned target dependency triples |
| 7. Learner Triple Overlap | pct aligned student dependency triples |
| 8. Token Match | pct token-identical token alignments |
| 9. Similarity Match | pct similarity-resolved token alignments |
| 10. Semtype Match | pct type-resolved token alignments |
| 11. Lemma Match | pct lemma-resolved token alignments |
| 12. Synonym Match | pct synonym-resolved token alignments |
| 13. Variety of Match (0-5) | sum of features 8-12 |
| 14. Target Answer ID | target answer id |
| 15. Student Answer ID | student answer id |

Table 3: CoMiC system features.

## 4 Extensions of the Baseline System

Stamatatos (2009) provides an extensive overview about approaches and stylometric features used in computerized authorship attribution. The features are divided into four subclasses. Table 4 based on (Stamatatos, 2009, page 3) lists all the features used, as well as their corresponding category (lexical/character/syntactic/semantic) and information about whether they are applied to one or two documents. If they are applicable to one document, then there exists a feature both for the student and for the target side in order to model the relation in this specific dimension of similarity, reflected in the prefix 'Student' or 'Target' in the feature names. Features applied to two documents are computed via cosine similarity between a vector for each answer holding the frequencies of the elements under consideration. The feature *all features interpolated* is a special overlap feature, for which first all frequencies of all feature extractors were added to one vector before the cosine similarity was applied (see Figure 1). The first $m$ entries in the vector are lexical features, followed by $n$ character features, etc.

The *SpellCorr* feature measures the token overlap between two texts using spelling corrected and surface forms. For each token, the system checks

| Feature | Description | # Docs |
|---|---|---|
| **lexical** | | |
| AvgWordLength | Average word length | 1 |
| TTR | Type-Token Ratio | 1 |
| WordUniFreq | Word Unigram frequency similarity | 2 |
| WordBiFreq | Word Bigram frequency similarity | 2 |
| WordTriFreq | Word Trigram frequency similarity | 2 |
| SpellCorr | Spell Corrected Unigram Matches | 1 |
| **character** | | |
| CharFreq | Character frequency similarity | 2 |
| UpperCharFreq | Uppercase character frequency similarity | 2 |
| LowerCharFreq | Lowercase character frequency similarity | 2 |
| DigitCharFreq | Digit character frequency similarity | 2 |
| LetterProportion | Proportion of letters (A-Za-z) in answer | 1 |
| UpperProportion | Proportion of uppercase letters in answer | 1 |
| LowerProportion | Proportion of lowercase letters in answer | 1 |
| CharBigramFreq | Character bigram frequency similarity | 2 |
| CharTrigramFreq | Character trigram frequency similarity | 2 |
| CharFourgramFreq | Character fourgram frequency similarity | 2 |
| CharFivegramFreq | Character fivegram frequency similarity | 2 |
| **syntactic** | | |
| POS | Part of Speech tag frequency similarity | 2 |
| Chunk | Chunk tag frequency similarity | 2 |
| NPChunk | Noun phrase chunk frequency similarity | 2 |
| PosBigram | POS tag bigram frequency similarity | 2 |
| PosTrigram | POS tag trigram frequency similarity | 2 |
| PosFourgram | POS tag fourgram frequency similarity | 2 |
| PosFivegram | POS tag fivegram frequency similarity | 2 |
| **semantic** | | |
| Synonym | Proportion of synonym-overlapping tokens | 1 |
| DepTriple | Proportion of dependency triple overlaps | 1 |
| **combination** | | |
| all features interpolated | all features combined | 2 |

Table 4: Authorship attribution features implemented in CoMiC.

whether the token or its lemma appears in a word list. If not, the system seaches the closest Levensthein match cosidering both the other document and the word list. All *.arff* feature files were generated with the same givenness constraints as the CoMiC baseline features and exported from there to WEKA.

## 5 Experimental Testing

The following orthogonal hypotheses were tested:

1. The accuracy for the learner language short answer assessment task increases when features from the domain of authorship attribution are added.

2. The accuracy for the plagiarism classification task increases when features from the short answer assessment system are added.

### 5.1 Method

The WEKA lazy iBk memory based learner with k=5-nearest neighbor search was run in a 10-fold cross validation setting. Following Dietterich (1998), the McNemar's test with $\alpha = 0.1$ is used in

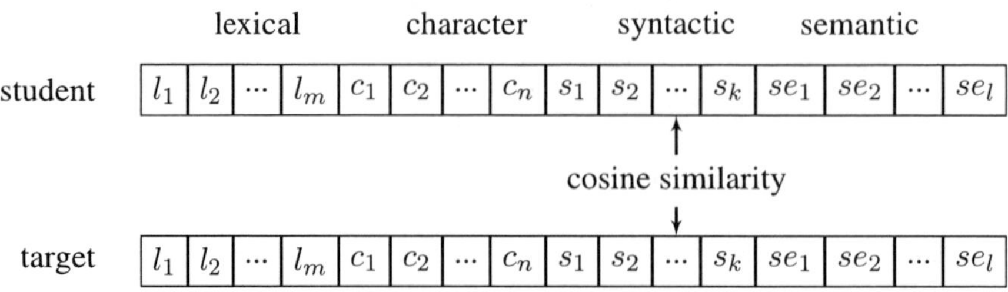


Figure 1: Interpolated textual similarity.

R to test whether an improvement over the baseline is statistically significant.

## 5.2 Results

Table 5 shows accuracies for the prediction of the semantic equivalence of learner answers and the prediction of plagiarism. For short answer assessment, the CoMiC features yielding an accuracy of 84.5% (KU) and 87.1% (OSU) are used as a baseline. For plagiarism detection, the set of all style features (Table 4, 84.2%) was used as the baseline. Table 5 shows that using only the baseline features from the other domain already yield significant improvements (92.6% for the WRC, 86.9% for CREG-1032-KU) over the baseline of in-domain features. Also the combination of both baseline feature sets yields improvements over the respective baseline. Even though the interpolated similarity feature on its own resulted in a surprisingly high accuracy for CREG-1032-OSU (87.9%), it only works in combination for the WRC corpus, resulting in the highest accuracy of all experiments (95.8%). Lexical features alone result in accuracies comparable to the baseline accuracies for both tasks. The character based features alone work better for short answer assessment, with even better results when combined with the baseline features. Semantic features have a higher impact for plagiarism detection, although for the CREG-1032-OSU data set, these features alone yield nearly the baseline accuracy.

**Feature Analysis.** The information gain of features was computed in WEKA with the InfoGainAttributeEval filter with default parameters. Table 6 shows the ten most informative features for each data set. The most informative features are mostly lexical or character-based and thus content-modeling features, where the most informative fea-

| Features | Data | | |
|---|---|---|---|
| | KU | OSU | WRC |
| **baselines** | | | |
| CoMiC | 84.5 | 87.1 | 92.6* |
| all style features | 86.9* | 86.0 | 84.2 |
| **baselines + new features** | | | |
| CoMiC + all style features | 85.6 | 87.7 | 90.5* |
| all features interpolated | 78.0 | 87.9 | 62.1 |
| CoMiC + all features interpolated | 84.3 | 87.2 | 95.8* |
| lexical features | 84.5 | 86.3 | 90.5* |
| CoMiC + lexical features | 84.4 | 88.2 | 88.4 |
| character features | 83.3 | 86.3 | 82.2 |
| CoMiC + character features | 85.7 | 87.7 | 83.2 |
| syntactic features | 67.4 | 69.0 | 80.0 |
| CoMiC + syntactic features | 84.3 | 85.1 | 87.4 |
| semantic features | 82.1 | 85.0 | 90.6* |
| CoMiC + semantic features | 83.8 | 87.0 | 91.6* |

Table 5: Results for the binary classification tasks. * denotes a significant improvement ($\alpha = 0.1$).

ture indicates the proportion of matched tokens when spelling-corrected versions are used. This is not surprising given the high surface variability in the corpora, and the design choices of the corpus creation to ignore form errors and focus on semantics.

## 6 Discussion and Related Work

Grieve (2007) provided an extensive comparison of quantitative authorship attribution methods for extrinsic plagiarism detection. The observation that word and character-based metrics are most successful for extrinsic plagiarism detection can be confirmed by the present study. Clough and Stevenson (2011) tested two methods for classifying the texts in their Wikipedia Reuse Corpus: n-gram overlap and longest common subsequence. They report on an accuracy of 80% for predicting all four labels, and an accuracy of 94.7% for the binary classification. The present work outperformed the already very accu-

| Rank | CREG-1032 | WRC |
|---|---|---|
| 1 | TargetSpellCorr | StudentSpellCorr |
| 2 | CharBigramFreq | Token Match |
| 3 | CharTrigramFreq | CharTrigramFreq |
| 4 | CharFourgramFreq | CharFourgramFreq |
| 5 | WordUniFreq | CharFivegramFreq |
| 6 | all features interpolated | TargetSpellCorr |
| 7 | Target synonym overlap | CharBigramFreq |
| 8 | CharFivegramFreq | StudentSynonym |
| 9 | StudentSpellCorr | WordUniFreq |
| 10 | TargetSynonym | TargetSynonym |

Table 6: Ten most informative features for the CREG-1032 and WRC data set.

rate system by Clough and Stevenson (2011) by almost one percent point with an accuracy of 95.8%. Zesch and Gurevych (2012) used a variety of content, structural, and stylistic features for the plagiarism classification task on the Wikipedia Reuse Corpus. They report an accuracy of 96.8% for the task of binary plagiarism classification. Meurers et al. (2011b) reported an accuracy of 84.6% for both the CREG-1032-KU and the CREG-1032-OSU data set with an early version of the CoMiC-DE system. Hahn and Meurers (2012) report an accuracy of 86.3% for the CREG corpus as a result of using the CoSeC system, which uses abstract semantic representations. Horbach et al. (2013) re-implemented the CoMiC system and tested the effect of considering the text instead of pre-defined target answers. In the best case, they reached an accuracy of 84.4% on the CREG corpus. Pado and Kiefer (2015) classified answers in the CREG corpus according to their similarity to a target answer. All answers above a threshold were classified as correct, resulting in an accuracy of 83.7% for CREG-1032. Ziai and Meurers (2014) made use of human-annotated information structural annotations for the CREG-1032-OSU data set. They obtained an accuracy of 90.3% for the CREG-1032-OSU data set for the CoMiC system. Rudzewitz (2015) augmented the CoMiC system with alignment weighting features measuring the importance of aligned elements with respect to the concrete task and general linguistic properties of aligned elements. This work reported an accuracy of 90.0% for the CREG-1032-OSU corpus. The difference of 1.2% to the present work warrants a combination of both approaches in future work.

## 7 Conclusions and Future Work

This article represents a pioneer work for linking the three research areas short answer assessment, authorship attribution, and plagiarism detection.

The experiments confirmed the hypothesis formulated in the introduction that these areas share a similar methodology in terms of frameworks, tasks, and features. It was shown that semantics-based features modeling aspects of content, especially robust character-based features, were most effective for both short answer assessment and plagiarism detection, and that the most informative features for both corpora were surprisingly similar. The experiments also made evident that already rather simple features can yield reasonable results for these tasks. Both research hypotheses formulated in section 5 could be confirmed, respectively the null hypothesis could be rejected: features from authorship attribution yielded significant improvements for the task of learner language assessment, and features from learner language assessment yielded significant improvements for the task of plagiarism detection. However, it has to be noted that not all features are strictly task-specific, and also applicable to other NLP tasks.

A comparison with related work showed that the results are comparable to current state-of-the-art approaches, although there is still room for improvement. Future work therefore will explore the usage of more features, more elaborate machine learning algorithms, and automatic feature selection techniques. In addition, more corpora from either domain will be used to obtain a broader evaluation perspective. Especially stylistic features modeling for example stopword patterns as well as longest common subsequence features are hypothesized to be beneficial for the task of plagiarism detection since they model stylistic rather than semantic properties.

## Acknowledgments

I would like to thank the three anonymous reviewers and Ramon Ziai for their insightful comments.

**References**

Stacey Bailey and Detmar Meurers. 2008. Diagnosing meaning errors in short answers to reading comprehension questions. In Joel Tetreault, Jill Burstein, and Rachele De Felice, editors, *Proceedings of the 3rd Workshop on Innovative Use of NLP for Building Educational Applications (BEA-3) at ACL'08*, pages 107–115, Columbus, Ohio.

Jason Baldridge. 2005. The OpenNLP Project. *URL: http://opennlp. apache. org/index. html,(accessed 25 August 2015)*.

Steven Burrows, Iryna Gurevych, and Benno Stein. 2015. The eras and trends of automatic short answer grading. *International Journal of Artificial Intelligence in Education*, 25(1):60–117.

Paul Clough and Mark Stevenson. 2011. Developing a corpus of plagiarised short answers. *Language Resources and Evaluation*, 45(1):5–24.

Walter Daelemans, Jakub Zavrel, Ko van der Sloot, and Antal van den Bosch, 2007. *TiMBL: Tilburg Memory-Based Learner Reference Guide, ILK Technical Report ILK 07-03*. Induction of Linguistic Knowledge Research Group Department of Communication and Information Sciences, Tilburg University, Tilburg, The Netherlands, July 11. Version 6.0.

Thomas G Dietterich. 1998. Approximate statistical tests for comparing supervised classification learning algorithms. *Neural computation*, 10(7):1895–1923.

David Gale and Lloyd S. Shapley. 1962. College admissions and the stability of marriage. *American Mathematical Monthly*, 69:9–15.

Jack Grieve. 2007. Quantitative authorship attribution: An evaluation of techniques. *Literary and linguistic computing*, 22(3):251–270.

Michael Hahn and Detmar Meurers. 2012. Evaluating the meaning of answers to reading comprehension questions: A semantics-based approach. In *Proceedings of the 7th Workshop on Innovative Use of NLP for Building Educational Applications (BEA-7) at NAACL-HLT 2012*, pages 94–103, Montreal.

Mark Hall, Eibe Frank, Geoffrey Holmes, Bernhard Pfahringer, Peter Reutemann, and Ian H. Witten. 2009. The weka data mining software: An update. In *The SIGKDD Explorations*, volume 11, pages 10–18.

Birgit Hamp and Helmut Feldweg. 1997. GermaNet – a lexical-semantic net for german. In *Proceedings of ACL workshop Automatic Information Extraction and Building of Lexical Semantic Resources for NLP Applications*, Madrid.

Andrea Horbach, Alexis Palmer, and Manfred Pinkal. 2013. Using the text to evaluate short answers for reading comprehension exercises. In *Second Joint Conference on Lexical and Computational Semantics (*SEM), Volume 1: Proceedings of the Main Conference and the Shared Task: Semantic Textual Similarity*, pages 286–295, Atlanta, Georgia, USA, June. Association for Computational Linguistics.

Vladimir I. Levenshtein. 1966. Binary codes capable of correcting deletions, insertions, and reversals. *Soviet Physics Doklady*, 10(8):707–710.

Detmar Meurers, Ramon Ziai, Niels Ott, and Stacey Bailey. 2011a. Integrating parallel analysis modules to evaluate the meaning of answers to reading comprehension questions. *IJCEELL. Special Issue on Automatic Free-text Evaluation*, 21(4):355–369.

Detmar Meurers, Ramon Ziai, Niels Ott, and Janina Kopp. 2011b. Evaluating answers to reading comprehension questions in context: Results for German and the role of information structure. In *Proceedings of the TextInfer 2011 Workshop on Textual Entailment*, pages 1–9, Edinburgh, July. ACL.

Joakim Nivre, Jens Nilsson, Johan Hall, Atanas Chanev, Gülsen Eryigit, Sandra Kübler, Svetoslav Marinov, and Erwin Marsi. 2007. MaltParser: A language-independent system for data-driven dependency parsing. *Natural Language Engineering*, 13(1):1–41.

Niels Ott, Ramon Ziai, and Detmar Meurers. 2012. Creation and analysis of a reading comprehension exercise corpus: Towards evaluating meaning in context. In Thomas Schmidt and Kai Wörner, editors, *Multilingual Corpora and Multilingual Corpus Analysis*, Hamburg Studies in Multilingualism (HSM), pages 47–69. Benjamins, Amsterdam.

Ulrike Pado and Cornelia Kiefer. 2015. Short answer grading: When sorting helps and when it doesn't. In *Proceedings of the 4th workshop on NLP for Computer Assisted Language Learning at NODALIDA*, page 43.

Björn Rudzewitz. 2015. Alignment Weighting for Short Answer Assessment. Bachelor's thesis, University of Tübingen.

Helmut Schmid. 1994. Probabilistic part-of-speech tagging using decision trees. In *Proceedings of the International Conference on New Methods in Language Processing*, pages 44–49, Manchester, UK.

Efstathios Stamatatos. 2009. A survey of modern authorship attribution methods. *Journal of the American Society for Information Science and Technology*, 60(3):538–556.

Peter Turney. 2001. Mining the web for synonyms: PMI-IR versus LSA on TOEFL. In *Proceedings of the Twelfth European Conference on Machine Learning (ECML-2001)*, pages 491–502, Freiburg, Germany.

Daniel Bär Torsten Zesch and Iryna Gurevych. 2012. Text reuse detection using a composition of text similarity measures. In *Proceedings of COLING*, volume 1, pages 167–184.

Ramon Ziai and Detmar Meurers. 2014. Focus annotation in reading comprehension data. In *Proceedings of the 8th Linguistic Annotation Workshop (LAW VIII, 2014)*, pages 159–168, Dublin, Ireland. COLING, Association for Computational Linguistics.

Ramon Ziai, Niels Ott, and Detmar Meurers. 2012. Short answer assessment: Establishing links between research strands. In *Proceedings of the 7th Workshop on Innovative Use of NLP for Building Educational Applications (BEA-7) at NAACL-HLT 2012*, pages 190–200, Montreal.

Sven Meyer Zu Eissen and Benno Stein. 2006. Intrinsic plagiarism detection. In *Advances in Information Retrieval*, pages 565–569. Springer.

# Sentence-Level Grammatical Error Identification
## as Sequence-to-Sequence Correction


Allen Schmaltz          Yoon Kim          Alexander M. Rush          Stuart M. Shieber

**Harvard University**

{schmaltz@fas,yoonkim@seas,srush@seas,shieber@seas}.harvard.edu



## Abstract

We demonstrate that an attention-based encoder-decoder model can be used for sentence-level grammatical error identification for the Automated Evaluation of Scientific Writing (AESW) Shared Task 2016. The attention-based encoder-decoder models can be used for the generation of corrections, in addition to error identification, which is of interest for certain end-user applications. We show that a character-based encoder-decoder model is particularly effective, outperforming other results on the AESW Shared Task on its own, and showing gains over a word-based counterpart. Our final model—a combination of three character-based encoder-decoder models, one word-based encoder-decoder model, and a sentence-level CNN—is the highest performing system on the AESW 2016 binary prediction Shared Task.


## 1 Introduction

The recent confluence of data availability and strong sequence-to-sequence learning algorithms has the potential to lead to practical tools for writing support. Grammatical error identification is one such application of potential utility as a component of a writing support tool. Much of the recent work in grammatical error identification and correction has made use of hand-tuned rules and features that augment data-driven approaches, or individual classifiers for human-designated subsets of errors. Given a large, annotated dataset of scientific journal articles, we propose a fully data-driven approach for

this problem, inspired by recent work in neural machine translation and more generally, sequence-to-sequence learning (Sutskever et al., 2014; Bahdanau et al., 2014; Cho et al., 2014).

The Automated Evaluation of Scientific Writing (AESW) 2016 dataset is a collection of nearly 10,000 scientific journal articles (over 1 million sentences) published between 2006 and 2013 and annotated with corrections by professional, native English-speaking editors. The goal of the associated AESW Shared Task is to identify whether or not a given unedited source sentence was corrected by the editor (that is, whether a given source sentence has one or more grammatical errors, broadly construed).

This system report describes our approach and submission to the AESW 2016 Shared Task, which establishes the current highest-performing public baseline for the binary prediction task. Our primary contribution is to demonstrate the utility of an attention-based encoder-decoder model for the binary prediction task. We also provide evidence of tangible performance gains using a character-aware version of the model, building on the character-aware language modeling work of Kim et al. (2016). In addition to sentence-level classification, the models are capable of intra-sentence error identification and the generation of possible corrections. We also obtain additional gains by using an ensemble of a generative encoder-decoder and a discriminative CNN classifier.

## 2 Background

Recent work in natural language processing has shown strong results in sequence-to-sequence trans-




*Proceedings of the 11th Workshop on Innovative Use of NLP for Building Educational Applications*, pages 242–251,
San Diego, California, June 16, 2016. ©2016 Association for Computational Linguistics

formations using recurrent neural network models (Cho et al., 2014; Sutskever et al., 2014). Grammar correction and error identification can be cast as a sequence-to-sequence translation problem, in which an unedited (*source*) sentence is "translated" into a corrected (*target*) sentence in the same language. Using this framework, sentence-level error identification then simply reduces to an equality check between the source and target sentences.

The goal of the AESW shared task is to identify whether a particular sentence needs to be edited (contains a "grammatical" error, broadly construed[1]). The dataset consists of sentences taken from academic articles annotated with corrections by professional editors. Annotations are described via insertions and deletions, which are marked with start and end tags. Tokens to be deleted are surrounded with the deletion start tag <del> and the deletion end tag </del> and tokens to be inserted are surrounded with the insertion start tag <ins> and the insertion end tag </ins>. Replacements (as shown in Figure 1) are represented as deletion-insertion pairs. Unlike the related CoNLL-2014 Shared Task (Ng et al., 2014) data, errors are not labeled with fine-grained types (article or determiner error, verb tense error, etc.).

More formally, we assume a vocabulary $\mathcal{V}$ of natural language word types (some of which have orthographic errors) and a set $\mathcal{Q} = \{\texttt{<ins>}, \texttt{</ins>}, \texttt{<del>}, \texttt{</del>}\}$ of annotation tags. Given a sentence $\mathbf{s} = [s_1, \ldots, s_I]$, where $s_i \in \mathcal{V}$ is the $i$-th token of the sentence of length $I$, we seek to predict whether or not the gold, annotated target sentence $\mathbf{t} = [t_1, \ldots, t_J]$, where $t_j \in \mathcal{Q} \cup \mathcal{V}$ is the $j$-th token of the annotated sentence of length $J$, is identical to $\mathbf{s}$. We are given both $\mathbf{s}$ and $\mathbf{t}$ for supervised training. At test time, we are only given access to sequence $\mathbf{s}$. We learn to predict sequence $\mathbf{t}$.

Evaluation of this binary prediction task is via the $F_1$-score, where the positive class is that indicating an error is present in the sentence (that is, where $\mathbf{s} \neq \mathbf{t}$)[2].

Evaluation is at the sentence level, but the paragraph-level context for each sentence is also provided. The paragraphs, themselves, are shuffled so that full article context is not available. A coarse academic field category is also provided for each paragraph. Our models described below do not make use of the paragraph context nor the field category, and they treat each sentence independently.

Further information about the task is available in the Shared Task report (Daudaravicius et al., 2016).

## 3 Related Work

While this is the first year for a shared task focusing on sentence-level binary error identification, previous work and shared tasks have focused on the related tasks of intra-sentence identification and correction of errors. Until recently, standard hand-annotated grammatical error datasets were not available, complicating comparisons and limiting the choice of methods used. Given the lack of a large hand-annotated corpus at the time, Park and Levy (2011) demonstrated the use of the EM algorithm for parameter learning of a noise model using error data without corrections, performing evaluation on a much smaller set of sentences hand-corrected by Amazon Mechanical Turk workers.

More recent work has emerged as a result of a series of shared tasks, starting with the Helping Our Own (HOO) Pilot Shared Task run in 2011, which focused on a diverse set of errors in a small dataset (Dale and Kilgarriff, 2011), and the subsequent HOO 2012 Shared Task, which focused on the automated detection and correction of preposition and determiner errors (Dale et al., 2012). The CoNLL-2013 Shared Task (Ng et al., 2013)[3] focused on the correction of a limited set of five error types in essays by second-language learners of English at the National University of Singapore. The follow-up CoNLL-2014 Shared Task (Ng et al., 2014)[4] focused on the full generation task of correcting all errors in essays by second-language learners.

As with machine translation (MT), evaluation of

---

[1]Some insertions and deletions in the shared task data represent stylistic choices, not all of which are necessarily recoverable given the sentence or paragraph context. For the purposes here, we refer to all such edits as "grammatical" errors.

[2]The 2016 Shared Task also included a probabilistic esti-

mation track. We leave for future work the adaptation of our approach to that task.

[3]http://www.comp.nus.edu.sg/~nlp/conll13st.html

[4]http://www.comp.nus.edu.sg/~nlp/conll14st.html

the full generation task is still an open research area, but a subsequent human evaluation ranked the output from the CoNLL-2014 Shared Task systems (Napoles et al., 2015). The system of Felice et al. (2014) ranked highest, utilizing a combination of a rule-based system and phrase-based MT, with re-ranking via a large web-scale language model. Of the non-MT based approaches, the Illinois-Columbia system was a strong performer, combining several classifiers trained for specific types of errors (Rozovskaya et al., 2014).

## 4 Models

We use an end-to-end approach that does not have separate components for candidate generation or re-ranking that make use of hand-tuned rules or explicit syntax, nor do we employ separate classifiers for human-differentiated subsets of errors, unlike some previous work for the related task of grammatical error correction.

We next introduce two approaches for the task of sentence-level grammatical error identification: A binary classifier and a sequence-to-sequence model that is trained for correction but can also be used for identification as a side-effect.

### 4.1 Baseline Convolutional Neural Net

To establish a baseline, we follow past work that has shown strong performance with convolutional neural nets (CNNs) across various domains for sentence-level classification (Kim, 2014; Zhang and Wallace, 2015). We utilize the one-layer CNN architecture of Kim (2014) with the publicly available[5] word vectors trained on the Google News dataset, which contains about 100 billion words (Mikolov et al., 2013). We experiment with keeping the word vectors static (CNN-STATIC) and fine-tuning the vectors (CNN-NONSTATIC). The CNN models only have access to sentence-level labels and are not given correction-level annotations.

### 4.2 Encoder-Decoder

While it may seem more natural to utilize models trained for binary prediction, such as the aforementioned CNN, or for example, the recurrent network

approach of Dai and Le (2015), we hypothesize that training at the lowest granularity of annotations may be useful for the task. We also suspect that the generation of corrections is of sufficient utility for end-users to further justify exploring models that produce corrections in addition to identification. We thus use the Shared Task as a means of assessing the utility of a full generation model for the binary prediction task.

We propose two encoder-decoder architectures for this task. Our word-based architecture (WORD) is similar to that of Luong et al. (2015). Our character-based models (CHAR) still make predictions at the word-level, but use a CNN and a high-way network over characters instead of word embeddings as the input to the encoder and decoder, as depicted in Figure 1. We follow past work (Sutskever et al., 2014; Luong et al., 2015) in stacking multiple recurrent neural networks (RNNs), specifically Long Short-Term Memory (LSTM) (Hochreiter and Schmidhuber, 1997) networks, in both the encoder and decoder.

Here, we model the probability of the target given the source, $p(\mathbf{t} \mid \mathbf{s})$, with an *encoder* neural network that summarizes the source sequence and a *decoder* neural network that generates a distribution over the target words and tags at each step given the source.

We start by describing the basic encoder and decoder architectures in terms of the WORD model, and then we describe the CHAR model departures from WORD.

**Encoder** The encoder reads the source sentence and outputs a sequence of vectors, associated with each word in the sentence, which will be selectively accessed during decoding via a soft attentional mechanism. We use a LSTM network to obtain the hidden states $\mathbf{h}_i^s \in \mathbb{R}^n$ for each time step $i$,

$$\mathbf{h}_i^s = \mathrm{LSTM}(\mathbf{h}_{i-1}^s, \mathbf{x}_i^s).$$

For the WORD models, $\mathbf{x}_i^s \in \mathbb{R}^m$ is the word embedding for $s_i$, the $i$-th word in the source sentence. (The analogue for the CHAR models is discussed below.) The output of the encoder is the sequence of hidden state vectors $[\mathbf{h}_1^s, \ldots, \mathbf{h}_I^s]$. The initial hidden state of the encoder is set to zero (i.e. $\mathbf{h}_0^s \leftarrow \mathbf{0}$).

**Decoder** The decoder is another LSTM that produces a distribution over the next target word/tag

---

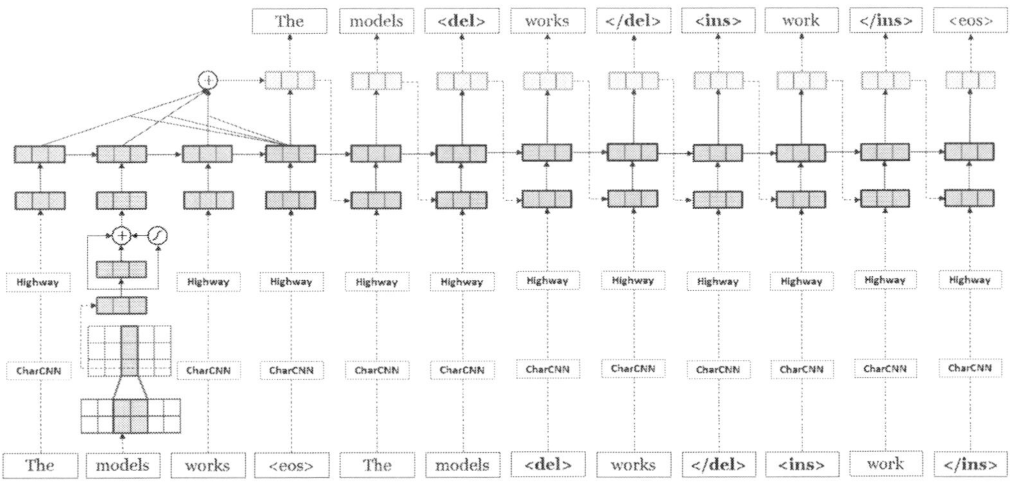


**Figure 1:** An illustration of the CHAR model architecture translating an example source sentence into the corrected target with a single word replacement. A CNN (here, with three filters of width two) is applied over character embeddings to obtain a fixed dimensional representation of a word, which is given to a highway network (in light blue, above). Output from the highway network is used as input to a LSTM encoder/decoder. At each step of the decoder, its hidden state is interacted with the hidden states of the encoder to produce attention weights (for each word in the encoder), which are used to obtain the context vector via a convex combination. The context vector is combined with the decoder hidden state through a one layer MLP (yellow), after which an affine transformation followed by a softmax is applied to obtain a distribution over the next word/tag. The MLP layer (yellow) is used as additional input (via concatenation) for the next time step. Generation continues until the <eos> symbol is generated.

given the source vectors $[\mathbf{h}_1^s, \dots, \mathbf{h}_I^s]$ and the previously generated target words/tags $\mathbf{t}_{<j} = [t_1, \dots t_j]$. Let

$$\mathbf{h}_j^t = \text{LSTM}(\mathbf{h}_{j-1}^t, \mathbf{x}_j^t)$$

be the summary of the target sentence up to the $j$-th word, where $\mathbf{x}_j^t$ is the word embedding for $t_j$ in the WORD models. The current target hidden state $\mathbf{h}_j^t$ is combined with each of the memory vectors in the source to produce attention weights as follows,

$$u_{j,i} = \mathbf{h}_j^t \cdot \mathbf{W}_\alpha \mathbf{h}_i^s$$
$$\alpha_{j,i} = \frac{\exp u_{j,i}}{\sum_{k \in [1,I]} \exp u_{j,k}}$$

The source vectors are multiplied with the respective attention weights, summed, and interacted with the current decoder hidden state $\mathbf{h}_j^t$ to produce a *context* vector $\mathbf{c}_j$,

$$\mathbf{v}_j = \sum_{i \in [1,I]} \alpha_{j,i} \mathbf{h}_i^s$$
$$\mathbf{c}_j = \tanh(\mathbf{W}[\mathbf{v}_j; \mathbf{h}_j^t])$$

The probability distribution over the next word/tag is given by applying an affine transformation to $\mathbf{c}_j$ followed by a softmax,

$$p(t_{j+1} \mid \mathbf{s}, \mathbf{t}_{<j}) = \text{softmax}(\mathbf{U}\mathbf{c}_j + \mathbf{b})$$

Finally, as in Luong et al. (2015), we feed $\mathbf{c}_j$ as additional input to the decoder for the next time step by concatenating it with $\mathbf{x}_j^t$, so the decoder equation is modified to,

$$\mathbf{h}_j^t = \text{LSTM}(\mathbf{h}_{j-1}^t, [\mathbf{x}_j^t; \mathbf{c}_{j-1}])$$

This allows the decoder to have knowledge of previous (soft) alignments at each time step. The decoder hidden state is initialized with the final hidden state of the encoder (i.e. $\mathbf{h}_0^t \leftarrow \mathbf{h}_I^s$).

**Character Convolutional Neural Network** For the CHAR models, instead of a word embedding, our input for each word in the source/target sentence is an output from a character-level convolutional neural network (CharCNN) (depicted in Figure 1). Our character model closely follows that of Kim et al. (2016).

Suppose word $s_i$ is composed of characters $[p_1, \dots, p_l]$. We concatenate the character embeddings to form the matrix $\mathbf{P}_i \in \mathbb{R}^{c \times l}$, where the $k$-th column corresponds to the character embedding for $p_k$ (of dimension $c$).

We then apply a convolution between $\mathbf{P}_i$ and a *filter* $\mathbf{H} \in \mathbb{R}^{c \times w}$ of width $w$, after which we add a bias and apply a nonlinearity to obtain a *feature map* $\mathbf{f}_i \in \mathbb{R}^{l-w+1}$. The $k$-th element of $\mathbf{f}_i$ is given by,

$$\mathbf{f}_i[k] = \tanh(\langle \mathbf{P}_i[*, k : k + w - 1], \mathbf{H} \rangle + b)$$

where $\langle \mathbf{A}, \mathbf{B} \rangle = \mathrm{Tr}(\mathbf{A}\mathbf{B}^T)$ is the Frobenius inner product and $\mathbf{P}_i[*, k : k + w - 1]$ is the $k$-to-$(k + w - 1)$-th column of $\mathbf{P}_i$. Finally, we take the *max-over-time*

$$z_i = \max_k \mathbf{f}_i[k]$$

as the feature corresponding to filter $\mathbf{H}$. We use multiple filters $\mathbf{H}_1, \dots \mathbf{H}_h$ to obtain a vector $\mathbf{z}_i \in \mathbb{R}^h$ as the representation for a given source/target word or tag. We have separate CharCNNs for the encoder and decoder.

**Highway Network**  Instead of replacing the word embedding $\mathbf{x}_i$ with $\mathbf{z}_i$, we feed $\mathbf{z}_i$ through a *highway network* (Srivastava et al., 2015). Whereas a multi-layer perceptron produces a new set of features via the following transformation (given input $\mathbf{z}$),

$$\hat{\mathbf{z}} = f(\mathbf{W}\mathbf{z} + \mathbf{b})$$

a highway network instead computes,

$$\hat{\mathbf{z}} = \mathbf{r} \odot f(\mathbf{W}\mathbf{z} + \mathbf{b}) + (\mathbf{1} - \mathbf{r}) \odot \mathbf{z}$$

where $f$ is a non-linearity (in our models, ReLU), $\odot$ is the element-wise multiplication operator, and $\mathbf{r} = \sigma(\mathbf{W}_r\mathbf{z} + \mathbf{b}_r)$ and $\mathbf{1} - \mathbf{r}$ are called the *transform* and *carry* gates. We feed $\mathbf{z}_i$ into the highway network to obtain $\hat{\mathbf{z}}_i$, which is used to replace the input word embeddings in both the encoder and the decoder.

**Inference**  Exact inference is computationally infeasible for the encoder-decoder models given the combinatorial explosion of possible output sequences, but we follow past work in NMT using beam search. We do not constrain the generation process of words outside insertion tags to words in the source, and each low-frequency holder token generated in the target sentence is replaced with the source token associated with the maximum attention weight. We use a beam size of 10 for all models, with the exception of one of the models in the final system combination, for which we use a beam of size 5, as noted in Section 6.

Note that this model generates corrections, but we are only interested in determining the existence of any error at the sentence-level. As such, after beam decoding, we simply check for whether there were any corrections in the target. However, we found that decoding in this way under-predicts sentence-level errors. It is therefore important to calibrate the weights associated with corrections, which we discuss in Section 5.3.

## 5   Experiments

### 5.1   Data

The AESW task data differs from previous grammatical error datasets in terms of scale and genre. To the best of our knowledge, the AESW dataset is the first large-scale, publicly available professionally edited dataset of academic, scientific writing. The training set consists of 466,672 sentences with edits and 722,742 sentences without edits, and the development set contains 57,340 sentences with edits and 90,106 sentences without. The raw training and development datasets are provided as annotated sentences, $\mathbf{t}$, from which the $\mathbf{s}$ sequences may be deterministically derived. There are 143,802 sentences in the Shared Task test set with hidden gold labels, which serve directly as $\mathbf{s}$ sequences.

As part of pre-processing, we treat each sentence independently, discarding paragraph context (which sentences, if any, were present in the same paragraph) and domain information, which is a coarse grouping by the field of the original journal (Engineering, Computer Science, Mathematics, Chemistry, Physics, etc.). We generate Penn Treebank style tokenizations of the input. Case is maintained and digits are not replaced with holder symbols. The vocabulary is restricted to the 50,000 most common tokens, with remaining low frequency tokens replaced with a special <unk> token. The CHAR model can encode but not decode over open vocabularies and hence we do not have any <unk> tokens on the source side of those models. For all of the encoder-decoder models, we replace the low-frequency target symbols during inference as discussed above in Section 4.2.

For development against the provided data with labels, we set aside a 10,000 sentence sample from the original development set for tuning, and use the remaining 137,446 sentences for validation[6]. The encoder-decoder models are given all 466,672 pairs of s and t sequences with edits, augmented with varying numbers of pairs without edits. The CHAR+SAMPLE and WORD+SAMPLE models are given a random sample of 200,000 pairs without edits for a total of 666,672 pairs of s and t sequences. The CHAR+ALL and WORD+ALL models are given all 722,742 sentences without edits for a total of 1,189,414 pairs of s and t sequences. For some of the final testing models, we also train with the development sentences. In these latter cases, all sequence pairs are used. In training all of the encoder-decoder models, as indicated in Section 5.2, we drop sentences exceeding 50 tokens in length.

We also experimented with creating corrected versions of sentences for the CNN. The binary CNN classifiers are given 1,656,086 single-sentence training examples, of which 722,742 are error-free examples (in which s = t), and the remaining examples are constructed by removing the tags from the annotated sentences, t, to create tag-free examples that contain errors (466,672 instances) and additional error-free examples (466,672 instances).

## 5.2 Training

Training (along with testing) of all models was conducted on GPUs. Our models were implemented with the Torch[7] framework.

**CNN** Architecture and training approaches were informed by past work in sentence-level classification using CNNs (Kim, 2014; Zhang and Wallace, 2015). A limited grid search on the development set determined our use of filter windows of width 3, 4, and 5 and 1000 feature maps. We trained for 10 epochs. Training otherwise followed the approach of the correspondingly named CNN-STATIC and CNN-NONSTATIC models of Kim (2014).

**encoder-decoder** Initial parameter settings (including architecture decisions such as the number of layers and embedding and hidden state sizes) were informed by concurrent work in neural machine translation and existing work such as that of Sutskever et al. (2014) and Luong et al. (2015). We used 4-layer LSTMs with 1000 hidden units in each layer. We trained for 14 epochs with a batch size of 64 and a maximum sequence length of 50. The parameters for the WORD model were uniformly initialized in $[-0.1, 0.1]$, and those of the CHAR model were uniformly initialized in $[-0.05, 0.05]$. The $L_2$-normalized gradients were constrained to be $\leq 5$. Our learning rate schedule started the learning rate at 1 and halved the learning rate after each epoch beyond epoch 10, or once the validation set perplexity no longer improved. The WORD model used 1000-dimensional word embeddings. For CHAR, the character embeddings were 25-dimensional, the filter width was 6, the number of feature maps was 1000, and 2 highway layers were used. The maximum word length was 35 characters for training CHAR. Note that we do not reverse the source (s) sequences, unlike some previous NMT work. Following the work of Zaremba et al. (2014), we employed dropout with a probability of 0.3 between the LSTM layers.

Training both WORD and CHAR on the training set took on the order of a few days using GPUs, with the former being more efficient than the latter. In practice, we used two GPUs for training CHAR due to memory requirements.

## 5.3 Tuning

Post-hoc tuning was performed on the 10k held-out portion of the development set. In terms of maximizing the $F_1$-score, this post-hoc tuning was important for these models, without which precision was high and recall was low. We leave to future work alternative approaches to this type of post-hoc tuning.

For the CNN models, after training, we tuned the decision boundary to maximize the $F_1$-score on the held-out tuning set. Analogously, for the encoder-decoder models, after training the models, we tuned the bias weights (given as input to the final softmax layer generating the words/tags distribution) associated with the four annotation tags via a simple grid search by iteratively running beam search on the tun-

---

[6]Note that the number of sentences in the final development set without labels posted on CodaLab (`http://codalab.org`) differed from that originally posted on the AESW 2016 Shared Task website with labels.

[7]`http://torch.ch`

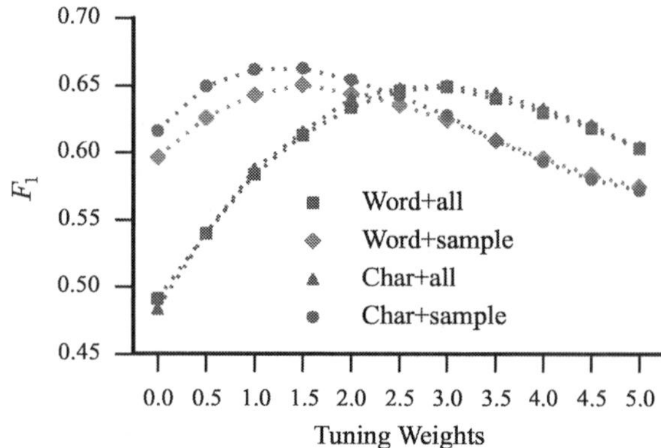

Figure 2: $F_1$ scores for varying values applied additively to the bias weights of the four annotation tags on the held-out 10k tuning subset.

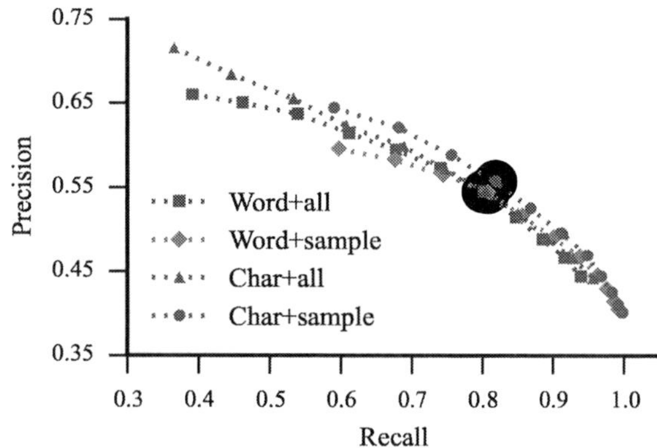

Figure 3: Precision vs. recall trade-off as the bias weights associated with the four annotation tags are varied on the held-out 10k tuning subset. The points yielding maximum $F_1$ scores are highlighted with black circles.

ing set. Due to the relatively high expense of decoding, we employed a coarse grid search in which the bias weights of the four annotation tags were uniformly varied.

## 6   Results

Results on the development set, excluding the 10k tuning set, appear in Table 1. Here (and elsewhere) RANDOM is the result of randomly assigning a sentence to one of the binary classes. For the CNN classifiers, fine-tuning the word2vec embeddings improves performance. The encoder-decoder models improve over the CNN classifiers, even though the latter are provided with additional data (via word2vec). The character-based models yield tangible improvements over the word-based models.

For consistency here, we kept the beam size at 10 across models, but subsequent analysis revealed that increasing the beam from 5 to 10 had a negligible effect on overall performance.

Tuning results appear in Figures 2 and 3, illustrating the importance of adjusting the bias weights associated with the annotation tags in balancing precision and recall to maximize the $F_1$ score. The models trained on all sequence pairs without edits, CHAR+ALL and WORD+ALL, perform particularly poorly without tuning these bias weights, yielding $F_1$ scores near that of RANDOM before tuning, which corresponds to a weight of 0.0 in Figure 2.

The official development set posted on CodaLab differed slightly from the original development set provided with labels, so we include those results in Table 2 for the encoder-decoder models. Here, evaluation is performed on the CodaLab server, as with the final test submission. The overall relative performance pattern is similar to that of the original development set.

A comparison of our results with other shared task submissions appears in Table 3. (Teams were allowed to submit up to two results.) Our submission, COMBINATION was a simple majority vote at the system level (for each test sentence) of 5 models[8]: (1) a CNN-NONSTATIC model trained with the concatenation of the training and development sets (and using word2vec); (2) a WORD model trained on all sequence pairs in the training and development sets with a beam size of 10 for decoding; (3,4) a CHAR+SAMPLE model trained on the training set, decoding the test set twice, each time with different weight biases (the two highest performing via the grid search over the tuning set) with a beam size of 10; and (5) a CHAR model trained on all sequence pairs in the training and development sets, with training suspended at epoch 9 (out of 14) and a beam size of 5 to meet the Shared Task deadline. For reference, we also include the CodaLab evaluation for just the CHAR+SAMPLE model trained on the training set with a beam size of 10, with the bias

---

[8]The choice of models was limited to those that were trained and tuned in time for the Shared Task deadline.

| Model | Data | Precision | Recall | $F_1$ |
|---|---|---|---|---|
| RANDOM | N/A | 0.3885 | 0.4992 | 0.4369 |
| CNN-STATIC | Training+word2vec | 0.5349 | 0.7586 | 0.6274 |
| CNN-NONSTATIC | Training+word2vec | 0.5365 | 0.7758 | 0.6343 |
| WORD+ALL | Training | 0.5399 | 0.7882 | 0.6408 |
| WORD+SAMPLE | Training | 0.5394 | 0.8024 | 0.6451 |
| CHAR+ALL | Training | 0.5400 | 0.8048 | 0.6463 |
| CHAR+SAMPLE | Training | 0.5526 | 0.8126 | 0.6579 |

**Table 1:** Experimental results on the development set excluding the held-out 10k tuning subset.

| Model | Data | Precision | Recall | $F_1$ |
|---|---|---|---|---|
| RANDOM | N/A | 0.3921 | 0.5981 | 0.4736 |
| WORD+ALL | Training | 0.5343 | 0.7577 | 0.6267 |
| WORD+SAMPLE | Training | 0.5335 | 0.7699 | 0.6303 |
| CHAR+ALL | Training | 0.5351 | 0.7749 | 0.6330 |
| CHAR+SAMPLE | Training | 0.5469 | 0.7803 | 0.6431 |

**Table 2:** Results on the official development set. Here, RANDOM was provided by the Shared Task organizers.

| Model | Data | Precision | Recall | $F_1$ |
|---|---|---|---|---|
| RANDOM | N/A | 0.3607 | 0.6004 | 0.4507 |
| KNOWLET | – | 0.6241 | 0.3685 | 0.4634 |
| NTNU-YZU | – | 0.6717 | 0.3805 | 0.4858 |
| HITS | – | 0.3765 | 0.948 | 0.5389 |
| UW-SU | – | 0.4145 | 0.8201 | 0.5507 |
| NTNU-YZU | – | 0.5025 | 0.7785 | 0.6108 |
| CHAR+SAMPLE | Training | 0.5112 | 0.7841 | 0.6189 |
| COMBINATION | Training+Dev+word2vec | 0.5444 | 0.7413 | 0.6278 |

**Table 3:** Final submitted results on the Shared Task test set. COMBINATION was our final submitted system. RANDOM was provided by the Shared Task organizers. For comparison, we have included the other team submissions from National Taiwan Normal University and Yuan Ze University (NTNU-YZU), the University of Washington and Stanford University (UW-SU), HITS (HITS), and Knowlet (KNOWLET). Teams were allowed to designate up to two final submissions. (The CHAR model trained on the combined training and development set had not finished training by the Shared Task deadline. As such, it was not submitted, but the partially trained model was included in COMBINATION.)

weights being those that generated the highest $F_1$-score on the 10k tuning set.

## 7 Discussion

Of particular interest, the CHAR+SAMPLE model performs well, both in terms of performance on the test set relative to other submissions, as well as on the development set relative to the WORD models and the CNN classifiers. It is possible this is due to the ability of the CHAR models to capture some types of orthographic errors.

The empirical results suggest that simply adding additional already correct source-target pairs when training the encoder-decoder models may not boost performance, ceteris paribus, as seen in comparing the performance of CHAR+SAMPLE vs WORD+SAMPLE, and CHAR+ALL vs WORD+ALL. We leave to future work alternative approaches for introducing additional correct (target) sentences, as has been examined for neural machine translation models (Sennrich et al., 2015; Gülçehre et al., 2015).

Our results provide initial evidence to support the hypothesis that training at the lowest granularity of annotation is a more efficient use of data than training against the binary label. In future work, we plan to compare against sentence classification using LSTMs (Dai and Le, 2015) and convolutional models that use correction-level annotations.

Another benefit of the encoder-decoder models is that they can be used to generate corrections (and identify locations of intra-sentence errors) for end-users. However, the added generation capabilities of the encoder-decoder models comes at the expense of considerably longer training and testing times compared to the CNN classifiers.

We found that post-hoc tuning provides a straight-forward means of tuning the precision-recall trade-off for these models, and we speculate (but leave to future work for investigation) that in practice, end-users might prefer greater emphasis placed on precision over recall.

## 8   Conclusion

We have presented our submission to the AESW 2016 Shared Task, suggesting, in particular, the utility of a neural attention-based model for sentence-level grammatical error identification. Our models do not make use of hand-tuned rules, are not trained with explicit syntactic annotations, and do not make use of individuals classifiers designed for human-designated subsets of errors.

For the encoder-decoder models, modeling at the sub-word level was beneficial, even though predictions were still made at the word level. It would be of interest to push this further to eliminate the need for an initial tokenization step, in order to generalize the approach to other languages, such as Chinese and Japanese.

We plan to examine alternative approaches for training with additional correct (target) sentences. Inducing artificial errors to generate more incorrect (source) sentences is also a direction we intend to pursue.

We leave for future work an analysis of the generation quality of our encoder-decoder models on the AESW dataset and the CoNLL-2014 Shared Task data, as well as user studies to assess whether performance is sufficient in practice to be useful, including the utility of correction vs. identification.

We consider this to be just the beginning of the development of data-driven support tools for writers, and many areas remain to be explored.

## Acknowledgments

We would like to thank the organizers of the Shared Task for coordinating the task and making the unique AESW dataset available for research purposes. The Institute for Quantitative Social Science (IQSS) and the Harvard Initiative for Learning and Teaching (HILT) supported earlier, related research that led to our participation in the Shared Task. Jeffrey Ling graciously contributed a torch-based CNN implementation of Kim (2014).

## References

Dzmitry Bahdanau, Kyunghyun Cho, and Yoshua Bengio. 2014. Neural machine translation by jointly learning to align and translate. *CoRR*, abs/1409.0473.

Kyunghyun Cho, Bart Van Merriënboer, Çağlar Gülçehre, Dzmitry Bahdanau, Fethi Bougares, Holger Schwenk, and Yoshua Bengio. 2014. Learning phrase representations using rnn encoder–decoder for statistical machine translation. In *Proceedings of the 2014 Conference on Empirical Methods in Natural Language Processing (EMNLP)*, pages 1724–1734, Doha, Qatar, October. Association for Computational Linguistics.

Andrew M. Dai and Quoc V. Le. 2015. Semi-supervised sequence learning. *CoRR*, abs/1511.01432.

Robert Dale and Adam Kilgarriff. 2011. Helping our own: The hoo 2011 pilot shared task. In *Proceedings of the 13th European Workshop on Natural Language Generation*, ENLG '11, pages 242–249, Stroudsburg, PA, USA. Association for Computational Linguistics.

Robert Dale, Ilya Anisimoff, and George Narroway. 2012. Hoo 2012: A report on the preposition and determiner error correction shared task. In *Proceedings of the Seventh Workshop on Building Educational Applications Using NLP*, pages 54–62, Stroudsburg, PA, USA. Association for Computational Linguistics.

Vidas Daudaravicius, Rafael E. Banchs, Elena Volodina, and Courtney Napoles. 2016. A report on the automatic evaluation of scientific writing shared task. In *Proceedings of the Eleventh Workshop on Innovative Use of NLP for Building Educational Applications*, San Diego, CA, USA, June. Association for Computational Linguistics.

Mariano Felice, Zheng Yuan, Øistein E. Andersen, Helen Yannakoudakis, and Ekaterina Kochmar. 2014. Grammatical error correction using hybrid systems and type filtering. In *Proceedings of the Eighteenth Conference on Computational Natural Language Learning: Shared Task*, pages 15–24, Baltimore, Maryland, June. Association for Computational Linguistics.

Çaglar Gülçehre, Orhan Firat, Kelvin Xu, Kyunghyun Cho, Loïc Barrault, Huei-Chi Lin, Fethi Bougares, Holger Schwenk, and Yoshua Bengio. 2015. On using monolingual corpora in neural machine translation. *CoRR*, abs/1503.03535.

Sepp Hochreiter and Jürgen Schmidhuber. 1997. Long short-term memory. *Neural Comput.*, 9(8):1735–1780, November.

Yoon Kim, Yacine Jernite, David Sontag, and Alexander M. Rush. 2016. Character-Aware Neural Language Models. In *Proceedings of AAAI*.

Yoon Kim. 2014. Convolutional neural networks for sentence classification. In *Proceedings of the 2014 Conference on Empirical Methods in Natural Language Processing (EMNLP)*, pages 1746–1751, Doha, Qatar, October. Association for Computational Linguistics.

Minh-Thang Luong, Hieu Pham, and Christopher D. Manning. 2015. Effective approaches to attention-based neural machine translation. In *Empirical Methods in Natural Language Processing (EMNLP)*, pages 1412–1421, Lisbon, Portugal, September. Association for Computational Linguistics.

Tomas Mikolov, Ilya Sutskever, Kai Chen, Greg S Corrado, and Jeff Dean. 2013. Distributed representations of words and phrases and their compositionality. In C. J. C. Burges, L. Bottou, M. Welling, Z. Ghahramani, and K. Q. Weinberger, editors, *Advances in Neural Information Processing Systems 26*, pages 3111–3119. Curran Associates, Inc.

Courtney Napoles, Keisuke Sakaguchi, Matt Post, and Joel Tetreault. 2015. Ground truth for grammatical error correction metrics. In *Proceedings of the 53rd Annual Meeting of the Association for Computational Linguistics and the 7th International Joint Conference on Natural Language Processing (Volume 2: Short Papers)*, pages 588–593, Beijing, China, July. Association for Computational Linguistics.

Hwee Tou Ng, Siew Mei Wu, Yuanbin Wu, Christian Hadiwinoto, and Joel Tetreault. 2013. The CoNLL-2013 shared task on grammatical error correction. In *Proceedings of the Seventeenth Conference on Computational Natural Language Learning: Shared Task*, pages 1–12, Sofia, Bulgaria, August. Association for Computational Linguistics.

Hwee Tou Ng, Siew Mei Wu, Ted Briscoe, Christian Hadiwinoto, Raymond Hendy Susanto, and Christopher Bryant. 2014. The CoNLL-2014 shared task on grammatical error correction. In *Proceedings of the Eighteenth Conference on Computational Natural Language Learning: Shared Task*, pages 1–14, Baltimore, Maryland, June. Association for Computational Linguistics.

Y. Albert Park and Roger Levy. 2011. Automated whole sentence grammar correction using a noisy channel model. In *Proceedings of the 49th Annual Meeting of the Association for Computational Linguistics: Human Language Technologies - Volume 1*, HLT '11, pages 934–944, Stroudsburg, PA, USA. Association for Computational Linguistics.

Alla Rozovskaya, Kai-Wei Chang, Mark Sammons, Dan Roth, and Nizar Habash. 2014. The Illinois-Columbia system in the CoNLL-2014 shared task. In *Proceedings of the Eighteenth Conference on Computational Natural Language Learning: Shared Task*, pages 34–42, Baltimore, Maryland, June. Association for Computational Linguistics.

Rico Sennrich, Barry Haddow, and Alexandra Birch. 2015. Improving neural machine translation models with monolingual data. *CoRR*, abs/1511.06709.

Rupesh Kumar Srivastava, Klaus Greff, and Jürgen Schmidhuber. 2015. Training very deep networks. *CoRR*, abs/1507.06228.

Ilya Sutskever, Oriol Vinyals, and Quoc VV Le. 2014. Sequence to sequence learning with neural networks. In *Advances in Neural Information Processing Systems*, pages 3104–3112.

Wojciech Zaremba, Ilya Sutskever, and Oriol Vinyals. 2014. Recurrent neural network regularization. *CoRR*, abs/1409.2329.

Ye Zhang and Byron Wallace. 2015. A sensitivity analysis of (and practitioners' guide to) convolutional neural networks for sentence classification. *CoRR*, abs/1510.03820.

# Combining Off-the-shelf Grammar and Spelling Tools for the Automatic Evaluation of Scientific Writing (AESW) Shared Task 2016


**René Witte** and **Bahar Sateli**
Knowlet Networks Inc.
Montréal, QC, Canada
http://www.knowlet.net



## Abstract

We applied two standard, open source tools for detecting spelling and grammar errors to the AESW 2016 shared task: *After the Deadline* and *LanguageTool*. The tools' output was combined with a Maximum Entropy machine learning model to classify each input sentence as requiring or not requiring any edits. This approach yielded the second-highest precision of 64.41% in the binary estimation task at AESW 2016, but also the lowest recall of 36.85%, resulting in an F-Measure of 46.34%.


## 1 Introduction

The *Automated Evaluation of Scientific Writing Shared Task* (AESW 2016) targeted the analysis of individual sentences, in order to assess whether or not a sentence as a whole requires editing or not (Daudaravicius et al., 2016). The long-term vision behind this task is to *"promote the development of automated writing evaluation tools that can assist authors in writing scientific papers"*.[1]

Our work in this area is similarly motivated by the idea of providing an interactive "virtual research assistant" that supports researchers in their daily tasks. Writing support includes providing interactive feedback on the quality of textual artifacts to academic authors. Such a support generally requires achieving high precision over recall, as tools with too many false positives tend to be ignored by authors. Additionally, providing salient feedback on detected mistakes – ideally together with suggestions for improvements – to the authors is an important feature. Stan-

dard, open source grammar and spelling tools have addressed these questions for quite some time, but are generally not focused on academic texts. Hence, we were interested in how well existing, general-purpose tools perform when applied to academic writing. In our experiments, we applied two well-known tools, *After the Deadline* and *LanguageTool* (described in Section 2.3), to the AESW data sets. Our hypothesis was that these two tools are *(i)* complementary to some degree, so that their combination can increase precision and/or recall; and *(ii)* a machine learning approach can combine the tools' output with additional syntactical context information, thereby attuning them to academic writing.

## 2 Methods

In this section, we discuss the setup of our AESW 2016 experiments.

### 2.1 Data and Task Description

Here, we briefly describe the datasets and tasks; for the full details, please refer to (Daudaravicius et al., 2016).

The input sentences were randomly selected from more than 9,000 journal articles across different domains (Computer Science, Physics, Human Sciences, etc.). The *training* and *development* data sets contain 256,389 and 31,732 sentences, respectively. Some sentences contain changes that were applied by professional editors, who are native English speakers. These sentences have inline <ins> and <del> tags that mark inserted and removed content, respectively. An example sentence is shown in Fig. 1.

The test data set (31,085 sentences) *"retain texts*

---

[1] AESW 2016, http://textmining.lt/aesw/index.html




*Proceedings of the 11th Workshop on Innovative Use of NLP for Building Educational Applications*, pages 252–255,
San Diego, California, June 16, 2016. ©2016 Association for Computational Linguistics

```
<sentence sid="3570.3">
 The enterprise aims to increase <del>in</del>
 <ins>the</ins> output (at the same time to
 reduce expenses) _MATH_ and to decrease
 <del>in</del><ins>the</ins> consumed
 <del>efforts</del><ins>effort</ins> _MATH_.
</sentence>
```

**Figure 1:** Example sentence in XML format from the AESW 2016 development set

*tagged with <del> tags and the tags are dropped. Texts between <ins> tags are removed."*[2]

The goal of the AESW tasks was to predict whether a given sentence as a whole requires editing – that is, individual insertions or deletions did not have to be annotated. Thus, the output for the two tasks was either a boolean feature (True meaning a sentence requires editing) or a probabilistic feature with a value in [0,1] (where "1" indicates that an edit is required).

## 2.2 Preprocessing

To facilitate cross-fold evaluations, we split all AESW data sets (development, training, and testing) into individual XML files containing 1000 sentences each.

For machine learning, each sentence from the development and training sets received an *edit* feature of True if it contained at least one <ins> or <del> tag, otherwise the *edit* feature was set to False. For training, content marked as 'inserted' (between <ins> tags as shown in Fig. 1) was removed from the texts. The <del> tags were likewise removed, but the content was retained, thereby showing a sentence's content before any changes performed by an editor. Note that this conforms to the format of the test set, as described above.

## 2.3 Writing Error Detection Tools

We experimented with two open source tools for writing error detection:

**After the Deadline (AtD)** detects spelling, grammar, and style errors (Mudge, 2010).[3] We used version atd-081310 in its default configuration for our experiments.

**LanguageTool (LT)** is another popular open source spelling and grammar tool,[4] which also supports multiple languages. We used version 3.2-SNAPSHOT from the LT GitHub repository[5] for our experiments.

## 2.4 Experimental Setup

To facilitate the combination of the individual results, we integrated both tools into a pipeline through the *General Architecture for Text Engineering* (GATE) (Cunningham et al., 2011). Each error reported by one of the tools is added to the input text in the form of an *annotation*, which holds a start- and end-offset, as well as a number of *features*, such as the type of the error, the internal rule that generated the error, and possibly suggestions for improvements, as shown in Figure 2.

Additionally, we added a number of standard GATE plugins from the ANNIE pipeline (Cunningham et al., 2002) to perform tokenization, part-of-speech tagging, and lemmatization on the input texts. Finally, annotations spanning placeholder texts in the sentences, such as _MATH_, were filtered out, as these were particular to the AESW data.

## 2.5 Machine Learning

In addition to applying the AtD and LT tools individually, we experimented with their combination through machine learning. Essentially, we follow a stacking approach (Witten and Frank, 2011) by treating the AtD and LT tools as individual classifiers and use them to train a model for assigning the output 'edit' feature to a sentence.

**ML Features.** Table 1 lists all features we derive from the input sentences. We experimented with different token root and category n-grams, including unigrams, bigrams and trigrams.

**ML Algorithms.** Training and evaluation were performed using the Weka[6] (Witten and Frank, 2011) and Mallet[7] (McCallum, 2002) toolkits. These were executed from within GATE using the *Learning*

---

[2] AESW 2016 Data Set, see http://textmining.lt/aesw/index.html#data

[3] After the Deadline, http://www.afterthedeadline.com/

[4] LanguageTool, https://languagetool.org/

[5] LanguageTool GitHub repository, https://github.com/languagetool-org/languagetool

[6] Weka, https://sourceforge.net/projects/weka/

[7] Mallet, http://mallet.cs.umass.edu/

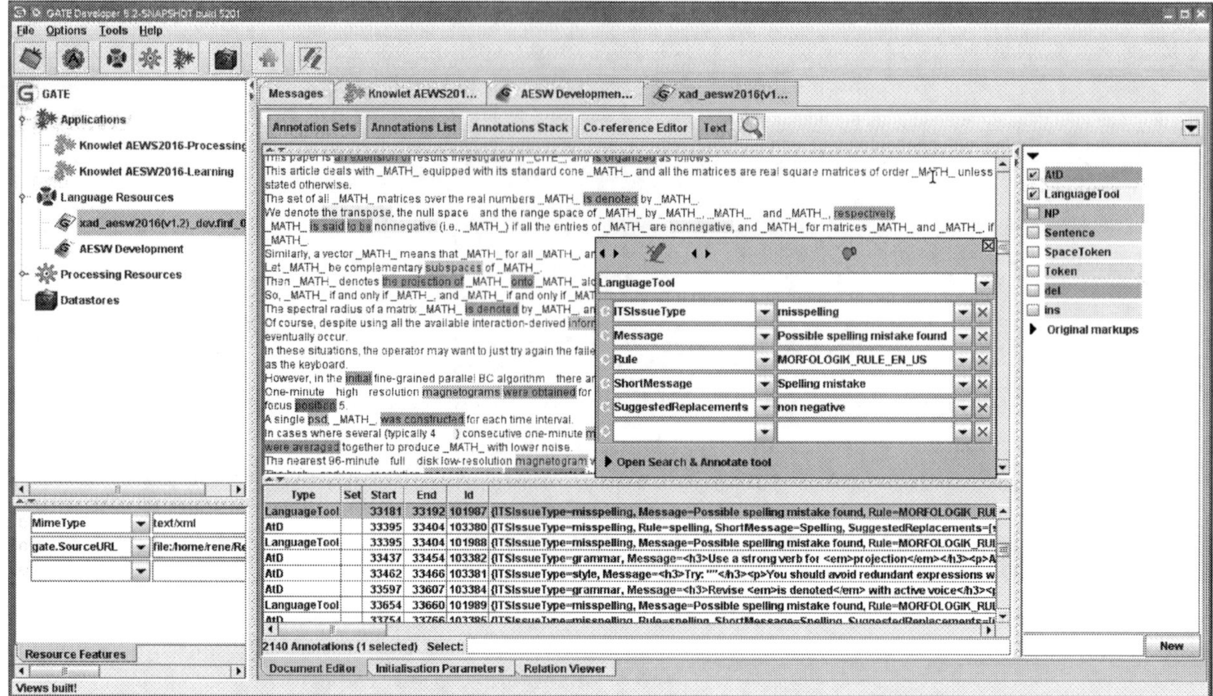

**Figure 2:** Combination of the writing analysis tools *After the Deadline* and *LanguageTool* in the GATE Developer GUI

| Feature | Description |
| --- | --- |
| Token.root | Morphological root of the token |
| Token.category | Part-of-speech tag for the token |
| LT.rule | Rule name as reported by LT |
| LT.string | Reported text (surface form) |
| AtD.rule | Rule name as reported by AtD |
| AtD.string | Reported text (surface form) |

**Table 1:** Machine Learning Features

*Framework Plugin.*[8] We experimented with a number of classification algorithms, including Decision Trees, Winnow, Naïve Bayes, KNN, PAUM, and Maximum Entropy. The latter generally performed best for the dataset and features, hence in this paper we only report the results from the MaxEnt model.

## 3   Results

In this report, we provide a summary of our system's results – for a complete description of all AESW 2016 results, please refer to (Daudaravicius et al., 2016).

---

[8]GATE Learning Framework Plugin, https://github.com/GateNLP/gateplugin-LearningFramework

**Baseline experiments.**   To establish a baseline, we ran the AtD and LT tools on the development set. Here, every sentence that had at least one error annotation received an edit feature of True. Table 3 shows the results as reported by the *Codalab* site[9] used in the competition.

| Tool | Precision | Recall | F-Measure |
| --- | --- | --- | --- |
| AtD | 0.4318 | 0.7448 | 0.5467 |
| LT | 0.4719 | 0.4739 | 0.4729 |

**Table 3:** Baseline experiments: Evaluation of the individual tools on the development set

**Feature analysis.**   We measured the impact of the various features shown in Table 1 on the classification performance. A selected set of results is shown in Table 2. Accuracy was calculated using Mallet with a three-fold cross-validation on the training data set. Generally, adding more features increased precision, but did not improve recall.

**Submitted run.**   For the submitted run, we retrained the MaxEnt classifier using the full fea-

---

[9]Codalab, http://codalab.org/

| Feature Set | Accuracy |
| --- | --- |
| AtD.rule, AtD.string, LT.rule, LT.string | 0.6261 |
| AtD.rule, AtD.string, LT.rule, LT.string, Token.root unigrams, Token.category unigrams | 0.6584 |
| AtD.rule, AtD.string, LT.rule, LT.string, Token.root bigrams, Token.category bigrams | 0.7300 |
| AtD.rule, AtD.string, LT.rule, LT.string, Token.root trigrams, Token.category trigrams | 0.8525 |

**Table 2:** Three-fold cross-validation of the MaxEnt classifier on the training data with different feature sets

ture set (using trigrams for both Token.root and Token.category) on both development and training set. The exact same configuration was used for the probabilistic task submission, using the classifier's confidence as the prediction value (with 1-confidence for sentences classified as not requiring edits). The results are summarized in Table 4.

| Tool | Precision | Recall | F-Measure |
| --- | --- | --- | --- |
| binary | 0.6241 (1) | 0.3685 (8) | 0.4634 (7) |
| probabilistic | 0.7294 (2) | 0.6591 (6) | 0.6925 (5) |

**Table 4:** Submitted runs for the AESW 2016 task on the test set (as reported by Codalab)

## 4 Conclusions

Based on our experiments, standard spell and grammar checking tools can help in assessing academic writing, but do not cover all different types of edits observed in the training data. In future work, we plan to categorize the false negatives and develop additional features to capture specific writing errors.

As the AESW 2016 task was performed on individual sentences, the results do not accurately reflect the interactive use within a tool: False positive errors, such as spelling mistakes reported for an unknown acronym, are counted for every sentence, rather than once for the entire document, thereby decreasing precision significantly when an entity appears multiple times. Also, document-level writing errors, such as discourse-level mistakes, cannot be captured with this setup – for example, use of acronyms before they are defined or inconsistent use of American vs. English spelling. Finally, while the sentence-level decision can be helpful in directing the attention of an editor to a possibly problematic sentence, by itself it does not explain *why* a given sentence was flagged or *how* it could be improved, which are important information for academic writers.


## References

Hamish Cunningham, Diana Maynard, Kalina Bontcheva, and Valentin Tablan. 2002. GATE: A Framework and Graphical Development Environment for Robust NLP Tools and Applications. In *Proceedings of the 40th Anniversary Meeting of the Association for Computational Linguistics (ACL'02)*.

Hamish Cunningham, Diana Maynard, Kalina Bontcheva, Valentin Tablan, Niraj Aswani, Ian Roberts, Genevieve Gorrell, Adam Funk, Angus Roberts, Danica Damljanovic, Thomas Heitz, Mark A. Greenwood, Horacio Saggion, Johann Petrak, Yaoyong Li, and Wim Peters. 2011. *Text Processing with GATE (Version 6)*. http://tinyurl.com/gatebook.

Vidas Daudaravicius, Rafael E. Banchs, Elena Volodina, and Courtney Napoles. 2016. A report on the automatic evaluation of scientific writing shared task. In *Proceedings of the Eleventh Workshop on Innovative Use of NLP for Building Educational Applications*, San Diego, CA, USA, June. Association for Computational Linguistics.

Andrew Kachites McCallum. 2002. MALLET: A Machine Learning for Language Toolkit. http://mallet.cs.umass.edu/.

Raphael Mudge. 2010. The Design of a Proofreading Software Service. In *Workshop on Computational Linguistics and Writing: Writing Processes and Authoring Aids (CL&W 2010)*.

Ian H. Witten and Eibe Frank. 2011. *Data Mining: Practical Machine Learning Tools and Techniques*. Morgan Kaufmann, 2nd edition.

# Candidate re-ranking for SMT-based grammatical error correction

**Zheng Yuan, Ted Briscoe** and **Mariano Felice**
The ALTA Institute
Computer Laboratory
University of Cambridge
`{zy249,ejb,mf501}@cam.ac.uk`

## Abstract

We develop a supervised ranking model to re-rank candidates generated from an SMT-based grammatical error correction (GEC) system. A range of novel features with respect to GEC are investigated and implemented in our re-ranker. We train a rank preference SVM model and demonstrate that this outperforms both Minimum Bayes-Risk and Multi-Engine Machine Translation based re-ranking for the GEC task. Our best system yields a significant improvement in I-measure when testing on the publicly available FCE test set (from 2.87% to 9.78%). It also achieves an $F_{0.5}$ score of 38.08% on the CoNLL-2014 shared task test set, which is higher than the best original result. The oracle score (upper bound) for the re-ranker achieves over 40% I-measure performance, demonstrating that there is considerable room for improvement in the re-ranking component developed here, such as incorporating features able to capture long-distance dependencies.

## 1 Introduction

Grammatical error correction (GEC) has attracted considerable interest in recent years. Unlike classifiers built for specific error types (e.g. determiner or preposition errors), statistical machine translation (SMT) systems are trained to deal with all error types simultaneously. An SMT system thus learns to translate incorrect English into correct English using a parallel corpus of corrected sentences. The SMT framework has been successfully used for GEC, as demonstrated by the top-performing systems in the CoNLL-2014 shared task (Ng et al., 2014).

However, the best candidate produced by an SMT system is not always the best correction. An example is given in Table 1.

Since SMT was not originally designed for GEC, many standard features do not perform well on this task. It is necessary to add new local and global features to help the decoder distinguish good from bad corrections. Felice et al. (2014) used Levenshtein distance to limit the changes made by their SMT system, given that most words translate into themselves and errors are often similar to their correct forms. Junczys-Dowmunt and Grundkiewicz (2014) also augmented their SMT system with Levenshtein distance and other sparse features that were extracted from edit operations.

However, the integration of additional models/features into the decoding process may affect the dynamic programming algorithm used in SMT, because it does not support some complex features, such as those computed from an n-best list. An alternative to performing integrated decoding is to use additional information to re-rank an SMT decoder's output. The aim of n-best list re-ranking is to re-rank the translation candidates produced by the SMT system using a rich set of features that are not used by the SMT decoder, so that better candidates can be selected as 'optimal' translations. This has several advantages: 1) it allows the introduction of new features that are tailored for GEC; 2) unlike in SMT, we can use various types of features without worrying about fine-grained smoothing issues and it is easier to use global features; 3) re-ranking is easy to implement, and the existing decoder does not need to be modified; and 4) the decoding process in SMT



*Proceedings of the 11th Workshop on Innovative Use of NLP for Building Educational Applications*, pages 256–266,
San Diego, California, June 16, 2016. ©2016 Association for Computational Linguistics

| | |
|---|---|
| Source | There **are** some **informations** you have asked me about. |
| Reference | There **is** some **information** you have asked me about. |
| **10 best list** | |
| 1st: | There are some information you have asked me about. |
| 2nd: | *There is some information you have asked me about.* |
| 3rd: | There are some information you asked me about. |
| 4th: | There are some information you have asked me. |
| 5th: | There are some information you have asked me for. |
| 6th: | There are some information you have asked me about it. |
| 7th: | There is some information you asked me about. |
| 8th: | There are some information you asked me for. |
| 9th: | There were some information you have asked me about. |
| 10th: | There is some information you have asked me. |

**Table 1:** In this example, there are two errors in the sentence (marked in **bold**): an agreement error (are → is) and a mass noun error (informations → information). The best output is the one with highest probability, which only corrects the mass noun error, but misses the agreement error. However, the *2nd*-ranked candidate corrects both errors and matches the reference (marked in *italics*). The source sentence and error annotation are taken from the FCE dataset (Yannakoudakis et al., 2011), and the 10-best list is from an SMT system trained on the whole CLC (Nicholls, 2003). More details about the datasets and system are presented in Section 3.

only needs to be performed once, which allows for fast experimentation.

Most previous work on GEC has used evaluation methods based on precision (P), recall (R), and F-score (e.g. the CoNLL 2013 and 2014 shared tasks). However, they do not provide an indicator of improvement on the original text so there is no way to compare GEC systems with a 'do-nothing' baseline. Since the aim of GEC is to improve text quality, we use the Improvement ($I$) score calculated by the I-measure (Felice and Briscoe, 2015), which tells us whether a system improves the input.

The main contributions of our work are as follows. First, to the best of our knowledge, we are the first to use a supervised discriminative re-ranking model in SMT for GEC, showing that n-best list re-ranking can be used to improve sentence quality. Second, we propose and investigate a range of easily computed features for GEC re-ranking. Finally, we report results on two well-known publicly available test sets that can be used for cross-system comparisons.

## 2 Approach

Our re-ranking approach is defined as follows:

1. an SMT system is first used to generate an n-best list of candidates for each input sentence;

2. features that are potentially useful to discriminate between good and bad corrections are extracted from the n-best list;

3. these features are then used to determine a new ranking for the n-best list;

4. the new highest-ranked candidate is finally output.

### 2.1 SMT for grammatical error correction

Following previous work (e.g. Brockett et al. (2006), Yuan and Felice (2013), Junczys-Dowmunt and Grundkiewicz (2014)), we approach GEC as a translation problem from incorrect into correct English.

Our training data comprises parallel sentences extracted from the Cambridge Learner Corpus (CLC) (Nicholls, 2003). Two automatic alignment tools are used for word alignment: GIZA++ (Och and Ney, 2003) and Pialign (Neubig et al., 2011). GIZA++ is an implementation of IBM Models 1-5 (Brown et al., 1993) and a Hidden-Markov alignment model (HMM) (Vogel et al., 1996). Word alignments learnt by GIZA++ are used to extract phrase-to-phrase translations using heuristics. Unlike GIZA++, Pialign creates a phrase table directly from model probabilities. In addition to default features, we add character-level Levenshtein distance to each mapping in the phrase table as proposed by Felice et al. (2014).

Decoding is performed using Moses (Koehn et al., 2007). The language models used during decoding are built from the corrected sentences in the learner corpus, to make sure that the final system outputs fluent English sentences. The IRSTLM Toolkit (Federico et al., 2008) is used to build n-gram language models (up to 5-grams) with modified Kneser-Ney smoothing (Kneser and Ney, 1995). Previous work has shown that adding bigger language models based on larger corpora improves performance (Yuan and Felice, 2013; Junczys-Dowmunt and Grundkiewicz, 2014). The use of bigger language models will be investigated at the re-ranking stage, as it allows us to compute a richer set of features that would otherwise be hard to integrate into the decoding stage.

## 2.2  Ranking SVM

The SMT system is not perfect, and candidates with the highest probability from the SMT system do not always constitute the best correction. An n-best list re-ranker is trained to re-rank these candidates in order to find better corrections. We treat n-best list re-ranking as a discriminative ranking problem. Unlike standard SMT, the source input sentence is also added to the candidate pool if it is not in the n-best list, since in many cases the source sentence has no error and should be translated as itself.

We use rank preference SVMs (Joachims, 2002) in the SVM$^{rank}$ package (Joachims, 2006). This model learns a ranking function from preference training examples and then assigns a score to each test example, from which a global ordering is derived. The default linear kernel is used due to training and test time costs.

Rank preference SVMs work as follows. Suppose that we are given a set of ranked instances $R$ containing training samples $x_i$ and their target rankings $r_i$:

$$R = \{(x_1, r_1), (x_2, r_2), ..., (x_l, r_l)\} \qquad (1)$$

such that $x_i \succ x_j$ when $r_i < r_j$, where $\succ$ denotes a preference relationship. A set of ranking functions $f \in F$ is defined, where each $f$ determines the preference relations between instances:

$$x_i \succ x_j \Leftrightarrow f(x_i) > f(x_j) \qquad (2)$$

The aim is to find the best function $f$ that minimises a given loss function $\xi$ with respect to the given ranked instances. Instead of using the $R$ set directly, a set of pair-wise difference vectors is created and used to train a model. For linear ranking models, this is equivalent to finding the weight vector $w$ that maximises the number of correctly ranked pairs:

$$\forall(x_i \succ x_j) : w(x_i - x_j) > 0 \qquad (3)$$

which is, in turn, equivalent to solving the following optimisation problem:

$$\min_w \frac{1}{2} w^T w + C \sum \xi_{ij} \qquad (4)$$

subject to

$$\forall(x_i \succ x_j) : w(x_i - x_j) \geq 1 - \xi_{ij} \qquad (5)$$

where $\xi_{ij} \geq 0$ are non-negative slack variables that measure the extent of misclassification.

## 2.3  Feature space

New features are introduced to identify better corrections in the n-best produced by the SMT decoder. We use general features that work for all types of errors, leaving L2-specific features for future work. These are described briefly below.

**A) SMT feature set:** Reuses information extracted from the SMT system. As the SMT framework has been shown to produce good results for GEC, we reuse these pre-defined SMT features. This feature set includes:

**Decoder's scores:** Includes unweighted translation model scores, reordering model scores, language model scores and word penalty scores. We use unweighted scores, as the weights for each score will be reassigned during training.

**N-best list ranking information:** Encodes the original ranking information provided by the SMT decoder. Both *linear* and *non-linear* transformations are used.

Note that both the decoder's features and the n-best list ranking features are extracted from the SMT system output. If the source sentence is not in the n-best list, it will not have these two kinds of features and zeros will be used.

**B) Language model feature set:** Raw candidates from an SMT system can include many malformed sentences so we introduce language model (LM) features and adaptive language model (ALM) features in an attempt to identify and discard them.

**LM:** Language models are widely used in GEC, especially to rank correction suggestions proposed by other models. Ideally, correct word sequences will get high probabilities, while incorrect or unseen ones will get low probabilities. We use Microsoft's Web N-gram Services, which provide access to large smoothed n-gram LMs built from web documents (Gao et al., 2010). All our experiments are based on the 5-gram 'bing-body:apr10' model. We also build several n-gram LMs from native and learner corpora, including the CLC, the British National Corpus (BNC) and ukWaC (Ferraresi et al., 2008). The LM feature set contains unnormalised sentence scores, normalised scores using *arithmetic mean* and *geometric mean*, and the minimum and maximum n-gram probability scores.

**ALM:** Adaptive LM scores are calculated from the n-best list's n-gram probabilities. N-gram counts are collected using the entries in the n-best list for each source sentence. N-grams repeated more often than others in the n-best list get higher scores, thus ameliorating incorrect lexical choices and word order. The n-gram probability for a target word $e_i$ given its history $e_{i-n+1}^{i-1}$ is defined as:

$$p_{n-best}(e_i|e_{i-n+1}^{i-1}) = \frac{count_{n-best}(e_i, e_{i-n+1}^{i-1})}{count_{n-best}(e_{i-n+1}^{i-1})} \quad (6)$$

The sentence score for the $s$th candidate $H_s$ is calculated as:

$$score(H_s) = \log(\prod p_{n-best}(e_i|e_{i-n+1}^{i-1})) \quad (7)$$

The sentence score is then normalised by sentence length to get an average word log probability, making it comparable for candidates of different lengths. In our re-ranking system, different values of $n$ are used, from 2 to 6. This feature is taken from Hildebrand and Vogel (2008).

**C) Statistical word lexicon feature set:** We use the word lexicon learnt by the IBM Model 4, which contains translation probabilities for word-to-word mappings. The statistical word translation lexicon is used to calculate the translation probability $P_{lex}(e)$ for each word $e$ in the target sentence. $P_{lex}(e)$ is the sum of all translation probabilities of $e$ for each word $f_j$ in the source sentence $f_1^J$. Specifically, this can be defined as:

$$P_{lex}(e|f_1^J) = \frac{1}{J+1}\sum_{j=0}^{J} p(e|f_j) \quad (8)$$

where $f_1^J$ is the source sentence and $J$ is the source sentence length. $p(e|f_j)$ is the word-to-word translation probability of the target word $e$ from one source word $f_j$.

As noted by Ueffing and Ney (2007), the sum in Equation (8) is dominated by the maximum lexicon probability, which we also use as an additional feature:

$$P_{lex-max}(e|f_1^J) = \max_{j=0,...,J} p(e|f_j) \quad (9)$$

For both lexicon scores, we sum over all words $e_i$ in the target sentence and normalise by sentence length to get sentence translation scores. Lexicon scores are calculated in both directions. This feature is also taken from Hildebrand and Vogel (2008).

**D) Length feature set:** These features are used to make sure that the final system does not make unnecessary deletions or insertions. This set contains four length ratios:

$$score(H_s, E) = \frac{N(H_s)}{N(E)} \quad (10)$$

$$score(H_s, H_1) = \frac{N(H_s)}{N(H_1)} \quad (11)$$

$$score(H_s, H_{max}) = \frac{N(H_s)}{N(H_{max})} \quad (12)$$

$$score(H_s, H_{min}) = \frac{N(H_s)}{N(H_{min})} \quad (13)$$

where $H_s$ is the $s$th candidate, $E$ is the source (erroneous) sentence, $H_1$ is the 1-best candidate (the candidate ranked $1st$ by the SMT system), $N(\cdot)$ is the sentence's length, $N(H_{max})$ is the maximum candidate length in the n-best list for that source sentence and $N(H_{min})$ is the minimum candidate length.

## 3 Experiments

### 3.1 Dataset

We use the publicly available FCE dataset (Yannakoudakis et al., 2011), which is a part of the CLC. The FCE dataset is a set of 1,244 scripts written by learners of English taking the First Certificate in English (FCE) examination around the world between 2000 and 2001. The texts have been manually error-annotated with a taxonomy of approximately 80 error types (Nicholls, 2003). The FCE dataset covers a wide variety of L1s and was used in the HOO-2012 error correction shared task (Dale et al., 2012). Compared to the National University of Singapore Corpus of Learner English (NUCLE) (Dahlmeier et al., 2013) used in the CoNLL 2013 and 2014 shared tasks, which contains essays written by students at the National University of Singapore, the FCE dataset is a more representative test set of learner writing, which is why we use it for our experiments. The performance of our model on the CoNLL-2014 shared task test data is also presented in Section 3.7.

Following Yannakoudakis et al. (2011), we split the publicly available FCE dataset into training and test sets: we use the 1,141 scripts from the year 2000 and the 6 validation scripts for training, and the 97 scripts from the year 2001 for testing. The FCE training set contains about 30,995 pairs of parallel sentences (approx. 496,567 tokens on the target side), and the test set contains about 2,691 pairs of parallel sentences (approx. 41,986 tokens on the target side). Both FCE and NUCLE are too small to build good SMT systems, considering that previous work has shown that training on small datasets does not work well for SMT-based GEC (Yuan and Felice, 2013; Junczys-Dowmunt and Grundkiewicz, 2014). To overcome this problem, Junczys-Dowmunt and Grundkiewicz (2014) introduced examples collected from the language exchange social

networking website Lang-8, and were able to improve system performance by 6 F-score points. As noticed by them, Lang-8 data may be too noisy and error-prone, so we decided to add examples from the fully annotated learner corpus CLC to our training set (approx. 1,965,727 pairs of parallel sentences and 29,219,128 tokens on the target side).

Segmentation and tokenisation are performed using RASP (Briscoe et al., 2006), which is expected to perform better on learner data than a system developed exclusively from high quality copy-edited text such as the Wall Street Journal.

### 3.2 Evaluation

System performance is evaluated using the I-measure proposed by Felice and Briscoe (2015), which is designed to address problems with previous evaluation methods and reflect any improvement on the original sentence after applying a system's corrections. An $I$ score is computed by comparing system performance ($WAcc_{sys}$) with that of a baseline that leaves the original text uncorrected ($WAcc_{base}$):

$$I = \begin{cases} \lfloor WAcc_{sys} \rfloor & \text{if } WAcc_{sys} = WAcc_{base} \\[2ex] \dfrac{WAcc_{sys} - WAcc_{base}}{1 - WAcc_{base}} & \text{if } WAcc_{sys} > WAcc_{base} \\[2ex] \dfrac{WAcc_{sys}}{WAcc_{base}} - 1 & \text{otherwise} \end{cases}$$

$$(14)$$

Values of $I$ lie in the $[-1, 1]$ interval. Positive values indicate improvement, while negative values indicate degradation. A score of 0 indicates no improvement (i.e. baseline performance), 1 indicates 100% correct text and -1 indicates 100% incorrect text.

In order to compute the $I$ score, system performance is first evaluated in terms of weighted accuracy ($WAcc$), based on a token-level alignment between a source sentence, a system's candidate, and a gold-standard reference:[1]

---

[1] TP: true positives, TN: true negatives, FP: false positives, FN: false negatives, FPN: both a FP and a FN (see Felice and Briscoe (2015))

$$WAcc = \frac{w \cdot \text{TP} + \text{TN}}{w \cdot (\text{TP} + \text{FP}) + \text{TN} + \text{FN} - (w + 1) \cdot \frac{\text{FPN}}{2}} \quad (15)$$

In Section 3.3 and 3.7, we also report results using another two evaluation metrics for comparison: $F_{0.5}$ from $M^2$ Scorer (Dahlmeier and Ng, 2012b) and GLEU (Napoles et al., 2015). The $M^2$ Scorer was the official scorer in the CoNLL 2013 and 2014 shared tasks, with the latter using $F_{0.5}$ as the system ranking metric. GLEU is a simple variant of BLEU (Papineni et al., 2002), which shows better correlation with human judgments on the CoNLL-2014 shared task test set.

### 3.3 SMT system

We train several SMT systems and select the best one for our re-ranking experiments. These systems use different configurations, defined as follows:

- GIZA++: uses GIZA++ for word alignment;

- Pialign: uses Pialign to learn a phrase table;

- FCE: uses the publicly available FCE as training data;

- + LD: limits edit distance by adding the character-level Levenshtein distance as a new feature;

- + CLC: incorporates additional training examples extracted from the CLC.

Evaluation results using the aforementioned metrics are presented in Table 2. As we mentioned earlier, a baseline system which makes no corrections gets zero F score. We can see that not all the systems make the source text better. Pialign outperforms GIZA++. Adding more learner examples improves system performance. The Levenshtein distance feature further improves performance. The best system in terms of the I-measure is the one that has been trained on the whole CLC, aligned with Pialign, and includes edit distance as an additional feature (*Pialign + FCE + CLC + LD*). The positive *I* score of 2.87 shows a real improvement in sentence quality. This system is also the best system in terms of GLEU and $F_{0.5}$ so we use the n-best list from this system to perform re-ranking.

### 3.4 SVM re-ranker

The input to the re-ranking model is the n-best list output from an SMT system. The original source sentence is used to collect a 10-best list of candidates generated by the SMT decoder, which is then used to build a supervised re-ranking model. For training, we use per-sentence I-measure values as gold labels.

The effectiveness of our re-ranker is proved by the results: performing a 10-best list re-ranking yields a statistically significant improvement in performance over the top-ranked output from the best existing SMT system.[2] The best re-ranking model is built using all features, achieving $I = 9.78$ (Table 3 #1). In order to measure the contribution of each feature set to the overall improvement in sentence quality, a number of ablation tests are performed, where new models are built by removing one feature type at a time. In Table 3, *SMT best* is the best SMT system output without re-ranking. *FullFeat* combines all feature types described in Section 2.3. The rest are *FullFeat* minus the indicated feature type.

The ablation tests tell us that all the features in the *FullFeat* set have positive effects on overall performance. Among them, the SMT decoder's scores are the most effective, as their absence is responsible for a 6.58 decrease in I-measure (Table 3 #2). The removal of the word lexicon features also acounts for a 2.13 decrease (#6), followed by SMT n-best list ranking information (1.46 #3), ALM (1.43 #5), length features (0.75 #7) and the LM features (0.22 #4). In order to test the performance of the SMT decoder's scores on their own, we built a new re-ranking model using only these features, which we report in Table 3 #8. We can see that using only the SMT decoder's scores yields worse performance than no re-ranking, suggesting that the existing features used by the SMT decoder are not optimal when used outside the SMT ecosystem. We hypothesise that this might be caused by the lack of scores for the source sentences that are not included in the n-best list of the original SMT system.

Looking at the re-ranker's output reveals that there are some L2 learners errors which are missed by the SMT system but are captured by the re-ranker - see Table 4.

---

[2] We perform two-tailed paired T-tests, where $p < 0.05$.

| Align | Setting | GLEU | M$^2$ | | | I-measure | |
|---|---|---|---|---|---|---|---|
| | | | P | R | F$_{0.5}$ | WAcc | I |
| Baseline | | 60.39 | 100 | 0 | 0 | 86.83 | 0 |
| GIZA++ | FCE | 61.42 | 36.66 | 16.97 | 29.76 | 83.24 | -4.14 |
| | + LD | 61.64 | 37.70 | 16.40 | 29.92 | 83.64 | -3.68 |
| | + CLC | 67.70 | 48.67 | **37.64** | 45.97 | 83.94 | -3.33 |
| | + CLC + LD | 67.98 | 49.87 | 37.16 | 46.67 | 84.42 | -2.78 |
| Pialign | FCE | 62.22 | 43.13 | 11.34 | 27.64 | 84.94 | -2.17 |
| | + LD | 62.19 | 43.07 | 11.17 | 27.41 | 85.00 | -2.11 |
| | + CLC | 70.07 | 62.37 | 32.19 | 52.52 | 87.01 | 1.38 |
| | + CLC + LD | **70.15** | **63.27** | 31.95 | **52.90** | **87.21** | **2.87** |

Table 2: SMT system performance on the FCE test set (in percentages). The best results are marked in **bold**.

| # | Feature | WAcc | I |
|---|---|---|---|
| 0 | SMT best | 87.21 | 2.87 |
| 1 | FullFeat | **88.12** | **9.78** |
| 2 | - SMT (decoder) | 87.25 | 3.20 |
| 3 | - SMT (rank) | 87.93 | 8.32 |
| 4 | - LM | 88.09 | 9.56 |
| 5 | - ALM | 87.93 | 8.35 |
| 6 | - word lexicon | 87.84 | 7.65 |
| 7 | - length | 88.02 | 9.03 |
| 8 | SMT (decoder) | 87.15 | 2.40 |

Table 3: Results of 10-best list re-ranking on the FCE test set (in percentages). The best results are marked in **bold**.

## 3.5 Oracle score

In order to estimate a realistic upper bound on the task, we calculate an oracle score from the same 10-best list generated by our best SMT model. The oracle set is created by selecting the candidate which has the highest sentence-level weighted accuracy (*WAcc*) score for each source sentence in the test set.

Table 5 #0-2 compares the results of standard SMT (i.e. the best candidate according to the SMT model), the SVM re-ranker (the best re-ranking model from Section 3.4) and the approximated oracle. The oracle score is about 41 points higher than the standard SMT score in terms of *I*, and about 5 points higher in terms of *WAcc*, suggesting that there are alternative candidates in the 10-best list that are not chosen by the SMT model. Our re-ranker improves the *I* score from 2.87 to 9.78, and the *WAcc* score from 87.21 to 88.12, a significant improvement over the standard SMT model. However, there

is still much room for improvement.

The oracle score tells us that, under the most favourable conditions, our models could only improve the original text by 44.35% at most. This also reveals that in many cases, the correct translation is not in the 10-best list. Therefore, it would be impossible to retrieve the correct translation even if the re-ranking model was perfect.

## 3.6 Benchmark results

We also compare our ranking model with two other methods: Minimum Bayes-Risk (MBR) re-ranking and Multi-Engine Machine Translation (MEMT) candidate combination.

MBR was first proposed by Kumar and Byrne (2004) to minimise the expected loss of translation errors under loss functions that measure translation performance. Instead of using the model's best output, the one that is most similar to the most likely translations is selected. We use the same n-best list as the candidate set and the likely translation set. MBR re-ranking can then be considered as selecting a *consensus* candidate: the least 'risky' candidate which is closest on average to all the likely candidates.

The MEMT system combination technique was first proposed by Heafield and Lavie (2010) and was successfully applied to GEC by Susanto et al. (2014). A *confusion network* is created by aligning the candidates, on which a beam search is later performed to find the best candidate.

The 10-best list from the best SMT system in Table 2 is used for re-ranking and results of using MBR re-ranking and MEMT candidate combination are

| System | Example sentences |
|---|---|
| Source | I meet a lot of people on **internet** and it really **interest** me. |
| Reference | I meet a lot of people on **the Internet** and it really **interests** me. |
| SMT best | I meet a lot of people on **the internet** and it really **interest** me. |
| SVM re-ranker | I meet a lot of people on **the Internet** and it really **interests** me. |
| Source | And they **effect** everyone's life directly or indirectly. |
| Reference | And they **affect** everyone's life directly or indirectly. |
| SMT best | And they **effect** everyone's life directly or indirectly. |
| SVM re-ranker | And they **affect** everyone's life directly or indirectly. |
| Source | Of course I will give you some more **detail** about the student conference. |
| Reference | Of course I will give you some more **details** about the student conference. |
| SMT best | Of course I will give you some more **detail** about the student conference. |
| SVM re-ranker | Of course I will give you some more **details** about the student conference. |

**Table 4:** Example output from SMT best and SVM re-ranker.

| # | Model | WAcc | I |
|---|---|---|---|
| 0 | SMT best | 87.21 | 2.87 |
| 1 | SVM re-ranker | 88.12 | 9.78 |
| 2 | Oracle | 92.67 | 44.35 |
| 3 | MBR | 87.32 | 3.71 |
| 4 | MEMT | 87.75 | 5.34 |

**Table 5:** Performance of SMT best, SVM re-ranker, oracle best, MBR re-ranking and MEMT candidate combination (in percentages).

presented in Table 5 #3-4. *SVM re-ranker* is our best ranking model (#1), *MBR* is the MBR re-ranking (#3) and *MEMT* is the MEMT candidate combination (#4). We can see that our supervised ranking model achieves the best *I* score, followed by MEMT candidate combination and MBR re-ranking. Our model clearly outperforms the other two methods, showing its effectiveness in re-ranking candidates for GEC.

### 3.7 CoNLL-2014 shared task

The CoNLL-2014 shared task on grammatical error correction required participating systems to correct all errors present in learner English text. The official training and test data comes from the NUCLE. $F_{0.5}$ was adopted as the evaluation metric, as reported by the $M^2$ Scorer. In order to test how well our re-ranking model generalises, we apply our best model trained on the CLC to the CoNLL-2014 shared task test data. We re-rank the 10-best correction candidates from the winning team in the shared task

(CAMB, Felice et al. (2014)), which were kindly provided to us for these experiments. After the shared task, there has been an on-going discussion about how to best evaluate GEC systems, and different metrics have been proposed (Dahlmeier and Ng, 2012b; Felice and Briscoe, 2015; Bryant and Ng, 2015; Napoles et al., 2015; Grundkiewicz et al., 2015). We evaluated our re-ranker using GLEU, the $M^2$ Scorer and the I-measure. Our proposed re-ranking model (SVM re-ranker) is compared with five other systems: the baseline, the top three systems in the shared task and a GEC system by Susanto et al. (2014), which combined the output of two classification-based systems and two SMT-based systems, and achieved a state-of-the-art $F_{0.5}$ score of 39.39% - see Table 6. We can see that our re-ranker outperforms the top three systems on all evaluation metrics. It also achieves a comparable $F_{0.5}$ score to the system of Susanto et al. (2014) even though our re-ranker is not trained on the NUCLE data or optimised for $F_{0.5}$. This result shows that our model generalises well to other datasets. We expect these results might be further improved by retokenising the test data to be consistent with the tokenisation of the CLC.[3]

## 4 Related work

The aim of GEC for language learners is to correct errors in non-native text. Brockett et al. (2006) first

---

[3]The NUCLE data was preprocessed using the NLTK toolkit, whereas the CLC was tokenised with RASP.

| System | GLEU | F$_{0.5}$ | I |
|---|---|---|---|
| Baseline | 64.19 | 0 | 0 |
| CAMB + SVM re-ranker | 65.68 | 38.08 | -1.71 |
| Susanto et al. (2014) | n/a | 39.39 | n/a |
| **Top 3 systems in CoNLL-2014** | | | |
| CAMB (Felice et al., 2014) | 64.32 | 37.33 | -5.58 |
| CUUI (Rozovskaya et al., 2014) | 64.64 | 36.79 | -3.91 |
| AMU (Junczys-Dowmunt and Grundkiewicz, 2014) | 64.56 | 35.01 | -3.31 |

**Table 6:** System performance on the CoNLL-2014 test set without alternative answers (in percentages).

proposed the use of a noisy channel SMT model for correcting a set of 14 countable/uncountable nouns which are often confusing for learners. Dahlmeier and Ng (2012a) developed a beam-search decoder to iteratively generate candidates and score them using individual classifiers and a general LM. Their decoder focused on five types of errors: spelling, articles, prepositions, punctuation insertion, and noun number. Three classifiers were used to capture three of the common error types: article, preposition and noun number. Yuan and Felice (2013) trained phrase-based and POS-factored SMT systems to correct 5 error types using learner and artificial data. Later, researchers realised the need for new features in SMT for GEC. Felice et al. (2014) and Junczys-Dowmunt and Grundkiewicz (2014) introduced Levenshtein distance and sparse features to their SMT systems, and reported better performance. In addition, Felice et al. (2014) used a LM to re-rank the 10-best candidates after they noticed that better corrections were in the n-best list. Similarly, for Chinese GEC, Zhao et al. (2015) confirmed that their system included correct predictions in its 10-best list not selected during decoding, so a re-ranking of the n-best list was clearly needed.

Re-ranking has been widely used in many natural language processing tasks such as parsing, tagging and sentence boundary detection (Collins and Duffy, 2002; Collins and Koo, 2005; Roark et al., 2006; Huang et al., 2007). Various machine learning algorithms have been adapted to these re-ranking tasks, including boosting, perceptrons and SVMs.

In machine translation, generative models have been widely used. Over the last decade, re-ranking techniques have shown significant improvement. Discriminative re-ranking (Shen et al., 2004), one of

the best-performing strategies, used two perceptron-like re-ranking algorithms that improved translation quality over a baseline system when evaluating with BLEU. Goh et al. (2010) employed an online training algorithm for SVM-based structured prediction. Various global features were investigated for SMT re-ranking, such as the decoder's scores, source and target sentences, alignments and POS tags, sentence type probabilities, posterior probabilities and back translation features. More recently, Farzi and Faili (2015) proposed a re-ranking system based on swarm algorithms.

## 5 Conclusions and future work

We have investigated n-best list re-ranking for SMT-based GEC. We have shown that n-best list re-ranking can be performed to improve correction quality. A supervised machine learning model has proved to be effective and to generalise well. Our best re-ranking model achieves an $I$ score of 9.78% on the publicly available FCE test set, compared to a 2.87% score for our best SMT system without re-ranking. When testing on the official CoNLL-2014 test set without alternative answers, our model achieves an F$_{0.5}$ score of 38.08%, an $I$ score of -1.71%, and a GLEU score of 65.68%, outperforming the top three teams on all metrics.

In future work, we would like to explore more discriminative features. Syntactic features may provide useful information to correct potentially long-distance errors, such as those involving subject-verb agreement. Features that can capture the semantic similarity between the source and the target sentences are also needed, as it is important to retain the meaning of the source sentence after correction. Neural language models and neural machine translation models might also be useful for GEC. It is worth trying GEC re-ranking jointly for larger context as corrections for some errors may require a signal outside the sentence boundaries, for example by adding new features computed from surrounding sentences. The n-best list size is an important parameter in re-ranking. We leave its optimisation to future research, but our upper bound for re-ranking the 10-best list of just over 40% suggests further improvements may be possible.

## Acknowledgements

We would like to thank Christopher Bryant for his valuable comments, Cambridge English Language Assessment and Cambridge University Press for granting us access to the CLC for research purposes, as well as the anonymous reviewers for their feedback.

## References

Ted Briscoe, John Carroll, and Rebecca Watson. 2006. The second release of the RASP system. In *Proceedings of the COLING/ACL 2006 Interactive Presentation Sessions*, pages 77–80.

Chris Brockett, William B. Dolan, and Michael Gamon. 2006. Correcting ESL errors using phrasal SMT techniques. In *Proceedings of the COLING/ACL 2006*, pages 249–256.

Peter F. Brown, Vincent J. Della Pietra, Stephen A. Della Pietra, and Robert L. Mercer. 1993. The mathematics of statistical machine translation: parameter estimation. *Computational Linguistics*, 19(2):263–311.

Christopher Bryant and Hwee Tou Ng. 2015. How far are we from fully automatic high quality grammatical error correction? In *Proceedings of the ACL/IJCNLP 2015*, pages 697–707.

Michael Collins and Nigel Duffy. 2002. New ranking algorithms for parsing and tagging: kernels over discrete structures, and the voted perceptron. In *Proceedings of the ACL 2002*, pages 263–270.

Michael Collins and Terry Koo. 2005. Discriminative reranking for natural language parsing. *Computational Linguistics*, 31(1).

Daniel Dahlmeier and Hwee Tou Ng. 2012a. A beam-search decoder for grammatical error correction. In *Proceedings of the EMNLP/CoNLL 2012*, pages 568–578.

Daniel Dahlmeier and Hwee Tou Ng. 2012b. Better evaluation for grammatical error correction. In *Proceedings of the NAACL 2012*, pages 568–572.

Daniel Dahlmeier, Hwee Tou Ng, and Siew Mei Wu. 2013. Building a large annotated corpus of learner english: the NUS Corpus of Learner English. In *Proceedings of the 8th Workshop on Innovative Use of NLP for Building Educational Applications*, pages 22–31.

Robert Dale, Ilya Anisimoff, and George Narroway. 2012. HOO 2012: a report on the preposition and determiner error correction shared task. In *Proceedings of the 7th Workshop on the Innovative Use of NLP for Building Educational Applications*, pages 54–62.

Saeed Farzi and Heshaam Faili. 2015. A swarm-inspired re-ranker system for statistical machine translation. *Computer Speech & Language*, 29:45–62.

Marcello Federico, Nicola Bertoldi, and Mauro Cettolo. 2008. IRSTLM: an open source toolkit for handling large scale language models. In *Proceedings of the 9th Annual Conference of the International Speech Communication Association*, pages 1618–1621.

Mariano Felice and Ted Briscoe. 2015. Towards a standard evaluation method for grammatical error detection and correction. In *Proceedings of the NAACL 2015*, pages 578–587.

Mariano Felice, Zheng Yuan, Øistein E. Andersen, Helen Yannakoudakis, and Ekaterina Kochmar. 2014. Grammatical error correction using hybrid systems and type filtering. In *Proceedings of the 18th Conference on Computational Natural Language Learning: Shared Task*, pages 15–24.

Adriano Ferraresi, Eros Zanchetta, Marco Baroni, and Silvia Bernardini. 2008. Introducing and evaluating ukWaC, a very large web-derived corpus of English. In *Proceedings of the 4th Web as Corpus Workshop (WAC-4)*.

Jianfeng Gao, Patrick Nguyen, Xiaolong Li, Chris Thrasher, Mu Li, and Kuansan Wang. 2010. A comparative study of Bing Web N-gram language models for Web search and natural language processing. In *Proceeding of the 33rd Annual ACM SIGIR Conference*, pages 16–21.

Chooi-Ling Goh, Taro Watanabe, Andrew Finch, and Eiichiro Sumita. 2010. Discriminative reranking for SMT using various global features. In *Proceedings of the 4th International Universal Communication Symposium*, pages 8–14.

Roman Grundkiewicz, Marcin Junczys-Dowmunt, and Edward Gillian. 2015. Human evaluation of grammatical error correction systems. In *Proceedings of the EMNLP 2015*, pages 461–470.

Kenneth Heafield and Alon Lavie. 2010. CMU multi-engine machine translation for WMT 2010. In *Proceedings of the Joint 5th Workshop on Statistical Machine Translation and MetricsMATR*, pages 301–306.

Almut Silja Hildebrand and Stephan Vogel. 2008. Combination of machine translation systems via hypothesis selection from combined n-best lists. In *Proceedings of the 8th Conference of the Association for Machine Translation in the Americas*.

Zhongqiang Huang, Mary P. Harper, and Wen Wang. 2007. Mandarin part-of-speech tagging and discriminative reranking. In *Proceedings of the EMNLP/CoNLL 2007*, pages 1093 – 1102.

Thorsten Joachims. 2002. Optimizing search engines using clickthrough data. In *Proceedings of the 8th ACM

*Conference on Knowledge Discovery and Data Mining (KDD)*, pages 133–142.

Thorsten Joachims. 2006. Training linear SVMs in linear time. In *Proceedings of the 12th ACM Conference on Knowledge Discovery and Data Mining (KDD)*.

Marcin Junczys-Dowmunt and Roman Grundkiewicz. 2014. The AMU system in the CoNLL-2014 shared task: grammatical error correction by data-intensive and feature-rich statistical machine translation. In *Proceedings of the 18th Conference on Computational Natural Language Learning: Shared Task*, pages 25–33.

Reinhard Kneser and Hermann Ney. 1995. Improved backing-off for M-gram language modeling. In *Proceedings of the IEEE International Conference on Acoustics, Speech, and Signal Processing*, pages 181–184.

Philipp Koehn, Hieu Hoang, Alexandra Birch, Chris Callison-Burch, Marcello Federico, Nicola Bertoldi, Brooke Cowan, Wade Shen, Christine Moran, Richard Zens, Chris Dyer, Ondřej Bojar, Alexandra Constantin, and Evan Herbst. 2007. Moses: open source toolkit for statistical machine translation. In *Proceedings of the ACL 2007 Interactive Poster and Demonstration Sessions*, pages 177–180.

Shankar Kumar and William Byrne. 2004. Minimum Bayes-Risk decoding for statistical machine translation. In *Proceedings of the NAACL 2004*.

Courtney Napoles, Keisuke Sakaguchi, Matt Post, and Joel Tetreault. 2015. Ground truth for grammatical error correction metrics. In *Proceedings of the ACL/IJCNLP 2015*, pages 588–593.

Graham Neubig, Taro Watanabe, Eiichiro Sumita, Shinsuke Mori, and Tatsuya Kawahara. 2011. An unsupervised model for joint phrase alignment and extraction. In *Proceedings of the ACL 2011*, pages 632–641.

Hwee Tou Ng, Siew Mei Wu, Ted Briscoe, Christian Hadiwinoto, Raymond Hendy Susanto, and Christopher Bryant. 2014. The CoNLL-2014 shared task on grammatical error correction. In *Proceedings of the 18th Conference on Computational Natural Language Learning: Shared Task*, pages 1–14.

Diane Nicholls. 2003. The Cambridge Learner Corpus - error coding and analysis for lexicography and ELT. In *Proceedings of the Corpus Linguistics 2003 Conference*, pages 572–581.

Franz Josef Och and Hermann Ney. 2003. A systematic comparison of various statistical alignment models. *Computational Linguistics*, 29(1):19–51.

Kishore Papineni, Salim Roukos, Todd Ward, and Wei-Jing Zhu. 2002. BLEU: a method for automatic evaluation of machine translation. In *Proceedings of the ACL 2002*, pages 311–318.

Brian Roark, Yang Liu, Mary Harper, Robin Stewart, Matthew Lease, Matthew Snover, Izhak Shafran, Bonnie Dorr, John Hale, Anna Krasnyanskaya, and Lisa Yung. 2006. Reranking for sentence boundary detection in conversational speech. In *Proceedings of the 2006 IEEE International Conference on Acoustics, Speech and Signal Processing*.

Alla Rozovskaya, Kai-Wei Chang, Mark Sammons, Dan Roth, and Nizar Habash. 2014. The Illinois-Columbia System in the CoNLL-2014 Shared Task. In *Proceedings of the 18th Conference on Computational Natural Language Learning: Shared Task*, pages 34–42.

Libin Shen, Anoop Sarkar, and Franz Josef Och. 2004. Discriminative reranking for machine translation. In *Proceedings of the NAACL 2004*.

Hendy Raymond Susanto, Peter Phandi, and Tou Hwee Ng. 2014. System combination for grammatical error correction. In *Proceedings of the EMNLP 2014*, pages 951–962.

Nicola Ueffing and Hermann Ney. 2007. Word-level confidence estimation for machine translation. *Computational Linguistics*, 33(1):9–40.

Stephan Vogel, Hermann Ney, and Christoph Tillmann. 1996. HMM-based word alignment in statistical translation. In *Proceedings of the 16th International Conference on Computational Linguistics*, volume 2, pages 836–841.

Helen Yannakoudakis, Ted Briscoe, and Ben Medlock. 2011. A new dataset and method for automatically grading ESOL texts. In *Proceedings of the ACL 2011*, pages 180–189.

Zheng Yuan and Mariano Felice. 2013. Constrained grammatical error correction using statistical machine translation. In *Proceedings of the 17th Conference on Computational Natural Language Learning: Shared Task*, pages 52–61.

Yinchen Zhao, Mamoru Komachi, and Hiroshi Ishikawa. 2015. Improving Chinese grammatical error correction using corpus augmentation and hierarchical phrase-based statistical machine translation. In *Proceedings of The 2nd Workshop on Natural Language Processing Techniques for Educational Applications*, pages 111–116.

# Spoken Text Difficulty Estimation Using Linguistic Features[*]

**Su-Youn Yoon** and **Yeonsuk Cho** and **Diane Napolitano**
Educational Testing Service
660 Rosedale Rd
Princeton, NJ, 08541, USA
syoon@ets.org

## Abstract

We present an automated method for estimating the difficulty of spoken texts for use in generating items that assess non-native learners' listening proficiency. We collected information on the perceived difficulty of listening to various English monologue speech samples using a Likert-scale questionnaire distributed to 15 non-native English learners. We averaged the overall rating provided by three non-native learners at different proficiency levels into an overall score of *listenability*. We then trained a multiple linear regression model with the listenability score as the dependent variable and features from both natural language and speech processing as the independent variables. Our method demonstrated a correlation of 0.76 with the listenability score, comparable to the agreement between the non-native learners' ratings and the listenability score.

## 1 Introduction

Extensive research has been conducted on the prediction of difficulty of understanding written language based on linguistic features. This has resulted in various readability formulas, such as the Fry readability index and the Flesch-Kincaid formula, which is scaled to United States primary school grade levels. Compared to readability, research into listenability, the difficulty of comprehending spoken texts,

has been somewhat limited. Given that spoken and written language share many linguistic features such as vocabulary and grammar, efforts were made to apply readability formula to the difficulty of spoken texts, rending promising results that the listenability of spoken texts could be reasonably predicted from readability formula without taking acoustic features of spoken language into account (Chall and Dial, 1948; Harwood, 1955; Rogers, 1962; Denbow, 1975; O'Keefe, 1971). However, linguistic features unique to spoken language such as speech rate, disfluency features, and phonological phenomena contribute to the processing difficulty of spoken texts as such linguistic features pose challenges at both perception (or parsing) and comprehension levels (Anderson, 2005). Research evidence indicated that ESL students performed better on listening comprehension tasks when the rate of speech was slowed and meaningful pauses were included (Blau, 1990; Brindley and Slatyer, 2002). Shohamy and Inbar (1991) observed that EFL students recalled most when the information was delivered in the form of a dialogue rather than a lecture or a news broadcast. The researchers attributed test takers poor performance on the latter two text types to a larger density of propositions, greater than that of the more orally oriented text type (p. 34). Furthermore, it is not difficult to imagine how other features unique to spoken language affect language processing. For example, prosodic features (e.g., stress, intonation) can aid listeners in focusing on key words and interpreting intended messages. Similarly, disfluency features (e.g., pause, repetitions) may provide the listener with more processing time and redundant in-

---

[*]We would like to thank to Yuan Wang for data collection, Kathy Sheehan for sharing text difficulty prediction system and insights, and Klaus Zechner, Larry Davis, Keelan Evanini, and anonymous reviewers for comments.



*Proceedings of the 11th Workshop on Innovative Use of NLP for Building Educational Applications*, pages 267–276,
San Diego, California, June 16, 2016. ©2016 Association for Computational Linguistics

| Source | Length (sec.) | Number of passages | % in the total sample | Set A | Set B | Set C |
|---|---|---|---|---|---|---|
| English proficiency tests for business purpose | 25 - 46 | 50 | 25 | 16 | 16 | 18 |
| English proficiency tests for academic purpose | 23 - 101 | 80 | 40 | 28 | 26 | 26 |
| News | 15 - 66 | 35 | 18 | 12 | 12 | 11 |
| Interviews | 30 - 93 | 35 | 18 | 11 | 12 | 12 |
| Total | | 200 | 100 | 67 | 66 | 67 |

**Table 1:** Distribution of speech samples

formation (Cabrera and Martínez, 2001; Chiang and Dunkel, 1992). Dunkel et al. (1993) stated that a variety of linguistic features associated with spoken texts contribute to task difficulty on listening comprehension tests. Thus, for a valid evaluation of the difficulty of spoken texts, linguistic features relevant to spoken as well as written language should be carefully considered. However, none of the studies that we were aware of at the time of the current study had attempted to address this issue in developing an automated tool to evaluate the difficulty of spoken texts using linguistic features of both written and spoken language. Lack of an automated evaluation tool appropriate for spoken texts is evidenced in more recent studies that applied readability formula to evaluate the difficulty of spoken test directions (Cormier et al., 2011) and spoken police cautions (Eastwood and Snook, 2012).

Recently, Kotani et al. (2014) developed an automated method for predicting sentence-level listenability as part of an adaptive computer language learning and teaching system. One of the primary goals of the system is to provide learners with listening materials according to their second-language proficiency level. Thus, the listenability score assigned by this method is based on the learners' language proficiency and takes into account difficulties experienced across many levels of proficiency and the entire set of available materials. Their method used many features extracted from the learner's activities as well as new linguistic features that account for phonological characteristics of speech.

Our study explores a systematic way to measure the difficulty of spoken texts using natural language

processing (NLP) technology. In contrast to Kotani et al. (2014)'s system for measuring sentence-level listenability, we predict a listenability score for a spoken text comprised of several sentences. We first gathered multiple language learners' perceptions of overall spoken text difficulty, which we operationalized as a criterion variable. We assumed that the linguistic difficulty of spoken texts relates to four major dimensions of spoken language: acoustic, lexical, grammatical, and discourse. As we identified linguistic features for the study, we attempted to represent each dimension in our model. Finally, we developed a multiple linear regression model to estimate our criterion variable using linguistic features. Thus, this study addresses the following questions:

- To what extent do non-native listeners agree with the difficulty of spoken texts?

- What linguistic features are strongly associated with the perceived difficulty of spoken texts?

- How accurately can an automated model based on linguistic features measuring four dimensions (Acoustic, Lexical, Grammatical, and Discourse) predict the perceived difficulty of spoken texts?

## 2   Data

### 2.1   Speech Samples

We used a total of 200 speech samples from two different types of sources: listening passages from an array of English proficiency tests for academic and business purposes, and samples from broadcast news and interviews which are often used as listening practice materials for language learners. Table 1 shows the distribution of the 200 speech samples by source and by random partition into three distinct sets A, B, and C for the collection of human ratings. Each set includes a similar number of speech samples per source.

All speech samples were monologic speech and the length of speech samples was limited to a range of about 23 to 101 seconds. All samples were free from serious audio quality problems that would have obscured the contents. The samples from the English proficiency exams were spoken by native English speakers with high-quality pronunciation and typical Canadian, Australian, British, or American accents. The samples from the news clips were part of 1996 English Broadcast News Speech corpus described in Graff et al. (1997). We selected seven television news programs and extracted speech samples from the original anchors. The interview samples were excerpts from interview corpus described in Pitt et al. (2005). They were comprised of unconstrained conversational speech between native English speakers from the Midwestern United States and a variety of interviewers who, while speaking native- or near-native English, are from unknown origins. We only extracted a monologic portion from the interviewee.

## 2.2  Human Ratings

A questionnaire was designed to gather participants' perceptions of overall spoken text difficulty, operationalized as our criterion variable. The questionnaire is comprised of five Likert-type questions designed to be combined into a single composite score during analysis. Higher point responses indicated a lower degree of listening comprehension and a higher degree of text difficulty. The original questionnaire is as follows:

1. Which statement best represents the level of your understanding of the passage?

    5) Missed the main point

    4) Missed 2 key points

    3) Missed 1 key point

    2) Missed 1-2 minor points

    1) Understood everything

2. How would you rate your understanding of the passage?

    5) less than 60%

    4) 70%

    3) 80%

    2) 90%

    1) 100%

3. How much of the information in the passage can you remember?

    5) less than 60%

    4) 70%

    3) 80%

    2) 90%

    1) 100%

4. Estimate the number of words you missed or did not understand.

    5) more than 10 words

    4) 6-10 words

    3) 3-5 words

    2) 1-2 words

    1) none

5. The speech rate was

    5) fast

    4) somewhat fast

    3) neither fast nor slow

    2) somewhat slow

    1) slow

The first three questions were designed to estimate participants' overall comprehension of the spoken text. The fourth question, regarding the number of missed words, and the fifth question were designed to estimate the difficulty associated with the Vocabulary and Acoustic dimensions. We did not include separate questions related to the Grammar or Discourse dimensions.

Our aim was to recruit two non-native English speakers of beginner, intermediate, and advanced proficiency and have them rate each set of speech samples. We were able to recruit 15 non-native English leaner representing various native language groups including Chinese, Japanese, Korean, Thai, and Turkish. Prior to evaluating the speech samples, participants were classified into one of the three proficiency levels based on the score they received on the TOEFL Practice Online(TPO). TPO is an online practice test which allows students to gain familiarity with the format of TOEFL, and we used a total score that was a composite score of four section scores: listening, reading, speaking, and writing. Each participant rated one set, approximately 67 speech samples. The participants were assigned to one of the three sets of speech samples with care taken to ensure that each set was evaluated by a group representing a wide range of proficiency levels. Table 2 summarizes the number of listeners at each proficiency level assigned to each set.

|        | Beginner | Intermediate | Advanced |
|--------|----------|--------------|----------|
| Set A  | 2        | 1            | 2        |
| Set B  | 1        | 1            | 3        |
| Set C  | 2        | 1            | 2        |

**Table 2:** Distribution of non-native listeners

All participants attended a rating session which lasted about 1.5 hours. At the beginning of the rating session, the purpose and procedures of the study were explained to the participants. Since we were interested in the individual participants' personal perceptions of the difficulty of spoken texts, participants were told to use their own criteria and experience when answering the questionnaire. Participants worked independently and listened to each speech sample on the computer. The questionnaire was visible while the listening stimuli were playing; however, the ability to respond to it was disabled until the speech sample had been listened to in its entirety. After listening to each sample, the participants provided their judgments of spoken text difficulty by answering the questionnaire items. The speech samples within each set appear in random sequence to minimize the effect of the ordering of the samples on the ratings. Furthermore, to minimize the effect of listeners' fatigue on their ratings, they were given the option of pausing at any time during the session and resuming whenever ready.

Before creating a single composite score from five Likert-type questions, we first conducted correlation analysis using the entire dataset. We created all possible pairs among five Likert-type questions and calculated Pearson correlations between responses to paired questions. The responses to the first four questions were highly correlated with Pearson correlation coefficients ranging from 0.79 to 0.92. The correlations between Question 5 and the other four questions ranged between 0.49 and 0.61. The strong inter-correlations among different Likert-type questions suggested that these questions measured one aspect: the overall difficulty of spoken texts. Thus, instead of using each response from a different question separately, for each audio sample, we summed each individual participant's responses to the five questions. This resulted in a scale with a minimum score of 5 and maximum score of 25, where the higher score, the more difficult the text. Hereafter, we refer to an individual-listener's summed rating an aggregated score.

Since our system goal was to predict the averaged perceived difficulty of the speech samples across English learners at beginning, intermediate, and advanced levels, we used the average of three listeners' aggregated scores, one listener from each proficiency level. Going forward we will refer to this average rating as the *listenability* score. The mean and standard deviation of listenability scores were 17.3 and 4.6, respectively. We used this listenability score as our dependent variable during model building.

## 3 Method

### 3.1 Speech-Based Features

In order to capture the acoustic characteristics of speech samples, we used speech proficiency scoring system, an automated proficiency scoring system for spontaneous speech from non-native English speakers. speech proficiency scoring system creates an automated transcription using an automated speech recognition (ASR) system and does not require a manual transcription. However, in this study, when generating features for our listenability model, we used a forced alignment algorithm to align the audio sample against a manual transcription in order to avoid the influence of speech recognition errors. This created word- and phone-level transcriptions with time stamps. The system also computes pitch and power and calculates descriptive statistics

| Dimension | Feature | Correlation with Average Human Difficulty Rating |
| --- | --- | --- |
| Acoustic | Speaking rate in words per second | −0.42 |
| | Number of silences per word | 0.25 |
| | Mean deviation of speech chunk | −0.30 |
| | Mean distance between stressed syllables in seconds | 0.25 |
| | Variations in vowel durations | −0.30 |
| Vocabulary | Number of noun collocations per clause | −0.27 |
| | Type token ratio | 0.33 |
| | Normalized frequency of low frequency words | −0.49 |
| | Average frequency of word types | −0.25 |
| Grammar | Average words per sentence | −0.38 |
| | Number of long sentences | −0.39 |
| | Normalized number of sentences | 0.45 |

**Table 3:** Correlation between linguistic features and listenability

such as the mean and standard deviation of both of these at the word and response level. Given the transcriptions with time stamps and descriptive features of pitch and power, speech proficiency scoring system produces around 100 features for automated proficiency scoring per input. However, because speech proficiency scoring system is designed to measure the non-native speaker's degree of language proficiency, and a large number of features assess distance between the non-native test takers' speech and the native speakers' norm. These features are not applicable to our data since all audio samples are from native speakers. After excluding these features, only 20 features proved to be useful for our study. The features were classified into three groups as follows:

- Fluency: Features in this group measure the degree of fluency in the speech flow; for example, speaking rate and the average length of speech chunk without disfluencies;

- Pause: Features in this group capture characteristics of silent pauses in speech; for example, the duration of silent pauses per word, the mean of silent pause duration, and the number of long silent pauses;

- Prosodic: Features in this group measure rhythm and durational variations in speech; for example, the mean distance between stressed syllables in syllables, and the relative frequency of stressed syllables.

## 3.2 Text-Based Features

Text-based features were generated on clean transcripts of the monologic speech using the text difficulty prediction system system. (Sheehan et al., 2014) The main goal of text difficulty prediction system is to provide an overall measure of text complexity, otherwise known as readability, an important subtask in the measurement of listenability. However, because of the differences between readability and listenability, only seven of the more than 200 linguistic features generated by text difficulty prediction system were selected for our model, four of which cover the Vocabulary construct and three of which cover our Grammar construct.

## 3.3 Model Building

Beginning with the full set of features generated by speech proficiency scoring system and text difficulty prediction system, we conducted a correlation analysis between these linguistic features and our human ratings. We used the entire dataset for correlation analysis due to the limited amount of available data. We selected our subset of features using the following procedure: first, we excluded a feature when its Pearson correlation coefficient with listenability scores was less than 0.25. In order to avoid collinearity in the listenability model, we excluded highly correlated features ($r \geq 0.8$). Next, the remaining features were classified into four groups (Acoustic, Vocabulary, Grammar, and Discourse) each containing the three features representing that dimension with the highest correlations. The final, overall set of features used in our analysis was selected to maximize the coverage of all of the combined characteristics represented by the overall constructs. For instance, if two features showed a correlation larger than 0.80, a feature whose dimension was not well represented by other features was selected. This resulted in a set of 12 features as presented in Table 3. We did attempt to develop a Coherence dimension using two features (the frequency of content word overlap and the frequency of casual conjuncts), but both were found to have insignificant correlations with the listenability score and thus were excluded from the model.

Model-building and evaluation were performed using three-fold cross-validation. We randomly divided out data into three sets, two of which were combined for training with the remaining set used for testing. For each round, a multiple linear regression model was built using the average difficulty ratings of three non-native listeners, one at each proficiency level, as the dependent variables and the 12 features as independent variables.

## 4   Results

### 4.1   Agreement among non-native listeners

In this study, we estimated the difficulty of understanding spoken texts based on self-reported ratings via Likert-type questions, similar to the approach taken by Kotani et al. (2014). Likert-type questions are effective in collecting the participants' impression for the given item and are widely used in survey research but are highly susceptible. Participants may avoid selecting extreme response categories (central tendency bias) or may choose the "easy" category more often to inflate their listening comprehension level. These distortions may result in shrinkage of the listenability score's scale. In particular, the second bias may be more salient for participants at low proficiency levels and cause a skew toward higher listenability scores. In order to examine whether any participant was subject to such biases, we first analyzed the distribution of response categories per each participant. Approximately 335 responses were available per participant (67 audio samples, 5 questions per sample). All participants made use of every response category, and 10 out of

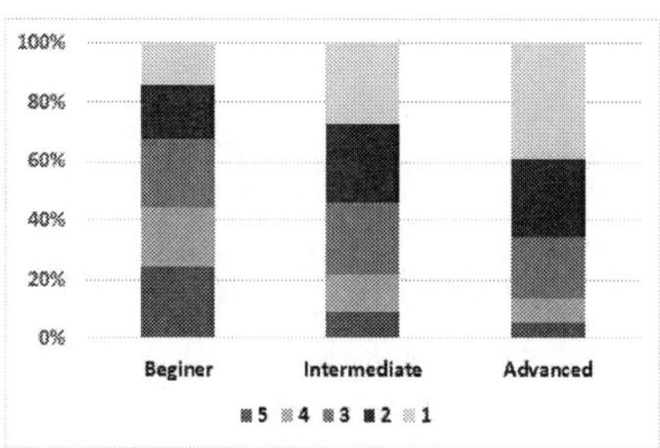



**Figure 1:** Distribution of Likert-type responses per proficiency group

15 participants used all categories at least 4% of the time. However, four participants rarely used certain response categories; two advanced learners and one intermediate learner used category "5" (most difficult) only 1%. On the contrary, one rater at the beginner level used category "1" (easiest) only for 1%. Due to the potential bias in these ratings, we tried to exclude them when selecting three listeners (one listeners per proficiency level) to use in calculating the listenability score; these advanced learners and this beginner learner were excluded, but the intermediate learner was included due to lack of an alternative learner at the same proficiency level.

Next, we examined the relationship between difficulty ratings and non-native listeners' proficiency levels. Figure 4.1 shows distribution of aggregated scores per proficiency group.

The aggregated score reflects the degree of comprehension by non-native listeners. The lowest response category indicated understanding of all words and possibly all main points, while the highest response category indicated that listeners failed to understand the main point, or they understood less than 60% of the contents. Beginners' scores were relatively evenly distributed; the proportion of response category "1" (easiest) was 14%, while the proportion of response category "5" (most difficult) was 24%. In regards to the high proportion of "5" responses by beginners, we would expect that, if there was a tendency on the part of the beginners to inflate their scores, the proportion of this category would be low. On the contrary, it was the most frequently selected category, demonstrating that the beginning listeners in this study did not seem to be inflating their ability to understand the spoken text.

Not surprisingly, as proficiency level increased, the listeners were more likely to judge the samples as easy, and the frequency of selecting categories representing difficulty decreased. The percentages of response category "5" selections were 24% for beginners, 9.1% for intermediate learners, and 5.3% for advanced learners.

Finally, we used Pearson correlation coefficients to assess the inter-rater agreement on the difficulty of spoken texts. The correlation analysis results between two listeners at the same proficiency level are summarized in second and third rows of Table 4. For the beginner group, the correlation coefficient for set B was unavailable due to the lack of a second listener. We also analyzed the agreement between all possible pairs of listeners across the different groups by calculating the Pearson correlation coefficient per pair and taking the average for each set (8 pairs for set A and C, 5 pairs for set B). The results are presented in the last row of Table 4.

Table 4 provides Pearson correlation coefficients.

| Group | Proficiency Level | A | B | C | Mean |
|---|---|---|---|---|---|
| Within Group | Beginner | 0.56 | - | 0.60 | 0.58 |
| | Advanced | 0.55 | 0.64 | 0.64 | 0.61 |
| Cross-Group | | 0.61 | 0.58 | 0.60 | 0.60 |

Table 4: Pearson correlations among non-native listeners' ratings

The non-native listeners showed moderate agreement on the difficulty of our selection of spoken texts. Within the same group, the Pearson correlation coefficients ranged from 0.55 to 0.64, and the average was 0.58 for the beginner group and 0.61 for the advanced group. The average correlation across groups was also comparable to the within-group correlation values, although the range of the coefficients was wider, ranging from 0.51 to 0.7.

Next, we evaluated the reliability of the listenability scores (the average of three non-native listeners' ratings) based on the correlation with the second listener's ratings not used in the listenability scores. Compared to correlations between individual listeners' ratings (Pearson correlation coefficients of within-group condition), there were increases in the Pearson correlation coefficients. The Pearson cor-

relation coefficient with the beginner group listener score was 0.65, and that with the advanced group listener score was 0.71; there was 0.07 increase in the beginner listener and 0.10 increase in the advanced listener, respectively. This improvement is expected since the listenability scores are averages of three scores and therefore a better estimate of the true score. We will use Pearson correlation coefficients of 0.65 and 0.71 as reference of human performance when comparing with machine performance.

## 4.2 Relationships Between Listenability Scores and Linguistic Features

We conducted a correlation analysis between our set of 12 features used in the model and the average listenability scores. A brief description, relevant dimension, and Pearson correlation coefficients with the listenability scores are presented in Table 3. Features in the Acoustic dimension were generated using speech proficiency scoring system based on both a audio file and its manual transcription. Features in both the Vocabulary and Grammar dimensions were generated using text difficulty prediction system and only made use of the transcription.

The features showed moderate correlation with the listenability scores, with coefficients ranging from 0.25 to 0.50 in absolute value. The best performing feature was the "normalized frequency of low frequency words" which measures vocabulary difficulty. It was followed by the "normalized number of sentences" which measures syntactic complexity and then the "speaking rate of spoken texts" from the Acoustic dimension.

## 4.3 Performance of the Automated System

Table 5 presents the agreement between ratings generated by our system and the human ratings. The model using both written and spoken features, "All", has a strong correlation with the averaged listenability score, with a Pearson correlation coefficient of 0.76. This result is comparable to the agreement between the average listenability score and those of the individual listeners (0.65 and 0.71). In order to evaluate the impact of different sets of features, we developed two models: a model based only on speech proficiency scoring system features (Acoustic dimension alone) and a model based only on text difficulty prediction system features (the Vocabulary and Grammar dimensions). The performance of the model was promising, but there was a substantial drop in agreement: a decrease of approximately 0.1 in the Pearson correlation coefficient from the observed for the model with both written and spoken features. Overall, the results strongly suggest that the combination of acoustic-based features and text-based features can achieve a substantial improvement in predicting the difficulty of spoken texts over the limited linguistic features typically used in traditional readability formulas.

| Feature Set | Correlation | Weighted Kappa |
|---|---|---|
| All | 0.76 | 0.73 |
| speech proficiency scoring system only | 0.67 | 0.64 |
| text difficulty prediction system only | 0.65 | 0.63 |

**Table 5:** Correlation between automated scores and listenability scores based on human ratings

## 5   Discussion

Due to the limited amount of data available to us, the features used in the scoring models were selected using all of our data, including the evaluation partitions; this may result in an inflation of model performance. Additionally, we selected a subset of features based on correlations with listenability scores and expert knowledge (construct relevance) but we did not use an automated feature selection algorithm. In a future study, we will address this issue by collecting a larger amount of data and making separate, fixed training and evaluation partitions.

In this study, we used non-native listeners' impression-based ratings as our criterion value. We did not provide any training session prior to collecting these ratings which were based on individual participants' own perceptions of the difficulty. The individual raters had a moderate amount of agreement on the difficulty of the spoken texts, but for use in training our model, the reliability of listenability scores based on the average of three raters was substantially higher. However, impression-based ratings tend to be susceptible to raters' biases, so it is not always possible to get high-quality ratings. Ratings from non-native learners covering a wide range of proficiency levels is particularly difficult. Obtaining a high-quality criterion value has been a critical challenge in the development of many listenability systems. To address this issue, we explored automated methods that improve the quality of aggregated ratings. Snow et al. (2008) identified individual raters with biases and corrected them using small set of expert annotations. Ipeirotis et al. (2010) proposed a method using the EM algorithm without any gold data: they first initialize the correct rating for each task based on the majority vote outcome, then estimated the quality of each rater based on the confusion matrix between each individual rater's ratings and majority vote-based answers. Following that, they re-estimated correct answers based on the weighted vote using the rater's error rate. They repeated this process until it converged. Unfortunately we found that it was difficult to apply these methods to our study. Both methods required correct answers across all raters (either based on expert annotations or majority voting rules). In our case, the answers varied across proficiency levels since our questions were in regards to the degree of spoken text comprehension. In order to apply these methods, we would have needed to define a set of correct answers per proficiency level. In the future, instead of applying these automated methods exactly, we intend to develop a new criterion value based on an objective measure of a listener's comprehension. We will create a list of comprehension questions specific to each spoken text and estimate the difficulty based on the proportion of correct answers.

Originally, responses of individual Likert-type question are ordinal scale data. The numbers assigned to different response categories express a "greater than" relationship, and the intervals between two consequent points are not always identical. For instance, for the Likert-type question using five response categories ("strongly disagree", "disagree", "neither disagree nor agree", "agree", and "strongly agree"), the interval between "strongly agree" and "agree" may not be identical to the interval between "agree" and "neither disagree nor agree". Thus, some analyses applicable to interval data are not appropriate for Likert-type data. On the contrary, the Likert-scale data is comprised of a series of Likert-type questions addressing one aspect, and all questions are designed to create one single composite score. For this type of data, we can use descriptive analysis such as mean and standard deviation and linear regression models. In this study, five Likert-type questions were designed to measure one aspect, perceptions of overall spoken text difficulty, and, in fact, responses to different questions were strongly correlated. Based on this observation, we treated our data as a Likert-scale data and conducted various analysis applicable to the interval scale data.

Our method was initially designed to assist with the generation of listening items for language proficiency tests. Therefore, we focused on spoken texts frequently used on such tests, so, as a result, the range of text types investigated was narrow and quite homogenous. Interactive dialogues and discussions were not included in this study. Furthermore, although effort was made to include a variety of monologues by adding radio broadcasts to our data sample, a significant portion of the speech samples were recorded spoken texts that were designed for a specific purpose, that is, testing English language proficiency. It is possible that the language used in such texts is more contrived than that of monologues encountered in everyday life, particularly since they do not contain any background noise and were produced by speakers from a narrow set of English accents. That having been said, our method is applicable within this context, and predicting the difficulty of monologues produced by native speakers with good audio quality is its best usage.

## 6 Conclusion

This study investigated whether the difficulty of comprehending spoken texts, known as *listenability*, can be predicted using a certain set of linguistic features. We used existing natural language and speech processing techniques to propose a listenability estimation model. This study combined written and spoken text evaluation tools to extract features and build a multiple regression model that predicts human perceptions of difficulty on short monologues. The results showed that a combination of 12 such features addressing the Acoustic, Vocabulary, and Grammar dimensions achieved a correlation of 0.76 with human perceptions of spoken text difficulty.


## References

John R Anderson. 2005. *Cognitive psychology and its implications*. Macmillan.

Eileen K Blau. 1990. The effect of syntax, speed, and pauses on listening comprehension. *TESOL quarterly*, 24(4):746–753.

Geoff Brindley and Helen Slatyer. 2002. Exploring task difficulty in esl listening assessment. *Language Testing*, 19(4):369–394.

Marcos Penate Cabrera and Plácido Bazo Martínez. 2001. The effects of repetition, comprehension checks, and gestures, on primary school children in an efl situation. *ELT journal*, 55(3):281–288.

Jeanne S Chall and Harold E Dial. 1948. Predicting listener understanding and interest in newscasts. *Educational Research Bulletin*, pages 141–168.

Chung Shing Chiang and Patricia Dunkel. 1992. The effect of speech modification, prior knowledge, and listening proficiency on efl lecture learning. *TESOL quarterly*, 26(2):345–374.

Damien C Cormier, Kevin S McGrew, and Jeffrey J Evans. 2011. Quantifying the degree of linguistic demand in spoken intelligence test directions. *Journal of Psychoeducational Assessment*, 29(6):515–533.

Carl Jon Denbow. 1975. Listenability and readability: An experimental investigation. *Journalism and Mass Communication Quarterly*, 52(2):285.

Patricia Dunkel, Grant Henning, and Craig Chaudron. 1993. The assessment of an l2 listening comprehension construct: A tentative model for test specification and development. *The Modern Language Journal*, 77(2):180–191.

Joseph Eastwood and Brent Snook. 2012. The effect of listenability factors on the comprehension of police cautions. *Law and human behavior*, 36(3):177.

David Graff, Zhibiao Wu, Robert MacIntyre, and Mark Liberman. 1997. The 1996 broadcast news speech and language-model corpus. In *Proceedings of the DARPA Workshop on Spoken Language technology*, pages 11–14.

Kenneth A Harwood. 1955. I. listenability and readability. *Communications Monographs*, 22(1):49–53.

Panagiotis G Ipeirotis, Foster Provost, and Jing Wang. 2010. Quality management on amazon mechanical turk. In *Proceedings of the ACM SIGKDD workshop on human computation*, pages 64–67. ACM.

Katsunori Kotani, Shota Ueda, Takehiko Yoshimi, and Hiroaki Nanjo. 2014. A listenability measuring method for an adaptive computer-assisted language learning and teaching system. In *Proceedings of the 28th Pacific Asia Conference on Language, Information and Computation*, pages 387–394.

M Timothy O'Keefe. 1971. The comparative listenability of shortwave broadcasts. *Journalism Quarterly*, 48(4):744–748.

Mark A Pitt, Keith Johnson, Elizabeth Hume, Scott Kiesling, and William Raymond. 2005. The buckeye corpus of conversational speech: Labeling conventions and a test of transcriber reliability. *Speech Communication*, 45(1):89–95.

John R Rogers. 1962. A formula for predicting the comprehension level of material to be presented orally. *The journal of educational research*, 56(4):218–220.

Kathleen M. Sheehan, Irene Kostin, Diane Napolitano, and Michael Flor. 2014. The textevaluator tool: Helping teachers and test developers select texts for use in instruction and assessment. *The Elementary School Journal*, 115(2):184 – 209.

Elana Shohamy and Ofra Inbar. 1991. Validation of listening comprehension tests: The effect of text and question type. *Language testing*, 8(1):23–40.

Rion Snow, Brendan O'Connor, Daniel Jurafsky, and Andrew Y Ng. 2008. Cheap and fast—but is it good?: evaluating non-expert annotations for natural language tasks. In *Proceedings of the conference on empirical methods in natural language processing*, pages 254–263. Association for Computational Linguistics.

# Automatically Extracting Topical Components for a Response-to-Text Writing Assessment


**Zahra Rahimi** and **Diane Litman**
Intelligent Systems Program & Learning Research and Development Center
University of Pittsburgh
Pittsburgh, PA 15260
{zar10,dlitman}@pitt.edu



## Abstract

We investigate automatically extracting multi-word topical components to replace information currently provided by experts that is used to score the Evidence dimension of a writing in response to text assessment. Our goal is to reduce the amount of expert effort and improve the scalability of an automatic scoring system. Experimental results show that scoring performance using automatically extracted data-driven topical components is promising.


## 1 Introduction

Automatic essay scoring has increasingly been investigated in recent years. One important aspect of writing assessment, specifically in source-based writing, is evaluation of content. Different methods have been used to assess the content of essays, e.g., bag of words (Mayfield and Rose, 2013), semantic similarity (Foltz et al., 1999; Kakkonen et al., 2005; Lemaire and Dessus, 2001), content vector analysis and cosine similarity (Louis and Higgins, 2010; Higgins et al., 2006; Attali and Burstein, 2006), and Latent Dirichlet Allocation (LDA) topic modeling (Persing and Ng, 2014).

These prior studies differ from our research in several ways. Much of the prior work does not target source-based writing and thus does not make use of source materials. Approaches that do make use of source materials are typically designed to detect only if an essay is on-topic. Our source-based assessment, in contrast, is also concerned with localizing in the student essay pieces of evidence that students provided from the source material. This is be-

cause our goal is to not only score an essay, but also to provide feedback based on detailed essay content.

Various kinds of source-based assessments of content (both in essay and short answering scoring) typically require some expert work in advance. Experts have provided reference answers (Nielsen et al., 2009; Mohler et al., 2011) or manually crafted patterns (Sukkarieh et al., 2004; Makatchev and VanLahn, 2007; Nielsen et al., 2009). Using manually provided information helps increase the accuracy of a scoring system and its ability to provide meaningful feedback related to the scoring rubric. But involving experts in the scoring process is a drawback for automatically scoring at scale.

Research to reduce expert effort has been underway to increase the scalability of scoring systems. A semi-supervised method is used to reduce the amount of required hand-annotated data (Zesch et al., 2015). Text templates or patterns are automatically identified for short answer scoring (Ramachandran et al., 2015). Content importance models (Beigman Klebanov et al., 2014) are used to predict source material that students should select.

In this paper, our goal is to use natural language processing to automatically extract from source material a comprehensive list of topics which include: a) important topic words, and b) specific expressions (N-grams with $N > 1$) that students need to provide in their essays. We call this comprehensive list *"topical components"*. Automatic extraction of topical components helps to reduce expert effort before the automatic assessment process. We evaluate the usefulness of our method for extracting topical components on the Response-to-Text Assessment (RTA)




*Proceedings of the 11th Workshop on Innovative Use of NLP for Building Educational Applications*, pages 277–282,
San Diego, California, June 16, 2016. ©2016 Association for Computational Linguistics

| | |
|---|---|
| **Excerpt from the article:** Many kids in Sauri did not attend school because their parents could not afford school fees. Some kids are needed to help with chores, such as fetching water and wood. In 2004, the schools had minimal supplies like books, paper and pencils, but the students wanted to learn. All of them worked hard with the few supplies they had. It was hard for them to concentrate, though, as there was no midday meal. By the end of the day, kids didn't have any energy. |
| **Prompt:** The author provided one specific example of how the quality of life can be improved by the Millennium Villages Project in Sauri, Kenya. Based on the article, did the author provide a convincing argument that winning the fight against poverty is achievable in our lifetime? Explain why or why not with 3-4 examples from the text to support your answer. |
| ***Essay with score of 4 on Evidence dimension:*** *I was convinced that* winning the fight of poverty is achievable *in our lifetime. Many people* couldn't afford medicine *or* bed nets to be treated for malaria *. Many* children had died *from this dieseuse even though it could be treated easily. But* now, bed nets are used in every sleeping site *. And the* medicine is free *of charge. Another example is that the* farmers' crops are dying *because they* could not afford the nessacary fertilizer and irrigation *. But they are now, making progess. Farmers* now have fertilizer and water *to give to the crops. Also with* seeds and the proper tools *. Third, kids in Sauri were not well educated. Many families* couldn't afford school *. Even at school there was* no lunch *. Students were exhausted from each day of school. Now,* school is free *. Children excited to learn now can and they do* have midday meals *. Finally, Sauri is making great progress. If they keep it up that city will no longer be in poverty. Then the Millennium Village project can move on to help other countries in need.* |

**Table 1:** An excerpt from the source text, the prompt, and a high-scoring essay with highlighted evidence (Rahimi et al., 2014).

(Correnti et al., 2012; Correnti et al., 2013).

RTA is developed to assess analytical writing in response to text (Correnti et al., 2013), e.g., making claims and marshalling evidence from a source text to support a viewpoint. Automatic scoring of the Evidence dimension of the RTA was previously investigated in (Rahimi et al., 2014). The Evidence dimension evaluates how well students use selected details from a text to support and extend a key idea. A set of rubric-based features enabled by topical components manually provided by experts were used in (Rahimi et al., 2014) to automatically assess Evidence.

In this paper, we propose to use a model enabled by LDA topic modeling to automatically extract the topical components (i.e., topic words and significant N-grams ($N \geq 1$)) needed for our scoring approach[1]. We hypothesize that extracting rubric-based features based on data-driven topical components can perform as well as extracting features from manually provided topical components. Results show that our method for automatically extracting topical components is promising but still needs improvement.

## 2  Data

We have two datasets of student writing from two different age groups (grades 5-6 and grades 6-8) that were written in response to one prompt introduced in (Correnti et al., 2013). The student essays com-

prising our datasets were obtained as follows. A text was read aloud by a teacher and students followed along. The text is about a United Nations project to eradicate poverty in a rural village in Kenya. After a guided discussion of the article, students wrote an essay in response to a prompt that required them to make a claim and support it using details from the text. A small excerpt from the article, the prompt, and a sample high-scoring student essay from grades 5-6 are shown in Table 1.

Our datasets (particularly essays by students in grades 5–6) have a number of properties that may increase the difficulty of the automatic essay assessment task. For example, the essays are short and many of them are only one paragraph (the median number of paragraphs for 5–6 and 6–8 datasets are 1 and 2 respectively). Some statistics about the datasets are in Table 2.

The RTA provides rubrics along five dimensions to assess student writing, each on a scale of 1-4 (Correnti et al., 2013). In this paper we focus only on predicting the score of the Evidence dimension[2]. The essays in our datasets were scored half by experts and the rest by trained undergraduates. The corpus of grades 5–6 and 6–8 respectively consist of 1569 essays with 602 of them double-scored, and 1045 essays with all of them double-scored, for inter-rater reliability. Inter-rater agreement (Quadratic Weighted Kappa) on the double-scored portion of

---

[1]Unlike much LDA-enabled work, we not only make use of topic words, but also expressions clustered to a set of topics.

[2]The other RTA dimensions are Analysis, Organization, Style, and MUGS (Mechanics, Usage, Grammar, Spelling).

| Dataset | | Mean | SD |
|---|---|---|---|
| 5–6 Grades | words | 161.25 | 92.24 |
| | unique words | 93.27 | 40.57 |
| | sentences | 9.01 | 6.39 |
| | paragraphs | 2.04 | 1.83 |
| 6–8 Grades | words | 218.90 | 111.08 |
| | unique words | 109.34 | 41.59 |
| | sentences | 11.98 | 7.17 |
| | paragraphs | 2.56 | 1.72 |

**Table 2:** The two dataset's statistics.

| Dataset | 1 | 2 | 3 | 4 | Total |
|---|---|---|---|---|---|
| 5–6 Grades | 471 (30%) | 594 (38%) | 334 (21%) | 170 (11%) | 1569 |
| 6–8 Grades | 250 (24%) | 434 (42%) | 229 (22%) | 132 (13%) | 1045 |

**Table 3:** Distribution of the Evidence scores.

the grades 5-6 and 6-8 corpora respectively are 0.67 and 0.73 for the Evidence dimension. The distribution of Evidence scores is shown in Table 3.

## 3 Extracting Topical Components

One way of obtaining topical components is to have experts manually create them using their knowledge about the text (Rahimi et al., 2014). An example subset of the components, provided by experts and used to extract the features mentioned in Section 4.2, are in Table 4. The excerpt from the text from which the "school" topic is extracted is shown in Table 1.

In this paper, we instead automatically extract the topical components. Our proposed method has 3 main steps: (1) using topic modeling to extract topics and probabilistic distribution of words, (2) using Turbo-Topic to get the significant N-grams per-topic, and (3) post-processing the Turbo-Topic output to get the topical-components.

The first step uses LDA topic modeling (Blei et al., 2003) which is a generative probabilistic model of a corpus. The basic idea is that documents are represented as random mixtures over latent topics, where each topic is characterized by a distribution over words. The output of the LDA algorithm is a list of topics. Each topic is a probability distribution over words in a vocabulary.

The second step feeds the posterior distribution output of LDA over words as an input to Turbo-Topic (Blei and Lafferty, 2009) to extract significant N-grams per-topic. In Turbo-Topic, the pos-

terior distribution output of LDA is used to annotate each word occurrence in the corpus with its most probable topic. It uses a back-off language model defined for arbitrary length expressions and a statistical co-occurrence analysis is carried out recursively to extract the most significant multi-word expressions for each topic. Finally, the resulting expressions are combined with the unigram list. One advantage of Turbo-Topic is the ability of finding significant phrases without the necessity of all words in the phrase being assigned to the topic by using the information of repeated context in the language model. For example, the N-gram "schools now serve lunch" can be distinguished as a significant N-gram for the topic "School" using the language model even if only the words "schools" and "lunch" are assigned to the topic "school" by LDA.

The third step uses the output of Turbo-Topic, which is a list of significant N-grams ($N \geq 1$) with their counts per-topic, to extract the topical components. To make different topics unique and more distinguishable, we decided to include each N-gram in only one topic. For this purpose, we use the count of N-grams in topics and assign each N-gram to the topic in which it has the highest count. The next issue is to remove the redundant information. If $A$ and $B$ are two N-grams in a topic and $A$ is a subset of $B$, we remove the N-gram $A$. After processing the output of Turbo-Topic, we divide it to a list of highly important words and a list of expressions per-topic. We use a cut-off threshold and only include the top N-grams based on their counts in each topic.

## 4 Experiments

We configure experiments to test the validity of the hypothesis that scoring models that extract features based on automatically extracted LDA-enabled topical components can perform as well as models which extract features from topical components manually provided by experts.

### 4.1 Experimental Tools and Methods

All experiments use 10 fold cross validation with Random Forest as a classifier (max-depth=5). We report performance using Quadratic Weighted Kappa, a standard evaluation measure for essay assessment. Paired student t-test with p-value $< 0.05$ is used to measure statistical significance.

| | Topic:Hospitals | Topic:Schools | Topic:Progress |
|---|---|---|---|
| a) Topic Words | care, health, hospital, doctor, disease | school, supply, fee, student, lunch | progress, four, serve, attendance, maintain |
| b) N-grams ($N > 1$) | Yala sub district hospital<br>no running water electricity<br>not medicine treatment could afford<br>no doctor only clinical officer<br>three kids bed two adults | kids not attend go school<br>not afford school fees<br>no midday meal lunch<br>schools minimal supplies<br>concentrate not energy | progress made just four years<br>water connected hospital<br>bed nets used every sleeping site<br>kids go school now<br>now serves lunch |

**Table 4:** A sub-list of manually extracted a) topic words and b) specific expressions for three sample topics. They are manually provided by experts in (Rahimi et al., 2014). Some of the stop-words might have been removed from the expressions by experts.

| | Topic: Hospitals | Topic: Schools | Topic: Progress |
|---|---|---|---|
| a) Topic Words | author, fight, hospital, yala, sub, 2015 | school, water, food, malaria, children, free | sauri, progress, made, student, project, better |
| b) N-grams ($N > 1$) | common diseases<br>win the fight against poverty<br>also has a generator for<br>district hospital<br>rate is way up<br>yala subdistrict hospital | school supplies<br>school fees and<br>afford it<br>food supply<br>midday meal<br>paper and | made amazing progress in just four years<br>lunch for the students<br>school now serves<br>water is connected to the<br>just 4 years<br>progress in just 4 |

**Table 5:** A sub-list of automatically extracted a) topic words and b) specific expressions for three sample topics. They are automatically extracted by the data-driven LDA-enabled model (see Section 3).

We compare results for models that extracted features from topical components with a baseline model which uses the top 500 unigrams as features (chosen based on a chi-squared feature selection method), and with an upper-bound model which is the best model reported in (Rahimi et al., 2014). The only difference between our model and the upper-bound model is that in our model the topical components were extracted automatically instead of manually.

To train LDA, we use a set of 591 not-scored essays (which are not used in our cross validation experiments) from grades 6-8, and the text. We use the LDA-C implementation (Blei et al., 2003) with default values for the parameters and seeded initialization of topics to a distribution smoothed from a randomly chosen document. The number of topics is chosen equal to the number of topics provided by experts ($K = 8$). The Turbo-Topic parameters are set as P-value = 0.001 and min-count = 10 based on our intuition that it is better to discard less. The cut-off threshold for removing less frequent N-grams is intuitively set to the top 20 most frequent N-grams in a topic.

### 4.2 Features

We use the same set of primarily rubric-based features introduced in (Rahimi et al., 2014) to score the Evidence dimension of RTA:

**Number of Pieces of Evidence (NPE):** based on the list of important words for each main topic.

**Concentration (CON):** a binary feature which indicates if an essay has a high concentration, defined as fewer than 3 sentences with topic words.

**Specificity (SPC):** a vector of integer values. Each value shows the number of examples from the text mentioned in the essay for a single topic.

**Word Count (WOC):** number of words.

We need the list of important words per topic to calculate the NPE and CON features, and the list of important expressions per topic to calculate SPC.

## 5 Results and Discussion

Sample extracted topical components are in Table 5. The shown topic labels (e.g. "Hospitals") were assigned manually by looking at the N-grams and are only for the purpose of better understanding the output. Qualitatively comparing the extracted topical components (Table 5) with the ones provided by experts (Table 4) suggests that the method presented in Section 3 can: (1) distinguish a lot of important N-grams that students were expected to cover in their essays as pieces of evidence, and (2) group related N-grams to topics. In fact, we were able to intuitively map our learned topics to 4 of the 8 manually-produced topics; 3 of these 4 mappings are shown in Table 5. However, while some of the automatically extracted topics are of a promising quality, there is still much room for improvement.

|   | Model | (5-6) [n=1569] | (6-8) [n=1045] |
|---|---|---|---|
| 1 | Unigram baseline | 0.52 | 0.49 |
| 2 | Unigram + WOC | 0.53 | 0.52 |
| 3 | Automatic (proposed) | 0.56(1) | 0.53(1) |
| 4 | Automatic (proposed) minus WOC | 0.54 | 0.51 |
| 5 | Manual (upper bound) | **0.62** | **0.60** |

**Table 6:** Performance of models using automatically extracted topical components, baseline models, and the upper-bound. Bold shows that the model significantly outperforms all other models. The numbers in parentheses show model numbers that the current model significantly outperforms.

We can think of several reasons for not being able to map all automatically extracted topics to the manually produced topics. First, the manually provided topics are based on an expert's knowledge of the text. Experts may expect some details in student essays and include these in the topic list, but students are not always able to distinguish these details to cover in their essays. In other words, the LDA-enabled model is data-driven while expert knowledge is not. If some details are not covered in our training dataset, the data-driven model is not able to distinguish them. Second, experts are able to distinguish topics and their important examples even from only a few sentences in the text. But, if topics and examples are covered in the essays by only a phrase or a few sentences, the data-driven model is not able to distinguish them as distinct topics. They will not be distinguished or will be included in other topics by our model. We also observed that some examples provided by experts are broken down to more than one N-gram in our model. For example, "less than 1 dollar a day" is broken down to two N-grams: "less than" and "1 dollar a day".

Table 6 presents the quantitative performance of our proposed model, where features for predicting RTA Evidence scores are derived using the automatically extracted topical components. The results on both datasets show that the proposed model (Model 3) significantly outperforms the unigram baseline (Model 1). However, the upper-bound model performs significantly better than all other models. There is no significant difference between the rest of the models. To better understand the role of word count (which is not impacted by topical component

extraction) in Model 3, we also created Models 2 and 4. Comparing Models 1 and 4, as well as Models 2 and 3, shows that the proposed model still outperforms unigrams after matching for use of word count or not. Although the improvement is no longer significant, unigrams are less useful than our rubric-based features for providing feedback. We also note that absolute performance is lower on the grade 6–8 dataset for all models, which could be due to the larger size of the 5–6 dataset. In sum, our quantitative results indicate that rubric-based Evidence scoring without involvement of experts is promising, yielding scoring models that maintain reliability while improving validity compared to unigrams. However, the gap with the upper bound shows that our topic extraction method still needs improvement.

## 6  Conclusion and Future Work

We developed a natural language processing technique to automatically extract topical components (topics and significant words and expressions per-topic) relevant to a source text, as our previous approach required these to be manually defined by experts. To evaluate our method, we predicted the score for the Evidence dimension of an analytical writing in response to text assessment (RTA) for upper elementary school students. Experiments comparing the predictive utility of features based on automatically extracted topical components versus manually defined components indicated promising performance for the LDA-enabled extracted topical components. Replacing experts' work with our LDA-enabled method has the potential to better scale rubric-based Evidence scoring.

There are several areas for improvement. We need to tune all parameters. We plan to examine using supervised LDA to make use of scores, or seeded LDA where a few words for each topic are provided. We should study how the size, score distribution, and spelling errors in training data impact topical extraction and scoring. We plan to examine generality by using other RTA articles and prompts. Finally, motivated by short-answer scoring (Sakaguchi et al., 2015), we would like to integrate features needing expert resources with other (valid) features.

## Acknowledgments

This research was funded by the Learning Research and Development Center. We thank R. Correnti, L. C. Matsumara and E. Wang for providing expert topical components and datasets, and H. Hashemi and the ITSPOKE group for helpful feedback.

## References

Y. Attali and J. Burstein. 2006. Automated essay scoring with e-rater v.2. *Journal of Technology, Learning, and Assessment*, 4(3).

Beata Beigman Klebanov, Nitin Madnani, Jill Burstein, and Swapna Somasundaran. 2014. Content importance models for scoring writing from sources. In *Proceedings of the 52nd Annual Meeting of the Association for Computational Linguistics (Volume 2: Short Papers)*, pages 247–252, Baltimore, Maryland, June.

David M Blei and John D Lafferty. 2009. Visualizing topics with multi-word expressions. *arXiv preprint arXiv:0907.1013*.

David M Blei, Andrew Y Ng, and Michael I Jordan. 2003. Latent dirichlet allocation. *the Journal of machine Learning research*, 3:993–1022.

Richard Correnti, Lindsay Clare Matsumura, Laura S Hamilton, and Elaine Wang. 2012. Combining multiple measures of students' opportunities to develop analytic, text-based writing skills. *Educational Assessment*, 17(2-3):132–161.

R. Correnti, L.C. Matsumura, L.H. Hamilton, and E. Wang. 2013. Assessing students' skills at writing in response to texts. *Elementary School Journal*, 114(2):142–177.

Peter W Foltz, Darrell Laham, and Thomas K Landauer. 1999. The intelligent essay assessor: Applications to educational technology. *Interactive Multimedia Electronic Journal of Computer-Enhanced Learning*, 1(2):939–944.

Derrick Higgins, Jill Burstein, and Yigal Attali. 2006. Identifying off-topic student essays without topic-specific training data. *Natural Language Engineering*, 12(02):145–159.

Tuomo Kakkonen, Niko Myller, Jari Timonen, and Erkki Sutinen. 2005. Automatic essay grading with probabilistic latent semantic analysis. In *Proceedings of the second workshop on Building Educational Applications Using NLP*, pages 29–36.

Benoit Lemaire and Philippe Dessus. 2001. A system to assess the semantic content of student essays. *Journal of Educational Computing Research*, 24(3):305–320.

Annie Louis and Derrick Higgins. 2010. Off-topic essay detection using short prompt texts. In *Proceedings of the NAACL HLT 2010 Fifth Workshop on Innovative Use of NLP for Building Educational Applications*, pages 92–95.

Maxim Makatchev and Kurt VanLahn. 2007. Combining bayesian networks and formal reasoning for semantic classification of student utterances.

E. Mayfield and C. Rose. 2013. Lightside: Open source machine learning for text. In M. D. Shermis and J. Burstein, editors, *A Handbook of Automated Essay Evaluation: Current Applications and New Directions*, pages 124–135.

Michael Mohler, Razvan Bunescu, and Rada Mihalcea. 2011. Learning to grade short answer questions using semantic similarity measures and dependency graph alignments. In *Proceedings of the 49th Annual Meeting of the Association for Computational Linguistics: Human Language Technologies*, pages 752–762.

Rodney D Nielsen, Wayne Ward, and James H Martin. 2009. Recognizing entailment in intelligent tutoring systems. *Natural Language Engineering*, 15(04):479–501.

Isaac Persing and Vincent Ng. 2014. Modeling prompt adherence in student essays. In *ACL (1)*, pages 1534–1543.

Zahra Rahimi, Diane J Litman, Richard Correnti, Lindsay Clare Matsumura, Elaine Wang, and Zahid Kisa. 2014. Automatic scoring of an analytical response-to-text assessment. In *Intelligent Tutoring Systems*, pages 601–610. Springer.

Lakshmi Ramachandran, Jian Cheng, and Peter Foltz. 2015. Identifying patterns for short answer scoring using graph-based lexico-semantic text matching. In *Proceedings of the 10th Workshop on Innovative Use of NLP for Building Educational Applications*, pages 97–106.

Keisuke Sakaguchi, Michael Heilman, and Nitin Madnani. 2015. Effective feature integration for automated short answer scoring. In *Proceedings of the 2015 Conference of the North American Chapter of the Association for Computational Linguistics: Human Language Technologies*, pages 1049–1054, Denver, Colorado, May–June.

Jana Z Sukkarieh, Stephen G Pulman, and Nicholas Raikes. 2004. Auto-marking 2: An update on the ucles-oxford university research into using computational linguistics to score short, free text responses. *International Association of Educational Assessment*.

Torsten Zesch, Michael Heilman, and Aoife Cahill. 2015. Reducing annotation efforts in supervised short answer scoring. In *Proceedings of the 10th Workshop on Innovative Use of NLP for Building Educational Applications*, pages 124–132.

# Sentence Similarity Measures for Fine-Grained Estimation of Topical Relevance in Learner Essays


**Marek Rei**
The ALTA Institute
Computer Laboratory
University of Cambridge
United Kingdom
`marek.rei@cl.cam.ac.uk`

**Ronan Cummins**
The ALTA Institute
Computer Laboratory
University of Cambridge
United Kingdom
`ronan.cummins@cl.cam.ac.uk`



## Abstract

We investigate the task of assessing sentence-level prompt relevance in learner essays. Various systems using word overlap, neural embeddings and neural compositional models are evaluated on two datasets of learner writing. We propose a new method for sentence-level similarity calculation, which learns to adjust the weights of pre-trained word embeddings for a specific task, achieving substantially higher accuracy compared to other relevant baselines.


## 1 Introduction

Evaluating the relevance of learner essays with respect to the assigned prompt is an important part of automated writing assessment (Higgins et al., 2006; Briscoe et al., 2010). Students with limited relevant vocabulary may attempt to shift the topic of the essay in a more familiar direction, which grammatical error detection systems are not able to capture. In an automated examination framework, this weakness could be further exploited by memorising a grammatically correct essay and presenting it in response to *any* prompt. Being able to detect topical relevance can help prevent such weaknesses, provide useful feedback to the students, and is also a step towards evaluating more creative aspects of learner writing.

Most existing work on assigning topical relevance scores has been done using supervised methods. Persing and Ng (2014) trained a linear regression model for detecting relevance to each prompt, but this approach requires substantial training data for all the possible prompts. Higgins et al. (2006) addressed off-topic detection by measuring the cosine similarity between tf-idf vector representations of the prompt and the entire essay. However, as this method only captures similarity using exact matching at the word-level, it can miss many topically relevant word occurrences in the essay. In order to overcome this limitation, Louis and Higgins (2010) investigated a number of methods that expand the prompt with related words, such as morphological variations. Ideally, the assessment system should be able to handle the introduction of new prompts, i.e. ones for which no previous data exists. This allows the list of available topics to be edited dynamically, and students or teachers can insert their own unique prompts for every essay. We can achieve this by constructing an unsupervised function that measures similarity between the prompt and the learner writing.

While previous work on prompt relevance assessment has mostly focussed on full essays, scoring individual sentences for prompt relevance has been relatively underexplored. Higgins et al. (2004) used a supervised SVM classifier to train a binary sentence-based relevance model with 18 sentence-level features. We extend this line of work and investigate unsupervised methods using neural embeddings for the task of assessing topical relevance of individual sentences. By providing sentence-level feedback, our approach is able to highlight specific areas of the text that require more attention, as opposed to showing a single overall score. Sentence-based relevance scores could also be used for estimating coherence in an essay, or be combined with a more general score for indicating sentence quality (Andersen et al., 2013).

283


*Proceedings of the 11th Workshop on Innovative Use of NLP for Building Educational Applications*, pages 283–288,
San Diego, California, June 16, 2016. ©2016 Association for Computational Linguistics

In the following sections we explore a number of alternative similarity functions for this task. The evaluation of the methods was performed on two different publicly available datasets and revealed that alternative approaches are required, depending on the nature of the prompts. We propose a new method which achieves substantially better performance on one of the datasets, and construct a combination approach which provides more robust results independent of the prompt type.

## 2 Relevance Scoring Methods

The systems receive the prompt and a single sentence as input, and aim to provide a score representing the topical relevance of the sentence, with a higher value corresponding to more confidence in the sentence being relevant. For most of the following methods, both the sentence and the prompt are mapped into vector representations and cosine is used to measure their similarity.

### 2.1 Baseline methods

The simplest baseline we use is a random system where the score between each sentence and prompt is randomly assigned. In addition, we evaluate the majority class baseline, where the highest score is always assigned to the prompt in the dataset which has most sentences associated with it. It is important that any engineered system surpasses the performance of these trivial baselines.

### 2.2 TF-IDF

TF-IDF (Spärck Jones, 1972) is a well-established method of constructing document vectors for information retrieval. It assigns the weight of each word to be the multiplication of its term frequency and inverse document frequency (IDF). We adapt IDF for sentence similarity by using the following formula:

$$IDF(w) = \log(\frac{N}{1 + n_w})$$

where $N$ is the total number of sentences in a corpus and $n_w$ is the number of sentences where the target word $w$ occurs. Intuitively, this will assign low weights to very frequent words, such as determiners and prepositions, and assign higher weights to rare words. In order to obtain reliable sentence-level frequency counts, we use the British National Corpus (BNC, Burnard (2007)) which contains 100 million words of English from various sources.

### 2.3 Word2Vec

Word2Vec (Mikolov et al., 2013) is a useful tool for efficiently learning distributed vector representations of words from a large corpus of plain text. We make use of the CBOW variant, which maps each word to a vector space and uses the vectors of the surrounding words to predict the target word. This results in words frequently occurring in similar contexts also having more similar vectors. To create a vector for a sentence or a document, each word in the document is mapped to a corresponding vector, and these vectors are then summed together.

While the TF-IDF vectors are sparse and essentially measure a weighted word overlap between the prompt and the sentence, Word2Vec vectors are able to capture the semantics of similar words without requiring perfect matches. In the experiments we use the pretrained vectors that are publicly available, trained on 100 billion words of news text, and containing 300-dimensional vectors for 3 million unique words and phrases.[1]

### 2.4 IDF-Embeddings

We experiment with combining the benefits of both Word2Vec and TF-IDF. While Word2Vec vectors are better at capturing the generalised meaning of each word, summing them together assigns equal weight to all words. This is not ideal for our task – for example, function words will likely have a lower impact on prompt relevance, compared to more specific rare words.

We hypothesise that weighting all word vectors individually during the addition can better reflect the contribution of specific words. To achieve this, we scale each word vector by the corresponding IDF weight for that word, following the formula in Section 2.2. This will still map the sentence to a distributed semantic vector, but more frequent words have a lower impact on the result.

### 2.5 Skip-Thoughts

Skip-Thoughts (Kiros et al., 2015) is a more advanced neural network model for learning distributed sentence representations. A single sentence

---

[1]https://code.google.com/archive/p/word2vec/

is first mapped to a vector by applying a Gated Recurrent Unit (Cho et al., 2014), which learns a composition function for mapping individual word embeddings to a single sentence representation. The resulting vector is used as input to a decoder which tries to predict words in the previous and the next sentence. The model is trained as a single network, and the GRU encoder learns to map each sentence to a vector that is useful for predicting the content of surrounding sentences.

We make use of the publicly available pretrained model[2] for generating sentence vectors, which is trained on 985 million words of unpublished literature from the BookCorpus (Zhu et al., 2015).

### 2.6 Weighted-Embeddings

We now propose a new method for constructing vector representations, based on insights from all the previous methods. IDF-Embeddings already introduced the idea that words should have different weights when summing them for a sentence representation. Instead of using the heuristic IDF formula, we suggest learning these weights automatically in a data-driven fashion.

Each word is assigned a separate weight, initially set to 1, which is used for scaling its vector. Next, we construct an unsupervised learning framework for gradually adjusting these weights for all words. The task we use is inspired by Skip-Thoughts, as we assume that neighbouring sentences are semantically similar and therefore suitable for training sentence representations using a distributional method. However, instead of learning to predict the individual words in the sentences, we can directly optimise for sentence-level vector similarity.

Given sentence $u$, we randomly pick another nearby sentence $v$ using a normal distribution with a standard deviation of 2.5. This often gives us neighbouring sentences, but occasionally samples from further away. We also obtain a negative example $z$ by randomly picking a sentence from the corpus, as this is unlikely to be semantically related to $u$.

Next, each of these sentences is mapped to a vector space by applying the corresponding weights and summing the individual word vectors:

$$\vec{u} = \sum_{w \in u} g_w \vec{w}$$

where $\vec{u}$ is the sentence vector for $u$, $\vec{w}$ is the original embedding for word $w$, and $g_w$ is the learned weight for word $w$.

The following cost function is minimised for training the model – it optimises the dot product of $u$ and $v$ to have a high value, indicating high vector similarity, while optimising the dot product of $u$ and $z$ to have low values:

$$cost = max(-\vec{u}\vec{v} + \vec{u}\vec{z}, 0)$$

Before the cost calculation, we normalise all the sentence vectors to have unit length, which makes the dot products equivalent to calculating the cosine similarity score. The $max()$ operation is added, in order to stop optimising on sentence pairs that are already sufficiently discriminated. The BNC was used as the text source, and the model was trained with gradient descent and learning rate 0.1.

We removed any tokens containing an underscore in the pretrained vectors, as these are used to represent longer phrases, and were left with a vocabulary of 92, 902 words. During training, the original word embeddings are left constant, and only the word weights $g_w$ are optimised. This allows us to retrofit the vectors for our specific task with a small number of parameters – the full embeddings contain 27, 870, 600 parameters, whereas we need to optimise only 92, 902.

Similar methods could potentially be used for adapting word embeddings to other tasks, while still leveraging all the information available in the Word2Vec pretrained vectors. We make the trained weights from our system publicly available, as these can be easily used for constructing improved sentence representations for related applications.[3]

## 3 Evaluation

Since there is no publicly available dataset that contains manually annotated relevance scores at the sentence level, we measure the accuracy of the methods at identifying the original prompt which was used to generate each sentence in a learner essay. While

---

[2]https://github.com/ryankiros/skip-thoughts

[3]http://www.marekrei.com/projects/weighted-embeddings

not all sentences in an essay are expected to directly convey the prompt, any noise in the dataset equally disadvantages all systems, and the ability to assign a higher score to the correct prompt directly reflects the ability of the model to capture topical relevance.

Two separate publicly available corpora of learner essays, written by upper-intermediate level language learners, were used for evaluation. The First Certificate in English dataset (FCE, Yannakoudakis et al. (2011)), consisting of 30,899 sentences written in response to 60 prompts; and the International Corpus of Learner English dataset (ICLE, Granger et al. (2009)) containing 20,883 sentences, written in response to 13 prompts.[4]

There are substantial differences in the types of prompts used in these two datasets. The ICLE prompts are short and general, designed to point the student towards an open discussion around a topic. In contrast, the FCE contains much more detailed prompts, describing a scenario or giving specific instructions on what should be mentioned in the text. An average prompt in ICLE contains 1.5 sentences and 19 words, whereas an average prompt in FCE has 10.3 sentences and 107 words. These differences are large enough to essentially create two different variants of the same task, and we will see in Section 4 that alternative methods perform best for each of them.

During evaluation, the system is presented with each sentence independently and aims to correctly identify the prompt that the student was writing to. For longer prompts, the vectors for individual sentences are averaged together. Performance is evaluated through classification accuracy and mean reciprocal rank (Voorhees and Harman, 1999).

## 4 Results

Results for all the systems can be seen in Table 1. TF-IDF achieves good results and the best performance on the FCE essays. The prompts in this dataset are long and detailed, containing specific keywords and names that are expected to be used in the essay, which is why this method of measuring word overlap achieves the highest accuracy. In contrast, on the ICLE dataset with more general and open-ended prompts, the TF-IDF method achieves

---

<sup></sup>[4]We used the same ICLE subset as Persing and Ng (2014).

|                      | FCE | | ICLE | |
|                      | ACC | MRR | ACC | MRR |
|----------------------|-----|-----|-----|-----|
| Random               | 1.8 | 7.9 | 7.7 | 24.4 |
| Majority             | 22.4 | 25.8 | 28.0 | 39.3 |
| TF-IDF               | **37.2** | **47.0** | 32.3 | 46.9 |
| Word2Vec             | 14.1 | 26.2 | 32.8 | 49.6 |
| IDF-Embeddings       | 22.7 | 33.9 | 40.7 | 55.1 |
| Skip-Thoughts        | 2.8 | 9.1 | 21.9 | 37.9 |
| Weighted-Embeddings  | 24.2 | 35.1 | **51.5** | **65.4** |
| Combination          | 32.6 | 43.4 | 49.8 | 64.1 |

**Table 1:** Accuracy and mean reciprocal rank for the task of sentence-level topic detection on FCE and ICLE datasets.

mid-level performance and is outranked by several embedding-based methods.

Word2Vec is designed to capture more general word semantics, as opposed to identifying specific tokens, and therefore it achieves better performance on the ICLE dataset. By combining the two methods, in the form of IDF-Embeddings, accuracy is consistently improved on both datasets, confirming the hypothesis that weighting word embeddings can lead to a better sentence representation.

The Skip-Thoughts method does not perform well for the task of sentence-level topic detection. This is possibly due to the model being trained to predict individual words in neighbouring sentences, therefore learning various syntactic and paraphrasing patterns, whereas prompt relevance requires more general topic similarity. Our results are consistent with those of Hill et al. (2016), who found that Skip-Thoughts performed very well when the vectors were used as features in a separate supervised classifier, but gave low results when used for unsupervised similarity tasks.

The newly proposed Weighted-Embeddings method substantially outperforms Word2Vec and IDF-Embeddings on both datasets, showing that automatically learning word weights in combination with pretrained embeddings is a beneficial approach. In addition, this method achieves the best overall performance on the ICLE dataset by a large margin.

Finally, we experimented with a combination method, creating a weighted average of the scores from TF-IDF and Weighted-Embeddings. The com-

| 0.382 | Students have to study subjects which are not closely related to the subject they want to specialize in . |
| 0.329 | In order for that to happen however , our government has to offer more and more jobs for students . |
| 0.085 | I thought the time had stopped and the day on which the results had to be announced never came . |

University, degrees, undergraduate, doctorate, professors, university, degree, professor, PhD, College, psychology

**Table 2:** Above: Example sentences from essays written in response to the prompt "Most University degrees are theoretical and do not prepare us for the real life. Do you agree or disagree?", and relevance scores using the Weighted-Embeddings method. Below: Most highly ranked individual words for the same prompt.

bination does not outperform the individual systems, demonstrating that these datasets indeed require alternative approaches. However, it is the second-best performing system on both datasets, making it the most robust method for scenarios where the type of prompt is not known in advance.

| two | -1.31 | cos | 3.32 |
| although | -1.26 | studio | 2.22 |
| which | -1.09 | Labour | 2.18 |
| five | -1.06 | want | 2.01 |
| during | -0.80 | US | 2.00 |
| the | -0.73 | Secretary | 1.99 |
| unless | -0.66 | Ref | 1.98 |
| since | -0.66 | film | 1.98 |
| when | -0.66 | v. | 1.91 |
| also | -0.65 | Cup | 1.89 |

**Table 3:** Top lowest and highest ranking words and their weights, as learned by the Weighted-Embeddings method.

## 5 Discussion

In Table 2 we can see some example learner sentences from the ICLE dataset, together with scores from the Weighted-Embeddings system. The method manages to capture an intuitive relevance assessment for all three sentences, even though none of them contain meaningful keywords from the prompt. The second sentence receives a slightly lower score compared to the first, as it introduces a somewhat tangential topic of government. The third sentence is ranked very low, as it contains no information specific to the prompt. Automated assessment systems relying only on grammatical error detection would likely assign similar scores to all of them. The method maps sentences into the same vector space as individual words, therefore we are also able to display the most relevant words for each prompt, which could be useful as a writing guide for low-level students.

Table 3 contains words with the highest and lowest weights, as assigned by Weighted-Embeddings during training. We can see that the model has independently learned to disregard common stopwords, such as articles, conjunctions, and particles, as they rarely contribute to the general topic of a sentence. In contrast, words with the highest weights mostly belong to very well-defined topics, such as politics, entertainment, or sports.

## 6 Conclusion

In this paper, we investigated the task of assessing sentence-level prompt relevance in learner essays. Frameworks for evaluating the topic of individual sentences would be useful for capturing unsuitable topic shifts in writing, providing more detailed feedback to the students, and detecting subversion attacks on automated assessment systems.

We found that measuring word overlap, weighted by TF-IDF, is the best option when the writing prompts contain many details that the student is expected to include. However, when the prompts are relatively short and designed to encourage a discussion, which is common in examinations at higher proficiency levels, then measuring vector similarity using word embeddings performs consistently better.

We extended the well-known Word2Vec embeddings by weighting them with IDF, which led to improvements in sentence representations. Based on this, we constructed the Weighted-Embeddings model for automatically learning individual weights in a data-driven manner, using only plain text as input. The resulting method consistently outperforms the Word2Vec and IDF-Embeddings methods on both datasets, and substantially outperforms any other method on the ICLE dataset.

## References

Øistein E. Andersen, Helen Yannakoudakis, Fiona Barker, and Tim Parish. 2013. Developing and testing a self-assessment and tutoring system. *Proceedings of the Eighth Workshop on Innovative Use of NLP for Building Educational Applications.*

Ted Briscoe, Ben Medlock, and Øistein Andersen. 2010. Automated Assessment of ESOL Free Text Examinations. Technical report.

Lou Burnard. 2007. Reference Guide for the British National Corpus (XML Edition). Technical report.

Kyunghyun Cho, Bart van Merrienboer, Caglar Gulcehre, Dzmitry Bahdanau, Fethi Bougares, Holger Schwenk, and Yoshua Bengio. 2014. Learning Phrase Representations using RNN Encoder-Decoder for Statistical Machine Translation. In *Conference on Empirical Methods in Natural Language Processing (EMNLP 2014).*

Sylviane Granger, Estelle Dagneaux, Fanny Meunier, and Magali Paquot. 2009. International Corpus of Learner English v2. Technical report.

Derrick Higgins, Jill Burstein, Daniel Marcu, and Claudia Gentile. 2004. Evaluating Multiple Aspects of Coherence in Student Essays. *Proceedings of the Human Language Technology Conference of the North American Chapter of the Association for Computational Linguistics.*

Derrick Higgins, Jill Burstein, and Yigal Attali. 2006. Identifying Off-topic Student Essays Without Topic-specific Training Data. *Natural Language Engineering*, 12.

Felix Hill, Kyunghyun Cho, and Anna Korhonen. 2016. Learning Distributed Representations of Sentences from Unlabelled Data. In *The 15th Annual Conference of the North American Chapter of the Association for Computational Linguistics: Human Language Technologies (NAACL-HLT).*

Ryan Kiros, Yukun Zhu, Ruslan Salakhutdinov, Richard S. Zemel, Antonio Torralba, Raquel Urtasun, and Sanja Fidler. 2015. Skip-Thought Vectors. In *Advances in Neural Information Processing Systems (NIPS 2015).*

Annie Louis and Derrick Higgins. 2010. Off-topic essay detection using short prompt texts. *NAACL HLT 2010 Fifth Workshop on Innovative Use of NLP for Building Educational Applications.*

Tomáš Mikolov, Greg Corrado, Kai Chen, and Jeffrey Dean. 2013. Efficient Estimation of Word Representations in Vector Space. *Proceedings of the International Conference on Learning Representations (ICLR 2013).*

Isaac Persing and Vincent Ng. 2014. Modeling prompt adherence in student essays. In *52nd Annual Meeting of the Association for Computational Linguistics (ACL 2014).*

Karen Spärck Jones. 1972. A Statistical Interpretation of Term Specificity and its Retrieval. *Journal of Documentation*, 28.

Ellen M. Voorhees and Donna Harman. 1999. Overview of the Eighth Text REtrieval Conference (TREC-8). In *Text REtrieval Conference (TREC-8).*

Helen Yannakoudakis, Ted Briscoe, and Ben Medlock. 2011. A New Dataset and Method for Automatically Grading ESOL Texts. In *Proceedings of the 49th Annual Meeting of the Association for Computational Linguistics: Human Language Technologies.*

Yukun Zhu, Ryan Kiros, Richard Zemel, Ruslan Salakhutdinov, Raquel Urtasun, Antonio Torralba, and Sanja Fidler. 2015. Aligning Books and Movies: Towards Story-like Visual Explanations by Watching Movies and Reading Books. *arXiv preprint.*

# Insights from Russian second language readability classification: complexity-dependent training requirements, and feature evaluation of multiple categories

**Robert Reynolds**

UiT: The Arctic University of Norway

Postboks 6050 Langnes

9037 Tromsø, Norway

`robert.reynolds@uit.no`

## Abstract

I investigate Russian second language readability assessment using a machine-learning approach with a range of lexical, morphological, syntactic, and discourse features. Testing the model with a new collection of Russian L2 readability corpora achieves an F-score of 0.671 and adjacent accuracy 0.919 on a 6-level classification task. Information gain and feature subset evaluation shows that morphological features are collectively the most informative. Learning curves for binary classifiers reveal that fewer training data are needed to distinguish between beginning reading levels than are needed to distinguish between intermediate reading levels.

## 1 Introduction

Reading is one of the core skills in both first and second language learning, and it is arguably the most important means of accessing information in the modern world. Modern second language pedagogy typically includes reading as a major component of foreign language instruction. There has been debate regarding the use of authentic materials versus contrived materials, where *authentic* materials are defined as "A stretch of real language, produced by a real speaker or writer for a real audience and designed to convey a real message of some sort" (Morrow, 1977, p. 13).[1] Many empirical studies have demonstrated advantages to using authentic materials, including increased linguistic, pragmatic, and discourse competence (Gilmore, 2007, citations in §3). However, Gilmore (2007) notes that "Finding appropriate authentic texts and designing tasks for them can, in itself, be an extremely time-consuming process." An appropriate text should arguably be interesting, linguistically relevant, authentic, recent, and at the appropriate reading level.

Tools to automatically identify a given text's complexity would help remove one of the most time-consuming steps of text selection, allowing teachers to focus on pedagogical aspects of text selection. Furthermore, these tools would also make it possible for learners to find appropriate texts for themselves.

A thorough conceptual and historical overview of readability research can be found in Vajjala (2015, §2.2). The last decade has seen a rise in research on readability classification, primarily focused on English, but also including French, German, Italian, Portuguese, and Swedish (Roll et al., 2007; Vor der Brück et al., 2008; Aluisio et al., 2010; Francois and Watrin, 2011; Dell'Orletta et al., 2011; Hancke et al., 2012; Pilán et al., 2015). Broadly speaking, these languages have limited morphology in comparison with Russian, which has relatively rich morphology among major world languages. It is therefore not surprising that morphology has received little attention in studies of automatic readability classification. One important exception is Hancke et al. (2012) which examines lexical, syntactic and morphological features with a two-level corpus of German magazine articles. In their study, morphological features are collectively the most predictive category of features. Furthermore, when combining feature categories in groups of two or three, the

---

[1] The definition of authenticity is itself a matter of disagreement (Gilmore, 2007, §2), but Morrow's definition is both well-accepted and objective.



*Proceedings of the 11th Workshop on Innovative Use of NLP for Building Educational Applications*, pages 289–300,
San Diego, California, June 16, 2016. ©2016 Association for Computational Linguistics

highest performing combinations included the morphology category. If morphological features figure so prominently in German readability classification, then there is good reason to expect that they will be similarly informative for Russian second-language readability classification.

This article explores to what extent textual features based on morphological analysis can lead to successful readability classification of Russian texts for language learning. In Section 2, I give an overview of previous research on readability, including some work on Russian. The corpora collected for use in this study are described in Section 3. The features extracted for machine learning are outlined in Section 4. Results are discussed in Sections 5 and 6, and conclusions and outlook for future research are presented in Section 7.

## 2  Background

The history of empirical readability assessment began as early as 1880 (DuBay, 2006), with methods as simple as counting sentence length by hand. Today, research on readability is dominated by machine-learning approaches that automatically extract complex features based on surface wordforms, part-of-speech analysis, syntactic parses, and models of lexical difficulty. In this section, I give an abbreviated history of the various approaches to readability assessment, including the kinds of textual features that have received attention. Although some proprietary solutions are relevant here, I focus primarily on work that has resulted in publically available knowledge and resources.

### 2.1  History of evaluating text complexity

The earliest approaches to readability analysis consisted of developing readability formulas, which combined a small number of easily countable features, such as average sentence length, and average word length (Kincaid et al., 1975; Coleman and Liau, 1975). Although formulas for computing readability have been criticized for being overly simplistic, they were quickly adopted and remain in widespread use today.[2] An early extension of

these simple 'counting' formulas was to additionally rely on lists of words deemed "easy", based on either their frequency or polling of young learners (Dale and Chall, 1948; Chall and Dale, 1995; Stenner, 1996). A higher proportion of words belonging to these lists resulted in lower readability measures, and vice versa.

With the recent growth of natural language processing techniques, it has become possible to extract information about the lexical and/or syntactic structure of a text, and automatically train readability models using machine-learning techniques. Some of the earliest attempts at this built unigram language models based on American textbooks, and estimated a text's reading level by testing how well it was described by each unigram model (Si and Callan, 2001; Collins-Thompson and Callan, 2004). This approach was extended in the REAP project[3] to include a number of grammatical features as well (Heilman et al., 2007; Heilman et al., 2008a; Heilman et al., 2008b).

Over time, readability researchers have increasingly taken inspiration from various subfields of linguistics to identify features for modeling readability, including syntax (Schwarm and Ostendorf, 2005; Petersen and Ostendorf, 2009), discourse (Feng, 2010; Feng et al., 2010), textual coherence (Graesser et al., 2004; Crossley et al., 2007a; Crossley et al., 2007b; Crossley et al., 2008), and second language acquisition (Vajjala and Meurers, 2012). The present study expands this enterprise by examining second language readability for Russian.

### 2.2  Automatic readability assessment of Russian texts

The history of readability assessment of Russian texts takes a very similar trajectory to the work related above. Early work was based on developing formulas based on simple countable features (Mikk, 1974; Oborneva, 2005; Oborneva, 2006a; Oborneva, 2006b; Mizernov and Graščenko, 2015).

Some researchers have tried to be more objective about defining readability, by obtaining data from expert raters, or from other experimental means, and then performing statistical analysis—such as linear regression, or correlation—to identify impor-

---

[2]The Flesch Reading Ease test and the Flesch-Kincaid Grade Level test are implemented in the proofing tools of many major word processors.

[3]http://reap.cs.cmu.edu

tant factors of text complexity (Sharoff et al., 2008; Petrova and Okladnikova, 2009; Okladnikova, 2010; Špakovskij, 2003; Špakovskij, 2008; Ivanov, 2013; Kotlyarov, 2015), such as lexical properties, morphological categories, typographic layout, and syntactic complexity.

To my knowledge, only one study has previously examined readability in the context of Russian second-language pedagogical texts. Karpov et al. (2014) performed a series of experiments using several different kinds of machine-learning models to automatically classify Russian text complexity, as well as single-sentence complexity. They collected a small corpus of texts (described in Section 3 below), with texts at 4 of the CEFR levels:[4] A1, A2, B1, and C2. They extracted 25 features from these texts, including document length, sentence length, word length, lexicon difficulty, and presence of each part of speech. No morphological features were included, despite the fact that morphology is the most challenging feature of Russian grammar for most language learners. Using Classification Tree, SVM, and Logistic Regression models for binary classification (A1-C2, A2-C2, and B1-C2), they report achieving accuracy close to 100%. It should be noted that no results were reported with more customary stepwise binary combinations, such as A1-A2, A2-B1, and B1-C2, which are more difficult— and more useful—distinctions. In a four-way classication task, they state that their results were lower, but they only provide precision, recall, and accuracy metrics for the B1 readability level during four-way classification, which were as high as 99%. Irregularities in reporting make it difficult to draw firm conclusions from their work, especially because their corpora covered only four out of six CEFR levels with no more than 60 data points per level.

## 3 Corpora

The corpora[5] in this study all use the same scale for rating L2 readability, the Common European Framework of Reference for Languages (CEFR). The six

---

<sup></sup>

[4]CEFR levels are introduced in Section 3.

[5]Some of the corpora used in this study are proprietary, so they cannot be published online. However, they can be shared privately for research purposes. With the exception of the two corpora from Karpov et al. (2014), all of the corpora were created and used for the first time in this study.

common reference levels of CEFR can be divided into three levels—Basic user (A), Independent user (B), and Proficient user (C)—each of which is subdivided into two levels. This yields the following six levels in ascending order: A1, A2, B1, B2, C1, and C2.[6] For all corpora, reading levels were assigned by the original author or publisher, so there is no guarantee that the reading levels between corpora align well.

Two subcorpora were used by Karpov et al. (2014). The CIE corpus includes texts created by teachers for learners of Russian. These texts are taken from a collection of materials kept in an open repository at `http://texts.cie.ru`. The second subcorpus used by Karpov et al. (2014) consists of 50 original news articles for native readers, rated at level C2.

The LingQ corpus (LQ) is a corpus of texts from `http://www.lingq.com`, a commercial language-learning website that includes lessons uploaded by member enthusiasts, with 3481 texts. Reading levels were determined by the member who uploaded each lesson.

The Red Kalinka (RK) corpus is a collection of 99 texts taken from 13 books in the "Russian books with audio" series available at `http://www.redkalinka.com`. These books include stories, dialogues, texts about Russian culture, and business dialogues.

The TORFL corpus comes from the Test of Russian as a Foreign Language, a set of standardized tests administered by the Russian Ministry of Education and Science. It is a collection of 168 texts that I extracted from official practice tests for the TORFL.

The Zlatoust corpus (Zlat) comes from a series of readers for language learners at the lower CEFR levels, with 746 documents.

The Combined corpus is a combination of the corpora described above. The distribution of documents per level is given in Table 1. Note that some corpora do not have texts at every reading level.

Table 2 shows the median document length (in words) per level in each of the corpora. The overall median document size is 268 words. Within each corpus, median document length tends to in-

---

[6]There is no consensus on how the CEFR levels align with other language evaluation scales, such as the ACTFL and ILR used in the United States.

| | All | A1 | A2 | B1 | B2 | C1 | C2 |
|---|---|---|---|---|---|---|---|
| CIE | 145 | 28 | 57 | 60 | – | – | – |
| news | 50 | – | – | – | – | – | 50 |
| LQ | 3481 | 323 | 653 | 716 | 832 | 609 | 348 |
| RK | 99 | 40 | 18 | 17 | 18 | 6 | – |
| TORFL | 168 | 31 | 36 | 36 | 26 | 28 | 11 |
| Zlat. | 746 | – | 66 | 553 | 127 | – | – |
| Comb. | 4689 | 422 | 830 | 1382 | 1003 | 643 | 409 |

**Table 1:** Distribution of documents per level for each corpus

crease with each level, with some exceptions. Tests were conducted with a modified corpus in which longer documents were truncated to approximately 300 words; classifier performance was slightly lower with this modified corpus.

| | All | A1 | A2 | B1 | B2 | C1 | C2 |
|---|---|---|---|---|---|---|---|
| CIE | 314 | 116 | 340 | 354 | – | – | – |
| news | 174 | – | – | – | – | – | 174 |
| LQ | 246 | 65 | 47 | 225 | 522 | 3247 | 436 |
| RK | 286 | 68 | 296 | 418 | 278 | 292 | – |
| TORFL | 158 | 55 | 160 | 196 | 238 | 146 | 284 |
| Zlat. | 344 | – | 122 | 345 | 414 | – | – |
| Comb. | 268 | 67 | 68 | 275 | 474 | 2621 | 313 |

**Table 2:** Median words per document for each level of each corpus

The overall distribution of document length is shown in Figure 1, where the x-axis is all documents ranked by document length and the y-axis is document length. The shortest document contains 7 words, and the longest document contains over 9000 words.

**Figure 1:** Distribution of document length in words

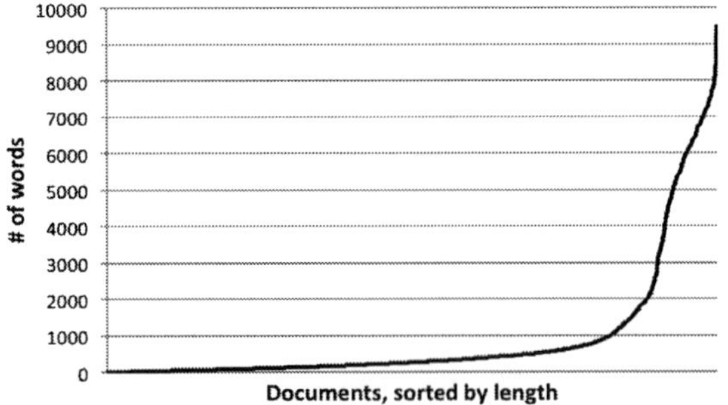


## 4 Features

In the following sections, I give an overview of the features used in this study, both the rationale for their inclusion, as well as details regarding their operationalization and implementation. I combine features used in previous research with some novel features based on morphological analysis. I divide features into the following categories: lexical, morphological, syntactic, and semantic.

### 4.1 Lexical features (LEX)

The lexical features (LEX) are divided into three subcategories: lexical variability (LEXV), lexical complexity (LEXC), and lexical familiarity (LEXF).

**LEXV** The lexical variability category contains features that are intended to measure the variety of lexemes found in a document. One of the most basic measures of lexical variability is the type-token ratio, which is the number of unique wordforms divided by the number of tokens in a text. Because the type-token ratio is dependent on document length, I included a few more robust metrics that have been proposed: Root TTR ($T/\sqrt{N}$), Corrected TTR ($T/\sqrt{2N}$), Bilogarithmic TTR ($\log T/\log N$), and the Uber Index ($\log^2 T/\log(N/T)$). For all of these metrics, a higher score signifies higher concentrations of unique tokens, which indicates more difficult readability levels.

**LEXC** Lexical complexity includes multiple concepts. One is the degree to which individual words can be parsed into component morphemes. This is a reflection of the derivational or agglutinative structure of words. Another measure of lexical complexity is word length, which reflects the difficulty of chunking and storing words in short-term memory. Depending on the particulars of a given language or the development level of a given learner, lexical complexity can either inhibit or enhance comprehension. For example, the word *neftepererabatyvajuščij (zavod)* 'oil-refining (factory)' is overwhelming for a beginning learner, but an advanced learner who has never seen this word can easily deduce its meaning by recognizing its component morphemes: *nefte-pere-rabat-yvaj-uščij* 'oil-re-work-IPFV-ing'.

Word length features were computed on the basis of characters, syllables, and morphemes. For each of these three, both an average and a maximum were computed. In addition, all six of these features were computed for both all words, and for content words only.[7] The features for word length in morphemes were computed on the basis of Tixonov's Morpho-orthographic dictionary (Tixonov, 2002), which contains parses for about 100 000 words. All words that are not found in the dictionary were ignored. In addition to average and maximum word lengths, I also followed Karpov et al. (2014) in calculating word length bands, such as the proportion of words with five or more characters. These bands are calculated for 5–13 characters (9 features) and 3–6 syllables (4 features). All 13 of these features were calculated both for all words and for content words only.

**LexF** Lexical familiarity features were computed to attempt to capture the degree to which the words of a text are familiar to readers of various levels. These features model the development of learners' vocabulary from level to level. Unlike the features for lexical variability and lexical complexity, which are primarily based on surface structure, the features for lexical familiarity rely on a predefined frequency lists or lexicons.

The first set of lexical familiarity features are derived from the official "Lexical Minimum" lists for the TORFL examinations. The lexical minimum lists are compiled for the four lowest levels (A1, A2, B1, and B2), where each list contains the words that should be mastered for the tests at each level. These lists can be seen as *prescriptive* vocabulary for language learners. Following Karpov et al. (2014), I computed features for the proportion of words above a given reading level.

The second set of lexical familiarity features are taken from the Kelly Project (Kilgarriff et al., 2014), which is a "corpus-based vocabulary list" for language learners. These lists are based primarily on word frequency, with manual adjustments made by professional teachers. Just like the features based on the Lexical Minimum, I computed the proportion of words over each of the six CEFR levels.

The third set of lexical familiarity features are based on raw frequency and frequency rank for both lemma frequency and token frequency.[8] For each of the four kinds of frequency data, I computed average, median, minimum, and standard deviation.

## 4.2 Morphological features (MORPH)

Morphological features are primarily based on morphosyntactic values, as output by an automatic morphological analyzer. The first three sets of features reflect simple counts of whether a morphosyntactic tag is present or what proportion of tokens receive each morphosyntactic tag. The first set of features expresses whether a given morphosyntactic tag is present in the document. A second set of features, expresses the ratio of tokens with each morphosyntactic tag, normalized by token count. A third set of features, the value-feature ratio (VFR), was calculated as the number of tokens that express a morphosyntactic value (e.g. past), normalized by the number of tokens that express the corresponding morphosyntactic feature (e.g. tense).

In the early stages of learning Russian, learners do not have a knowledge of all six cases, so I hypothesized that texts intended for the lowest reading level might be distinguished by a limited number of attested cases. Similarly, two subcases in Russian, partitive genitive and second locative, are generally rare, but are overrepresented in texts written for beginners who are being introduced to these subcases. Two features were computed to capture these intuitions: the number of cases and the number of subcases attested in the document.

Following Nikin et al. (2007; Krioni et al. (2008; Filippova (2010), I calculated a feature to measure the proportion of abstract words. This was done by using a regular expression to test lemmas for the presence of a number of abstract derivational suffixes. This feature is normalized to the number of tokens in the document.

### 4.2.1 Sentence length-based features (SENT)

The SENT category consists of features that include in their computation some form of sentence length, including words per sentence, syllables per sentence, letters per sentence, coordinating conjunctions per sentence, and subordinating conjunc-

---

[7]The following parts of speech were considered content words: adjectives, adverbs, nouns and verbs.

[8]Lemma frequency data were taken from Ljaševskaja and Šarov (2009) (available digitally at `http://dict.ruslang.ru/freq.php`), which is based on data from the Russian National Corpus. The token frequency data were taken directly from the Russian National Corpus webpage at `http://ruscorpora.ru/corpora-freq.html`.

tions per sentence. In addition, I also compute the type frequency of morphosyntactic readings per sentence. This category also includes the traditional readability formulas: Russian Flesch Reading Ease (Oborneva, 2006a), Flesch Reading Ease, Flesch-Kincaid Grade Level, and the Coleman-Liau Index.

### 4.3 Syntactic features (SYNT)

Syntactic features for this study were primarily based on the output of the `hunpos`[9] trigram part-of-speech tagger and `maltparser`[10] syntactic dependency parser, both trained on the SynTagRus[11] treebank. Using `maltoptimizer`,[12] I found that the best-performing algorithm was Nivre Eager, which achieved a labeled attachment score of 81.29% with cross-validation of SynTagRus.

Researchers of automatic readability classification and closely related tasks have used a number of syntactic dependency features which I also implement here (Yannakoudakis et al., 2011; Dell'Orletta et al., 2011; Vor der Brück and Hartrumpf, 2007; Vor der Brück et al., 2008). These include features based on dependency lengths (the number of tokens intervening between a dependent and its head), as well as the number of dependents belonging to particular parts of speech, in particular nouns and verbs. In addition, I also include features based on dependency tree depth (the path length from root to leaves).

### 4.4 Discourse/content features (DISC)

The discourse/content features (DISC) are intended to capture the broader difficulty of understanding the text as a whole, rather than the difficulty of processing the linguistic structure of particular words or sentences. One set of features are based on *definitions* (Krioni et al., 2008), which are a set of words and phrases that are used to introduce or define new terms in a text. Using regular expressions, I calculate definitions per token and definitions per sentence.

Another set of features is adapted from the work

of Brown et al. (2007; 2008), who show that logical propositional density—a fundamental measurement in the study of discourse comprehension—can be accurately measured purely on the basis of part-of-speech counts.

One other feature is based on the intuition that reading dialogic texts is generally easier than reading prose. This feature is computed as the number of dialog symbols[13] per token.

### 4.5 Summary of features

As outlined in the preceding sections, this study makes use of 179 features. Many of the features are inspired by previous research of readability, both for Russian and for other languages. The distribution of these features across categories is shown in Table 3.

| Category | Number of features |
|---|---|
| DISC | 6 |
| LEXC | 42 |
| LEXF | 38 |
| LEXV | 7 |
| MORPH | 60 |
| SENT | 10 |
| SYNT | 16 |
| Total | 179 |

**Table 3:** Distribution of features across categories

## 5 Results

The machine-learning and evaluation for this study were performed using the `weka` data mining software (Hall et al., 2009). Based on preliminary tests, the Random Forest model was selected as the classifier algorithm for the study.[14] All results reported below are achieved using the Random Forest algorithm with default parameters. Unless otherwise specified, evaluation was performed using ten-fold cross validation.

Results are given in Table 4. *Precision* is a measure of how many of the documents predicted to be at a given readability level are actually at that level (true positives divided by true and false positives).

---



[9]`https://code.google.com/p/hunpos/`
[10]`http://www.maltparser.org/`
[11]`http://ruscorpora.ru/instruction-syntax.html`
[12]`http://nil.fdi.ucm.es/maltoptimizer/index.html`

[13]In Russian, -, –, — and : are used to mark turns in a dialog.

[14]Other classifiers that consistently performed well were NNge (nearest-neighbor with non-nested generalized exemplars), FT (Functional Trees), MultilayerPerceptron, and SMO (sequential minimal optimization for support vector machine).

*Recall* measures how many of the documents at a given readability level are predicted correctly (true positives divided by true positives and false negatives). The two metrics are calculated for each reading level and weighted averages are reported for the classifier as a whole. The *F-score* is a harmonic mean of precision and recall. *Adjacent accuracy* is the same as weighted recall, except that it considers predictions that are off by one category as correct. For example, a B2 document is counted as being correctly classified if the classifier predicts B1, B2, or C1. The baseline performance achieved by predicting the mode reading level (B1)—using `weka`'s ZeroR classifier—is precision 0.097 and recall 0.312 (F-score 0.149). The OneR classifier, which is based on only the most informative feature (corrected type-token ratio), achieves precision 0.487 and recall 0.497 (F-score 0.471). The Random Forest classifier, trained on the full Combined corpus with all 179 features, achieves precision 0.69 and recall 0.677 (F-score 0.671), with adjacent accuracy 0.919.

| | Precis. | Recall | F-score |
|---|---|---|---|
| ZeroR | 0.097 | 0.312 | 0.149 |
| OneR | 0.487 | 0.497 | 0.471 |
| RandomForest | 0.690 | 0.677 | 0.671 |

**Table 4:** Baseline and RandomForest results with Combined corpus

A confusion matrix is given in Table 5, which shows the predictions of the RandomForest classifier. The rows represent the actual reading level as specified in the gold standard, whereas the columns represent the reading level predicted by the classifier. Correct classifications appear along the diagonal. Table 5 shows that the majority of misclassifications are only off by one level, and indeed the adjacent accuracy is 0.919, which means that less than 10% of the documents are more than one level away from the gold standard.

## 5.1 Binary classifiers

Evaluation was performed with binary classifiers, in which the datasets contain only two adjacent readability levels. Since the Combined corpus has six levels, there are five binary classifier pairs: A1-A2, A2-B1, B1-B2, B2-C1, C1-C2. The results of

| | A1 | A2 | B1 | B2 | C1 | C2 |
|---|---|---|---|---|---|---|
| A1 | **234** | 120 | 48 | 0 | 0 | 0 |
| A2 | 41 | **553** | 192 | 17 | 0 | 0 |
| B1 | 16 | 76 | **1130** | 90 | 5 | 5 |
| B2 | 1 | 57 | 311 | **478** | 83 | 4 |
| C1 | 1 | 20 | 66 | 98 | **394** | 6 |
| C2 | 0 | 3 | 40 | 58 | 9 | **78** |

**Table 5:** Confusion matrix for RandomForest, all features, Combined corpus. Rows are actual and columns are predicted.

the cross-validation evelution of these classifiers is given in Table 6. Red Kalinka and LQsupp (the second largest subcorpus of LingQ)—which were judged to be the most reliable subcorpora—were also examined individually.

| | | A1-A2 | A2-B1 | B1-B2 | B2-C1 | C1-C2 |
|---|---|---|---|---|---|---|
| Comb. | prec. | 0.821 | 0.857 | 0.817 | 0.833 | 0.894 |
| | recall | 0.821 | 0.857 | 0.811 | 0.831 | 0.897 |
| | F-score | 0.812 | 0.855 | 0.806 | 0.826 | 0.892 |
| RK | prec. | 0.967 | 0.943 | 0.832 | 0.837 | – |
| | recall | 0.966 | 0.943 | 0.829 | 0.792 | – |
| | F-score | 0.965 | 0.943 | 0.828 | 0.730 | – |
| LQsupp | prec. | 0.911 | 0.806 | 0.955 | 0.914 | 0.926 |
| | recall | 0.903 | 0.806 | 0.956 | 0.915 | 0.924 |
| | F-score | 0.901 | 0.806 | 0.954 | 0.912 | 0.924 |

**Table 6:** Evelution metrics for binary classifiers: RandomForest, all features

As expected, because the binary classifiers' are more specialized, with less data noise and fewer levels to choose between, their accuracy is much higher.

One potentially interesting difference between binary classifiers at different levels is their learning curves, or in other words, the amount of training data needed to approach optimal results. I hypothesized that the binary classifiers at lower levels would need less data, because texts for beginners have limited possibilities for how they can vary without increasing complexity. Texts at higher reading levels, however, can vary in many different ways. To adapt Tolstoy's famous opening line to *Anna Karenina*, "All [simple texts] are similar to each other, but each [complex text] is [complex] in its own way." If this is true, then binary classifiers at higher reading levels should require more data to reach the upper limit of their classifying accuracy. This prediction was tested by controlling the number of documents used in the training data for each binary classifier, while tracking the F-score on cross-validation. Results of this experiment are given in Figure 2.



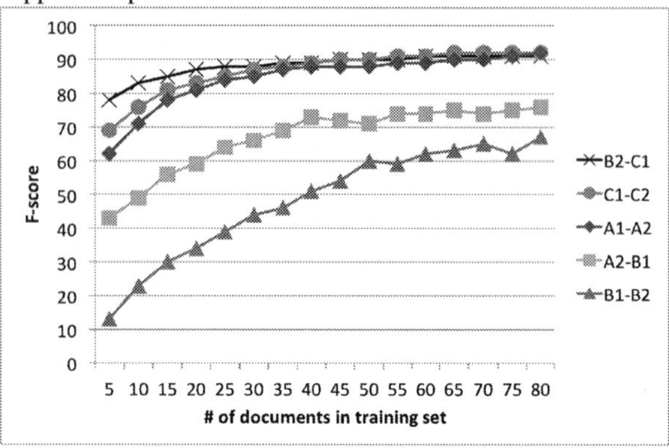

**Figure 2:** Learning curves of binary classifiers trained on LQ-supp subcorpus

The results of this experiment support the hypothesized difference between binary classifier levels, albeit with some exceptions. The A1-A2 classifier rises quickly, and begins to level off after seeing about 40 documents. The A2-B1 classifier rises more gradually, and levels off after seeing about 55 documents. The B1-B2 classifier rises even more slowly, and does not level off within the scope of this figure.

Up to this point, the data confirm my hypothesis that lower levels require less training data. However, the B2-C1 and C1-C2 classifiers buck this trend, with learning curves that outperform the simplest binary classifier with very little training data. One possible explanation for this is that the increasing complexity of CEFR levels is not linear, meaning that the leap from A1 to A2 is much smaller than the leap from C1 to C2. The increasing rate of change is explicitly formalized in the official standards for the TORFL tests. For example, the number of words that a learner should know has the following progression: 750, 1300, 2300, 10 000, 12 000 (7 000 active), 20 000 (8 000 active). This means that distinguishing B2-C1 and C1-C2 should be easier because the distance between their respective levels is an order of magnitude larger than the distance between the respective levels of A1-A2, A2-B1. Furthermore, development of grammar should be more or less complete by level B2, so that the the number of features that distinguish C1 from C2 should be smaller than in lower levels, where grammar development is a limiting factor.

## 6  Feature evaluation

As summarized in Section 4.5, this study makes use of 179 features, divided into 7 categories: DISC, LexC, LexF, LexV, MORPH, SENT, and SYNT. Many of the features used in this study are taken from previous research of related topics, and some features are proposed for the first time here. Previous researchers of Russian readability have not included morphological features, so the results of these features are of particular interest here.

In this section, I explore the extent to which the selected corpora can support the relevance and impact of these features in Russian second language readability classification. One rough test for the value of each category of features is to run cross-validation with models trained on only one category of features. In Table 7, I report the results of this experiment using the Combined corpus.

| Category | # features | precision | recall | F-score |
|---|---|---|---|---|
| DISC | 6 | 0.482 | 0.482 | 0.477 |
| LexC | 42 | 0.528 | 0.532 | 0.514 |
| LexF | 38 | 0.581 | 0.573 | 0.567 |
| LexV | 7 | 0.551 | 0.552 | 0.546 |
| MORPH | 60 | 0.642 | 0.627 | 0.618 |
| SENT | 10 | 0.478 | 0.479 | 0.474 |
| SYNT | 16 | 0.518 | 0.533 | 0.514 |
| LexC+LexF+LexV | 87 | 0.652 | 0.645 | 0.639 |

**Table 7:** Precision, recall, and F-score for six-level Random Forest models trained on the Combined corpus

The results in Table 7 show that MORPH, has the highest F-score of any single category, with an F-score just 0.053 below a model trained on all 179 features. True comparisons between categories are problematic because the number of features per category varies significantly.

In order to evaluate the usefulness of each feature as a member of a feature set, I used the correlation-based feature subset selection algorithm (CfsSubsetEval) (Hall, 1999), which selects the most predictive subset of features by minimizing redundant information, based on feature correlation.

Out of 179 features, the CfsSubsetEval algorithm selected 32 features. Many of the features selected for the optimal feature set are also among the top 30 most informative features according to information gain. However, the morphological features—which had only 7 features among the top 30 for information gain—now include 14 features, which indicates that although these features are not as informative, the information that they contribute is unique.

A classifier trained on only these 32 features with the Combined corpus achieved precision 0.674 and recall 0.665 (F-score 0.659), which is only 0.01 worse than the model trained on all 179 features.

## 7 Conclusions and Outlook

This article has presented new research in automatic classification of Russian texts according to second language readability. This technology is intended to support learning activities that enhance student engagement through online authentic materials (Erbaggio et al., 2010). I collected a new corpus of Russian language-learning texts classified according to CEFR proficiency levels. The corpus comes from a broad spectrum of sources, which resulted in a richer and more robust dataset, while also complicating comparisons between subsets of the data.

**Classifier performance**   A six-level Random Forest classifier achieves an F-score of 0.671, with adjacent accuracy of 0.919. Binary classifiers with only two adjacent reading levels achieve F-scores between 0.806 and 0.892. This is the first large-scale study of this task with Russian data, and although these results are promising, there is still room for improvement, both in corpus quality and modeling features.

In Section 5.1, I showed that binary classifiers at the lowest and highest reading levels required less training data to approach their upper limit. Beginning with the lowest levels, each successive binary classifier learned more slowly than the last until the B2-C1 level. I interpret this as evidence that simple texts are all similar, but complex texts can be complex in many different ways.

**Features**   Among the most informative individual features used in this study are type-token ratios, as well as various measures of maximum syntactic dependency lengths and maximum tree depth. However, as a category, the morphological features are most informative. When features with overlapping information are removed using correlation-based feature selection, the resulting set includes 14 MORPH features, 8 SYNT features, 4 LEXV fea-

tures, 3 LEXF features, and 2 LEXC features, and 1 DISC feature. Models trained on only one category of features also show the importance of morphology in this task, with the MORPH category achieving a higher F-score than other individual categories.

Although the feature set used in this study had fairly broad coverage, there are still a number of possible features that could likely improve classifier performance further. Other researchers have seen good results using features based on semantic ambiguity, derived from word nets. Implementing such features would be possible with the new and growing resources from the Yet Another RussNet project.[15]

Another category of features that is absent in this study is language modeling, including the possibility of calculating information-theoretic metrics, such as surprisal, based on those models.

The syntactic features used in this study could be expanded to capture more nuanced features of the dependency structure. For instance, currently implemented syntactic features completely ignore the kinds of syntactic relations between words. In addition, some theoretical work in dependency syntax, such as catenae (Osborne et al., 2012) and dependency/locality (Gibson, 2000) may serve as the basis for other potential syntactic features.

**Applications**   One of the most promising applications of the technology discussed in this article is a grammar-aware search engine or similar information retrieval framework that can assist both teachers and students to identify texts at the appropriate reading level. Such systems have been discussed in the literature (Ott, 2009), and similar tools can be created for Russian language learning.

## Acknowledgments

I am indebted to Detmar Meurers and Laura Janda for insightful feedback at various stages of this project. I am grateful to Nikolay Karpov for openly sharing his research source files. I am also thankful to the CLEAR research group at UiT and three anonymous reviewers for feedback on an earlier version of this paper. Any remaining errors or shortcomings are my own.



---

[15]http://russianword.net/en/

# References

Sandra Aluisio, Lucia Specia, Caroline Gasperin, and Carolina Scarton. 2010. Readability assessment for text simplification. In *Proceedings of the NAACL HLT 2010 Fifth Workshop on Innovative Use of NLP for Building Educational Applications*, pages 1–9.

Cati Brown, Tony Snodgrass, Michael A. Covington, Ruth Herman, and Susan J. Kemper. 2007. Measuring propositional idea density through part-of-speech tagging. poster presented at Linguistic Society of America Annual Meeting, Anaheim, California, January.

Cati Brown, Tony Snodgrass, Susan J. Kemper, Ruth Herman, and Michael A. Covington. 2008. Automatic measurement of propositional idea density from part-of-speech tagging. *Behavior Research Methods*, 40(2):540–545.

Jeanne S. Chall and Edgar Dale. 1995. *Readability revisited: the new Dale-Chall Readability Formula*. Brookline Books.

Meri Coleman and T. L. Liau. 1975. A computer readability formula designed for machine scoring. *Journal of Applied Psychology*, 60:283–284.

Kevyn Collins-Thompson and Jamie Callan. 2004. A language modeling approach to predicting reading difficulty. In *Proceedings of HLT/NAACL 2004*, Boston, USA.

Scott A. Crossley, David F. Dufty, Philip M. McCarthy, and Danielle S. McNamara. 2007a. Toward a new readability: A mixed model approach. In Danielle S. McNamara and Greg Trafton, editors, *Proceedings of the 29th annual conference of the Cognitive Science Society*. Cognitive Science Society.

Scott A. Crossley, Max M. Louwerse, Philip M. McCarthy, and Danielle S. McNamara. 2007b. A linguistic analysis of simplified and authentic texts. *The Modern Language Journal*, 91(1):15–30.

Scott A. Crossley, Jerry Greenfield, and Danielle S. McNamara, 2008. *Assessing text readability using cognitively based indices*, pages 475–493. Teachers of English to Speakers of Other Languages, Inc. 700 South Washington Street Suite 200, Alexandria, VA 22314.

Edgar Dale and Jeanne S. Chall. 1948. A formula for predicting readability. *Educational research bulletin; organ of the College of Education*, 27(1):11–28.

Felice Dell'Orletta, Simonetta Montemagni, and Giulia Venturi. 2011. Read-it: Assessing readability of Italian texts with a view to text simplification. In *Proceedings of the 2nd Workshop on Speech and Language Processing for Assistive Technologies*, pages 73–83.

William H. DuBay. 2006. *The Classic Readability Studies*. Impact Information, Costa Mesa, California.

P Erbaggio, S Gopalakrishnan, S Hobbs, and H Liu. 2010. Enhancing student engagement through online authentic materials. *International Association for Language Learning Technology*, 42(2).

Lijun Feng, Martin Jansche, Matt Huenerfauth, and Noémie Elhadad. 2010. A comparison of features for automatic readability assessment. In *In Proceedings of the 23rd International Conference on Computational Linguistics (COLING 2010), Beijing, China*.

Lijun Feng. 2010. *Automatic Readability Assessment*. Ph.D. thesis, City University of New York (CUNY).

Anastasija Vladimirovna Filippova. 2010. *Upravlenie kačestvom učebnyx materialov na osnove analize trudnosti ponimanija učebnyx tekstov [Managing the quality of educational materials on the basis of analyzing the difficulty of understanding educational texts]*. Ph.D. thesis, Ufa State Aviation Technology University.

Thomas Francois and Patrick Watrin. 2011. On the contribution of MWE-based features to a readability formula for French as a foreign language. In *Proceedings of Recent Advances in Natural Language Processing*, pages 441–447.

Edward Gibson. 2000. The dependency locality theory: A distance-based theory of linguistic complexity. *Image, language, brain*, pages 95–126.

Alex Gilmore. 2007. Authentic materials and authenticity in foreign language learning. *Language teaching*, 40(02):97–118.

Arthur C. Graesser, Danielle S. McNamara, Max M. Louweerse, and Zhiqiang Cai. 2004. Coh-metrix: Analysis of text on cohesion and language. *Behavior Research Methods, Instruments and Computers*, 36:193–202.

Mark Hall, Eibe Frank, Geoffrey Holmes, Bernhard Pfahringer, Peter Reutemann, and Ian H. Witten. 2009. The weka data mining software: An update. In *The SIGKDD Explorations*, volume 11, pages 10–18.

Mark A Hall. 1999. *Correlation-based feature selection for machine learning*. Ph.D. thesis, The University of Waikato.

Julia Hancke, Detmar Meurers, and Sowmya Vajjala. 2012. Readability classification for German using lexical, syntactic, and morphological features. In *Proceedings of the 24th International Conference on Computational Linguistics (COLING)*, pages 1063–1080, Mumbay, India.

Michael Heilman, Kevyn Collins-Thompson, Jamie Callan, and Maxine Eskenazi. 2007. Combining lexical and grammatical features to improve readability measures for first and second language texts. In *Human Language Technologies 2007: The Conference of the North American Chapter of the Associa-*

*tion for Computational Linguistics (HLT-NAACL-07),* pages 460–467, Rochester, New York.

Michael Heilman, Kevyn Collins-Thompson, and Maxine Eskenazi. 2008a. An analysis of statistical models and features for reading difficulty prediction. In *Proceedings of the 3rd Workshop on Innovative Use of NLP for Building Educational Applications at ACL-08*, Columbus, Ohio.

Michael Heilman, Le Zhao, Juan Pino, and Maxine Eskenazi. 2008b. Retrieval of reading materials for vocabulary and reading practice. In *Proceedings of the Third Workshop on Innovative Use of NLP for Building Educational Applications (BEA-3) at ACL'08*, pages 80–88, Columbus, Ohio.

V. V. Ivanov. 2013. K voprocu o vozmožnosti ispol'zovanija lingvističeskix xarakteristik složnosti teksta pri issledovanii okulomotornoj aktivnosti pri čtenii u podrostkov [toward using linguistic profiles of text complexity for research of oculomotor activity during reading by teenagers]. *Novye issledovanija [New studies]*, 34(1):42–50.

Nikolay Karpov, Julia Baranova, and Fedor Vitugin. 2014. Single-sentence readability prediction in Russian. In *Proceedings of Analysis of Images, Social Networks, and Texts conference (AIST)*.

Adam Kilgarriff, Frieda Charalabopoulou, Maria Gavrilidou, Janne Bondi Johannessen, Saussan Khalil, Sofie Johansson Kokkinakis, Robert Lew, Serge Sharoff, Ravikiran Vadlapudi, and Elena Volodina. 2014. Corpus-based vocabulary lists for language learners for nine languages. *Language resources and evaluation*, 48(1):121–163.

J. P. Kincaid, R. P. Jr. Fishburne, R. L. Rogers, and B. S Chissom. 1975. Derivation of new readability formulas (Automated Readability Index, Fog Count and Flesch Reading Ease formula) for Navy enlisted personnel. Research Branch Report 8-75, Naval Technical Training Command, Millington, TN.

A. Kotlyarov. 2015. Measuring and analyzing comprehension difficulty of texts in contemporary Russian. In *Materials of the annual scientific and practical conference of students and young scientists (with international participation)*, pages 63–65, Kostanay, Kazakhstan.

Nikolaj Konstantinovič Krioni, Aleksej Dmitrievič Nikin, and Anastasija Vladimirovna Filippova. 2008. Avtomatizirovannaja sistema analiza složnosti učebnyx tekstov [automated system for analyzing the complexity of educational texts]. *Vestnik Ufimskogo Gosudarstvennogo Aviacionnogo Texničeskogo Universiteta [Bulletin of the Ufa State Aviation Technical University]*, 11(1):101–107.

O. N. Ljaševskaja and S. A. Šarov. 2009. *Častotnyj slovar' sovremennogo russkogo jazyka (na materialax Nacional'nogo Korpusa Russkogo Jazyka) [Frequency dictionary of Modern Russian (based on the Russian National Corpus)]*. Azbukovnik, Moscow.

Ja. A. Mikk. 1974. Metodika razrabotki formul čitabel'nosti [methods for developing readability formulas]. *Sovetskaja pedagogika i škola IX*, page 273.

I. Ju. Mizernov and L. A. Graščenko. 2015. Analiz metodov ocenki složnosti teksta [analysis of methods for evaluating text complexity]. *Novye informacionnye texnologii v avtomatizirovannyx sistemax [New information technologies in automated systems]*, 18:572–581.

Keith Morrow. 1977. Authentic texts in ESP. *English for specific purposes*, pages 13–16.

Aleksej Dmitrievič Nikin, Nikolaj Konstantinovič Krioni, and Anastasija Vladimirovna Filippova. 2007. Informacionnaja sistema analiza učebnogo teksta [information system for analyzing educational texts]. In *Trudy XIV Vserossijskoj naučno-metodičeskoj konferencii Telematika [Proceedings of the XIV pan-Russian scientific-methodological conference Telematika]*, pages 463–465.

Irina Vladimirovna Oborneva. 2005. Matematičeskaja model' ocenki učebnyx tekstov [mathematical model of evaluation of scholastic texts]. In *Informacionnye texnologii v obrazovanii: XV Meždunarodaja konferencija-vystavka [Information technology in education: XV international conference-exhibit*.

Irina Vladimirovna Oborneva. 2006a. Avtomatizacija ocenki kačestva vosprijatija teksta [automation of evaluating the quality of text comprehension]. No longer available on internet.

Irina Vladimirovna Oborneva. 2006b. *Avtomatizirovannaja ocenka složnosti učebnyx tekstov na osnove statističeskix parametrov [Automatic evaluation of the complexity of educational texts on the basis of statistical parameters]*. Ph.D. thesis.

Svetlana Vladimirovna Okladnikova. 2010. Model' kompleksnoj ocenki čitabel'nosti testovyx materialov na etape razrabotki [a model of multidimensional evaluation of the readability of test materials at the development stage]. *Prikaspijskij žurnal: upravlenie i vysokie texnologii*, 3:63–71.

Timothy Osborne, Michael Putnam, and Thomas Groß. 2012. Catenae: Introducing a novel unit of syntactic analysis. *Syntax*, 15(4):354–396.

Niels Ott. 2009. Information retrieval for language learning: An exploration of text difficulty measures. ISCL master's thesis, Universität Tübingen, Seminar für Sprachwissenschaft, Tübingen, Germany.

Sarah E. Petersen and Mari Ostendorf. 2009. A machine learning approach to reading level assessment. *Computer Speech and Language*, 23:86–106.

I. Ju. Petrova and S. V. Okladnikova. 2009. Metodika rasčeta bazovyx pokazatelej čitabel'nosti testovyx materialov na osnove ekspertnyx ocenok [method of calculating basic indicators of readability of test materials on the basis of expert evaluations]. *Prekaspijskij žurnal: upravlenie i vysokie texnologii*, page 85.

Ildikó Pilán, Sowmya Vajjala, and Elena Volodina. 2015. A readable read: Automatic assessment of language learning materials based on linguistic complexity. In *Proceedings of CICLING 2015- Research in Computing Science Journal Issue (to appear)*.

Mikael Roll, Johan Frid, and Merie Horne. 2007. Measuring syntactic complexity in spontaneous spoken Swedish. *Language and Speech*, 50(2):227–245.

Sarah Schwarm and Mari Ostendorf. 2005. Reading level assessment using support vector machines and statistical language models. In *Proceedings of the 43rd Annual Meeting of the Association for Computational Linguistics (ACL-05)*, pages 523–530, Ann Arbor, Michigan.

Serge Sharoff, Svitlana Kurella, and Anthony Hartley. 2008. Seeking needles in the web's haystack: Finding texts suitable for language learners. In *Proceedings of the 8th Teaching and Language Corpora Conference (TaLC-8)*, Lisbon, Portugal.

Luo Si and Jamie Callan. 2001. A statistical model for scientific readability. In *Proceedings of the 10th International Conference on Information and Knowledge Management (CIKM)*, pages 574–576. ACM.

Jurij Francevič Špakovskij, 2003. *Formuly čitabel'nosti kak metod ocenki kačestva knigi [Formulae of readability as a method of evaluating the quality of a book]*, pages 39–48. Ukrainska akademija drukarstva, Lviv'.

Jurij Francevič Špakovskij. 2008. Razrabotka količestvennoj metodiki ocenki trudnosti vosprijatija učebnyx tekstov dl'a vysšej školy [development of quantitative methods of evaluating the difficulty of comprehension of educational texts for high school]. *Naučno-texničeskij vestnik [Instructional-technology bulletin]*, pages 110–117.

A. Jackson Stenner. 1996. Measuring reading comprehension with the lexile framework. In *Fourth North American Conference on Adolescent/Adult Literacy*.

A. N. Tixonov. 2002. *Morfemno-orfografičeskij slovar': okolo 100 000 slov [Morpho-orthographic dictionary: approx 100 000 words]*. AST/Astrel', Moskva.

Sowmya Vajjala and Detmar Meurers. 2012. On improving the accuracy of readability classification using insights from second language acquisition. In Joel Tetreault, Jill Burstein, and Claudial Leacock, editors, *In Proceedings of the 7th Workshop on Innovative Use of NLP for Building Educational Applications*, pages 163–173, Montréal, Canada, June. Association for Computational Linguistics.

Sowmya Vajjala. 2015. *Analyzing Text Complexity and Text Simplification: Connecting Linguistics, Processing and Educational Applications*. Ph.D. thesis, University of Tübingen.

Tim Vor der Brück and Sven Hartrumpf. 2007. A semantically oriented readability checker for German. In Zygmunt Vetulani, editor, *Proceedings of the 3rd Language & Technology Conference*, pages 270–274, Poznań, Poland. Wydawnictwo Poznańskie.

Tim Vor der Brück, Sven Hartrumpf, and Hermann Helbig. 2008. A readability checker with supervised learning using deep syntactic and semantic indicators. *Informatica*, 32(4):429–435.

Helen Yannakoudakis, Ted Briscoe, and Ben Medlock. 2011. A new dataset and method for automatically grading ESOL texts. In *Proceedings of the 49th Annual Meeting of the Association for Computational Linguistics: Human Language Technologies - Volume 1*, HLT '11, pages 180–189, Stroudsburg, PA, USA. Association for Computational Linguistics. Corpus available: `http://ilexir.co.uk/applications/clc-fce-dataset`.

# Investigating Active Learning for Short-Answer Scoring


**Andrea Horbach**
Dept. of Computational Linguistics
Saarland University
Saarbrücken, Germany
andrea@coli.uni-saarland.de

**Alexis Palmer**
Leibniz ScienceCampus,
Dept. of Computational Linguistics
Heidelberg University
Heidelberg, Germany
palmer@cl.uni-heidelberg.de



## Abstract

Active learning has been shown to be effective for reducing human labeling effort in supervised learning tasks, and in this work we explore its suitability for automatic short answer assessment on the ASAP corpus. We systematically investigate a wide range of AL settings, varying not only the item selection method but also size and selection of seed set items and batch size. Comparing to a random baseline and a recently-proposed diversity-based baseline which uses cluster centroids as training data, we find that uncertainty-based sampling methods can be beneficial, especially for data sets with particular properties. The performance of AL, however, varies considerably across individual prompts.


## 1 Introduction

Methods for automatically scoring short, written, free-text student responses have the potential to greatly reduce the workload of teachers. This task of automatically assessing such student responses (as opposed to, e.g., gap-filling questions) is widely referred to as short answer scoring (SAS), and automatic methods have been developed for tasks ranging from science assessments to reading comprehension, and for such varied domains as foreign language learning, citizenship exams, and more traditional classrooms.

Most existing automatic SAS systems rely on supervised machine learning techniques that require large amounts of manually labeled training data to achieve reasonable performance, and recent work (Zesch et al., 2015; Heilman and Madnani, 2015; Horbach et al., 2014; Basu et al., 2013, among others) has begun to investigate the influence of the quantity and quality of training data for SAS. In this paper we take the next logical step and investigate the applicability of active learning for teacher workload reduction in automatic SAS.

As for most supervised learning scenarios, automatic SAS systems perform more accurate scoring as the amount of data available for learning increases. Particularly in the educational context, though, simply labeling more data is an unsatisfying and often impractical recommendation. New questions or prompts with new sets of responses are generated on a regular basis, and there's a need for automatic scoring approaches that can do accurate assessment with much smaller amounts of labeled data ('labeling' here generally means human grading).

One solution to this problem is to develop generic scoring models which do not require re-training in order to do assessment for a new data set (i.e. a new question/prompt plus responses). Meurers et al. (2011) apply such a model for scoring short reading comprehension responses written by learners of German. This system crucially relies on features which directly compare learner responses to target answers provided as part of the data set, and the responses are mostly one sentence or phrase. In this work we are concerned with longer responses generated from a wide range of prompt types, from questions asking for list-like responses to those seeking coherent multi-sentence texts (details in Section 3). For such questions, there is generally no single best response, and thus the system cannot rely on comparisons to a single target answer per question. Rather systems

301


*Proceedings of the 11th Workshop on Innovative Use of NLP for Building Educational Applications*, pages 301–311,
San Diego, California, June 16, 2016. ©2016 Association for Computational Linguistics

need features which capture lexical properties of responses to the prompt at hand. In other words, a new scoring model is built for each individual prompt.

A second solution involves focused selection of items to be labeled, with the aim of comparable performance with less labeled data. Zesch et al. (2015) investigate whether carefully selected training data are beneficial in an SAS task. For each prompt, they first cluster the entire set of responses and then train a classifier on the labeled instances that are closest to the centroids of the clusters produced. The intuition – that a training data set constructed in this way captures the lexical diversity of the responses – is supported by results on a data set with shorter responses, but on the ASAP data set, the approach fails to improve over random selection.

The natural next step is to use active learning (AL, Settles (2012)) for informed selection of training instances. In AL, training corpora are built up incrementally by successive selection of instances according to the current state of the classifier (a detailed description appears in Section 4). In other words, the machine learner is queried to determine regions of uncertainty, instances in that region are sampled and labeled, these are added to the training data, the classifier is retrained, and the cycle repeats.

Our approach differs from that of Zesch et al. (2015) in two important ways. First, rather than selecting instances according to the lexical diversity of the training data, we select them according to the output of the classifier. Second, we select instances and retrain the classifier in an incremental, cyclical fashion, such that each new labeled instance contributes to the knowledge state which leads to selection of the next instance.

Sample selection via AL involves setting a number of parameters, and there is no single best-for-all-tasks AL setting. Thus we explore a wide range of AL scenarios, implementing a number of established methods for selecting candidates. We consider three families of methods. The first are uncertainty-based methods, which target items about which the classifier is least confident. Next, diversity-based methods aim to cover the feature space as broadly as possible; the cluster-centroid selection method described above is most similar to this type of sample selection. Finally, representativeness-based methods select items that are prototypical for the data set at hand. Our results show a clear win for uncertainty-based methods, with the caveat that performance varies greatly across prompts.

To date, there are no clear guidelines for matching AL parameter settings to particular classification tasks or data sets. To better understand the varying performance of different sample selection methods, we present an initial investigation of two properties of the various data sets. Perhaps unsurprisingly, we see that uncertainty-based sampling brings stronger gains for data sets with skewed class distributions, as well as for those with more cleanly separable classes according to language model perplexity.

In sum, active learning can be used to reduce the amount of training data required for automatic SAS on longer written responses without representative target answers, but the methods and parameters need to be chosen carefully. Further investigation is needed to formulate recommendations for matching AL settings to individual data sets.

## 2   Related work

This study contributes to a recent line of work addressing the question of how to reduce workloads for human graders in educational contexts, in both supervised and unsupervised scoring settings.

The work most closely related to ours is Zesch et al. (2015), which includes experiments with a form of sample selection based on the output of clustering methods. More precisely, the set of responses for a given prompt (using both the ASAP and Powergrading corpora) are clustered automatically, with the number of clusters set to the number of training instances desired. For each cluster, the item closest to its centroid is labeled and added to the training data. This approach aims at building a training set with high coverage of the lexical variation found in the data set. The motivation for this approach is that items with similar lexical material are expressed by similar features, often convey the same meaning and in such cases often deserve the same score. By training on lexically-diverse instances, the classifier should learn more than if trained on very similar instances. Of course, a potential danger is that one cluster may (and often does) contain lexically-similar instances that differ in small but important details, such as the presence or absence of negation.

For the ASAP corpus (which is also the focus of our experiments), the cluster-centroid sampling method shows no improvement over a classifier trained on randomly-sampled data. An interesting outcome of the experiments by Zesch et al. (2015) is the highly-variable performance of classifiers trained on a fixed number of randomly-sampled instances; out of 1000 random trials, the difference between the best and worst runs is considerable. The highly-variable performance of systems trained on randomly-selected data underscores the need for more informed ways of selecting training data.

A related approach to human effort reduction is the use of clustering in a computer-assisted scoring setting (Brooks et al., 2014; Horbach et al., 2014; Basu et al., 2013). In these studies, answers are clustered through automatic means, and teachers then label clusters of similar answers instead of individual student responses. The approaches vary in whether human grading is actual or simulated, and also with respect to how many items in each cluster graders inspect. The value of clustering in these works has no connection with supervised classification, but rather lies in the ability it gives teachers both to reduce their grading effort and to discover subgroups of responses that may correspond to new correct solutions or to common student misconceptions.

In the domain of educational applications, AL has recently been used in two different settings where reduction of human annotation cost is desirable. Niraula and Rus (2015) use AL to judge the quality of automatically generated gap-filling questions, and Dronen et al. (2014) explore AL for essay scoring using sampling methods for linear regression.

To the best of our knowledge, AL has not previously been applied to automatic SAS. Our task is most closely related to studies such as Figueroa et al. (2012), where summaries of clinical texts are classified using AL, or Tong and Koller (2002) and McCallum and Nigam (1998), both of which label newspaper texts with topics. Unlike most other previous AL studies, text classification tasks need AL methods that are suitable for data that is represented by a large number of mostly lexical features.

## 3   Experimental setup

This section describes the data set, features, and classifier used in our experiments.

### 3.1   Data

All experiments are performed on the ASAP 2 corpus, a publicly available resource from a previous automatic scoring competition hosted by Kaggle.[1]. This corpus contains answer sets for 10 individual short answer questions/prompts (we use the terms interchangeably) covering a wide range of topics, from reading comprehension questions to science and biology questions. Each answer is labeled with a numeric score from 0.0-2.0/3.0 (in 1.0 steps; the number of possible scores varies from question to question), and answer length ranges from single phrases to several sentences. Although scores are numeric, we treat each score as one class and model the problem as classification rather than regression. This approach is in line with previous related work as well as standard AL methods.

For each prompt, we split the data set randomly into 90% training and 10% test data. We then augment the test set with all items from the ASAP "public leaderboard" evaluation set. Table 1 shows the number of responses and label distributions for each prompt. Some data sets (i.e. answer set per prompt) are clearly much more imbalanced than others.

### 3.2   Classifier and features

In line with previous work on the ASAP data, classification is done using the Weka (Hall et al., 2009) implementation of the SMO algorithm.

For feature extraction, all answers are preprocessed using the OpenNLP sentence splitter[2] and the Stanford CoreNLP tokenizer and lemmatizer (Manning et al., 2014). As features, we use lemma 1- to 4-grams to capture lexical content of answers, as well as character 2- to 4-grams to account for spelling errors and morphological variation. We lowercase all textual material before extracting ngrams, and features are only included if they occur in at least two answers in the complete data set.

This is a very general feature set that: (a) has not been tuned to the specific task, and (b) is sim-

---

[1]https://www.kaggle.com/c/asap-sas
[2]https://opennlp.apache.org/

| prompt | #answers | training 0.0 | 1.0 | 2.0 | 3.0 | #answers | test 0.0 | 1.0 | 2.0 | 3.0 |
|---|---|---|---|---|---|---|---|---|---|---|
| 1 | 1505 | 331 | 389 | 474 | 311 | 724 | 152 | 208 | 225 | 139 |
| 2 | 1150 | 150 | 289 | 422 | 289 | 554 | 86 | 137 | 190 | 141 |
| 3 | 1625 | 385 | 913 | 327 | - | 589 | 145 | 322 | 122 | - |
| 4 | 1492 | 571 | 803 | 118 | - | 460 | 190 | 232 | 38 | - |
| 5 | 1615 | 1259 | 291 | 37 | 28 | 778 | 594 | 138 | 27 | 19 |
| 6 | 1617 | 1369 | 143 | 60 | 45 | 779 | 644 | 73 | 41 | 21 |
| 7 | 1619 | 837 | 405 | 377 | - | 779 | 390 | 195 | 194 | - |
| 8 | 1619 | 501 | 418 | 700 | - | 779 | 224 | 204 | 351 | - |
| 9 | 1618 | 390 | 661 | 567 | - | 779 | 195 | 312 | 272 | - |
| 10 | 1476 | 261 | 688 | 527 | - | 710 | 110 | 348 | 252 | - |

**Table 1:** Data set sizes and label distributions for training and test splits. '-' indicates a score does not occur for that data set.

ilar to the core feature set for most other SAS work on the ASAP data. In preliminary classification experiments, we also tried out features based on skip ngrams, content-word-only ngrams, and dependency subtrees of various sizes. None of these features resulted in consistently better performance across all data sets, so they were rejected in favor of the simpler, smaller feature set.

## 4 Parameters of Active Learning

The core algorithm we use for active learning is the standard setting for pool-based sampling (Settles, 2010); pseudocode is shown in Figure 1.

---

**The AL algorithm**

---

split data set into *training* and *test*
select seeds $s_0, s_1, ..., s_n \in training$
request labels for $s_0, ...s_n$
$labeled := \{s_0, s_1, ..., s_n\}$
$unlabeled := training \backslash \{s_0, s_1, ..., s_n\}$
while *unlabeled* $\neq \emptyset$:
    select instances $i_0, i_1, ..., i_m \in unlabeled$ *
    $unlabeled = unlabeled \backslash \{i_0, i_1, ..., i_m\}$
    request labels for $i_0, i_1, ..., i_m$
    $labeled = labeled \cup \{i_0, i_1, ..., i_m\}$
    build a classifier on *labeled*
    run classifier on *test* and report performance
* according to some sample selection method

---

**Figure 1:** Pseudocode for general, pool-based active learning.

The process begins with a pool of unlabeled training data and a small labeled seed set. At the start of each AL round, the algorithm selects one or more instances whose label(s) are then requested. In simulation studies, requesting the answer means revealing a pre-annotated label; in real life, a human annotator (i.e. a teacher) would provide the label. After newly-labeled data has been added to the training data, a new classifier is trained, run on the remaining unlabeled data, and the outcomes are stored. For uncertainty sampling methods, these are used to select the instances to be labeled in the next round. The classifier's performance is evaluated on a fixed test set. The efficacy of the item selection method is evaluated by comparing the performance of this classifier to that of a classifier trained on the same number of randomly-selected training instances.

In the following, we discuss the main factors that play a role in active learning: the item selection methods that determine which item is labeled next, the number of seed instances for the initial classifier and how they are chosen, and the number of instances labeled per AL cycle.

### 4.1 Item selection

The heart of the AL algorithm is (arguably) item selection. Item selection defines how the next instance(s) to be labeled are selected, with the goal of choosing instances that are maximally informative for the classifier. We explore a number of different item selection strategies, based on either the uncertainty of the classifier on certain items (*entropy*, *margin* and *boosted entropy*), the lexical *diversity* of the selected items, or their *representativeness* with respect to the unlabeled data.

**Random Baseline.** We use a standard random sampling baseline. For each seed set, the random baseline results are averaged over 10 individual random runs, and evaluations then average over 10 seed sets, corresponding to 100 random runs.

**Entropy Sampling** is our core uncertainty-based selection method. Following Lewis and Gale (1994), we model the classifier's confidence regarding a particular instance using the predicted probability (for an item $x$) of the different labels $y$, as below.

$$x_{selected} = \text{argmax}_x \left( -\sum_i P(y_i|x) log P(y_i|x) \right)$$

Classifier confidence is computed for each item in the unlabeled data, and the one with the highest entropy (lowest confidence) is selected for labeling.

**Boosted Entropy Sampling** Especially for very skewed data sets, it is often favourable to aim at a good representation of the minority class(es) in the training data selected for AL. Tomanek and Hahn (2009) proposed several methods for selecting the minority class with a higher frequency. We adopt their method of boosted entropy sampling, where per-label weights are incorporated into the entropy computation, in order to favor items more likely to belong to a minority class. Tomanek and Hahn (2009) apply this technique to named entity recognition, where it is possible to estimate the true label distribution. In our case, since we don't know the expected true distribution of scores, for each AL round, we instead adapt label weights using the distribution of the current labeled training data set.

**Margin Sampling** is a variant of entropy sampling with the one difference that only the two most likely labels (instead of all three or four) are used in the entropy comparison. As a result, this methods tends to select instances that lie on the decision border between two classes, instead of items at the intersection of all clasess.

**Diversity Sampling** aims to select instances that cover as much of the feature space as possible, i.e. that are as diverse as possible. We model this by selecting the item with the lowest average cosine similarity between the item's feature vector and those of the items in the current labeled training data set.

**Representativeness Sampling** uses a different intuition: this method selects items that are highly representative of the remainder of the unlabeled data pool. We model representativeness of an item by the average distance (again, measures as cosine similarity between feature vectors) between this item and all other items in the pool. This results in selection of items near the center of the pool.

Note that these selection methods are somewhat complimentary. While entropy and margin sampling generally select items from the decision boundaries, they tend to select both outliers and items from the center of the distribution.

Representativeness sampling never selects outliers but only items in the center of the feature space. Diversity sampling selects items that are as far from all other items as possible, and in doing so covers as much of the feature space as possible, with a tendency to select outliers.

### 4.2 Cluster Centroid Baseline

Another interesting baseline for comparison are classifiers trained on cluster centroids, as proposed by Zesch et al. (2015). Following their approach, we use Weka's k-means clustering to cluster the data, with $k$ equal to the desired number of training instances. From each cluster, we extract the item closest to the centroid, build a training set from the extracted items, and learn a classifier from the training data. This process is repeated with varying numbers of training items: the first iteration has 20 labeled items, and we add in steps of 20 until reaching 200 labeled items. We then add data in steps of 50 until we reach 500 labeled items, and in steps of 100 until all data has been labeled. Note that this approach does not directly fit into the general AL framework. In AL, the set of labeled data is increased incrementally, while with this approach a larger training set is not necessarily a proper superset of a smaller training set but may contain different items.

### 4.3 Seed selection

The seed set in AL is the initial set of labeled data used to train the first classifier and thus to initialize the item selection process. The quality of the seeds has been shown to play an important role for the performance of AL (Dligach and Palmer, 2011). Here we consider two ways of selecting seed set items.

First is the baseline of *(a) random seed selection*. Random selection can be suboptimal when it produces unbalanced seed sets, especially if one or more classes are not contained in the seed data at all or – in the worst case – the seed set contains only items of one class. Some of the ASAP data sets are very skewed (e.g. questions 5 and 6, see Table 1) and carry a high risk of producing such suboptimal seeds via random selection.

The second condition is *(b) equal seed selection*, in which seed items are selected such that all classes are equally represented. We do this in an oracle-like condition, but presumably teachers could produce a balanced seed set without too much difficulty by scanning through a number of student responses. Of course, this procedure would require more effort than simply labeling randomly-selected responses.

The number of items in the seed set is another important AL parameter. While a larger seed set provides a more stable basis for learning, a smaller seed set shows benefits from AL at an earlier stage and requires less initial labeling effort. In the *small seed set* condition, and for both random and equal selection methods, 10 individual seed sets per prompt are chosen, each with either 3 or 4 seeds (corresponding to the number of classes per prompt). We repeat this process for the *large seed set* condition, this time selecting 20 items per seed set.

### 4.4 Batch size

Batch size determines how many instances are labeled in each AL round. This parameter is especially relevant with the real-world application of SAS in mind. In real life, it may be inconvenient to have a teacher label just one instance per step, waiting in between labeling steps for retraining of the classifier.

On the other hand, sampling methods benefit from smaller batch sizes, as larger batches tend to contain a number of similar, potentially redundant instances. To combine the benefits of the two settings, we use *varying batch sizes*. To benefit from fine-grained sample selection, we start with a batch size of one and keep this until one hundred instances have been labeled. We then switch to a batch size of 5 until 300 instances have been labeled, and from then on label 20 instances per batch.

For comparison, we also run experiments where 20 instances are labeled in every AL step before a new classification model is learned, in order to investigate whether the potentially inconvenient process of training a new model after each individual human annotation step is really necessary.

## 5 Results

We now investigate to what extent active learning, using various settings, can reduce the amount of training data needed for SAS.

### 5.1 Evaluation of Active Learning

We evaluate all of our SAS systems using Cohen's linearly weighted kappa (Cohen, 1968). Each result reported for a given combination of item selection and seed selection methods is the average over 10 runs, each with a different seed set. The seed sets remain fixed across conditions.

In order to evaluate the overall performance of an AL method, we need to measure the performance gain over a baseline. Rather than computing this at one fixed point in the learning curve, we follow Melville and Mooney (2004) in looking at averaged performance over a set of points early in the learning curve. This is where AL produces the biggest gains; once many more items have been labeled, the differences between the systems reduces. We slightly adapt Melville and Mooney's method and compute the average percent error reduction (that is, error reduction on kappa values) over the first 300 labeled instances (18-26% of all items, depending on the size of the data set).

### 5.2 Experiment 1: Comparison of different item selection methods

The first experiment compares the different item selection methods outlined in Section 4.1, using small seedsets and varying batch sizes.

To give a global picture of differences between the methods, Figure 2 shows the learning curves for all sample selection methods, averaged over all prompt and seed sets. Especially in early parts of the learning curve until about 500 items are labeled, uncertainty-based methods show improvement over the random baseline. Both representativeness and diversity-based sampling perform far worse than random. On average, the systems trained on cluster centroids perform at or below the random baseline,

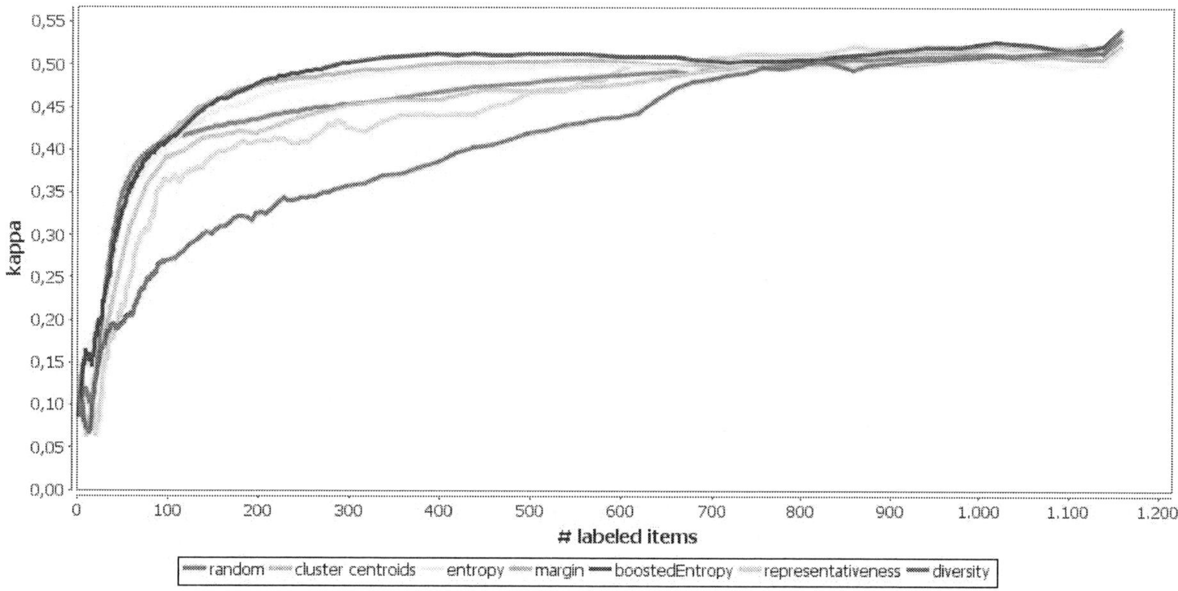


**Figure 2:** AL performance curves compared to two baselines: random item selection and cluster centroids. All results are averaged over all prompts and seed sets.

confirm the findings of Zesch et al. (2015) (though in a slightly different setting).

The picture changes a bit when we look at the performance of AL methods per prompt and with different seed selection methods. Table 2 shows the percent error reduction (compared to the random baseline) per prompt and seed selection method, averaged over the first 300 labeled items. Most noticeable is that we see a wide variety in the performance of the sample selection methods for the various prompts. For some - most pronouncedly prompt 2, 5, 6 and 10 - there is a consistent improvement for uncertainty sampling methods, while other prompts seem to be almost completely resistent to AL. When looking at individual averaged AL curves, we can see some improvement for prompts 7 to 9 that peaks only after 300 items are labeled. For prompt 3, none of the AL methods ever beats the baseline, at any point in the learning process. We also observe variability in the performance across seed sets for one prompt, as can be seen from the standard deviation.

The question of which AL method is most effective for this task can be answered at least partially: if any method yields a substantial improvement, it is an uncertainty-based method. On average, boosted entropy gives the highest gains in both seed selection settings. Comparing random to equal seed selection, performance is rather consistently better when AL starts with a seed set that covers all classes equally.

| prompt & seeds | entropy | margin | boosted entropy | diversity | represen- tativeness |
|---|---|---|---|---|---|
| 1 Equal | -0.58 (5.8) | -0.05 (4.5) | -0.51 (4.0) | -30.53 (1.3) | -14.04 (2.8) |
| 2 Equal | 5.61 (5.1) | 3.82 (7.4) | **6.75** (6.5) | -24.40 (0.5) | 0.88 (1.7) |
| 3 Equal | -2.42 (3.0) | -2.18 (5.1) | -2.32 (3.2) | -27.10 (0.9) | -11.34 (2.7) |
| 4 Equal | -3.40 (7.5) | **1.44** (2.3) | -2.41 (6.6) | -14.67 (1.8) | -10.15 (5.8) |
| 5 Equal | 12.67 (2.5) | **15.38** (2.8) | 12.25 (6.6) | -15.50 (2.7) | -9.44 (11.9) |
| 6 Equal | 21.49 (5.9) | 22.70 (3.3) | **24.39** (2.6) | -16.47 (4.9) | -10.29 (3.5) |
| 7 Equal | -1.49 (6.8) | -2.36 (6.4) | -2.97 (5.5) | -4.85 (1.4) | **0.65** (1.2) |
| 8 Equal | -4.41 (8.6) | **0.26** (4.5) | -2.31 (5.3) | -9.71 (1.5) | -9.16 (4.3) |
| 9 Equal | -2.91 (5.4) | -0.84 (9.1) | **3.32** (5.3) | -0.88 (5.5) | -9.10 (5.6) |
| 10 Equal | 7.97 (6.6) | 8.33 (6.7) | **10.88** (6.3) | 10.31 (3.7) | -4.92 (5.0) |
| avg | 3.25 (5.7) | 4.65 (5.2) | **4.71** (5.2) | -13.38 (2.4) | -7.69 (4.4) |
| 1 Random | -4.24 (6.3) | -2.98 (8.0) | -0.33 (2.6) | -30.81 (2.2) | -13.10 (3.7) |
| 2 Random | 4.28 (5.7) | 2.98 (7.6) | **6.14** (3.2) | -21.37 (1.1) | -0.82 (2.4) |
| 3 Random | -11.41 (7.3) | -5.82 (7.3) | -5.52 (9.5) | -26.13 (2.6) | -11.13 (2.5) |
| 4 Random | **0.18** (7.8) | -5.09 (9.8) | -1.73 (7.5) | -11.13 (2.2) | -11.11 (2.8) |
| 5 Random | 8.92 (5.0) | **12.93** (3.9) | 10.86 (4.8) | -41.56 (16.0) | -2.20 (5.3) |
| 6 Random | 19.66 (3.9) | **21.13** (3.6) | 19.29 (2.1) | -42.53 (26.6) | -11.41 (2.9) |
| 7 Random | -4.21 (7.8) | 0.39 (5.4) | -4.24 (7.6) | -4.22 (1.8) | **0.56** (2.3) |
| 8 Random | -1.63 (7.3) | -0.52 (7.0) | -0.54 (4.3) | -10.19 (0.5) | -6.18 (3.7) |
| 9 Random | -2.78 (6.9) | -4.35 (7.1) | -3.53 (6.3) | -3.17 (5.4) | -10.46 (6.1) |
| 10 Random | 4.89 (9.6) | 7.74 (7.2) | **10.95** (5.0) | 10.94 (3.4) | -3.01 (3.2) |
| avg | 1.37 (6.7) | 2.64 (6.7) | **3.13** (5.3) | -18.02 (6.2) | -6.89 (3.5) |
| all | 2.31 (6.2) | 3.65 (5.9) | **3.92** (5.2) | -15.70 (4.3) | -7.29 (4.0) |

**Table 2:** Performance for each combination of prompt and seed selection method, reporting mean percentage error reduction on kappa values and SD compared to the random baseline.

| Seeds | entropy | margin | boosted |
|---|---|---|---|
| Random – large seeds | 1.45 | 2.72 | 2.57 |
| Random – small seeds | 1.36 | 2.63 | 3.12 |
| Equal – small seeds | **3.25** | **4.65** | **4.71** |

**Table 3:** Error reduction rates over random sampling for different seed set sizes, averaging over all prompts.

| Seeds | entropy | | margin | | boosted | |
|---|---|---|---|---|---|---|
| Equal | -1.11 | (3.25) | 3.78 | (4.65) | 2.12 | (4.71) |
| Random | 0.04 | (1.36) | 2.60 | (2.63) | 0.93 | (3.12) |
| All | -0.53 | (2.30) | 3.19 | (3.64) | 1.53 | (3.92) |

**Table 4:** Error reduction rates over random sampling for large batch size and small seed sets, averaging over all prompts. Scores from the varying batch size setup appear in parentheses.

## 5.3 Experiment 2: The influence of seeds

Experiment 1 shows a clear benefit for using equal rather than random seeds. In a real life scenario, however, balanced seed sets are harder to produce than purely random ones. One might argue that using a larger randomly-selected seed set increases the likelihood of covering all classes in the seed data and provides a better initialization for AL, without the additional overhead of creating balanced seed sets.

This motivates the next experiment, in which learning begins with seed sets of 20 randomly-selected labeled items, but otherwise follows the same procedure. We compare the performance of systems intialized with these larger seed sets to both random and equal small seed sets, considering only the more promising uncertainty-based item selection methods, and again using varying batch sizes.

Table 3 shows the results. We can see, that the performance for margin and entropy sampling is slightly better than the small random seed set (curiously not for boosted entropy), but it is still below that of the small equal seed set. However, the trend across items is not completely clear. We still take it as an indicator that seeds of good quality cannot be outweight by quantity.

## 5.4 Experiment 3: The influence of batch sizes

In experiment 1 we used varying batch sizes that learn a new model after each individual labeled item in the beginning and allow larger batches only later in the AL process. In a real life application, larger batch sizes might be in general preferrable. Therefore we test an alternative setup where we sample and label 20 items per batch before retraining.

Table 4 presents results for uncertainty-based sampling methods, averaged over the first 300 labeled instances. Compared to the varying batch size setup (numbers in parentheses), performance goes down, indicating that fine-grained sampling really does provide a benefit, especially early in the learning process. Where larger batch sizes may lead to selection of instances in the same region of uncertainty, a smaller batch size allows the system to resolve a certain region of uncertainty with fewer labeled training instances.

## 6 Variability of results across datasets

On average, it is clear that uncertainty-based active learning methods are able to provide an advantage in classification performance over random or cluster-centroid baselines. If we look at the result for the different prompts, though, it is equally clear that AL performance varies tremendously across data sets for individual prompts.

In order to deploy AL effectively for SAS, we need to better understand *why* AL works so much better for some data sets than for others.

In Table 2 we see that AL is especially effective for prompts 5 and 6. Cross-referencing Table 1, it becomes clear that these are the two ASAP prompts with the highest degree of class imbalance. Figure 3 shows the changes in the distribution of the individual classes among the labeled data for prompt 6 as AL (here with entropy item selection) proceeds. We see clearly that uncertainty sampling at early stages selects the different classes in a way that is more balanced than the overall distribution for the full data set and thus increases the classifier's accuracy in labeling minority class items. For comparison, a plot for random sampling would ideally consist of four lines parallel to the x axis, and both diversity and representativeness sampling tend to select items from the majority class, explaining their bad performance.

Class imbalance explains some of the variable performance of AL across prompts, but clearly there is more to the story. Next, we use language model (LM) perplexity (computed using the SRILM toolkit (Stolcke, 2002)) as a measurement of how similar

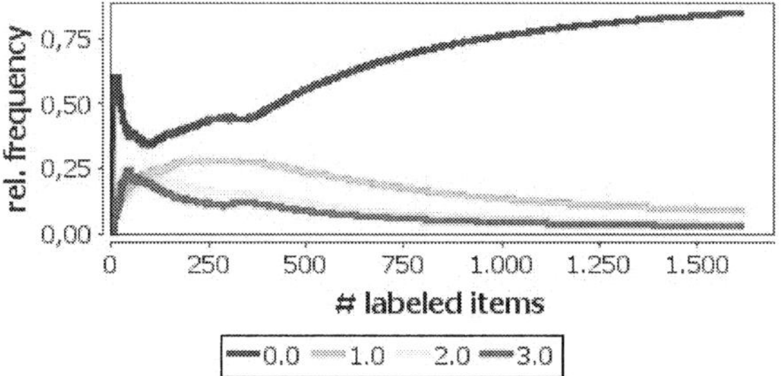

**Figure 3:** Distribution of individual classes among the labeled data for prompt 6, using entropy sampling.

the classes within a prompt are to one another. We measure this per class by training a LM on the items from all other classes (for the same prompt) and then compute the average perplexity of the target class items under the "other-classes" LM. Higher average perplexity means that the items in the class are more readily separable from items in other classes.

| prompt | score 0.0 | score 1.0 | score 2.0 | score 3.0 |
|--------|-----------|-----------|-----------|-----------|
| 1      | 156       | 46        | 27        | 45        |
| 2      | 104       | 48        | 52        | 56        |
| 3      | 44        | 23        | 64        | -         |
| 4      | 78        | 59        | 55        | -         |
| 5      | 970       | 88        | 52        | 49        |
| 6      | 907       | 76        | 60        | 44        |
| 7      | 338       | 117       | 45        | -         |
| 8      | 535       | 70        | 47        | -         |
| 9      | 633       | 127       | 56        | -         |
| 10     | 304       | 49        | 39        | -         |

**Table 5:** Average perplexity per prompt and class under LMs trained on all "other-class" items from the same prompt.

Table 5 shows the results. We see that for those answers that work well under AL, again prominently prompts 5 and 6, at least some classes separate very well against the other classes. They show a high average perplexity, indicating that the answer is not well modeled by other answers with different scores. In comparison, for some other data sets where the uncertainty curves do not clearly beat random sampling, especially 3 and 4, we see that the classes are not well separated from each other. They are among those with the lowest perplexity across scores.

This result, while preliminary and dependent on knowing the true scores of the data, suggests that uncertainty sampling profits from classes that are well separated from one another, such that clear regions

of uncertainty can emerge. An intriguing future direction is to seek out other approaches to characterizing unlabeled data sets, in order to determine: (a) whether AL is a suitable strategy for workload reduction, and (b) if so, which AL setting will give the strongest performance gains for the data set at hand.

## 7  Conclusion

In this study, we have investigated the applicability of AL methods to the task of SAS on the ASAP corpus. Although the performance varies considerably from prompt to prompt, on average we find that **uncertainty-based sample selection** methods outperform both a random baseline and a cluster centroid baseline, given the same number of labeled instances. Other sample selection methods capturing diversity and representativeness perform well below the baselines.

In terms of seed selection, there is a clear benefit from an **equal seed set**, one that covers all classes equally. A small equal seed set is preferable even to a larger but potentially unbalanced seedset. In addition, we see benefits from a **variable batch size** setting over using a larger batch size. It is beneficial to proceed in small steps at the beginning of learning, selecting one item per run, and only move to larger batch sizes later on.

We see two interesting avenues for future work. First, the influence of the quality of seed set items with respect to the coverage of classes raises the question of how best to select - or even generate - equally distributed seed sets. One might argue whether an automated approach is necessary: perhaps an experienced teacher could easily browse through the data in a time-efficient way to select clear examples of low-, mid-, and high-scoring answers as seeds.

The second question is the more challenging and more important one. The variability of AL performance across prompts clearly and strongly points to the need for better understanding how attributes of data sets affect the outcome of AL methods. A solution for predicting which AL settings are suitable for a given data set is an open problem for AL in general. Further steps in this direction need to be taken before AL can be reliably and efficiently deployed in real life assessment scenarios.

# 8 Acknowledgements

We want to thank the three anonymous reviewers for their helpful comments.

Andrea Horbach is funded by the Cluster of Excellence "Multimodal Computing and Interaction" of the German Excellence Initiative. Alexis Palmer is funded by the Leibniz ScienceCampus *Empirical Linguistics and Computational Language Modeling*, supported by the Leibniz Association under grant no. SAS-2015-IDS-LWC and by the Ministry of Science, Research, and Art (MWK) of the state of Baden-Württemberg.

# References

Sumit Basu, Chuck Jacobs, and Lucy Vanderwende. 2013. Powergrading: A clustering approach to amplify human effort for short answer grading. *Transactions of the Association for Computational Linguistics*, 1:391–402.

Michael Brooks, Sumit Basu, Charles Jacobs, and Lucy Vanderwende. 2014. Divide and correct: Using clusters to grade short answers at scale. In *Proceedings of the First ACM Conference on Learning @ Scale Conference*, L@S '14, pages 89–98, New York, NY, USA. ACM.

Jacon Cohen. 1968. Weighted kappa: nominal scale agreement with provision for scaled disagreement or partial credit. *Psychol Bull.*, (70):213–220.

Dmitriy Dligach and Martha Palmer. 2011. Good seed makes a good crop: accelerating active learning using language modeling. In *Proceedings of the 49th Annual Meeting of the Association for Computational Linguistics: Human Language Technologies: short papers-Volume 2*, pages 6–10. Association for Computational Linguistics.

Nicholas Dronen, Peter W. Foltz, and Kyle Habermehl. 2014. Effective sampling for large-scale automated writing evaluation systems. *CoRR*, abs/1412.5659.

Rosa L Figueroa, Qing Zeng-Treitler, Long H Ngo, Sergey Goryachev, and Eduardo P Wiechmann. 2012. Active learning for clinical text classification: is it better than random sampling? *Journal of the American Medical Informatics Association*, 19(5):809–816.

Mark Hall, Eibe Frank, Geoffrey Holmes, Bernhard Pfahringer, Peter Reutemann, and Ian H. Witten. 2009. The WEKA Data Mining Software: An Update. *SIGKDD Explor. Newsl.*, 11(1):10–18, November.

Michael Heilman and Nitin Madnani. 2015. The impact of training data on automated short answer scoring performance. *Silver Sponsor*, pages 81–85.

Andrea Horbach, Alexis Palmer, and Magdalena Wolska. 2014. Finding a tradeoff between accuracy and rater's workload in grading clustered short answers. In *Proceedings of the 9th Language Resources and Evaluation Conference (LREC)*, pages 588–595, Reykjavik, Iceland.

David D. Lewis and William A. Gale. 1994. A sequential algorithm for training text classifiers. In *Proceedings of the 17th Annual International ACM SIGIR Conference on Research and Development in Information Retrieval*, SIGIR '94, pages 3–12, New York, NY, USA. Springer-Verlag New York, Inc.

Christopher D. Manning, Mihai Surdeanu, John Bauer, Jenny Finkel, Steven J. Bethard, and David McClosky. 2014. The Stanford CoreNLP natural language processing toolkit. In *Association for Computational Linguistics (ACL) System Demonstrations*, pages 55–60.

Andrew McCallum and Kamal Nigam. 1998. Employing EM and Pool-Based Active Learning for Text Classification. In *Proceedings of the Fifteenth International Conference on Machine Learning*, ICML '98, pages 350–358, San Francisco, CA, USA. Morgan Kaufmann Publishers Inc.

Prem Melville and Raymond J. Mooney. 2004. Diverse ensembles for active learning. In *Proceedings of 21st International Conference on Machine Learning (ICML-2004)*, pages 584–591, Banff, Canada, July.

Detmar Meurers, Ramon Ziai, Niels Ott, and Janina Kopp. 2011. Evaluating Answers to Reading Comprehension Questions in Context: Results for German and the Role of Information Structure. In *Proceedings of the TextInfer 2011 Workshop on Textual Entailment*, pages 1–9, Edinburgh, Scottland, UK. Association for Computational Linguistics.

Nobal Bikram Niraula and Vasile Rus. 2015. Judging the quality of automatically generated gap-fill question using active learning. In *Proceedings of the Tenth Workshop on Innovative Use of NLP for Building Educational Applications*, pages 196–206, Denver, Colorado, June. Association for Computational Linguistics.

Burr Settles. 2010. Active learning literature survey. *University of Wisconsin, Madison*, 52(55-66):11.

Burr Settles. 2012. *Active Learning*. Synthesis Lectures on Artificial Intelligence and Machine Learning. Morgan & Claypool.

Andreas Stolcke. 2002. SRILM - An Extensible Language Modeling Toolkit. pages 901–904.

Katrin Tomanek and Udo Hahn. 2009. Reducing class imbalance during active learning for named entity annotation. In *in K-CAP 09: Proceedings of the fifth international conference on Knowledge capture*, pages 105–112. ACM.

Simon Tong and Daphne Koller. 2002. Support vector machine active learning with applications to text classification. *J. Mach. Learn. Res.*, 2:45–66, March.

Torsten Zesch, Michael Heilman, and Aoife Cahill. 2015. Reducing annotation efforts in supervised short answer scoring. In *Proceedings of the Building Educational Applications Workshop at NAACL*.

**Association for Computational Linguistics**
209 N. Eighth Street
Stroudsburg, Pennsylvania 18360

ISBN 978-1-5108-2525-3